Christopher Lee is a writer, historian and broadcaster, best-known for writing the radio history series *This Sceptred Isle* for the BBC. Lee was the first Quatercentenary Fellow in Contemporary History and Gomes Lecturer at Emmanuel College, Cambridge. He researched The History of Ideas at Birkbeck, University of London. He has written nearly thirty books and more than one hundred radio plays.

THIS SCEPTRED ISLE

CHRISTOPHER LEE

CONSTABLE · LONDON

Constable & Robinson Ltd
55-56 Russell Square
London WC1B 4HP
www.constablerobinson.com

First published in the UK by BBC Books, 1997

This updated edition published by Constable,
an imprint of Constable & Robinson Ltd., 2012

A copy of the British Library Cataloguing in
Publication data is available from the British Library

ISBN 978-1-84529-994-1

Printed and bound in the UK

1 3 5 7 9 10 8 6 4 2

For
Charlie, George and Elizabeth

Contents

Author's Note

British Isles appears to be a late sixteenth-century phrase, some-times attributed to John Dee. Please accept the inaccuracy of British Isles when used in the work for periods earlier than the Elizabethans. It is convenient and hopefully offends no one. I have used BC as a personal preference to BCE although some readers may prefer the latter. I have also, with acknowledgement to the Venerable Bede, used Anno Domini.

Timeline

2.4–2.1 billion years BC	Huronian Glacial (Ice) Age
850–630 million years BC	Cryogenian Ice Age
460–430 million BC	Andean-Sahara Ice Age
360–260 million BC	Karoo Ice Age
*c.*2 million–*c.*10,000 BC	Old Stone Age (Palaeolithic)
*c.*10,000 BC–*c.*5,500 BC	Middle Stone Age (Mesolithic)
*c.*5,500–*c.*2,500 BC	New Stone Age (Neolithic)
3,150 BC–1,200 BC	The Seven Bronze Ages
*c.*1,200 BC–*c.*580 BC	Iron Age
55 BC	Caesar's first exploratory invasion
54 BC	Caesar's second invasion opposed by Cassivellaunus
AD 43	Conquests starts and Caratacus defeated at the Medway
61	Invasion of Wales and slaughter of the Druids; rebellion of Boudicca
75–7	Julius Agricola, Roman governor of Britain
84	Battle of Mons Graupius (Romans defeat Picts led by Calgacus)
*c.*122–30	Hadrian's Wall
166	The first Christian church in England
293	Division of Roman Empire
304	Martyrdom of St Alban
306–37	Constantine the Great
410	Withdrawal of Roman legions and the virtual end of Roman rule; beginning of the Dark Ages
449	Angles, Saxon and Jute invaders; Hengist and Horsa; St Patrick in Ireland

476	Defeat of last Roman Emperor Romulus Augustulus by the German, Odoacer
477	Ælle conquers Sussex
494	Jutes conquer Kent
518	King Arthur defeat Saxons at Mount Badon
c.550	St David's Mission to Wales
563	Columba establishes the Iona community
597	St Augustine lands in Kent
c.607	The first St Paul's Church in London
635	Lindisfarne monastery
664	Synod of Whitby
c.685	Foundation of Saxon Winchester Cathedral
731	*Book of Kells*
c.783	Offa's Dyke
787	Start of Danish raids
829	Egbert, overlord of England
c.840	Dublin built by Danes
c.850	Kenneth MacAlpin, first King of Scotia
871	Alfred the Great
c. 891	*The Anglo-Saxon Chronicle*
924	King Athelstan
939	Edmund I
959	King Edgar
978	Corfe Castle and Edward the Martyr
978	Æthelred (Ethelred) the Unready
991	Ælfric's *Life of the Saints*
994	Danes besiege London
c.1000	Offshore and deep-sea fishing starts
1002	St Brice's Day Massacre
1007	Danegeld
1016	Cnut
1017	England split into four earldoms
1034	Duncan I of Scotland
1035	Harold I of England
1039	Gruffudd ap Llywelyn

1040	Harthacnut
1040	Macbeth, King of Scots
1042	Edward the Confessor
1058	Malcolm III Canmore, King of Scots
1064	Earl Harold's homage to William of Normandy
1066	Harold II and Battle of Hastings; King William I; Hereward the Wake
1067	First Marcher Lord (Hereford); Tower of London started
1079	Norman Winchester Cathedral started
1086	*Domesday* started
1087	William Rufus; Rhys ap Tewdwr
1093–7	Donald III Bane, King of Scots
1097	Edgar, King of Scots
1100	Henry I; marries Matilda
1107	Alexander I, King of Scots
*c.*1110	Miracle Plays first performed (Dunstable)
1120	*White Ship*; death of Henry I's son, William
1124	David I
1135–54	King Stephen
1138	David I invades England
1153	Malcolm IV, King of Scots
1154	Henry II; Adrian IV – only English Pope
1165	William, the Lion of the Scots
1166	Rory O'Connor drives Dermot MacMurrough from Ireland
*c.*1167	Foundation of Oxford University
1170	Strongbow lands in Ireland; murder of Becket
1177	John Lackland, titular Lord of Ireland; founding of Belfast
1179	The Grand Assize
1189	Richard I, Coeur de Lion
1190	Massacre of Jews, York
*c.*1191	Lord Mayor of London (Henry fitz Ailwin)

1194	Richard I ransomed
1199	King John; Wars in France over English possessions
1209	Cambridge University
1214	Alexander II of the Scots
1215	Magna Carta; First Barons' War; Louis of France invades England
1216	Henry III; Forest Charter
1218	Llywelyn ap Iorwerth; Treaty of Worcester
1220	Salisbury Cathedral
1225	Magna and Forest Charters re-issued
1227	Henry III declared of age
1242	Battle of the Saintes
1249	Alexander III of the Scots
1258	Provisions of Oxford
1264	Second Barons' War
1266	Treaty of Perth. Norway cedes Western Isles and Isle of Man
1267	Llywelyn ap Gruffudd, Prince of Wales
1271	Marco Polo travels to China
1272	Edward I
1278	Jews arrested for gold-clipping
1279	Statute of Mortmain limiting church landowning
1286	Margaret, Queen of Scots
1290	Expulsion of Jews
1292	John Balliol, King of Scots
1295	Model Parliament
1297	William Wallace defeats English at Stirling Bridge
1305	William Wallace executed
1306	Robert I, King of Scots
1307	Edward II
1308	Edward II weds Isabella of France
1309	Papacy to Avignon
1310	Lords Ordainers
1312	Gaveston executed
1314	Bannockburn

1318	Despensers
1325	Queen Isabella flees to France
1326	Isabella and Roger de Mortimer imprison Edward II
1327	Edward II assassinated; Edward III
1329	David II, King of Scots
1337	Hundred Years War begins
1340	Battle of Sluys
1346	Battle of Crécy
1347	Calais
1348	Order of the Garter
1356	Poitiers
c.1362	William Langland's *Piers Plowman*
1376	Death of Edward, the Black Prince
1377	Richard II
1378	The Great Schism splits Church
1381	Peasants' Revolt
1388	Otterburn
1390	Robert III, King of Scots
c.1390	Chaucer's *Canterbury Tales*
1399	Death of John of Gaunt; Bolingbroke seizes crown
1399	Henry IV
1400	Richard II murdered(?)
1401	First Lollard Martyr
1403	Percy's Revolt; Henry Percy killed at Shrewsbury
1406	James I of Scots
1409	Owen Glyndŵr
1411	Foundation of Guildhall in London
1413	Henry V
1415	Agincourt
1420	Treaty of Troyes; Paston Letters
1422	Henry VI
1429	Joan of Arc at Orléans
1437	James II of Scots
1450	Cade's Rebellion
1453	End of Hundred Years War; *Gutenberg Bible*

1455	Wars of the Roses begin
1460	James III of Scots
1461	Edward IV
c.1474	Caxton prints first book in English
1483	Richard III
1485	Henry VII; founding of the Yeomen of the Guard
1488	James IV of Scots
1492	Christopher Columbus reaches America
1509	Henry VIII marries Catherine of Aragon
1513	James V of Scots
1519	Charles V, Holy Roman Emperor
1527	Henry VIII fails in attempt to divorce Catherine of Aragon
1533	Henry VIII marries Anne Boleyn; Cranmer, Archbishop of Canterbury
1536	Henry VIII marries Jane Seymour; Wales annexed to England
1540	Henry VIII marries and divorces Anne of Cleves; marries Catherine Howard
1540	Henry VIII, King of Ireland
1542	Mary, Queen of Scots
1547	Edward VI
1549	First *Book of Common Prayer*
1553	Mary I
1556	Cranmer executed
1558	Elizabeth I
1561	Mary, Queen of Scots returns to Scotland from France
1562	British slave trade starts
1567	James VI, King of Scotland
1571	First anti-Catholic Penal Law
1580	Drake's circumnavigation
1587	Mary, Queen of Scots executed
1596	Robert Cecil, Secretary of State
1600	British East India Company incorporated

1601	Essex executed
1603	James I
1603	Ralegh treason trial and imprisonment
1611	Authorized Version of the Bible
1616	Death of William Shakespeare
1618	Ralegh executed; Thirty Years War starts
1625	Charles I
1632	Lord Baltimore granted patent for the settlement of Maryland
1641	The Grand Remonstrance issued
1642	Civil War starts; Battle of Edgehill
1643	Battle of Newbury
1644	Battle of Marston Moor
1645	New Model Army established
1649	Charles I executed; massacres at Wexford and Drogheda
1651	Charles II crowned at Scone; Hobbes' *Leviathan* published
1655	Jamaica captured
1658	Cromwell dies
1660	Charles II; Declaration of Breda; Pepys begins his diary
1662	The Royal Society; Boyle's Law
1666	Fire of London
1670	Hudson's Bay Company
1673	Test Act
1678	Bunyan's *Pilgrim's Progress*
1685	James II
1689	William III and Mary II
1690	Battle of the Boyne
1692	Massacre of Glencoe
1694	Bank of England
1695	Bank of Scotland
1702	Queen Anne
1704	Battle of Blenheim; capture of Gibraltar
1707	Union with Scotland
1714	George I

1719	Daniel Defoe's *Robinson Crusoe*
1722	Walpole, first Prime Minister
1727	George II
1740	War of Austrian Succession; Arne composes 'Rule Britannia'
1742	Handel's *Messiah*
1746	Battle of Culloden
1751	Clive captures Arcot
1755	Dr Johnson's *Dictionary*
1756	Seven Years War
1759	General Wolfe dies at Battle of Quebec
1760	George III
1765	Stamp Act; Hargreaves' spinning jenny
1767	Revd Laurence Stone's *Tristram Shandy*
1768	Royal Academy of Arts founded
1772	Warren Hastings, first Governor General of Bengal
1773	Boston Tea Party
1774	Priestley isolates oxygen
1775	American Revolution – Lexington and Concord
1776	American Declaration of Independence
1779	Captain Cook killed in Hawaii
1780	Gordon Riots; Epsom Derby
1781	Battle of Yorktown
1783	Pitt the Younger PM
1788	Regency Crisis
1789	French Revolution
1792	Tom Paine's *The Rights of Man*
1799	Napoleon
1801	Union with Ireland
1805	Trafalgar
1807	Abolition of Slave Trade Act
1815	Waterloo
1820	George IV
1828	University of London founded
1829	Catholic Emancipation Act

1830	William IV
1832	First Reform Act
1833	Abolition of slavery in British colonies Act
1834	Houses of Parliament burned down
1836	Births, Marriages & Deaths Act
1837	Queen Victoria
1838	Public Records Office founded
1839	Bed Chamber Crisis; Opium War
1840	Prince Albert; Treaty of Waitangi
1843	Joule's First Law
1844	Rochdale Pioneers; first telegraph line in England
1846	Repeal of Corn Laws
1847	Marks and Engels' *The Communist Manifesto*
1849	Punjab conquered
1850	Public libraries; Tennyson, Poet Laureate
1854	Crimean War; British Medical Association founded
1855	*Daily Telegraph* founded; Palmerston PM
1857	Sepoy Rebellion (Indian Mutiny); Trollope's *Barchester Towers*
1858	Canning, first Viceroy of India
1859	Darwin's *On the Origin of Species*
1861	Prince Albert dies; American Civil War
1865	Abraham Lincoln assassinated
1867	Second Reform Act; first bicycle
1868	TUC
1869	Suez Canal opened; *Cutty Sark* launched
1870	Death of Dickens
1876	Victoria made Empress of India
1880	Gladstone PM
1881	First Boer War
1884	Third Reform Act

1885	Gordon dies at Khartoum
1887	Queen Victoria's Golden Jubilee
1891	Elementary school fees abolished
1895	Salisbury PM
1896	*Daily Mail* founded
1898	Omdurman
1899	Second Boer War
1900	Elgar's *Dream of Gerontius*
1901	Edward VII
1903	Suffragettes
1904	Entente Cordiale
1908	Borstal opened
1909	Old Age Pensions
1910	George V
1914	Irish Home Rule; First World War
1916	Lloyd George PM
1918	RAF formed from Royal Flying Corps; Marie Stopes
1919	John Maynard Keynes' *Economic Consequences of the Peace*
1920	Black and Tans; Anglican Church in Wales disestablished
1921	Irish Free State
1922	Bonar Law PM
1923	Baldwin PM
1924	First Labour Government (MacDonald PM); Baldwin PM; Lenin dies
1925	Britain joins Gold standard
1926	General Strike
1928	Women over twenty-one given vote
1929	The Depression; MacDonald PM
1931	National Government; Statute of Westminster
1932	British Union of Fascists
1933	Hitler
1935	Baldwin PM
1936	Edward VIII; George VI; Spanish Civil War
1937	Chamberlain PM

1938	Austria annexed by Germany; Air Raid Precautions (ARP)
1939	Second World War
1940	Battle of Britain; Dunkirk; Churchill PM
1942	Beveridge Report; fall of Singapore and Rangoon
1944	Butler Education Act; Normandy allied landings
1945	Attlee PM; Germany and Japan surrender
1946	UN founded; National Insurance Act; National Health Service
1947	India Independence; Pakistan formed
1948	Railways nationalized; Berlin Airlift; Ceylon (Sri Lanka) independence
1949	NATO; Irish Independence; Korean War
1951	Churchill PM
1952	Elizabeth II
1955	Eden PM; Cyprus Emergency
1956	Suez Crisis
1957	Macmillan PM
1958	Life Peerages; EEC
1959	Vietnam War; Fidel Castro
1960	Macmillan's Wind of Change speech
1963	Douglas-Home PM; De Gaulle veto on UK EEC membership; Kennedy assassination
1964	Wilson PM
1965	Southern Rhodesia UDI
1967	Pound devalued
1969	Open University; Northern Ireland Troubles; Robin Knox-Johnston first solo, non-stop sailing circumnavigation
1970	Heath PM
1971	Decimal currency in UK
1972	Bloody Sunday, Northern Ireland
1973	Britain in EEC; VAT

1974	Wilson PM
1976	Callaghan PM; first Concorde passenger flight
1979	Thatcher PM; Rhodesian Settlement
1982	Falklands War
1985	Mikhail Gorbachev; Global warming – British report hole in ozone layer
1986	Chernobyl; Reagan–Gorbachev Zero missile summit
1987	Wall Street Crash
1988	Lockerbie
1989	Berlin Wall down
1990	John Major PM; Iraq invades Kuwait
1991	Gulf War; Helen Sharman first Briton in space; Tim Berners-Lee first website; collapse of Soviet Communism
1992	Maastricht Treaty
1994	Church of England Ordination of Women; Channel Tunnel opens
1995	British forces to Sarajevo
1996	Dolly the Sheep clone
1997	Blair PM; Diana Princess of Wales dies; Hong Kong returns to China
1998	Rolls-Royce sold to BMW; Good Friday Agreement
1999	Scottish Parliament and Welsh Assembly elections
2001	Terrorist attacks on New York
2002	Elizabeth the Queen Mother dies
2003	Second Gulf War
2004	Asian Tsunami
2005	Freedom of Information Act; Prince of Wales and Camilla Parker-Bowles wed; terrorist attacks on London
2006	Queen's eightieth birthday
2007	Ministry of Justice created; Brown PM
2008	Northern Rock collapse

2009	Market crash; banks partly national-ized; MPs expenses scandal
2010	Cameron PM. First post-Second World War British Coalition Government

Acknowledgements

No book writes itself. Even revised versions and updates rely on people who encourage and those who help as a matter of course or because it is something they do every day, even without knowing who the author is or seeing the bigger picture. In these times, we should thank the people who compile and post piles of information on the internet. Yet, I still cannot bring myself to use the World Wide Web as a research tool – one day, I suppose, but not yet. Sitting on a library committee during 2010, I found myself arguing for the purchase of a reference work rather than relying on readers to download. I was surprised by the depth of argument for the internet version. There is something very special about handling paper and turning pages – and anyway, who needs pop-ups and cookies in their lives? Maybe it is generational.

It's not surprising then that this author would say a huge thank you to the always patient staff at the British Library's Rare Books and Music Reading Room. Also, to the Senate Library at the University of London and the Institute for Historical Research. Thanks are ever due to the careful research of Nick Beale. To the many who advised I am in debt and grateful even if I do not mention all of them by name. Some must be known. Hazhir Teimourian encouraged me over his good lunches and said keep going when I wondered if I was doing the right thing. My editor, Andreas Campomar, helped by never rushing me when good Catholic guilt inside me insisted that I was falling behind the run rate. We both tacitly understood that I would be watched over by Howard Watson – an exceptional copy editor with the confidence an author too often needs (well at least this one does). My biggest Thank You letter is to my sometime publisher, now my agent and always my friend, Christopher Sinclair-Stevenson who has never sent nor received an email or made a mobile telephone call, and does not care that Google is a verb.

Introduction

The original edition of *This Sceptred Isle* was generously received at seemingly every level. It set out to explain the story of these, the British islands. Later volumes covered the twentieth century and, most importantly, the origins, growth and end of British colonial and imperial history. Put together, the three books suggested the character of the people who became the modern-day British and to some extent the making of Britishness. However, the three volumes were never intended to define Britishness nor specifically trace its progress. Three separate volumes could not do that to my satisfaction. The task in this single volume therefore is firstly to tell the whole story from the Romans to the twenty-first century, including stronger emphasis from the seventeenth century on colonial and imperial history, and to make all the connections with institutions and changing industrial and social characteristics that produce, in loose terms, that which we call Britishness. I have long believed that Britishness as others would see it is an image created inadvertently by Winston S. Churchill during the Second World War. Consequently, anomalies occur when, for example, we consider that Britishness is not exclusively British. Moreover, British may have a number of definitions; not all those definitions may be compatible with the term's popular, even universal, image. Yet it would appear that it is nonsense to suggest anyone can be British; surely, the first qualification is to be English, Scots or Welsh. The province of Northern Ireland, founded as recently as 1921, is in the United Kingdom but not part of Great Britain; is it then denied a Britishness status? Certainly a large part of its population would not easily embrace membership of the Britishness club.

Yet there is no exclusivity to Britishness. In theory you simply need to adopt the language, the mannerisms and the style – that is the superficial make-up of being British. The Anglo-Saxon connection between the United States, Australia, New Zealand and the United Kingdom is an obvious language-based transfer of identity.

If there is a determining factor to identifying Britishness it is the history of the British Isles. It is the tracing of the growth and composition of the peoples of these islands, together with the institutions that influence the character of those peoples and determine the social and political patterns and securities of their lives, that suggest Britishness is an evolving characteristic. Moreover, the British have absorbed and in many cases chosen the influences on the tones of their societies since Saxon times. This fortune (and let us suppose for a moment that this is what it is) is quite unlike the times of those living on Continental Europe; their ancestry has been crisscrossed by armies and migrating populations. Consequently, influences on their national character, including their language and customs, have been imposed rather than chosen.

This book is an attempt to trace the ancestry of the British within these islands and to see the influence of institutions such as law and church on the creation of what we call Britishness. In doing so, we shall begin to see ourselves as many others see us. In a mirror, image is misleading; that is the first clue to what is, or is not, Britishness.

CHAPTER ONE

700,000 BC–AD 570

The average person may easily have difficulty in remembering what people, tribes and invaders came first to these islands. Danes before the Saxons? Saxons before the Normans? When was Alfred? When was Boudicca or as some prefer, Boadicea? (See the Timeline at the beginning of this book for the answers). What most people do remember is that the Romans came before them all. Perhaps that is why the arrival of the Romans in our islands in 55 BC is often the beginning of British taught history and so ignores the obvious point that the Britons were waiting for them and knew all about Caesar and his ilk as they had fought in the Roman armies. Here then is the simplest reminder that the active and diverse human history of the British Isles began long before the Romans.

The most obvious clue to life before the Romans is that most classrooms once had memorable images of Romans meeting savage Britons painted in blue woad. Caesar wrote. '*Omnes vero se Britanni vitro inficiunt, quod caeruleum efficit colorem*' – 'All the British colour themselves with glass, which produces a blue colour.' There is no original source that the Britons painted themselves with leaf dye from the plant *Isatis tinctoria* but that is the popular story. That dye, still produced today in the British Isles, is the colouring from the same plant grown since the Neolithic period in the Middle East – about 9,000 BC. So someone brought it to these lands long before the Romans came. However, we start our story of this island and the making of its people tens of thousands of years before woad because human beings lived in Britain 700,000 years ago. Flint tools found in Pakefield, Suffolk, and voles' teeth tell us this is so.[1]

---

1 Professor Chris Stringer, Department of Palaeontology, Natural History Museum, London, in *Nature*, 2005.

Of course, our human timeline since 700,000 has been broken many times. The gaps were caused by not one but many natural phenomena including uncivilizing depths of cold in the ice ages. Yet, the debris of societies was preserved by those freezing ages. For example, we know that around 30,000 years ago the descendants of the earliest creatures of *Homo sapiens* were here as hunter-gatherers.

During the past one million years there have been at least ten ice ages in the northern hemisphere; they occurred approximately every 100,000 years. These phenomena appear to have been caused by changes in the orbit of the earth around the warming sun.[2] Today we predict catastrophic rises in sea levels as global warming melts the polar ice caps. So it is easy to understand that during the ice ages the opposite happened; there were mountain ranges made of ice. Temperatures gradually dropped and so sea levels ebbed – perhaps by as much as 400 feet – and faces of the earth were carved by advancing glaciers that created much of the land shapes we know today. The last cold period, which we commonly refer to as the Ice Age, started about 70,000 years ago and ended about 10,000 years ago; we say 'about 10,000 years' because it was not a matter of waking one morning to find the snow gone – this was no cold snap. At the same time that the glaciers receded, an important stage of human civilization was occurring in an area of the Middle East that roughly coincides with modern Syria and Iraq. It was here that farming began. People grew and harvested their food rather than nomadically hunting and gathering. When men farm they have to settle to tend the crops. Settlements provide the fundamental stability for a society to emerge as well as cultural comfort. Hence the cradle of civilization was born in the Middle East.

It took another 4,000 to 5,000 years before farming reached these shores and as societies changed from exclusively hunter-gathering to farming some therefore stayed in one area and so gradually created settled tribal regions. Of course, Britain did not overnight turn into a society that stayed put. Some were ever on the move and indeed that is how and why farming spread. Nor must we think in modern terms of change. There was nothing of the trend about the growth of

---

2   This has been known since the seventeenth century largely due to the work of Johannes Kepler (1571–1630).

farming. The gradual shift of the majority from hunting and gathering to food growing probably took as long as it is now from the growth of Christianity – easily 2,000 years.

Although people lived in these islands before the great freeze, as far as we can tell, no one lived here during that period. So when the ice went, the people who arrived in the islands were not necessarily descendants of those who lived here before. Important? Yes, because it gives us a better idea of all our origins and to even better remember that until about 8,500 years ago (so, after the Ice Age) we were not islanders. What we now call the North Sea was then dry land. By 5,000 BC the water levels had risen to create our islands. Because the British lands were surrounded by water then it followed that development of the islands was likely to be later than that of, for example, eastern Continental Europe. That is a generalization, but not out of place in our story. This period is called Neolithic which can be translated from two Greek words *neos* (new) and *lithos* (stone) – thus Neolithic is New Stone Age. Because of what was going on in settled farming, it is sometimes called the Agricultural Age and is seen as a 'culturally more dramatic threshold than our more recent Agricultural Revolution'.[3] Yet, if we look at the New Stone Age or Agricultural Age in the British Isles, we would probably date it c.5,500 BC–c.2,500 BC. But the same age in the region where Europe meets Asia started not c.5,000 BC but c.10,000 BC. The three larger reasons for this late start were the distances from the origins of change in the Middle East; climate; and resettlement that came from two distinct directions. When the migration started, it appears to have been mainly a pincer movement. One migration came along the southern European-Balkan corridors then up the western coast of Europe. The second claw in the migratory pincer was from the near neighbours of northwestern Europe.

Agriculture followed by settled farmers (as opposed to herdsmen who would follow the grazing) is in evidence in East Anglia as early as 6,300 years ago. It took hundreds of years for the Agricultural Revolution to spread throughout the islands from the south, the east and the west as far north as the Orkneys.[4] What is not so clear is the answer to the threefold question of the consequence of the introduction

---

3   Stephen Oppenheimer, *The Origins of the British* (London: Robinson, 2007), 197.
4   The Skara Brae settlement is an exceptional example of preserved Neolithic society.

of the new society: Were the influences of the new cultures spread by
the migrants from Continental Europe or by the indigenous population? Did the new farming produce a diet and a less vulnerable
lifestyle that preserved the indigenous population? Is the language
that we speak today developed from migrations or from what already
existed? In very crude terms: did the people who lived in these
islands absorb the migrants or did the visitors gradually take over?

There was also in these migration patterns an obvious source of
identification: people on the move carry with them the utensils they
need to cook and feed. So, from about 3,000 BC there arrived in
Britain the simplest utensil: the beaker. It could be used to drink
from, eat from and, in some form, to cook in. Beaker history is one
of the more fruitful forms of archaeology because beakers had
regional characteristics including decoration and many artefacts
have survived. Even fragments tell us much about population origins,
growths and progression. Beakers were brought from the near northern Continental Europe. The migrations from the Continent into the
islands between 3,000 BC and 2,000 BC gave us evidence of a society
that took great care in the burial of its dead. Earlier burials were
communal affairs but about 3,000 BC the northern European trend for
individual graves spread across the Continent and over the seas to
the British Isles. With the gradual adoption of single graves came the
practice of a more personal morbid liturgy that included provisions
for another place. The departed took utensils for the next journey.
So, in excavations in Wiltshire-cum-Wessex, the ritual centre of
England during the Neolithic and Bronze ages[5] there is good evidence
of what have become known as beaker graves including those of
travellers from north-west Continental Europe. Others arrived from
Iberia, suggesting a quite different migratory passage to the north-
west European visitors. For example, according to Professor Barry
Cunliffe, Maritime Bell Beaker culture that may have originated in
what is now Portugal brought to these shores trading networks, metal
working and even language.[6]

Here then we have some idea that the traceable origins of the
British are to be found following the big thaw in the Middle Stone
Age period after 10,000 BC. The period between, say, 13,000 BC and

5   Oppenheimer, *The Origins of the British*, 272.
6   Barry Cunliffe, *Facing the Ocean: The Atlantic and Its Peoples* (Oxford: OUP, 2004), 218–19.

5,500 BC saw the migrations of hunter-gatherers crossing mainland Europe from the Caucuses, while northwards along the Atlantic coast came the Franco-Iberian travellers still besieged by the ice. As the ice melted, these islands were formed because the sea levels rose and from 5,500 BC the Neolithic or Agricultural Age people who were looking to settle and farm began arriving from as far away as the Middle East, the Balkans, across the Mediterranean and along the Atlantic Iberian coastline; eventually they were followed by the Anglo-Saxons from Germany and the Lowlands and then the Vikings. So by the time the Romans arrived, just a generation or so before the birth of Christ, the society of the Britons was established; hunter-gatherers may have lived here but the general make-up of the Britons suggested that they were farmers, people who would stick to one area and form into groups that became large groups that became communities that became regional tribes of inter-related, settled people. It was also a society that was not isolated and had even fought with the Romans on the Continent.

Julius Caesar (100 BC–44 BC) came to Britain, islands on the very edge of the known world, on 26 August 55 BC. This was not the great invasion that would govern our island society. Caesar had come prepared but not prepared enough. He had 10,000 men when he landed near Deal on the Kent coast and fought off the harassing Britons. But to properly invade, Caesar needed far more men, cavalry and all the logistical people and equipment that sustain an advancing army. Many times, these islands have been protected from invaders by the weather. So it was at the end of that July 55 BC when his cavalry tried to land without understanding tides (tides rarely happen in the Mediterranean). At the end of that month there was a full moon, which produces extreme tides.

The landing was not entirely a failure. Caesar achieved three objectives. He understood that he had the wrong sort of vessels to transport his invasion; he knew what forces he needed to beat the Britons; and his expedition was seen in Rome as a great success. He returned to northern Italy and prepared a new fleet of specially designed warships and transports that could be sailed or pulled with great oars. Caesar had, in effect, designed the first landing craft – vessels that could run right on to the beaches of Britannia and so make it simpler to get stores, men and horses ashore. The obvious question remained: did he really need to land on these islands? After all, they posed no military threat to this general who had all but conquered Gaul, as France was then called. The answer is that Caesar had to maintain his authority and ambition and so he had to command, to defend and to conquer. Caesar was vulnerable. He had many enemies in Rome who wanted him to return to face charges levied at him years before when he was a consul. Those accusations included debt even though he had paid his creditors with treasure seized when he had sacked Spain. In Rome prosecutions for crimes were rarely pursued against victorious military heroes, thus Caesar remained above the law so long as he continued to conquer. Thus, he had no option but to plot and plan to exploit his reputation and power that came from his undoubted brilliance as a general and as a politician. This was the man who shortly would be the first emperor of Rome and called Pater Patriae (Father of the Country) and the man seen by one of his more famous political enemies, Cicero, as having a 'calm and kind nature; delight in great minds; he listens to right and just requests and doesn't care about the careerist's ones; he is clever and forward-looking . . . I admire his dignity and justice and intelligence'. Here was the man who came, for the second time, to conquer Britain. He would not succeed. It would take another 100 years before the real conquest under the auspice of Claudius in AD 43 would mean the Romanization of Britain. But in 54 BC the invasion under Caesar would be enough to inspire the idea for 2,000 years and more that it was indeed Julius who conquered the Britons.

The Romans would not have understood the people of Britain as the English. The English came very much after the Romans; the people they knew were Celts with a common language: Celtic. Celtic place names were so well established that the Romans simply Romanized them. Also, this was not a land of savages although the people were capable of behaving what we would think of as savagely. By 54 BC many had farms and therefore settled into hamlets and even villages. Hedges and boundaries suggest a form of regular and marked ownership of land and the river valleys were becoming more populated because of this organized agriculture. The beginnings of industrial pottery, a common language and what are now called Gallo-Belgic coins suggest that Caesar was right when he said that the people in the lowland areas, broadly what are now called the South-East and Midlands, were infiltrated by those from the

Continent. At the end of July 54 BC Caesar was also ready to infiltrate from the Continent. Across the narrow seaway, the Britons knew he was coming. These Britons had fought in Gaul alongside Caesar's men. They knew of what he was capable, and what he might do with that capability. Some of the tribes sent envoys to Caesar; they didn't want to fight. Also, many of them were at war with each other so there was much to gain from making peace with the Romans and even promising to

Caesar returned to Britain with 800 warships of troops, cavalry and supplies. It was a well-structured invasion and occupation force but not without opposition. The Britons, or some of them, had united under a leader called Cassivellaunus, who may have been the King of the Catuvellauni. The Catuvellauni were the strongest of the southern tribes and had settled in what is now Hertfordshire. They were resilient and inventive, especially in the way they deployed their chariots when fighting. Cassivellaunus had many enemies. There were other tribes who hated his tribe; there were other leaders who hated him. It is thought that one of these tribes, the Trinovantes who lived in Essex, entered into a pact with Caesar. Other tribes joined this arrangement and so Cassivellaunus now fought Romans in front of him and treachery behind. Eventually peace was negotiated and Britons were taken hostage. Victory for Caesar? It was never to be as simple as that. Winter was approaching: there was no way in which an invading army could in those times find ready-made shelter and the Romans had no way in which they could resupply the huge cohorts needed to maintain the territory they had taken. Worse still, there was a revolt in Gaul. So Caesar left Britain taking his British prisoners with him. And that was it. Caesar's flirtation with Britain was just that, a flirtation. In ten years he would be murdered, and a century would pass before the Emperor Claudius would once more attempt to subjugate the tribes of Britain.

But the time between Caesar's withdrawal in 54 BC and the Roman return in AD 43 was not a dark age for islanders. From the top of what is now Scotland south to the Kent coast there were more than twenty large tribes. Some of the names became famous: the Iceni in East Anglia, the Catuvellauni in the East Midlands and Essex, the Parisi in Yorkshire, the Silures in Wales and the Brigantes, probably in the Pennines. Strabo, writing in the first-century BC in the fourth of his seventeen-volume *Geographica*, tells us that the Britons exported cattle, hides, grain, slaves, gold and silver and, apparently, hunting dogs. In return, they imported wine and oil and glass. And most of this trade was with the prosperous South-East. So, even 2,000 years ago, there was a north-south divide in Britain.

Some ninety years after Julius Caesar's departure, the Emperor Claudius was persuaded by an exiled Briton that it would be politically to his advantage to return to Britain. His name was Bericus. This was nearly a century after Caesar's campaigns – seen as triumphs. Yet if ever there were to be an example of how the British Isles were believed to be on the edge of the world and mysteriously dangerous then, at about the time of Christ, the proposed invasion showed this ignorance and fear. Plautius was ordered to prepare and execute the invasion of Britain from his base in Gaul, France. Cassius Dio, in his early third-century AD version of Roman history, describes what happened: 'Plautius undertook this campaign, but had difficulty in inducing his army to advance beyond Gaul, for the soldiers were indignant at the thought of carrying on a campaign outside the limits of the known world and would not yield in obedience.'

Even after 100 years and much trading beyond their shores, these islands were still at the edge of the 'known' world. But the Romans invaded once more and this time they found that the Britons weren't expecting them. Tacitus wrote that although the Britons had many military strengths, they were not a cohesive force:

> Once they owed obedience to kings; now they are distracted between the warring factions of rival chiefs. Indeed nothing has helped us more in fighting against their very powerful nations than their inability to co-operate [with each other]. It is but seldom that two or three states unite to repel a common danger; thus, fighting in separate groups, all are conquered.

But the Britons did fight back in a way that Churchill might have applauded men when another darkest hour had been reached. They had learned there was little point in taking on the Romans at their own game. Instead, they hid in the forests and the swamps. Cassius Dio suggests that the resistance was not long lived.

Plautius had a great deal of trouble searching them out; but when at last he did find them, he first defeated Caratacus and then Togodumnus . . . After the fight of these kings, he advanced father and came to a river. The barbarians thought that the Romans would not be able to cross it without a bridge and bivouacked in rather careless fashion on the opposite bank; but he [Plautius] sent across a detachment of Germans who were accustomed to swim easily in full armour.

The following year it was safe for the emperor, Claudius to cross the Channel and join the Roman legions on the banks of the Thames and so (with elephants) lead the victory – with all that meant in Rome.

Taking command, and enjoining the barbarians who were gathered at his approach, he defeated them in battle and captured Camulodunum [Colchester], the capital of Cynobellinus. He deprived the conquered of their arms [took the surrender] and handed them to Plautius, bidding him also subjugate the remaining districts. Claudius now hastened back to Rome sending ahead news of his victory. The Senate on hearing of his achievement gave him the title Britannicus and granted him permission to celebrate a triumph.

But back in Britain Caratacus (sometimes Caractacus) resisted and as Tacitus wrote, Caratacus had become a hero and not just among his own people: 'His reputation had gone beyond the islands, had spread over the nearest provinces, and was familiar in Italy itself where the curiosity to see what manner of man it was that had for so many years scorned our power.' He had resisted the might of Roman power for six years, hiding in the Welsh borders and may have succeeded if it had not been for British treachery. He was not defeated by Ostorius (the successor to Plautius) but handed over to him by the queen of the northern tribe, the Brigantes. Also, the Romans saw this man as the fierce warrior from the furthest point in their known world. That alone made him a figure of much curiosity.

While the king's humble vassals filed past, ornaments and neck rings and prizes won in his foreign wars were borne in parade; next his brothers, wife and daughter were placed on view; finally, he himself. The rest stooped to unworthy entreaties dictated by fear; but on the part of Caratacus not a downcast look nor a word requested pity.

Arrived at the tribunal, he spoke as follows: 'Had my lineage and my rank been matched by my moderation in success, I should have entered this city rather as a friend than as a captive. My present lot, if to me a degradation, is to you a glory. If I were dragged before you after surrendering without a blow, there would have been little heard either of my fall or your triumph; punishment of me will be followed by oblivion; but save me alive, and I shall be an everlasting memorial to your clemency.'

And so he was. Caratacus was freed. The Romans struck his chains and those of his family but he was not to return to Britain. Caratacus, or so the chronicles tell us, remained in honourable captivity. That was hardly the end of the story of that invasion. The most gruesome slaughter and the conquest were yet to come.

The centre of Roman Britain was Camulodunum (Colchester). The idea was that Britain, or at least part of it, should become a province within the Roman Empire. But this was difficult to achieve. The Britons were warlike and because there were some twenty-three tribal regions, it was impossible to get overall agreement, or even an understanding, with more than a few of them. The south and the east were the most easily controllable. The Romans had large forces there, they had set up their capital at Colchester and there were good trade routes through Essex and Kent. The uplands of Britain presented a bigger problem. In AD 54 Claudius died and his stepson, Nero became emperor. The death of another leader, this one in Britain, left a longer lasting impression upon British history and folklore. Her name was Boudicca and she was the widow of the King of the Iceni in East Anglia. Boudicca had been flogged and abused, as had her daughters, by the Romans. She and her tribe sought terrible revenge for this outrage.

The Romans had no more than 20,000 men in Britain in four legions: two were thirty days' march away on the farther side of Wales, one was not much closer in Gloucester and the last was 120 miles away, at Lincoln. Boudicca led her warriors through East Anglia to the capital at Colchester. They attacked with uncompromising fury and massacred every Roman and every person in the pay or appropriating the style of the Roman occupation. None was spared. Word had been sent to Lincoln where the Roman Ninth Legion was in camp. Their commander, Petilius Cerialis, saddled his cavalry but could only move south at the pace of his infantry. Boudicca, still covered in blood from her gruesome work at Colchester, set out to meet the Ninth Legion and fell upon the infantry. The Romans were slaughtered. Cerialis escaped with his cavalry. But when the Roman, Suetonius, whose job it was to defend London and its people, heard that Boudicca had cut down the Ninth Legion and Cerialis was in flight and was now heading south to what would one day be Britain's capital, he abandoned London. Boudicca carried on and found London empty of troops and so her warriors butchered anyone they found. They next turned their vengeance on St Albans, then called Verulamium. No quarter was shown. The simplicity of the thirty-five words of Tacitus tells everything: 'They wasted no time in getting down to the bloody business of hanging, burning and crucifying. It was as if they feared that retribution might catch up with them while their vengeance was only half-complete.'

But for the Romans, and the reputation of Suetonius, all was not lost. Reinforced, he marched to the Midlands where Boudicca had amassed 230,000 troops. Suetonius had 10,000 Romans. That number would be sufficient because at last the Romans were fighting in their own style, not Boudicca's. She had been successful when her tribesmen fought as marauders and terrorists. Now, Boudicca was to fight on Roman terms, which was a foolish mistake. The Romans were at the top of a slope and they enticed the Britons on. When they came, the Romans launched their javelins, then charged with their legionaries and cavalry, then forced the Britons back on their carts and their families who were behind them. They slaughtered the cart horses so there was no escape and then massacred the Britons, the ancients, their women, their children. As for Boudicca, she was finished and could expect no sweet charity and wanted none. She is said to have poisoned herself. Her surviving followers were cut down and Nero sent extra troops across the Channel to terrorize the other tribes. The vengeance of Boudicca had unsettled the Romans so that they now took no chances. Dead Britons were relatively less dangerous. Their grieving kith and kin were philosophical in the aftermath of sword and fire.

Diplomacy took over where military action had not always maintained the peace and the south never again rose against the Romans. There were battles to come, men to die and there were those Britons who preferred death to subjugation. But it was also true that Britain had embarked upon a civilized way of life that lasted for 350 years. The Romans ruled Britain for nearly 400 years and they gave the Britons their first written historical descriptions. They recorded their versions of what was happening and the names of people who were making it happen. But when the Romans started to leave Britain in AD 410 – recalled to defend Rome – many of those who could write went with them, as did the imperial incentive to keep records, and so there are few contemporary written accounts of what was going on in Britain for many years.

Exactly what followed the Roman exodus is very difficult to verify. There is a long period in the history of these islands that can never be accurately written. Instead we rely on, for example, a sixth-century monk called Gildas the Wise.[7] Most of what he wrote was a religious tract, but in it there is at least a sense of the story of this period. Gildas suggests that the Anglo-Saxons began arriving in the 470s because they were imported as mercenaries and that other mercenaries were bought to defend against them. Gildas tells us it was a time of misery and of the rising of a great tyrant, who was probably Vortigern – although Gildas did not name him. Vortigern was on the side of the Britons. He hired mercenaries to defend the Britons against the Anglo-Saxons who were led by Hengist and Horsa. There was a great victory at a place called Mons Badonicus. Gildas felt this victory was important because it brought peace for perhaps half a century.

> Then all the councillors, together with that proud tyrant Gurthrigern [Vortigern], the British king, were so blinded, that, as a protection to their country, they sealed its doom by inviting in among them the fierce and impious Saxons, a race hateful both to God and men, to repel the invasions of the northern nations . . . What palpable darkness must have enveloped their minds – darkness desperate and cruel! Those very people whom, when absent, they dreaded more than death itself, were invited to reside, as one may say, under the selfsame roof. Foolish are the princes, as it is said, of Thafneos, giving counsel to unwise Pharaoh. A multitude of whelps came forth from the lair of this barbaric lioness, in three cyuls, as they call them, that is, in three

---

7   Gildas Badonicus, a Celtic monk writing in the 540s to denounce the wickedness of his times.

ships of war, with their sails wafted by the wind and with omens and prophecies favourable, for it was foretold by a certain soothsayer among them, that they should occupy the country to which they were sailing three hundred years, and half of that time, a hundred and fifty years, should plunder and despoil the same. They first landed on the eastern side of the island, by the invitation of the unlucky king, and there fixed their sharp talons, apparently to fight in favour of the island, but alas! more truly against it. Their motherland, finding her first brood thus successful, sends forth a larger company of her wolf-ish offspring, which sailing over, join themselves to their bastard-born comrades. From that time the germ of iniquity and the root of conten-tion planted their poison amongst us, as we deserved, and shot forth into leaves and branches.[8]

All England, it would have appeared, was leaves and branches. In this period, the middle of the fifth century, there were great forests almost everywhere. The Weald at that time ran from Kent to Hampshire: 120 miles long and 30 miles deep. Where there wasn't forest, there were often marshlands. There were roads, almost 5,000 miles of them, left by the Romans yet the towns were crumbling. It would be called urban decay today and it had started before the Romans left. The Britons, and the Saxon invaders, were rarely stone masons; they left no record of knowing much about repairing the buildings and cared even less. The great Saxon churches, many surviving today, came much later.

If we have doubts about Gildas, we have fewer doubts about the importance of the clues to this period found in *The Anglo-Saxon Chronicle* and the *Historia Ecclesiastica Gentis Anglorum, The Ecclesiastical History of the English People* by the Venerable Bede – the first British historian. Here, and among archaeological records, are found the few traces of Saxon heritage and the names that make up the history of these islands: Hengist, Horsa, Penda, Æthelberht slaughtered by Offa, St Augustine, Eric Bloodaxe, Edward the Confessor, his son Harold and, the greatest mystery of all Saxon history, King Arthur and Camelot. If we have an ounce of romantic history then, along with Robin Hood, Arthur is the one we really want to believe in. There was a warrior king, or chieftain, who did

8   J. A. Giles (ed.), *Six Old English Chronicles* (London: Henry G. Bohn, 1848).

great deeds but no one is quite sure who he was. In the fifth century mercenaries came from northern Europe, supposedly to help the Britons. But they started to help themselves to Britain. Later, according to, among others, the ninth-century Welsh scholar Nennius, they were sent packing. And Arthurian hopefuls would say that it may have been Arthur who defeated them. He is found in early bardic literature collectively called *Mabinogion* and developed in the late twelfth-century romances of Chrétien de Troyes – he gave us Lancelot. Writers usually relied upon hearsay. Even if Arthur was a minor king who fought twelve battles that defeated the barbarians, it may not have been so important in sixth-century Britain. In a country which accepted raiding, violence and its dreadful consequences as a matter of course, twelve battles over a couple of years would not have been remarkable.

According to Nennius, who was writing *c*.830 (see the *Historia Brittonium*), Arthur's last battle took place on Mount Badon and although its location remains unknown, by cross-checking other events, including the birthdays and the deaths of chroniclers, it seems that this final – the twelfth – battle took place between 490 and 503. So hopefully for Arthurians, a mighty knight did live and fight towards the end of the fifth century who defeated invaders and was seen as a chivalrous saviour.

The Venerable Bede (673–735), an altogether more reliable chronicler, provides an exact date for another figure of the time, Columba, in his *Historia Ecclesiastica*.

> In the year of our Lord 565, there came into Britain a famous priest and abbot, a monk by habit and life, whose name was Colomba, to preach the word of God to the provinces of the northern Picts; who are separated from the southern parts by steep and rugged mountains.

Bede's steep and rugged mountains are the Grampians and Columba was sent to convert those who lived to the north of them. It seems that the southerners had already been converted by a Briton, Bishop Ninian, who had learned his theology in Rome. Columba's arrival coincided with the beginnings of what became the Ionan community. Bede is quite certain of Columba's origin.

Columba came into Britain in the ninth year of the reign of Bridus [accession 557 according to Bede],[9] who was the son of Meilochon, and the powerful king of the Pictish nation, and he converted the nation to the faith of Christ, by his preaching and example. It is true they followed uncertain rules in their observance of the great festival [Easter], wherefore they only practised such works as piety and chastity as they could learn from the prophetical, evangelical, and apostolical writings. The manner of keeping Easter continued among them for the space of 150 years, till the year of our Lord's incarnation 715.

So a carefully crafted journal gives us the dates of a Scottish king: Bride (Bridius), the son of Meilochon. Ninian and Columba measured men in their God's image and there were none who could not be saved and Easter, whether or not it was celebrated according to synodical decree, was the most important event in their year and preached forgiveness of sins. Perhaps there was spiritual and temporal fairness abroad in these islands but there was wickedness and violence too. There was also a new conflict that would end, once more, with the defeat of the Britons. This time, the English, who did not come from England, would be the victors.

---

9   See also *Life of Saint Columba* by Abbot Adomnán (627–704).

CHAPTER TWO
570–886

E nglish is the most common international language of the twenty-first century. It remains a living language whose origins tell us so much about the earliest years of our identity. Equally, discovering the story of those early years is made complicated by the unfamiliar styling of what became common English and the context in which it might have been used – and therefore its sometimes obscure meaning. So when thinking of the Venerable Bede, we have to see how difficult it is for some of us to read the English words. But were they English? Also, what clue does the language or the dialect give us to the make-up of the peoples of these islands during this important period after the Romans and before the Normans?

To judge a nation from a collection of societies it is useful to turn to the list of languages spoken in that 'country'. So it is with our story of the early Middle Ages. We would like to see if there are clues to modern English which has more words than any other language and is the second most spoken language in the world (three-quarters of letters are addressed in English). In Bede's seventh- and eighth-century England this was far from so. The earliest language that we know about in the British Isles was Celtic. That does not mean that all of the people in these islands spoke Celtic. Certainly the northern (Scottish and Cumbrian) and western (Irish, Welsh and Cornish) peoples have spoken Celtic or Celtic dialogues for 2,000 years. Surviving inscriptions suggest this is so. Clearly, a form of Celtic may have been spoken more broadly across the whole of the British Isles, but with the arrival of the German tribes during the fifth century, many if not most of those Celts were pressed further and further to the west until the Celts and their language survived only in the far west – Wales, Cornwall, the north-west (Cumbria), Ireland and Scotland. After the fifth century, there is not much evidence that Celtic was a strong language in the rest of England. Then what replaced it?

The Jutes, the Angles and the Saxons crossed into England during the fifth century. Because they overpowered the indigenous population, their languages survived and were used wherever they settled and ruled. Because the Angles came from Engle and because these Germanic people were the dominant invaders of the time, their language was adopted more easily. It was called Engllisc, and so English. The obvious geographical connection with the Angles today is East Anglia. The realm (if that is not too grand a title) of the East Angles was established by bringing together the 'north fulk' and the 'suth fulk'; this was between AD 550 and AD 600, about 150 years after the Roman armies had been recalled from Britain to defend Rome. It was not virgin soil upturned or grazed. The Saxons were in what are now the eastern counties before the arrival of the Angles; they were there with the Romans and existed by an understanding and sometimes by treaty or covenant (Latin: *foedus*) who were expected to respond to a Roman call to arms. A tribe that had this responsibility (and the protection of the Romans) was known as a Foederatus. From this and its Latin root we get the modern word federation. We also see the origin of feudal (*feodum* – fee). Is this important to an understanding of the British? The answer must be yes because we then begin to see something of our origins that we can identify in the twenty-first century.

Language always suggests that the group (not necessarily a nation) speaking that language dominates a region and, importantly, shows us what influences press themselves on that group. So when we come to English, we have to think in terms of Old English, Middle English and Modern English. When we see where (roughly) these groups start, then we can also recognize some of the man influences on our ancestors.

Celtic was spoken in parts of these islands before the Romans arrived. Celtic did not survive as a dominant language because the people who spoke it did not survive in sufficient numbers to dominate the islands and all the people. Old English had its origins in the Indo-European languages that produced the mixture of Germanic dialects and languages. So we start with the thought that Old English did not appear from tribal languages already in the British Isles but from the invasions and migrations from Continental Europe. That language, Old

English, was spoken and, importantly, written by about AD 700. But there was not one language. There were four main dialects: Kentish, Mercian, Northumbrian and, perhaps most interestingly, West-Saxon. Old English is sometimes referred to as Anglo-Saxon and early West-Saxon was the language that would have been used by Alfred the Great (849–99). Alfred was a great warrior but we should not forget that he was a considerable scholar. During times that his sword was still, Alfred translated Latin texts including those of Bede and particularly *Liber Regulae Pastoralis* ('Pastoral Care' or 'Pastoral Rule'), written by Pope Gregory the Great sometime in the 590s. Maybe this scholarly reputation is one – if not the main – reason that West-Saxon became the regular form of written language of that period.

The written word was not set in linguistic stone. The very fact that there are traces that Angles settled in the 470s in the once Roman stronghold of Caerwent (Venta Silurum) suggests that the language even at this stage was mixing dialects and origins that were Celtic and Roman, as well as the Germanic tongues. There are fifth-century Anglo-Saxon inscriptions that give an idea of the style of language and the regional variations. Up to the ninth-century invasions of the Vikings the Northumbrian dialects dominated English culture. Within another hundred years West-Saxon English, both written and spoken, seems to have become the official language of the islands although dialects did not disappear and use of the Scandinavian alphabet, the Runic or Younger Futhark, dates from *c*.AD 750 to 1500. By the time of the Battle of Hastings (1066) Old English was a mix of Anglo-Saxon, Norse, Danish and Latin. In fact, when English exasperates non-English speakers because of the same word having slightly different meanings, then the inconvenience may be traced to this early, Old English concoction. With the Norman Invasion and the introduction of Norman French, the language became more complex. Some Germanic plurals survived (e.g. feet, teeth) but the French style of adding an 's' for a plural was to dominate and, of course, further confuse with, for example, the French 'qu' replacing 'cw' and so on. Thus, with such a collection of dialects and languages, by the time of the Norman invasion the die was cast that one day (as now) English would become the language with the biggest vocabulary in the world.

With the invasion, Norman French became the language of the court and cultured classes, and this remained so for 150 years. In fact, Henry IV (1367–1413) was the first monarch of England since the Conquest whose first language was English. By then Old English (c.700–c.1066) had become Middle English and the dialect of Chaucer *et al.*, spoken in and about the capital, London, had replaced West-Saxon as the 'official' language. By Shakespeare's time (he invented some 1,600 words) Middle English was giving way to what we would more easily recognize as Modern English. The great periods of exploration and global reconnaissance culminating in the 1700s meant that Modern English was taking in words from all over the world to such an extent that it is difficult to imagine a sentence uttered today on any subject that does not include a couple of words with foreign origins. Moreover, the common language that we saw at the start of this chapter, with its origins in the tongues of invaders, did not remain in these islands. Apart from Chinese, more people speak, write and officially communicate in English than any other language. Equally, spot the number of words in that sentence with foreign origins. Even Bede had no 'pure' form of his language.

The Venerable Bede was taken into a monastery in Jarrow in the late seventh century, probably just before his tenth birthday, and it was in this monastery in the north-east of Britain that he wrote that book on which much of our knowledge of early England relies: the aforementioned *Historia Ecclesiastica Gentis Anglorum* or *The Ecclesiastical History of the English People*.

In the year 449, Marcian being made emperor with Valentinian, ruled the empire for seven years. The nation of the Angles, or Saxons, being invited by the aforesaid king, arrived in Britain . . . those who came over were of the three most powerful nations of Germany: Saxons, Angles, and Jutes. From the Jutes are descended the people of Kent and the Isle of Wight, and those in the province of the West-Saxons who are to this day called Jutes, seated opposite the Isle of Wight. From the Saxons, that is the country which is now called Old Saxony, came the East-Saxons, the South-Saxons and West-Saxons. From the Angles, that is the country which is called Anglia, are descended the East-Angles, the Middle-Angles, the Mercians, all the races of the Northumbrians, that is, of those nations that dwell on the north side of the river Humber, and the other nations of the English. The first two commanders are said to have been Hengist and Horsa.

According to Bede, Ælle was the 'bretwalda', or ruler, of Britain. 'Bret' means Britain; 'Walda' means ruler. So Ælle was the first of seven kings who claimed the kingdoms south of the Humber, probably in the final quarter of the fifth century. The concept of kings and kingdoms was not new, but from whence came the migrant warriors, there were no kings. These same warriors in England claimed heritage from fantastical gods and gradually by wealth or success in battle or both they attracted the finest followers. But how would these men at arms be rewarded? The kings had no money so they promised or gave the only honour and reward they could: land. By sword they could take land or if there was no need to take it, then they could declare it in the king's name. That land they gave to the loyalist, bravest and most reliable followers. Here we have the seeds of what we now call the landed gentry – mighty men, close to the monarch with titles to land given by the monarch. Everything those men had, including their titles and positions, were owed to the monarch. Here were the beginnings of aristocracy as we know it today. But there was more than one king because, geographically, there had to be. There were limitations on the way fifth- and sixth-century people could travel. Also, no one now had an army that could be structured to subjugate the whole island race and the Saxons were migrating, not enlarging an existing empire. Nevertheless, it is warfare that propels nations, however fragmented. And it was war in the year 577 that expanded the hold of the Saxons over the defending Britons.

In the 570s and 580s, the southern Britons had been subjugated by the English – those who lived in the southern counties as they are now called – who made up the Sutangli, or Southern Angles, or Southern English. And this north–south divide affected the history of this island race. As the historian, Sir Frank Stenton, points out, 'From the age of the migrations down to the Danish wars of the ninth century, the peoples south of the Humber were normally subject to the authority of a common overlord.' The term 'common overlord' means that different parts were ruled by a sort of underlord or lesser king. Here we have an idea of the development of British rule and ruled: kingship. In return for allegiance, the king would give and protect so it was hardly fanciful that the Pope understood what was happening in this once provincial holding of Rome.

The Anglo-Saxon Chronicle tells us that in the year 595, 'Pope Gregory sent Augustine to Britain with very many monks who preached God's word to the English nation.' But they were nervous. They thought the land of the Britons thoroughly barbarous and that none of their lives would be spared. They were still on the other side of the Channel when Augustine and his evangelists decided to go no further. But Pope Gregory wrote to Augustine and his brethren.

> Gregory, the servant of the servants of God, to the servants of our Lord. For as much as it had been better not to begin a good work than to think of desisting from that which has been begun, it behoves you, my beloved sons, to fulfil the good work which by the help of our Lord, you have undertaken. Let not, therefore, the toil of the journey nor the tongues of evil speaking men, deter you; but with all possible earnestness and zeal perform that which, by God's direction you have undertaken; God keep you in safety my most beloved sons.

Pope Gregory's letter worked. Augustine and his nervous monks trudged on and eventually crossed to the Isle of Thanet. But what they needed was protection and that could only come from the local king. The king was Æthelberht. 'Æthel' means, more or less, nobly born. Æthelberht was not a Christian. We would not expect him to have been. He worshipped Thor, the god of thunder. He had thought of converting, not because he felt any spiritual need, but for a political reason. His wife, a Frankish princess, whose name was Bertha, was a Christian. Kent, recognized by the Romans as the most civilized part of the land of the Britons, was the one place where a Christian revival would be most likely to take hold. Æthelberht sensed that it might not be such a bad idea to go with the mood of the people. And so Æthelberht became the first 'English' king to convert to Christianity. For Augustine it was, perhaps, a heaven-sent opportunity. It was not wasted. He converted Æthelberht (Ethelbert) who was overlord (not king) of the southern regions that extended to the West Country. By conversion, Æthelberht hoped to use that influence with other converted chiefs to extend his lordship over more of England. There was no king of England at this time.

To consolidate his position, in fact both their positions, Æthelberht and Augustine called a conference of the Christian bishops. It was doomed from the start, partly because the bishops did not like to be told what to and especially because Augustine displayed a tactless self-assurance, maybe arrogance. There was a second conference. It failed as the first had. Worse than that, the gathering broke up with Augustine threatening war and making sure that the lot of Rome would be thrown behind Æthelberht and the English. Of course, there was no war. It was never likely, but Augustine achieved the development of Christian belief in these islands. And he began training a clergy who would go out and achieve many of the things that this arrogant messenger from Rome had hoped for himself. As to some extent heathenism declined and Christianity prospered there rose the question of whose version of Christianity should rule – Augustine's or the northern Celtic. The issues were quite basic: how should Easter be observed? Should the tonsure – a symbol of church doctrine – be worn? It was symbolism that would continue in other regions – including 500 years later in Ireland – where the Catholic Church as then it was felt its authority threatened.

In today's world of headlines and superlatives, the matter of the tonsure would be described as splitting public opinion. In the seventh-century British Isles, the issue was one of authority rather than for the people. Authority at that time was the king, the bret-walda, of the East Angles, Redwald. We know little of Redwald other than he was the son Tytila and died in or about 627 and may have been the bretwalda in the Sutton Hoo ship-burial. It is also thought that he killed Æthelfrid, bretwalda of Northumbria, in 616 and so returned the throne to Edwin (616–32). Edwin was the over-lord of the realm of England with the exception of Kent and so the mightiest king the region had seen. It was Edwin's generalship and persuasion that set the map that was to become England and over which the Wessex kings would one day rule. There is a further aspect of Edwin's rule that we should note: he was an atheist but he married a Christian princess from Kent. When his princess left Canterbury for York, there travelled with her Paulinus who, by making that journey, would become the first missionary of Rome to northern England. Edwin worshipped idols. That meant he had courtiers, henchmen and priests who did the same. Paulinus converted Edwin – or at least he baptized him. However, for the King to say, 'I give my life to Christ', is one thing; to carry with him these vital allies towards a religion that was relatively new in the kingdom was not only an act of faith, in early England it was also a political decision. He had to carry his realm with him. And that's exactly what he did.

The other princes and bretwaldas did not send cards. After all, Edwin's new alliance with Kent was a destabilizing factor in the fierce world of tribal and national politics. For example, in 633 Penda, the heathen King of Mercia, connived an alliance with Cadwallon of north Wales (himself a declared Christian). The task was to unseat Edwin and the increasingly powerful kingdom of Northumbria. Penda may have had little in religious common with Cadwallon, but they had similar interests towards Edwin. At a treacherous battle of Doncaster, the mighty Edwin was slain and his head displayed above the ramparts of York. The Christian and Saxon warriors mourned Edwin and wished fury brought down on his killers. Oswald became leader of the Christian warriors. In just twelve months he had marched on and destroyed Cadwallon in what would become the last battle between Saxons and Britons.

In these times, there were no deciding battles – only settled scores. The fundamental issues were about Christianity and which version to adopt persisted. And, at this time in the island's history, any prolonging of differences could mean war. What might be done to settle, not military outrages, but matters of high faith and constitutional (in seventh-century terms) ambitions? The answer was the Synod of Whitby in 663. The question put was simplicity itself: should what had become the British version of Christianity follow what we may now call Rome, or should the expression of Christianity be found in the monastic orders in these islands? All matters religious are, and have been, a collection of compromises. The Church of Northumbria was to follow Rome. It was inevitable that Mercia would follow suit as the kings of Mercia now ruled England south of the Humber (as opposed to north of the Humber – Northumbria). That is how it remained for eighty years.

Æthelbald, King of Mercia from 716, called himself 'rex Britanniae', which was the Latin for the Saxon English title, bretwalda, ruler of Britain. But this wasn't an idle boast. *The Anglo-Saxon Chronicle* tells us that he was fighting, and winning, as far away as Somerton in Somerset. That meant that Æthelbald controlled a huge chunk of Wessex. One indication of that control was that he could buy and sell land as he wished. He was the strongest figure in southern Britain. In spite of his confessions of faith, he was barbaric and everyone, including the Church, knew that and could do little about it. No other king had ruled so masterfully and for so long. But then it came to an end. In 757, after forty-one years on his throne, Æthelbald was murdered by his own bodyguard. The result was a civil war in the Midlands. It didn't last a full year and when it was done the new king of the Mercians was Offa (750?–96), one of the most famous names of this period and a contemporary of Charlemagne (741–814).

Charlemagne was the most celebrated of the Frankish rulers. The Franks were the post-Roman barbarians of what we now know as Belgium, France, Germany, the Netherlands and Switzerland. It was Charlemagne who inspired the rethinking of kingship, whereby in return for allegiance the leader protects those who follow him or her. His extension of this thought was better called the right to rule. It was his belief that the monarch could not rule by half measure and therefore should rule both his State and the Church within that State. Here was the basis for the contest between State and Church that would continue long after his empire's passing. Although barbaric and indeed largely illiterate, Charlemagne inspired learning and such a close relationship with Rome that, on Christmas Day 800, Pope Leo III crowned Charlemagne emperor of what would become the Holy Roman Empire. Given that Leo III had called for Charlemagne's help the previous year when he was in danger of being usurped, the coronation was the least gift of the Holy Father. Given the power and the uncompromising ambition of Charlemagne, the relationship with the king of the English (not of England) tells us much about the importance of Offa. Charlemagne had wanted one of his sons to marry one of the daughters of Offa. Offa's reaction was that the process of diplomatic relations had to be two-way. If he was to take Charlemagne's son as an in-law, then one his Offa's sons should marry one of Charlemagne's daughters. If this seems petty diplomacy, it was not. The marriage of sons and daughters among monarchs was a powerful symbol of diplomatic relations if not lasting unity.

Offa could not live in peace; few monarchs of any sort did. After all, he came by the throne because his predecessor, his cousin Æthelbald, was murdered. Symeon of Durham, albeit writing in the early twelfth century, noted in his *Historia Regum* that in 771, Offa 'subdued by arms the people of the Hestingi'. Hestingi was modern Hastings and the final battle in that bloody campaign against the

Hestingi took place at Otford close by what is modern Sevenoaks. Offa's power certainly spread beyond these island shores even if they were less recognized north of the Humber. Also, we must remember that Offa was of the time when declarations of religious faith had more than pious symbolism: he saw himself as the defender of the faith. And it was here that a single incident that marked Offa as particularly relevant to our history occurred. Offa had his son anointed as King of Mercia and consecrated – this was probably the first time that an English king had been consecrated and, therefore, it was the moment that marked a religious dimension to the English throne.

Offa remains famous for one great work, his earthwork: the dyke. His battles against the Welsh eventually claimed parts of Powys and it was to build an obvious and presumably recognizable (to both Welsh and English) border that Offa constructed his monument. Yet we should recognize the force of this monarch who held Mercian power throughout south England and certainly had a direct influence in the northern parts. Moreover, we can tell something of Offa's reputation beyond the British shores when we remember that Pope Adrian I described Offa as the King of the English – not of England as a land or State, but of the people. Also, Offa negotiated treaties on equal terms with Charlemagne who would become emperor. Therefore Offa's reputation must go far beyond the creation of a dyke.

By AD 796 Offa was dead and the Vikings were about to arrive. The Romans had begun to leave early in the fifth century and the Angles, the Jutes and the Saxons together became the English after the Romans left. At the end of the 700s the Vikings arrived from Scandinavia: the Swedes, Norwegians and Danes. Imagine for a moment the confusion of their arrival. There was not huge invasion – just three vessels. Their purpose, we should think, would be apparent. But three ships? Surely they had no strength in numbers nor evil purpose. There were too few for that. The reeve (sheriff) should have been confused. What was he expected to think of these strangers? *The Anglo-Saxon Chronicle* tells us – and what happened next. The year was AD 789.

In this year Beorhtric took to wife Eadburh, daughter of King Offa. And in his days came first three ships of Norwegians from Horthaland; and then the reeve rode hither and tried to compel them to go to the royal manor, for he did not know what they were: and then they slew him. These were the first ships of the Danes to come to England.

The Vikings arrived first at Portland in Dorset. They killed many and then withdrew. A small incident, but important to the inhabitants of these islands: this landing and these murders were the beginnings of the age of the Vikings. They returned in 793, as *The Anglo-Saxon Chronicle* records:

> In this year terrible portents appeared over Northumbria and miser- ably frightened the people there; these were exceptionally high winds and flashes of lightning and fiery dragons were seen flying in the air. A great famine soon followed these signs; and a little after that in the same year on the eighth day of January the harrying of the heathen miserably destroyed God's church in Lindisfarne.

When more raiders arrived not so far away at Jarrow the following year, the locals were ready for them. Those they captured they put to terrible and agonizing death so that the raiders who escaped took home to Denmark the story of vicious and uncompromising island- ers. But these were vicious and uncompromising times. This was probably a small group from a much larger fleet of long ships. They sailed on to the north of Scotland and landed. They set up encamp- ments in Caithness and Sutherland, in the Orkneys and Shetland. They went on to Ireland and eventually conquered a small commun- ity and it is thought that their Viking king, Olaf, founded what is now called Dublin.

In AD 865 the great invasion of the east coast of England started. And the pickings were great. England was proud of its Christianity and the Church had thrived. The people believed that all they had to do was to pay for the absolution of their many sins. And pay they did. So in the churches and monasteries were stored great treasures and the Vikings were delighted. None more so than Ivar Ragnarsson, known as Ivar the Boneless, so named because he may have suffered from a form of osteogenesis imperfecta.[1] There is no sure way to confirm this. If it seems unlikely that a warrior of such bloodthirsty

---

1   Frank. R. Donovan (author), Sir Thomas D. Kendrick (consultant), *The Vikings* (New York, NY: Horizon Caravel Books, 1964), 44–5.

fame would suffer from something akin to brittle bone disease, then that is reason to doubt his condition. However, this reason for his name has persisted.[2] His father was Ragnar Lodbrok, who was captured by Ælla, the King of Northumbria, and thrown into a pit of poisonous adders to die. When the four sons of Ragnar Lodbrok heard this, each swore the vengeance known as Blood-Red Eagle. The killer of their father should be captured, his flesh and ribs cut and turned back so that the avenging son could tear out the living lungs – or so legend has it. However, whatever its form, no son took this oath of revenge more seriously than Ivar the Boneless.

More importantly to our story, the defeat of Ælla at York in 866 and all that followed marked the end of the kingdom of Northumbria as the dominant regional power. Although in later times, the Percy family would hold the fortunes of the monarchy and the State in its hands, after the 860s, northern England was never again so import-ant in the military and constitutional make-up of the British Isles. And what happened to the Boneless? It is not recorded with any certainty, but in the surviving fragments of the eleventh-century Middle Irish *Fragmentary Annals of Ireland*, it may be construed that Ivar the Boneless died in Dublin in 873. By that time, the English were celebrating one of the most famous leaders from these islands, Alfred the Great.

Alfred is an early monarch known by most people, few of whom are quite sure what he did apart from trying to keep the Danes at bay by paying them not to fight him – which is where the expression 'Danegeld' comes from – and supposedly being the founder of the British navy. And of course, Alfred burned the cakes. Much of what we know of Alfred comes from Asser's *Life of King Alfred*, written in 893. Asser was a Welsh monk from St David's who became Bishop of Sherborne (now in Dorset). He was an acolyte of Alfred's and employed to revive theological understanding in Wessex. Inevitably there are those who would question the authority and authorship of Asser's *Life of Alfred*, but for most it is accepted as a reasonable account of this famous monarch even though it sings his praises louder than some might. His graphic accounts of skirmishes

---

2   See also the Old Norse vernacular saga poem *Háttalykill*, attributed to Rögnvaldr Kali Kolsson of Orkney.

and battles (most battles were really skirmishes) are detailed and necessarily in praise of his king.

> In the year of our Lord's incarnation 849, was born Alfred, king of the Anglo-Saxons, at the royal village of Wanating [Wantage], in Berkshire, which country has its name from the wood of Berroc, where the box-tree grows most abundantly. His genealogy is traced in the following order. King Alfred was the son of king Ethelwulf, who was the son of Egbert, who was the son of Elmund, was the son of Eafa, who was the son of Eoppa, who the son of Ingild. Ingild, and Ina, the famous king of the West-Saxons, were two brothers. Ina went to Rome, and there ending this life honourably, entered the heavenly kingdom, to reign there for ever with Christ.

Alfred's life was committed to fighting and making peace if he could by paying off the Danish invaders. Before becoming king himself, he helped his brother Æthelred, King of Wessex, in his struggle against the Danes. Asser is quite certain of the mood of looting and pillaging led to slaughter and retribution:

> In the year of our Lord's incarnation 871, which was the twenty-third of king Alfred's life, the pagan army, of hateful memory, left the East-Angles, and entering the kingdom of the West-Saxons, came to the royal city, called Reading, situated on the south bank of the Thames, in the district called Berkshire; and there, on the third day after their arrival, their earls, with great part of the army, scoured the country for plunder, while the others made a rampart between the rivers Thames and Kennet on the right side of the same royal city. They were encountered by Ethelwulf, earl of Berkshire, with his men, at a place called Englefield; both sides fought bravely, and made long resistance. At length one of the pagan earls was slain, and the greater part of the army destroyed; upon which the rest saved themselves by flight, and the Christians gained the victory.

Feeling triumphant and not a little brave by their victory, Æthelred and his brother Alfred fell upon the Danes at Reading and gutted those they found outside the stronghold. But the Danes counter-attacked and the men of Wessex, Asser's Christians, broke ranks and turned tail.

Roused by this calamity, the Christians, in shame and indignation, within four days, assembled all their forces, and again encountered the pagan army at a place called Ashdune, which means the 'Hill of the Ash'. The pagans had divided themselves into two bodies, and began to prepare defences, for they had two kings and many earls, so they gave the middle part of the army to the two kings, and the other part to all their earls. Which the Christians perceiving, divided their army also into two troops, and also began to construct defences. But Alfred, as we have been told by those who were present, and would not tell an untruth, marched up promptly with his men to give them battle; for king Æthelred remained a long time in his tent in prayer, hearing the mass, and said that he would not leave it, till the priest had done, or abandon the divine protection for that of men. Now the Christians had determined that king Æthelred, with his men, should attack the two pagan kings, but that his brother Alfred, with his troops, should take the chance of war against the two earls. Things being so arranged, the king remained a long time in prayer, and the pagans came up rapidly to fight. Then Alfred, though possessing a subordinate authority, could no longer support the troops of the enemy, unless he retreated or charged upon them without waiting for his brother. At length he bravely led his troops against the hostile army, as they had before arranged, but without awaiting his brother's arrival; for he relied in the divine counsels, and forming his men into a dense phalanx, marched on at once to meet the foe. And when both armies had fought long and bravely, at last the pagans, by the divine judgment, were no longer able to bear the attacks of the Christians, and having lost great part of their army, took to a disgraceful flight. One of their two kings, and five earls were there slain, together with many thousand pagans, who fell on all sides, covering with their bodies the whole plain of Ashdune. The whole pagan army pursued its flight, not only until night but until the next day, even until they reached the stronghold from which they had sallied. The Christians followed, slaying all they could reach, until it became dark.

Shortly after Easter 871, Æthelred died and was buried at Wimborne Minster. Alfred was now king, but in miserable times. Within a month he was fighting the Danes just outside Salisbury, at Wilton. His losses were horrific. According to *The Anglo-Saxon Chronicle*, after that battle at Wilton there were at least nine major campaigns against the Vikings in the south. And, says the *Chronicle*, 'In the course of this year were slain nine earls and one king; and this year the West Saxons made peace with the host.'

Made peace? Alfred bought them off with the Danegeld. The Vikings moved for the winter to London and it is here that coins with the Danish king, Hafdan, on one side and the monogram of London on the other first appeared. The Vikings were intent on staying, if not in London, in England. But there was not going to be peace for the Saxons and the Danes. Certainly King Alfred didn't think so. *The Anglo-Saxon Chronicle* tells us that in 875 Alfred, 'sailed out to sea with a fleet and fought against seven ships' companies and captured one of them and put the others to flight'. But there was little long-term victory. His armies were dispersed and many in Wessex thought he had deserted them for France or even that he was dead. In fact Alfred, not yet 'The Great', was in hiding and reduced to foraging for food. And it is here that we come to Asser's version of the burning buns. It is now 878:

Alfred, king of the West-Saxons, with a few of his nobles, and certain soldiers and vassals, used to lead an unquiet life among the wood-lands of the country of Somerset, in great tribulation; for he had none of the necessaries of life, except what he could forage openly or stealthily, by frequent sallies, from the pagans, or even from the Christians who had submitted to the rule of the pagans.

But it happened on a certain day, that the countrywoman, wife of the cowherd, was preparing some loaves to bake, and the king, sitting at the hearth, made ready his bow and arrows and other warlike instruments. The unlucky woman espying the cakes burning at the fire, ran up to remove them, and rebuking the brave king, exclaimed:

Ca'sn thee mind the ke-aks, man, an' doossen zee 'em burn? I'm boun thee's eat 'em vast enough, az zoon az 'tiz the turn.

The blundering woman little thought that it was king Alfred, who had fought so many battles against the pagans, and gained so many victories over them.

But the Almighty not only granted to the same glorious king victories over his enemies, but also permitted him to be harassed by them, to be sunk down by adversities, and depressed by the low estate of his followers, to the end that he might learn that there is one Lord of all things, to whom every knee doth bow, and in whose hand are the hearts of kings; who puts down the mighty from their seat and exalteth the humble; who suffers his servants when they are elevated at the summit of prosperity to be touched by the rod of adversity, that in their humility they may not despair of God's mercy, and in their prosperity they may not boast of their honours, but may also know, to whom they owe all the things which they possess.

In today's terms, Alfred became a guerrilla fighter. And then came a massive and decisive engagement when Alfred gathered his Saxons together, filled with a new spirit.

The Danish army remained in camp at Chippenham for that summer of 878. Twelve months on they were gone to East Anglia. But a new Viking army sailed for England and camped at Fulham. By 886 the Danes dominated the high ground including the capital. Alfred and the West Saxons were emboldened. They marched on London slashing and slaying as they went. Into the city they marched, burning and slaughtering and took it from the invaders.

Alfred, King of the Anglo-Saxons, after the burning of the cities and the slaying of the people, honourably rebuilt the city of London and made it again habitable. He gave it into the custody of his son-in-law, Æthered, earl of Mercia, to which king all the Angles and Saxons, who before had been dispersed everywhere, or were in captivity with the pagans, voluntarily turned and submitted themselves to his dominion.

This date, 886, is important because for the first time London became the centre for resistance to England's enemies. It meant also that at this point Alfred could claim the title 'The Great'; he was the great leader, obeyed, with the exception of the Dane lands (see Chapter 3) by all the English-speaking peoples.

CHAPTER THREE
886–1065

A lfred the Great made an uneasy truce with the Vikings – or the Danes – in the late 800s, the last years of his life. The map of England, Scotland and Wales looked something like this: Wales was much as it is now. Wessex was a triangle with one corner in Land's End, another in North Foreland on the far Kent coast and the top corner on the north-west coast near Liverpool. In that corner is what was called English Mercia. The rest, including East Anglia, was Danish, known as Danelaw. Danelaw's northern boundary was a squiggly line from the North Sea coast, about thirty miles south of Durham, across to the Cumbrian coast. The cauldron of peace bought in bribes (Danegeld), inter-marriages and baptisms were about to boil over. However, the fire was lit, not in England, but on the Continent where the Viking raiders were at war and here the timing is sensitive to the impending death of the Viking king, Guthrum, who lived in England. In 878, Guthrum had been defeated by Alfred, but spared. What is more, Alfred had converted Guthrum to Christianity and was his godfather; there followed a sort of peace that was closer to a truce than a settlement for all time. Here, *The Anglo-Saxon Chronicle* notes that the era was about to end.

> And Guthrum, the northern king, whose baptismal name was Athelstan, passed away. In the year 892 the great host . . . went again from the kingdom of the East Franks westward to Boulogne and were there provided with ships, so that they crossed in one voyage, horses and all, and they came up into the mouth of the Lympne [pronounced Limn] with 250 ships. The river flows out from the forest; they rowed their ships up as far as the forest, four miles from the entrance to the estuary and there stormed a fort within the fen; occupying it were a

few peasants and it was half built. Then soon after this, Haesten came with eighty ships into the mouth of the Thames and made himself a fort at Milton Regis.

Milton Regis is still there, now a, suburb of Sittingbourne and there is no great forest. But back to the battle. Three points emerge. First, Alfred once again offered gold to the invaders. This was a common practice. It was partly common sense, a recognition that if gold could buy peace then why not buy it. Second, Alfred, having paid up and so delayed the attack, persuaded the Viking King, Haesten, to have his two young sons baptized. And third, King Alfred was, perhaps, in failing health because he gave way to a younger leader, Edward, his twenty-two-year-old son. Alfred also had an ally, the young Mercian prince, Æthelred. The Vikings, as expected, broke their oaths of peace and Edward and Æthelred prepared for battle.

Alfred's men chased the Danes, fought them near Aldershot and chased them again until they reached the Thames, across which the Danes escaped, for the moment. At Benfleet, they captured Haesten's wife and two sons. Alfred ordered their return, an act of clemency for which he was much criticized. And the Danes? They were free but instead of attempting to take English Mercia, they roamed and pillaged Wales before returning to the safety of East Anglia and then the Thames estuary. The long-term result was a stalemate. Thanks to earlier Viking successes, the Danes were always going to be able to rely on support in Northumbria and East Anglia. Alfred was never going to get any more support than he had. Peace was impossible. And so it was that Alfred's kingdom was still at war when he died, in 901 according to the monk Florence of Worcester (although the accepted date is 899).[1] Alfred had ruled for almost twenty-nine years. His son, Edward, succeeded him and this led to a split with his cousin Æthelwald, who turned to the Vikings of Northumberland for help. The Vikings were happy to oblige. In 902, Eric, their king, and Æthelwald headed south and attacked Wiltshire. When Edward in turn attacked the Danes in East Anglia he could hardly have anticipated that in spite of many of his men, especially those from Kent,

---

1   Florence of Worcester died in 1118. His *Chronicon ex Chronicus* is the earliest English chronicle from the time of the Creation. Much of the work is based on the writings of an Irish monk, Marianus Scotus (d.1082).

being butchered by the Danes, his cousin and the Danish king would be among the dead. The new King of the Danes, Guthrum II, made peace with the King of Wessex through a treaty in 886. True, the peace did not last long. When it broke in 910, it was to the detriment of any ambitions the Danes had of ruling more of England. At Tettenhall in Staffordshire, the Danes were vanquished so much so that the Danish lands of East Anglia and the English Midlands were at last vulnerable to the English soldiers.

At this point, we have to remind ourselves just how powerful were the Viking holdings in Britain. At about this time, 900, the south of England was Wessex. The Midlands stretched from the course of the Thames north-westerly to the coast at about what is now Liverpool. This Midlands region was called Mercia. Only the western part of Mercia was English territory. Moreover, the rest of England – Cambridgeshire, East Anglia, Lincolnshire, Nottinghamshire, Derbyshire, the whole of Yorkshire and Lancashire, Cumbria, Durham and Northumberland, in our geographical terms – was all the so-called Viking Conquests.

The Mercians were ruled not by kings but by ealdormen, from the Old English 'Elder Man', a term that had all but disappeared by the eleventh century when it developed from the same root into the altogether more important title 'eorl', which was eventually earl. The ealdormen openly acknowledged King Edward of Wessex as their liege. When Alfred died and Edward became king, the Ealdorman of Mercia was Æthelred. He had married Alfred's first child, (and so Edward's sister) Æthelflaed. She had inherited the Alfredian Wessex genes of being a thoughtful and very tough leader. In about 902, her husband Æthelred became seriously ill and effectively handed over the rule of the Mercians to her. She ruled wisely as her husband's regent for almost a decade, opposing the Vikings and building fortresses until his death in 911 when she was acclaimed by the Mercians as 'Myrcna hlaefdige', Lady of the Mercians. Brother and sister had become a powerful and thoughtful alliance against the Vikings. The Lady of the Mercians administered the land of her people and led them in battle to great success, particularly when she took Derby – a strategic fortress – from the Danes. It was only a matter of time and opportunity before she would take the war into Viking territory and that meant heading north into Cumbria and across the Solway Firth. When she died in the summer of 918 at home in Tamworth, Æthelflaed was, as the *Annals of Ulster* noted, a famous queen of the Saxons.[2] The siblings had conquered the five boroughs of Danelaw and when Edward, now without his sister, pressed north there was little to stop him. Both the north and Wales were the outposts of the Britons, not the English, but the Welsh princes declared for Edward and soon the task started by Alfred the Great was completed. Then, in 924, Edward died and in 925, the year that St Dunstan was born, Edward's son, the remarkable Athelstan, who had served his squiredom at the court of his aunt Æthelflaed, came to the throne. If it is at all possible to say who the first king of all England was, then that person was Athelstan.

It is said that Alfred had known that, one day, his grandson would be king and that he had cloaked the child in scarlet and then invested him with the Royal Saxon sword with a golden hilt, the symbol of regal dignity. Athelstan was the first King of Wessex who was truly part of the Mercian aristocracy. His father wasn't. Certainly Alfred the Great wasn't. So Athelstan held a unique position, one of great respect, when he joined with Mercians against Northumbria – still known as Danelaw and still an alien territory to the southern kingdom. Sensibly and with the style of the times, Athelstan began his reign by seeking accord with the Danelaw leaders. That way of peace was never likely and in 926 Athelstan marched on Yorkshire. Rapidly, Northumbria, the monarchs of Strathclyde and the Scots and even the Welsh princes agreed Athelstan to be their lord. Once more, peace was unreal and uneasy truce likely.

Ten years earlier, Athelstan had defeated the late father of King Olaf of Dublin. Now, in AD 937, Olaf sought revenge. Thus he gathered the Vikings and Celts, including Scots (led by Constantine, King of the Scots) and Strathclyde Britons, into a motley alliance of Christian and pagan forces. It was a bloody affair even by the standards of the bloody day. Olaf's armies lost five kings and seven earls; any hope that the Celts may have had of ridding the British Isles of Saxons lay silent with them. It is called the Battle of

---

2   F. T. Wainwright, 'Aethelflaed, Lady of the Mercians', in Peter Clemoes (ed.), *The Anglo-Saxons; Some Aspects of their History and Culture presented to Bruce Dickins* (London: Bowes & Bowes, 1959), 53–69.

Brunanburh but where the battle took place is unknown. One strong claimant is Brinkburn in Northumberland. What we do know is that it inspired *Brunanburh*, the first epic verse in our language – Saxon English – in 937:

Her Aethelstan cyning, eorla dryhten,
beorna beag-giefa, and his brothor eac,
Eadmund aetheling, ealdor-langetir
geslogon aet saecce sweorda ecgun
ymbe Brunanburh. Bord-weall clufon,
heowon heathu-linde hamora lafum
eaforan Eadweardes, swa him ge-aethele waes
fram cneo-magnum thaet hie aet campe oft
with lathra gehwone land ealgodon,
hord and hamas. Hettend crungon,
Scotta leode and scip-flotan,
faege feollon. Feld dennode
secga swate sithan sunne upp
on morgen-tid, maere tungol,
glad ofer grundas, Godes candel beorht,
eces Dryhtnes, oth seo aethele gesceaft
sag to setle. Thaer laeg secg manig
garum agieted, guma Northerna
ofer scield scoten, swelce Scyttisc eac,
werig, wiges saed.

West-Seaxe forth
andlange daeg eorod-cystum
on last legdon lathum theodum,
heowon here-flieman hindan thearle
mecum mylen-scearpum. Mierce ne wierndon
heardes hand-plegan haeletha nanum
thara-the mid Anlafe ofer ear-gebland
on lides bosme land gesohton,
faege to gefeohte. Fife lagon
on tham camp-stede cyningas geonge,
sweordum answefede, swelce seofone eac
eorlas Anlafes, unrim herges,
flotena and Scotta. Thaere gefliemed wearth
North-manna brego, niede gebaeded,
to lides stefne lytle weorode;
cread cnear on flot, cyning ut gewat
on fealone flod, feorh generede.
Swelce thaere eac se froda mid fleame com
on his cyththe north, Constantinus,
har hilde-rinc. Hreman ne thorfte
meca gemanan; he waes his maga sceard,
freonda gefielled on folc-stede,
beslaegen aet saecce, and his sunu forlet
on wael-stowe wundum forgrunden,

In this year King Aethelstan, Lord of warriors,
ring-giver to men, and his brother also,
Prince Eadmund, won eternal glory
in battle with sword edges
around Brunanburh. They split the shield-wall,
they hewed battle shields with the remnants of hammers.
The sons of Eadweard, it was only befitting their noble
descent from their ancestors that they should often
defend their land in battle against each hostile people,
horde and home. The enemy perished,
Scots men and seamen,
fated they fell. The field flowed
with blood of warriors, from sun up
in the morning, when the glorious star
glided over the earth, God's bright candle,
eternal lord, till that noble creation
sank to its seat. There lay many a warrior
by spears destroyed; Northern men
shot over shield, likewise Scottish as well,
weary, war sated.

The West-Saxons pushed onward
all day; in troops
they pursued the hostile people.
They hewed the fugitive grievously from behind
with swords sharp from the grinding. The Mercians did
not refuse hard hand-play to any warrior
who came with Anlaf over the sea-surge
in the bosom of a ship, those who sought land,
fated to fight. Five lay dead
on the battle-field, young kings,
put to sleep by swords, likewise also seven
of Anlaf's earls, countless of the army,
sailors and Scots. There the North-men's chief
was put to flight, by need constrained
to the prow of a ship with little company;
he pressed the ship afloat, the king went out
on the dusky flood-tide, he saved his life.
Likewise, there also the old campaigner through flight
came to his own region in the north--Constantine--
hoary warrior. He had no reason to exult
the great meeting; he was of his kinsmen bereft,
friends fell on the battle-field,
killed at strife: even his son, young in battle, he left
in the place of slaughter, ground to pieces with wounds.

geongne aet guthe. Gielpan ne thorfte
beorn blanden-feax bill-gesliehtes,
eald inwitta, ne Anlaf thy ma;
mid hira here-lafum hliehhan ne thorfton
thaet hie beadu-weorca beteran wurdon
on camp-stede cumbol-gehnastes,
gar-mittunge, gumena gemotes,
waepen-gewrixles, thaes hie on wael-felda
with Eadweardes eaforan plegodon.

That grizzle-haired warrior had no
reason to boast of sword-slaughter,
old deceitful one, no more did Anlaf;
with their remnant of an army they had no reason
to laugh that they were better in deed of war
in battle-field--collision of banners,
encounter of spears, encounter of men,
trading of blows--when they played against
the sons of Eadweard on the battle-field.

Gewiton him tha North-menn naegled-cnearrum,
dreorig darotha laf, on Dinges mere
ofer deop waeter Dyflin secan,
eft lra lang aewisc-mode.
Swelce tha gebrothor begen aetsamne,
cyning and aetheling, cyththe sohton,
West Seaxna lang, wiges hremge.
Leton him behindan hraew bryttian
sealwig-padan, thone sweartan hraefn
hyrned-nebban, and thone hasu-padan,
earn aeftan hwit, aeses brucan,-
graedigne guth-hafoc, and thaet graege deor,
wulf on wealda.

Departed then the Northmen in nailed ships.
The dejected survivors of the battle, at Dinges
mere sought Dublin over the deep water,
to return to Ireland, ashamed in spirit.
Likewise the brothers, both together,
King and Prince, sought their home,
West-Saxon land, exultant from battle.
They left behind them, to enjoy the corpses,
the dark coated one, the dark horny-beaked
raven and the dusky-coated one,
the eagle white from behind, to partake of carrion,
greedy war-hawk, and that gray animal
the wolf in the forest.

Ne wearth wael mare
on thys ig-lande aefre gieta
folces gefielled beforan thissum
sweordes ecgum, thaes-the us secgath bec,
eald uthwitan, siththan eastan hider
Engle and Seaxe upp becomon,
ofer brad brimu Britene sohton,
wlance wig-smithas, Wealas ofercomon,
eorlas ar-hwaete eard begeaton.

Never was there more slaughter
on this island, never yet as many
people killed before this
with sword's edge: never according to those
who tell us from books, old wisemen,
since from the east Angles and Saxons came up
over the broad sea. Britain they sought,
Proud war-smiths who overcame the Welsh,
glorious warriors they took hold of the land.

None now doubted Athelstan's credentials as a leader of his land and not simply his people. He was styled *Rex totius Britanniae*. Athelstan was recognized as a true European monarch and not simply an island chief. By marriage and political interest the house of Alfred, his son Edward the Elder, and Athelstan were bound with events in mainland Europe. The first Saxon King of the Germans, Henry the Fowler, had attempted an alliance with Athelstan and it was as a result of this approach that Athelstan's sister, Edith, married Henry's eldest son Otto. Thus, England and Germany became tied in all sorts of events, many of which had a direct influence on English ecclesiastical history and the reform of the monastery system. Small points, perhaps, but reminders that history takes its time and does not directly rest on the outcome of battles.

Athelstan died in 939, just two years after Brunanburh. His half-brother, the eighteen-year-old Edmund, lived only for a further six years but in that time put down all tests of his authority and the rule of his late brother's kingdom. Edmund and his successor Edred protected the legacy of Athelstan, which was a more united kingdom with an organization of courts and councils on a much wider basis. The result was that regional selfishness, while not disappearing, was at least tempered and therefore the unity of the land was more likely. Yet the island was not a Saxon, certainly not an English, entity. The Vikings had arrived more than a century before Athelstan's death. Their influence had changed, not disappeared. For example, the eastern counties of England had deep-running Danish blood even though that had not yet led to an attempt to usurp the new authority of the Saxon monarchy. But the Vikings had not renounced all claims on violent intrusion.

There now appeared the most fearsome Viking leader. And he had the name to go with it: Eric Bloodaxe. He was Norwegian and had been the king in his homeland until he was deposed and did what many of his luckless predecessors had done: sailed for England and the Northumbrian coast where his Viking country-men lived, and where there was a desire to kick out the Saxons and join the Vikings who lived in Dublin to establish one big Viking state.

The Northumbrian Vikings welcomed Eric. King Edred, Alfred the Great's grandson and a chip off the Saxon block, did not. Edred fought and burned his way through the region and, instead of fighting Eric Bloodaxe, threatened the Northumbrians with earthly damnation. He meant to kill them all and burn their towns. So, the Northumbrians turned against Eric. But Eric Bloodaxe returned with stronger forces and once again called himself King. And for a time it worked. But Eric Bloodaxe was killed with his son and his brother at the Battle of Stainmore, on the heights overlooking what is now called Edendale. *The Anglo-Saxon Chronicle* dismisses it in a single entry: 'AD 954: In this year the Northumbrians drove out Eric, and Eadred succeeded to the Northumbrian kingdom.'

It is true that Eric Bloodaxe had united the Vikings of Dublin and York, but he had failed to establish a kingdom that could rival the English. After he died it was no longer possible for a single invader, no matter how strong and resourceful, to begin a completely new dynasty to rule England. In 955, a twelve-year-old boy, Edgar, became King of Mercia. His brother, Eadwig (sometimes, Edwy), was about three years older and he became King of Wessex. Wessex was the senior kingdom in England. But Eadwig died a couple of years later and Edgar, only just into his teens, also became King of Wessex, Mercia and Northumberland. Edgar's coronation was the first to have a written Order of Service, and it is the basis of the one used today. Edgar's reign was not the record of slaughter and gore normally associated with kings of this period. One of the finest historians of the Saxons, Sir Frank Stenton, noted that 'It is a sign of Edgar's competence as a ruler that his reign is singularly devoid of recorded incident.'[3] It is true also that he was never called upon to defend his people against intruders nor uprisings. Edgar's reign was one of peaceful rebuilding of the sometimes very vulnerable mix of societies and defending the peaceful State that his immediate ancestors had fought so hard for. And he would be remembered for the way in which he supported the new cultural identity of the State, particularly in the way of English monastic life.

The figure behind the crown at the time was the man who became St Dunstan. He was a nobleman born in 925. At the age of eighteen he was created Abbot of Glastonbury, for centuries past and centuries to come, an important church. It was from Glastonbury that Dunstan helped to rebuild English monastic orders. He had been banished from England by Edgar's eldest brother Eadwig. Eadwig was easily distracted and on his coronation day he left the anointing celebrations to amuse himself with a woman and her daughter. He was found, in flagrante delicto, by the bishop, Dunstan. The King was upset, the woman was upset, the daughter was upset and Dunstan ended up in exile, and the daughter ended up married to the King. But a couple of years later, when Edgar became King of Wessex, the historical partnership between Edgar and the now restored Dunstan began.

Edgar became King of Wessex in 959 when he was sixteen but chose not to assume the throne until he believed he was mature in mind and moral thought. In those days, a man could not be ordained a priest until he was thirty. So we should not separate Edgar's religious foundation from his reign and the timing of his coronation as late as Whit Sunday at Bath in 973: Edgar was thirty in 973. With Dunstan as his tutor, Edgar based his whole thinking on theology and so the religious communities became important and different than during the reign of many other rulers. Equally, Edgar's authority was different. It came not from the crown he wore, but from the religious significance of anointment. In the coronation order written by Edgar with Dunstan, the importance of the ceremony was not the placing of the crown on the new king's head, but the solemn moment of anointment. This was not simply piety. That act set the king apart from other men.

Shortly after his coronation, the eight kings in Britain (Kenneth, King of Scots; Malcolm, King of Cumbrians; Maccus, King of Islands; Dufnal; Siferth; Huwal; Jacob and Juchil) arrived on the same day at the foot of Edgar's throne at Chester to beg he should accept their allegiance and their acknowledgement of his supremacy. Even with such fealty, Edgar was not long for his throne. As one of the earliest poems in *The Anglo-Saxon Chronicle* tells us, he died in the seventh month of 975, and terrible times were to come: 'His son, a stripling, succeeded then to the throne; the name of the prince of earls was Edward. Then the praise of the Ruler fell away everywhere throughout the length and breadth of Mercia, and many wise servants of God were expelled.'

Edgar had married twice and Edward was his son by the first marriage. But Edward's mother died and in 964 Edgar married again. His new wife was a widow of the Ealdorman of East Anglia. Her name was Ælfthryth and the surviving son she bore Edgar was Æthelred who was to become known as the Unready. Edward was visiting his step-mother Ælfthryth and his half-brother Æthelred at their home at Corfe Castle in Dorset. On 18 March, he arrived, dismounted, was surrounded by his step-mother's servants and held while he was repeatedly stabbed until he was dead. So the finger points to Ælfthryth, but nothing is known for certain. What is known is that within a month her son, Æthelred, was crowned in Edward's place. The King has been described as 'a child, a weakling, a vacillator, a faithless, feckless creature'.[4] Churchill is

---

4   W. S. Churchill, *A History of the English-speaking Peoples* (ed. Christopher Lee, London: Cassells, 1999).

a little unkind. Æthelred the Unready has had an unfair press. Unready comes from '*unraed*', meaning ill-counselled rather than not ready.

What is not in doubt is that in 980 the Viking raiders returned. They sailed across from Ireland – their western stronghold – and attacked Chester. Others landed along the south coast from Kent to Cornwall. They had strongholds in France and some on the Isle of Wight. The memorable confrontation was in the Essex seaport Maldon. Danish Vikings on one side of the river met English Saxons on the other. The Vikings demanded gold, otherwise threatening the English with a storm of spears. The Essex alderman, a man called Byrhtnoth, refused. He pledged to defend the land of his prince, Æthelred. A writer of the time tells us that Byrhtnoth cried that 'The heathen shall fall in the war. Not so likely shall you come by the treasure: point and edge [in other words, spear and sword] shall first make atonement, grim warplay, before we pay tribute.' Æthelred again resorted to Danegeld, a common practice after Alfred. But Æthelred could not be certain that his money would buy safety because he had within his ranks many Danish mercenaries. He is said to have ordered the slaughter of all Danes living in the south. Whether or not this story is exaggerated hardly matters because many Danes were indeed killed. The attacks on the Danes living in England started on 13 November, St Brice's Day, 1002. At Oxford, Danes took refuge in a church, which was burned down. The dead included Gunhilde, the sister of Sweyn I, King of Denmark, known as Sweyn Forkbeard. It is reasonable to think that the Danish king invaded England the following year to seek revenge although there is no primary source material to confirm this.

The carnage and the massacres were without parallel. For four gruesome years, from Norwich and Thetford in East Anglia to the downs of Kent, to the upper reaches of the Thames, to Exeter in the West Country, limbless, violated, sightless victims of Viking anger were piled high. The slaughter stopped only when, predictably, Æthelred paid more bribes. This time the price was 36,000 pounds of silver – probably three years of the national income. But it was not enough. Sweyn did leave but he returned. *The Anglo-Saxon Chronicle* tells what happened next. The year was 1011 and the host described by the chronicler was the Danish invader:

The king and his counsellor sent to the host, and craved peace, promising them tribute and provisions on condition that they should cease their harrying. They had East Anglia, Middlesex, Oxfordshire, Hertfordshire, Buckinghamshire, Bedfordshire, Kent, Sussex, Surrey and Hampshire . . . then they besieged Canterbury. And there they seized the Archbishop and kept the Archbishop as their prisoner. Then the host became greatly incensed against the Bishop, because he was not willing to offer them more money and forbade any ransom to be given for him. Moreover they were very drunk. Then they took the Bishop and led him to their tribunal and pelted him to death with bones and the heads of cattle; and one of them smote him on the skull with the iron of an axe so that he sank down and his holy blood fell upon the earth and his holy soul was sent forth to God's kingdom

If we find this so horrifying an account of how marauders dealt with a hostage in the eleventh century, then we may pause to consider our own times in the twenty-first century – exactly 1,000 years on. The act of hostage-taking has not much changed; nor has the motive. Nor have the likely consequences for a prisoner when a demanded ransom is not paid. The difference between the times of King Alfred and those of Æthelred was that where Alfred used gold and the edge of his sword to bring about peace, Æthelred relied on the Danegeld. Consequently money was hard to come by. So much had been paid out that it probably took Æthelred's counsellors a great deal of time before they could find enough to satisfy the invaders. Æthelred's time was running low. Moreover, a new moment in British history was approaching. We would be hearing of a great imperial king, Cnut, and not hearing much of a remarkable woman, Emma of Normandy, who would be mother of two kings and wife of two kings. First the arrival of Cnut.

Cnut was the son of Sweyn Forkbeard and in 1013 he accompanied his father on raids into England. They penetrated deeply and proceeded the conquest of the monarchy. Sweyn's forces were so powerful that the five boroughs of Danelaw capitulated, as did Oxford and Winchester. London held firm, but that was no matter because it soon fell and Sweyn was accepted as lord of West Mercia – a traditional Wessex stronghold. Æthelred left the country. He really had no choice. Sweyn had usurped his authority so he took refuge with his brother-in-law, the Duke of Normandy, with his wife Emma, the duke's younger sister. Emma was one of those too often mislaid links in Saxon history; a half century on, her link to England would bring William to Hastings: Emma of Normandy was to be the mother of Edward the Confessor.

It was at this point that Sweyn, instead of enjoying the fruit of his campaign, died. He had been King of Denmark for nearly thirty years and had spent much of that time raiding England, especially after the killing of his sister Gunnhild during the massacre of St Brice's Day, 1002. He had been king of Danish England for only forty days or so when he had a fall from his horse and on 3 February 1014 he died at his home and headquarters, Gainsborough. The English returned to their exiled monarch, Æthelred, with petitions that he should return to England with his bride, Emma of Normandy. There is no evidence that he wanted to return, but it could be that Emma displayed her ambition sufficiently enough to persuade him to do so. But the line and loin of Sweyn Forkbeard ran strongly and deeply in young Cnut. He decided that he would claim the English throne for Denmark. Equally, the blood of famous lineage flowed through Wessex veins. Æthelred may have found testing times too much, but his son brought, for a short moment, the style and vigour that Alfred himself would have found inspiring. This was Edmund, who would be dubbed Ironside for his exploits. It was Edmund, barely freed from his teenage years, who gathered a loyal band to harry and strike the invaders. When Æthelred died in 1016, Edmund became king. He was successful and in two years had built a reputation for his exploits. Then, at the mere age of twenty-two, Edmund died. How and why, we are uncertain. It was as if the Wessex line had snapped. The counsellors and burghers believed no fate would will them to victory and they abandoned their pedigree and gave their allegiance to Cnut.

Cnut promised to rule for all men's good. Yet there was still the ambition of Emma of Normandy with which to contend. Æthelred was dead; Edmund Ironside was dead; but Emma's sons weren't. And their father was Æthelred. The counsellors of the English had agreed to abandon the family of Æthelred from its royal line, in other words, its claim to the throne. But kings don't stay kings if they rely on paper agreements. Cnut saw just one way out of this dilemma;

marry the opponent. So Cnut married Emma. But he already had a wife and a son. He packed them off first to the north and made his wife his queen there, and then later he made her Regent of Norway. Emma and Æthelred's sons were not allowed to live in England – nothing was left to chance – and by 1016 they were living in Normandy.

Cnut was King of Denmark and conqueror of Norway. Soon he controlled everything from the entrance to the Baltic Sea down to the Bay of Biscay. His was a real and large empire with England its headquarters. And so Cnut's was a careful and wary reign of assurance and cajoling, but interestingly he did all this from England. He liked the climate, the way of life and the laws and institutions that Edgar had established. Cnut would have liked to have ruled in the style of Edgar, regarding his reign as seventeen years of relative peace. Cnut was a holy-minded man who now hoped for the blessing of wisdom. He developed a system that we would now call devolved government. People had more responsibility for their affairs, but were not independent. Cnut did not want England to go back to warlords and so, for example, in Cnut's England a very real Danish relationship between the throne and the people who were in charge of the regions developed. And, in the English hierarchy, the Danish title of earl emerged. The earl was appointed by the king. So, the interests of the king would override those of the region. This was a change in the way that England was governed.

By 1030 or so, the Danish earls had disappeared. Cnut's chief advisers then seemed to be Godwine (often Godwin), Earl of Wessex, and Leofric, Earl of Mercia, both Anglo-Saxon. Here we have another important clue in the historical detective story. The rivalry of these two families, Godwine's and Leofric's, meant it was now quite impossible that England would be united against the Normans when they invaded in 1066. When, in 1035, Cnut died, his empire became leaderless because no one could separate ambition from constitutional sense. He had three sons, but none was impressive; certainly not one of them had the notion that something other than brawn was necessary to rule effectively. The Wessex line was always a possibility through another two sons of Emma of Normandy (by Æthelred): Edward the Albino and Alfred the Innocent. They were living in exile in France and one of them, Alfred, immediately on Cnut's death travelled to England. Enter the amazingly ambitious Earl Godwine of Wessex. Albert was intercepted, his courtiers killed; he was blinded and destined to spend his days ineffectual in an Ely monastery. We are getting close to the events that led to 1066 and more than that. Cnut had wanted his son Harthacnut (Emma was his mother) to succeed him as King of England and Denmark. But there was a war on Denmark's borders and he simply couldn't leave for England. Godwine and Emma said Harthacnut should be declared King, even if he stayed in Denmark. But Leofric, Godwine's rival, proposed that another son of the late King should be regent. (Leofric's teenage wife, by the way, was Lady Godiva.) His name was Harold. This was Harold I. The Saxons called him Harold Harefoot. By 1037, Harthacnut was still in Denmark. Harold Harefoot was recognized as King and Emma went into exile, in Flanders. Godwine, being Godwine, now supported Harold. But Harold didn't last long and as soon as he was dead Harthacnut arrived to claim the throne. But like all of Cnut's sons, he died at about the age of twenty-five. *The Anglo-Saxon Chronicle* suggests the King was in drink: 'The year 1042: in this year Harthacnut died as he stood at his drink and he suddenly fell to the ground with a horrible convulsion; and those who were near took hold of him, but he never spoke again, and passed away on June 8.'

Edward the Albino (later the Confessor) was the only choice as successor as far as Emma was concerned, although the arrangement did not quite work in her favour: 'The year 1043: in this year Edward was consecrated King in Winchester on the first day of Easter with great ceremony. Soon in this same year the King had all the lands which his mother owned confiscated for his own use, and undertook from her all that she possessed.' Why so harsh with his old mother? Very simply, they did not get on. Edward thought she had always favoured his brother and she had established a cabal of influence that could have been used against him. These were classic signs of a dowager attempting to be the real power and to even rule. Her confidant in all this, or so Edward thought (probably rightly), was the Archbishop of Canterbury, Stigand. Edward took no chances and so confiscated everything Stigand owned or laid claim to. Moreover, it was clear that Earl Godwine was determined to be the real kingmaker. It was far from simple for the Wessex earl. Edward was never a hard and ruddy character. He was an albino, which added a sense of mystery, and he was also a pious man who felt unsafe in his newly given realm, which was why he brought his own Norman priests and administrators into his court and why land was given to Norman families who would protect him.

The introduction of Normans into the court and realm of Edward the Confessor is a further reminder that just as Caesar was not the first Roman seen by the Britons, so William the Conqueror was hardly the first Norman in England. The Normans were already established when, in 1066, Duke William landed at Pevensey. The Normans who followed Edward to England were increasingly suspicious of Godwine and his ambitions for his sons. However, Godwine grew more powerful with Edward on the throne, even though the King regarded him with great suspicion and still saw him as the man behind the death of his brother, Alfred. Alfred's elder sons became earls. One of them, Swein, stretched family loyalties when he seduced an abbess and murdered his cousin, one of the King's earls. Edward publicly declared him to be 'nithing', meaning 'a man without any honour'. Swein fled to Flanders. Yet, Godwine was not invulnerable, especially as the accusations about Albert never went away. In 1051, the Normans convinced Edward that Godwine's evil act could no longer be ignored. Godwine was driven into exile.

It was about now that the story of the right of William of Normandy to the English throne becomes obvious. With Godwine away, William visited England and, so it would seem, talked to Edward about the succession. There is no evidence to hand that William had a promise that he would succeed Edward. Yet, let us consider three points: although there were Norwegian claims – and they would be enforced with bloody consequences – Edward's nephew's son, Edgar, was the blood line to the throne, but was too young and had no support to defend the claim. Secondly, the other contender for the throne of England was the Godwine family. Edward was perhaps a ditherer but he had made it clear that he still had his suspicions (perhaps solid belief) that the Godwines had intercepted his brother Albert. The Godwines were in exile. Thirdly, Edward felt comfortable with his Normans. He would be advised by his Normans at court that the Godwines had to be stopped and that William was the natural and blood successor, even invoking the family connection through his disgraced mother.

So on balance, if we want to take an opinion, the likelihood is that Edward would at the very least have indicated that he favoured William as his successor even if he did not make promises. All this is important when considering the reasons for the invasion and the utter changes these islands were to experience after the invasion of 1066.

However, the Godwines did not give up a throne so easily and they succeeded in their ambition. In 1052, Godwine returned from exile with an army raised in Flanders. With his son, Harold Godwineson, Godwine forced Edward to give back his authority in England. Godwine died shortly after his return and Harold succeeded to the authority his father had won from Edward. Then, in January 1066, Edward died and by his death set in train the invasion. This, from *The Anglo-Saxon Chronicle*:

> King Edward came to Westminster towards Christmas [1065] and there had the abbey church consecrated which he himself had built to the glory of God, St Peter, and all God's saints; the consecration of the church was on Holy Innocents' Day [28 December]. He passed away on the vigil of the Epiphany and was buried on the Epiphany [6 January]. Here in the world he dwelt for a time in royal majesty, sagacious in counsel; a gracious ruler for twenty-four years . . . And so Edward died and with him the line of the Saxon Kings.

The boy who should have been King on Edward's death was Edgar. He was the son of the King's nephew. But he was in no position to lead the nation, certainly not to defend it, especially as it was certain that Duke William of Normandy and the King of Norway would each claim the crown for himself. The English had to decide between a respect for the royal line and the need to be protected. Harold was unique. No one man, other than the King himself, had ever been so popular and so powerful throughout the land.

Yet one irony remained. On his deathbed, Edward warned of the great evil that was about to sweep his land. But the Archbishop of Canterbury encouraged Harold to ignore the warnings. This was nothing more, he said, than the ramblings of an ancient robbed of his wits. The Archbishop was that great ecclesiastical survivor, Stigand. But the warnings were true and the spirit of Edward ruled English hearts for centuries, so much so that it wasn't until the fourteenth century that the people abandoned Edward as the nation's patron saint for the mythical St George. And while England mourned, Duke William of Normandy made ready for sea.

CHAPTER FOUR

1066–87

Edward the Confessor died on 5 January 1066. The Battle of Hastings took place later that same year, on 14 October. But what happened in that ten-month gap before the start of the Norman Conquest? We should really know because this was the last successful invasion of these islands.

The first point to make is that the Normans weren't French in the way that the term is understood today. Their origins were in Scandinavia. Under a vigorous warrior king, called Rollo, the Vikings had settled in northern France a century-and-a-half before William the Conqueror was born. During the years before the invasion, Normandy was a land of ambitious, well-ordered, often uncompromising peoples and it had something of a structured society, but it wasn't as far advanced in statehood as England. Leaders in England were beginning to take quite seriously the business of government by bureaucracy rather than by battleaxe.

The England of 1066 usually appears as some pastoral canvas about to be slashed by a Norman vandal. Considering the internal strife and the ambitions of lords and minor lords it was hardly a land of undisturbed peace. Nor was it a State able to defend itself against a carefully planned invasion. There was no English fleet other than a few ships which the king could requisition. Also, gathering enough soldiers to reinforce the monarch's professional fighters was a complicated task. At the core of Saxon physical authority was the 'thegn', part of the system of nobility (nowhere near as complex as it was to become towards the end of the Middle Ages). The Anglo-Saxon aristocracy was a simple rank structure that could be assessed according to what twenty-first century Britain might call death duties, known in the eleventh century as *heriot*. The most powerful in society (and not many of them) were the earls. The next in line was the person who was committed to the king and had land supplied by the king; in return this person supplied the king with a small army. He was the king's thegn, a term that later translated into count. The median thegn did not get his land from the king but from a senior figure such as an earl. At whatever level, a thegn held his land in return for military service. Peasants also had obligations, but it was often difficult to decide how far that obligation went. And unlike the system across the Channel, England didn't have a complex of castles as defensive points in any county or region.

So, in spite of the structure of obligation, the omens were not good for Harold, especially as he faced enemies on two fronts: his half-brother Tostig, who hated him and had aligned himself with King Hardrada III of Norway; and William of Normandy, who believed the English crown belonged to him. If there were two enemies, it was inevitable there would be two fronts and so two battles. Hardrada was the last of the Cnut-inspired northern kings determined to rule England. With a considerably larger fleet than Harold of England could have mustered, Hardrada arrived off the north-east coast in the summer of 1066 and sailed up the Humber. The local earls, Edwin and Morcar, had little chance against the fierce and well-organized invaders. *The Anglo-Saxon Chronicle* provides the gruesome detail:

> Earl Edwin and Earl Morcar had gathered as great a force as they could; but a great number of the English were either slain or drowned or driven in flight, and the Norwegians had possession of the place of slaughter. After the battle King Harold [Hardrada] and Earl Tostig entered York and received hostages from the borough and provisions. Then meanwhile came Harold the King of the English on the Sunday to Tadcaster and there drew up his household troops in battle order and on Monday marched through to York. The King of Norway and Earl Tostig and their force had gone beyond York to Stamford Bridge. Then Harold, King of the English, came upon them unawares beyond the bridge. And that day no side gave quarter. There were slain Harold the Fairhead [Hardrada], the King of the Norwegians, and Earl Tostig and the remaining Norwegians were put to flight until some of them reached their ships, some were drowned, others burned to death and thus perished in various ways so many that there [were] few to survive. And the English had possession of the place of slaughter.

Edwin and Morcar may have been defeated at the first battle (20 September) but before they went down, they must have taken many of the invaders with them. Therefore, when Harold arrived he was fighting a much weakened army of Hardrada and Tostig. Equally, that battle had also taken its terrible toll on Harold's allies and so they could not raise many troops, certainly not fresh ones, and march with Harold to Sussex where he was to meet William of Normandy who had landed at Pevensey beach on the morning of Thursday, 28 September 1066. He had come to claim the throne of England for himself from Harold, who would become the last king of the Old English.

It is easy to see why William believed he had a right to the English throne. Emma of Normandy, who had been married to King Cnut, and also to Æthelred the Unready by whom she had the son who became Edward the Confessor, was also the sister of Robert, Duke of Normandy. William was the illegitimate son of Robert. In addition, Harold was not of the royal line, and he had agreed that when Edward died he would support William's claim to the throne. As the bastard son of Robert, William was not able to secure as Duke of Normandy until he was twenty, in 1047, thirteen years after his father had died. William had to fight for his inheritance and the experience hardened him.

It was also during this period, on the Continent, but not in Britain, that warfare began to change. The chain-mailed knight appeared and more thought was given to fortifications, cavalry tactics (instead of simply using horses for transportation) and disciplined armies, which in some cases had not been seen since Roman times. William of Normandy emerged as a proper general, not just a general by right. He brought together disparate soldiery, including peasants and mercenaries, and welded them into formidable fighting units. So they proved, north of the Pevensey coast at a place which hardly had a name, but is now a town called Battle.

In just seven days Harold had marched the 200 or so miles from Stamford Bridge in the north-east to Sussex. On the way, he gathered what forces he could. But there were few. When he arrived at the slope called Senlac Hill on 13 October 1066, Harold II of England surely must have known that promised soldiers would arrive too late, if at all. Eight miles away, the Normans made ready. Harold's foot-soldiers formed up at the top of the slope behind a wall of shields. The shields, even when buffeted and cut through could be reformed and, but for discipline, Harold might have had the day though surely not the battle. William needed to break down the shields and the best way was to get the Saxons to do it for him. The Normans appeared to be in retreat. The Saxons sensing the chance of victory broke ranks and chased after the Normans, who were withdrawing and not retreating as Harold's men soon found out. William sent in his cavalry to slice through the ill-armed Saxons and then to deal with what was left of the shield-bearers.

Harold died, according to the Bayeux Tapestry, from an arrow through the eye. In truth it would seem that he was cut down by Norman cavalry. William, who had three horses killed under him, survived and camped upon the battlefield. There is a general and easily concluded notion that the Battle of Hastings decided the fate of the English nation. And that's probably true. But on Senlac Hill that 14 October 1066 night, when a purple robe was wrapped about King Harold's naked body, and William of Normandy began to count the cost of that day's slaughter, no one knew that for sure. Here was a moment in history that hindsight sees with clarity. At the time, few – Saxon nor Norman – had such clear vision. There were pockets of resistance, but with the exception of Hereward the Wake in East Anglia, they were never as organized as had been the vengeful Boudicca against the detested Romans. For example, when Saxon rebels on nearby Romney Marsh attacked and slaughtered a band of Normans, William sent his knights and took terrible revenge. The Kentish opposition melted. William marched on London but was wise enough not to assault the capital. Instead he laid waste to its borders and settlements; the smoke from burning thatch and carcasses was enough warning to the people of that town. William then followed the Thames and then towards Wallingford and Berkhampsted. The Saxons, once proud nobles with their clergy in tow, bent at the knee.

Some of the English believed they could raise another army. But they needed a leader. They chose Edgar the Æthling. The choice did not amount to much. William was to be crowned that Christmas Day at Westminster and that was that. But even in such stark circumstances there was still a sense of constitutional decorum to be observed. Can we really imagine that a ruthless invader chose to stick to the constitutional rules? We are told that the people at the coronation had to show that they freely accepted him as King. But not all spoke Saxon English and not all spoke French. So the question was put to them in two languages. The commotion of their responses echoed about the building. Outside, William's guards could only hear roaring and shouting. They thought the crowd inside must have turned upon William. So they panicked and set fire to the surrounding buildings. But when all had calmed, and presumably the fires had been put out, the ceremony continued and the Crown of England was William's. One point from this story is worth remembering when we explore the next 200 years: Henry IV (1367–1413) was probably the first English king after the Norman invasion to use English as a first language. The previous twelve monarchs – William I, William Rufus, Henry I, Stephen, Henry II, Richard I (Coeur de Lion), John, Henry III, Edward I, Edward II, Edward III and Richard II – all appeared to have used French as their first language.

The physical legacy of the period is seen in castles and churches, but especially castles. One of the first was by the Thames, which was some indication of the importance of London and the fear that towns could be the centre of an uprising. Soon William replaced the castle with his lasting visible monument: the Tower of London. The castle of London and the taxes William imposed marked the start of his steady conquest of these islands.

But conquest does not necessarily mean control. It's true that six months after the Battle of Hastings William felt confident enough to return to Normandy. But it was three years before Chester fell. And he had to make sure he was not going to be overthrown while he was away. So, he made Bishop Odo, his half-brother, Earl of Kent, installed him in Dover Castle and left him in charge along with William fitz Osbern, who was his most trusted steward. Then, having decided to go, he took to Normandy the very people who might lead an uprising once his back was turned. It was as much as he could do, but eleventh-century rebellion was never far from the minds of those who lived not close to court, but in the marches of England's still Saxon civilization. However many flowers are thrown for conquering soldiers, many bear the thorns of distrust and rebellion. And for two decades at least after William's coronation, the Normans remained invaders and so always on watch, always vulnerable to cunning as well as hothead rebels. One such rebel in the Cambridgeshire fens was Hereward the Wake.

So little is known of Hereward that there's a temptation to add him to the same gallery as King Arthur and Robin Hood. But he was real enough. He came from Lincolnshire and he was one of the aforementioned thegns – those who held land in return for military service. Today he'd probably be called a freedom fighter or guerrilla. A modern-day William would call him a terrorist. He doesn't appear to have been a nobleman, which makes it hard to understand why so many followed him. There is, however, in a near contemporary document called *De Gestis Herwardi*, a description of the man. We're told he had yellow hair and large grey eyes, one of them slightly discoloured. He had great and sturdy limbs and none was his equal in daring and braveness. The most romantic of all ideas is that his mother might have been Lady Godiva and his father Leofric of Mercia. It is known that for years Hereward led a rebellion in the southern part of East Anglia and that when Ely fell he escaped into the Fens. After that, like the less real figures of King Arthur and Robin Hood, Hereward's name became a symbol of resistance to evil authority.

However, the King's next major rebellion came not from the Saxons, but from his own people. It happened in 1075 and was a product of the disaffection of Norman knights across a line from East Anglia through the Midlands to the Welsh Marches. There was one particular Saxon sympathizer to the revolt. He was Waltheof Siwardson, a figure who would achieve something close to martyrdom. He was the first Earl of Northampton, and Earl of Huntingdon and Northumberland. As matter of political convenience and in the manner of the day, William the Conqueror had given one of his nieces in marriage to Waltheof. In 1075, the Revolt of the Earls began and the others enticed Waltheof into the plot – perhaps because his extensive lands across the Midlands would be valuable in raising armies to repel the inevitable retaliation from William, who was then in Normandy. Waltheof never appears to have been a willing rebel. In fact he went to London and confessed his part to the seemingly everlasting Archbishop of Canterbury, Lanfranc. Lanfranc advised him to go to Normandy, take plenty of expensive gifts and confess all to William. He did. William, for the moment surprisingly, did nothing about Waltheof but sent his forces against the other earls. The rebels enlisted the help of the Danes, but it all came to nothing even though the conflict was renewed in Normandy itself. Whether or not Waltheof was actually betrayed by his wife Judith has never been conclusively set out. Whatever the circumstances, William now had Waltheof arrested and prepared for execution. Legend is a fine tickler of history's duller moments. The executioner was impatient (so runs the story) and brought down his axe as Waltheof was praying the Lord's Prayer and had reached the exhortation, 'and lead us not into temptation'. It is said that from the head rolling across the floor came the clear words, 'but deliver us from evil'.

It is thought that he was the only noble to be executed by King William. Yet, even in these cruel times, this death penalty of someone of such high rank, who had, incidentally, given himself up to William, was regarded as harsh, even unjust. The Saxon population may have wanted revenge (Waltheof was regarded as an Englishman), but not this. Waltheof became a martyr. The medieval legend has it that the guilt of Waltheof's execution hovered over the King for the rest of his life.

William was King of England for twenty-one years and much of that time was spent in bringing the two societies together. The Saxon aristocracy learned Norman French. The two peoples mingled and married. Perhaps many longed for the days of Saxon England, but most accepted they were gone forever and, anyway, for most had not been so marvellous that they should have created a national nostalgia. But if the conquered society was to live in some sort of harmony then it had to have basic rights. And these rights developed over long periods. There were laws for estate workers. A cowherd was, usually, entitled to the milk of an old cow after she was newly calved. A shepherd's due was twelve nights' dung at Christmas; he also got one lamb a year, a bellwether's fleece and a bowl of buttermilk throughout the summer, And slaves, the lowest of all workers, were to be given food at Christmas and Easter and a strip of land they could plough and tend. A female slave was given three pence or one sheep for winter's food. There was also an indication that the Normans exacted clear penalties from those who offended this new society. An early twelfth-century document called *Textus Roffensis* gives some idea of what were known as the Laws of King William, particularly those to protect his Norman followers.

I will that all the men whom I have brought with me, or who have come after me, shall be protected by my peace and shall dwell in quiet. And if any one of they [*sic*] shall be slain, let the lord of his murderer seize him within five days; if he cannot, let him begin to pay me fort-six marks of silver so long as substance avails. And when his substance is exhausted, let the whole hundred in which the murder took place pay what remains in common. And if the murderer were caught, and if he were an Englishman, then the Laws of William the Conqueror were quite clear as to what happened next.

If a Frenchman shall charge an Englishman with perjury or murder or theft or homicide or 'ran', as the English call rapine, which cannot be denied, the Englishman may defend himself as he shall prefer, either by the ordeal of hot iron or by wager of battle. But if the Englishman be infirm let him find another who will take his place. If one of them shall be vanquished, he shall pay a fine of forty shillings to the King. If an Englishman shall charge a Norman and he be unwilling to prove his accusation either by ordeal or by wager of battle, I decree, nevertheless, that the Norman shall acquit himself by valid oath.

Details of the preceding and following periods may be found in documents such as *Textus Roffensis*, which allow us to see the importance of what we could easily describe as 'civilized behaviour'. It is all too easy to think about these early Middle Ages as an era of the sword, rape, pillage, disease and vicious intrigue. There was, of course, plenty of that too and the idea of settling an argument by 'wager of battle' supports the coarser view of the period. But we should read *Textus Roffensis* or more properly, *Textus de Ecclesia Roffensi per Ernulphum episcopum* – 'The Book of the Church of Rochester through Bishop Ernulf' – as a two-volume memorandum of what was right and what was wrong, what was proper and what was improper. This tells us something we need to know about that period immediately after the Conquest: the debate and open conflict between the English Church and the Normans. The laws and agreements also tell us that Normans and English did indeed compromise on so much that might easily have turned them to civil war. Our earlier observation about differing languages is perfectly represented in this document of more than 200 vellum leaves (in the archive of Rochester Cathedral); *Textus Roffensis* so often explains that the contrasting Romance language and laws of the invaders could find compromise with the equally established English language and laws.

The most famous of the books of the Conqueror's period is
Domesday. A contemporary chronicler wrote that the book was to be
called *Domesday* because 'It spared no man, but judged all men
indifferently, as the Lord in that great day will do.' The idea of
Domesday came to William at Christmas in 1085. It is today seen as
a book that lists who owned what in Norman England. Even estate
agents use the term *Domesday* to suggest the antiquity of the village
in which they're selling a house. But *Domesday* was more than a
description of the second half of the eleventh century. *Domesday* is
a legal document; it is the most thorough record of lawyers and
jurors supplying legal information and is, therefore, a legal text of
what was the law of the 1080s, revealing how and why the laws of
England moved inexorably to what became Common Law – the
legal principles followed by judges by understanding custom and
precedent. *Domesday* was to be William's last great achievement.
The survey, the great reckoning, was born out of crisis at home and
abroad. But William of Normandy's influence was more lasting in
England than anywhere else. He changed the way the English lived,
the laws that governed them and the course of their history. He did
so ruthlessly.

There was one particular aspect which made his rule different
from any that had gone before. It determined the development of
feudalism and, in some sense, it applies to this day. William said that
whatever loyalty a person had to his immediate lord, his protector,
then that person's allegiance to the monarch must always be greater.
His reign was the more remarkable considering the conflicts in his
own family and in particular, in Normandy, where his Queen,
Matilda, ruled in his absence. However, to some in England he
seemed to be spending more and more time in his homeland. For
example, between 1077 and 1080, William was not in England at all.
The dukes of Normandy were powerful in France and successive
French kings were determined to weaken them. The weakness was,
not unusually, in family feuding.

Matilda tried to control the fortunes of Normandy from her seat at
Rouen. Their son, Robert, was a feckless, high-spending youth who
proved disloyal by conspiring with the French King to unseat his
father. Robert eventually stood shoulder to shoulder with Philip of
France, but the conflict that was inevitable was between father and
son. They met in combat beyond the walls of the castle at Gerberoi.

Robert, strong and reckless and little wondering at the significance of the duel charged his father full-tilt and wounded and unhorsed William. If it had not been for one of William's English knights, Tokig of Walligford, Robert would have slain his father then and there. Instead, there was a temporary truce although that was not the end of conflict for the increasingly tempestuous Robert. He broke with his two brothers, William Rufus and Henry, both of whom would also be King one day. And even when there was reconciliation it was never for long. That was the way of powerful families. The twelfth-century William of Malmesbury (the son of a Norman father and English mother) thought it simply the way of Normans. In his opinion they 'envy their equals; they wish to vie with their superiors; and they plunder their subjects'. Equally, William of Malmesbury (who was a monk) thought it well that the Normans had revived religion and that 'you might see churches rise in every village . . . monasteries built after a style unknown before'. But overall, William's view was that Normans were scheming, often brutal and at the same time civilized, whatever that might have meant at the time. But let us not condemn the Normans as the only brutalizers in eleventh-century Britain.

In 1080, the Northumbrians killed the Norman Bishop of Durham and, we're told by one of the chroniclers, another 100 died with him. And in that same year, the Earl of Moray was killed by an army of Scots. These islands were unstable and would have probably been so even without an invasion. Equally, the Conquest engendered powerful interests in opposition to William, often emboldened by his forced absence defending Normandy. For example, the Scottish kings had never accepted the lines drawn between England and Scotland. They defended their prejudice to the death. So did the clique that had survived Harold at Hastings, including Edgar the Æthling, a great survivor who indeed was to outlive William. He was now related by marriage to Malcolm the Bighead, the Scottish King. Malcolm had become King when he beat Macbeth (the real Macbeth) in 1057. He too outlived, and out-harried, William who spent so much time sorting out his family quarrels. As his days grew dim, William agreed that his son William Rufus would succeed him as king of England and that Robert would rule as Duke of Normandy in their homeland. At first the Conqueror refused to make Robert the Duke of Normandy, but the priests pressed the dying King to change his mind. One of the monks at the St Gervase Priory recorded William's words at the time:

> Since he has disdained to come here himself it is with your witness and the will of God that I shall act. With my testimony I declare that I forgive him all the sins he has committed against me and I grant him the whole Duchy of Normandy. He has learned to take advantage of my leniency and now he has brought down his father's grey hairs in sorrow to the grave.

In Book VII of the *Historia Ecclesiastica* of Orderic Vitalis (1075–c.1142), the author tells of William's final confession:

> I treated the native inhabitants of the kingdom with unreasonable severity, cruelly oppressed high and low, unjustly disinherited many, and caused the death of thousands by starvation and war, especially in Yorkshire . . . In mad fury I descended on the English of the north like a raging lion, and ordered that their homes and crops with all their equipment and furnishings should be burnt at once and their great flocks and herds of sheep and cattle slaughtered everywhere. So I chastised a great multitude of men and women with the lash of starvation and, alas! was the cruel murderer of many thousands, both young and old, of this fair people.

William the Conqueror died on 9 September 1087, commending himself to the Virgin Mary. Immediately after the rattle had sounded, the wealthy left to protect their interests. The poorer, or so Orderic claimed, 'seized the arms, vessels, clothing, linen, and all the royal furnishings, and hurried away leaving the king's body almost naked on the floor of the house'.

For those who had lived under Edward the Confessor, then through the spring, summer and early autumn of 1066 under Harold and finally through the two decades of William, it had all been a terrible period. Nothing but conflict and conquest. Nothing but change. The last of the Saxon lords and landowners suffered more than the peasant class. All had to live beneath the rule of a foreign king. There could have been little consolation in the improved bureaucracy of the governing of the country. And

England could only look forward to more conflict as the barons played a dangerous game with the division of the Anglo-Norman inheritance between the warring brothers: Robert in Normandy and the new King, William Rufus.

CHAPTER FIVE

1087–1165

In 1087 William Rufus became king because his dying father wished it and because one of the most influential men in England, Archbishop Lanfranc, approved. Lanfranc was an Italian who had arrived in Normandy at the monastery of Bec in 1042. He had been responsible for the education of the Conqueror's sons so, more than anyone, Lanfranc understood William Rufus. Lanfranc's authority came from the Conqueror himself who made him Archbishop of Canterbury. It was he who rebuilt the great cathedral in that place. Almost no important political decision was taken in England without his approval. Equally, bishops respected their own power as much as an archbishop's and exercised it. In these times, few expected a transition of power without rebellion and without obvious plotting. The Bishops Odo, Geoffrey and William, along with Earl Roger, harried and ransacked farms and estates of any they thought owned any allegiance to the new king. As *The Anglo-Saxon Chronicle* recorded:

> The Bishop of Durham did as much damage as he could everywhere in the North, Bishop Odo, who was the instigator of these troubles, went to his earldom in Kent and his men laid waste the lands of the King and the Archbishop, and all the spoil was taken into his castle at Rochester.

The King promised new and fair tax laws, he promised new hunting rights and almost anything else he could think of. Although there was no way he could, or would, keep these promises, he managed to get a large army on his side and he besieged Rochester Castle. But Odo had escaped, ironically to Pevensey where the Conqueror, his half-brother, had landed in 1066. But, eventually, the King won the day. Bishop Odo and the rest went into exile in Normandy. Odo never came back. He died at Palermo on his way to take part in a Crusade.

This English rebellion was not simply land grabbing or due to dislike of the King. It was just one episode in the conflict between the sons of the Conqueror. Robert fought William. William fought them all. And Henry, the youngest son, was sometimes on one side, sometimes on the other.

England at this time was a society governed by ruthlessness, greed and poor kingship. When Lanfranc died, in 1089, there was no longer any restraint on the treacherous instincts of William Rufus. The sons of the Conqueror deserved each other, even if the people deserved something better. This was a family so much at war that at one point, Robert and William joined against their younger brother Henry. But events far from Normandy and Winchester were once more to divert the flow of rivalries.

In 1096 Robert decided to go on a Crusade, an expensive business. So William played pawnbroker and Robert hocked Normandy to him for 10,000 silver marks. Ironically, thirty-two years after the Battle of Hastings, Robert of Normandy and the still surviving Edgar the Æthling, the great-nephew of Edward the Confessor, joined forces against a common enemy: the Turks at Antioch. Robert led his warriors on land and Edgar commanded a grand fleet. This is really nothing more than an aside, but it is a reminder that history is not simply a string of dates: some characters who at the time appear to have little more than a walk-on part can, and often do, turn up again later in pivotal parts. Kings often play little part in history other than to hold court to the more powerful history-makers. So it was with William II, William Rufus.

William of Malmesbury wrote that the day before he died, Rufus dreamed that a surgeon was letting his blood and the stream flowed so high that it clouded out the daylight. A monk warned that he should not hunt the next day, but Rufus, having drunk a great deal, did go into the forest. Then came the accident. An attendant called Walter Tirel shot the King with an arrow. William of Malmesbury reported that a few countrymen recovered the body and took it on a cart to the cathedral at Winchester, the blood dripping from it all the way. Three days after the death of Rufus, Henry had seized the Treasury at Winchester and crowned himself King. He needed to take the throne as quickly as he dared while his brother Robert was still away on the Crusade.

Proving a quick-witted politician, Henry introduced a coronation charter that, among other things, declared that he (Henry) would right all the wrongs of William Rufus's reign. He needed also to consolidate his rule throughout the islands and, partly for this reason, he married Matilda, the granddaughter of Edmund Ironside, the son of Æthelred the Unready who had been King of England before Cnut. She was, therefore, the niece of the seemingly ever-present Edgar the Ætheling. Good Queen Maud, as Matilda became known, was, more importantly, the daughter of Malcolm Canmore, King of the Scots, who had been killed in England. The marriage did two things: in theory at least, it gave Henry a respectability that was convenient and it neatly tied a knot with the Scottish kings. But for the moment, Henry had a wee family difference. His brother, Robert, wanted his blood. For six years Henry had to defend William the Conqueror's deathbed promise that he would be King of England. He could not really do that effectively in England itself. He had to fight in Normandy but could not do that until he had properly established his English throne so that it was safe for him to cross the Channel without fear of being usurped while away.

The two brothers met in battle at Tinchebrai in September 1106. Henry, with an army enhanced with Saxon warriors, vanquished his brother Robert, Duke of Normandy. Robert was imprisoned in England where he would have less chance of raising a rebellion. Henry was not only King of England, he was now in full control of Normandy. Effectively, the administrative capital of Normandy was handed from Rouen to London. There is a footnote to the Battle of Tinchebrai: the Saxons in Henry's army regarded the battle as revenge for Hastings. It would be an exaggeration to suggest that Tinchebrai was so important that it started the process that would lead to the Hundred Years War, but its significance should not be ignored. Henry did not have a settled kingdom. For example, the Scots, under King David, had driven Henry's armies as far south as Lancashire. The Scots were perhaps never to be as strong again and when David succeeded his brother, Alexander, as King of all Scotland in 1124, he became an important figure in the holding together of these islands from the north to the south.

Henry was wise enough to understand that throughout his reign he would have to reflect the changes in his kingdom and so he introduced many long-lasting reforms of existing systems; at the same time, he took nothing, certainly not unity, for granted, especially when tragedy settled on the family.

On 25 November, Henry's legitimate son and heir, seventeen-year-old William, was sailing in a vessel called *White Ship* from Normandy back to England, a frequent enough voyage. In the Seine estuary, the vessel struck a rock. How? Bad weather and, according to some reports, the ship's company had taken drink. Whatever the reason, William perished. Apart from the personal tragedy, Henry was faced with a dilemma over succession because there was no other natural male heir to the throne. He nominated his daughter, the Empress Matilda (1102–67) although it was never sure that she would succeed. Medieval succession and accession were rarely simple and agreeable affairs. Matilda, like her mother known as Maud, had been married off when she was just eight to the Emperor Henry V in Germany. The Emperor died in 1125 and three years on, the now twenty-six-year-old Matilda married the fourteen-year-old Geoffrey Martel of Anjou. It was not a happy match, but it produced the future Henry II of England and here, in this marriage, was the start of the Plantagenet history of Britain.

Before his accession much happened, including the Laws of King Henry I. By later standards, these laws were hardly laws at all. Jurisprudence was not contained in an Act of Parliament for there was no such thing. These Laws of Henry I were simply passed to his judges by hand or even by word of mouth. In them there was a clear statement that Edward the Confessor's memory would be honoured. This was so important to the period and the fogged memory of nostalgia. Henry understood this and did not want to give any impression of breaking with the past, particularly with the ways and the image left by Edward the Confessor. At the time, the Confessor was so blessed in English memory, that it was in this century, the twelfth, that he was canonized. St Edward became the patron saint of the English peoples and remained so until the Hundred Years War.

We are at one of the many milestones on the road to Britishness and identity. Henry raised the usefulness of the minor aristocracy by making them middle management administrators and, of course, making certain that the bureaucracy was in place to be administered. For the most part, there basic institutional framework existed even when it was not exploited for any good, never mind that of the commoners. Importantly (and maybe because so much money had to be raised for wars) it was Henry I who developed the Norman idea of the Exchequer, although it was Henry II who put it on a more bureaucratic footing. The name Exchequer comes from the chequered cloth spread on a table to make accounting simpler to follow. Henry I's officials and sheriffs had to account for income and expenditure twice a year when the Exchequer was audited at Easter and Michaelmas.

Naturally, the administration of the islands was not the king's personal task. In Henry I's time, the secretary of state who made the existing institutions, particularly the financial audit, more efficient was a bishop, Roger of Salisbury (1065–1139), a true son of the Conquest. So powerful and trusted was this bishop, that for three years (1123–6) he ruled England while Henry was abroad, where his daughter Matilda and her husband, Geoffrey of Anjou, were at the centre of a rebellion against him. They both wanted him to give them fortresses and acres to substantiate their claim to the throne on his death. Henry did not, partly because he now preferred Stephen, his nephew. He was in Normandy in December 1135, arguing once more with Matilda, when he died at Lyons-la-Forêt. The distance helped Stephen claim the throne. Henry's corpse was embalmed and carried to Reading where it was buried in the monastery church of which he had been the most valued patron.

For almost thirty-six years Henry had ruled England and, for twenty-nine of them, Normandy. But although he had managed to hold back his enemies, he had never satisfied them and never brought them on his side. The barons had suffered because of what they saw as his dictatorial style. Yet it says something for his reign that he survived for so long, especially as the baronage was, on many occasions, at breaking point. *The Anglo-Saxon Chronicle* records that, 'He was a good man, and was held in great awe. In his days no man dared to wrong another. He made peace for man and beast.' But after Henry's death there was to be little peace. Henry was barely embalmed when Stephen – his nephew, the Count of Blois, Champagne and Chartres, and, by his mother, a grandson of William the Conqueror – had the throne of England.

Stephen was consecrated on Christmas Day, 1135. According to the twelfth-century chronicler, Walter Mapp (1140– *c.*1209), a clerk in the Royal Household, Stephen did not fit the template of his, often cruel, predecessors. This is perhaps why the prospects for civil war and anarchy were so strong. One of Stephen's first decisions was to revive the holding of a court, a levee. King Henry had more or less abandoned these gatherings because he thought they were too costly, but this was Stephen's first chance to receive oaths of loyalty. And so the most important people in England gathered at the royal court where they were required publicly to display allegiance to the new King. However, a significant figure missing from that gathering was Robert of Gloucester, an important ally of Matilda.

Robert's support was so crucial to Stephen's future that the court was adjourned until Robert could be present. After considerable negotiations, Robert pledged his loyalty to the King. But he laid down conditions and Stephen was forced to accept this qualified homage. For a while there was uneasy peace. There were small rebellions, but these were dealt with. Stephen crossed to Normandy where there were further uprisings, but when he got back, it was to face anarchy. The Scots were invading from the northern counties, the Welsh were in rebellion but, most dangerously, Robert of Gloucester was preparing for war. The oath of homage was broken. In the early years of his reign Stephen lost the support of the three essential elements of his strength: the baronage, who were sure that this was the long-awaited moment to press their claims; the novel civil service now also began to stand aside from the new King; and much of the Church was against him. King David of Scotland, persuaded of the English decay, crossed the border and laid claim to Northumbria. The Archbishop of York advanced against him with the support of the northern counties and, in a murderous battle at Northallerton, the Archbishop and his forces repulsed and slaugh-tered the invaders. This reverse, far from discouraging the malcontents, was the prelude to civil war.

Moreover, in 1139, Matilda arrived in England to claim her inher-itance including, she thought, the throne. She was not without support, particularly from the bishops. Stephen could not fend off the rebellion. Certainly he was unable to bring together the forces of those who had sworn allegiance to him at court. At the Battle of Lincoln, Stephen was captured and jailed, and Matilda for nearly a year virtually ruled England. But rebellion produced too many factions that held good and so England dissolved into not its first civil war, and not its last.

This was a war of many of the barons who had been dominated by the late king. It was also a chance for the Scots to reclaim territory in England that they believed to be theirs. As ever, the people suffered. Contemporary witnesses write that there was unspeakable cruelty. There was famine: dogs and horses were eaten, and thousands upon thousands starved to death. Stephen was incarcerated at Lincoln but within nine months he was released and was probably more popular than ever. Thanks to her often arrogant and unfeeling behaviour, Matilda had made few friends among the English. So when, in 1145, Stephen's forces scored a great victory at Faringdon in Berkshire, everyone understood that Matilda's fortunes had ebbed and so indeed those of the Church that had once stood as her ally. Then came one of those step-changes in any nation's history. A new monarch upon whom the expectations were as awkward as the crown of statehood was about to be anointed. The process started when the leader of Matilda's faction, Robert of Gloucester, died in 1147. Who would lead for Matilda? The answer: her son, Henry Fitz-Empress. Fitz means 'son' while 'Empress' reflected his mother's title through her first marriage to Henry V, Holy Roman Emperor. The emblem of his father Geoffrey of Anjou's house was the *Planta Genesta*, the broom. And so Henry would now become known as Henry Planta Genesta, Henry Plantagenet.

In 1147 Henry was a teenager, just fifteen, and six weary years were to pass before he could claim the throne. By that time, the architects of anarchy as well as loyal opposition would be dead, so would King David of Scotland and so would Stephen's eldest son, Eustace. He died pillaging the abbey estates of Bury St Edmunds, and was hardly mourned. After this, the people, the bishops and the magnates, tired of war, persuaded Stephen to adopt Henry as his son and therefore his heir. Fourteen months later, in 1154, Stephen was dead and Henry Plantagenet arrived to claim his throne.

Henry's royal bloodline flowed from William the Conqueror and, on his grandmother's side, from the Anglo-Saxons. To the English people the young Henry Plantagenet represented a hope of strong, peaceful government. They had suffered the consequences of anarchy while lords and masters had attempted to regain from Stephen the influence they had lost during the reign of Henry I. There had been famine, cruelty and uncertainty. And now there was a renewal of kingship and a reminder that the King of England was also the ruler of Normandy. In fact, England was a single colony in Henry's empire that ran from the outer islands of Scotland all the way south to the Pyrenees. It is this constant reminder that England was part of a wholly owned geopolitical conglomerate of States, factions and national and dialectic interests that should stay with us for another two centuries and more so that we can understand the process of civil war, as well as the England versus France rivalry, which led to the Hundred Years War that lasted from 1337 to 1453.

When we judge the historical and lasting contribution of one period on the centuries and people that and who followed, then we should gather the spirit and value of the rule of Henry II. Walter Mapp, in his notebook *Of Courtiers' Trifles*, tells that Henry II was:

A little over medium height, a man blessed with sound limbs and a handsome countenance, one upon whom men gazed closely a thousand times, yet took occasion to return. In physical capacity he was second to none, lacking no courtesy, well read to a degree both seemly and profitable, having a knowledge of all tongues from the coasts of France to the river Jordan, but making use of only Latin and French [here again, the king of England who spoke only in French]. In making laws and in ordering the affairs of government he showed discrimination, and was clever in devising new and undiscovered legal procedure; he was easy to approach, modest and humble; though vexed by the importunity of suitors and litigants and provoked by injustice, he bore all in silence. Nevertheless he was ever on his travels, and in this respect he showed little mercy to his household which accompanied him. He had great experience of dogs and birds and was a very keen follower of hounds; in night-watches and labours he was unremitting.

It is also said that Henry never sat down unless it was to eat or ride.[1]

Here was the simple insight into the first ruler of the House of Plantagenet, the father of Richard Coeur de Lion and King John, and the husband of Eleanor of Aquitaine (1122–1204). Eleanor's own position was not simply as the daughter of the Duke of Aquitaine and

---

1   In particular, see Richard Barber, *Henry Plantagenet: A Biography of Henry II of England* (London: Boydell Press, 1964).

therefore a political bride. She had been married to King Louis VII for fourteen years. She was beautiful, full of life. Louis was unbending, worthy, pious. Eleanor once said she was married to a monk, not a king. On one occasion, Pope Eugenius III actually ordered them to sleep in the same bed. The result was, or seems to have been, the birth of a child – but only a daughter and kings, especially French kings, needed a son and heir. This Eleanor had not managed and so in 1152 the marriage was annulled; she immediately married Henry II and bore him five sons – William (who died as an infant), Henry, Richard, Geoffrey and John. She eventually joined forces with Richard against her husband, was imprisoned and stayed there until Henry II's death in 1189.

Medieval kings were rarely ordinary although, given the strife of the times, that is what most would have wished for. Henry was not in that mould. This was the king who destroyed the Adulterine Castles built by barons as bases for their pillage of surrounding hamlets, villages and townships, and who reclaimed the lands given away by Stephen to raise money. Here was the man who sent his knights to Canterbury to rid him of Thomas à Becket, and who sent his Norman knights from Pembroke to Ireland and so started the long English agony of Irish occupation. It was this king who owned more land in France from Anjou to Poitevin to Normandy than the King of France but who was a subject of that monarch.

The power of the monarchy over these lands may have been impressive but Henry II needed wise administrators and his own genius to manage such vast tracts with their own histories, feudal customs and practices and all of which had to have a common bureaucracy and jurisprudence. He established the Exchequer as the central financial control. He deported mercenaries, brought the baronage under sharper if not absolute control and gradually regained royal authority over England. He established what is now the jury system and what was until recently the assize and grand assize courts. Henry II was a confident, intelligent king and a man full of energy. He needed to be. His first task was, naturally, to re-establish central government rather than rely on the feudal system, with the power in the hands of the barons. And, apart from his Continental empire, Henry inherited unresolved business closer to home. He needed to give some order to his relationship with Ireland, Scotland and Wales. The Scots had never regained the dominance achieved under King David I, who had died in 1153. They'd gained control of the northern counties from a weak king suffering civil war and David's successors could not hold them against a strong and well-organized Henry.

The new King of Scotland, Malcolm, paid homage to Henry and Scotland did not regain its independence until Richard I came to the throne. As for Ireland, Henry immediately considered an invasion. Probably the objection of his mother, who influenced many of his ideas, prevented this. But he did have one supporter for an expedition: the Pope. He saw it as a way of bringing Ireland under the direct influence of the Holy See, but that came later, after the death of Becket, and largely at the request of the Irish themselves. Of immediate concern to Henry was Wales.

In 1157, Henry II launched an expedition against the Welsh prince, Owen Gwynedd. It was a disaster. A truce was agreed. Henry's attempts to subjugate north and then south Wales continued to fail. And it wasn't until the peace of 1171 that he was content to leave the Welsh princes to get on with their own affairs. They visited England, they settled their nation's differences, they celebrated their peace with music and verse. And in 1176, at the festival of Christ's Mass, they gathered in the newly built Cardigan Castle for the first Eisteddfod. By then, and far away from bards and musicians, Henry's efforts to reform England were taking shape. In this, Henry II was defeated. But these were the beginnings of a remarkable reign that was to last more than three decades. It was a period of war, legal reform, the invasion of Ireland and the building of a palace in Dublin; a period of the break-up of his marriage, the rebellion of his sons, his own final anguish and the humiliation and the death of Thomas Becket.

CHAPTER SIX
1166–89

Henry II is usually remembered for three things: he was the first Plantagenet king; he developed the idea of the assizes; and, of course, Thomas Becket was martyred.

At the age of seventeen, three years before he became King of England, Henry became Duke of Normandy. His interests, responsibilities and complicated relationships with France dominated much of his private and public life. His education prepared him to rule with more than the two strong arms and courage of the double-handed swordsman. He was taught by the poet, Peter of Saintes. At the age of nine he began his studies in Bristol, where he was influenced by the scientist Adelard of Bath. He was instructed in ethics by William of Conches. Little wonder then, that as Henry II, he should be remembered more for his administrative genius and moral agonies rather than his military achievements and failures in France.

William fitz Stephen describes the London of Henry II in his *Materials for the Life of Thomas Becket* as the capital of England and one which, he says, 'extends its glory farther than all the others and sends its wealth and merchandise more widely into distant lands'. He adds that, 'It is happy in the healthiness of its air; in its observance of Christian practice; in the honour of its citizens; in the modesty of its matrons.' He says that the Tower of London is fixed with mortar, 'tempered by the blood of animals'. He describes the Palace of Westminster as a 'building incomparable in its ramparts and bulwarks'.

Obviously this picture of London, of which any tourist board would be proud, doesn't reflect the fact that England as a whole was less than well ordered. One aspect of twelfth-century society in need of reform was the law. Henry Plantagenet's chief justice, Rannulf Glanvill, supervised the setting out of the first comprehensive record of legal procedure: it was based on a new system of juries and writs. The assizes were developed.

'Assize' comes from the old French word for 'sitting'. A jury sat to assess. And the writ meant, in theory at least, that a man could appeal to the king to put right a wrong of that man's lord and master. The record of the Assize of Clarendon is the first big piece of Henry II's legislation and the earliest document of his major administrative changes. The date is 1166, a hundred years after the Norman Conquest:

> And let anyone who shall be found accused or notoriously suspect of having been a robber or murderer or thief. Or a receiver of them, since the lord King has been King, be taken and put to the ordeal of water. And if the lord of the man who has been arrested shall claim him by pledge within the third day following his capture, let him be released on bail with his chattels until he himself shall stand trial . . . And when a robber or murderer or thief has been arrested, let the sheriffs send word to the nearest justice that they have arrested such men, and that the justices shall send word back to the sheriffs informing them where they desire the men to be brought before them.

So bail may be set, and dates set for hearings. It sounded very fair. However there were a few zero-tolerance (as we would now have it) ideas. Anyone, for example, caught red-handed didn't get a trial. Nor did a person who admitted guilt, even if they denied it later. And the law now attached great importance to a suspect's criminal record or even local knowledge, that the accused was a villain.

These are just a few of the laws from the Assize of Clarendon. The law was set out so that no one could have any doubts. The community was expected to maintain the law. Moreover, the law was there to be seen to be done, which meant that punishment was clear-cut and sometimes gruesome:

> Let him go to the ordeal of the water. And if he fails let him lose one foot. And for the sake of stern justice he shall likewise lose his right hand with his foot, and he shall abjure the realm, and within forty days be banished from the kingdom.

Henry II was trying to make sure that the law was not simply legal memory. He wanted documents to which one could refer to and which could be amended. The law was becoming articulate and, therefore, an institution. And that other institution, the Church, watched with more than a little interest. Just as Henry was bringing secular reforms in his kingdom, so the Roman Church had been reinvigorated, by the late Pope Gregory VII. Pope Gregory believed that the King's single religious role was total obedience to the Church. Conflict between Church and State was inevitable and that inevitability was clearly expressed by Becket.

Thomas Becket was a month away from his thirty-sixth birthday when Henry II came to the throne in 1154. Henry was barely twenty-one. Thomas Becket was born in London, the son of a merchant from Rouen. As a student he had never excelled. In fact, his Latin was so poor that on one occasion, at the Council of Tours, he was so ashamed that he refused to preach. Even as Archbishop, he had a tutor who would explain the complicated theology of the scriptures. But by the time he became a minister in Henry II's household, he was already Archdeacon of Canterbury and Provost of Beverley. It was thanks to the then Archbishop, and his mentor, Theobald, that Becket became Chancellor of the King's household. Theobald's hope was that Becket would guard the interests of the Church. Instead, he became the King's secretary, diplomat and even judge, and was won over by the glamour of court life so much that he often took the King's side rather than that of the Church. No wonder then that when the archbishopric of Canterbury fell vacant, the King made every effort to have Becket elected. Henry believed that if his friend were Chancellor and Archbishop, then the ambitions of the Church in State affairs would be curbed. Some in the Church were cautious about the appointment and the King's emissary; Richard of Luce tried to reassure the clergy that the friendship of King and Chancellor could only mean harmony, not division. Richard of Luce also reminded the gathered clergy of the consequences of not accepting the King's wishes: 'The King is most zealous in everything which concerns the things of God and displays the most utmost devotion towards the holy Church, especially towards this Church of Canterbury, which he recognizes in all humility, loyalty and filial affection as his particular mother in the Lord.'

At last, with one dissenting opinion from Bishop Gilbert of London (who probably wanted to be Archbishop himself), the clergy accepted Becket as the new Archbishop of Canterbury. Becket would not have it that he would be the King's man. He threw away his credentials to the King's court. He was now the Pope's courtier, not Henry's – although the Pope was markedly uneasy about what would be seen as a schism between London and Canterbury.

The open quarrel between the two former friends began as soon as Henry returned from Normandy in January 1163. Becket successfully opposed Henry's demand for customary dues to be paid into the royal Exchequer. He excommunicated one William of Eynesford without consulting the King, as in theory he should have done. He protected clerks and clergy from the full punishment under the law even when some were charged with rape, murder and theft. The King claimed, at the Council of Westminster, the right to punish clerks. The bishops hesitated. Becket told them to stand firm. Henry then confiscated lands owned by Becket from his days as Chancellor. A meeting was arranged between King and Archbishop but what could have been reconciliation became recrimination. And Becket did not have the full support of the clergy, nor of the one person he expected to be sympathetic to his stand against the throne: the Pope, Alexander III. The Pope did not wish to anger the King, nor could he entirely ignore his Archbishop. His decision was to advise Becket to give way to Henry. Henry then made what appears to have been a mistake: he attempted to revoke the promise made by King Stephen that the State should be subservient to the Pope. He published this attempt to put back the clock in 1164, in what was called the Constitutions of Clarendon. Becket was ordered to appear before the Great Council. He would not recognize the king's supremacy and claimed the protection of Rome and God.

That Council was held at Northampton. Becket faced charges of contempt of court, of wrongful use of money that had passed through his hands when he was Chancellor and of wrongfully borrowing money and using the King's name as a guarantor. He was found guilty.

On the fourth day of the Council, the Archbishop offered the King 2,000 marks in compensation. But Henry refused. He was determined to destroy his former friend. The bishops were divided. Becket was shamed and vilified and that night he escaped, first from Northampton, and then from England, into exile. Many churchmen were glad that he was gone. Confrontation with the monarch was a dangerous game, as the Pope knew. Becket became vindictive and on Whit Sunday, 1166, excommunicated a whole bench of bishops. The bishops and clergy complained to the Pope and denounced Becket's declaration as uncanonical and unlawful. It was a quarrel that would have tested the powers of the cleverest diplomat. And here is the irony. Previously, Henry would have had the perfect envoy to resolve such a delicate matter: Becket himself.

But then, six years after Becket's exile, something happened that would eventually bring them together: Henry wanted his son crowned as his successor during his own lifetime. Becket, still Archbishop of Canterbury, should have been the person to officiate. Henry said that the Archbishop of York should stand in for him. The Pope said no. Henry ignored the Pope's ruling. To Becket this was an outrage. The Pope was bound to support him, and so was Louis VII of France, who was in a position to threaten Henry's French possessions. Henry relented. The two men met and according to Henry of Bosham were reconciled with Becket honouring his monarch and, in the sight of all there present, humbly prostrated himself at the King's feet.

That was on 22 July 1170. On 15 October the King issued a proclamation of reconciliation. But the difference was deeper rooted than a proclamation. The next month Becket, still in France and preparing to return to England, suspended the Archbishop of York and once again excommunicated the Bishops of London and Salisbury. On 1 December he landed at Sandwich in Kent and rode to Canterbury. The excommunicated bishops sailed for Normandy, where the King was. Their advice, or so we are told by Becket's friend, William fitz Stephen, in his *Materials for the Life of Thomas Becket*, was blunt, 'My lord, while Thomas lives, you will not have peace or see good days.' Four knights, eager to win Henry's favour, left the court for Canterbury.

It was 29 December 1170. The knights, Reginald Fitz-Urse, William de Traci, Hugh of Morville and Richard Brito, arrived at Canterbury and demanded to see Becket whom they accused of plotting to remove the crown from the King's son. Becket denied it and treated the knights with contempt. 'Cease your threats,' he said, 'and still your brawling. I put my trust in the King of Heaven. I have not come back to flee again. Here shall he who wants me find me.' Becket threatened to excommunicate all who disobeyed the Church. The knights sprang to their feet. One shouted at him, 'We declare that you have spoken in peril of your head.' The knights left but Becket knew they would be back. His clergy pleaded with him to escape. 'It is not meet to make a fortress of the house of prayer,' said Becket in reply. The knights returned and the clergy deserted Becket, hiding among the altars of the vast cathedral. But three remained, including Edward Grim, who wrote down what happened. A translation is in Grim's *Vita S. Thomae, Cantuariensis Archepiscopi et Martyris*:

The invincible martyr – seeing that the hour which would bring the end to his miserable mortal life was at hand and already promised by God to be the next to receive the crown of immortality – with his neck bent as if he were in prayer and with his joined hands elevated above – commended himself and the cause of the Church to God, St Mary, and the blessed martyr St Denis. He had barely finished speaking when the impious knight, fearing that [Becket] would be saved by the people and escape alive, suddenly set upon him and, shaving off the summit of his crown which the sacred chrism consecrated to God, he wounded the sacrificial lamb of God in the head; the lower arm of the writer was cut by the same blow. Indeed [the writer] stood firmly with the holy archbishop, holding him in his arms – while all the clerics and monks fled – until the one he had raised in opposition to the blow was severed. Behold the simplicity of the dove, behold the wisdom of the serpent in this martyr who presented his body to the killers so that he might keep his head, in other words his soul and the church, safe; nor would he devise a trick or a snare against the slayers of the flesh so that he might preserve himself because it was better that he be free from this nature! O worthy shepherd who so boldly set himself against the attacks of wolves so that the sheep might not be torn to pieces! and because he abandoned the world, the world – wanting to overpower him – unknowingly elevated him. Then, with another blow received on the head, he remained firm. But with the third the stricken martyr bent his knees and elbows, offering himself as a living sacrifice, saying in a low voice, 'For the name of Jesus and the protection of the church I am ready to embrace death.' But the third knight inflicted a grave wound on the fallen one; with this blow he shattered the sword on the stone and his crown, which was large, separated from his head so that the blood turned white from the brain yet no less did the brain turn red from the blood; it purpled the appearance of the church with the colours of the lily and the rose, the colours of the Virgin and Mother and the life and death of the confessor and martyr. The fourth knight drove away those who were gathering so that the others could finish the murder more freely and boldly. The fifth – not a knight but a cleric who entered with the knights – so that a fifth blow might not be spared him who had imitated Christ in other things, placed his foot on the neck of the holy priest and precious martyr and (it is horrible to say) scattered the brains with the blood across the floor, exclaiming to the rest, 'We can leave this place, knights, he will not get up again.'

The night passed in lamentation and mourning. The single most shocking event in the twelfth-century Christian world had occurred. The Christian ruler of a Christian nation had ordered the assassination of his Archbishop because that Archbishop had stood up for his belief that no one, not even a king, was above the law of the Church and therefore God. The rights and wrongs of the tale are irrelevant. That is how the event was seen by the majority. Becket was a martyr and within two years he was canonized. Churches were dedicated to his name. In the Holy Land the order of the knights of St Thomas of Acre was instituted. As far north as Iceland the life of the martyr appeared in sagas. He became the subject of iconography. Thomas Becket frescoes appeared in Rome. In his name antiphons were sung with psalms.

For two years Henry II was ostracized. But he recovered. He was, after all, a king and he had done at least symbolic penance. The symbol of his recovery was Ireland. The story that Henry II invaded Ireland to enlarge his empire is only a small part of the beginnings of the Anglo-Irish condition – often seen as a difficult one from whichever shore of the treacherous sea it is viewed.

The beginning of the story may lie with Nicholas Breakspear of St Albans who became Pope Adrian IV and still the only English pontiff albeit for a short time (1154–9). He was not much regarded in Ireland, not because he was English but because the Irish did not much care for any doctrine of papal authority, particularly supremacy. The Irish Church was dominated by the monasteries, much to Rome's annoyance because that monastic existence had no need for

Rome. The monasteries influenced the running of the Church and doctrine in Ireland, and took small notice of custom other than their own. For example, the See of Armagh was hereditary (family patronage being a powerful influence) and therefore in need of broods. It is not surprising, then, that eight of its bishops appear to have been married and had children, and did not even have to be ordained. Even considering the sentiments and conditions of the times, the bishops of Armagh led eccentric livings.

Looking over maps and charts in his papal room, it is not unlikely that Pope Adrian could see that geography held an answer to the aggravation. The British Isles, as we shall still call them, was from Rome's distance an obvious collection of land and peoples with no hard reason to live separately from each other. If England came under Rome's dominion, then so should the whole collection of islands, including Ireland. Adrian therefore made this official by issuing a papal bull, 'Laudabiliter', which gave Henry II authority over Ireland and therefore brought it into Rome's map of Catholic holdings. In future, it was up to Henry II, or any other monarch for that matter, to make sure that Ireland did not break away.

The matter came to something long after Adrian IV's passing in 1159. The King of Leinster, Dermot MacMurrough was deposed by the King of Connaught, Rory O'Connor. It took MacMurrough nearly two years to find Henry who was seemingly far away looking after his French interests. Henry gave permission of some of the Norman knights castled in Pembrokeshire to go to the rescue. It was a difficult decision, which Henry monitored very carefully. The Norman knights, led by Richard de Clare, known as Strongbow, landed in 1170 and were successful in restoring the Irish monarch to his Leinster throne. But Henry, probably rightly, then guessed that the Norman knights might stay, marry into the Irish royalty and aristocracy and so build a potential stronghold that would eventually threaten his kingdom. He could have had no doubt of this when MacMurrough died in 1171 leaving Leinster to Strongbow.

With the dubious authority of Adrian's Laudabiliter, Henry landed at Waterford on 17 October 1171. He took with him nearly 5,000 knights and archers. It took 400 ships from Bristol to transport men, stores and even siege towers. Only the kings of Tyrone and

Tyrconnell refused to pay homage to Henry. This didn't bother him. He moved to Dublin, built a palace, entertained the princes and very soon the submission of the Irish Church followed. Within a year, Henry, supported by the Pope, was recognized as Lord of Ireland. The Pope made it clear to the bishops that they must support Henry in his work of subduing what he called, 'this barbarous and uncouth race, ignorant of divine law'.

However, Henry failed to understand the triad of interests that existed. Anglo-Norman barons fought each other. The Irish fought among themselves and against the barons. And third, intermarriage founded a new class: the Anglo-Irish. Despite this Henry Plantagenet, restored to papal favour after Becket's death, was now one of the most powerful rulers in Europe.

Although he may have for a brief moment brought his reputation up high, he was beside himself with the treachery and scheming of his own family. His sons, Henry (who died of dysentery in 1183), Richard, Geoffrey and John, wanted power and, to get it, only the death of their father would do. Eleanor, Henry II's Queen, drove their ambition. They rejoiced even when their father imprisoned his wife for her treason. They promised one day to free her, but really gave little sign that they meant it. During 1173 and 1174, they had the help of disaffected barons and they rebelled. At the right moment Philip II Augustus of France (1165–1223) joined with them. The French monarch was to be remembered as the man who broke the spirit and the influence of the Angevin empire, from which Henry II, as Henry Plantagenet, came. In 1188, his son Richard, who ruled Aquitaine, defeated him at Le Mans with the support of King Philip. Henry II was defeated by his sons and stepped away from the struggle life had dealt. 'Shame, shame on a conquered king,' he is said to have uttered before his death and, perhaps, that shame was the sadness that he, the monarch, had sired such treacherous sons.

The chronicler, Gerald of Wales, tells us that Henry, 'uttering words of dire calamity, the herald of his own confusion, passed away, overwhelmed and oppressed with grief rather than succumbing to a natural death'. At his burial, there was not, says Gerald, 'a ring for his finger, a sceptre for his hand or crown for his head; scarcely any insignia of royalty but what had been begged for the purpose'.

Henry II, the lawmaker, the gatherer of lands and riches, died on 6 July 1189. Only one son, Geoffrey, was at his deathbed. In cloisters and chancels, news of Henry's miserable end was recited and, with it, the pronouncement that this was God's vengeance delivered upon Henry Plantagenet, murderer of Thomas Becket.

CHAPTER SEVEN
1189–99

Henry II's eldest surviving son, Richard, succeeded him in 1189. Richard I (1157–99) was to rule for just ten years, mostly *in absentia*. But in that decade he built a naval town, Portsmouth, on the south coast; drew up the first Articles of War; sold Scotland its independence; led a great Crusade; and would be called Richard Coeur de Lion.

And yet this was the man who rejected the peace efforts of Pope and bishops and, with the King of France, defeated his own father in battle; the man who, once the campaign was done, forced the dying King, his father, into accepting humiliating terms and who wasted little time in mourning. And yet, Richard is probably remembered as a man of great chivalry. That can only be because he is Richard Coeur de Lion, Richard the Lionheart, the crusader hero of European medieval history. He captured Messina and Cyprus, where he married Berengaria of Navarre (*c.*1170–1230), and defeated the feared Saladin. He was kidnapped, held to ransom and only briefly returned to England.

So Richard I was an absentee landlord. He freed his mother, Queen Eleanor, whom Henry II had imprisoned for encouraging Richard's and John's rebellion. Eleanor became Richard's representative in England. He also made peace with his late father's supporters, partly because it was in his nature to do so, but mainly because he did not want a palace coup while he was away. He also intended to install himself as Duke of Normandy. Richard was also generous to his two surviving brothers who had not always shown loyalty to him. To Geoffrey he gave the vacant Archbishopric of York and to the youngest son, John, he gave Isabel, the third daughter of the Earl of Gloucester, as well as lordships, castles and six entire counties: Devon, Cornwall, Dorset, Somerset, Nottingham and Derby. John was already Lord of Ireland. When Richard finally arrived in England, in the summer of his father's death, he was received with great delight by the people. But within four months, and having been crowned at Westminster, he was gone again. The Crusades were an expensive business. Money had to be raised at phenomenal levels and so he sold Berwick and Roxburgh to King William I of Scotland for 10,000 silver marks. He had also to agree tenuous truces with warlords, princes and kings of Europe. The whole of Europe was seemingly fighting for influence and lands and the Pope sent emissaries throughout Europe pleading with princes and kings to stop fighting each other and turn their efforts towards the certain evil that threatened Christendom: Saladin. Richard responded to the Pope's call to 'Take the Cross', the expression used to go on the Crusade. He and Philip of France, although engaged in open conflict with each other, resolved to 'Take the Cross' together.

Richard led his army to within twelve miles of Jerusalem, but that was as close as he ever came to victory. As did so many enemies in war, Richard became increasingly friendly with the man he was fighting, Saladin. They met and discussed ways in which Jerusalem might be partitioned. Nevertheless the Crusade was doomed, largely because of the disunity among its leaders. Richard was forced to set out for home, hurried by news that his own kingdom was in a state of near anarchy. It was on this journey back to England that he was kidnapped. Richard had sailed from Acre on 9 October 1192 but he was shipwrecked, and he tried to head home by land. This meant going through the region of Vienna controlled by Duke Leopold of Austria, a man with whom Richard had quarrelled during the Crusade. Leopold captured Richard in December and kept him prisoner until the following February. He then sold him to the Holy Roman Emperor, Henry VI, who demanded 150,000 marks ransom. To get some idea of the enormous sum this ransom represented, it was considered to be almost twice the normal annual revenue of the English estate. There is ever skulduggery in medieval lore. King Philip of France and Richard's brother John offered the Holy Roman Emperor the same amount of ransom if he gave them Richard rather than set him free for England. However, the Emperor honoured his agreement with Richard and the King returned home on 13 March 1194. The ransom had all but impoverished his people, but they cheered him and his fame.

John made little secret of his treachery and attempted to raise
another rebellion. However, war had now started against Philip of
France and Richard crossed the Channel to defend his possessions.
He was never to return to England. It may have been the case that
sensitive and State appointments still had to be approved by the
King and, accordingly, delegations would be sent from England to
find the King at some camp or siege to get his instruction. For day-
to-day administration of his realm, Richard relied on good and
faithful servants. One such person was the Archbishop of
Canterbury and Chief Justice, Hubert Walter, the man who had
been in charge of raising the ransom for Richard's release. He had
been a student at Bologna and a judicial and administrative clerk in
the household of Henry II (whose system of law and government
required the King's authority, but not necessarily always his presence). He now had a reputation as a clear-sighted and loyal servant
of the absent King. Hubert Walter's career in the household of
Henry II was a sensitive training ground for the task he took on: the
assurance that what we would call central government would work
in medieval England. It is in Walter's administration that we find
the role of the coroner emerging as a public servant whose office
would survive any interludes of maladministration down the
centuries.

There had been mention of the office of coroner as early as the
late ninth and early tenth centuries although it has never been clear
what powers the coroner would have other than as 'crowner' to
preserve the authority of crown property, especially the collection of
any death duties. The coroner as we would think of him or her in the
twenty-first century dates quite specifically from September 1194
when Walker established the office, or at least put it on a proper
constitutional and legal footing. It was also about this time that the
civic bureaucracy was strengthened to include the office of Mayor of
London. The first 'Lord' Mayor of London appeared in about 1191,
a man called Henry fitz Ailwin. The importance of this new machinery of administration is clear: the king was no longer the single
guarantor of law and order. But the law, the administration and the
genius of Hubert Walter could not lessen Richard's demands for
funds for his war against Philip of France and his treacherous brother,
John. And it was the need to finance this campaign that led to the
death of the King.

In 1199, while laying siege to a castle at Châlus in France, Richard was hit in the neck by an arrow. He probably died from gangrene. He knew that he would not last and so made those about him swear allegiance to John (1166–1216), his brother and the favourite son of their father, Henry II. It is also said that on his deathbed, Richard pardoned the archer who had fired the fatal bolt. Much good it did either of them. Richard died in considerable discomfit and the archer was flayed alive. This was, after all, still the twelfth century.

CHAPTER EIGHT
1199–1216

The barons had strengthened their position during Richard I's reign in spite of the celebrated administration reforms and curbs of Hubert Walter. They certainly did not like the crown taking extra powers and demanding money to fight wars. They were always ready to confront the new King, John. John had been known as John Lackland for the obvious reason that he actually possessed no great acreage, which is why Henry II, his father, had declared him Lord of Ireland. He had divorced his first wife, Avice of Gloucester. Avice (known as Isabel) gave John no heir, so he divorced her. She later married twice, the second time to one of the most powerful men in the history of the time, Hubert de Burgh (d.1243), who negotiated with the barons on behalf of King John and who led a small flotilla to defeat an invading French fleet in the Channel in 1217. The king's second wife was Isabella of Angoulême, the mother of the future Henry III and Richard, Earl of Cornwall (1209–72). If John personally lacked land, he most certainly was a landless monarch when Philip II Augustus precipitated the loss of the English territories in France – Anjou, Brittany, Maine and Normandy.

How did this all come about after such a relatively stable inheritance? When John became King he immediately did what all heirs did in those days; he took control of the Treasury. Then he rode to Rouen and his investiture as Duke of Normandy. Next, he crossed the Channel, and on Ascension Day John was crowned King of England at Westminster. Not everyone applauded. Moreover, he did not have much support on the Continent. Matters were hardly improved when he married Isabella. She was supposed to have married Hugh the Brown of Lusignan. The House of Lusignan was insulted and John was too arrogant to pay them off, which was the normal way of going about these matters, and the family laid a formal complaint at the court of Philip, who gleefully summoned John to court. John, through his French titles, was a vassal of the French King. So under French law he should have answered the summons but he refused to go. That was how the lands were confiscated.

King John then had to face Arthur of Brittany (son of John's brother Geoffrey) who now attempted to kidnap Eleanor, the King's mother and his own grandmother. John rescued her and, most controversially, took Arthur prisoner. Arthur, aged sixteen, was perhaps the most serious threat to John's own throne and he was sent to prison first at Falaise and then Rouen. It is said that John's knights went to Rouen and castrated Arthur who died of shock during the crude surgery. The Bretons went into great revolt at the news of the murder of their duke. Philip of France watched as others withdrew their support from John. But Normandy was not ready to fall for the French King. It was rich, there were many loyal to John and reinforcements could be brought from England. But John was not an inspired leader. He appealed to Pope Innocent to rule against Philip of France. It came to nothing and then, in December 1203, John returned to England and by Midsummer's Day, 1204, all that England had left of the Duchy of Normandy were the Channel Islands.

It was now, in 1205, that Eleanor died. She had almost single-handedly protected John's interests as best she could in France. Of equal seriousness, Hubert Walter died. It was not in John's gift to appoint the Archbishop of Canterbury. Pope Innocent III chose Cardinal Langton as the new Archbishop. King John, who preferred John de Gray, Bishop of Norwich, retaliated against the decision by seizing Church lands. In 1208, the Pope responded by laying England under an interdict, which meant that the whole country had been excommunicated. For six years, the churches remained closed. People couldn't be given a Christian baptism, marriage or burial. John seized more property. The Pope excommunicated him. Philip of France was delighted: he was all ready to invade England. After all, with England outside the Church, such an adventure would be regarded as a Crusade. Instead of openly fighting the Pope, John suggested that England should be a fiefdom of Rome. The Pope was delighted. He accepted England and then returned the country to John to keep it safely as his vassal. Moreover, if the French attacked England, they would be attacking the Pope. That could not be done. As for Stephen Langton, he saw Rome taking over the English see.

That could not happen, he thought, and so became an enemy of the very Vicar of Christ who had originally appointed him to Canterbury.

This was a very clever strategy by John, but if he was normally that astute, he should have been able to protect himself from the barons. He could not. They were the constitutional grandchildren of Henry II's reforms. They now felt the time had come to make sure that arbitrary rule by one king could never again usurp the custom and law of the land and its peoples, especially if those peoples included the barons. Who would lead the barons? Stephen Langton, of course.

The result of all this was the Great Charter, Magna Carta. At St Paul's Cathedral, Archbishop Langton produced the first list of demands and read it aloud to the barons. The barons took up the cry and promised they would enforce the liberties contained in that document. This was the start of the fight for what would be known as the Articles of the Barons and, eventually, the first Magna Carta (there were to be many). Most of the barons were not after removing the monarchy nor all its powers. They wanted to safeguard their own positions in the future when a new monarch with a leaning towards despotism or even a madman might be king.

The first document of the barons' demands was short and drafted after a meeting at Runnymede. It is perhaps the most momentous single document in the history of these lands. Without it, there would have been no Magna Carta, no Great Charter. And we have it still, the very parchment that was at Runnymede: there are two copies in the British Museum, one in Salisbury Cathedral and one in Lincoln Cathedral. The parchment of forty-nine Articles begins with the simple statement: 'These are the articles which the Barons ask for and the Lord King grants.'

The Charter reflects feudal law and feudal custom. The taxes (aids and scutage) are feudal, so too are the ways of raising and paying debts. The assizes were to be held more often; the liberty of the Church was to be respected. However, this is not an old document irrelevant to our twenty-first century times. We should today ever remember the original words and sentiment of Article 39:

No free man shall be arrested or imprisoned or disseised [legally disposed] or outlawed or exiled or victimized in any other way, neither will we attack him or send anyone to attack him, except by lawful judgment of his peers or by the law of the land.

On this Article alone rests much of what most in Britain in the twenty-first century believe as their rights and protection from a police state. In the thirteenth century, Magna Carta promised the concept that any man shall be entitled to trial by the due process of the law.

In theory, the Charter's great achievement was to establish that no one, not even a king was above the law. If he attempted to override the law, there now existed a process 'To distrain and distress him in every possible way'. Curiously, Magna Carta had little immediate constitutional significance and some petty and cruel barons even attacked officers of the Royal Household who tried to implement the Charter.

With the barons having got the Charter, it might seem that there could be little reason for war. That supposes John felt fine about the Charter. He did not. It assumes that the barons felt fine about the King. They did not. What they really wanted was to rid themselves of the King. The recalcitrant barons were not republicans and, remember, the English aristocracy was also 'French', which was why a case could be made for calling the thirteenth- and fourteenth-century Hundred Years War a civil war, not simply a conflict between France and England. So, we should not be surprised that the barons called upon Louis, the son of King Philip of France, to lead them against John and, if he was successful, to become king. Furthermore, the Scots led by Alexander and the Britons led by Llewellyn would join with the barons. So would the towns of London, Winchester and Worcester. The south-east Channel ports, the Cinque Ports of Rye, Winchelsea, Hastings, Hythe, Sandwich and Dover, if not for the barons, were subject to them. Clearly John was not enormously popular, but nor was he alone. Individuals, including William the Marshal, the Earl of Pembroke, could bring their troops. It was an altogether bloody affair. Louis was on his way from France and the Cinque Ports safely in command of his sponsors, but John took Rochester and with the help of money and mercenaries, mostly pillaging Flemings, at least held his ground, while his mercenaries laid waste to it. Louis, meanwhile, had landed and taken Winchester and Southampton, so in effect had control of key points in England with his supporters holding even more.

By Christmas 1215 John had reached Nottingham; by early January 1216 he was in York; and by the middle of the month he was as far north as Berwick. The new Scottish King, Alexander II, encouraged by the northern barons, raided across the border. For nearly two weeks, John's troops struck into the lowlands, punishing the Scottish King by harrying his people. John then turned and marched south with his foreign mercenaries, who plundered their way through Lincolnshire and then East Anglia. The Flemings were not the only criminals of war. Local barons and squires used the war as an excuse to kill, maim, steal and land-grab. These travesties actually helped the King. He needed money to continue the war and so instead of physical punishments he imposed massive fines: 1,000 pounds from York and Beverley; 80 silver marks from Thirsk; another 100 from Melton Mowbray. Within three months King John had reconquered the north of his country. And then came the end, as described by one John de Erley, a squire of William the Marshal:

> Finally, he the King, made his way towards Lindsey. On the way he was seized by illness. He was forced to stop at Newark. With him were the Bishop of Winchester, John of Monmouth, Walter Clifford, sire Roger, John Marshal and a number of other men of high rank. Feeling his illness growing worse, King John said to them: 'My Lords, I must die; I cannot hold against this illness.'

The best evidence suggests that over-tiredness, too much food and too much wine left King John with dysentery. He died on 18 October 1216, exactly 150 years, almost to the day, after another king, Harold, had perished defending his realm against the invasion. John was dead and therefore so was one of the main reasons for the war. John's successor was his son, Henry, who was nine years old. The barons had no quarrel with Henry. Rome and the de facto ruler after John's death, William the Marshal, who would become a reluctant regent, decided that constitutional precedence must be followed, otherwise the ambition of others for the throne would send the realm into even bloodier civil war. Henry was crowned at Gloucester on 28 October 1216 and began a remarkable reign of more than half a century.

As for Louis of France, he still believed he could be King of England. In the winter of 1216 he returned to France for reinforcements and many of his English supporters deserted. On 20 May 1217, the remaining barons and Louis were defeated in the narrow streets of the Battle of Lincoln or the Fair of Lincoln, as it became known. Three months later the reinforcements raised by Blanche of

Castile, Louis's wife, put to sea under the command of the royalist traitor, Eustace the Monk. Royalist sailors came alongside the French ships, threw quicklime into the eyes of the French crews and seized the vessels. The intended invasion was over.

CHAPTER NINE
1217–72

Henry III was king for fifty-six years. For the first ten of them he was too young to rule. England was ruled by a Regency and was in need of firm government. When the nine-year-old Henry became King in 1216, England was still engaged in the Barons' War. After Louis's defeat (cushioned by 10,000 silver marks) all the King's men started to put Henry's house in order. Three of these were William the Marshal, Stephen Langton, the Archbishop of Canterbury, and Hubert de Burgh. However, they didn't unquestioningly support the Crown. So, in 1216, we have the young King, formidably protected by Church, State, Treasury and sword. At first, William the Marshal and Guala, the Papal Legate, managed the task. But within two years of Henry's coronation Guala left England. The following year, William the Marshal died.

So it was that Hubert de Burgh became the Justiciar, the chief officer of the realm. Hubert de Burgh had the full support and counsel of the Archbishop, Stephen Langton. And both led Henry to the point, in 1227, when he could confidently declare himself of age and rule his kingdom. Henry may not have been held responsible for his father John's misadventures with finances and the authority of the monarch, but he was hardly without his violent critics. The country was not well run; there was hopeless fiscal management at the highest levels; there was particular anger at the intrusion into court and bureaucracy of foreigners, all favourites of Henry and of his wife, Eleanor of Provence (c.1223–91), whom he wed in 1236. The fact that Henry rebuilt Westminster in the name of Edward the Confessor meant presumably that he wished to be seen as a devout king. In piety there is little retribution for grievance.

The next twenty-four years were uneasy years. The relationship between the young King and the barons was rarely anything but unsettled. When he was a child, Henry's Regency had to consult the barons. Once he became King, Henry, naturally, ruled in his own style and through the hand-picked servants of the Crown. The barons preferred the old way. Also, the barons believed that his Queen's relations encouraged the King to think too much about his French claims. That meant spending money. It meant taxes and loans. And many of the barons no longer had direct interests in France. They also knew that Magna Carta, no matter how many times it was revised and reissued (it wasn't a one-off document but more like a modern Act of Parliament which may be amended), wasn't enough to control the King and force him to consult them on important matters, not even through the Great Council.

In theory the Great Council was a sort of Privy Council. But because the King could call anyone he liked to it, and therefore not call anyone he didn't like, it did not have much power. Neither did the barons, or so they thought. In 1258 there was a constitutional confrontation, and it went on for seven years. The immediate result was the Provisions of Oxford.

The Provisions of Oxford were reforms rather than rules. They were issued by a committee appointed by the Oxford Parliament in 1258 (the Parliament sat in different places, not Westminster as today). It was in this year that the word 'Parliament' entered the language. The word comes from the Norman French, meaning a gathering to talk about important matters, to parley. It was a direct development of the Curia Regis, the royal court of the Norman kings. They were nothing like the modern Parliaments with Speakers, a government party, an opposition front bench or chief whips. Instead, the thirteenth-century Parliaments were the more important sessions of the Great Council.

The Provisions of Oxford, drawn-up by a committee of twenty-four sound men, contain a series of oaths which illustrate something of the importance of the new Council of Fifteen and its Parliaments. For example:

There are to be three Parliaments a year. The first on the octave is Michaelmas. The second, the morrow of Candelmas. The third, the first Holy day of June, that is to say, three weeks before St John's Day.

Power to appoint the Council would be chosen not by the monarch but by the Earl Marshal, Hugh Bigod, John Mansel and the Earl of Warwick instead:

> And they are to have authority to advise the King in good faith on the government of the kingdom and all things pertaining to the King or to the kingdom, and authority to amend and redress all the things they see need to be redressed and amended. And authority over the chief Justiciar, and over all other people. And if they cannot be present, what the majority does shall be firm and established.

Here, then, one more tablet in the mosaic of the image and heritage of the British. The king would have executive power but would share a considerable part of it with the Council of Fifteen and the Justiciar – the word came from the medieval Latin, *justiciarius*, from which comes justice. It was also, certainly by Norman times, the title held by the king's chief minister. By Henry II, the title *justiciarius totius Angliae* was exclusive given to his chief minister. The role is not easy to define but, for example, Elizabethan secretaries of state such as William and Robert Cecil, had a similar function. There was also a further tablet in that mosaic of the British. The Provisions of Oxford were written in French, Latin and in English. There may seem little remarkable in that, but, for a hundred years, English had not been used as an official language. So perhaps this tells us how important the Provisions of Oxford were: they were intended to have the widest possible readership. Moreover, this was just another step in constitutional reform. In 1259 the Provisions of Oxford were reinforced by the Provisions of Westminster.

One of the names that appears in these Provisions, clearly and unswervingly is on the side of the earls and barons. He was the Norman Lord Simon, Earl of Leicester, remembered as Simon de Montfort (*c*.1208–65). He was undoubtedly the leader of the baronial opposition to the King. In 1230 Simon had arrived in England to claim the Earldom of Leicester by way of his grandmother. The Plantagenet kings had refused Frenchmen the right of hereditary title in English lands for obvious reasons – such refusal reduced the chances of a 'Frenchman' raising a rebellion against the throne. Given the times, this was not an unlikely event. Simon was not, at first appearances, a likely usurper of the King's authority. He was said to be pious and this slightly softened Henry's suspicions – but only slightly. De Montfort was busy at court and married Eleanor, the sister of Henry III, in 1238 and received his earldom in 1239. The marriage was not a matter of course, for Eleanor was supposed to be in chastity as part of her mourning for her late husband, William the Marshal, the Earl of Pembroke, who had died seven years earlier. Many of the barons expressed deep anger at the wedding and Henry, although not necessarily under any obligation to do so, defended his sister and his new brother-in-law.

Mainly because of his dubious ways of raising money, the ever poor de Montfort was forced into exile and, with his reputation still that of a man of some piety, joined the 1240 Crusade. He governed Gascony from 1248, when the intrigue of the King's courtiers led to him being accused of being a brutal lieutenant governor of Gascony and its peoples. He was dragged to Westminster in the spring of 1252 to stand trial against these accusations. The commission could find no evidence strong enough to convict him. So firm was the judgment that the court had to promise de Montfort financial compensation as a wrong defendant against such serious charges. The money was important but de Montfort's deeper anger was directed at Henry's court, the royal party as we could now call these cohorts. It did not help the King's case that the compensation was not paid.

It is now that we come back to the Provisions of Oxford. In 1258, we find de Montfort's name among a list of seven barons who demanded that the King should send abroad his generally detested Poitevin half-brothers and at the same time observe strictly the terms of the Provisions of Oxford, reforming his household to enable this.

Simon de Montfort became increasingly powerful. He struck up an understanding with the King's son, Edward, who was emerging as one of the first political princes in English history and one who believed he was being excluded by the royal party from his rightful role of being part of the governing of his country. Young men rallied to Edward. They knew that he would be King one day and they believed him to be more trustworthy than his father. But the difference between Simon de Montfort and the young Prince Edward was this: Simon believed that through the Council – the Parliament – the King could be controlled. Edward saw the Council as a group of advisers, nothing more.

King Henry became suspicious of the alliance between his son and de Montfort, even though their differences were obvious. Henry sent Edward into exile, but he was not a good enough leader to keep control of his kingdom as it headed for civil war. His dilemma deepened when Richard de Clare, Earl of Gloucester, his finest and probably most loyal general, died in July 1262. De Montfort was once more in exile in France but was ensconced in the protection of the French court of Louis IX who was hardly Henry III's ally but was equally unwilling to support a movement that threatened monarchy, as de Montfort would shortly find out.

De Montfort was by now on firmer legal and constitutional grounds as well as leading an increasingly uncompromising baronial group against the King. Henry had followed neither the spirit nor the letter of the Provisions. De Montfort now returned to England and demanded the Parliament use its authority to observe the Provisions with considerable force of arms. Henry persuaded de Montfort to allow the French King to decide who was right and who was wrong. De Montfort thought he had an ally in Louis IX, but Louis would agree with nothing that questioned absolute, even divine, royal power. He sat with the evidence at the Mise (judgment and writ) of Amiens in 1264. Louis not only rejected the terms of the Provisions but ruled that Henry III's full and earlier powers should be restored. This was not at all what the barons had expected. The barons draw their swords and on 14 May 1264 defeated King Henry at the Battle of Lewes.

Lewes was the start of the Second Barons' War. With the King and Edward captured, De Montfort was, in effect, ruler of England. But he had no ambitions to replace Henry, nor Edward. With the Bishop of Chichester and Gilbert de Clare, the new Earl of Gloucester, Simon de Montfort governed England in the name of the King. But the alliance was short-lived because the new Earl of Gloucester had the same instincts as his father: he was a royalist. Throughout 1265 Simon de Montfort's position weakened. Gloucester's doubts were made more public and, when Prince Edward escaped from de Montfort in May, Gloucester went with him. Edward, singing the praises of Magna Carta, not the Provisions of Oxford, raised an army in the Welsh Marches. Effectively, Edward was uniting the barons under his and not de Montfort's slogan of reform. Anything de Montfort said or did now appeared to be nothing more than personal rather than constitutional ambition.

Militarily de Montfort was weakened and forced to retreat into Wales. His son, the younger Simon, had raised troops from the south-east, but they never reached the elder de Montfort. Instead, Edward's army demolished them near Kenilworth. De Montfort could not know this and pressed on in the belief that he would be reinforced at any moment. When his army arrived at Evesham in August 1265, it was clear that he stood quite alone. The Welsh were beaten back and de Montfort killed. Yet his rebellion had not died with him. True, his followers were stripped of their properties; but a guerrilla campaign began in England. Supporters of the dead de Montfort became known as the Disinherited. They became outlaws. They hid in hills and in forests including the great forest of Sherwood. It was clear that the king had to make provisions for the grievance otherwise he would ever be at civil war and always in danger of being deposed and the authority of his crown with him.

When the next legal reform provision, the Statute of Marlborough of 1267, was drawn up it may have been so that the King could once again choose his own advisers, councillors and servants, but the causes of the original de Montfort supporters were evident in that document. Magna Carta was invoked. (Note how often this happened in English history: Magna Carta was the only authority for reform.) Regular Parliaments were to be held:

Provisions made at Marlborough in the Presence of our Lord King Henry, and Richard King of the Romans, and the Lord Edward eldest Son of the said King Henry, and the Lord Ottobon, Legate in England

In the Year of Grace, One thousand two hundred sixty-seven, the two-and-fiftieth Year of the Reign of King Henry, Son of King John, in the Utas of Saint Martin, the said King our Lord providing for the better Estate of his Realm of England, and for the more speedy Ministration of Justice, as belongeth to the Office of a King, the more discreet Men of the Realm being called together, as well of the higher as of the lower Estate: Provided, agreed, and ordained, that whereas the Realm of England of late had been disquieted with manifold Troubles and Dissensions; for Reformation whereof Statutes and Laws be right necessary, whereby the Peace and Tranquillity of the People must be observed; wherein the King, intending to devise convenient Remedy, hath made these Acts, Ordinances, and Statutes underwritten, which he willeth to be observed for ever firmly and inviolably of all his Subjects, as well high as low.

... It was Provided and established and with full consent ordained, That (whereas the Realm of England having been of late depressed by manifold Troubles and the evils of Dissensions, standeth in need of a Reformation of the Laws and Usages, whereby the Peace and Tranquillity of the People may be preserved, whereto it behoved the King and his liege Men to apply an wholesome Remedy,) the Provisions, Ordinances, and Statutes underwritten, should be firmly and inviolably observed by all the People of the same Realm, as well high as low, for ever.

And here we have the case of Distress. It means no one could settle grievances – personal, financial or whatever – other than through the Crown: in other words, only through the courts. This protection and definition of distress was so important and it would remain vital in British law into the twenty-first century:

Of wrongful Distresses, or Defiances of the King's Courts. Punishment for unlawful Distresses:

Whereas at the time of a Commotion late stirred up within this Realm, and also sithence, many great Men, and divers other, refusing to be justified by the King and his Court, like as they ought and were wont in Time of the King's noble Progenitors, and also in his Time; but took great Revenges and Distresses of their Neighbours, and of other, until they had Amends and Fines at their own Pleasure; and further, some of them by the King's Officers, nor suffer them to make Delivery of such Distresses as they had taken of their own Authority; It is Provided, agreed, and granted, that all Persons, as well of high as of low Estate, shall receive Justice in the King's Court; and none from henceforth shall take any such Revenge or Distress of his own Authority, without Award of our Court, though he have Damage or Injury, whereby he would have amends of his Neighbour either higher or lower.

And upon the foresaid Article It is Provided and granted, that if any from henceforth take such Revenges of his own Authority, without Award of the King's Court as before is said, and be convict thereof, he shall be punished by Fine, and that according to the

Trespass; and likewise if one Neighbour take a Distress of another without Award of the King's Court, whereby he hath Damage, he shall be punished in the same wise, and that after the Quantity of the Trespass; and nevertheless sufficient and full Amends shall be made to them that have sustained Loss by such Distresses.

Distresses shall not be driven out of the County. Distresses shall be reasonable.

None from henceforth shall cause any Distress that he hath taken, to be driven out of the County where it was [taken]; and if one Neighbour do so to another of his own Authority, and without Judgment, he shall make Fine, as above is said, as for a Thing done against the Peace; nevertheless, if the Lord Presume so to do against his Tenant, he shall be grievously punished by Amerciament.

Moreover, Distresses shall be reasonable, and not too great; and he that taketh great and unreasonable Distresses, shall be grievously amerced for the Excess of such Distresses . . . It shall be lawful for no Man from henceforth, for any manner of cause, to take Distresses out of his Fee, nor in the King's Highway, nor in the common Street, but only to the King or his Officers, having special authority to do the same.

We should not ignore the Statute of Marlborough of 1267. Here, medieval England, was once more making provision for a common ideal of its people that would survive to our own times.

In 1272, Henry died. He had played little part in government during his latter years. That governance he had left to his son, Edward. But when his father died, Edward was abroad on the Crusade. It took him nearly two years to return to England. This could have been a time of further rebellion and crown seeking; instead, the smooth governing of England continued because, although the reforms had led to civil war, they were nevertheless well-founded and well-respected. And here is an irony: Simon de Montfort's reforms, or his ideas for them, would not die with him. And the person responsible for his death, the new King, Edward I, continued to implement them.

CHAPTER TEN
1272–1307

Henry III was buried in the dearest object of his life, his new abbey at Westminster. He was sixty-five in November 1272, when he died, which was not a bad age for the Middle Ages. A man who reached sixty-five might well have mourned most of his childhood friends not because people naturally had short lives, but because many of the causes of death were not yet understood. Men knew how to wield swords but few scalpels. Science moved slowly but social change stepped up its pace. With change came some sinister events.

For example, for the first time there were signs that land would become a commodity. Until this period, the buying and selling of vast tracts of land was not a commercial proposition as today we would understand it. The feudal system – through both baron and monarch – had kept land in tight ownership. Yet there was now in England a small group who understood that to own land meant financial as well as social power. Here we have the usurers, the moneylenders and therefore the opportunity seized to persecute the Jews of England. The Jews were blamed for turning the richer into debtors (even though they had always been in debt) and, at this period, for buying up great tracts of the islands' heritage, that is, the land. Behind all this debate was the place of the moneylender. The Church and the state had for centuries been caught in terribly unanswered questions about moneylending. Therefore it was easy to blame the Jews who themselves were not always in agreement what they should be doing under their own laws:

If thou lend money to any of my people, even to the poor with
   thee, thou shalt not be to him as creditor, neither shall you lay upon
him interest. (Exodus 22: 24)

Thou shalt not lend upon interest to thy brother; interest of money, interest of victuals, interest of anything that is lent upon interest. Unto a foreigner thou mayest lend upon interest; but unto thy brother thou shalt not lend upon interest; that the Lord thy God may bless thee in all that thou puttest thy hand unto, in the land thou goest in to possess it. (Deuteronomy 23: 20)

Here was the Jewish code which apparently sat easily with the Christian Church making it clear that it was wrong (if not illegal) to lend money and demand interest on that loan from the needy and the poor. The Church went as far as to declare that since no one should be harmed, then usury should be banned.

At the same time, the Church was a lender to its own clergy because the clergy had to pay taxes to Rome and had to borrow money to do so – from Rome itself. Rome did very well out of lending through bankers (it never leant its own money because it did not until the fourteenth century have the structure to do so) and depositing its own money. The monasteries did as well because the monks acted as middlemen between the borrower, the lender and the papal bankers, for example, the Medicis in Florence. Further complications were partly to do with banking and even a question of development. For example, the Church was not allowed to charge interest unless the loan repayment was overdue and this made greater strains on the lack of financial structures and greater reliance on the banking families. A second example was expressed by Pope Innocent IV (1243–54). He was totally convinced that the future of agriculture was the future of the nations. Because not much investment went into agriculture because lending was so expensive, he then regarded usury as an evil. So the Church in Britain continued its 'ban' on lending and interest payments. This, of course, is oversimplified and further study will tell a great deal of the depth of loans and borrowing in this period of British life.[1]

The consequence of theological and social practice in Britain in the late thirteenth century, and indeed beyond, had something to do

---

1   P. Cleary, *The Church and Usury* (Dublin: M. H. Gill & Son, 1914); J. Gilchrist, *The Church and Economic Activity in the Middle Ages* (London: Macmillan 1969); E. S. Tan, 'An empty shell? Rethinking the Usury Laws in Medieval Europe', *Journal of Legal History*, 23: 3 (December 2002), 177–96.

with the Church's anti-Semitism. The Church and the State saw most moneylending as a Jewish activity. The Jews argued that they satisfied a need and reminded Church and State that it was a form or survival because Jews were not allowed to have a profession (banking was not considered a profession until well into the nineteenth century) and they were not allowed to be landowners, only leaseholders. They did, however, know how to deal in money. The people did not. The Jews were growing richer and the people owed them money. Here then was the basis, as ever, for mistrust. So distinct was this general suspicion that when Pope Honorius (1216–27) honoured a Jew, he answered criticism by saying he had been able to do so because this particular Jew was not a moneylender. This attitude of distinguishing good Jews from bad Jews was really a means for the English Church to separate Christians from non-Christians. The Jews, first brought to England by William the Conqueror to finance his invasion, became objects of hate.

There were even hysteria-based stories that the Jews sacrificed children. The animosities and the British anti-Semitism spread. In 1189 there were widespread massacres of Jews including 150 in York. Jews, accused of coin clipping (to steal the silver) were hanged. By the second half of the thirteenth century feeling was so high against the Jews that, in 1275, the Statute of Jewry was issued during the Michaelmas Parliament at Westminster.

Statute of Jewry
1275

Forasmuch as the King hath seen that divers evils and the disinheriting of good men of his land have happened by the usuries which the Jews have made in time past, and that divers sins have followed thereupon albeit that he and his ancestors have received much benefit from the Jewish people in all times past, nevertheless, for the honour of God and the common benefit of the people the King hath ordained and established, that from henceforth no Jew shall lend anything at usury either upon land, or upon rent or upon other thing.

And that no usuries shall run in time coming from the feast of St Edward last past. Nothwithstanding the covenants before made shall be observed, saving that the usuries shall cease. But all those who owe debts to Jews upon pledge of moveables shall acquit them between this and Easter; if not they shall be forfeited. And if any Jew shall lend at usury contrary to this Ordinance, the King will not lend his aid, neither by himself or his officers for the recovering of his loan; but will punish him at his discretion for the offence and will do justice to the Christian that he may obtain his pledges again.

And that the distress for debts due unto Jews from henceforth shall not be so grievous but that the moiety [part] of lands and chattels of the Christians shall remain for their maintenance; and that no distress shall be made for a Jewry debt upon the heir of the debtor named in the Jew's deed, nor upon any other person holding the land that was the debtor's before that the debt be put in suit and allowed in court.

And if the sheriff or other bailiff by the King's command hath to give Saisin to a Jew be it one or more, for their debt, the chattels shall be valued by the oaths of good men and be delivered to the Jew or Jews or to their proxy to the amount of the debt; and if the chattels be not sufficient, the lands shall be extended by the same oath before the delivery of Saisin to the Jew or Jews, to each in his due proportion, so that it may be certainly known that the debt is quit, and the Christian may have his land again; saving always to the Christian the moiety of his land and chattels for his maintenance as aforesaid, and the chief mansion.

And if any moveable hereafter be found in possession of a Jew, and any man shall sue him the Jew shall be allowed his warranty if he may have it; and if not let him answer therefore so that he be not therein otherwise privileged than a Christian.

And that all Jews shall dwell in the King's own cities and boroughs where the chests of the chirographs of Jews are wont to be.

And that each Jew after he shall be seven years old, shall wear a badge on his outer garment that is to say in the form of two tables joined of yellow fait of the length of six inches and of the breadth of three inches.

And that each one, after he shall be twelve years old pay three pence yearly at Easter of tax to the King whose bond-man he is; and this shall hold place as well for a woman as for a man.

And that no Jew shall have the power to infeoff another whether Jew or Christian of houses, rents, or tenements, that he now hath, nor to alien in any other manner, nor to make acquittance to any Christian of his debt without the special licence of the King, until the King shall have otherwise or ordained therein.

And forasmuch as it is the will and sufferance of Holy Church that they may live and be preserved, the King taketh them under his protection, and granteth them his peace; and willeth that they be safely preserved and defended by his sheriffs and other bailiffs and by his liege man, and commandeth that none shall do them harm or damage or wrong in their bodies or in their goods, moveable or immovable, and they shall neither plead not be impeaded in any court nor be challenged or troubled in any court except in the court of the King whose bondmen they are; and that none shall owe obedience, or service or rent except to the King or his bailiffs in his name unless it be for their dwelling which they now hold by paying rent; saving the right of Holy Church.

And the King granteth unto them that they may gain their living by lawful merchandise and their labour, and that they may have inter-course with Christians in order to carry on lawful trade by selling and buying. But that no Christian for this cause or any other shall dwell among them. And the King willeth that they shall not be reason of their merchandise be put to lot and soot nor in taxes with the men of the cities and boroughs where they abide; for that they are taxable to the King as his bondmen and to none other but the King.

Moreover, the King granteth unto them that they may buy houses and castilages in the cities and boroughs where they abide, so that they hold them in chief of the King; saving unto the lords of the fee their services due and accustomed. And that they may take and buy farms or land for the term of ten years or less without taking homages or fealties or such sort of obedience from Christians and without having advowsons of churches, and that they may be able to gain their living in the world, if they have not the means of trading or cannot labour; and this licence to take land to farm shall endure to them for fifteen years from this time forward.

Jews were to cease usury; they now had to live in effectual ghettos and were restricted in how far they could travel; and any Jew over the age of seven had to wear the yellow star of David on the sleeve. This racial identification predated by eight centuries, therefore, the distasteful practice adopted elsewhere in Europe. On the brighter side for the Jews, the King did promise to protect them with equal rights of any other in his realm. But the restrictions on what the Jews could do meant that many became poverty-stricken and left England. For those who waited, expulsion came in 1290. It was inevitable. Apart from social discrimination, the spread of the Italian banking system made it easier for the barons and feudal rulers to get money. The Jews who managed to continue to trade for the limited period allowed had less money to lend and therefore they could not compete so easily with the rates of the bankers. Then, two years after the Statute of Jewry, Edward I seized all Jewish property and took it into Crown ownership. Anyone who had borrowed from a Jewish usurer now owed that debt to the Crown. It could not end there. In July 1290, Edward I published the Edict of Expulsion and Jews were given until 1 November 1290 to leave England or be imprisoned and even executed. Most Jews, perhaps 3,000, had to leave. Others stayed and some secretly returned. None professed their faith for fear of death.

Not only for the Jews was the England of Edward I a period of quickly changing fortune. Margaret was about to become Queen of Scotland, to be quickly followed by John Balliol. The Welsh, once more, revolted against the English. Llywelyn ap Gruffudd, Prince of Wales, was killed and Dafydd, who succeeded his brother Llywelyn, was captured and executed. And as the century drew to an end, the Scot William Wallace defeated the English at Stirling Bridge, only to be vanquished the following year at Falkirk before escaping to France.

The population of England had doubled since the Conquest. By now it was probably about three million. The villages had grown, split into three or four communities, and the land that had been ravaged by the Conqueror was restored. Towns thrived. Newcastle became the centre of the only big coalfield of the time. Lynn (later King's Lynn) became the port for the Fens, Hull for York. It was a land of exporters and importers: wool (the equivalent of modern-day oil to the finances of medieval England) was sent to Flanders where the best weavers were to be found; corn went to Norway and to France; and fish to the Continent. In return came timber, French and Italian wines, currants, jewels, ginger and peppers. Peppers were so important that tradesmen had banded together to form the Guild of Pepperers in 1180. As we shall see later, by the sixteenth century peppers and spices became the focus for the huge investments in Asian commercial exploration that led to the founding of the East India Company and, with sugar, were responsible for the building of the British Empire. The twelfth-century pepperers became merchants and they started dealing 'en gros' – hence the word, grocers.

But this was not a wealthy and sophisticated society. Most people were peasants and while they were no worse off than at the time of *Domesday*, there's little evidence that their lot had much improved. Magna Carta and social and legal reform did not make people wealthier. The rich were richer and the divide between the haves and have-nots was greater. Perhaps the biggest change came from the King himself. Edward I set out to remove as much corruption as was convenient so to do. His principal reformer was his Chancellor, the Bishop of Bath and Wells Robert Burnell, who built what is still the chapel of Wells Cathedral, to which his remains were taken after his death at Berwick. Burnell was to be an indispensible figure at Edward's court and had looked after his interests during the interregnum between Henry II's death and Edward's enthronement.

Burnell was born *c.*1239 in Shropshire and became a clerk in the royal chancery. It was there that he learned the vagaries of administration as well as the formal style and script of court writing. It was from the chancery that he joined Edward's household and became his personal clerk (we would probably describe him as a private secretary) at the end of 1264. Six years later, Burnell, surely for services to Edward, was appointed Archdeacon of York. In fact, Edward wanted him to be Archbishop of Canterbury, but the canons frustrated even the King's wishes (and then the Pope frustrated theirs by appointing his own man, Robert Kilwardby).

But Burnell was not denied promotion and in April 1275 he was consecrated Bath and Wells. It may have been expected that Edward could now be in a position to have Bishop Burnell elected to Canterbury, but perhaps because he kept a mistress rather publicly, Pope Nicholas III turned him down. Burnell was not to be remembered as a Bishop but as the King's Chancellor. He restructured the way in which the important departments of State worked and it was he who established the department of Chancery and the treasury, the Exchequer, in London. As well as organizing the King's household, Burnell made sure that his own house was in good order, particularly financially. When he died in October 1292, he was said to have eighty manor houses throughout the country, particularly in Worcester, Kent and Surrey. He needed to leave a good legacy; like many clergy of the time in eccentric orders of chastity he fathered many children. However, Burnell should be remembered not as a man of fortune and office but as someone who above all things looked after the interests of his King.

But Edward's personal world had changed for the worse. His wife, Eleanor of Castile, had died, as had his mother, Eleanor of Provence, and his two eldest sons. The loss of his wife was particularly sad for him. He was clearly in love with her; it had not been a medieval marriage of convenience. Eleanor had been with Edward on his Crusade in 1270. In 1290 she died at Hadby in Nottinghamshire. Her body was brought to London and that last journey can be traced because Edward built crosses everywhere the cortège stopped. He built them at Lincoln, Grantham, Stamford, Geddington, Northampton, Stony Stratford, Woburn, Dunstable, St Albans, Waltham and, perhaps most famously, in London at Charing Cross. The word Charing comes from the Saxon word '*cierring*' that means a bend or a turn – in this case the bend in the River Thames. Charing was a hamlet at the entrance of the royal mews of the Palace of Westminster. The cross was made of oak, but later replaced by a marble monument. It eventually fell to ruin and was replaced again after the Commonwealth of Cromwell in 1675 by a statue of the mounted Charles I.

Four years after Eleanor's death and still in mourning, Edward went to war with France. He would seem to have been forced into that war, as what had gone before suggested that he had not wanted war. Edward had come to an arrangement – a token surrender of the English garrisons in Gascony – so that the French King, Philip IV, known as Philip the Fair (1268–1314) could show that his position of overlord was recognized. The matter did not rest. The token surrender became absolute. Edward had to raise money for the campaign and even needed to justify it. He did so by calling together a council, a Parliament that imposed heavy taxes on an already impoverished people. The winter of 1294 was a winter of open discontent. The nation muttered against the King. The Welsh rebelled. The Scots renewed an alliance with France. The barons and earls grew openly against him. Entries in the record of Walter of Guisborough give some idea of the heated debate with the king.

> The king held his Parliament near at Salisbury where he asked certain
> of the magnates to cross over to Gascony. They began to excuse
> themselves. And the king was very angry and threatened some of
> them, that either they went or he would give their lands to others who
> were willing to go. And many were offended at this and a split began
> to appear between them.

The Earl of Hereford and the Earl Marshal said they would gladly go if the King marched with them. But the King wanted them to march without him. A bitter argument flared up and the Earl Marshal walked out.

The two Earls, Hereford and the Earl Marshal, joined by many magnates and more than thirty picked banners, grew into a multitude. They numbered 1500 men on armed horses ready for war and the King began to fear them. They went off to their own lands, where they would not allow the King's servants to take either wool or hides or anything whatever out of the ordinary or to exact anything from anyone against his will. Indeed they forbade them entry to their lands.

Edward I sailed for Flanders but the recalcitrant earls and barons rode into London and demanded that Magna Carta and extensions and protocols covering taxes on wool and hides (which Edward was exacting to pay for the war), liberties of the clergy and people, and much more, should be accepted by the King. Edward by that time was in Ghent. He accepted the principles, but acceptance and observance are different matters. Eventually, at another Parliament, this time held at Lincoln, solemn agreement was reached. The agreement was more than simple triumph. Here was a point of constitutional principle that declared the King did not have total power and could not therefore order his knights and nobles to ride with him into war. If they did not want to go, then they could argue their case. This was not a triumph for the barony, more the establishment of case precedent. The second consequence of the challenge to the monarch's authority was that it led to the eventual change in the structure, purpose and manner of an army. If the King could not rely on the barons to send soldiers on demand, then a new type of army had to evolve. It did not happen overnight, but here was the beginning of the professional army, a standing group of soldiers paid for their services rather than being obliged to go to war under the feudal system. The third precedent to evolve over time was that after this confrontation, it became clear that the King would have to accept that his powers were no longer unquestioned and that in future Parliament would have to be asked to give its authority in such major issues as tax raising and making war.

Since the end of the twelfth century, the English kings had fought their own clergy, barons and earls. The clergy refused to accept that, in matters spiritual, kings were above the Church. The barons were protecting their own interests. But there was a constant in the conflict between monarch, people, Church and baronage. It was this: the English kings were devoted to protecting their interests in France. It was, after all, where they came from. And their magnates had land, titles and families across the Channel. So for a long time after the Conquest it was easy for the king to convince his nobles, and therefore their exchequers, to fight for him in France. But by the second half of the thirteenth century, fewer of the English magnates were directly tied to Continental lands. The king's difficulty then was to persuade them to come up with the money, as well as the soldiers, for overseas expeditions.

By the closing years of the thirteenth century, successive kings had been so obsessed with their French campaigns that they had never properly dealt with the threat closer to home. It began in Scotland and, more immediately, in Wales. The king's sentries at the Scottish and Welsh borders were the Marcher Lords. The Marches (from the Norman French *marche* as an edge) were the borders, often imprecisely denoted between two States, but not necessarily two peoples. The Marcher Lords had an enormous responsibility of keeping the order in the borders, but they also held two particular forms of power. Firstly, because they had considerable armed resources for their duty, they could with impunity raid either side of the border for their own gains – here was a good use of the medieval term 'robber baron'. Secondly, as powerful barons, they continuously suggested a threat to the monarch himself. Edward was not the first or the last king to assume that the Marcher Lords could easily be the source of palace revolution.

As for the people the Marcher Lords were there to contain the Welsh, in particular; they rarely had need to raid into England. When they were pursued by the Marchers, then the Welsh had the advantage of home turf, or rather home granite. They knew better than the barons the often treacherous terrain on their sides of the borders. Moreover, like the Scots, geography had a great deal to do with the character of the Welsh and their relations with the English. Warring Welsh chieftains had long had the tactic of being able to withdraw to the hills and mountains, and even across the sea to Ireland. Their biggest disadvantage was not so much the power of the Marcher barons; like the Scots, the Welsh were often at each other's throats. Neither in Wales nor in Scotland was there a national purpose. Why?

Mainly because there may have been an identifiable nation but there was no State as we understand the term. Certainly, we cannot claim that in most medieval States there was anything as definable as national purpose. One nation could detest another, but marshalling that detestation and prejudice into an uncompromising force was quite another thing. What brought a nation to war as a cohesive force was leadership behind the strength of the ruler with one obvious faculty being obligation either to monarch or feudal lord. There was no such obligation and sense of national strength among Scots and certainly not among the Welsh where local jealousies were apparently stronger than some claim of Welsh unity. Even when great Welsh lords such as Rhys ap Tewdwr or Owen Gwynedd commanded the country, family feuds dissipated resolve.

This variable sense of unity of the Welsh was, of course, a conundrum for the English. There could be no single opponent. No single standard could be struck and no one surrender to be received. Edward had need of patience. He had to accept that it would always be a land never quite subjugated but neither could any campaign be abandoned. Edward knew this was to be a drawn-out campaign. It has a particular interest to us today as it was probably the patch in military history that the feudal system of supplying soldiers under obligation began to be replaced by the establishment of paid armies; here then, in the late thirteenth century, was the birth of the professional army in England and coincidentally the appearance on the battlefield of the longbow, the most devastating battlefield weapon and ironically one which was developed not in England, but south Wales.

The first thing Edward did was to establish a base at Chester. Then, just as a modern general would have to do, Edward set up a line of communications. He cut a road through the wooded coastline to Aberconwy. He sent his fleet round to Anglesey and his Marcher Lords in from the east and south. It took time, it was bloody, but it worked. Within two years of the signing of a treaty at Aberconwy, much of the Welsh holdings were being organized on an English county system. All seemed settled but all was not.

On Palm Sunday, 1282, the Welsh attacked. Daffyd, the brother of Llywelyn ap Gruffudd, the self-proclaimed Lord of Aberffraw and Prince of Wales, invaded Cardigan and captured Aberystwyth. Early in December, Llewelyn left north Wales, where he was safe, for the Upper Wye Valley. He was killed, not in some great battle, but at what might have been, except for his death, an insignificant skirmish close to Builth Wells in 1282. Six months later, Dafydd was betrayed to the English and executed. Following this, the Statute of Rhuddlan declared that the land held by the Princes of Gwynedd using the umbrella of Princes of Wales (hence Wales has always been a principality) were now part of England or English rule. But this was not the whole of Wales as we know the land. Some of it in the south from Pembrokeshire (where the Norman knights had held sway since the eleventh century) to the south Wales border with England was already ruled by the Marcher barons. If Edward regarded himself as the conqueror of the Welsh, it was something of an illusion and it would be more than two centuries before Wales was incorporated into union with England, with representation in the Parliament. However, at the closing of the thirteenth century and the opening of the fourteenth century, the closest of all Anglo–Welsh constitutional ties became fixed. In Carnarvon Castle the English King's son, Edward, was born during the same year as the Statute of Rhuddlan was proclaimed, 1284. Seventeen years later, in 1301, this Edward became the first English Prince of Wales. One day he too would be king.

Edward I assumed he had Wales. He did not have Scotland. He never had Scotland and never would even though it was the strongest military ambition of his reign. It was possible, of course, that the brutal animosities of the Scots and English could be settled at the altar rather than the battlefield. When in 1286 Alexander III died his heir was his granddaughter, a toddler of three, Margaret, known as the Maid of Norway. It was an obvious hope that Edward I's son would take her as his bride, and thus bring the two kingdoms together. In 1290, Margaret was sent for from Norway. She perished during the stormy crossing. Who would have the throne of Scotland? It came down to Robert Bruce (1210–95) or John Balliol (1250–1313).

Balliol had hardly been in Scotland as a landowner. Most of his holdings were in England and France, not so unusual in the thirteenth and fourteenth centuries. Whatever his powers, Balliol would always be caught between two demands: those of Edward his King and the Scottish chieftains who by all means were determined to resist the demands of the English monarch. Robert Bruce's credentials were altogether more credible because he was the young brother of William the Lion whom many had regarded as heir from 1237 to

1241. We can see then the splintered and shattered claims of the various petitioners for the Scottish throne. None was certain and straightforward. For the English monarch this was no local matter to be decided by the Scots themselves and curiously, considering what was to follow, the Scots themselves believed Edward should have an interest in the future of the Scottish throne.

Ever since the ninth century and the conquests of the Picts by the Scots, the kings of the Scots had regarded a lot of what is now northern England as fair game. Had the Scots been less clannish and had they avoided their own internal jealousies, then perhaps the lands of the Scots might have expanded. But it was never to be. Under the true kingship of David I during the first half of the twelfth century, the Scots achieved recognition for his claims to the English northern counties. But by the time of Alexander II in 1237, those claims were abandoned by the Treaty of York, in return for yet more contrived family relations, payment in silver as compensation for English broken promises and a few thousand acres of land. But by the time of the question of succession, relations were sound and Edward I was called upon to arbitrate between the claims for the Scottish throne.

The act of arbitration was a sensible idea because unless there was some peaceful acceptance of a new monarch, then Scotland would probably go to civil war. Edward I's reputation for legal and constitutional wisdom was everything in this matter. Edward insisted before arbitration that he would expect that whoever took the crown would submit to his (Edward's) authority and that, to confirm that authority and Scottish acceptance of it, castles would be given to the English monarch. It was under these circumstances that Edward, hardly unexpectedly, picked John Balliol. Balliol was ostensibly a puppet monarch, or was expected to be. The Scottish barons knew this and so instituted a twelve-man council to advise their monarch – to make sure that he did not lose sight of Scottish interests. We need at this point to understand that Edward I was also Duke of Aquitaine and so was a vassal of the French monarch, Philip IV, Philip the Fair, who would later become his brother-in-law when he married Philip's sister, Marguerite, after the death of his beloved wife Eleanor of Castile. The 1290s were not good years for the relationship between the English and French monarchs. This relationship perished to the point that within forty years the two States would embark on what became the Hundred Years War. That war, as we shall see, came about because of trade

– especially the specialist wool trade to Flanders, the extent of English lands in France and, for our immediate understanding, the long alignment of France against the English.

Returning to the period of selecting a new Scottish king, it was at this stage that Philip IV insisted that Edward pay more taxes (which he could only do by taxing his own people English and Scots) and obey a summons to the French court. Edward by this time was totally absorbed in what was going on north of his border. Philip either used this as an excuse or really did regard it Edward's refusal to attend him as an enormous slight. Whatever the real reason or opportunity, Philip stripped Edward of his titles to his French possessions and, to make sure that Edward was vulnerable on two fronts, made a secret arrangement to support the Scots, led by the man Edward had placed on the Scottish throne. Military hostilities were inevitable and therefore even greater taxes on all the people, whether breeched or kilted.

Edward was furious. He demanded that Balliol meet him at Berwick but the Scottish baronage told their King not to go. The time for consultations was over. Edward regarded the Scots' defiance and alignment with France as an act of war. He unsheathed his swords and marched on Berwick and, in an act of savagery, sacked the once peaceful town. Thousands were slaughtered and the town surrendered. Balliol had no option but to renounce his allegiance to Edward I. At Dunbar in April 1296 they met in battle. Balliol was defeated and taken prisoner. He gave his kingdom to Edward who held him prisoner and eventually released him in France. By that time, Balliol was no threat although his son, Edward Balliol, was to claim the Scottish throne. Bruce was never going to be the man to hold Scotland, never mind northern England. He gave up his claim on the throne to his later generations. The hero of Scotland at this stage then was not Balliol or Bruce. It was William Wallace (1270–1305).

Wallace appears in our history in September 1297 when he and Andrew Moray (d.1297), one of Scotland's unsung warriors who had that summer kept his lands in north-eastern Scotland from the British, joined forces. Balliol was in captivity but still King. Wallace now led Balliol's army to Stirling Bridge and in a terrible, bloody affair defeated the English and so, for a moment, had Scotland back for the Scots and his monarch. He went on to raid the northern counties of England and was such a hero (the Scots had few at the time) was appointed guardian of Scotland in the King's absence. His celebrity was not to last for that generation. The deciding battle took place at Falkirk on 22 July 1298. Wallace made a simple and centuries-old mistake: instead of fighting the advancing forces in a series of disrupting skirmishes, he fought in open battle. His cavalry fled. Wallace had relied on his spearmen, but Edward had brought his longbow-men from Wales. They fired volley after volley at the Scottish schiltrons (circles of spearmen) until there were more dead and wounded than standing.

It was now the time of a second Bruce. The earlier Robert grew too old for the challenge and his son, Robert, Earl of Carrick (1253–1304), took up the gauntlet. He did not have long to claim back the throne and so passed the duty to his son, another Robert. It was this Robert who became known as Robert the Bruce (1274–1329).

To say Robert the Bruce was an opportunist may seem a little unfair considering the fickle loyalties of the age. Yet this Bruce had actually fought on Edward I's side against his own King, Balliol. Then he changed sides when Wallace looked like being successful in 1297. Between 1302 and 1305 Bruce bent his knee in submission to Edward. His ambitions were higher. One of those who deserted Wallace was thought to have been John III Comyn, Lord of Badenoch (c.1270–1306). We cannot know the truth of this, but he clearly had enemies especially when he was appointed joint guardian of Scotland with Bruce the younger. In 1304 he helped to arrange a truce with Edward I. It is at this point that, with the help of the bishops, Robert the Bruce sought an agreement that he should be King. Comyn was his only opposition. In February 1306 the two men met at the Church of the Grey Friars at Dumfries. What caused their differences to become violent disagreement is not really known (although Bruce wanted to attack the English, Comyn did not; and both wanted to be King). Bruce stabbed Comyn and another knight finished him off. Bruce was crowned King. For the mythical storyteller, Bruce is recalled because after he was defeated that same year, 1306, he fled to Rathlin Island off the Antrim coast, and the legend has it that while there he watched a spider trying, again and again, to climb a single slender strand, and that the spider's eventual success inspired the Bruce to return to Scotland and continue to fight. Edward, now too weak to ride, was carried to do battle once more against the rebellious Scots. But in 1307 he died on the road as the rebellion continued. Bruce is sometimes recorded as the best of Scottish kings.

CHAPTER ELEVEN
1307–30

Edward's legacy is rarely doubted. Winston S. Churchill had him as 'a master-builder of British life, character, and fame'. He laid the basis of taxation through Parliament, established a documented and efficient administrative process and made clear the laws of his kingdom. And he did most of this without excessively offending an aristocracy that was becoming increasingly class conscious. Equally, Edward left the country in debt because of his wars on two fronts – France and Scotland. He left the matter of the monarch's standing as the Duke of Aquitaine unsettled. And this could, and would, threaten the peace of Europe.

He also left an heir, Edward II (1284–1327), who may be described as a feckless prince whose obsession for Piers Gaveston, son of Sir Arnaud de Gaveston (or Gabeston), a Gascon knight who had seen service with Edward I, was to bring about anarchy and war.

As Prince of Wales, Edward had become infatuated with Gaveston. Immediately he became King, Edward made his young friend Earl of Cornwall. When the King went to France to marry Isabella, the twelve-year-old daughter of Philip IV, he left Gaveston as 'keeper of the realm', effectively ruler of England. At the coronation on 25 February 1308, it was Gaveston who carried, in procession, the crown and the sword of St Edward. It was Gaveston who was described as being dressed more like the god Mars than a mere mortal. After the coronation, Isabella's kinsmen returned to France. They took with them a story that Edward loved Gaveston more than his Queen. The movement against Edward grew. At its head was Henry, the Earl of Lincoln. The barons would stand for no more of this domination by the King's favourite. An ordinance was presented to Edward, demanding that dignity be returned to the Crown. Indiscretion was one thing but allowing the object of that indiscretion to become a powerful figure in the governance of the realm was quite another. In other words, Gaveston must be banished.

At the April Parliament the barons forced the King to agree to their wishes. But Edward could not bear to lose his friend for so long. He appointed him his Lieutenant in Ireland and, when the time came for his sailing from Bristol, Edward was there to see him off. But even this temporary exile did not settle the aristocracy's long list of grievances. When that list was presented, in 1309, Edward agreed to reforms but in return demanded the recall of Gaveston.

The counter-balance to Edward II's self-indulgence was the establishment in 1311 of the Lords Ordainers. This was a committee of twenty-one lay, ecclesiastical and lordly representatives led by the grandson of Henry III, Thomas Plantagenet, Second Earl of Lancaster (1278–1322). The task of the Ordainers was simple: to safeguard the State – by which they meant the aristocracy – from the anticipated excesses of Edward II. It was this group that penned the forty-one articles which have become known as the Ordinances of 1311. The Ordinances, among other things, declared that the King was not to leave the realm without the consent of the barons, was not to appoint a keeper of the realm (as he had Gaveston), was not to appoint whomsoever he wished as senior officials, and that all officials had to take an oath to uphold the Ordinances.

Perhaps Gaveston was all the things the barons said he was. He was also a scapegoat for Edward's weaknesses and lack of kingship. Gaveston was exiled, yet again, this time to Flanders. And, yet again, he returned. In May of that year, 1312, Lancaster, the leader of the Ordainers, raised his army against the king and his favourite at Newcastle. The pair escaped south and Gaveston was trapped in Scarborough Castle, thinking perhaps that the King would safeguard him. Gaveston was too sure of his royal protection. He understood the King himself could not defend him but he had been promised the safety of the Earl of Pembroke. Neither could save Gaveston. The Ordainers had him under siege in Scarborough Castle and so Gaveston made terms. His mistake was to believe that the Ordainers spoke with one voice. A group led by one of their number, the Earl of Warwick, captured and executed Gaveston at Blacklow Hill on Lancaster's estate near Warwick. It would be no great comfort to the King's friends that years later he would have Lancaster executed. Their immediate worry was the King's sanity. Yet there was another factor in that event at Blacklow Hill. Some of the barons may have had their way, but the effect of Gaveston's execution was the utter distraction of Edward and disunity among the Lords Ordainers. Nevertheless, by and large the barons had the changes they had wanted.

The King's reason may have been questioned, but he remained King and thus still possessed significant powers, and he was going to need them for wars awaited him. There was still France to war against and always there was unfinished and costly business in the north. Taxes were raised along with grumpiness from reluctant donors. Edward had no mind of this. He raised an army of more than 20,000 foot soldiers, archers and gentlemen armoured cavalry, and in 1314 set against the Scots led still by Robert the Bruce who had learned to deploy and defend his much smaller force. The lesson of Falkirk was not lost. The two armies met at Bannockburn on 24 June 1314. The story of what happened at Bannockburn has been told in verse and chronicle. None could have imagined Edward's defeat. Many of his soldiers, such as the archers from Wales and the foot soldiers from the Midlands and the north-west, were experienced and in little hurry to get into battle with what they saw as a well-organized enemy positioned with flanks covered and deeply dug defiles to disrupt the cavalry. Moreover, Edward's forces needed time to reconnoitre and reconsider their tactics against such a well dug-in if much smaller force. In fact, the King's nephew, the Earl of Gloucester, wisely said that the troops should be rested for a day after their long march. Edward would have none of this. He accused Gloucester of cowardice. The young Earl immediately and foolishly led his cavalry against the massed schiltrons – those oblong hedges of Scottish shields and pikes – and was killed. It was the way of this battle. So close was the hand-to-hand combat that many of the English fell to their own archers, who were not able to aim with any accuracy. As the English retreated they did so in confusion into their own ranks of reinforcements. The Scots followed and cut them down. Not until the fourteenth-century wars in France would chivalry be so butchered.

Bruce himself was a hero and sent his troops to raid and kill in northern England and destroy great swathes as far south as Yorkshire. Edward's own authority was reduced even further. After Bannockburn he was unpopular and very much reliant upon his closest officials.

The growing aristocracy wanted control of the inner cabinet of the King's advisers – the King's wardrobe – without either destroying the monarchy or bringing about the downfall of the bureaucracy so necessary for the running of State affairs. Edward very quickly found himself at the contemptuous mercy of his own people, particularly the group of Lords Ordainers still led by Thomas Lancaster who was becoming the power of the realm rather than the King. However, Lancaster may have held the power but he did not have the confidence of all the barons. It may have been that many of them did admire their King, and they certainly protected the establishment of their monarchy and the embryo civil service so important to the future of the country and its governance. In time there was a very practical as well as constitutional questioning of Lancaster's hold on the ring of power.

From the autumn of 1315, Lancaster's authority had been unchallenged. He had control of the country's administration. He gave instructions to the Chancellor, made appointments and even issued pardons. He was Steward of England. And while all this was going on, the people were suffering a famine. For three years torrential rains ruined the harvests of Europe from as far north as Scotland and Russia, south to Italy. In England, men murdered for food. Cannibalism was recorded. Prices rose by as much 800 per cent in one year. Families fought each other. Counties were in rebellion. Thomas not only had a revolt in his own county, but his wife, Alice de Lacy (1281–1348; incidentally an indirect ancestor of Sarah Ferguson, the former wife of the present Prince Andrew) left him and took up with Sir Ebulo Lestrange (whom she later married) thus starting a private war with Yorkshire. Lancaster, inflicting the nation with his incompetent stewardship, was not the man to resolve the nation's troubles. Loosening his grip was, however, hardly an easy matter.

In all the disorganization of the King's realm, there emerged a new grouping, a middle party. It was led by the Earl of Pembroke, who had fallen from the King's favour after Bannockburn, and included the bishops. They saw good reason in their aims for administrative reform, particularly the changes they thought necessary to the King's household itself. Not surprisingly, this did not please Edward II. He turned to Hugh Despenser and his son, also Hugh, for whom the king showed signs of infatuation. It became clear that the baronage would never accept the Despensers especially if it proved to be so that the younger Hugh had taken the place of Piers Gaveston in the King's heart. Hugh the elder had long been an unquestioning royalist. He'd been a loyal servant of the King's father, Edward I. Also, he'd been the only baron to support Gaveston during the move to get rid of him in 1308; and he was by Edward's side at the retreat from Bannockburn. Hugh the younger had been a member of Edward's household while he was still Prince of Wales. He'd married Eleanor, the King's niece. The Despensers were certainly no more opportunists than Lancaster and his supporters, but the clue to the great opposition to them is in their rank. The Despensers may have gained lands, titles and influence, but they were not from one of the great families. In the medieval pecking order only the important landowning families could expect any right to influence the King. Here was a qualification for influence that would survive into the nineteenth century. In 1321 the King bowed to the demands of the baronage to dispense with the Despensers, but Edward could not live without the affections of the young Hugh and father and son had returned the following year. It was this same year that with renewed guile and support, Edward had taken the war to Thomas of Lancaster, captured and beheaded him.

However, tragedy was waiting for Edward II. His wife, Isabella, disgusted by her husband's passion for Hugh Despenser, became the lover and confederate of Roger de Mortimer, one of the chief Marcher Lords against the king, who had escaped to France. Isabella had gone to France to negotiate the restoration to England of Gascony – seized by her brother, Charles IV of France. Worse was to come. In 1324, perhaps with Despenser's authority, Isabella's estates were sequestrated. There was also a rumour that the young Hugh was attempting an annulment of her marriage to the King. Isabella needed a triumph to establish some authority within the claim of Gascony. She called for their son, also Edward, to be sent to honour and show allegiance to Gascony. This was simply a ruse to get the young Edward away from his father and, shortly after the prince's arrival, Isabella and her now lover, Roger de Mortimer (who had made a name as Justiciar in Ireland), gathered an army led by exiled English malcontents. To cement the force, Isabella had betrothed her four-teen-year-old son, the heir to the throne, to the Count of Hainault's daughter, Philippa, in return for soldiers. In 1326 the rebels sailed for

Harwich and the Isabella–Mortimer axis was triumphant. The two Despensers were captured and they were executed at Hereford. Now, the rebels turned on the King.

Edward II is said to have been murdered in Berkeley Castle when red-hot pokers were inserted and his bowels burned out. In an age of gruesome histories it is, for some, an attractive tale. There really is no evidence for this flimsy notion other than an unauthenticated account, which suggests that Edward II suffered an unusual form of execution, in a version of the *Brut Chronicle*:

> When that night the king had gone to bed and was asleep, the traitors, against their homage and their fealty, went quietly into his chamber and laid a large table on his stomach and with other men's help pressed him down. At this he woke and in fear of his life, turned himself upside down. The tyrants, false traitors, then took a horn and put it into his fundament as deep as they could, and took a pit of burning copper, and put it through the horn into his body, and oftentimes rolled therewith his bowels, and so they killed their lord and nothing was perceived.

Whatever the method of execution, Edward II had few friends to mourn his going, but there were plenty who mourned the act of regicide and the method of power changing. There was little they could do about it. Edward was murdered because of his foolishness. He was weak, without political imagination or intelligence. He lacked dignity and most certainly appears to have been a thoughtless monarch. And, in reality, he was no longer King when he was imprisoned. He'd already been forced to abdicate and in his place his young son was crowned as Edward III, who erected a fine monumental mausoleum for his father.

The English monarchy was now threatened by the most serious events since the Conquest. For three years after the death of Edward II, England was effectively ruled by the Queen's lover, Roger de Mortimer. Let us consider not so much a phenomenon of reign, but the unusual consequences of the time. Firstly, Isabella and Mortimer had no constitutional authority even by the standards of medieval power and certainly could not command the whole support of the nobility – the basis of all rule. Secondly, the precarious and doubtful basis for their rule meant Mortimer and Isabella were effectively constitutional outlaws and therefore had to sell authority and political silver to stay in power. The French and Scots were not slow to capitalize on this vulnerability to seemingly forgo so many of the claims the English had on their northern and southern neighbours, especially in Scotland. It was at this stage that the triumph of Robert the Bruce was complete and the historical shame of Isabella and Mortimer was also complete. The couple gave up English claims on Scotland and recognized Bruce as King of the North. There were two treaties, Edinburgh, in March 1328, and its protocol of ratification, Northampton.

The Treaty of Northampton was decided when 100 Scottish knights had been asked to a Parliament to talk peace. The Scots were probably ready to reach an understanding and the documents of the settlement had been written, or at least drafted, under the influence of Bruce himself at the abbey at Holyrood. But the young King Edward III appears to have seen the treaty as a total humiliation. An extract from the fourteenth-century *Chronicle of Lanercost*[1] makes clear the belief that he really wanted nothing to do with what he saw as a shameful document, especially as it committed future kings to acknowledge Scotland's independence. It was also yet another document to be blessed by royal intermarriage:

Acting on the pestilent advice of his mother and Sir Roger Mortimer (they being the chief controllers of the King, who was barely 15 years old) he was forced to release the Scots by his public deed from all exaction, right, claim or demand of the Overlordship of the Kingdom of Scotland on his part, and from any homage to be done to the Kings of England. He restored to them also that piece of the Cross of Christ which the Scots call the Black Rood. But the people of London would in no wise allow to be taken away the Stone of Scone, whereon the Kings of Scotland used to be set at their coronation at Scone. All these objects, the illustrious King Edward [Edward I] son of Henry, had caused to be brought away from Scotland when he reduced the Scots to his rule. Also the aforesaid young King gave his younger sister, my lady Joan of the Tower, in marriage to David, son of Robert de Brus [Bruce], King of Scotland, he then being a boy five years old.

---

1   *The Chronicle of Lanercost, 1272–1346* (tr. Sir Herbert Maxwell, Bt, Glasgow: MacLehose, 1913).

[Joan of the Tower, about seven years old] All this was arranged by the King's mother, the Queen of England, who at this time governed the realm. The nuptials were solemnly celebrated at Berwick on the Sunday before the feast of St Mary Magdalene.

We should not underestimate the anger expressed by people outside the baronage – what we may today call 'public opinion'. Certainly there was a widespread belief that Isabella and Mortimer were usurpers; by itself, that state could have been tolerated. What was harder to carry was the burden of incompetence, corruption and Mortimer's arrogance towards the barons, particularly in the Welsh Marches. We would do well to remember that the Marcher Lords held special powers. Mortimer had contrived to declare himself Justice of Wales, a life appointment. He then, in the autumn of 1328, declared himself to be Earl of March, a title that had to be confirmed by the Parliament of nobles. One of the most influential of those barons was missing from the count – Henry Lancaster, the brother of the Lancaster executed on orders of Edward II. The Lancastrians were in revolt. Mortimer had enough support to put it down, for the moment, largely because, as ever, the barons looked to their individual interests rather than collectively ganging up. Still, with a little more thought, Mortimer could have survived. But the power of the barons, on occasions, could be overwhelming. The idea that the aristocracy held power while the King held only high office could be seen to have more than an ounce of truth to it. Mortimer's downfall was due to two particular events: King Edward III began to rebel and Edmund Woodstock (1301–30), the late King's half-brother (son of Edward I and Queen Marguerite) and now the Earl of Kent, believed Edward II may be alive. He had been a supporter of Lancaster, his cousin, but when Mortimer and his troops attacked Lancaster's lands and invaded the Earldom of Leicester, Kent deserted him. Isabella and Mortimer had long decided that Kent was dangerous. He had friends; he had influence; he was fickle. There's evidence that Isabella and Mortimer instructed their agents to drop hints, to lay false evidence, which they knew Kent would pick up. The opening lines of *Chronicon Galfridi le Baker de Swynbroke*[2] describe how easily the ploy, an elaborate one, succeeded.

---

2   Geoffrey Baker, *Chronicon Galfridi le Baker de Swynbroke* (ed. Sir Edward Maunde Thompson, Oxford: Clarendon Press, 1889).

Certain men pretended that King Edward, lately murdered, was living magnificently in Corfe Castle [Dorset] but never wished to be seen by day. Wherefore they caused dancing to take place on many nights on the walls and turrets of the castle, bearing before them tapers and torches so they might be seen by the yokels of the countryside, as if they guarded within some great king . . . The Earl of Kent therefore sent a Dominican friar to find the truth of the matter who, thinking that he had corrupted the doorkeeper of the castle by bribes, was himself deceived. He was led in to hide by day and to see by night the person whom he wished to see. At night he was brought into the hall and there he saw, as he thought, Edward the King's father, sitting splendidly at supper. He told the Earl of Kent what he believed he had seen. The earl therefore swore, in the presence of some whom he not to have trusted, that he would work to release his [half] brother from prison.

The story of the plot spread and Edmund Kent was arrested and charged with treason because he had told the 'wrong' people that he intended to get the man he believed to be Edward II out of his prison at Corfe Castle. The living king, Edward III, who really wanted nothing much to do with this affair, held his court at Winchester where Kent was tried and sentenced to execution. This was a thoroughly unpopular verdict. It is sometimes said that the only person who would act as executioner was a convicted murder who stepped up on the understanding that he himself would be set free. Lancaster and his supporters quickly realized that unless they seized some sort of initiative, then they too would be victims of the treachery of Isabella and Mortimer. Young Edward assumed his powers of monarchy in October 1330 protected by the Earl of Lancaster. It was this step-stage that signalled the end of the events and eventually the execution of Mortimer. The remaining Kents were now treated as they should have been, as part of the new royal family.

Mortimer's treasonable act was that of having assumed the throne, albeit with the equally treacherous Isabella. But she was saved by her son, now Edward III. Towards the end of her long life, Isabella became a nun and was buried in a Franciscan church at Newgate. Despite the realm of Isabella and Mortimer being undermined by the coming of age of Edward III, Parliament had assumed a growing importance and the views of knights and burgers of the kingdom were listened to. Public opinion and the emergence of a Parliament which would – very slowly, but increasingly – represent the common view became important. Chroniclers began to write about 'the Commons'.

CHAPTER TWELVE

1331–76

A change of reign is a common time to identify an exceptional movement, almost a flurry of constitutional, political and therefore social change in a nation-state. In our modern times, British monarchs do not influence such movements even when their behaviour raises constitutional eyebrows. Political appointees – prime ministers and US presidents most certainly do have the powers to change a nation's direction. Until the seventeenth century, English monarchs had this influence and used it. The long and vigorous reign of Edward III, and several years after it, was one such time. The Hundred Years War began. The Black Prince won his spurs at the Battle of Crécy. The Order of the Garter was founded. The Black Death came and went. William Langland's *Piers Plowman* was written. The first Stuart King of Scotland came to the throne. Richard II came to the English throne. The Peasants' Revolt took place. Wat Tyler died and John of Gaunt was born. The Scots beat the English at Otterburn. And Chaucer finished *The Canterbury Tales*. And all this happened in the sixty years between 1337 and 1397. Edward III reigned until 1377.

Immediately, we can see that Edward III continued the policies of not his father, but his grandfather, Edward I. These were not necessarily peaceful arrangements for the country. The thorn that was Robert the Bruce and Edward II's ignoble defeat at Bannockburn on 24 June 1314 still niggled the English, even though Bruce was dead. David II of Scotland, who had come to the throne in 1329 after Bruce's death, was young, inexperienced and in a regency. Edward Balliol saw his chance, defeated David's followers at Dupplin Moor and had himself crowned. Edward III could not tolerate this uprising and launched an army against the Scots at Halidon Hill. Balliol had little power to resist and gave up Berwickshire and much of the surrounding region. While not every Scot would have supported Balliol, all Scotland was set against the English incursion. As for David, he fled to France in 1334. He stayed there for seven years while the French court encouraged the Scots in rebellion against England.

The English therefore were more than usually annoyed with the French. This is important because English kings had found it hard to get much support, especially financial help, from the barons every time they wanted to fight the French. But something was about to happen that would encourage the English magnates to dig deeply into their pockets. Edward III was about to embark on what would be known as the Hundred Years War. There were four apparent reasons for the war.

Firstly, the English, through Edward's mother, the disreputable Isabella of France, had until 1331 claimed the vacant French throne as Kings of England and France (the French House of Valois claimed the throne as Kings of France). Secondly, the French disputed the rights of the English over English areas of France – for example, Gascony. Thirdly, there was the French encouragement for the Scots against the English and the by now King of France, Philip VI, encouraged a force to invade Scotland on behalf of the exiled David. Fourthly, perhaps the most important of the reasons to go to war: wool. Wool in the fourteenth century was the equivalent of oil in the twenty-first century. It was the commodity that could tip the economy. The English produced wool but sent much of it to the superior weavers and markets of Flanders. They therefore tried to control Flanders. The French refused to sit by and let the English have such domination. The Flemish merchants and towns particularly valued the English wool trade. Without it, they would have been in terrible financial straits.

In 1337, Philip of France confiscated Gascony and Edward III dusted off his claim to the French throne. And to keep people and Parliament on his side, Edward III published his manifesto, telling everyone the reasons for the coming war:

These are the offers made to the King of France by the King of England to avoid war. First the King sent to France various solemn messages, begging him to return to him lands which he is withholding from him; but the King of France did nothing, until at last, he promised that if the King of England would come in his own person, he would do him justice, grace and favour.

Philip at first refused to see Edward, then took even more of Edward's possessions. Edward then claimed that he made the ultimate offers to the French monarch, offers which even casual students of this period will find familiar.

First the marriage of his eldest son, now Duke of Cornwall, with the daughter of the King of France, without taking anything for the marriage. The marriage of his sister, now Countess of Guelders, with his son, together with a very great sum of money. The marriage of his brother, the Earl of Cornwall, with any lady of the royal blood.

Because the King of England was given to understand that the King of France wished to undertake a Crusade to the Holy Land, and wished to have him in his company, the King of England offered to go with a large force with him in the Crusade; provided that, however, before he set off, the French King should make him full restitution of all his lands.

Then he offered to go with him on condition that, before he went, the French King should restore half, or a certain part of his lands. Then that he would go with the French King if he would make such a restitution on his return from the Holy Land. But the King of France would accept none of these offers; but, seeking his opportunities, busied himself in aid and maintenance of the Scots, the enemies of the King of England, attempting to delay him from the Scottish War, so that he would have no power to pursue his rights elsewhere.

This was the war made memorable by Crécy, Agincourt and the Maid of Orléans, Joan of Arc. Less often told is the story of the Battle of Sluys. It took place on 24 June 1340. It is thought by many military historians to have been the grizzliest battle of the whole Hundred Years War. It certainly was the main naval engagement and, importantly, it was commanded by the king himself. Edward sailed from the River Orwell on 22 June with 200 vessels and was reinforced by Admiral Sir Robert Morley's squadrons of about fifty ships. Within the king's squadron was his wife, Philippa of Hainault and her ladies-in-waiting, one of whom was killed in the battle. From a letter to his son, Edward the Black Prince, the King believed the

French had 190 sailing ships in company with mercenary Genoese galleys when the two fleets formed up in the estuary inlet between Flanders and Zeeland before the town of Sluys. The French fleet was in the defensive position and so, with the naval tactics of the day, lay their ships chained together in three (or perhaps four) lines. Remember, this was not Trafalgar. There were no seventy-four pounders to fire broadsides in 1340. Edward sailed with the sun behind him and his bowmen fired salvo after salvo into the French fleet – jammed to the gunwales with fighting men. This was a battle of arrows and uncompromising, hand-to-hand combat. *The Chronicle of Geoffrey le Barker*, a friar at Osney Priory, tells us:

> An iron shower of quarrels from crossbows and arrows from long-bows brought death to thousands . . . Stones hurled from the turrets of masts dashed out the brains of many . . . In the morning, the Normans were defeated . . . the number of the enemy killed and drowned exceeded 25,000. Of the English, 4,000 were slain.

It was a terrible triumph and perhaps its awesome spectacle was one of the reasons Edward III failed to capitalize on the victory by imme-diately taking the war ashore. If he had, the English may never have been driven from France, as indeed they were, and the war would not have dragged itself through decades and changing crowns.

When the land war did commence the English reached the walls of Paris on 12 July 1346. Philip of France, perhaps thinking that Edward intended to by-pass Paris and head on to Gascony, had an uncertain start, but he had superior forces and the English withdrew. The war then continued in country which became grimly familiar in the early years of the twentieth century – Amiens, the Somme, Picardy, Abbeville – until the two armies fought themselves to a standstill, with the English lucky to escape defeat. But they still could not get back to the Channel coast without another fight on 26 August: Crécy.

On the French side, which included kings and princes, the blind King of Bohemia claimed the right to command the first division and even prophesied that he would be killed in battle. He was. The King of Majorca, so confident of victory for the French, claimed that when the battle was over, he had the right to have Edward III as his pris-oner. But when others took up this demand for selective prisoners,

Philip of France was worried that they were over-confident. He ordered that the great banner of Oriflamme should be flown. This was the banner of St Denis, traditionally blessed by the Abbot of St Denis before a war. Once flown, no prisoners were to be taken. Edward responded by unfurling his banner of the Dragon to remind everyone, especially the French, that the English under his command would give no quarter.

> About sundown, the first charge was made by the French with resounding trumpets, drums and kettle-drums with strident clarions; and with shouting almost like thunder, the cross-bow men of the French advanced, but none of their quarrels reached the English. At the tremendous clamour of the cross-bow men, the English archers were called forth and riddled their adversaries with arrows. When they saw their cross-bow men were not harming the English, the French men-at-arms mounted on warhorses, rode down the cross-bow men, standing to the number of 7000 between them and the English, crushing them under the feet of their horses, rushing forward to show . . . how brave they were. So anguished were the cries of pain from the trampled that those in the rear of the French thought it was the English who were being slain. Upon hearing all this, the French pressed forward on the heels of those in front; in this ill-considered ardour, the most conspicuous were raw young knights, in whom the army abounded, all panting for the honour of capturing the King of England.[1]

Edward was not going to make the same mistake as the French. His archers, superior to the French crossbow-men, were set along the flanks so that they shot across from the sides of his army. And perhaps remembering the experience of the Scottish campaigns, when English knights tumbled and were slain in pits, the English now quickly dug holes in front of their positions.

> The French became confused, fighting with the English men-at-arms, they were beaten down with battle-axes, lances and swords,

---

1   Geoffrey le Baker, *Chronicles* (ed. Herbert Bruce, Cardiff: W. Lewis, 1918); Geoffrey Baker, *Chronicon Galfridi le Baker de Swynbroke* (ed. Sir Edward Maunde Thompson, Oxford: Clarendon Press, 1889).

and in the middle many Frenchmen were crushed to death without any wound but by the weight of the numbers. In such a woeful encounter, Edward of Woodstock [Black Prince] the King's eldest son, being then sixteen years old, showed his valour to the French, piercing horses, laying low the riders, shattering helmets and breaking spears, helping his men, and showing an example to all. The French repeatedly changed their front line, bring up fresh hordes. These continual accessions of strength kept the Prince and his companions so closely engaged that the great mass of the enemy compelled him to fight on his knees. Then someone rode to the King, his father, imploring help. He was sent with twenty knights to help the Prince, and found him and his men leaning on spears and swords, and taking breath and resting quietly on long mounds of corpses . . . the total number of knights and men of superior dignity killed in this battle exceeded 4000.[2]

No one counted the lesser people slain. Geoffrey le Baker's account, written three decades after the event, is based on a description given him by Thomas de la More, a knight at Crécy. How accurate it is, we cannot tell for certain, but contemporary notes suggest the terrible battle was no less horrific than he described.

In the morning King Philip of France and a small retinue escaped to Amiens. They left behind them the bodies of the King of Bohemia, the Counts of Blois, Flanders, Alençon, Harcourt, Auxerre, Aumale, Savoy, Moreuil, Nevers and many more. And Geoffrey le Baker recounts, if his word can be relied upon, that only forty English died in the two days of fighting. Edward reached Calais by the beginning of September and laid siege to the city for nearly a year. No matter the effort, the siege came near to failure and, in the winter, his soldiers wanted the warmth of their homes not the continually bitter wet lowland of northern France. But Edward held fast and starved the people of Calais into submission.

When Edward returned from France, he officially founded what has been called the 'most brilliant inspiration of the Age of Chivalry', the Order of the Garter. The idea seems to have come to him at the end of a grand tournament at Windsor in 1344, two years before Crécy. He is said to have been so inspired by the occasion that he

---

2   Baker, *Chronicles*; Baker, *Chronicon*.

swore to set up if not a new Camelot, then his own Round Table of his closest knights. How the garter became a symbol of this order is disputed, but it may well have had something to do with the Countess of Salisbury and the siege of Calais. Edward was in love with the countess and, at a celebration ball at the end of the siege of Calais, the countess is said to have dropped her garter. The King picked it up and bound it to his knee. The whole court knew of his love for the countess and there was much 'sniggering and tittering'. The King is said to have rebuked them with '*Honi soit qui mal y pense*'. The Garter became the symbol, the French became the motto.

The Order of the Garter was dedicated to St George, who replaced Edward the Confessor as patron saint of England in 1348, but no saint could protect the people from a catastrophe in that same year.

The Black Death infiltrated England and for twenty or so years: it came, went, returned, retreated, returned again and went. It was terrible. Between 1348 and 1350, the plague killed one-and-a-half million people of a total population of four million. Between one-quarter and one-third of the population of Europe perished in those two years of shrouds.

The England to which the plague arrived was a changing but not always happy land. It was a land of wood, corn and beasts. Wood was used as the main source of fuel, building and manufacturing. There were great hardwood forests throughout the kingdom and there were corn belts in East Anglia and the south Midlands even then. There were large herds and flocks of livestock. Large beasts were needed to cart goods and to plough. Dairy farming was increasing and sheep, apart from their value in the lucrative wool trade, were invaluable as a source of manure for grain cultivation. But this was not an idyllic rural England. Floods, which had covered much of Europe, brought famine to a peasantry already weakened by indifferent nutrition and the demands of war. Sheep were drowned in their thousands. Crops, in spite of efforts to improve yields, were often poorly grown and disappeared. Prices dropped.

One result was that big landlords rented off parcels of farms, therefore tenant farming increased even if it was at subsistence level. The people lived in small groupings. Towns were small. Probably only London and York had populations of more than 10,000. Yet hamlets and villages were so well established that most of the rural communities that exist today existed in the fourteenth century.

The conditions in which people lived, their general constitution, their ignorance of preventative medicine, the entire lack of antidotes and, most of all, the viciousness of the plague all meant that life for many in the middle of the fourteenth century was miserable. The effects of the plague were devastating and the consequences far reaching. In some places, there were too few to bury the many dead. Fields were piled with dead livestock and a yeoman could die within a week of catching the disease. None was invulnerable. One of the grander victims was Edward III's wife, Philippa. She died in 1369 in what would have been the third of the plagues. Half the clergy in Winchester, Norwich, Ely and Exeter died. Many of the houses and mansions of England became uninhabited and fell into ruin. Villages emptied. Labourers and servants, those most vulnerable to the plague, died in such great numbers that the estates could not be worked. Landlords had to give up rents from tenants and waive penalties for non-payment. There was no one to pay. There was also a feeling among the people that their Church and their God had betrayed them. Thus covens and sects emerged to blame and purge their fellows and the institutions – the Church certainly – that had claimed their allegiance in return for sure protection. People stricken to the last ounce of living felt betrayed and needed a reason why. None could give it. But if nearly a third perished, then two-thirds survived. Survivors married, some for a second time, and they had children. But, in 1360, when the plague returned – albeit in a weaker form – those very children would have been the most vulnerable. Indeed, this plague's main victims appear to have been children. Eight years later there was a further outbreak, and a decade later yet another, this time mainly in the north of the country.

It is hopeful proposition that calamity makes men see reason. Yet history records that man rarely has enough death. It should not surprise us therefore that in spite of the seeping calamity of the plague, by 1355 the war with France was back in full and bloody swing. The Black Prince defeated the French at Poitiers the follow-ing year, and captured a rather foolhardy John II of France. In 1357, the King of Scotland, David II, who had been under arrest in the Tower for ten years, was released. The inspirations of the times are revealed by *Piers Plowman*, written around 1362 by Long Will, or

William Langland as he was also known. It is full of high towers of truth, dungeons of wrong, bribery, reason and conscience. It was, probably, an accurate reflection of fourteenth-century England: a people intermittently at war – from lowly Welsh archer to the highest born including the dear sons of Edward's queen, the often forgotten Philippa.

Philippa had been brought from Hainault and married off to Prince Edward in 1328, when he was barely sixteen and she was just a child. His bride grew into a loving and loyal regal figure who was committed to her husband and the family. She bore Edward fourteen children, two of whom died in infancy. The seven surviving sons and five daughters were married off, and well. The sons were seemingly as warlike and sporting as their father, most famously Edward the Black Prince, who had commanded with such distinction at Crécy, and John, Earl of Leicester, Lincoln and Derby, and Duke of Lancaster. He was born in Ghent and thus known as John of Gaunt (1340–99) .

When the Hundred Years War resumed, it was no surprise to find these two princes in the line, but not always in the same one, as in the late summer of 1356 when John of Gaunt was fighting the King of France, John II in Normandy. There had been a master plan that the two brothers, one from the south and one from the north, would meet on the Loire. John of Gaunt was facing the King of France in the north at the time that Edward the Black Prince was advancing from Aquitaine. Edward's soldiers, including the Gascons, burned and pillaged as far as the Loire at Tours. He tried to take the great castle of Tours, but it did not fall to siege. King John II, by then at Chartres, advanced as fast as his depleted army could to meet the Black Prince, perhaps wishing to avenge the terrible defeat at Crécy. Edward wisely withdrew, but not fast enough. John II, having abandoned his slowest moving infantry, caught up with the Prince southwest of Poitiers. Edward relied on the defensive tactics that had been so successful at Crécy – but this time with the addition of a wood and a brook as natural defence obstacles. He also deployed his baggage train as a further obstacle to a direct enemy charge. On his flanks, Edward set his longbowmen. The French sent knights, cavalry and pikemen in the belief they could destroy Edward's archers. When the French charged, the archers fired. Down went French chivalry. Their infantry followed on. The fog of war is nothing to the uncertainty and panic in battle where few well laid plans survive the first fifteen minutes. So it was at Poitiers. When Edward's reserve cavalry attacked the French from behind, uncertainty and the jumble of death caused immovable panic.

The French were devastated, then defeated and John II was captured. The price for his return was yet another king's ransom, three million gold crowns, said to have been twice France's annual income. John II was released to return to France from London but gave his honour to return if he could not encourage his exchequer and his aristocracy to raise the bail. He did find a third of the ransom and to help pay it a new French coin was minted: the franc. On this reduced payment, John II was released from London but had to give two of his sons, various aristocrats and people of some importance from each of the main towns of France as hostages in London. When one of the sons, the Duke of Anjou, decided he could no longer be doing with the indignity of being a hostage and escaped, John returned to England and that's where he died, in 1364.

The Battle of Poitiers was in 1356. Four years on, 8 May 1360 the two sides signed the Treaty of Brétigny. It was a treaty of peace like so many of the period. It was really a truce, albeit one that lasted nine years. Within the treaty, Edward gave up his claim to the throne of France and the Duchies of Touraine and Normandy, the latter of particular significance since 1066. On the other hand, Edward achieved a surer footing in Aquitaine. Edward III had probably expected the French Crown for himself, and although he still had the French King in the Tower, he could no longer bargain from such strength as he once thought.

Moreover, constant war meant the monarch had to repeatedly ask for money to fight those battles, most of which achieved very little for the English. Worse still for the king, if he wanted money then he had to listen to the demands of petitioners. There was a system of petitioning that allowed even a minor matter to come before the monarch, but the monarch might also be a petitioner, particularly in the most constant of regal grievances: money, or lack of it. If the King wanted to go to war, then he had to call Parliament together to hear his petition. Parliament did not sit as it does in the twenty-first century, only gathering when the monarch called it. The more the King was at war, the more Parliament had to be called together. Therefore, there was in theory more opportunity for the common petitions to be heard; they were often made in the hope that the Crown through Parliament would compensate for grievances or, better still, right the apparent wrongs that had cause grievance. The common people held similar grievances and so collective petitioning became the style of the day and the commoners could petition as a formal and, to some extent under Edward III, influential collective body and voice. The two groups, the aristocrats (the Lords) and the ordinary people (the Commoners) remained quite separate and clearly the upper house retained the upper hand and would do so for five centuries. It is from this period, the fourteenth century, that we can see the real distinctions between the Houses of Parliament, the Lords and Commons, and many of the offices of State that were formed then are recognizable today.

Of all today's positions of dignity with origins in the fourteenth century, there came the single most important office in the country after the monarch: in 1377 Sir Thomas Hungerford became the first Speaker designate. Yet, we should not get the idea that the rule of Edward III meant a rush for democracy nor Parliamentary debate. The Parliament met relatively rarely and it certainly did not have to meet in London, and frequently did not. Furthermore, for its members and interested parties it was an expensive and elaborate business to attend Parliament. Eyre and Spottiswoode's *English Historical Documents* includes a record of the expenses of four representatives who travelled from London to a Parliament at Cambridge. It details the sorts of comforts politicians of the day expected:

Expenses incurred in attending Parliament by Adam Bamme, Henry Vanner, William Tonge, and John Clenhound:

In the first place: for timber and carpentry, tillers and daubers, in preparing the house for their lodging, as well as the chambers in the hall, buttery, kitchens and stables; and for making stools and forms throughout, and for carting out the rubbish, such house being quite ruinous; for payment made good to the man of the house for the said lodging, six pounds nine shillings.

Also for firewood, charcoal, turf and sedge, five pounds thirteen shillings.

Also, for the hire of horses, and for hay and oats, and for straw for the beds, as well as for litter for the horses; and for horse shoeing, twelve pounds fifteen shillings and sevenpence.

And for expenses incurred in riding on horseback to Cambridge and back; and for carriage of wine and all harness thither and back, seven pounds sixteen shillings and eightpence.

Also, two pipes of red wine taken thither from London, and for other wine bought at Cambridge, nine pounds two shillings. Also, for clothes for them and their servants, arrayed in like suit, twenty-two pounds and fifteen shillings.

Also, expenditure at Cambridge throughout the time of the Parliament on bread, ale, flesh-meat, fish, candles, sauce, the laundry man, and in gifts to minstrels of the King and of other lords, together with divers other outlays made, twenty-three pounds, five shillings and ninepence.

There may be those interested in the 2009 debate on MPs' expenses who may think there is little new under the Parliamentary sun and that mid-fourteenth century Members of Parliament had modest needs. Certainly, English society during the second half of the fourteenth century was unlikely to be aware of the costs and expenses of those who did not really represent them. It was true also that English society then appeared exhausted and concerned only with the constant drudge of survival in an island where the effects of the Black Death lingered.

The Church, never much of a comfort to ordinary people, only an accuser, was hardly an example to follow. Schism and corruption had the Pope now established in Avignon and seen as anti-English, or at least pro-French. From 1305 to 1378, seven popes (Clement V, John XXII, Benedict XII, Clement VI, Innocent VI, Urban V and Gregory XI) sat at Avignon. Each of them was French.[3] The leaders of the church lived as princes. It was the Oxford theologian, John Wyclif, who emerged as the man who led the renewal of Christianity. Wyclif committed the unthinkable: the translation of the Bible into English in 1382.

England had changed step. The old order was changing throughout the land including the disappearance of its heroes. The Black Prince, the heir to the throne, died, a sad, broken figure in 1376, no longer the dashing prince in black armour. The King, an increasingly

---

3   P. N. R. Zutschi, 'The Avignon Papacy', in M. Jones (ed.), *The New Cambridge Medieval History*, *Volume VI* c.*1300*–c.*1415* (Cambridge: Cambridge University Press, 2000), 653–73.

unheroic figure in his widowhood and approaching dotage, took up with Alice Perrers, a former lady-in-waiting to Queen Philippa, a political intriguer and, some say, a person who took the very rings from her husband's dying fingers.

In 1377 Edward III had been King for more than fifty years. In his time he was an adventurer, unscrupulous and vain. He was certainly dissipated, and maybe his pre-senile dementia was the price he paid. Yet he honoured the chivalrous and warrior hopes of his country. He built a military reputation for England and he balanced Church and Parliament, often not very well, but he corrupted neither. Fourteenth-century English men and women liked him. His first wife, Philippa, was devoted to him. His sons did not intrigue against him and John of Gaunt, still in his thirties, had taken on many of the regal responsibilities, often with a deviousness that is kindly called politics. Edward III died, at sixty-five years old, a lonely figure but seemingly his people of England mourned his passing.

CHAPTER THIRTEEN
1377–99

Richard II (1367–1400) came to the throne in 1377. He was just ten years old, and the eleventh King of England since William the Conqueror, almost 300 years earlier. Richard wasn't supposed to be King at all. The Black Prince, Edward III's eldest son, should have been King, but he died the year before his father and Richard was the Black Prince's eldest son. And so it was Richard who swore that he would solemnly preserve the laws and customs conceded by ancient and devout kings before him. It was John of Gaunt, Duke of Lancaster, and the King's uncle, who carried the ceremonial sword, Curtana, at the coronation. As a symbol, Curtana, was, and has remained, all-important in the coronation procession. It is a blunted sword, the sword of mercy. Therefore the bearer of Curtana also carried the authority of the King's highest prerogative: mercy. The importance was not lost on those gathered at the coronation.

It was John of Gaunt who became Steward of England and ran the Regency for the boy-king. But John of Gaunt was unpopular with the businessmen of the City of London, the hierarchy of the clergy and the Commoners of Parliament. He led the anti-clerical party in England. Fundamentally, he was trying to re-establish the authority of the Crown and the Royal Family. In 1371, six years before Edward III's death, John of Gaunt managed the removal of both the Chancellor and the Treasurer: the charge was maladministration. Their replacements were less efficient and even more corrupt. Five years later, Parliament – known as the Good Parliament of 1376 – attacked the government and, in particular, Gaunt's cronies. But Gaunt had another Parliament called, fixed it by packing it with his supporters and reversed all the decisions of the Good Parliament. John of Gaunt was able to use Parliament for his own purposes because, in the fourteenth century, Parliaments were councils, meetings that were called only by the monarch, usually to get money.

The England of the late 1370s and early 1380s was leaderless, overtaxed and at war, and not very successfully so. A dull war that celebrates nothing has few compensations for those at home and brings opportunity to protest that dues and poll taxes are unfair. The poll tax had been levied 150 years earlier. It comes from the medieval word 'polle' or head. The fourteenth-century poll tax had traumatic effects. People avoided paying for every member of the family and when the returns showed that less had been collected than anticipated, household assessments were made: a sort of fourteenth-century means test. Furthermore, since 1351, the Statute of Labourers had frozen wages to pre-Black Death rates. This Statute and the new poll tax were the root causes of what is now the Peasants' Revolt which occurred in 1381 when the common men marched through Essex and Kent and by the Medway towns, pausing only to burn records and fine houses, seize the castle at Rochester and release the imprisoned John Ball and Wat Tyler. From both banks of the Thames the revolters converged on the City of London on 13 June 1381 and waited for the fourteen-year-old King Richard to hear their grievance.

Richard called everyone together at Smithfield, or Smooth-field, as it was. And by St Bartholomew's, a house of Church canons, he stopped. In front of him on the east side were the people, the Commoners, led by Wat Tyler (also, Tyghler). This had not been a peaceful protest. They had burned down John of Gaunt's manor house (the Savoy) by the Thames, captured the Tower of London and executed the Archbishop of Canterbury, Simon of Sudbury, and the Treasurer, Sir Robert Hales. The Mayor, William Walworth, called the watch-commanders of the City of London's twenty-four wards and instructed them to tell everyone to arm themselves and rush to the King's side at Smithfield. It is said that Wat Tyler strutted. He approached the king in a haughty fashion, but told the King that if he agreed their demands then he would have 40,000 more friends among the Commoners than afore. Richard is said to have agreed that the Commoners would get their demands but that Tyler had to take his people back to their counties.

At this stage, it is also said that a courtier described Tyler as a liar and thief and that Tyler drew his dagger. Walworth pounced and had

Tyler arrested. Tyler struck the Mayor with his dagger, but Walworth wore good armour, drew his cutlass and cut Tyler about the neck and head. An attendant leapt towards Tyler and stabbed at him. In front of the Commoners, Tyler fell from his pony mortally wounded and calling on the people to come to his aid and revenge. They did not. He was taken to the poor hospital but the Mayor had him dragged out and beheaded him. The head was topped on a pikestaff and shown to the people, who supposedly fell like men discomforted crying to the King for mercy. The King cancelled the promised reforms and so the Peasants' Revolt failed to achieve its objectives; although it did kill, for the moment, the poll tax. But the uprisings of 1381 showed just how much the people had lost confidence in those who governed them. Kingship, along with Tyler, lay cold.

At the same time the influence of a new aristocracy – one that had been developing for at least a generation – was growing. A handful of families, all connected by blood with the throne – Lancaster, York, Gloucester, Cornwall and Clarence – were beginning to make their mark. Yet it was still the King's court and his royal judges who restored order when the feudal classes lost their nerve and, by 1389, the King was in his early twenties and, at last, had begun to rule for himself.

The revolt of the aristocracy came about after John of Gaunt had left England to pursue his claim to the kingdom of Castile, a claim he thought himself entitled to through his second wife, Constance of Castile, the heiress daughter of Pedro the Cruel. He left his son, Henry Bolingbroke, in charge of his English estates, which he had inherited when his first wife, Blanche of Lancaster, died. Thomas of Woodstock, Duke of Gloucester, the youngest and most ambitious brother of the absent John of Gaunt, joined forces with the young Henry Bolingbroke, John de Mowbray, Earl of Nottingham, and the Earls of Arundel and Warwick, and marched on London. They called themselves the Lords Appellant and accused Richard's closest advisers, particular his Chancellor Michael de la Pole, of treason.

Another of those accused, Robert de Vere, Duke of Ireland, raised an army in Cheshire and marched to the King's rescue. They didn't get very far. Just before Christmas Day, 1387, troops led by Gloucester and Bolingbroke scattered them at Radcot Bridge in Oxfordshire. The Lords Appellant were in command and, in February 1388, they summoned what became known as the Merciless

Parliament. It was a good name. Little mercy was shown to five of Richard's friends: Sir Robert Tresilian, the chief justice of the King's Bench, and the Lord Mayor of London, Sir Nicholas Brember, were hanged, drawn and quartered. The other three escaped to the Continent. Then came the lull none had expected. During it, Richard contemplated ways for revenge. The barons had to be very careful. By and large, Richard was popular. Richard, still a young man, remember, called his barons and magnates together. He questioned them about his authority. He wanted to know if they accepted that at the age of twenty-two he should not have the same rights of determination of any other man in his realm – to reach his majority at twenty-one. The barons, apparently unnerved, agreed that Richard had equal rights and more than any in his kingdom. Richard had heard the words for which he had hoped. He declared that it was time for him to throw off his tutors and appoint his own advisers. Richard was now King in his own land and for the next eight years, England was well and quietly governed.

John of Gaunt returned from Castile and perhaps his still-great presence reduced the influence of the Lords Appellant. In 1394, John of Gaunt went to Ireland. The English domain, known as the Pale, was yet again under threat. The 1366 Statute of Kilkenny forbade English settlers to inter-marry or adopt Irish customs or language. But the English authority ran only around Dublin, including Meath, Louth and Kilkenny. Certainly by the sixteenth century, this area was commonly known as the Pale, as was the English area around Calais. Hence anything outside the domain was 'beyond the Pale'. For all his weaknesses, Richard saw that the difficulties of Ireland had as much to do with the English administration as with the eccentric and sometimes barbarous behaviour of the Irish themselves. He also saw Ireland as a source of support.

In the same year, 1394, Richard's wife, Anne of Bohemia, died. Two years later he married Isabella, the seven-year-old daughter of the French King, Charles VI. This political marriage sealed a thirty-year truce with France and a secret clause meant that, should Richard be opposed at home, France would come to his aid. Richard II needed little help at this point. He searched for revenge. In January 1397, the King sensed the blood of Gloucester and Arundel. The latter, and others that Richard regarded as his henchmen, were executed. Gloucester was taken under guard, ostensibly into exile at Calais.

But there he was murdered. Richard assaulted the opposing aristocracy and the constitutional process that had supported its rampage. Parliament was frightened of him and stripped away the great constitutional rights of the thirteenth century.

And then, it seems, Richard lost his reason. John of Gaunt died in February 1399 and instead of allowing Henry Bolingbroke to inherit his father's vast estates by proxy, Richard took them over. Totally oblivious to the probable consequences, Richard then set off on an expedition to Ireland, leaving his kingdom unguarded. Henry of Lancaster (as now Bolingbroke was) saw this foolhardiness and landed in Yorkshire to claim his father's estate. He had the sure support of the northern barons including the formidable Northumberland. It took valuable time for Richard to hear of Henry Lancaster's landing and the support he had gained. By the time Richard arrived back from Ireland, he must have known what a hopeless task he had to regain his authority. He had little choice but to submit to Henry. He returned to his capital as a prisoner.

Many still mourn Richard II as a romantic figure, but it was the job of the King to stand between oppression and the people. Between 1389 and 1397 Richard protected his people well, but later he hounded them for revenge and corrupted the role of Parliament. He usurped the judiciary and he acted in the belief that the very lives of his people were subject to his every whim. That was not kingship. That was tyranny.

CHAPTER FOURTEEN
1399–1454

By the end of the fourteenth century, the Plantagenets had ruled England for almost 250 years. There had been eight kings, beginning with Henry II and ending, in 1399, with Richard II. But now the dynasty, although still Plantagenet, was to splinter: first the House of Lancaster, then the House of York, each of which could trace its line to the original Plantagenet monarch, Henry II. For the next sixty or so years, England was ruled by the House of Lancaster, the three Henrys, beginning with Richard's successor Henry Bolingbroke, who was to be Henry IV and would rule for fourteen years. In that time Owen Glyndŵr began the war for Welsh independence and defeated the English at Pilleth and then mysteriously disappeared; the King crushed a rebellion led by Richard Scrope, the Archbishop of York, and then had him executed; the first James became King of the Scots; and the first Lollard religious reformer was martyred by burning at Smithfield.

From the first day of his reign, Henry IV had to accommodate his supporters. After all, to attempt to overthrow a king is high treason. To fail is death. Therefore, his backers demanded their rewards and Henry needed their continuing support. It was by no means an easy succession for the House of Lancaster and its complications clouded the reigns of all three Lancastrian Kings. Also, when Henry came to the throne Richard II was not dead, he was merely in prison.

Richard II was a prisoner in Pontefract Castle and as the general bitterness towards him began to wilt, the weakness of Henry's government became more obvious. In January 1400 some of the nobles tried to rise in favour of the imprisoned Richard. They failed, but as long as Richard remained alive the greater chance there was of him becoming a rallying figure. It is generally said that he was starved to death, but one contemporary writer believed that Henry sent one of his knights, Sir Peter Exton, to kill Richard. But even then it was necessary to display Richard's body at St Paul's Cathedral to convince the people that he was really dead.

Henry was now faced with demands from the Church to restrain the excesses of the Lollards. The Lollards, who got their name from a medieval Dutch word meaning 'mutter', as in praying, were religious reformers and followers of the late John Wyclif. They did not believe in transubstantiation and they believed the clergy indulged in excesses. John Wyclif had translated the Bible into English; he believed that everyone who wanted to read the Testaments should be able so to do. The simplest way to deal with the Lollards, said the Church, was officially to declare them heretics. And so, in 1401, a Statute of enormous significance was published, written to deal with what its draughtsmen called 'the innovations and excesses of the Lollards'. *The Statute De Heretico Comburendo* made it legal in England to take anyone convicted of heresy and burn him, or her, at the stake:

> If any person refuses to abjure heresy so that according to the holy canons he ought to be handed over to the secular court, the sheriff shall receive the said persons, all of them, after such sentence has been promulgated, and cause them to be burned in a high place, so that such punishment may strike with fear the minds of others[1] and by this no such wicked doctrine and heretical and erroneous opinions shall be sustained or in any way suffered.

In 1401 the burning began. It would seem that Henry IV supported the Statute only partly because of his religious orthodoxy; the greater pressure was political. Henry's debts of loyalty were still being paid.

Henry also faced war with both Scotland and Wales. The Scots had renewed their alliance with France and, led by the Earl of Douglas, had destroyed the English force and captured young Hotspur, Henry Percy, the son of the First Earl of Northumberland. Henry IV advanced north as far as Edinburgh and then had to return south. The Welsh were on the move. *The Chronicle of Adam of Usk*, of autumn 1401, tells the story.

---

1 An early reference to which we have in Voltaire's *Candide*: '*Dans ce pay-ci, il est bon de tuer de temps en temps un amiral pour encourager les autres.*'

Owen Glyndwr, all north Wales and Cardigan and Powis siding with
him, sorely harried with fire and sword the English who dwelt in
those parts, and their towns. Wherefore, the English invading those
parts with a strong power, and utterly laying them waste and ravaging
them with fire, famine and sword, left them a desert, not even sparing
children or churches, and they carried away into England more than
1000 small children of both sexes to be their servants. Yet the same
Owen did no small hurt to the English, slaying many of them and
carrying off the arms, horses, and the tents of the King's eldest son,
the Prince of Wales, which he bore away for his own use to the mountain fastness of Snowdon.

The Welsh harried, the Scots harried; but for Henry, the villain was
in his own land and that villain was inevitably a Percy. The Percys
ruled the north, were the lords of the Northern Marches and, most
importantly, were the Northumberlands. Chief thorn in Henry's mind
was the Earl's son Hotspur. As Lords of the Marches, the Percys had
long protected the borders from the Scots and not always in the
king's interest but in their own as well. But if we think the individual
ambition to protect their own lands from the raiders was justification
to be suspicious of the Percys, then we should look deeper. The
Percys had, after all, joined with Henry when he had landed in
Yorkshire to claim his rights as John of Gaunt's son. King Henry's
suspicion fell upon Hotspur's brother-in-law, Edmund Mortimer. He
had hired out soldiers to Glyndŵr. The king's suspicion could not be
ignored. Hotspur rose to challenge that charge and declared against
the King. The romantic figure of Hotspur was to die; at the battle of
Shrewsbury on 21 July 1403, Henry IV killed him.

Hotspur's father had no alternative but to bow at the knee. But he
did not bow his heart. Others joined him in rebellion including the
considerable figure of the Archbishop of York, Richard le Scrope
(1350–1405). Scrope had been moved from Lichfield to York by
Richard II in 1398. He was, as Archbishop of the Northern Province,
close to the Percys. Nevertheless, he does not appear in the lists of
rebellion when Henry IV overthrew Richard II. No one could be
apolitical in such a high office, but Scrope was not, by reputation of
his history a plotter. It is true that he officiated at Henry's coronation,
but by then that may have been prudence rather than politics. One
respectable theory is that old Northumberland, seeking revenge for

the death of Hotspur, convinced Scrope that the King was not to be supported. Scrope, with the nineteen-year-old Lord Mowbray, found himself leading a not very good army under the general command of Northumberland. At some point, Northumberland abandoned them. At Shipton Moor Scrope was confronted by a superior royalist army. He ended up first in Pontefract Castle, then at his own palace, Bishopsthorpe. Archbishop Arundel warned the King that, as a clergyman, Scrope should be tried for treason only by Parliament or the Pope himself. Henry ignored the ecclesiastic plea and Scrope was executed on 8 June 1405. The execution of a priest was normally unforgiveable. But we are here, at a moment of great schism in the Church. If there had been only one Pope at the time, Henry IV would probably have been excommunicated for Scrope's execution. But the schism in the Church had left a Pope in Rome and a Pope in Avignon. Henry supported the Roman Pope, but if he punished Henry, the King might defect to Avignon. So, although the Church protested, Henry remained its child.

By 1408 the Earl of Northumberland was dead, killed in battle against the King's men at Bramham Moor, and Henry's England was free from uprising if not from malcontents. But the King had leprosy. It was agreed among the courtiers, the Bishop of Winchester and Henry's eldest son, also Henry, that the King should abdicate. Henry would never agree to that, but his stubbornness hardly mattered. He returned to the capital and died at Westminster in 1413. Henry IV left behind a country lacking unity and woefully in debt, and therefore dependent upon the goodwill and mercy of its magnates.

The new King, a young man of twenty-five, almost immediately led his country towards the one thing that might have brought order and even unity: war with France. Before that could get under way, Henry V had to demonstrate if not magnitude then a sense of pragmatism. He proclaimed a pardon for old adversaries; he made a deal with the Scots for the release of Hotspur's offspring and declared him Earl of Northumberland; he pardoned his cousin Edmund Mortimer who had connived with Scrope; he spectacularly brought what were said to be the remains of Richard II to London and had them placed with honour in Westminster Abbey; and, most wisely, he promised Parliament that whatever he had in mind, only Parliament could give the ultimate authority to a law being enacted. Henry V thus got his funding for his expeditionary force to France.

In 1415, Henry and his archers were on the road to Agincourt. Even in the medieval age, national unity tended to be a consequence of foreign war, but only as long as the foreign war was won and didn't cost too much in gold or in lives. Also, in this particular case, the English King had lucrative, and family, possessions and titles in France, and, like his forebears, he wished to fight to maintain or increase them. Moreover, the French had aligned themselves with the Scots and even with the Welsh. And Henry V appeared to believe in a sense of divine support, if not right. He seemed convinced that it was his task to conquer France and then lead soldiers from both nations on the great Crusade to recover Jerusalem.

And so Henry claimed his right to the throne of France. The French were weak from civil conflict between the Burgundians and the Orléanists, the Royalists. The latter offered Henry a large part of Aquitaine, 850,000 crowns and Catherine, the daughter of King Charles VI. Henry was also negotiating with the Burgundians to let him enter France in safety, and he promised that he would take their side against the Orléanists if they would support his claim to the throne. On 11 August, in what was a considerable naval fleet, Henry began transporting 10,000 men across the Channel. Within the month, Harfleur was overcome. Not all was so easy with his large army. As is so often the case in the theatre of war, there were many more casualties from disease than wounds. Henry pared his army and sent thousands back to the English south coast. Then with some 1,000 knights and soldiers and 4,000 archers, he began the trek to Calais – the English stronghold on the northern coast.

When they arrived close by Agincourt, this small English force was met by at least six times that number of French cavalry, foot-soldiers and crossbowmen. There were perhaps 20,000 French cavalry and footsoldiers, although one chronicler says there were, eventually, 60,000 French soldiers, but it would not have been possible to organize them all as a fighting force in that small area. There was parley during which Henry offered to return Harfleur. The French wanted him to give up all claim to the throne of France. This he would not do. Battle was joined. Henry's bowmen pierced the confusion of French horsemen and foot soldiers and left them dead. Those captured stood and waited philosophically and maybe in relief, for this was medieval warfare when knights could easily be taken and then returned shortly after a ransom according to rank was paid. But then came the most unchivalrous calamity. The English feared they had been attacked from the rear and so ordered the prisoners to be slaughtered. It was a massacre of terrible proportions. The battlefield was a terrible French charnel house open to the skies. The English lost perhaps fewer than 300, the French, maybe 6,000, including slaughtered prisoners. The English army was so weakened by the campaign that it struggled to reach the safety of Calais. In the following month, November 1415, Henry V returned to England. He was the hero the nation had longed for.

However, Henry's own ambitions were not realized and for the next two years he set out to overcome Normandy by siege and steady attrition. An agreement was reached that Henry would indeed marry Catherine, the daughter of Charles VI, and at Charles' death, Henry would become King of France. Henry and Catherine were married in June 1420. But by now Henry was desperate for a conclusion to the war. He took just one day's honeymoon before he returned to the conflict. Exhausted, and vulnerable to disease, he was dead two years later. The hero, the wise and true Englishman, Henry V, left a united England and a miserable France. But the cost of victory had to be paid long after the bells finished chiming, and the new King, Henry VI, was but nine months old.

Physically, Henry VI was weak. Mentally, he was probably simple; on some occasions, obviously so. He never much changed during his forty or so years on the throne. And when he was fifty, he was murdered.

Henry V had wanted his brother, the good Duke Humphrey of Gloucester, to be Regent of England but the magnates of England had other ideas. They wanted the chance to run the country without a king, without a strong leader. Gloucester was given the title Protector, but the country was really in the hands of an aristocratic council and the seemingly inevitable struggle for influence. Henry VI never had the measure of this council. As for the war in France, Parliament took the view that the longer the war, the more campaigns to finance; the more territory gained, the more to administer, the greater the costs. And because the territories were so ravaged by war, they were quite incapable of generating anything for their own upkeep, never mind supporting the English forces and camp followers.

The infant Henry VI knew little of this. Seven years later, in 1429, he was thought old enough to be crowned King of England. There was nothing special about the coronation. The English were used to boy-kings. They were also used to going to war. The coffers were usually bare but, however reluctantly, the business of intrigue and defending lands continued. The English were being held up on the southward march through France by the Armagnac possession of Orléans. Under the Earl of Salisbury they laid siege to the town. It wasn't much of a siege. The English force was weak, badly supplied and in bad mood when the Earl himself was killed.

It was at this siege that Joan of Arc made her famous appearance. She had, so it was said, a vision and she heard voices. And in March 1429, Joan of Arc went to the court of the Dauphin and told him of those voices and the message that he would be crowned King in Rheims. But first she had to deal with the English who, depleted and war-weary, fell back at Orléans. Joan of Arc then led the still scepti-cal Dauphin through Champagne, took Troyes and Châlons, and, on 17 July, as the voices had promised, the Dauphin was crowned King Charles VII in Rheims Cathedral.

The Maid of Orléans believed her mission completed. She wanted no more of war. She wanted to go home but the court would not let her. In May 1430 she was captured by the Burgundians and sold to the English for 10,000 gold francs. The French King made no attempt to rescue her. She was burned to death on 30 May 1431. Four years on, Burgundy had abandoned the English for France. The war was a simple line of retreat for the English. In 1449 the French took Rouen and then defeated the English at Castillon in 1453. The Hundred Years War was effectively at an end, which was just as well because two years later, the English were at war with themselves in the Wars of the Roses.

The conflict was a war of dynasties. On one side was the Beaufort family, bastard descendants of John of Gaunt and therefore Lancastrians (as was the King). On the other side was the King, Henry VI – kindly, soft, soon to be judged insane – and his new bride, Margaret. She was the seventeen-year-old Margaret of Anjou, married to Henry in a two-year truce with France. Margaret was a remarkable woman. She championed the Beauforts, set herself against the Duke of Gloucester, had him arrested and, so many believe, arranged his death.

The politics were complex but the ambitions were simple. The factions that had, at the start of the King's reign, fought for control of the government, now fought for the throne. Against this background, the country was in turmoil for another reason. In 1450 the Kentish rebellion led by Jack Cade was protesting against the government's incompetence and oppressive taxes. His demands were prefaced by his plea that the monarch would rule honourably and that his people would defend the nation as the sovereign willed. But this peaceful and reasonable declaration is misleading. Cade and his henchmen believed that the King was surrounded by evildoers – persons of malice, he declared. He implied that the King broke the law at his will, but followed this with the satire that this surely could not be so because the King had sworn an oath that he would rule honourably. As to the sense of uprising that was abroad in the whole land, Cade said that the rumour-mongers at court were saying that the people were out to destroy the King's friends and, after that, then the King himself and, once that was done, bring the good Duke of York to the throne:

> We will that all men know we blame not all the lords, nor all those that are about the king's person, nor all gentlemen nor yeomen, nor all men of law, nor all bishops, nor all priests, but all such as may be found guilty by just and true inquiry and by the law. We will that it be known we will not rob, nor plunder, nor steal, but that these defaults be amended, and then we will go home.[2]

This sounded reasonable. In practice, rebellion rarely replaces unreason with reason. In Cade's rebellion, local grievances were brought out and displayed as part of the uprising. Barons and bishops were beheaded. Poles bore the heads of the once comfortable.

Cade's uprising was a simple, violent illustration of the breaking down of law and order. The anger towards those who governed was great enough to spark violence and a belief that demands would

---

2   James Gairdner, *Three Fifteenth-century Chronicles, with Historical Memoranda by John Stowe* (London: Camden Society, 1880).

be met. Cade's rebellion began on the day William Aiscough (or Ainscough), Bishop of Salisbury, was murdered by his own parishioners at Edington, suggesting local grievances as well as support for Cade's wider rebellion. Another bishop, Adam Moleyns, Bishop of Chichester, was murdered by sailors in Portsmouth when he arrived to give them their backpay. The sailors were angry because the Bishop confessed to another's crime. He admitted (or so they said) that the late Duke of Suffolk had plotted for a French invasion, that he had sold the French details of English defences and had been bribed to prevent English armies going to France. The navy, or possibly a pirate, caught up with Suffolk and beheaded him in a long boat. As for Cade, he was eventually chased off and killed during a skirmish at Heathfield in Sussex in 1450.

Then, in 1453, the King went mad, or that is the lore of it. The King found his memory gone on too many occasions and his nature that of a child. What could be done? Queen Margaret saw her role as Protector of the Lancastrian cause. Yet it would be hard for her to raise forces to enforce that claim. Then, on 13 October of that year she gave birth, or so it was said, to a son who would be next in line to the Lancastrian throne. But there were suspicions that the new prince, Edward, Prince of Wales, was not the King's son. However, it was also clear that the King was incapable of ruling. The power of the Duke of York – father of the future Richard III – in the Council was sufficient that, in March 1454, he, and not Queen Margaret, was declared Protector. For more than a year, he was monarch in all but title. But then, in 1455, the King recovered his wits. Queen Margaret was ready to do battle. So was York. By May of that year the Queen's closest ally, Edmund, Duke of Somerset, was killed, and the King was taken prisoner. Margaret's screams for revenge echoed about the House of Lancaster. The Wars of the Roses had started.

CHAPTER FIFTEEN

1455–85

The Wars of the Roses spread over thirty years. But they weren't, as is sometimes imagined, one long war. Nor did anyone at the time call it this. The common title was introduced in the nineteenth century in Sir Walter Scott's novel set in the Middle Ages, *Anne of Geierstein, or The Maiden of the Mist* (1829). There is an oblique reference to roses in Shakespeare's *Henry IV, Part 1*, but nothing more than that. The idea that the roses were the only symbols does not stand up. The protagonists wore the various symbols of their leaders. Who fought is supposedly a simple matter but it too has its ambiguities. On one side was the House of Lancaster; on the other, the House of York; but the houses of York and Lancaster came from the same dynasty, the same family tree: the Plantagenets. And just because there were Yorkists and Lancastrians did not mean that the wars were between Yorkshire and Lancashire. Just as in modern times, noble titles had little to do with places.

Henry VI was of the House of Lancaster. The Lancasters commanded the Crown lands, for example, the Duchy of Cornwall. And they had all the Lancastrian earldoms: Lancaster itself, Derby, Lincoln, Leicester, Hereford and Nottingham. The other families who supported them gave them Somerset, Surrey, East Anglia and Devon. Then, with the Percys and the elder Nevilles in the Lancastrian camp, they had control of the northern strongholds.

The Yorkist strength was in the Mortimer family, and their lands were mainly on the Welsh borders, the Marches. They had strong support in Kent, some in Norfolk, and, because of the younger Nevilles, they had the Earl of Warwick and Salisbury, and the estates of Wiltshire and the southern Midlands.

An aspect of the build-up to this confrontation not to be disregarded was the fact that the King had come to the throne when he was only nine months old. Therefore the barons who ran the country on his behalf had, inevitably, become very powerful and factious. Maladministration, corruption and incompetent government were rife in England and all the main players had personal ambitions. None of these reasons, by themselves, account for the Wars of the Roses, but put them together and civil war seemed inevitable. Like the beginning of many conflicts, there was a peace of sorts, almost a phony war. Then, in the summer of 1460, the Earl of Warwick commanded the Yorkists against the Lancastrians of Henry VI at Northampton. Henry VI was on good ground, but he was deserted by Lord Grey of Ruthven who saw the lie of future land. Henry was captured but treated as monarch and put under house custody in London while Richard, the Duke of York, became *de facto* monarch. This of course, would have meant York succeeding to Henry on the latter's death. Queen Margaret had other ideas and York's days were truly numbered. Margaret was ensconced at Harlech Castle and she had troops in the north of England. She marched them on York where the two sides met in a terrible and uncompromising battle at Wakefield on 30 December 1460. York was killed. The Queen's army marched south, beat Warwick on the way, and released the King. That should have been that: the House of Lancaster was back on the throne and the Yorkists were humiliated. But it wasn't. The late Duke of York's eldest son, Edward, the Earl of March, hoisted his father's banner and joined with the bruised Warwick in Oxfordshire. Together they entered London in triumph.

A week after he arrived in London, the Earl of March was ruling England and the Queen was heading north. Edward caught up with her at Towton Field in Yorkshire at the end of March 1461 and, in a snow blizzard, slaughtered hundreds of Lancastrians. Henry VI escaped with his life, but not his throne. The twenty-year-old Duke of York was crowned Edward IV and one-third of the estates in England changed hands.

By 1465, Queen Margaret was penniless in France and King Henry VI was in the Tower. But the new King, Edward IV, was mysteriously reluctant to commit himself to his kingmaker's marriage plans for him. This kingmaker was Richard Neville, the Earl of Warwick – of the Neville family who were more or less running the country at the time – and he could see the political advantages of marrying the King to a French princess. He made all the diplomatic arrangements only to discover, belatedly, that his King was already married. Warwick was outraged. Edward, even though he was a Yorkist, had married Elizabeth Woodville, the widow of the Lancastrian, Lord Grey. Inevitably Warwick and Edward IV clashed.

In the summer of 1469 a rebellion broke out in the north. The contrived complaint was high taxes and favouritism. While this was going on, the marriage between Clarence (the King's brother) and Isabella (Warwick's daughter), which had been forbidden by the King, took place at Calais. Clarence and Warwick returned to England met the Royalists in battle at Edgecote. The King, trying to rally his scattered forces, was captured. Warwick now had two Kings at his mercy as Henry VI was still a prisoner. The Yorkists' sense of alarm that their own king was now also a prisoner divided them. As for the King, he decided, or was advised to decide, that the best thing for everyone including himself was to pardon his enemies and proclaim promises to be a better ruler. On that note he was freed, but it all meant little. Within a few months, there was another rising, this one in Lincolnshire. This time the King survived and Warwick and Clarence, who were now exposed, left England. In France, Louis XI forced Warwick to negotiate with the exiled Queen, Margaret of Anjou. She agreed to a marriage between her son, Prince Edward, and Warwick's daughter, Anne Neville. Their plan was that Margaret's son would one day be king and Warwick's daughter queen. But first they had to get rid of Edward IV and restore the imprisoned Henry VI to the throne.

Richard Neville, Earl of Warwick, and the Duke of Clarence, Edward IV's brother, landed at Dartmouth. Much of southern England welcomed Warwick who marched on London and freed Henry VI from the Tower, where he had been imprisoned for five years, and restored him to the throne. Edward IV fled the country.

But Warwick had made a serious mistake. He'd promised Clarence that he would be King. But a freed Henry, and the real chance of an heir, greatly lessened Clarence's chances. When Warwick had made him this promise, Clarence had deserted his brother, Edward IV, but now when Edward IV returned to fight Warwick, Clarence deserted his ally and rejoined his brother. Warwick's army was defeated and that was the end of the kingmaker. He was killed along with his brother, Lord Montague. As Warwick was dying, Queen Margaret was landing with her army and the young Edward, Prince of Wales, at Weymouth. The two sides met at Tewksbury. Margaret's army was defeated. Out came the axe, off came the heads of the Prince of Wales and Margaret's supporter, Edmund, Duke of Somerset. Edward IV then returned to London, dragged out the hapless King Henry VI and beheaded him. A fifteenth-century royal soap opera perhaps, but the Wars of the Roses were still not yet done. Edward IV had seven children, two of them boys and with the king only forty years old, there was plenty time for his heirs to develop and for the oldest boy, Edward, one day to be Edward V. That was the theory in 1483 and it may have worked had not the King died after a very short illness. The princes were vulnerable. There had to be a protectorate and the protector, by request of the late monarch, was to be his brother, Richard of Gloucester.

Richard of Gloucester's reputation has been too darkly drawn. Equally, he had a royal duty as protector to protect not only the heirs of the late King and their guardians but, most importantly, the State itself. Others had done this in other circumstances and had done so honourably and successfully. These were, as the Wars of the Roses suggest, difficult, even exceptional times. At what point Richard planned to be King is uncertain. But within a few weeks he was. He first arrested Earl Rivers and Sir Richard Grey, accusing them of plotting. They were the young prince's minders. Grey was Edward's half-brother. Two weeks later, doubting the support of Lord Hastings, who was allied to Edward IV's children, he had him beheaded and also imprisoned the Archbishop of York and the Bishop of Ely, the Treasurer. Meanwhile he'd lodged the twelve-year-old Edward V in the Tower, soon to be joined by his younger brother, Richard of Shrewsbury.

All Richard had to do now was convince Parliament, and the people, that the late King Edward IV's marriage to Elizabeth Woodville (the Queen and father of his children) was invalid and therefore their heirs had no right to the throne. Richard's chaplain, Ralph Shaa, was sent to St Paul's Cross in London to preach the sermon that would explain the Church's view. He vowed the princes were not rightfully heirs to the throne and that the late King had not been the legitimate son of the Duke of York, but that Richard of Gloucester most certainly was and that therefore it followed that

Richard had greater right to the throne than had the late King's heir. It should have been a solemnly received occasion. After all, the good Doctor Shaa was held in fine regard. The public regard for the chaplain was now stained. Few, if any, at St Paul's Cross believed him. Richard saw the need for stronger advocacy. The Duke of Buckingham was sent to the Guildhall and so to Parliament to demand that Richard should be accepted as King. A few said yes, many kept their peace.

Richard was not unduly put out by this lack of spontaneous popular approval. Parliament was the important body, not the people. Two days later, Richard, Duke of Gloucester, was proclaimed King Richard III. However, from the day of his coronation, there is a sense that the new King was not trusted by his people, nor by many of his magnates including Buckingham who had so vigorously championed Richard's cause but now feared to be seen as his ally, probably anticipating events. It is said that Richard ordered the death of the princes in the tower. Do we really know this to be true? Sir James Tyrell (c.1450–1502) is said to have been the willing servant of Richard and paid two assassins to smother the princes as they slept. Many believe the evidence offered by Sir Thomas More that Tyrell later confessed. A combination of More's claim and the Shakespearian version of their death in *Richard III* pins the deed on Tyrell and the instigation on Richard. It would be good to know the truth, but it is better not to believe that we do.

It is important to know also that there was a general rising of public anger when news of the death of the princes filtered abroad. The Duke of Buckingham was conspiring against Richard with the Countess of Richmond who, as a Beaufort, was a descendant of John of Gaunt and therefore in the Lancastrian line of Edward III. She'd married the Earl of Richmond, who was now dead. Their son (and Buckingham's second cousin) Henry Tudor was now Earl of Richmond and in exile in Brittany after a previous Lancastrian loss. Buckingham raised forces for a rebellion but his troops deserted him and he became a fugitive. He was soon captured and executed along with others within his conspiracy.

Richard may have had the throne, but in April 1484, when his son and only heir died, Henry Tudor, the Earl of Richmond, nevertheless became the next heir to the Crown. Richmond gathered about him former Ricardian supporters who sensed they had been on the wrong side. Richard would have to fight for his throne.

On 17 August 1485 the King, with 10,000 well-disciplined troops, set forth towards Leicester at the head of his army. Richmond's forces were rebels and the wild card, or unknown factor, was Lord Stanley's forces. The King, doubtful of him, had held his son and threatened to behead him if his father failed to support the royal standard. But Stanley, at the last moment, joined Richmond. It is said that Richard lost many supporters who fled or simply stood and did not fight. None could accuse Richard of uncertainty or coward-ice. He led from the front and may have survived as Richmond was falling back. At perhaps Richmond's weakest moment, he was saved by the arrival of his supporter William Stanley and, some say, 3,000 men. Stanley's arrival and rescue changed the course of British history. Richard's remaining supporters saw the game was up.

Richard's fate is described by Polydore Vergil in his *Anglica Historia*, which chronicled the reign of Henry VII, as Henry Tudor, Earl of Richmond, was to become.

> King Richard was killed in the thickest press of his enemies. Many forbore to fight who came to the field with King Richard for awe and for no good will, but destruction of that prince whom they hated. The body of King Richard, naked of all clothing, and laid upon a horse's back, with arms and legs hanging down both sides was brought to the abbey at Leicester, a miserable spectacle in good truth, and was buried there two days afterwards without any pomp or solemn funeral.

And that was the Battle of Bosworth. It was 1485 and the end of the Wars of the Roses.

CHAPTER SIXTEEN
1485–1515

The story of Tudor England began in 1485, when the twenty-eight-year-old Welshman, Henry Tudor, was crowned Henry VII at the Battle of Bosworth. This tall, blue-eyed, thin-haired young man with black teeth was to rule for almost twenty-four years. He would leave a curious legacy of contradictions; he was devout and had an uncompromising sense of justice but was also said to be avaricious. In spite of what was to follow during Henry's time on the throne, few of his people would have noticed the difference in the months, or even years, following that victory on Bosworth Field. England had yet to recover from the Black Death, which reached these islands nearly a century-and-a-half earlier. Before the plague the population was between four and five million. Yet now it was not much more than two-and-a-quarter million. A stagnant population gives a false prosperity. Food prices are kept low, or even fall, because there's little or no increase in demand. Also, if the population is slow to recover, then so is whatever industrial life it supports.

As for the King, Henry VII was preoccupied with the uncertainty of his own position. Richard III had got rid of most other contenders for the throne. Henry had also been smart enough to declare himself King before the Battle of Bosworth began, so all the losers were easily branded as traitors. When Parliament confirmed his right to the Crown, he married Elizabeth of York, Edward IV's daughter. Henry was a member of the House of Lancaster but this marriage satisfied most of those Yorkists who had joined Henry against Richard, not for Henry's sake, but because of their hatred of Richard. So a new dynasty, the Tudors, had begun. It did so with all the uncertainties that come with violent change. Richard still had some friends, although not at court. His sister, as one example, was the Duchess of Burgundy who sponsored the pretenders Lambert Simnel and Perkin Warbeck, who claimed he was the second prince of the Tower. Warbeck may have been an imposter but he had powerful enough anti-Henrican supporters to keep his claim going for seven years before he was stretched and hanged at Tyburn. Among Warbeck's sponsors were mischief-makers and true enemies of the Crown stretching from Austria to Flanders and up from Burgundy.

Warbeck also found some support in Ireland, which had provided a continuing sense of insecurity for almost every monarch since Henry II. The malcontents among the Irish baronage remind us that both Lancastrian and Yorkist sympathies were to be found within the important Anglo-Irish families. It was important to England who controlled Ireland. And controlling Ireland meant controlling more factions than there were in England and not taking for granted either their loyalties or the power of the recent innovation, the true cannonball. Nor could Scotland be brought to heel by the threat of smithereens. Medieval England was seemingly in a state of perpetual warfare with the Scots, made worse (for the English) by the alliance between Scotland and France. So Henry tried to resolve the differences between Scotland and England before he tackled Ireland.

The logical route to some sort of truce was marriage; in 1503 Henry married off his daughter Margaret Tudor to James IV of Scotland (1473–1513). This was a successful marriage and James even named one of his best warships after her. The Stuarts had in James IV one of their most celebrated monarchs, a man of guile and courage and culture. It was this monarch who introduced the first Scottish printing press (1505). He was, like many royals, a fluent linguist and spoke Flemish, French, German and Spanish, as well as Latin, of course. He was also the last Scottish monarch fluent in Gaelic. He was also the last king in these islands to die in battle. He died because he led an invasion of England at Flodden Edge in Northumberland on 9 September 1513 and was defeated by the ancient Thomas Howard, the Earl of Surrey. Moreover, 10,000 of his Scottish warriors perished with him that day. But that was the time of Henry VIII. Henry VII, having made some sort of peace by marriage with Scotland, now turned his attentions on France. He besieged Boulogne, yet again, and the French (who were also at war with the Spanish and the Holy Roman Empire) had to buy him off. The practice of Danegeld was not one confined to the hapless tenth-century Saxons of Æthelred.

At home, Henry VII was doing what many of his predecessors failed to do: putting the State books in order. Polydore Vergil said he was avaricious, but the St Andrews historian, John Guy, described Henry as the best businessman ever to sit on the English throne. Perhaps the two go together. Certainly the first Tudor monarch should be remembered as a King who, instead of introducing revolutionary systems into the administration of the state, made the old ones work better, especially when there were those in the baronage who would have had it otherwise. Henry also used wealth, and others' lack of it, to control officials, sometimes the courts and often the nobility itself – but then he felt he had to. The seventeenth-century idea that government was based on its army, or the nation's nobility, was true for Henry VII. He had no permanent army but he certainly had a ruling aristocracy and he knew how to control it, and therefore how to steady his country and keep his Crown, and his head.

Henry VII ruled for nearly quarter of a century. In that time he formed the Yeomen of the Guard (1485); Christopher Columbus 'discovered' America (1492); King's College, Aberdeen, was founded (1494); John Cabot received the Royal Licence to explore the other side of the Atlantic (1496); weights and measures were standardized (1496); Erasmus visited England (1499); building work started on Holyrood House (1500); the heir to the throne, Prince Arthur, married Catherine of Aragon (1501) and then died the following year; and the year after that (1503) Catherine was engaged to marry the new heir to the throne, Arthur's brother, Prince Henry.

In 1509, Henry VII died and Prince Henry became Henry VIII and immediately married Catherine. He was just eighteen years old; his bride was twenty-four. It is worth speculating that if Prince Arthur had lived to be King, Henry would probably have become a priest. However, there is no doubt that Henry VIII cared very much for the trappings of monarchy. There was, certainly in his earlier years, something about him that would have been at home in ancient Rome. And the new King was aware of the European Renaissance which was now reaching northern Europe. But most of all, especially given his temperament, Henry was aware of exploration. This, after all, was the time of Columbus and Cabot, and the Atlantic was opening to adventure. Yet the new King could hardly afford to become a merchant venturer and may not have had the commercial vision of his father. Nor, for entirely domestic reasons, could Henry VIII afford to spread his overseas ventures in a way he might have done. King Henry's immediate ambitions lay not so much with the New World, but within the old one, especially the near Continent.

By joining forces with gunners and infantry of the Austrian army, Henry began to achieve his ambition to conquer once more parts of France that he saw as British by rights. Nowhere was his success more heralded than in 1513 at the Battle of the Spurs – so named because the speedy retreat of the French meant, supposedly, that many of the cavalry lost their spurs. If England rejoiced at the news from the battlefield at Guinegate, there was not much joy for the Scots. This was the time of Flodden Edge.

The lasting English historical figure of Sir Thomas Wolsey came to prominence during this time. He had been in royal service with Henry's father, had been master of Magdalen College, Oxford, and had been made almoner (the distributor of alms) to Henry's Royal Household. Henry VIII needed someone who would carry out his wishes in such an uncompromising way that Henry would be allowed to get on with his pastimes, his music, his hunting, his pleasures. However, not until he was satisfied with Wolsey did he allow his back to be turned by these distractions. At that stage, Henry persuaded the Pope to create Wolsey as Papal Legate in England. That done, Wolsey sat above all ecclesiastical authority in the land. The English Church, therefore, was controlled by one of its number, who was also a royal servant. Cardinal Wolsey, as he was titled, was detested by many under him. They found him arrogant, fiercely efficient and, because of his wide patronage, immensely powerful. Once he had also been appointed Lord Chancellor and Chief Councillor, Wolsey's powers were absolute. Parliament rarely met and under his instigation the Court of Star Chamber (so named because it sat in the Star Chamber at the Palace of Westminster) became busy. Henry VII had used the Court to exercise royal power. Wolsey saw the sense of this and now used it for ministerial power. Interrogation by Star Chamber was often just, but very often ruthless; hence the survival into the twenty-first century of the expression 'star chamber' – implying the discarding of the niceties of the law.

CHAPTER SEVENTEEN

1516–46

The popular highlights of Henry VIII's reign concern his wives and break from Rome. Yet we should not forget the greater influences of the European cultural and religious questioning that was spreading from Continental Europe. Henry VIII did not invent the mood that caused the break with Rome. The greater religious tapestry will show us that the discordant notes in the Church were sounded not by the English King, but by the great sixteenth-century movement, the Reformation. The Reformation was the religious and therefore also political demand that the Roman Catholic Church should be reformed – hence the term Reformation. The result was the emergence of Protestantism and non-Roman Catholic Churches not just in England, but in Europe. In the 1520s the ideas of Martin Luther spread from the Continent to the British islands and thus the burning of Protestant martyrs began. Moreover, Catholicism was equated with France and Spain and therefore the suspicions of those old enemies were encouraged. By the 1540s Calvinism had started to replace even Lutherism.

This, too, was the period of the European Renaissance, the revival of art and letters based on classical forms and classical models. It had begun in Italy and was now spreading into northern Europe. One of the first effects in England was Christian humanism. The humanists offered biblical piety and the study of the Greek New Testament including the texts from Desiderius Erasmus who was finishing his *Novum Instrumentum*, a new version of the New Testament. He published tracts against the superstitions of Catholicism and thus the Pope.

Having escaped the frustrations and considerable anger of the Church in Amsterdam, Erasmus came to the comparative freedom of Cambridge to finish his New Testament and, as part of the 'new learning', indeed an important figure in it, he was embraced by the new scholars in England, including Thomas More and John Colet. The Dean of St Paul's, Colet had been to Italy, mastered Greek, wrote of divine truths and the importance of original texts, and preached of Church reform from within and spiritual revival. Thomas More's *Utopia*, published in 1516, presented an imaginary society of pagans and suggested that Christians could learn from such wretches. More, of course, was to go to the Tower eventually and his head would be hung over London Bridge.

Perhaps the first signs of the change of fortunes of those trusted by Henry came with the slide of Wolsey. Already doubted by Henry because of his part in the failure of further policies towards the French, Wolsey now found himself vulnerable to the King's ambition to get rid of his wife, Catherine of Aragon. We will not rehearse the stories of the six wives – Catherine of Aragon, Anne Boleyn, Jane Seymour, Anne of Cleves and the last two Catherines, Howard and Parr. However, Catherine of Aragon, the widow of Henry's late brother Arthur whom Henry had married, is a special case. Catherine was ageing; Anne Boleyn was not. The religious and political objections to this first discard created a highly charged atmosphere at court and set in place the increasing determination of Henry to have his way. Opposition came from very powerful people other than the learned bishops of England. They included Charles V, the Emperor of the Habsburgs. Italy had fallen to the Habsburgs and the Pope, although he needed Henry on his side, more or less had to do whatever Charles V wanted. The importance of Charles V was that his aunt was Catherine of Aragon. Wolsey was told to negotiate a solution. Wolsey failed and his stock fell. He was eventually arrested for high treason. As for Henry VIII and Anne Boleyn, they married in secrecy and on 7 September 1533 the future Queen Elizabeth was born.

After all the agonies, the diplomatic and military risks, Henry had not the male heir he so desperately wanted, but another daughter. It is said that in his anger he went to stay at the house of Sir John Seymour. There he fell in love with Sir John's daughter, Jane. Anne Boleyn's days were numbered, and before their daughter Elizabeth reached her third birthday, Anne was accused (perhaps falsely so) of treasonous adultery and was beheaded with a double-edged sword at the Tower.

The decision to abandon Catherine of Aragon was followed by a whirlwind of legislation. The Acts of Appeals discarded the Pope's right to rule in English Church lawsuits. The Act of Supremacy made the English monarch the supreme head of the Church of England. And the Treasons Act made it a high treasonable offence, that is, punishable by execution, to deny the monarch's supremacy. The Act against the Pope's authority, the Act of Reformation, was to come.

The administrative and constitutional revolution was led by Henry, with the help of Thomas More, against the doubts of John Fisher, the Bishop of Rochester. When both More and Fisher rebelled and refused to swear to the supremacy of the King, they fell. Rome appointed Fisher a cardinal. Henry had him executed in June 1535 (More, the following month) and sent his head to Rome so that the Vatican could fit Fisher with his cardinal's hat. Thomas Cranmer, the Archbishop of Canterbury, and Thomas Cromwell stood by the King. By the following year Henry was married to Jane Seymour, perhaps the truest love of his life. The marriage lasted but eighteen months. The new Queen died apparently under crude surgery, after the birth of their son, the future Edward VI. For the moment Henry's grief had to be set aside. Other affairs, those of State, were calling. The need to replenish his Treasury was uppermost in his mind and the obvious source was the fount of the greatest wealth in the land: the Church.

Henry VIII wished to suppress the 400 or so small monasteries which were in any case in decline and whose endowments were, in Henry's view, wasted on intellectually shabby monks. This wording, from the 1536 Act of Parliament, makes very clear that there was not much regard for the smaller houses, as the monasteries were known:

Forasmuch as manifest sin, vicious, carnal and abominable living is daily used and committed amongst the little and small abbeys, priories, and other religious houses of monks, canons, and nuns, where the congregation of such religious persons is under the number of twelve persons, whereby the governors of such religious houses and their convents, spoil, destroy, consume, and utterly waste as well their churches, monasteries, priories, principal houses, farms, granges . . .

And so it goes on. To the lawmakers, under the will of the monarch, the small monasteries were to be closed and the inmates – and this is often forgotten – were to be transferred to 'great and honourable monasteries of religion in this realm, where they may be compelled to live religiously for reformation of their lives'. Equally, this was not a simple religious intent to clean up the small monasteries and convents. The Act here simply reflects the intent to provide a public and moral justification of what was to follow.

For our purposes it is important to reflect that even Henry felt a need to justify what he was about to do – or what Thomas Cromwell (*c*.1485–1540) was to do on his behalf. Between 1536 (the date of the above Act) and 1540, the monasteries were suppressed and their contents became the King's. Cromwell, Henry's first minister, was thorough. He had served Wolsey well and had learned his craft and courtiership under that man without particularly envying the trappings of the office of first minister. He understood the need to reform and so took each department in what was still a medieval Royal Household and set them on the road to becoming what we would today call Departments of State. For that remarkable distinction, Cromwell is often forgotten. In 1536 the Privy Council replaced the King's Council as a sort of executive board of advisers and governors. It enforced policy, made sure the law courts worked – or tried to – and managed the economy. Through this system Cromwell began the financial reforms of England which eventually distanced the financing of royalty – what is now called the Civil List – from that of government.

Cromwell's main task, though, was to oversee the break up of the monasteries: the Dissolution. Monasteries often owed their allegiance to institutions outside England but this now contravened Henry's supreme power over the Church. Moreover, if Henry were to keep the nobility on his side, he had to make sure, with Cromwell's help, that they were looked after. The best way to do that was with patronage and money.

The events of the 1530s had a profound effect on the practice of religion: England was still a Catholic nation. Yet the access of worshippers to religious texts, and certainly the Bible, was severely controlled. The elders of the Church including the conservative laity believed the texts and testaments were dangerous documents, even subversive in the wrong hands and so should only be read by priests. However, the Tyndale and Coverdale translations of the Bible were appearing as early as 1535. Cromwell saw the inevitability of translated texts and ordered that Bibles in English (rather than Latin) should be available and read in churches everywhere, including the north of England where there was so much rebellion by the laity. There was also an adjunct to this uneasiness – tax collecting. There was a conservative reaction to what was happening under Henry and Cromwell, and this included the so-called, but very short-lived, Pilgrimage of Grace in which the rebellious captured Henry's tax commissioners. The King would not have this. Some 250 leaders of the Pilgrimage were executed.

It was at this point that Henry ordered the printing of more copies of the Bible, its reading in churches and its availability for parishioners to read it for themselves. It is this Bible that, through its revisions, including the King James Version, exists in the twenty-first century in parish churches throughout England. Henry the theologian and uncompromising religious revisionist did not rest his reputation in the pews. There was little holy in what remained of the reign of this Henry, once trained in the priesthood. His plundering of the institutions of the monasteries, 560 of them, continued until there was no booty left. The cost of wars that followed in the 1540s probably wiped out the financial gains and the material losses were obvious: the melting of fine jewellery and ornaments, the wanton destruction of Gothic buildings and the shredding of libraries.

Cromwell did much to ease the consequence of constitutional and philosophical vandalism, but even he was eventually thrown to his enemies and to execution. Anne of Cleves, Henry's fourth wife, was indirectly responsible for Cromwell's death. Cromwell had encouraged the marriage as a means of creating a union with the north German Lutheran princes, the best hope of an alliance on the Continent. But the marriage was never consummated – Henry thought Anne plain and uninteresting – and the failure of Cromwell's match-making made him vulnerable. The Duke of Norfolk, who detested Cromwell, plotted against him. For good measure, Norfolk encouraged one of his nieces to display much of her talents before the King. Henry fell for Catherine Howard's charms and listened to her uncle's poisonous words. He married the niece and on 28 July 1540 Cromwell was executed. The twenty-two-year-old Catherine may have been pretty and sparkly eyed, but she perhaps would have done better to keep her charms for her very middle-aged liege. Instead, she dallied with her cousin, Thomas Culpeper, and in February 1542 her head dropped into the same executioner's basket that had fielded the blindfolded head of Anne Boleyn.

Eighteen months later, Catherine Parr was Queen and nurse to Henry. Henry had long suffered from an enormous ulcer in his leg. Even his largely ceremonial armour had to be shaped to cope with the increasing pain. Craftsmen and tailors were not, however, able to cope with his increasing rages, perhaps gingered by his illness. Nor was it possible to calm his antagonism against Scotland and France.

Henry wanted war with France, but he understood that given the long alliance with Scotland, France would always be in a strong position to encourage the Scots to raid England should Henry's army cross the Channel in any great numbers. Indeed, Henry understood, even if he resisted, the notion that bringing England, Scotland, Ireland and Wales into some form of reasonable coexistence was a foremost responsibility of any King of England. The easiest part of this task, to some extent set in motion by Cromwell, was to achieve unity with Wales. In 1543, the year of Henry's marriage to Catherine Parr, the Act for the Government of Wales was passed. This meant that Wales was now under English law, including the system of administration by counties. From that date, twenty-four Welsh Parliamentary representatives would be sent to Westminster, and new Courts of Great Session were established to oversee the judiciary. It is from this date that the Welsh language would appear to have reached its most popular point. By the end of the Tudors, hastened by the introduction of English legal and commercial documentation and the accompanying officialdom, the language was on its way to a minority status from which it never recovered. Religious texts, including the Welsh Bible of 1588, are in the Late Modern Welsh, but the population was never large enough to support an expanding language and with the influx of foreign tradesmen and workers – certainly during the late eighteenth and early nineteenth centuries – the Welsh language was overwhelmed by English. None of this was of concern to Henry VIII whose preoccupations were with events east, south and north of the Welsh border.

He had captured Boulogne but the Holy Roman Emperor Charles V, his supposed ally, was at the same time making a separate treaty with King Francis. The outcome for Henry was a treaty of sorts which allowed Boulogne to remain English for eight years from 1546, but was then to be handed back, complete with new fortifications. The cost of this to England was enormous. At the same time, everything was going wrong for Henry in Scotland. Raids by English forces, and in particular the attack on Edinburgh, only united the Scots against him. So now Henry had exactly what he had tried so hard to avoid: war with Scotland and France at the same time.

Since the execution of Cromwell, Henry, perhaps arrogantly, had believed that he could be his own chief minister, leaving the everyday running of the country to the Privy Council. Although increasingly ill, he was never up to this grand scheme. Nevertheless, Henry seemed satisfied that he could hold apart the rival factions – the radicals of Thomas Cranmer, and the old guard of his Secretary Stephen Gardiner, the Bishop of Winchester, and the Duke of Norfolk. All three supported Henry, but for different reasons. But the question in the minds of everyone at court was simple: who would become Protector to the young King Edward when Henry VIII died? These were ever turbulent times. In 1545, the French had set ashore and burned Brighton, although it was then a relatively unimportant fishing village called Brighthelmstone. The following year the truce was signed with France, but peace did not settle easily in the fast ailing Henry's England, where religious dissension lingered on. Anne Ayscough (sometimes Askew, 1521–46) was tortured for confession then burned as a heretic. The same year, George Wishart (c.1513–46) preached in favour of Calvin and he too was executed. There were bloodier years to come, but King Henry VIII would not see them. He died the following year, 1547.

He had ruled since 1509 and his reign is remembered as the time of the break with Rome, of six wives, of savage persecution, torture and execution. Yet the English Church was in need of reform and throughout Europe there was a revolt against papal authority. The Reformation, the new thinking, Erasmus and Luther would have meant change was inevitable whoever ruled England.

With Henry gone, England needed a strong man at the centre of power to fend off the threat of constitutional and political implosion. Instead, the nation now had a weakling nine-year-old King and the vacillating Edward Seymour, Duke of Somerset, as his Protector.

CHAPTER EIGHTEEN
1547–58

The new monarch was the son of Henry VIII and Jane Seymour, and was titled Edward VI (1537–53). There was no doubt in the minds of his people that, although England was under a Regency – for two years, Edward's uncle, Edward Seymour, Duke of Somerset, was Lord Protector – the young king was a Protestant. This was important because the court needed a clear distinction that would not revive the Catholic persuasion. However, this could not prevent the disturbances in the realm that had travelled over from Henry's reign. There were ruptions in East Anglia where Robert Ket led a rebellion against land closures and in the West Country where rioters attacked Exeter. It was Edward Seymour's inability to cope with these disturbances, which became crises for the State that made him so vulnerable to other ambitions at court. The Ket rebellion was a case in point.

It was John Dudley, Earl of Warwick, who marched to Ket's camp to suppress the uprising; but when a small urchin spoke and gestured rudely the boy was immediately shot. The murder enraged Ket's followers and fighting began. Around 3,500 peasants were killed and there were no wounded. Ket was hanged at Norwich Castle. Warwick, strengthened by his management of the incident, became the leader of the opposition and his party, the Lords in London, met to take measures against the Protector. Warwick was now virtual ruler of England and none of any standing supported Somerset. In January, 1552, he was executed.

Warwick created himself Duke of Northumberland, restructured the Privy Council and, instead of calling himself Protector, he became Lord President of the Council – a title that survives into the twenty-first century. Northumberland also tidied up England's silly wars and turbulences, returned Boulogne to the French and withdrew English soldiers from Scotland. He had aligned himself with the Protestant cause and this decision had long-lasting results. For when Cranmer published the second edition of his *Book of Common Prayer* in 1552, it had to be approved by Parliament and supported by the Acts of Uniformity. It was from this point that the authority of the Church of England became reliant upon Parliament, and it still does. For good measure, Northumberland imprisoned a dissenting voice, the Bishop of Winchester, Stephen Gardiner, a man hardly impressed with the Protestant persuasion.

So the laity triumphed over the Church. But Northumberland had an immediate constitutional conundrum, a puzzle that would result in his own death. Edward VI, always a sickly youth, was dying. Mary, the daughter of Henry VIII's first wife, Catherine of Aragon, was the constitutional successor, followed by Elizabeth, daughter of Anne Boleyn. But Mary was a Catholic. Northumberland persuaded the dying Edward VI to disinherit Mary and Elizabeth in favour of Lady Jane Grey (1537–54), the teenage daughter of the Marquess of Dorset and the granddaughter of Henry VIII's younger sister, Mary. Jane Grey was a devout Protestant and so fitted the ideal of what Northumberland desired as monarch. She was, reluctantly, married off in 1553 to Northumberland's son, Lord Guildford Dudley.

On Edward's death, Jane Grey was proclaimed queen. It was 9 July 1553. The Crown was not really hers, nor would it be. The Catholic following was not vanquished. Mary Tudor's soldiers routed Northumberland's following. Northumberland was executed and there was little to protect the Protestant factions (as opposed to the true followers) from Mary's revenge. She released the deposed Bishop of Winchester, Stephen Gardiner, from the Tower and made him Lord Chancellor. Even allowing for the biased record writing of a later time, between them, the Queen and Gardiner – and after him the Papal Legate, Cardinal Reginald Pole – were probably responsible for more than 200 people being burned at the stake. The Queen's single ambition was reunion with Rome. Jane Grey and her husband were executed in 1554. As for the Queen, Mary married her cousin, the future Philip II of Spain, in spite of her denial of a request that could have changed British history: Philip, or his advisers, demanded the execution of the young Elizabeth. She was, they pointed out, in line to the throne and therefore a threat. Mary refused and they had to make do with Elizabeth's imprisonment.

Gardiner died in 1555 and Cardinal Pole became Archbishop of Canterbury after Cramner was removed from office. Pole was an exiled Catholic who had been forced to leave England in 1532. He published an attack on Henry's anti-papal ideas in 1536 and, because he was out of the country, his mother, the Countess of Salisbury (and a one-time governess to Queen Mary) was executed in his place. As for Philip, he was seen as a sinister figure largely because of the reputation of the Inquisition. Simon Renard, the Holy Roman Emperor's ambassador, described the situation in a letter to his Emperor, dated 3 September 1554: 'The Spaniards are hated . . . Only ten days ago, the heretics tried to burn a church in Suffolk with the entire congregation that was hearing Mass inside'.

When in March 1556 the aged Thomas Cranmer was executed, the Protestant rebellion took greater heart and determination. Cranmer's end was no more pitiful than that of the other martyrs. He was, with Nicholas Ridley, one of the most important theologians of the Reformation. It was Cranmer who insisted that the people should understand that Christ exists in faith, not in material symbols such as bread and wine. His original arrest would seem to have been because of Queen Mary's need to avenge his part in the divorce of her mother, Catherine of Aragon. But he had to be shown as a traitor to the throne or better still as a heretic. There followed long months of interrogation to prove his heresy. Eventually Cranmer appears to have lost his nerve – a crude summary perhaps of the interminable questioning, humiliation and continuing threat of death to which he was subjected. Ironically, he was not the power throughout the land that he once had been, but he was still a symbol of persecution to the Catholics and therefore the Marian court.

During his final days, Cranmer was taken from prison and lodged under house arrest with the Dean of Christ Church at Oxford. Between January and February 1556, he recanted his beliefs and acknowledged the authority of the Crown and the Pope. On 9 March Cranmer published his fifth so-called recantation in which he repudiated the doctrine of Luther and accepted Catholicism as the one Church. He received his requested absolution and went to Mass. This would not save him. He wrote a final recantation which was published on 18 March. Then came the drama that meant surely there would be no last stay of execution. At the University Church, Oxford, Cranmer delivered a homily that had been approved, but at the end of it he declared that the Pope was Antichrist. He had rejected all the documents he had signed, all the statements made in his name. He was dragged away along Brasenose Lane to the site in front of Balliol College where both Hugh Latimer, Church of England Chaplain to Edward VI, and Ridley had been burnt at the stake. There, 150 faggots of furze and 100 faggots of wood were stacked; Cranmer was stripped to his long white shirt and bound by the waist to the stake. As the flames grew Cranmer stretched his arm into the fire and cried, 'This hand hath offended.' It was 21 March 1556.

Queen Mary wanted Cranmer a Catholic or no Cranmer at all. She had her way. Two years on, she too would be dead.

CHAPTER NINETEEN
1558–87

In 1558, Mary I, known as Bloody Mary, died. She had reigned for five tempestuous years and tried to reverse the Reformation. She failed. She also could not prevent another war with France and in her last year she lost the English possession across the Channel, Calais.

And so, in 1558, Queen Elizabeth I came to the throne. Her country was poor, Scotland and France threatened England's peace, the banks of Antwerp threatened the nation's stability and many in Catholic Europe saw Elizabeth as a usurper. They believed Mary Queen of Scots (1542–87), the daughter of James V of Scotland and Mary of Guise who was now to be wed to the heir to the French throne (later Francis II), to be rightful heir to the Crown of England. Little wonder then that many in 1558 thought Elizabeth would not last very long. But Elizabeth took after her father, Henry VIII. She was experienced enough – perhaps sharpened is a better description – to understand the dangers of dogmatism, from whichever side of the religious divide it appeared. She had been threatened with beheading, had been locked in the Tower and was then made prisoner at Woodstock. Her mother had been executed and, for at least the past five years, Elizabeth had been seen as a direct threat to Queen Mary Tudor. However, Elizabeth did not stand alone. She had William Cecil, the man who would be judged by some as the finest civil servant of the whole century, as her Secretary of State. Moreover, she made it clear that Protestantism would continue under her stewardship as head of the English Church. That was never to be such a simple matter; the bishops, and most of the people who cared, were still Catholics. Perhaps if some arrangement could have been made with Rome that would have proved a better security for England and its monarch, then it would have been seriously pursued. But the then

Pope, Paul IV, believed that princes and kings should grovel to papal authority.

If there is any Christian persuasion in England unlike Catholicism, then it is non-conformism – that is, those worshippers who refuse to conform to the liturgy and style of the Church of Rome and what had now become an established Church of England. It was in Elizabeth's time that the Puritans emerged to question not simply the monarch's standing in ecclesiastical matters, but the very style of the established Church. Here was the basis for what would follow in the coming centuries – Cavaliers versus Roundheads, Tories versus Whigs. Elizabeth was truly trying to bring about an obvious unity within the country's Church of England's religious order. It was never going to be easy especially as the distinctions between the mighty Church and high-minded Church were inevitably irreconcilable. On one side, the Church of England had its origins and contemporary practice well defined by papist custom and law. The Puritanical streak was harder to fathom; describing what it was against, rather than precisely what it was for, is an easier way of defining Puritanism. Puritans were the extreme Protestants. Their theology was largely based on Calvinism. Puritans wanted a sparer, less ritualistic Church of England.

In 1558 the Continent was dominated by two opposing Catholic powers: the Valois monarchy of France and the Habsburg Empire, with Philip of Spain at its head. But there were signs of a truce, and if that were to happen, then the Pope might encourage them both to join in a Crusade – against the English. After all, in Catholic eyes, the English throne was now occupied by the daughter of the two people who caused the break with Rome: Henry VIII and Anne Boleyn. She represented a serious threat to Catholicism.

So for Elizabeth to maintain her religious balancing act, whatever measures were taken to defend the throne must also reflect what was going on elsewhere in Europe. And Elizabeth's own view was that she mustn't be seen to be fanatically Protestant because of the threat from Rome, and because of the disquiet of some of her own people who were still mostly Catholics. At the same time, she mustn't be seen to be leaning towards Rome, or she would not be able to contain the Protestant and Puritan opposition.

In 1559 the Acts of Supremacy and Uniformity were passed. The Act of Uniformity laid down the use of common prayer, divine service and the administration of the sacraments. It was, in some senses, a compromise. For the Protestants it didn't go far enough. It implied, to take just one example, the wearing of Catholic vestments. As the Scottish reformer John Knox remarked, 'She that now reigneth over them is neither good Protestant nor yet resolute Papist.' The 1559 Acts had some uncompromising warnings for churchmen who failed to conform to the letter of the *Book of Common Prayer*. A first offending priest would be fined one year's profit from his benefice and could even spend six months in prison. A second offence would mean a year in prison. A third offence would signify serious intent to defy the State and so a priest would, or could, be imprisoned for life.

The Acts of Supremacy and Uniformity were passed by Parliament, significantly without the consent of any of the churchmen; here was a clear demonstration of William Cecil's abilities. He was the sixteenth-century version of a twenty-first century robust government chief whip. The whole matter was concluded in 1563 with the definition of Church doctrine: the Thirty-Nine Articles, which were based on Cranmer's first draft completed as long ago as Edward VI's time. Eight years later, the Subscription Act made it unlawful for clergy not to subscribe to the Articles.

Elizabeth's establishing of the Church in law – that is, the Established Church – prevented a religious civil war similar to the one running through France at the time. It also set the course for what is now called the Anglican Church as the mainstay of the Elizabethan State. That settled, the court turned its attention to the next important matter: the continuation of the dynasty. In other words, finding a husband for the Queen. The tradition of primogeniture in the preferment of monarchy made so much sense. A natural and undisputed succession of rights and monarchy removed many of the prospective causes of conflict and turmoil in any nation-state. The nation needed a successor to the Queen, therefore the Queen had to have a husband and then issue, preferably a son. Would the court have stood by and waited for natural selection? Hardly. There was talk of her marrying her deceased sister Mary's husband, Philip II of Spain. That would have been a reasonable political marriage; it would have meant also being involved in the Continental rivalries that would have done little good to England. There was always Robert Dudley, her handsome favourite who was the son of the Duke of Northumberland. She believed, however, that there was little hurry. Yet in October 1562 Elizabeth seemed to be dying of small-pox. The Protestants feared, once more, a Catholic succession. They need not have worried. Their Queen recovered, but the Commons reminded her that she had a duty to marry and she must carry out that duty. If not abroad, then at home.

However, her closest advisers had another concern – Mary Stuart. Mary had inherited the title of Queen of the Scots as a baby when her father James V died shortly after the Battle of Solway Moss in 1542. Since the age of six to eighteen she had lived in France, spoke French and Latin and probably could not understand the native Scots, but they most certainly understood what she represented. So when she fled to England from Scotland (following the suspicious death of her husband Lord Darnley) in 1568, Elizabeth and her advisers felt more threatened than welcoming. Elizabeth imprisoned Mary in Tutbury Castle. The castle walls could not restrain the danger that many believed accompanied Mary. That danger was not simply her poten-tial as a rival: she was a rallying point for English Catholics. The Counter-Reformation of Europe understood well the symbolism of the imprisoned Catholic queen. None understood this more than Francis Walsingham, effectively Elizabeth's head of intelligence. He understood that even if Mary Stuart had no ambitions for the English throne, she could be used as an excuse to plot against Elizabeth. If the plot to bring down the monarch and Protestantism succeeded, the cause of all Protestants in Europe would be fragile. Nowhere was the division of faith and persuasion more evident in Europe than in England itself. Northern England was mainly Catholic, the south mainly Protestant; and, in 1569, the Northern Rebellion began. It was the start of some seven years of instability in Elizabethan England. And England's relationship with Catholic Spain was strained almost to the point of war, partly because Cecil had ordered the seizure of Spanish treasure ships on their way to the Netherlands.

At the same time the Pope, tired of what he saw as English disobedience, excommunicated Elizabeth in 1570 and issued an order that loyal Catholics should get rid of her. The conflict between the Netherlands and Spain became a rallying banner for Englishmen against Catholicism and Spain, and they volunteered to defend the Netherlands. In Elizabeth's government there were strong differ-ences of opinion. The cause was accepted, but not England's military commitment to it. But when the leader of the Dutch Protestants was assassinated the cause was revived. This was followed, in 1585, by Philip II of Spain seizing all the English ships in his ports and making plans to invade England. So the rapidly evolving differences between Spain and England were inevitably leading to war, and encouraged the ever-present threat of internal plotting on behalf of Mary Stuart against Elizabeth Tudor. Mary Stuart could never have hoped to survive whatever the personal feelings of Elizabeth. The Queen's court cared for the survival of the State and that State could only survive as a Protestant realm. Mary was accused and found guilty of treason. It was up to Elizabeth to sign the death order. She could have refused. Or could she? She signed. She may have been saddened after the event, but we should not believe that she had misunderstood what she was doing. On 8 February 1587, Mary Queen of Scots was executed at the second attempt of the axeman.

The England of this period was not utterly inward-looking and absorbed by its own calamities. This was, after all, the age of British discovery beyond the dreams of most, if not those of Francis Drake. It was also an age that was to leave a lasting stain on the conscience of the English societies of the nineteenth, twentieth and twenty-first centuries. That stain was slavery. The English were slow into this trade. The Portuguese had been the leaders of the West African slaving expeditions for close on a century before the British arrived in the region.

Elizabeth I herself was personally involved in the slave trade. In 1567, along with Lord Robert Dudley and the Earl of Pembroke, she backed John Hawkins' third voyage to the west coast of Africa to fill his six ships with 500 Africans. He then set sail on the trade winds to the West Indies to sell his human cargo to the Spanish. Elizabeth, remembering the rich pickings of the previous trips, lent him two of her ships, the *Jesus of Lubeck* and the *Minion*. He had also four smaller vessels including the *Judith*, commanded by his nephew, Francis Drake. The prospects were fine. The conclusion was disastrous.

The Spanish governor had said settlers should not buy slaves from Hawkins but the Englishman knew that they wanted African slaves and were willing to pay about 160 pounds on the black market for a half-decent specimen. However, in San Juan de Ulúa, now called

Veracruz, in the Gulf of Mexico, Hawkins and Drake ran into trouble with the Spanish fleet. Many of his sailors were slaughtered and one of the Queen's ships, the *Jesus of Lubeck*, was lost. Only fifteen of the 200 crew of her other vessel, the *Minion*, made it back to England. What had started as a colonial trading venture would indirectly lead to one of the most famous dates in English history, 1588 and the Spanish Armada (see Chapter Twenty).

It was in this same period that we can see the beginnings of what was to become England's first official colony in North America. The man at the centre of this exploration was neither Drake nor Hawkins, but Humphrey Gilbert, who had gained a reputation as a commander in Ireland by sticking victims' heads on poles during his campaign to subdue the Irish. In 1578, Gilbert was granted letters patent to mount an expedition to North America. This authority from the Queen was not conclusive because the wording was cautious. Gilbert was told that he should: 'Discover search find out and view such remote heathen and barbarous lands countries and territories not actually possessed of any Christian prince or people and . . . to have hold occupy and enjoy to him his heirs and assignees for ever.' On Monday 5 August 1583 Humphrey Gilbert took St John's harbour in Newfoundland for Elizabeth I and 200 leagues in every direction for his heirs, and with that he established the first English colony in North America. Unfortunately he went down with his ship on the return voyage.

We have in Elizabethan history a dazzling gallery of adventurers. As well as Drake, Hawkins and Gilbert, there was Walter Ralegh. He was Gilbert's half-brother and continued the pursuit of colonization on behalf of Elizabeth. At fourteen he was a student at Oxford. At fifteen he was fighting in France. He became the Queen's favourite, then not, then again, then in her final year (but not under her reign) he was sentenced to death for treason, but sent instead to the Tower. He stayed there for thirteen years, was released in 1616 but executed in 1618. He wrote the *History of the World* and founded the Poets' Club. Apart from the cloak, the puddle and the Queen, Ralegh remains a doublet-and-hose figure forever fighting the Spanish and, of course, supposedly bringing to England tobacco, potatoes and the possession of Virginia in North America. Ralegh made it clear that empire was possible. Two centuries on and Nelson made the expansion of empire certain.

In 1584, when Elizabeth told Ralegh he had a six-year monopoly on searching out what would be called Virginia, it was undoubtedly for colonization. This contradicts the idea that the British got an empire by accident. The letters patent were clearly titled:

Granted by the Queen's Majesty to Master Walter Ralegh, now knight, for the discovering and planting of new lands and coun-tries . . . reserving always to us, our heirs and successors, for all services and duties and demands, the fifth part of all the ores of gold and silver that from time to time and at all times after such discovery, subduing and possessing, shall be gotten and obtained. All which lands, countries, and territories shall be for ever be holden of the said Walter Ralegh, his heirs and assignees of us our heirs and successors by homage and by the said payment of the said fifth part

By now Ralegh was Elizabeth's favourite, but there were plenty enemies at court that would have been only too pleased to see him away for a few months and he was far from liked in the country. Elizabeth had made him wealthy by giving him monopolies over the broadcloth and wine trades. He was using some of his money to fit out ships for explorations when he got his letters patent and the vessels sailed on 27 April 1584.

In fact, it was his captains Arthur Barlowe and Philip Amadas who discovered (from a European viewpoint) what was to be called Virginia. They landed first on an island off what we know as the North Carolina coast:

After thanks given to God for our safe arrival thither we manned our boats and went to view the land next adjoining and to take possession of the same in the right of the Queen's most excellent Majesty as rightful Queen and Princess of the same . . . This island had many goodly woods full of deer, conies, hares and fowl even in the midst of summer in incredible abundance . . . we remained by the side of this island two whole days before we saw any people of the country. The third day we espied one small boat having in it three persons.

This epistle, written by Barlowe, goes on to describe a veritable Eden – perhaps in the late sixteenth century that strip of coastline was an Eden, but it certainly is not now and we should be wary of this account. The contents might not have been quite truthful as Ralegh wanted to use Barlowe's letter to convince Elizabeth and her court that the discovery should be followed up and money poured into the venture. It certainly worked. Ralegh could, for the moment, do no wrong. On 6 January following the voyage, he was dubbed Sir Walter and his heraldry was registered as Arms of Walter Ralegh Knight Lord and Governor of Virginia.

The following year, Ralegh wanted to lead his new venture to Virginia but the Queen insisted he stayed by her side. Sir Richard Grenville led the expedition along with Ralph Lane, whose instruction was to stay on and command the colony: 108 men were left in Virginia under his command. In April 1586, Ralegh sent Grenville back to Virginia with food and equipment for the settlement at Roanoke at the southern end of Chesapeake Bay. But Grenville went treasure-hunting among Spanish ships. It was only an unexpected visit from Sir Francis Drake, after he had sacked the Spanish holdings of San Domingo, Cartagena and Saint Augustine in the Caribbean, that saved the colonists. In fact, most of them abandoned the colony during a great storm and boarded Drake's ships. When Drake and the settlers arrived back in Plymouth towards the end of July 1586, there was a general air of gloom: these were not men full of brave deeds and tales of a promised land. Nonetheless, English America was born and a sense of colonization had taken over from those who would simply explore for its own sake. Those who had seen Virginia had seen the future, or so they said. On 7 January 1587 a man called John White was named governor of Ralegh, Virginia, and a proper colonization was underway, with colonists including husbands, wives and children setting sail for the New World.

But not Ralegh. He remained at home in Durham House, a London house given to him by Elizabeth. He became occupied with schemes to defend his own position in the court of the Queen. This was 1587, when little was normal in royal circles. It was the year of Elizabeth's great misery, the beheading of the Queen of Scots. Ralegh was an easy target for all the factions and the envy of others at court. He also had to contend with the latest arrival at court, Anne Boleyn's great nephew, the nineteen-year-old Robert Devereux, the Earl of Essex (1565–1601), who had caught the Queen's attention.

Ralegh felt dejected if not rejected. His position was perhaps helped by Spain because the court was increasingly concerned that the sea war with Spain was gaining a speed of its own. Drake, rather famously, had sailed from England that spring with a truly motley crew. We should set aside images from the paintings of scruffy but well-disciplined crews and Jolly Jack Tar. Drake had mutineers, convicts, rogues and vagabonds, as well as a few good sailors, aboard his ships. When they reached Cadiz he sailed right in, raided and burned thirty Spanish ships, and sailed out again without the loss of a single man. He then sailed to Sagres in southern Portugal, sacked a church, moved on to pillage the Azores and was home in time for tea. Most importantly for England was that his singeing of the ships in Cadiz had made it impossible for the Spanish Armada to sail that year, 1587. But it would do so within twelve months. While the American colonists waited for supplies and Ralegh waited for preferment, England waited for war.

CHAPTER TWENTY
1588–1602

In 1588 Philip II envisaged a land battle with England. The Armada was simply the armed transport for the Duke of Parma's forces. Towards the end of July 1588 the Armada appeared off the Lizard, Cornwall. In a crescent-shaped flotilla, it headed up the Channel. Drake, a yapping sea-dog, attacked the Armada from astern, but the Spanish fleet maintained its discipline and made for the French coast opposite Dover. It was supposed to make a rendezvous with the Duke of Parma's forces from the Netherlands. The fleet anchored, but couldn't get its ships into port. No one had worked out the depth of water against the deep draft of the vessels.

During the nights of 28 July and 7 August, the English sent in fire-ships – small, old vessels loaded with explosives and burning barrels on their bows. The Spanish flotilla scattered. The English fleet pounded it, sinking four ships, but damaging many more. A south-west gale drove the survivors into the North Sea, to escape as best they could around the north of Scotland.

So, the Armada was one of the most decisive battles of our history. But it did not decide the war between Spain and England. It did not, as Drake had dreamed it would, bring down the Spaniards or cut off their fleets from the riches in the Americas. And neither Catholicism nor Protestantism was any stronger for this decisive battle. The result was that here was proof, in this naval tourney, that the ambitions of one power to impose religious dogma on another could not rely on force to achieve it. That was the legacy of the engagement in the Channel in 1588.

Elizabeth was moody and she was cautious to the point of indecisiveness. Importantly, she could not shed her three great burdens: the security of her nation; the constantly emptying Treasury; and her succession. The rivalry amongst her courtiers hardly helped. In the late 1590s, Walter Ralegh and Robert Devereux, the Earl of Essex, were rivals, adventurers and heroes who first charmed the Queen, then didn't. Essex was the younger, brasher one who, having been given his head, lost it – forever. Ralegh and Essex both went to fight the Spaniards at Cadiz and they were both successful, but they came home without much booty. Booty and not glory pays for victories. Nevertheless, Essex was seen as a heroic figure, which was fine for his reputation but not entirely good for his plans to woo his sovereign: the Queen feared he would become more popular than she. However, he was promoted and, with Ralegh in a subordinate position, Essex was given command of a fleet sent to fight a new Armada in the Azores. It was an ill-planned and ill-executed venture and only the weather saved Essex's ships from defeat and all that that would have meant for England. Essex was forced to leave the court. His letters and pleas did little to restore his standing.

And then came a chance for redemption, or so he thought. The Queen wanted him to go to Ireland. Ever since Henry II, Ireland has been a complex and sometimes bloody setting for English misfortune. A popular view might be that the English should never have involved themselves in that place. At Henry II's time that was not such an easy option and so the rarely happy relationship was made. It was no different in Elizabeth's sixteenth century. Henry VIII had called himself King of Ireland but no English monarch really had any authority other than what he or she could impose with cutlass or gun. The Irish tribal aristocracy were given English titles, but that was never a gesture that would bring harmony for the two peoples. Moreover, largely Catholic Ireland and largely Protestant England could hardly meet without suspicion and for the English there was the persistent and justifiable suspicion that Catholic French and Catholic Spanish thrones would take Ireland's side. It was with such support from the Spanish that the Earl of Tyrone, Hugh O'Neill, was leading yet another rebellion against English rule.

In April 1599, Essex (not Elizabeth's first choice; she wanted Lord Mountjoy) was sent to Ireland in command of one of the largest English forces every seen in that island. Essex was not particularly bright and he may have spent too much time seeking glory (which success in Ireland was hardly likely to bring), but he knew the enormity of his task. His orders were to subdue Ulster and therefore Hugh O'Neill. But Essex turned south, to Leinster. He needed time to gather his forces together and for the weather to improve. His Leinster tactic was publicly criticized by his enemies in London; they said he should have confronted O'Neill. Essex was probably right in doing what he did. Apart from knocking his troops into a fighting force that was to his liking in conditions that were not, the march south allowed him to assess what was needed for the greater campaign. Foolishly, he sent his assessment to Elizabeth and added that the war would take a great deal of expensive time. He also criticized her for favouring Ralegh. The Queen was furious. Robert Cecil, the Queen's Secretary of State who had succeeded his father William Cecil's position of authority, was delighted. Cecil believed that Essex could usurp him in his place as Queen's counsel. The Ireland episode would disprove this.

A furious exchange of letters shuttled across the Irish Sea between Essex and his sovereign. Rumours of Essex giving away knighthoods by the helmet-full and pocketing spoils, but not getting on with the task of subduing Tyrone, only added to the Queen's fury. Eventually she told Essex that he had to remain in Ireland until the north was put down. But Essex's army was in no state to take Tyrone.

At the Lagan River, the two men, Essex and Tyrone, met. A fortnight's truce was agreed. It gave Tyrone fourteen days to regroup and Essex thought that, with this agreement, he was free to return to London. He was desperate to get back there because he knew that only his personal pleading would satisfy his Queen that he was her champion and her loyal subject. However, Essex was doomed. He was tried before the Council, found guilty of desertion and confined to his house. Charles Blount, Lord Mountjoy, was given the task of subduing Tyrone. In 1601 Essex was executed for treason, having marched on London in an attempt to force an audience with Elizabeth. Meanwhile, Cecil could get on with his work preparing for the succession and his private belief that only James VI of Scotland should succeed Elizabeth as monarch of England. This was court politics. On the streets and in the countryside, the people had a more everyday worry: poverty.

There was increased wealth in late Elizabethan England, but the beneficiaries were the middle men, the merchants. It's been estimated that as many as 40 per cent of the population survived at below subsistence level; thousands of families were 'on the Parish', that is, in need of support. And there was starvation, especially in the remoter parts of the country. As early as 1536 Poor Laws had been introduced. They offered relief, but with an insistence that the so-called 'sturdy' beggars should be made to work and whipped to do so. There was genuine pity but also a very real fear of beggars: 'Hark, hark, the dogs do bark, the beggars are coming to town', warned the rhyme. Some made begging their profession. In larger places, notably Ipswich and London, a sixteenth-century workless traveller might be better off living on handouts than looking for work.

CHAPTER TWENTY-ONE
1603–25

On 24 March 1603, before dawn, Elizabeth I died by the banks of the Thames at Richmond Castle. James VI of Scotland was to become James I of England. It was the end of the Tudor dynasty. But people don't go to bed as Elizabethans and wake up as Stuarts in the sense that their circumstances are any different. The larder was just as full or empty as it was the night before. Society evolves. It does not suddenly change. A nation wears the same clothes, washes the same dishes and cheers the new monarch from the same rooftops as the ones from which it mourned the last. So why was a Scottish King now King of England?

James I was the son of Mary Queen of Scots and her second husband, Lord Darnley. He became James I of England as a result of the Treaty of Berwick, which he and Elizabeth had signed in 1586, after almost four years of plot, counter-plot and rebellion. The two monarchs agreed that they would respect each other's religions, be allies, help if the other were to be invaded and, more importantly from Elizabeth's point of view, neither side would help anyone who threatened the other. So Elizabeth signed the treaty because it meant that Scotland would no longer help France, which was of immense importance to England. James got £4,000 a year out of it from the English, plus an understanding that Elizabeth would block any move in the English Parliament to oppose James's claim to the English throne, as long as he waited until after her death. If Elizabeth had chosen to, she could have easily, and with considerable support, broken that understanding but she didn't. James did nothing to spoil the arrangement. Even the year following the treaty's signing, when his mother was executed by Elizabeth, he said nothing. Nothing, as Cecil knew, had to be left to chance.

The first true indication throughout the kingdom that Elizabeth I was nearing death was when Cecil gave orders that all dissidents should be arrested, that the capital should have its guards doubled and that the strategically important cities of England should have their soldiery put on high alert. For three weeks in March 1603 England stood on its guard. Some stood nervously; after all, the woman they had honoured was their patron. On her death, they would be friendless where it mattered most – their offices, status and even their estates would be forfeited. One who worried for his future was her kinsman, Sir Robert Carey.[1]

At forty-two, Carey was the Lord Warden of the Middle Marches, the border with Scotland. He would weep at Elizabeth's passing. Prudently, he would contrive to be the messenger of her death and be first to bend in homage to James VI of Scotland – unless Cecil could stop him, which he most certainly would attempt to do.

In March 1603, Carey, believing the border country to be secure and quiet, felt it safe to leave the security of the wild country in the hands of his deputies. He was fearful that he would lose his position when Elizabeth died. Just as many would rush to James's side to renew or gain patronage, so at this point others rode to Richmond Palace in case final and lasting favour might be gained from the dying monarch. Carey also travelled to the court. He left a note of those final hours and his determination to take the news to James VI in Scotland and so secure his patronage:

On Wednesday, 23 March, she grew speechless. That afternoon, by signs, she called for her [Privy] Council: and by putting her hand to her head, when the king of Scots was named to succeed her, they all knew he was the man she desired should reign after her. At about six at night, she made signs for the Archbishop [Whitgift] and her Chaplains to come to her. At which time, I went in with them; and sat upon my knees full of tears to see that heavy sight. Her Majesty lay upon her back; with one hand in the bed, and the other without.

The end was hours away. Those left with their monarch prayed for this life and for the next. Archbishop Whitgift told her that her time had come and examined her in faith. She answered by blinking.

---

1   Later, Earl of Monmouth. His account of Elizabeth's death and his ride to inform James was written as late as 1627 and kept in private until Lord Cork allowed it to be published in 1759. A copy is to be found in the British Library.

Also there was Carey's sister, Eleanor (called Philadelphia in some documents at the time), married to Lord Scrope. Lady Scrope was a key actor in the drama that was to immediately follow Elizabeth's death. After prayers had been exhausted, Elizabeth was left with her ladies-in-waiting. Carey went to his lodging and gave orders to someone in the Coffer's Chamber to call him if Elizabeth's end looked close. He gave the porter an angel (a gold coin) to let him back in at any time.

In the early moments of Thursday 24 March, Elizabeth turned her face to the wall and died. There was blessed relief, but work to be done. The Privy Council had given orders that no one should be allowed in or out of Richmond Palace without a Council Warrant. Fortunately for the story, one of the Council, Sir Edward Wotton, met Carey and took him inside the Palace.

The word had got about that Carey intended to ride north and the Council, under Cecil's instructions, told him not to move without permission. He was trapped inside. Cecil did not want him spreading the news, especially to James. However, Carey's brother, George, Lord Hunsdon, was in the Palace and he bluffed his way out, with Carey at his side. There were factions within the Council and more importantly, in spite of Cecil's authority, there was for certain individuals and families much to lose and gain by following their own instincts for survival and position. Carey escaped Richmond, found a horse from the royal stable and turned for London.

> I took horse between nine and ten o'clock and that night rode to Doncaster [162 miles from London and 235 miles from Edinburgh].
>
> The Friday night [26 March] I came to my own house at Widdrington [99 miles from Edinburgh] and took order with my Deputies [of the Middle Marches] to see the Borders kept in quiet and that the next morning the king of Scotland should be proclaimed king of England at Widdrington, Morpeth and Alnwick.
>
> Very early on Saturday [27 March 1603] I took horse for Edinburgh and came to Norham about twelve noon, so that I might well have been with the king at supper time; but I got a great fall by the way and my horse with one of his heels gave me a great blow on the head, that made me shed much blood. It made me so weak that I was forced to ride a soft pace after: so that the king was newly gone to bed by the time I knocked at the gate.

I kneeled by him and saluted him by his title 'England, Scotland, France and Ireland'. He gave me his hand to kiss; and bade me welcome.

After he had long discoursed of the manner of the Queen's sickness, and of her death, he asked, what letters I had from the [Privy] Council. I told him None and acquainted him how narrowly I had escaped from them. And yet I brought him a blue ring from a Lady that I hoped would give him assurance of the truth I reported. He took it, and looked upon it and said 'It is enough. I know by this you are a true messenger.'

This is the famous story of the secret ring. It is sometimes said that the ring was taken from Elizabeth's dead finger and given to Carey. Documents in the Carey papers suggest that James had kept a long correspondence with Lady Scrope, Carey's sister. In this source, it is said that the ring was not on Elizabeth's finger but that James had sent Lady Scrope a sapphire ring with instructions to return it to him as a sign that Elizabeth was dead. It is said that she threw the sapphire to her brother from a window at the Palace and so began his journey. Was it worthwhile to Carey in his effort to maintain his titles and offices? At first, yes it was. James was naturally grateful. He looked after Carey and gave him into the care of Lord Home (an ancestor of Alec Douglas-Home, the twentieth-century Foreign Secretary and Conservative Prime Minister) and announced that he would carefully consider any reward Carey thought reasonable for his effort. Carey knew exactly what he wanted and so James gave Carey the title of Gentleman of the Bedchamber.

How Carey could ever have imagined that Cecil would let him off lightly, or that the King would fight his corner against Cecil, is hard to fathom. Cecil told the King that Carey should be dismissed and the King agreed. No one, not even a kinsman of Elizabeth, put anything over a Cecil.

On 24 March James was proclaimed monarch by the 'Lords Spirituall and Temporall' who made up the Privy Council. The seventeenth-century wording of that first proclamation reflected the sense of uncomplicated achievement of Robert Cecil: 'James the sixt king of Scotland, is now by the death of our late Soveraigne, Queene of England of famous memorie, become also our Onely, Lawfull,

Lineall and Rightfull Liege Lord, James the first, king of England,
France[2] and Ireland, defender of the faith.'[3]

The final lines of the proclamation announced, as ever, the
complete loyalty of every courtier, noble, justice, sheriff and bailiff,
constable and whoever came to mind and that those of the highest
and the lowest of authority would ever be at hand to assist:

> Ayding and assisting from time to time in all things that are or shalbe
> necessary for the preventing, resisting, and suppressing of any disor-
> derly assemblies, or other unlawfull Acte or Attempt, eithe rin worde
> or deede, against the publique peace of the Realme, or any way preju-
> diciall to the Right, honour, State or Person, of our only Undoubted
> and deere Lord and Soveraigne that now is James the first king of all
> the said Kingdomes, as they will avoyd the perill of his Majesties
> heavie indignation, and their owne utter ruine and confusion

The welcome for the new monarch had to be tempered by the real
or contrived sorrow for the passing of the old one. The obedience
and love of the people for Elizabeth had waned during her final
years. Some had been anxious that her passing should not be
delayed. Elizabeth had not thought to apologize for the unconscionable time she was taking to find an exit from her sovereign
duties. When she went, the mourning dresses were worn, but so
was the indifference on the sleeves of even her close courtiers. The
delicate mask between sadness and joy was exquisitely demonstrated in Thomas Millington's opening sentence describing the
procession of James VI south to London: 'James had his kingdom.
He now had to ride south to claim it.'

There is an odd parallel with James VI and some Eastern European
States at the end of the twentieth century. Once free of their former
frontiers, many East Europeans saw Western Europe as a honey-pot.
For years they had been impressed by the post-war economic miracle

---

2   British monarchs would call themselves King or Queen of France until the eighteenth century
even though the British sport of needling the French continued.
3   *Fidei Defensor*: the title seemed incongruous inasmuch that it was given by Pope Leo X in
1521 to Henry VIII before Rome felt inclined to revise its judgement of the English King. It was a
papal recognition of Henry's book. *Assertio septem sacramentorum*, an unequivocal attack on
Martin Luther. Parliament recognized the title in 1544 and it is retained to the present day, marked
on British coins as F.D.

and the richness of their West German cousins, French, Italian and British. There had to be plenty of money in the West and surely one only had to ask for it. The Scottish court in 1603 was penniless and draughty. The English throne, surely, sat in the middle of a honey-pot. James could not believe anything else. He had sensed the wealth and touched much of it. Travellers' tales alone encouraged him and his courtiers to believe that the Palace of Whitehall housed the Promised Land. He was not the only one who sensed richness.

Knights and sundry gentlemen were arriving in Edinburgh by the hour. They had come not, as so often in the past, to contest authority, but to pledge their allegiances and their hopes of preferment. One of the first to arrive from England was John Paiton, the son of the Lieutenant of the Tower of London, Sir John Paiton. The Tower represented constabular authority of the capital. Since William the Norman, the Tower had cast its own authority across the minds of even the most powerful, although its sinister reputation owed some-thing to a sense of pragmatism that would persist among the English nomenklatura until the eighteenth century. The significance of Paiton's arrival was not lost on James. Perhaps then, James felt a little more assured when, on Thursday 31 March 1603, he was proclaimed King of England, Scotland, Ireland and France at the Market Cross in Edinburgh. That night bonfires were lit in Scotland and burned brightly beyond dawn the next day. With James as King of Scotland, and staying at his castle in Scotland, then the nation had a leader with whom any would-be enemy, usurper or diplomatic opportunist would first have to reckon. Yet if James were going south to England and, worse still, to London, was it not true that Scotland was not at all gaining authority and kudos, but was losing a monarch and therefore power? James, of course, because of his nature, was inclined to construe any sense of gloom about his departure as a feeling of sadness for him personally. Rather magnanimously James assured his people that he would always love them even though far away and he would make a point of visiting Scotland once every three years. The truth was that most members of James's court were simply longing to get away to London and its promise of everything Edinburgh did not have: good living, authority and, more import-antly, a bottomless Exchequer to pay for it all – or so they thought.

Cecil had already supposed that it was going to be more costly to run the Scottish King than it had been to support the English Queen.

Elizabeth was often known for her meanness, perhaps a euphemism for being broke. There was trouble enough in the State without Scottish hands in the nation's bullion. On the journey south James had knighted 300 good men – that is, those on whom he could count if everything went terribly wrong. At Cambridge he rested on 28 April because this was the day of Elizabeth's funeral.

Elizabeth's corpse was embalmed and bound in waxed cotton. The lead coffin was brought after two days, the body placed in it and left for a further five days. Elizabeth's remains were then taken to the river at Richmond, placed upon a torch-lit barge and carried to Westminster where they lay in private state at the Palace of Whitehall. Westminster Hall was hung with mourning cloths and banners and the casket removed there. It was the King's duty, not the Church's, nor Cecil's, to give the orders for her funeral. He, of course, wanted to get it over very quickly so that he could get into his capital. Arrangements for royal funerals take time. Even kings-in-waiting must learn patience. Thus, it was not until 28 April that the coffin was borne by a hearse drawn by four horses draped in black mourning velvet to Westminster Abbey.

Atop the coffin was a life-size model of the Queen. It was fully robed and crowned; in one wax hand the orb, in the other the sceptre of State. Six earls held her regal canopy above the wax doll. Behind the hearse, again in a tradition observed even today, the Master of Horse led the Queen's riderless but saddled horse. Elizabeth's chief mourner, the Marchioness of Northampton, was followed by a column of noblewomen each, like the Marchioness, black-cloaked and hooded. Behind them followed almost 1,300, similarly dressed in black. Here was her realm, representative of the highest peerage and office to more than 200 of the very poor. The City of London followed with their Lord Mayor and, bringing up at the rear, the halberdiers of the Gentlemen Pensioners headed by the doomed captain of their guard, Ralegh.

Thousands in the street watched and wept as the image of their late sovereign passed. The coffin was carried into the abbey, and her Archbishop, Whitgift, read the service. The coffin was, that afternoon of 28 April, taken to the vault in the Henry VII Chapel and placed with the casket of Mary, the Queen's sister. Then came the final act of the symbolism of authority: the most senior of Elizabeth's courtiers, her Gentlemen, stepped to the vault and each snapped his white stick of office and tossed the broken rod on to the coffin. Their duty discharged. Her authority ended. James mounted for London. The people started to gather in greater numbers than ever.

On 3 May, James moved on to Theobalds, Robert Cecil's house in present-day Hertfordshire. The great officers of State gathered with their monarch: the Lord Treasurer, the Lord Keeper, the Lord Admiral and the now, King's Council. It was time to mix and match his Privy Councillors. Scottish nobles were added to the Council, including the Earl of Mar, the Duke of Lennox, the Treasurer of Scotland Sir George Home and Lord Kinloss, now to be Master of the Rolls. Of the English, he picked (or had recommended to him by Cecil) Lord Thomas Howard (whom he trusted as one who had warned him of the devilment of some – notably Ralegh) as Lord Chamberlain. He managed to find time to create another twenty-eight knights. Many of these knighthoods did not bring power, but the recipients already had some at least and, of course, they did bring, for the moment, unquestionable loyalty.

Hordes in their thousands had gathered around Theobalds to catch sight of the new monarch. The people had rightly mourned and so now they celebrated their good fortune at having a quiet transition. Yet again we have to remember how people would have lived during this period. While lives were simpler than those in later centuries, certainly the twentieth, there was a need to recognize rank for what it could provide. The symbolism of leadership is very important, particularly in a society ruled so distinctly. If Elizabeth was indeed the last monarch to command the absolute obedience of her people, then this thought suggests that the people quite liked the idea of being obedient. The people's obeisance was not to a constitutional convention and thus it relied heavily on the personality not of the monarchy, which was accepted, but the monarch, which sometimes was not. As that personality faded so the people waited anxiously for a new era. By March 1603 they had waited long enough. By the end of April the torches of welcome were lit both in James's honour and the expectations of the people.

The sheriff and livery of Middlesex greeted James as he approached the capital, just as the sheriffs of each county had met him at the Borders to hand him with dignity to the next sheriff in accordance with Cecil's instructions. Finally, James was met as he came to London by Sir Robert Lee, the Lord Mayor, who still had five months of his office to run, and 500 velvet-cloaked and gold-chained attendants. Even now this was not the moment to enter the city. This new pageant rode across the fields to Charterhouse and the home of Lord Thomas Howard. Here James rested for three days, but found the energy to eat sumptuously and dub 130 more people as knights. From Charterhouse the procession on the fourth day approached the Thames at Aldergate and there James embarked on the royal barge accompanied by a flotilla of cadet vessels. It appears that he had intended to land at Whitehall, but the coxswain overshot so James went on to the Tower – always a disturbing thought for monarchs. He gazed on the great cannon and then landed at King's Stairs where Sir Thomas Conisby, Gentleman Usher of the Privy Chamber, presented James with the sword of the city. James stayed the night in the Tower, relaxed in the knowledge that he was master of all he had at last surveyed and everything that he had not. His island peoples were going much further than he, James, had ever imagined. The transition from Tudors to Stuarts was coincidental with the step-change of British commercial exploration and exploitation that would establish holdings in Asia that would be remembered, more than anywhere else, as the beginnings of the British Empire.

By the end of the Tudors, in 1603, relations in Europe had changed or were changing and the expansion of colonial ideas was fixed in British minds. From 1603, we can talk about the British rather than just the English because in that year the new monarch, James I, coined the constitutional use of the phrase, Great Britain. James I made a priority the first year of his reign to stop the war between Spain and Britain. It was fruitless in the military and constitutional sense. It was far too expensive. It frustrated imperial ambition.

Britain now saw the wider horizons more clearly. For example, when in 1587 Drake had captured the Portuguese ship, the *San Felipe*, he had, apart from the fortune on board, come across the logs and navigational charts that literally opened his eyes to the secrets so jealously guarded by the Portuguese trading in the East Indies. In the 1590s these secrets were so exposed that when the ships fitted out by Sir John Lancaster began returning to England with exotic cargoes from the Far East, investors lined up to finance what would become the English East India Company.

If Stuart England under its first monarch was a dour society, the whole period of Stuart dynasty was far more important in the nation's imperial history than the seemingly more romantic Elizabethan age. The years between the start of the Stuarts in 1603 and the Hanoverians in 1714 was the founding century of the counting house that was the British Empire. For example, twelve of the thirteen American colonies[4] were established in that period. In the West Indies, the British-held islands produced enormous wealth, mainly through sugar plantations. Lancaster's East India Company overwhelmed anything that the Dutch, and before them the Portuguese, had managed in Asia. By the time the Hanoverians arrived the first British Empire was established and the Treaty of Utrecht (1713–14) that followed the Duke of Marlborough's victories in Europe would simply consolidate that imperial holding.

This first stage of empire building had much to do with the ability to fight for what the British wanted and more importantly it had a lot to do with the British character which reflected the nation's religious intolerance and commercial greed. If we examine religious bigotry at the highest level of governance of Britain we would see its contribution to the establishment of colonial communities in North America. A more liberal society in Britain, and therefore in British character, might easily have dulled imperial ambitions – apart from probably saving Charles I from execution. Take one example, the Pilgrim Fathers went to America in 1620 not because they preferred the social and agricultural climate, but because of persecution in England and dissatisfaction with the prospects of a new life in the Lowlands. They were not the founders of New England, but they did constitute about a third of the 102 people who sailed in the *Mayflower* for North America and built the colonial town of New Plymouth, Massachusetts.

New England was already well on its way to being established. When Captain John Smith (1580–1631, he of the Princess Pocahontas story) arrived in 1614 on the north-eastern seaboard, it was to him, literally, a new England. By then, the colonial terms planting and plantation, nurtured in Ireland, were now in common usage. Smith, for example, in 1616 wrote a treatise called *A True Relation of Virginia since the First Planting of that Colony*. Here in the name

---

4   Connecticut, Delaware, Georgia, Massachusetts, Maryland, New Hampshire, New Jersey, New York, North Carolina, Pennsylvania, Rhode Island, South Carolina and Virginia.

Virginia we have the true colonial spirit and determination that somewhere should be established in the image of the motherland. Once preconception, classical reference and occasion (for example, the relief in rounding a headland thus Cape of Good Hope) are exhausted then it is quite a good idea for the explorer to give his or her patron's name to a discovery.

The phenomenon of British migration to a newer world was, in its earlier days, almost entirely a mercantile adventure and hardly an expansion of territory to satisfy regal vanity and certainly not a national and European movement. Most Europeans, even by the late sixteenth century, did not think very much at all about the New World. This was not an intellectual blind spot. Europeans were then quite sophisticated. Their manner and intellectual development had created well-defined strata in Western Europe. A class system based on aristocracy was developing. 'Old' families already existed. Religious persuasion had an academical foundation. Yet explorers were hardly likely to excite the deeper interests of sixteenth-century Western Europeans. There was no discovery of magical societies with high levels of sophistication, of classical learning, of enlightened cultural dimension. Gold and savagery made an interesting commercial portfolio but there was no new Rome to be glimpsed.[5] Therefore, we might cautiously suppose that there was hardly an intellectual dimension to the early exploration and establishment of Empire.

As we have seen earlier, the British arrived quite late into the exploration of potential colonies, preoccupied as they were with their European uncertainties and Ireland, and because, for the most part, the English were broke and quite unable, or certainly unwilling, to finance big expeditions. This lack of capital was to be a theme of the British Empire throughout its history. Thus, a further irony of the biggest occupation of the globe by one nation is that the British managed to do so even when they were living beyond their means. They could never really afford their Empire. This of course, did not stop trading companies amassing fortunes. However, the lead to Empire had to come from commerce. So it is not surprising that until the latter half of the sixteenth century, the English interest in the

---

5   For more on this see Karen Ordahl Kupperman (ed.), *America in European Consciousness, 1493–1750* (Chapel Hill, NC: University of North Carolina Press, 1995).

New World was by and large represented by fishermen. They looked for no colonial catch and hardly interested themselves beyond the seaboard of the Newfoundland Banks.[6]

The early traders and settlers looked in two directions: westerly for sugar and easterly for spice. It is here that we have a very Eurocentric definition. The Old World is today an American observation about Europe, the place from which, until recently, most of their ancestors came.[7] However, for Europeans in the sixteenth century, the Old World lay across the Arabian Sea to the Spice Islands, the Indian sub-continent, Cathay and Japan. Here lay sophisticated societies with temples, cultures, orthodoxy and architecture that even predated much of Europe. Therefore, it roused the intellectual curiosity of European travellers and those to whom they reported their discoveries. The Americas never managed to excite that intellectual interest.

There were no tales coming back from the Americas of great palaces, silks and tapestries, no enchantment of music and literature, no rumours of provocative philosophy. No tinkling fountains on marble. The main attraction of America was threefold: a belief in often false travellers' tales of riches, a determination not to be left behind and, very importantly, as a refuge for those who wanted a new life.

This latter point should not be ignored when we remember the strong sense of Protestant determination of those who left for America from England and became its founding fathers. The Pilgrim Fathers were a different form of colonial settler: for them New Plymouth was a new life for they wanted nothing to do with the one they had left behind. They were the seventeenth-century equivalent of the twenty-first-century asylum seekers. There are times when in the twenty-first century we have tried to analyse the motives and influences of modern American society in international affairs. The birthmark of Protestantism is an arrogant and surefooted belief that it is the right and godly ordained way of life; so it was the driving ethic within the greatest colony of the first British Empire.

---

6   See D. and A. Quinn, *New American World: A Documentary History of North America to 1612, Volume 1* (New York, NY: Arno Press, 1974–9), pp. 91–120, 159–226.

7   The Asian and Hispanic pattern of immigration is changing the traditional view of origins in the United States.

If we accept that the English were not overly interested in the idea of building an empire but were forever conscious of the activities of their traditional adversaries, the French and Spanish, then we have to wonder at what stage it was that the indifference towards expanding commercially and politically into the New World was replaced by a concern that certainly the Spanish were building areas of interest that could threaten the English.

About three-quarters of the way through the sixteenth century differences among the major European States (and we should include the English in this sweep) became obvious. We only have to consider the circumstances that led to the Spanish Armada. More directly was the plight of the Huguenots. They had been persecuted in Europe and so great numbers sought refuge outside of Continental Europe. Franco-English Huguenots crossed the Atlantic in the 1570s and settled, for a while, in Florida. Little wonder that the Protestants there used the Florida coast and the cays to attack the Spanish galleons, which represented, of course, their former persecutors. The Spanish were not going to stand for this for very long and it was a pretty easy task to bombard the settlement and then land marines to sack it. There is some irony that is easily recognizable in international situations today; it seems unlikely that until the Spanish plundered the Huguenot settlement that the English started to make sensible assessments of how much commercial benefit the Spaniards were drawing from the region. The Spanish conflict with the Huguenots took place in the 1570s. The Spanish conflict with the English followed and continued until 1604 when James VI and I, made a sort of peace with Spain.

In the meantime, the geography of the Americas was slowly being recognized. America itself was seen as a continent which, in the late sixteenth century, was an incentive to investors who wondered what lay beyond the eastern seaboard. Yet there was still no rush to discover riches, partly because it was too costly to mount expeditions; secondly, the capabilities were few and thirdly, they needed royal as well as banking approval. The discovering of riches and territorial claims (apart from traditional and family claims in France) was a relatively unexplored system to the English. Nevertheless, the main incentive as it was for the whole of the colonial experience remained commercial and this began to sort itself into a procedure of recording journeys, registering claims and appealing for patents. How could this be any other way? To mount an expedition, to risk capital investment never mind lives, cost a lot of money. It had to be supported by Royal Assent in the form of a patent or charter bearing the monarch's signature.

None would invest a sixpence or a reputation unless there was a very good chance of huge financial gain. While we should not disregard the sense of adventure, everyone was into the business of colony-making for the simple reason that it was a business. The adventurers and entrepreneurs that built the two British Empires between the late fifteenth and early twentieth centuries were morally and commercially no different from those who built international commercial empires in the twentieth and twenty-first centuries. Money ruled and without it very little other than poetry and cubism was created.

If we accept the mercantile instincts of the original explorers without, for the moment, any judgement of how it was exercised we will find more revealing the first records of English travellers to this new world. There were chroniclers, just as there are today competing sections of the media (growing almost daily from the beginning of the sixteenth century), and of course academic and commercial published analysis. To write up an assessment of what existed and what was possible for future ventures gave authors some distinction as well as commercial possibilities. Whatever their reasoning and motives we have only to look at the records of, for example, Samuel Purchas (1577–1626) in his *Purchas, His Pilgrims*, to sense the very real adventure.[8]

Having said that, the English as a nation seemed indifferent to colonization outside of Ireland until the late sixteenth-century exploits of Humphrey Gilbert, as explored in Chapter Nineteen. Gilbert had been heavily involved in Elizabeth I's attempts to protect the Protestant Huguenots from the French Catholics before he turned his attention to exploration. He wanted to find a safe route to China by heading West, while Francis Drake was being encouraged to look for Australia. The excitement of exploration and riches was growing at an unprecedented rate among investors in Western Europe. There was now a convincing stream of information arriving in England

---

8   Purchas was a travel writer whose works include *Purchas his Pilgrimage or Relations of the World in all Ages*, which was published in 1613. The following year, Purchas became rector of St Martin's Church, Ludgate, London.

that riches were to be found and profits made. Also, there was a large element at Elizabeth's court who encouraged the likes of Drake, Gilbert and Hawkins because they saw this as a way of robbing the Spanish. Elizabeth became convinced that the way to get at the Spaniards and Catholicism was not through hopeless and prohibitively expensive land skirmishes but by attacking the Spaniards at the source of their new wealth – their empire. Little wonder that the court could see the sense, especially economically, of the English having their own empire.

After Gilbert's adventure of founding a colony in Newfoundland and Ralegh's settlement of Virginia, English attention turned towards the West Indies. This curved archipelago stretching north of Trinidad for some 500 miles was always to figure greatly in British history. The first proper settlement was made in 1623 when a Captain Warner, decided that St Kitt's, towards the north of the Leeward Islands, would be a very good place to grow tobacco, which was becoming if not a staple crop then a very good export to England.

Barbados was occupied by 1627 and although it is not much bigger than the Isle of Wight became a dumping ground for slaves and as a place of deportation, long before Australia was used. For example, those wretches not hanged by the infamous Judge Jeffreys after the Monmouth uprising in 1685 and the Bloody Assizes were deported. About 800 of them were sent to Barbados, which was almost entirely a huge sugar plantation and therefore a lucrative port of call for the slave traders. Almost the entire workforce had been kidnapped from Africa. Further south was Trinidad, held by the French until the British won it at the end of the Seven Years War. It too was a slave island of sugar plantations and cocoa. Neighbouring Tobago had a similar history and was used by Daniel Defoe as the island for *Robinson Crusoe*. What of the natives of these islands? Most of them were slaughtered by the Spaniards. Jamaica, one of the inner Caribbean islands, is typical of the region as it was first occupied by the Spanish, raided by British pirates, fought over and by the 1660s was a well established colony. It has always had a chequered social and political history. One of its early governors, in the 1670s, was the supposedly reformed buccaneer, Captain Henry Morgan.

In 1664 Jamaica was an example of potentially good colonial administration with a form of elective government established. This was no thriving democracy. After all, if there was not much in

England why should there have been in the colonies? One answer was the more subjective form of government of the occupied islands. Another was the fear of what the non-white population might do. A third was the realization that no colonial administration, no matter how much the idea of colonial image and code was transplanted, could fully implement the wishes of London political thought in an altogether different colonial community. So there was an uneasy relationship between the governor and the partially elected assembly which was restricted to the white settlers, and certainly not the slaves.

Not all the British occupations in the Caribbean were among the islands. The seas had been lucrative waters for British pirates raiding Spanish ships and settlements. Since the coming of James VI of Scotland to the throne of England, there had been great effort to end the wars between England and Spain. This conflict had nagged away at the British economy, which was in a parlous state. It took quite a time for James to make it clear that a ban on piracy had to form part of the solution to end the wars. Buccaneering had an official status at the beginning of the seventeenth century. It was a legitimate part of warfare as well as a lucrative one. Pirates were often better sailors than the King's own navy and their ships were better kitted out. A sea battle would often find privateers taking part alongside the navy like some maritime militia. However, the pirates were not in the business of fighting the Spaniards for heroic or loyal reasons: they were in it for the money. They were often royally backed. The expeditions to establish colonies, with the few exceptions of those involving the exploited and persecuted, were all about money. Why not? There was nothing disgraceful in these ambitions. The idea that local populations would be overwhelmed did not raise the same moral questions as they may in the twenty-first century. In today's global business ways, international corporations and governments sometimes cause terrible wounds on vulnerable societies, so there's little moral high ground to choose between.

The seventeenth-century pirates who worked the Caribbean would continue to do so as larger than life marine poachers and certainly pull in more than the occasional pheasant. Many of them retired as wealthy men and by the 1640s they could be found in British Honduras and Guiana living in some style. In fact, Honduras was largely found and sustained by these retired corsairs. This coastline in the seventeenth century had a lot in common with some strips of the twenty-first century Spanish coast, populated by gold-medallioned British men, some of whom had been on first-name terms with British justice.

These occupations and purposes of the British interest in the Caribbean were very much part of the first British Empire which was established as a new venture and experience. Apart from Ireland there was no history of colonialism and certainly not colonial admin-istration necessary to consolidate the complex systems needed to rule from a distance. The fourteenth- and fifteenth-century British administrations in northern France cannot be seen in the same context. The 'overseas' colonial system, therefore, had its origins in what the last of the Tudors and early Stuarts thought possible and profitable. The need to bring some formality to the settlements of this time was encouraged by the consequences of the continuing British, mainly English, conflict with Catholic France. In the sixteenth century, the French Huguenot admiral, Gaspard de Coligny expounded a tactical doctrine that appealed to the English when he encouraged that the Spanish should be attacked in the West Indies. Coligny's ambition was more than incursion into the Spanish commercial grounds of the Caribbean. Militarily the Spanish would have to reinforce their garrisons in the West Indies. This in turn would weaken them in Europe. It was a fundamental fact of military life that would survive the centuries, even to the twenty-first century when the British military became overstretched because of too varied commitments abroad.

The English connection to the Huguenots, who they had supported by sending troops to Normandy in 1562, continued to nurture the seeds of colonial expansion. Coligny, then Governor of Le Havre, decided that some of the Huguenots should flee the travails in France and sail for Florida, or Terra Florida as it was then known. The expe-dition sailed in February 1562 with the ambition to call Florida 'New France'. The English trusted and knew well the commander of that expedition, Jean Ribault. He landed at what we call South Carolina and set up a stockade in the name of King Charles IX, thus calling it Charlesfort, which is now Charleston. In the summer he sailed for France, but with the debacle of the English effort and the Huguenots' surrender to the Catholics, Ribault did not stay in France and went to his natural haven, England. He then published in English his account of the setting up of a mini-colony in Florida. Thomas Stukely, fascinated by Ribault's story, persuaded Elizabeth that all the rumours of Florida being if not paved, then seamed, with gold were true. In turn this led to Martin Frobisher (1535?–94) embarking on the first of his three voyages in search of a north-west passage to the Indies, and gold, in 1576. He failed in both missions, but dignified himself commanding the *Triumph*, alongside Drake in the *Revenge* and Hawkins in the *Victory*, in the defeat of the Spanish Armada in 1588. The importance of Frobisher is the way that he reflected not so much the sense of exploration – the original reason for his voyages – but the fact that they were all inevitably supported for commercial gain. Who else but entrepreneurs would finance them? No one else had money.

We should not get the idea that the commercial interests of this period were based only on grandiose schemes. When, as early as the fourteenth century, sailors had returned from the Newfoundland Banks with stories of enormous shoals of fish, the consistent and largely unsung group of voyagers were the fishermen.

Certainly by the second half of the sixteenth century a large West Country investment was going into the provisioning and fitting out of fishing vessels heading for the north-west Atlantic. The Newfoundland Banks and the areas beyond presented problem and opportunity. The dilemma was the distance involved. It certainly meant that the British fishermen had to dry and salt their catch. The English preferred to do this ashore whereas the French and Portuguese tended to fish in the grounds and stayed at sea by loading and barrelling the catch with salt. The French and Portuguese therefore stayed at sea longer than the British.

The British established drying bases on shore, which they fitted out with salt stages. Unlike the French, the British did not fish from the large vessels that had brought them across the Atlantic. Instead they put out from the shore in smaller vessels, often single-masted, with a very basic dipping lug sail and perhaps a small steadying sail on a mizzen mast towards the stern. These small but sturdy boats were called shallops. The importance in this distinction in fishing styles is obvious; the English by having their drying sheds and stages ashore were establishing small colonies. By doing this they were building important bases for the expansion of empire. Again we see the economic rather than the constitutional widening of British influence.

French vessels would come into the same harbours, particularly St John's, but the British made greater efforts to establish their lordship over these fishing havens. The French in the meantime went where the British were not: the estuary of the St Lawrence Seaway.

Uneasily perhaps, but commercially sensible, the French and the British tried to coexist with a minimum amount of conflict. It was the same sort of relationship that we would see between the two nations in India, when French and British commercial instincts and expediency all but ignored the fact that in another part of the world their two nations were at war. This 'peace' was not to last, but it showed that it was not only the British who were in the business of empire strictly for profits. This economic reasoning was not seen as a cynical motive even though today all those who do not run major businesses might curl a lip or two. Our twenty-first-century view that imperialism is a sour word and a euphemism for the British asset-stripping poorer peoples is rather different than the perspective in the sixteenth and seventeenth centuries. Times were different and commercial motives unexceptional. Moreover, a nation the size of Britain would have been bankrupt without its colonies.

G. L. Beer, in *Origins of the British Colonial System 1578 – 1660*, emphasizes the fact that Britain's colonial exploration during this period was built very much on the social and economic advantages. It was even thought that in spite of England having a population of no more than four million, colonization would alleviate England of what was seen as a surplus population. Certainly by 1600 there was little evidence that English agriculture could develop further to feed even so few people. The population was growing or, more accurately, was recovering from the devastation of the fourteenth-century Black Death. It must seem amazing today to hear that there was a strong view in Elizabeth's and James I's England that the country was overpopulated.

In 1600, London had about 200,000 people living in it, yet it wasn't much bigger in area than the present City of London. Other cities were by today's standards extremely small in area. Big cities outside of London were few. Norwich and Bristol are the most noticeable. Manchester, for example, was then not much more than a village or a hamlet. The difficulty was the way people lived in cramped and dirty conditions and the increasing numbers of very able-bodied men out of work. One result was a growing tendency to vagrancy and certainly to violence, while overcrowding, in 1603, was largely responsible for the death of more than 37,000 Londoners from a recurring epidemic of plague. It was not surprising that in the 1580s we find Richard Hakluyt, George Peckham and Christopher Carleill promoting the idea that a good reason for England to become a colonial entrepreneur was so that the vagrants, wastrels, unemployed and convicts could be sent off as settlers to North America, particularly to the growing colony of Newfoundland.

These were not casual observations and suggestions. They were hypotheses richly promoted not just at the end of the sixteenth century; as we know, transportation of convicts to Australia continued well into the nineteenth century. Sending convicted men, women and children to America only finished in 1788 because the British lost the colony.

Mercantilism in England was not dissimilar to what centuries later we would call protectionism. The principle was to export as much as possible and at the same time restrict foreign imports. That was all right for national commodities or easily manufactured goods. Basic food stuffs and anything that prospered in an English climate could be controlled. This is why we should not get so caught up in the glamour of believing that the likes of Hawkins, Ralegh and Drake were doing so well for England by plundering the silver, gold and jewels of Spanish galleons. Even more than these sparkling treasures, England really needed those things that it wanted every day right across the country and which could not be obtained in a temperate climate. So the real treasures to be brought back were commodities such as salt, sugar, peppers, sub-tropical fruits and spices. Peppers, for example, were first used as medicines. When, in the sixteenth century, the merchants in the East put up the price of spices on the Antwerp market, the English were prompted to sail East to establish their own trade, thus peppers were the origins of the Raj. The British Empire would be built on these needs and not territorial and constitutional aggrandizement and certainly not Spanish precious metals. For the British, El Dorado would be on the commodity markets, not the bullion exchanges.

We can then judge the importance of a letter from Ralph Lane, the first governor of Virginia, to Richard Hakluyt, written on 3 September 1585, when he says, 'what commodities so ever Spain, France, Italy or the East parts do yield unto us, in wines of all sorts, in oils, in flax, in resins, pitch, frankincense, currants, sugars, and suchlike, these parts do abound with the growth of them all'.

Richard Hakluyt, in his *A Discourse of Western Planting*, was of the opinion that Virginia could supply everything that the English would otherwise have to trade for in southern Europe, Africa and the Far East. There were also commodities to be had in North America which were far from exotic. Timber and cordage, so necessary for an English maritime nation in its building of ships from keel to mast-head, were mightily expensive. Much of the timber was coming from the Baltic, but the King of Denmark was imposing swingeing taxes. How much better to establish a colony and bring it home from the new Dominions? For good measure there was always the hope that the bullion the Spanish had so easily found further south might also be mined in similar tonnage by the British to the north. Yet this remained a hope that would be a bonus. The more long-term thinkers knew that there was gold in timber.

The commercial instincts were not one-sided or one-way. The attraction was to go to the new colonies and bring back, at a big profit, goods. The entrepreneurs also judged, quite rightly, that colonists who settled these new lands would be a wonderful market for goods made in England. Ask a man to dig in Virginia and he had to have a shovel. They made shovels in Sheffield. Thus, the entrepreneurs and governing council would profit from getting imports without paying high duties from other countries and would further profit by selling more manufactured goods to the very people they had sent or encouraged to the colony. Moreover, this increased trade had to be carried so there would be a need for more ships: the ship-yards would do good business and the shipowners even more.

Here then was a perfect example of the simplest economic rule of supply and demand. Even more than that, it was the establishment over a relatively short period of a new form of economics and a new economy for the British. This was British Empire plc.

Was this the beginning of the British rape of colonized lands and people? We might as well ask if the agricultural system, from its manorial and feudal beginnings, was a rape of these lands and an exploitation of the poorest people? The answer is yes, of course it was. The exploitation of black and coloured peoples is now unforgivable. So too was the medieval exploitation of the English, Scottish and Irish peasantry. The codicil is that commercial and colonial development, even in its most parochial form, was ever thus and not all the poor remained poor as a result. Perhaps this fundament of economic thinking had not sunk in when Elizabeth was on the throne, but there is no doubt that she would never have lent her seal to a voyage unless she would show a profit. Elizabeth was continuously broke. She did not need an empire to look good in her biographies. She wanted money, goods by the shipload and a system that stopped the Spanish and French getting them before she did. Elizabeth had bright men (seemingly) who would exploit this need: thus the backing for men such as Ralegh and Drake.

The one constant in the exploration of the American eastern seaboard was led by the fishermen. Here were touchable profits. No one could doubt the money to be made from fisheries. The relatively easy relationship between the English and the French continued. The French wanted to push further in to what became Canada. Trading hides and oils as well as fish was equably profitable and made a sensible economic diversion when the fish could only be taken seasonally. The French, led by Samuel de Champlain, 'conquered' the St Lawrence River in 1603 and established their province of Quebec in 1608. They were firmly in Canada. The English – most of the initiatives were from England at that time – and later the British concentrated their efforts further south in Virginia, despite the disaster of the first settlement. At the vanguard were the explorers. Behind them were the enormously influential figures of the merchant venturers, people like Sir Thomas Smythe.

The Smythes and their wider family had become rich through landowning and wise stewardship of their own and royal holdings. Smythe's mother was the daughter of Sir Andrew Judd, who had been a sort of business manager for Henry VIII. The commissions and patronage were considerable. Smythe's father was called Customer Smythe. The name 'Customer' came from the fact that he was the collector of Elizabeth's customs dues and had raked in a considerable fortune as his commission.

At a time when the cloth trade was once more taking off, Thomas Smythe backed it and reaped the rewards. Instead of buying ships he

saw there was far more money to be made without any risk whatsoever by victualling them. Also he was wise enough to believe that
although there were short-term profits to be made from warfare,
longer term investments showed a better return in peacetime. By the
end of the sixteenth century, when peace was breaking out over
Europe, Smythe was making even more money. Little wonder that
after his experiences of quietly piling fortune upon fortune in, for
example, the Levant, he became one of the original proposers for the
East India Company to bring back the millions of pounds worth of
cargo from the Spice Islands.

The coincidence of the death of Elizabeth and the end of the war
with Spain was based on sound economic sense. The influence of
Essex on the Queen prohibited peace negotiations with Spain.
When he was sent to Ireland in 1599, the more peacefully and
legitimately trading courtiers were able to persuade the Queen that
it was time to explore the possibility of peace with Spain. This was
an important step in the commercial and subsequent colonial plans
of the English. Certainly, people like Smythe and John Lancaster,
leader of the English East India project, were keen that the talks
with the Spanish, which took place that year at Boulogne, should
result in a diplomatic trade in concessions and permissions. The
English said, for example, that they would tell their people not to
enter any Spanish or Portuguese plantation or colony but reserve
the right to make their own excursions into non-plantations. Hence
the insistence in Elizabethan petitions and permissions that explorers should not attempt to colonize where Christian princes already
ruled.

Here was a diplomatic definition of where a country could trade
and also an origin of colony. The English were saying that to have
any title to distant lands then a country should have established some
colonial structure. In other words we come back to the idea of creating a community in the image of the occupying power socially,
constitutionally and legally. The French supported this idea. The
Spaniards, who of course had most to lose, did not. This is why
England remained at war with Spain until the death of Elizabeth and
the translation of James VI of Scotland to the throne of England.
King James's immediate priority, even before his coronation in the
summer of 1603, was to bring the wasteful war with Spain to an end.
In May 1604 Spanish diplomats went to London.

The English once more demanded that they should be free to trade with the Spanish possessions in the East as well as the West Indies. The English also insisted that the Spanish recognized that the English, or anyone else for that matter, had the right to colonize any land that was not occupied by another power – never mind the local people; they did not matter. Here was an attempt to agree international law – which in those days did not much exist – with regards to imperial and colonial exploration. The English were saying that internationally the main powers, England, France, Portugal, Spain and the Dutch (often it depended on who owned the Dutch at the time), had the right to establish a colony in 'undiscovered' territory and that the land should have a legally recognized status. For example, an English flag planted in Virginia meant that the other exploring powers should keep their hands off and recognize that it was as much English territory as, say, Wessex or Northumberland. As a reminder that the English were very late getting into the business of colonialism on a structured scale the Spaniards argued from strength and saw absolutely no reason why they should accept these demands.

Nevertheless, this was an attempt to have peace between the English and the Spaniards. The English wanted to expand colonial business. The Spaniards wanted James I to call off his pirates. He had done so, but in spite of his proclamation, the Spanish galleons were still plundered. It was all very well for James to issue a proclamation, but the people it was aimed at, the privateers, were hardly likely to see it for months. Many of them would not even know that James had issued it. When his authority was enforced, this did not mean the end of piracy. James never quite approved of corsairs because it antagonized the Spanish and therefore made his country vulnerable to attack. Certainly, his successor, Charles I, had no difficulties with piracy. Robert Rich, the second Earl of Warwick (1587–1658), obtained in March 1627 a liberal privateering commission from Charles I. He had eight ships with which to attack the Spaniards. In fact, he headed for Brazil hoping to seize Spanish bullion galleons but totally missed the fleet. However, during the following two years, Rich, still under the same authority from Charles I, was successful. The prizes to be gained were often small fortunes. A privateer did not simply sail for home, share the spoils on the quarterdeck and then head ashore to the nearest inn to celebrate. The distribution was complex. The King or his agent would expect a cut and various officials would attempt to take their commission. Rich certainly found this in the 1628 and 1629 pirate expeditions. It took twelve years of legal wrangling before he finally got what he thought were his just percentages.

Although the English did not get their way with the Spanish, they got some form of treaty – the Treaty of London, 1604. It was an anodyne document but it was the beginning of the legalities of English, or by that time British, imperial history.

The sensitivities should not be underrated. It was all right for the English to sail to a port in Spain to trade. It was not necessarily all right for that same vessel to sail into a Spanish possession in the East or West Indies. Why should this have been? One answer reflected the fundamental reason for having a colony. If an English ship sailed into Lisbon or Seville it might be selling goods from England and buying something from Spain or Portugal such as wine or leather. This would be unexceptional trade. The exceptional trade would be in the colonies where, say, the Spaniards were exclusively mining silver and there was a risk that the British ship was usurping the exclusive rights of the Spaniards. Multiply that scenario across the world of possessions and the very real possibilities of making individual deals with the locals and then establishing trading companies along the coast followed by stockades, and it is little wonder that the Spaniards believed that to let an English ship into an existing colony would threaten the commercial and military authority there.

The Spanish opposition to anybody trying to trade with, for example, their American colonies was not going to be pushed aside by the English. In fact, Spain maintained this opposition until the independence of those colonies in the 1800s. Also, the Spanish Empire was by then (the early seventeenth century) established. With the exception of Brazil (mostly Portuguese), the Spanish Latin American Empire stretched from Florida to Buenos Aires. We have only to remind ourselves that apart from Brazil, Spanish remains today the familiar language from Miami to the tip of South America and through many Caribbean islands. By the London conference of 1604, the Spanish influence was everywhere except Brazil, Guiana, the Lesser Antilles and North America. In North America the Spanish controlled most of Florida up to about thirty degrees of latitude north, with the capital of that colony at St Augustine. In theory, therefore, the rest of the Americas were still to be fought over. The

Dutch had a go at Brazil but were not very successful. If nothing else the Treaty of London had cleared the air so that the non-Iberian empire builders knew exactly what was up for grabs and so made preparations to grab.

But where was the money coming from? The excursions during the past forty years including the most successful of all, the East India Company, had been largely private ventures. The Crown had no money. In fact, the monarchy was so poor that almost the only time it called Parliament together was to ask for money, usually to go to war. The monarchy did have one commodity – people. The question of how to feed and control the ambitions of the people was rarely satisfied.

The theme of redistributing some of the British population to the colonies came up time and again. Therefore, to raise the money the Privy Council approved the idea of public stock companies. The Crown would appoint commissioners and it would be their role to finance or find the finance for the expeditions of the 'peopling and discovering of such countries as may be found most convenient for the supply of those defects which the realm of England most requireth'.[9] Most certainly, the whole thing had to be done in the name of the monarch at that time, James I. With the King's endorsement the venture was far more likely to attract public investment. Also, it was a formal warning to foreign powers that if a venture were to be attacked, especially one of its settlements, then this would be an attack on the monarch, on England, and therefore would invite official retaliation and even warfare. This was the way forward to sending people to known lands, to discover new ones, to farm and export whatever they found and, of course, to raise much needed customs dues on the produce of these colonies.

Smythe and other underwriters in the City had a forty-year tradition of making money out of explorations. These were the originators of the Muscovy Company, the Levant Company and the East Indian Company; these people saw that profits were to be made for individuals and also the practical advantages for England in finding goods and materials that were not controlled by the two Iberian states. The explorers and the Bristolian slave traders were

---

9   A. Brown, *The Genesis of the United States* (Boston, MA/New York, NY: Houghton Mifflin, 1899), pp. 37–42.

looking for new grounds ashore while those who had backed the Newfoundland Banks' fishermen looked for more stocks at sea. By this time Ralegh was far from being able to do anything to join in this exploration, including of Virginia. He was locked up in the Tower of London having been found guilty of treason in November 1603, condemned to be hanged, drawn and quartered but sent to prison instead just moments before his execution.[10] It was to Virginia that the new interest in exploration turned.

In 1606, Ralegh's nephew, George Ralegh, and Richard Hakluyt were given the patent to start colonies in Virginia. Walter Ralegh saw this as an opportunity for freedom and asked the King to release him from prison so that he too could sail for Virginia. Queen Anne (James's wife) was a supporter of Ralegh, but even she was unable to persuade James and his advisers to release him. By then, they would have preferred him dead. James could see nothing but trouble on any horizon upon which Ralegh stood, especially if there should be Spanish interest at hand. Although Queen Anne supported the voyages to Virginia, they were strictly commercial and therefore private ventures. However, they came under the single protection of a royal patent – the exploration was in the King's name and thus in theory protected from the likes of Spanish disruption.

Uniquely, a Royal Council for Virginia was created. A dozen or so trustees were appointed by the King. This Council would have the power to administrate the land between thirty-four degrees and forty-five degrees north of latitude. At last Virginia was to have the formal structure which, once more we should note, reflected our definition of a colony: the Council would issue on behalf of the monarch instructions or orders.[11] The first Council instructions for Virginia set out the commercial, bureaucratic and legal (including judicial) system to be imposed on the territory. Just as the colony had to reflect the mother country, so the legal distribution of land was to be as it was in England. The colonialists were not allowed to issue

---

10   Ralegh was tried for treason mostly on the evidence of Lord Cobham. Both men were to be executed. They were saved and sent to the Tower, partly perhaps because the mood of the people had swung in Ralegh's favour by reason of the way the trial was conducted and in spite of the fact that Ralegh had been one of the most detested men in Britain at the start of the trial. Ralegh was eventually executed in 1618 after failing to find El Dorado and attacking Spanish settlements.

11   The terminology 'instructions' survives to this day. For example, orders to the armed services at home and abroad are issued through DCIs, defence council instructions.

their own patents on who owned what land. Only the Crown could do that in England and only the Crown could do that in Virginia. It is this emphasis right the way through the history of the British Empire that shows that a colony was almost a shire county. The rules could not be bent until some self-government had been granted.

Each colony would form a council which would have the power to elect its own president and to nominate people to hold patents on the land. This council could, in just the same way as a local authority in England, create bye-laws to suit local conditions. However, it could only do this as long as the purpose and spirit in the law in England was not usurped.

This was not control-freakery by the Crown or the Privy Council. It was simply that this new colonialism was breaking new ground. Until then, apart from the Anglo-Normans and the Channel Islands and Ireland, English settlement abroad had been nothing more than the medieval concept of occupation rather than colonialization. Winning a battle against the French and taking territory was one thing; expanding England to, say, America as an identifiable extension of the State was quite new.

Thus, with all the flexibility of commercial and economic development, the settlers remained very English even to the extent of preserving their rights as Englishmen and women (mainly men) as loyal subjects of the Crown. Indeed, they emphasized this preservation of rights as a matter of self protection. Yet legal definitions and constitutional dignity were not sufficient to make a success of opening up new territory. The success or otherwise of the colonies would depend on four conditions: the local environment being able to support settlers; the determination of the settlers; the financial support behind them; and the distance they were from Spanish and, later, French interests.

On 20 December 1606 Sir Christopher Newport, commanded three ships (the *Discovery*, *Godspeed* and *Susan Constant*) as they sailed from England to Virginia to test these conditions. The tactical and strategic sense of this new expedition was based on two perceptions: the landing had to be benign and fruitful and, secondly, it had to be out of arm's reach of the Spanish.

They arrived in Virginia in May 1607. By then, James VI of Scotland had been James I of England for four years. So the first settlement in Virginia of this new expedition was called James Fort and then James Town. It sat on a peninsula in the mouth of the Chesapeake. It was not a very good place to build a stockade. Diseases, including malaria, wafted across from the swamps as did the local Indians with similar effect. This first settlement was in peril when Newport left about a hundred of the settlers to build up the community and clear the forests while he returned to England for supplies and to try to arrange a regular supply line.

Once more here is a reminder of the sheer physical difficulty of establishing the basics of a colony. An image of settlers being able to live off the land and give thanks for the first harvests, while vessels docked with the latest luxuries, is far removed from the truth surrounding the early empire builders. Supplies would not magically arrive from England. Time and again, records show that an elder of the settlement had to return to England, raise cash or credit, negotiate contracts and only then, maybe months later, sail for the settlement *and* find it – navigation was sometimes indifferent. Given these difficulties, supplies often arrived very late or even too late. When Newport returned from England just a few months later, half the settlers were dead.

We might have thought that the lessons were easily learned. Not so. In August 1607 the Plymouth colony was founded. This was the second of the settlements. Again, the tactical importance of being at the mouth of a river influenced its siting. Fort St George was built on the north bank of the estuary of the Kennebec River. It was called the Plymouth colony because it was named after the Plymouth Company that financed it. Unlike the more famous organizations, the East India Company, the Muscovy Company and the Levant Company, the Plymouth Company was underfunded and dreadfully organized. There seemed to be an impression that it was easy enough to fit out a ship, get would-be settlers to put some money up and hope for the best. There was a desperation behind this and so many of the other earlier schemes to settle America. Often we come back to crew lists and passenger manifests that appear to show that many of the settlers were economic, political or religious refugees. At the start of the seventeenth century, however, there was no national and social security system to ease their way into a new life. Instead, they found themselves in a beautiful but largely unwelcoming society. So it was at Fort St George. The Plymouth Company simply did not have the organization or the money to keep supplies sailing from

Devon to North Virginia. The mini-colony collapsed just a year after it was founded.

James Town, after its earlier setbacks, was better financed and certainly better led. The money and suppliers came through a London stock company and the settlers had now chosen a new leader, Captain John Smith.

Smith is an example of an early seventeenth-century soldier of fortune who is hardly known beyond the historical footnotes of that period, yet he was a truly remarkable adventurer. Some of those adventures have been questioned and even those proven to be correct still seem far-fetched. Smith was born in Lincolnshire in January 1580 (1579 in the old dating system). At the age of sixteen, following his father's death, Smith went to Continental Europe as a mercenary soldier. For probably two years he served in the French army in its war against Spain. When that was over he joined the rebels of the Low Countries. By 1600 he had returned home and tried to read as much military history and science as he could. He had seen how well-motivated forces could fail simply because they did not understand enough about warfare. He saw military science as the study of logistics – which he regarded as one of the most essential elements of warfare – and the proper use of reconnaissance and the deployment of forces suitable to the terrain and opponents. This obvious condition of warfare was not always understood by even the highest ranking officers, many of whom had high command through social distinction and little else. Communication was often poor, warfare was not a military science, there were no military academies and often soldiers at even the most senior levels failed to display as much intelligence as they did élan. A good example of this failure to be able to adapt to the environment and differing enemies was to be the initial undoing of British forces in their war against France in Canada in the eighteenth century and against the Patriots in the War of American Independence.

Shortly after about 1600, Smith is said to have fallen overboard during a voyage to Italy, but was rescued by a pirate for whom he worked out his gratitude. Eventually he got to Italy and then headed north and east, becoming a mercenary for the Archduke of Austria. He claimed a further series of startling adventures (many of which are partially supported from other sources) including killing three Turkish gladiators while in the service of Sigismund Bathori, the

Prince of Transylvania. His young luck seems to have run out shortly after this; Smith was captured and sold as a slave. He next appeared in England in 1605 telling the story of how two years earlier he had killed his slavemaster to escape home via Morocco – in itself an extraordinary story.

The next stage of his career brought him into the colonial rather than the mercenary history of Britain. Smith was among the 105 people who on 19 December 1606 sailed from the Thames near Deptford to be the founding settlers of Virginia. In many ways Smith, who was listed in the original manifest as a planter, was exactly what the early colonists needed. He was an adventurer, a soldier, an organizer and, with a history that must have hardened him to most conditions and circumstances, an uncompromising and determined fortune hunter.

Remembering that the motives of the settlers were mixed and that many of them were vagabonds, it was hardly a surprise that Smith should emerge as leader. He was never a dull administrator and the most unlikely adventures continued to involve him. It was Smith who was famously captured by Indians and supposedly released because of the personal intervention of Pocahontas. Whether or not the story is true is of no consequence other than it is typical of the tales that surrounded this remarkable man. In 1608 Smith proved he had another talent. He charted most of the Chesapeake coastline and bay, travelling, or so he said, 3,000 miles to provide himself with detailed charts, outlines and soundings. Smith attracted as much controversy and animosity as he did adventure. Therefore, it was inevitable that he would fall out with or be chased out by the cabal that ran the colony. He moved his attentions to New England and to produce the first coastal chart of the area. It seems inevitable that Smith was captured by the French and, as he had done a decade or so earlier, found himself serving as a mercenary for his captors until he was set free, probably in 1617. That was really the end of his colonial career. When he returned to London he occupied most of his time as a chart- and map-maker, something of a tame ending to the life of an extraordinary adventurer. He died in 1631.

We can see from Smith's story much of the uncertainties of early colonization, especially in Virginia. He was no Robert Walpole or William Pitt the Younger. He did not have to be. Smith's wild experience together with his grasp of leadership made him exactly the person needed to attempt to mould whatever talents were to be found in the motley of settlers in James Town. They were gradually producing a system of proper settlement rather than finding themselves under siege from the elements and the indigenous population.

Because of Smith's leadership the settlers were split into groups and each group had a responsibility. Some provided subsistence crops. This meant they had to clear the ground and learn from what was already planted. Here was some cooperation between the newcomers and the people who already lived there. The Indians showed them how to cultivate what was for the colonists a completely new crop, maize, or at least sometimes they did. We should avoid the impression of innocent natives kindly tutoring ignorant colonists. Often, animosities were cruelly expressed, not least of all because of the latent fears of settlers with instincts to cuff, or worse, their authority over the people whose land they took. Smith was the lynchpin in this founding colony. He had learned that resourcefulness and survival could only be accomplished by living off the land about him and wherever possible with the local people. In that way, reliance on supplies that might never come was minimized. Undoubtedly he was a despot. Equally surely he was a successful despot and it was probably his energies and uncompromising nature that saw the James Town settlement to its feet when it might easily have perished during the dreadful winter months of 1608 and 1609. Smith's success and the failure at Fort St George provided a high and low point of that exploration of Virginia. The success and failure demonstrated to the financiers in the West Country and London that in spite of earlier promises there were no quick fortunes to be made in this business of colonizing Virginia.

Those people who supported with money and political clout the great colonial adventure were becoming very critical of the 1606 Royal Charter – the authority by which men and women could go out and claim land in the name of the King and thus protect themselves in that same name. However, the Charter did not provide an authority with the power to recruit colonists and finance and establish the supply lines that were, as we have seen, at the beginnings of any settlement. James I had been badly advised. It was a time of political in-fighting at his court, which was just three years old.

The magnates who wanted the Charter either scrapped or revised were men of wealth and experience. They were nominally led by Sir Thomas Smythe. He and his friends could show that commercial nous, with a seal of government approval, could make almost all things commercially possible. Here was the forerunner of the late twentieth-century idea of PPP – public private partnership. Government gives authority for something it wants done to perhaps a conglomerate which then takes the profits. In 1609, the merchants petitioned the Crown for a new partnership and charter. James agreed and the Treasurer and Company of Adventurers and Planters of the City of London for the First Colony in Virginia was established. It is generally called the London Company.

Just as John Smith had taken over and steadied the trembling James Town settlement with absolute authority, Smythe became treasurer of the London Company and in a similar manner ran it for the next eight years. Here we have a reminder that it was the Smythes and Smiths, with their harsh discipline and, above all, their commercial instincts and ambitions, who were building the Empire, not the more familiar names surrounding the King and his court.

Smith was a hard man at the coal face of Empire. Smythe was equally hard, but no frontiersman. Smythe insisted upon hard leaders to be sent to the colonies. Equally, these men were not allowed to do what Smith had done – to make his own rules as he went along. Accordingly, in the spring of 1609 when the experienced soldier, Sir Thomas Gates, was appointed to be the London Company's man in the colony, he was given explicit instructions on how he should, within an advisory council, maintain discipline together with commercial and constitutional law. However, the explicit planning and prudence of Smythe and Gates had not catered for an unpredictable enemy – the weather.

They got as far as the Bermuda islands which were called, with good reason, the Isles of Storms by the Spanish. Gates had sailed in an expedition led by Sir George Somers aboard his ship, *Sea Venture*. They had left England on 15 May 1609 and two months later were wrecked off Bermuda. Here was the origin of the opening of Shakespeare's *The Tempest*, written in 1611 (although not published for a decade), and the line, 'still vex'd Bermoothes'. Somers, Gates and the few survivors, including William Strachey who wrote an account of the wreck, spent the winter months building two vessels, which they launched the following spring. They sailed into James Town on 23 May 1610. The following month they were followed in by supplies brought by Thomas West, Lord De La Warr.

When Somers and his rather bedraggled and far from imperial group arrived, it was to no rapturous welcome. The colony was starving to death. West's arrival was prompted by Smythe who feared for his investment. West was given absolute authority to declare martial law over the colony. He had, as a soldier, learned all about bringing into line recalcitrant civilians as well as soldiers during his successful campaigns in the Netherlands. He now put them to great effect. No one was allowed to desert. Every man had to work for the benefit of the whole community. Each who obeyed these rules would be looked after by that community. Thus none would starve. The laws had hardly been put into place when West died in 1611. Another soldier, Sir Thomas Dale, who was equally austere and uncompromising, took over. The system of rigorous, even brutal, communal regulation had worked well in a small community. The logic that escaped Smythe and the London Company was that in a larger, expanding and increasingly healthy plantation there was less hope of everyone sticking to the rules. Of necessity, a frontiersman was a hardened individual. He and, less often, she were either scurrilously or moralistically single-minded. These sorts of people rarely took kindly to authority that did not suit them and, often, no authority at all.

The independence seemingly bred into the sort of people that wanted a new start in life, and their immediate descendants, would time and again confound the thinking and ambitions of those comfortable in London. The reasons behind the War of American Independence a century-and-a-half later lay in that very sense of independence and the distance of London from the Americas – both geographically and temperamentally.

For the moment, however, Dale successfully drew the settlers together. He was in command of a colonial triptych. The military policing sought to guarantee the security of the settlers as well as protecting the London Company's interests including the stores which contained the lifeblood of the colony. The second group was that of the indentured colonists. These were mostly craftsmen and labourers who had been given free passage by the Company to Virginia. In return they had to work for everyone just as an indentured apprentice would work for a craftsman. They would not be free men. In their spare time these indentured workers would be allowed to build up a private holding until eventually it was possible for them to join the third group, the free men. These were the free farmers. They had paid to take passage on the immigrant ships. When the free farmers arrived they were given twelve acres each to cultivate as tenants for one year. After that, still as tenants, they had to pay rent. So they had twelve months to turn virgin soil to upturned profit. Here was the basis of the future of Virginia as a colony: a careful and profitable cultivation by colonialists who had a direct interest in the future of the colony.

By 1617 Dale had gone from Virginia to put his experience to good use with the East India Company, which was still a fledgling concern. His successor, Sir George Yeardley, continued his work on the basis that by now the supply system was working. The legal, military and constitutional divisions were properly exploited to the local good and not just to the theoreticians' demands. Yet both in the colony and in the holding company in London expectations had to be adjusted.

The British long believed that Virginia would supply many, if not all, the goods that came from southern Europe. Given the political uncertainties within Continental Europe, the British rightly believed that secondary sources should be found for everything from potash and wine to naval stores. Also, by maintaining a navy in the western Atlantic, Virginia could be a good storing point for the ships and men. However, Virginian settlers and the London Company needed more than this. The West Indies possessions had lucrative sugar crops. What might there be in Virginia? There was one possibility to make Virginia a commercial success – tobacco.

Regarding tobacco as a noxious drug is not a recent development. It was considered a terrible narcotic even in the early seventeenth century, so much so that James I issued a proclamation condemning smoking. He hated it. For twenty years or so, tobacco had been in England classed as an illicit drug in the way that 400 years later cannabis was rated. There was then a high customs and excise duty put on tobacco import (which has never been removed). Most of the tobacco came from Spanish plantations in the West Indies. In the early days of the colony, tobacco was certainly not envisaged as a staple crop for Virginia, but very soon it was realized that the climate was perfect and tobacco plantations were created. By 1617, tobacco had become Virginia's biggest export. Because of the craving of British smokers and the limited amount of imports, the Virginian planters were able to charge high prices. They could then use the money to buy, from England, the manufactured goods they needed and regarded as luxuries, thus creating a good market for British manufacturers. The importance of this use of tobacco profits was that the stockholders of the London Company did not always have to pay for the manufactured goods the planters needed and therefore the Company was more profitable and so attracted more investment. Also, the planters were gaining financial independence. Economic independence was an essential prerequisite for self-determination.

Colonial expansion was now unstoppable. The spreading of the fledgling empire was not confined to the hinterland and littoral states of America. The shipwrecked colonists who had taken refuge on Bermuda had, if nothing else, excited the idea that the fertility and easy access to wildlife made it an obvious target for colonists.

This was an important aspect of expansion because, as we have seen, it was about this time under James I that the experiment to plant the confiscated acres of Ulster with Scots and English was taking place. The immediate consequence was that the capital, manpower and enthusiasms necessary to expand the Virginia and island colonies were diverted to the Ulster experiment, it being closer and seemingly less risky. After all, why risk crossing an ocean to the relative unknown?

As mentioned, when Gates had been forced to take refuge among the Isles of Storms, his second-in-command, but leader of the voyage, was Sir George Somers (1554–1610). Somers was a celebrated and respected sea-dog adventurer who had sailed with Ralegh. Now the shipwrecked Somers, claimed Bermuda for England, although the Spanish had already found the islands. In fact, before they were renamed Bermuda, they were known as the Somers Islands. He was already dead when, in 1615, members of the Virginia Company running the American colony set up a new venture called the Company of the Plantation of the Somers Islands. Once more Sir Thomas Smythe was its leading member. Navigators were sent to survey the many islands and atolls that made up Bermuda. As an incentive for investment, the members of the company would each have an island named after them. The biggest stockholders were also given the tenancies of large tracts of land.

The template that had been successful thus far in Virginia was used in Bermuda. Each major tenant in the Company was given land on the understanding that he could afford to pay for indentured labour, get those workers to the islands and support them. So began in 1615 the history of the oldest surviving British colony.

The Spanish did not like this. They had discovered the islands and believed they had some territorial rights over that part of the ocean. They most certainly did not like the way that these Somers Islands were used as a jumping off point to harass Spanish shipping. However, by this time, 1615–20, the Spanish were no longer a threat to anyone unless provoked. A pattern was emerging of colonial interests. The Spanish had enough to look after with their American commitments south of St Augustine in Florida. The more interesting competition, part of which would eventually involve open warfare and animosities of culture and language that would survive into the twenty-first century, was being created much further north. The protagonists were the French, the English and, to a lesser extent, the Dutch.

The Dutch and the English were sending expeditions along the American coastline to the colder climes north of Virginia. The French had already gained strong footholds in this region. When the English routed the French colony around Port Royale on the Acadian peninsula and captured Jesuit missionaries in 1613, the Franco–English battle for the control of large swathes of North American territory, including what was to become Canada, had finally started. One of the most memorable leaders of that North American exploration had been Henry Hudson (1550–1611). Hudson was a sailor and a good navigator. At the age of fifty-seven he put to sea with just eleven crew in a small vessel called, appropriately, the *Hopewell*. He was supported by the Muscovy Company and tasked with finding not a north-westerly but north-easterly sea passage across the polar region to China. He got as far as Spitzbergen. The following year, 1608, he was blocked by ice off Novaya Zemlya. It was the year after that, 1609, that Hudson was working for the Dutch East India Company. This time he sailed in a north-westerly direction and reached the Davis Strait. Sailing on a southerly course, he then came across the estuary and then back into the mouth of a huge river. This was what is now called the Hudson River which he navigated and charted as far as the present Albany in New York State, some 150 miles from the mouth. In the spring of 1610 he sailed in the *Discovery*, rounded the southern tip of Greenland and crossed the Davis Strait which separates Greenland from Baffin Island, and then navigated through the narrows between Resolution Island and Button Island (the pincers which form the entrance to Hudson Strait). In June he entered the great inland sea named after him, Hudson Bay.

That winter, the *Discovery* was trapped in the ice. By the spring there was considerable desperation, with some of the crew accusing Hudson of keeping too much of the food for himself, his twelve-year-old son and a couple of officers. As the ice melted, Hudson, his son and his seven officers were put overboard in an open boat. They were never seen again. Henry Hudson's name lived on in the seaways he charted and in one of the great North American trading companies, the Hudson's Bay Company, which was still trading in one form or another four centuries on.

Hudson was employed by the Dutch East India Company and the Dutch, as well as the French and British, were very much in evidence as fishermen off the Newfoundland Banks. They were also expanding their fur trade. Dutch colonialism was as instinctive as any nation's and we might remember that the celebrated base of Dutch exploration forty years on was the colony of New Netherlands and its capital New Amsterdam; later, New York State and New York City. This concentration for fur, fish and navigable rivers in the north-east did not distract the British from wider interests. The fact, for example, that tobacco was to be grown in Virginia, was largely due to the success the English had with growing tobacco in Guiana (later Guyana). In other words, there was never a moment when the British confined themselves to one region and once they controlled the sea lanes, following the Battle of Trafalgar in 1805, the British economic curiosity literally knew few bounds.

The British had tried to settle Guiana on a number of occasions, never really successfully. Sir Walter Ralegh was an enthusiast and passed on his ideas to Robert Harcourt. It was Harcourt who with a small force planted Guyana between the Amazon and Orinoco rivers in King James's name in 1609–10, although the expedition was sponsored by Henry, Prince of Wales (1594–1612). The Dutch were already there and Harcourt appears to have attempted to follow their example of setting up small trading posts to do business with South American Indians. But he was never properly funded, in spite of his patron, and, although he used the Virginia colony as an example for administration and had the backing of the King, he could not interest enough investors.

Ralegh could not lead the expedition because he was still in the Tower. That Harcourt had the royal patronage of Prince Henry was almost certainly to do with Henry's total admiration for Ralegh. Henry was almost obsessed with Ralegh's stories of glorious Elizabethan conquests. After all, Ralegh was the last person who was directly associated with the Tudor heroes, including Drake and Sir Philip Sidney. He had been a close friend of the poet, Edmund Spenser. He had been to the mysterious corners of the new colonies. Intriguingly, it has never been certain that King James knew of his son's virtual infatuation, or if he was aware that Harcourt had been inspired by his friend Ralegh; if the King had known the Ralegh–Harcourt connection, it seems less than likely that he would have signed a warrant for the expedition in his name. No expedition, or so it seemed, could escape Ralegh's shadow. When Harcourt landed on the bank of the Waipoco River in May 1609, the local chief claimed Ralegh as a friend. Harcourt had to spend considerable time avoiding telling Ralegh's Central American friends that the great man was in prison for treason. There were even rumours that a second expedition was to be sent, with Ralegh in command. King James was not amused.

In spite of using Virginia as an example for so many ventures, a lot of the exploration seems to have been piecemeal. It is true there was enormous competition between the five European states of exploration, Great Britain (as James I liked to call his kingdom), Spain, Portugal, the Netherlands and the longest lasting of Britain's competitors, France. It was as if the new adventurers were uncertain of what it was they were trying to do. The need to colonize was first and foremost based upon the commercial opportunities. There was also the instinct to stake out territorial claims for strategic purposes and before other countries did so. Thirdly, each country understood perfectly that it was not self-sufficient and therefore national economies needed the resources a colony might bring and, as important, the markets they would provide.

The adventurers, opportunists and active investors had seized opportunities rather than becoming involved in long-term low-equity projects, but there were some obvious examples where settlement and sustained trade in the colonies might be profitable: for example, whaling, and there was also walrus hunting in the Davis Strait. Fishermen also proved to be natural long-term colonizers. It seemed usual enough that the fishermen off the Newfoundland Banks would want to keep the grounds and the small landing harbours for themselves. Their form of colonialism had nothing to do with a greater vision of imperial Britain. Instead it was a reflection of the colonial purpose of economic expansion. The people who owned the boats, and therefore the fishermen, quite liked the idea of colonizing the shores and keeping foreign fishermen away from the grounds, literally colonizing the fishing banks. On the other hand, it made some seafaring sense for the boats to sail from England on an annual or seasonal basis. This was partly due to the weather, shoal migration and spawning. On deeper examination, here was an illustration of the limitations of industry. To set up exclusive rights and to maintain some colonial rule over them in the Newfoundland ports would stretch the resources of the fishing managers and their funds. If they put too much effort into establishing themselves in Newfoundland then they could end up having less control over the management of the returning catches and the supply services and distribution in English ports. They could be edged out of the English harbours and end up as not much more than distant traders. This debate began at the beginning of the seventeenth century as the fishing industry expanded, along with the earliest perceptions of what an empire might do economically for its investors, not for Britain. That debate was still under way in the second half of the nineteenth century.

James I's administrators saw the Newfoundland fishing industry as a vital economic asset. More than that, the admirals saw in the 9,000 or so British fishermen a perfect recruiting ground for the navy. These fishermen were expected to supply more than 60 per cent of the ships' companies in the Royal Navy. So we have the focus of the so-called government of Britain emphasizing the economic as well as the strategic value of Newfoundland as a money-making exercise, as well as a proving ground for the navy. Even though the war with Spain was over, officially at least, by 1604 there was no doubt that the navy still needed men and Britain, which had adjusted to James I's perception that he ruled at God's command, now was getting towards the idea that it was also God's will that the British should rule the waves. This was to be a recurring theme into the twentieth century, not that Britain did rule the waves, but that it was divine judgement that they should. Thus, the expansion of the Empire so much relied on what naval doctrine later came to call the protection of the sea lanes.

To achieve the objective of this, in 1610 it was decided to build on the original claim of territory by Humphrey Gilbert in the sixteenth century with a new charter, sponsored by Sir Francis Bacon.[12] It was entitled 'The Treasurer and Company of Adventurers and Planters of the City of London and Bristol for the Colony or Plantation of Newfoundland'.

Bacon was one of the most exciting and excitable characters of the early seventeenth-century reign of James I. He was a scholar, scientist, essayist, administrator and almost anything else that would curry favour and advance his ambitions. If this makes his character a difficult one to admire then so be it. However, his breadth of examination, thinking and achievement was enormous. He understood the distinctions of patronage and the advantages to be gained from them. Not surprisingly, he expressed delight in almost any opinion of the King. He played to James's gallery and championed Church reform (a cause dear to James's heart), the bringing together of the interests of the monarch and Parliament (another cause dear to James's heart) and, most shrewdly, the Union of Scotland and England (the cause *most* dear to James's heart).

In the first year of his reign, 1603, James included Bacon in the list of 300 knights bachelor he dubbed and made him commissioner for the Union of England and Scotland. Bacon had a reputation among some of being a flatterer, especially within earshot of the monarch. Yet his brilliance might have been the only medal he needed. (Bacon's academic writings, particularly the *Advancement of Learning*, and his various theses on common law and usages should not be overlooked when trying to understand how England worked during the reign of James I.) His interest in the colonies went further than constitutional and legal lengths. His scientific curiosity led him to identify one of the problems for settlers and traders: how was meat to be kept other than salting? This experiment was his undoing. Bacon believed it would be possible to refrigerate meat. His rigorous belief that theoretical science was valueless without practical experiment led him in 1626 to take a hen and stuff it with snow to see what would happen if the flesh temperature was lowered.

---

12   Baron Verulam of Verulam, later, Viscount St Albans (1561–1626). He was nephew of William Cecil, Lord Burghley, and although he turned against him enjoyed the patronage of the Earl of Essex.

He kept on doing it. Unfortunately he discovered one of the by-products of refrigeration. During this experiment with fowls and buckets of snow, Bacon caught a cold and died.

This, then, was a man of enormous imagination and political significance in the governance of England and it was he who became the main sponsor and champion in government circles of the plantation and colony of Newfoundland. What made the Newfoundland Company so different was that although it used the experiences in Virginia as a colonial example for laws, commercial and social order, it unusually allowed one group carte blanche. The fishermen were free to go about their business as they would. In the rest of the world, the four nation peoples of the British Isles were also at sea, spreading a global business that would prove far more profitable than the banks fisheries.

The England to which James I came, in 1603, was a land of about four million people. The combined population of Scotland, Ireland and Wales was probably about half that. The birthrate might have been greater but for crude contraception, simple celibacy and a trend towards later marriages and therefore fewer child-bearing years. But in spite of this social change, the population survival rate in the first half of the seventeenth century was greater than the previous 100 years. The impact of disease and starvation lessened, and the increased population demanded growth in agricultural production, but that never really kept up with consumption, with the result that food prices rose at almost double the rate of wages. More people now bought their food than grew it, and therefore more of their income went on basic needs than before. The result was a decline in living standards. There was also greater pressure on government to look after its people. Yet government was not always able, or competent, to do so. Such new ideas meant raising funds. And it wasn't a good time for that.

James I's confrontation with Parliament was postponed until the winter of 1604 because of a plague. But when James I's first Parliament met it went on until the end of 1610, more than six years. After that, it didn't meet again for three years. James often reminded his Parliament that it had been established after kings and that he didn't depend on its members for his authority. However, Parliament provided James's only way to gain the funds he needed. This in turn gave its members the chance to tackle him on greater subjects, and that is what annoyed him, especially as he wasn't as good as Elizabeth had been at using his ministers to manipulate the political system.

At the heart of Parliament's role were the two functions: law-making and sorting grievances. The two could go together and, to give an idea of the influence of Parliament, more than half the laws came not from the King's ministers, but from the members. Still, the King's main interests were the ways in which he could get money out of Parliament.

In that first gathering there were 467 Members in the House of Commons. Many of them were inexperienced and had no under-standing of what they were trying to do, other than to do it as noisily as possible. The King described one session as a gathering without any control that 'voted without order, nothing being heard but cries, shouts, and confusion'. And, for good measure, he noted that the real problem was the gaggle of lawyers who tried to dominate every-thing. He wanted rid of them. It was a popular view. Just a few years before James came to the throne, Shakespeare wrote: 'The first thing we do, let's kill all the lawyers.'

But James I had greater problems than the problem of lawyers. One of the legacies of the Elizabethan reign was the Roman Catholic conundrum. When James became King there were, or so it is thought, about 40,000 Catholics in England. He told his closest adviser, Robert Cecil, that he would 'never allow in my conscience that the blood of any man shall be shed for diversity of opinions of religion'. Which is not quite what he meant.

James I accepted that some people were Catholics, and that as long as they didn't grow in numbers and cause trouble, they should remain so. But their priests, especially the Jesuits, he called 'firebrands of sedition' and, in February 1604, he ordered them out of England. He had a similar attitude towards the Puritans. The general people were fine; it was the zealots among them whom he refused to tolerate.

This, on the face of it, was a more relaxed attitude to the different religious persuasions in England, and Catholics started to be more public about their beliefs. The Archbishop of York, Matthew Hutton, had no doubts of the dangers of this when he told Cecil that the Catholics (Papists he called them), 'have grown mightily in number, courage, and influence. 'Tis high time to look unto them.' Cecil took note and spoke to the King, and a year later James claimed that he disliked Catholics so much that he'd rather be childless than risk his son becoming one. The differences might have been left at that, and the Catholics would have been safe, had it not been for a group of the very zealots James feared.

The Gunpowder Plot of 1605, a failed attempt to assassinate the King at the State Opening of Parliament, confirmed everything the Catholics' harshest critics had believed about them. By the next year, Parliament, apparently having settled the matter of gouty members, banned Catholics from living anywhere near London, from holding public or official office, and allowed James to take over two-thirds of the lands owned by Catholics. Most important of all, Catholics were to swear an oath of allegiance to the crown.

There was one part of this oath that had been drafted by James himself. The Powder Traitors, as they were called, had to publicly swear that neither the Pope, nor his agents, had any right to try to depose the King or invade his territories. But what happened if the Pope, in his supreme position, gave Catholics absolution from this declaration? James, or his advisers, had thought of that and added an almost impossible provision, impossible if you happened to be a Catholic. James believed, or said he believed, that as the earth hadn't a single monarch, then even though he was willing to accept that the Pope was the Prince of Bishops, Princeps Episcoporum, he was no more than that. Rome was not the holder of the only truth.

As early as January 1604 the Protestants, led by Bishop Bancroft, and the Puritans met the King at a special conference at Hampton Court. James had been brought up by Calvinists, and he disliked them. Nevertheless, the Puritans saw what they thought was an opportunity to persuade the King of the merits of their case.

The Puritans consisted of the so-called 'low church', clergy who wanted to be rid of the more ceremonial features of Rome. Apart from vestments, they objected also to genuflexion, to making the sign of the cross over a child at its baptism, to confirmation and even to wedding rings. They also wanted competent priests who were learned and who lived in the parishes, instead of the long-time practice of giving livings to men who never went near the parish, yet collected a stipend and often an income from glebe (lands that formed part of a clergyman's benefice).

The bishops, fearful that the Puritan leaders would have their way with the new King, came up with a plan to load the forthcoming conference with moderate Puritan speakers rather than zealots. The result was a few changes with which the bishops could agree and certain disappointments for the Puritan leaders but, most of all, a declaration that brought non-conformist ministers into some sort of line. There were few moments of accord in that conference; but the leader of the Puritan delegation, the president of Corpus Christi, Oxford, Dr John Reynolds, came up with a suggestion that particularly gained the King's attention and whose results have had a lasting effect. Reynolds had wanted four points of knowledge. Church doctrine should be preserved in a pure form according to what the Puritans saw as God's word. Ministers, or pastors, should be worthwhile characters and learned and should replace in each and every parish many of the duffers of the Established Church. He wanted also a better administration of the Church. He was not alone in this matter and the bishops shifted uneasily and at times pompously. His final point was that the *Book of Common Prayer* should be more pious. In fact, the Puritan notion was that it had very little to do with the Bible and should therefore be either rewritten or tossed out.

The bishops thought the Puritan demands, which of course they were not hearing for the first time, to be worth little consideration. James had little patience with Reynolds' intervention. James had grown up with dissent all about him. He saw his task as the new monarch of both countries as maintaining stability and thus being able to rule with fewer difficulties. He knew very well that any suggestion that he approved of the rewriting of the *Book of Common Prayer* would have the opposite effect. Religious infighting had no history of stability as an outcome. A more imaginative project was the wording of the Bible itself. The matter of the Geneva Bible was not on the conference agenda. There is little evidence to suggest that when James called the conference in October 1603 he intended to do much about that Bible. However, the Puritans, just as the Scottish Protestants had, regarded the Geneva Bible as the definitive translation. Yet he, James, did not think much of it and was not inclined to the Puritan view that it should become the King James Version of the Bible; in other words, authorized. Authorization would have meant that the Geneva Bible would be the official work and therefore held in every church. So how was he to at least partly cheer up the Puritans who had gone to the conference at Hampton Court with so many hopes and looked like going away with very little? The bishops would sit smugly knowing that it had gone their way and that James had protected their prayer book. So what could be done for the Puritans? There had to be some backstairs negotiations.

The Bishop of Durham, Toby Matthew, who had preached to James's delight in his cathedral when the new monarch first set foot in England, recorded that the Puritans wanted 'one only translation of the bible'. This single work would be considered authentic and therefore the only one at the lecterns. Moreover, everyone knew that a Roman Catholic version of the New Testament, and soon the Bible, was being prepared by priests at Douai and Rheims. No matter the schisms within the Protestant Church in England there was one matter that could bring them all together. Not a single one at the conference could bear the thought of any Roman Catholic influence. Puritan and established Churchmen could unite against the Catholics. How much better to have a new translation in place? Thus it was not the King, nor the bishops, but John Reynolds who publicly proposed a new translation of the Bible. The politicking of Hampton Court was successful. James declared that the scholars of Oxford and Cambridge should begin work on a translation that would be 'made of the whole Bible, as consonant as can be to the original Hebrew and Greek and this to be set out and printed without any marginal notes and only to be used in all churches of England in time of Divine service'.

The Puritans had not really got what they wanted. Equally, the Established Church was not convinced that the King was wholly with them and not inclined to the Puritans. James, who died in 1625, is not remembered for much in English history. His legacy is not in high diplomacy but the King James Version of the Bible is still read in the twenty-first century.

CHAPTER TWENTY-TWO
1625–39

In 1625 Charles I came to the throne at the age of twenty-five. His father was James I, his mother, Anne of Denmark. The court in which he was brought up was a place of crudeness, immorality and harsh debate. Charles, apparently, was shy and artistic, and he stammered.

Towards the end of his father's life, Charles effectively co-ruled with George Villiers, the Duke of Buckingham. It was Buckingham who arranged the entrance of Charles into the French royal family with his marriage to Henrietta Maria. Charles and his wife were happy. They had seven children, including the future Charles II and James II. Maryland in America was named after Queen Henrietta Maria. And when he became King, Charles was welcomed by the people and by Parliament. But not for long. The confrontation that was to come was not simply a case of a new King not understanding what Parliament wanted and how much it might be given. Charles was not a stranger to Parliament. James I had sent his son to the Lords in 1621 as part of his education. The Prince was there to learn the ways of the House so that when he became King, he would understand its workings and its importance, and protect it.

And certainly, when he did become King, Parliament was generous towards him. But in one particular matter, it was ungenerous. Parliament wanted rid of George Villiers, Duke of Buckingham, the King's closest adviser. Perhaps most frustrating for Buckingham's critics – and they stretched across every corridor, every courtyard and every bench of the agitated Parliament – was Charles's friendship with Buckingham and his belief that his friend had the good of the State at heart. Parliament blocked the supply of money to the King until he agreed to get rid of Buckingham. Charles regarded this as an affront – which it probably was – and dissolved Parliament, but not before Parliament had impeached Buckingham. Within twelve months of being on the throne, Charles had moved from being a liked and informed member of the Lords to being a King on a terrible collision course with that same institution. The King blamed what he called the 'violent and ill-advised passions of a few members of the House'. Sir Dudley Carleton, Secretary of State and Member of the Commons, said that in other countries monarchs had started to get rid of their elected bodies when they saw 'the turbulent spirits of their Parliaments'. The implication was clear: for the King to support Parliament then Parliament had to be worthwhile for the King. If it wasn't, then the King would look elsewhere for counsel.

But first he had to look elsewhere for money. He and his Council tried to insist on what was called 'a Force Loan' – a tax without Parliament's approval. Charles went to the law for approval but the judges turned him down and many very senior people in the land refused to pay this illegal tax. He had to summon Parliament and said he would make compromises as long as Buckingham's impeachment was dropped. He got a promise of some money, enough to carry on his war with Spain (as part of the Thirty Years War), but not unless he agreed to certain rights that Parliament knew he was trampling. Freemen were not be arrested unless they had been accused of law-breaking. The writ of habeas corpus was sacrosanct. If, after arrest, no evidence was offered against a freeman, then he should be set free or bailed. No freeman's property could be taxed without Parliament's approval. Charles believed that the way Parliament had behaved, and the way he had responded, would win him the affection of the people. But Sir Edward Coke, the man who had been responsible for the prosecutions of Elizabeth's one-time favourites, Essex and then Ralegh, and who had prosecuted the Gunpowder Plotters, urged the House to frame the Petition of Right. The King knew exactly what this meant.

This 1628 Petition threatened the Royal Prerogative. It emphasized the common freedoms of the people and started by citing the law from Edward I's time by which no tallage or aid shall be laid or levied by the King without the consent of magnates and freemen. Nor did the Petition miss a point of great vexation in seventeenth-century England. The militia and sailors were often billeted on civilians. Civilians did not like this. Also, there were times when soldiers, usually a motley lot, many of them mercenaries, were guilty of the cruellest misdemeanours, but escaped the law because they claimed the protection of martial law. Charles could see no way ahead in this debate and instead dismissed the Houses and, with Buckingham, planned an expedition to La Rochelle where Protestant Huguenots were besieged. At least that was the plan. But Buckingham was assassinated by one of his own men before his ship ever left Portsmouth harbour.

In 1640 Charles, under enormous pressure, summoned another Parliament. It sat for twenty years and so it is little surprise that it became known as the Long Parliament. He called the Parliament to order after his defeat in the Bishops' War (1639–40), which came about because Charles insisted that the Scots adopt the Anglican Church. The main influence on Charles was William Laud (1573–1645) who had been Archbishop of Canterbury since 1633. Perhaps Charles should have listened to James I, who had a sceptical opinion of clergymen. He was a restless spirit and, said James, one who 'cannot see when matters are well, but loves to bring things to a pitch of reformation floating in his brain'. It was Laud's insistence that the Scots use the English *Book of Common Prayer* that became the first of three steps to war with the bishops. The Scots took one look at it, and believed it to be the work of the Pope. The second mistake was that Charles planned to confiscate Scottish Church lands taken by Scottish nobles since the Reformation. The result was predictable: the nobility turned against him. Charles probably had no idea that what had started out as a simple idea of Laud's would end in open revolt, but the leaders of the revolt either believed, or found it convenient to believe, that what was happening was an attempt to impose Popery on Scotland. And the third mistake, with Parliament still not yet called, was made by the Marquess of Hamilton who was sent to Scotland by Charles to act as conciliator. He demanded, in 1638, that the General Assembly of Scotland, which had set itself against the King's order, should be dissolved. Hamilton was determined to use force, when none was necessary, in order to get his way. But force had to be paid for and only Parliament could raise that sort of money. If Charles was going to fight the Scots, he needed money for an army (the monarchy didn't have an army of its own) so he also needed official backing from the people. And there was only one place to acquire official backing: Parliament. However, the Scots were not about to wait to see what Charles would or wouldn't do.

The supporters of the Assembly were known as Covenanters, and in the powerful lowlands there was a strong Covenanters' army and, more important than that, it had been reinforced by reserves of war-hardened warriors from Scottish soldiers fighting for the Protestant cause in Germany. The inevitable outcome was a war of sorts in which Scotland saw how strong it was and capitalized on its alliance with France. Good sense did not prevail.

Sir Thomas Wentworth (1593–1641), the soon-to-be-created first Earl of Strafford, advised the King that war with Scotland was the way forward. Sir Thomas was an autocrat, quite ruthless, close to Archbishop Laud and, in 1632, as Lord Deputy of Ireland, had sought to make Ireland English in all its forms. More important to Charles, Wentworth had an Irish army of 8,000 men.

And so, after nearly eleven years of believing he could do without Parliament, Charles was forced to issue writs for elections to a new session: he needed money to raise and pay for troops. And his chances of avoiding confrontation with Parliament were not helped by his loving, devoted but Catholic Queen.

Henrietta Maria's closest adviser was, ironically, a Scotsman called George Con. He had been sent by the Pope to act as Papal Legate to the Queen's court. Henrietta Maria and Con made it clear they believed that Catholics were the natural supporters of the King. They even tried to raise Catholic troops from the Spanish enclaves of the Netherlands. The Catholic Earl of Nithsdale raised Scottish Roman Catholics for the King and, in Ireland, the Earl of Antrim said he too would raise an army. Many believed that Charles was too influenced by Rome, and that was his greatest single weakness.

Whatever the truth, all the help promised by Scottish Catholics and Irish peers did not save Charles. The Scots crossed the border. They were in possession of Northumberland and of Durham. And their great allies, the Parliamentary and Puritan party, watched and encouraged them from London. The King, whether he liked it or not, was being led towards the most historically important Parliament ever faced by an English monarch. And as England, in 1640, prepared for the Long Parliament, the public axeman numbered the days of Wentworth, and then of Archbishop Laud.

CHAPTER TWENTY-THREE
1640–49

Until King Charles I was forced to call the Parliament of 1640, he had governed England without Parliament for eleven years and he was constitutionally within his rights. Charles ruled through his King's Council, as a sort of Cabinet, and the period became known as the Personal Rule. But, as discussed, Parliament had to be assembled because Charles needed money to put down the Scottish Rebellion. The first Parliament of 1640 became known as the Short Parliament. It lasted for three weeks in April. But under the leadership of a Puritan called John Pym (c.1584–1643), who had encouraged the Scots in their war, Parliament wanted to discuss eleven years of grievances before giving Charles his money. And then John Pym pressed for a petition to the Lords to rid England of the 'most decrepit age of Popery'. He attacked the King's demands for money. And Charles, in frustration, or anger, or both, and against Strafford's advice, dissolved Parliament. But by November 1640, because he was defeated in the second Bishops' War, Charles was forced to summon Parliament (The Long Parliament). It was the fifth Parliament of Charles's reign, and his last. It was also the last from some of his closest friends.

The new Parliament contained formidable political figures and not time-servers. The two most immediately prominent were Pym and John Hampden (1594–1643). Pym, a Puritan, was first noticed because he had been part of the impeachment of Buckingham in 1626. By the Long Parliament, he had become a clever fixer and unifier when others might have given up the purpose of the opposition to the King. The opposition were essentially dividing into two camps: those trying to avoid civil war and those pleading the cause of republicanism. Hampden was less compromising. He would not tolerate what he saw as the dictatorial power assumed by the King.

The pair of them had a primary target before aiming at the King himself. The man to bring before the House was Strafford, the person with the most devastating influence on the King.

Thomas Wentworth, the First Earl of Strafford, had been an opponent of the King inasmuch he could not accept his general policies. But Charles cared for his advice and, among other offices, gave him the lord deputyship of Ireland in 1632 where he earned a reputation as an uncompromising proponent of an Ireland wholly ruled by England in the English manner and without any trace of Irish authority, nor even identity. When the Bishops' Wars began in Scotland in 1639, Charles brought back Wentworth from Ireland to advise him how to deal with the rebellion. Wentworth's advice, accepted by Charles and Laud, was that the only language understood by the Scots was the shrieks of anguish from their fellows once the bloodiest swords and guns of the English slashed and struck their terror. Moreover, Wentworth had his Irish army – traditionally well trained in bloody conflict. For his troubles, he was given an earldom, hence Strafford. But by then, 1640, Parliament could call Strafford and others to account. It was Pym who masterminded the impeachment of Strafford. Strafford was charged with treason. But treason is a crime against the Crown, and he had been working on behalf of Charles. Pym simply produced an idea of constructive treason, which he described as 'against the being of the law' as opposed to the rule of the law.

Parliament nearly accepted the Pym version, but many peers felt uneasy that they were being asked to commit one of their number for a crime which was not recognized as a crime. And there were a few at least who saw that what was happening to Strafford could easily happen to them. The speech which Strafford gave in his defence touched the very hearts of the doubters. It was the speech of a man fighting for his life, who but days earlier had decided the lives of others.

> My lords, the shedding of my blood may make a way for the tracing of yours. If every word, intention, circumstance of yours be alleged as treasonable, not because of statute, but a consequence, a construction, heaved up in a high rhetorical strain . . . I leave it to your lordships' consideration to foresee what may be the issue of so dangerous, so recent precedencies. These gentlemen [Pym *et al.*] tell

me they speak in defence of the Commonweal against their arbitrary treason; for if this latitude is admitted, what prejudice shall follow to the King, to the country, if you and your posterity be disabled by the same from the greatest affairs of the Kingdom.

There may have been some in the Lords moved by Strafford's plea, but not in the Commons. Seeing the difficulty before them, the Commons continued with an Act of Attainder. In simple terms, this meant that any allegation could be declared without the need for a formal trial. By this time, many Members had gone home – perhaps because they wanted no part in what was happening. The Act was passed and Charles – with enormous misgivings – gave his royal assent. Strafford was executed, the first of Charles's ministers to fall victim to Parliament's – and Pym's – revenge. Laud was impeached in 1640, but then inconveniently found not guilty by the Lords, which meant another Bill of Attainder in the Commons. He was eventually executed. The Lord Keeper and the Secretary of State both escaped death by fleeing to the Continent.

The Commons then passed a Bill banning bishops from Parliament. The Lords resented this, not so much for the loss of bishops, but more because the House of Commons was telling them what to do. The Lords threw out the Bill. Then Parliament, after much discussion, presented a Bill which guaranteed that there couldn't be more than a three-year gap between Parliaments. This second of three Triennial Acts of that time was a direct challenge to the King who considered that he alone decided when Parliament should be called.

Strafford's execution triggered an action in Ireland that perhaps the Parliamentarians had not quite anticipated. He had been a harsh ruler of Ireland. Now, those left in command were helpless to contain the uprising of Irish people that followed. Landowners were killed. Conflicting interests ended with much spilled blood. The King's Lord Justices retaliated with a vengeance that not even Strafford would have employed. To describe it as mass slaughter, certainly of many Irish males from troubled places, would be an exaggeration, but that was how it seemed at the time to the Irish. The Puritans warned that slaughter also would be the way in England if the Catholic persuasion were to overcome the established Church. From the north came a joining of clans to invade England (although this is something of an over-simplification). From the King came demands for funds to fight the invaders. England was a country in certain turmoil. Thus, we should discard the illusion that the Civil War started simply because Parliament argued with the King. The more complicated picture is an amalgamation of the Scots invading England, to be defended by a penniless monarch; Parliament having to be called to get that money; Parliament, led by Pym, seeing an opportunity to put right eleven years of dissatisfaction; the destruction of the King's inner cabinet by the zealous Pym (who, incidentally was mixed up in some shady commercial deals, so was hardly the Puritan goody some pretended him to be); and then the Irish rebellion.

The story is further complicated because by the autumn of 1641, Pym's support was not as strong as it had been at the start of the Parliament. And the King's supporters were gathering their strength. A document called the Grand Remonstrance, which told the King where Parliament stood, and where the Parliamentarians thought he should stand, was put to the vote. Pym and his colleagues thought that would sort the Parliamentarians from the Royalists. On 22 November 1641, the Grand Remonstrance was put to the vote. The debate was furious. As one Member remarked, 'We had like to have sheathed our swords in each other's bowels.' In the Commons, the Member for Cambridge, Oliver Cromwell, the future Lord Protector of England, awaited the outcome. It is said that he told a friend that if Parliament lost the vote, then he would leave England forever. The Parliamentarians won, but only just. They secured 159 votes; the Royalists 148. The King's supporters had stood by him and a majority of eleven was not sufficiently convincing for the Parliamentarians.

Charles offered Pym the job of Chancellor of the Exchequer. Pym turned it down. Charles made opposition Lords members of his Privy Council. Pym's people accused them of becoming closet Royalists. And so by the end of 1641, the Parliamentarians – the Pymites – and the Royalists were quietly getting their forces together. And then the King lost his nerve. Taunted and goaded by Queen Henrietta, he decided to prosecute five of his principal opponents – including Pym and Hampden – for treason. It was 4 January 1642. The King, and 300 to 400 swordsmen, later known as the Cavaliers, went down to the House of Commons to demand the surrender of the five. But Pym and his colleagues had been warned, and they were not in the Commons.

A crowd that included guild and trade apprentices then gathered outside Charles's palace in London. This crowd had been roused and there is no evidence that it was a spontaneous gathering. It was the pudding-basin haircuts of the apprentices that later gave the Parliamentary forces their name: the Roundheads. Whatever the circumstances, the protest was enough to scare the King and his court to leave London for the safer environs at Hampton Court. During the early months of 1642 Charles still thought he could agree terms of his constitutional role but on one essential point Crown and Commons were wide apart: Parliament wanted the King to surrender his sovereignty over Church and State. Charles could never agree to that. In late August 1642, the King raised his royal standard in Nottingham. This was the formal declaration of war.

Oxford University melted down its gold and silver to pay for the King's war effort. The Queen sold many of the crown jewels and escaped to the Low Countries where she recruited for Charles. By the end of the autumn, Charles had an army of more than 12,000 foot soldiers and 4,000 cavalry. The Roundheads had more. The popular view is that Cromwell was to the fore in starting the war. He was not. In autumn 1642, Oliver Cromwell was not the leader of the Parliamentary Army. He was a Fens colonel organizing the cavalry of the Army of the Eastern Association commanded by the second Earl of Manchester. Only later did Cromwell become supreme commander. Equally, his family were hardly obscure. He was distantly related to the famous Thomas Cromwell, Henry VIII's chief minister: his great-grandfather was a nephew of Thomas Cromwell.

Oliver Cromwell was born in Huntingdon on 25 April 1599 – that put him about eighteen months older than the King. His parents were local gentry who had done quite well when monastery lands had been taken from the Church. He spent a year at Sidney Sussex College, Cambridge, which was a Puritan college. He probably only left because his father died. Oliver had been the Member of Parliament (MP) for Cambridge in Charles's third Parliament, followed by both the Short and the Long Parliaments. He supported John Pym and he condemned Strafford and Laud. He spoke vigorously, sometimes cruelly, against the suppression of the rights of the common man. He appeared against Anglicans and (of course) Catholics. But it's difficult to label Cromwell simply as a Puritan because of his own contradictions. As he said, 'I can tell you what I would not have, though I cannot, what I would.' What is clear is that once he decided that he was doing 'God's work' then he did so tirelessly and single-mindedly. And perhaps that was one of the secrets of his military success. He believed that a soldier who prayed best fought best.

At the outset the Parliamentary rebellion claimed to fight for the King, and their commanders had instructions to rescue the King from his malicious advisers and counsellors. But by the autumn, the Parliamentary forces, instructed by German officers, were full of the passion of their cause.

The King's advantages and support was mainly in the north and West Country. The Parliamentarians were in London and the south and eastern counties. This meant the Parliamentarians had the King's capital and so Charles had to take it back. They clashed at Edgehill on 23 October 1642: Charles and his nephews Prince Rupert and Prince Maurice on one side, and Robert Devereux, the Earl of Essex and son of his namesake, Elizabeth I's favourite, on the other. This is often described as the first major battle of the Civil War but it ended, at best, indecisively, even though both sides claimed victory. The Parliamentarians, perhaps sensing the enormity of what was happening, offered terms. Charles, maybe over-confident after the battle, rejected any idea of peace. He wanted more than his capital back. He wanted his country. On he marched and met Parliamentarians again, this time at Turnham Green on the outskirts of London. He had to retreat and withdrew as far as Oxford which became the Royalist headquarters.

There were three armies for the King: Charles's own command at Oxford; the Duke of Newcastle's command in Yorkshire; and in the south-west, that of Ralph Hopton (1596–1652), a Puritan by instinct and birth but with a sense that Parliament should not control the militia. Then there were the Scots. They were against the King, which is why Charles – having to spread his resources – was defeated at Marston Moor near York in July 1644. The anti-Royalists at Marston had three commanders: the Scottish Earl of Leven (1582–1661); Sir Thomas Fairfax (1612–71); and Edward Montagu, the Earl of Manchester (1602–71). Charles's army was led by Prince Rupert. None of the commanders was very good. Prince Rupert was the lesser and 4,000 or so of his men were killed. The King no longer held the north of England and he had little chance of reaching and taking London.

By June 1645 Fairfax and Cromwell had under their command the recently formed New Model Army. This superior force, along with more thoughtful tactics and organization, led to yet another defeat for the King, this time at Naseby. Worse was to come for Charles. Oxford, effectively his capital, fell in June 1646. By then the Scots had already taken Charles's personal surrender at Newark. Any thoughts he had that he was safe in Scottish hands were dispelled when they handed him to the Parliamentarians in January 1647.

Now was the time, if ever there were to be one, for the two sides to reach a truce and more. That could not take place and Charles escaped across the Solent to the Isle of Wight and once again hoped to find a solution with the Scots. He did, in December 1647 get Scottish promises of support. They in turn were promised that he would bring Presbyterianism to England. With hope, the Royalists rose again and this became a sort of second Civil War. But it was not much of one. Cromwell and Fairfax were truly in command. That year, 1648, the Scots invaded England in support of the Stuart King, but they were routed at Preston. Charles was captured and brought before a High Court that called 'Charles Stuart, that man of blood, to account for the blood he had shed and mischief he had done to his utmost against the Lord's cause and the people in these poor nations'. Charles refused to recognize the court and would not speak in his own defence. It would have made little difference. His death warrant was already written and was simply waiting for its signature.

It was snowing on 30 January 1649 when Charles Stuart was beheaded in front of the Banqueting House in London that his father, James I, had commissioned Inigo Jones to build.

CHAPTER TWENTY-FOUR
1649–60

England became a Republic in January, 1649. The monarchy, the House of Lords and the Anglican Church were abolished. The Great Seal of England was thrown aside and a new one minted: on one face it had a map of England, on the other, the House of Commons. Scotland was integrated, Ireland savaged. Adultery became punishable by death. War was declared on the Dutch. The Sergeant at Arms, Edward Denby, with his trumpeters and outriders, went about London announcing that whosoever shall proclaim a new King in this nation of England shall be a traitor and suffer death.

Parliament had taken the legal murder of the King (for that's what some believed it to have been) most seriously, and understood perfectly that its authority would have to be enforced by the sternest of means. Cromwell's name had been on the King's death warrant but at this stage in 1649 he was not the all-powerful leader usually depicted. The first task was to decide who should govern England. It would be a Council of State of forty-one men of highest authority including, sometimes reluctantly, lawyers. If the Republicans thought they had to contend only with a loyalist rump, that was to ignore a simple fact of moving from one system to another: those who might have quietly agitated for rights under the old system often seize the moment of change to campaign even more for their rights, lest they be overlooked. Thus, the Council knew all about the Levellers.

John Lilburne (1614–57), the leader of the Levellers, had been jailed in 1638 for smuggling Puritan pamphlets into England. When he was released, he naturally enough fought on the side of the Parliamentarians. But he never settled at that. He was a rebel and so was sent back to prison, then exile. The Levellers were in some ways what the twentieth century would have called Socialists, Radicals or even Communists. As their name suggests, they wanted social justice to the extent that everyone should be at the same level in society. The next stage of that proposition was an elected Parliament. The views of the Levellers, as found in their *Agreement of the People* in 1647, would not be satisfied until the late nineteenth century. The Levellers should not be confused with the Diggers. This was a small, and short-lived, group of people who wanted to have an agriculture commune – a sort of kibbutz in England. The Diggers leader, Gerrard Winstanley (1609–60) was a true Christian 'communist', a seventeenth-century Marxist-Leninist as his *Law of Freedom in a Platform* published in 1652 and dedicated to Cromwell made clear. He opposed the idea of monarchy and landowners and wanted redistribution of wealth – and no wealthy. Cromwell had more urgent, and ruthless, matters on his mind. He may have set aside the Levellers, the Diggers and even a monarch, but the Irish Question was less easily answered.

Cromwell was determined that not only would he crush the Irish leaders in the military sense, but he would do it so bloodily that it would send shivers of submission through the consciousness of the remainder of the people. And Ireland wasn't united: there were factions and creeds, families for the Crown, families against it and families against each other.

The Protestant Royalists, led by the Marquess of Ormonde, were once a well-organized troop of perhaps 12,000 men, but when Cromwell arrived in Ireland, Ormonde was weak. Yet he still attempted to defend the towns of Wexford and Drogheda. After the battle in September 1649 Cromwell wrote to the President of the Council of State, John Bradshaw:

> It hath pleased God to bless our endeavours at Drogheda. After battle we stormed it. The enemies were about 3,000 strong in the town. We refused them quarter. I believe we put to the sword the whole number of the defendants. I do not think thirty of the whole number escaped with their lives. This hath been a marvellous great mercy. I do not believe that any officer escaped with his life, save only one lieutenant, who I hear, going to the enemy, said that he was the only man that escaped of all the garrison. The enemy upon this were filled with much terror. And truly I believe this bitterness

will save much effusion of blood, through the goodness of God. Dublin 16 September 1649.

Cromwell gave thanks to God for everything that had happened, according to his belief that a soldier who prayed fiercely, fought fiercely. Meanwhile, in Scotland the late King's eldest son had been proclaimed King of Great Britain, France and Ireland. One of the conditions of support for the Royalist cause was that the newly proclaimed King, Charles II, should support the Presbyterian cause. This was a terrible condition, especially as it tacitly condemned his mother, a devout Catholic, as an idolater. But the Scottish Commissioners, who demanded of the King more than he could give in his heart, were determined to succeed, and they did. And it was from this moment that Cromwell understood that once he was done with Ireland, he would have to fight on the Scottish borders.

Just twelve months after the massacre of Drogheda, Cromwell's forces left 3,000 Scots dead at the Battle of Dunbar. The remainder fled. The Scots rallied under Charles II's banner. At Scone they crowned him King, and followed him across the border. Cromwell let them. He watched their supply columns stretch, and he knew that the English Royalists would be of little use. In 1651, one year on from Dunbar and two years on from Drogheda, Cromwell defeated the Scots at Worcester. The King escaped and hid in a tree, and so spawned hundreds of public houses called the Royal Oak. Eventually he made his escape to Holland.

By now, Cromwell, the commander of the army but not yet of the country, saw the signs that the army's coming battle was with neither Royalist nor Irish opponents, but with Parliament itself. The army was no longer the servant militia of the great families and princes. It had, since Naseby, been a standing army, a national army. Cromwell understood the power it represented and the potential danger in its leaders.

From the moment the Rump Parliament (the group of Long Parliamentarians who kept their seats and announced that England was to be a Commonwealth) ordered the execution of Charles I, its actions, unwittingly and with hindsight, led to the Restoration of the monarchy. Instead of taking bold decisions, Parliament, in its incompetence, became reactionary. The law, local administration and financial management were largely unchanged, and the weaknesses in them were never overcome. And so the republic was run by the committee. Cromwell, the most powerful personality of the time, was seeking Parliament's revenge in Ireland, putting down the rebellion in Scotland and defeating the royalists at Worcester. It was the Rump Parliament that struggled ineffectively with the day-to-day conundrums of government.

Cromwell wanted a God-fearing reform of society. Parliament was incapable of delivering so Cromwell called together an assembly of 140 like-minded, supposedly saintly, souls who became known as Members of the Barebones Parliament, named after one of its number, a preacher called Praisegod Barbon. For five months they pontificated, sniped and sneered. They swept aside legislation and replaced it with little that was practical and even less that was popular, especially with the Church, property owners and the army. Eventually the army decided to get rid of the 'Saints'. It didn't work. The hard-head Republicans wanted to rip the constitution apart. But Cromwell fiercely protected the principle of the 1653 Instrument of Government – the only written constitution Britain ever had – and determined that the Republicans should go. The Instrument of Government was designed to establish a Protectorate and to create a balance between the army and Parliament. Cromwell was declared Lord Protector on 16 December 1653, but he found, having rid himself of the Republican zealots, that he still did not have the control he wanted so he dissolved Parliament.

A series of Royalist plots were attempted, including a popular one known as Penruddock's Rising. None was successful, but in 1655 Cromwell decided to split England and Wales into eleven districts, each to be run by a Major-General, a rank devised in the New Model Army in 1642. Almost without visible opposition, the Major-Generals policed, taxed and administered with a Puritan zeal that Cromwell respected. They raised taxes for the war against Spain and they raised the numbers in the Lords to nod through the Bills and money-raising legislature that Cromwell needed. Thus, by 1657 Cromwell had a clearly more agreeable, although not an entirely satisfactory, Parliament which produced an amended constitution called 'A Humble Petition and Advice'. This allowed Cromwell to name his successor and to choose his own council of rulers. (So much for the starting point of modern democracy.)

The Humble Petition and Advice also offered Cromwell the Crown, and there is some evidence that he liked the idea of becoming King so that he could continue what he saw as the Lord's work. The idea that an English Republic would wish to go back to monarchy should not be surprising. Monarchy was presumably dynastic, therefore with all the obvious historical difficulties in mind, the people did like the laws of succession and accession. Moreover, a monarch represented the people: in return for allegiance, the monarch would protect the people from its enemies – foreign invaders and government. This did not mean, as everyone was aware, that a king or queen would instigate benign (if not divine) rule. In these circumstances, should Cromwell be King, the twitch of regicide could easily be at his collar just as it had been for the previous incumbent. Cromwell, who had such distinct views on how society should behave, who could be ruthless (as the Irish had discovered at the massacre at Drogheda), who could bend and break the constitution when it suited, was incapable of taking that final step to the throne. For weeks and weeks, in conference after conference, the Lord Protector produced little more than page after page after page of speeches imperfectly punctuated with indecision, with references to the apostles, to the Psalms and always to God's will. But it was not until one Friday afternoon in May 1657 that Cromwell could bring himself to give Parliament his answer to their question: would he be King, or wouldn't he? Answer came in the usual rambling way Cromwell seemed incapable of avoiding: no. No, he would not accept the Crown. Behind his refusal was, as ever, the army, particularly the lower orders who did not like the regalia of monarchy. It is doubtful that Cromwell could have held the army's loyalty if he had accepted the Crown. Thanks to Cromwell, there was a well-trained army and it could turn on anyone and devour them; there was no institution in the land capable of stopping it from doing so.

But the important point here is not so much that Cromwell did or did not become King, but that a large and important group understood that kingship once more mattered to the survival of society. Cromwell understood it clearly. This offer of the Crown to Cromwell was, therefore, an admission that at some stage the monarchy would be restored. It was also recognition that Cromwell's weakness was partly based on the decision to execute Charles I. It may be an over-simplification, but Parliament, in its unsophisticated practice of politics and constitution, did not know how to exercise lasting power. Hence the irony: the real reason for offering Cromwell the Crown was to curb the very power that he had used to enforce his vision. He would protect the people for as long as the good Lord gave him the breath and strength to do so. Maybe, the Lord's attention wandered for, on 3 September1658, on the anniversaries of the terrible massacre at Drogheda, the Battle of Dunbar and the Battle of Worcester, the Lord Protector died.

The great experiment, the Commonwealth, the Republic, died with Cromwell; not officially or immediately, of course, but without Oliver Cromwell it ran out of steam. Cromwell's son, Richard, took over as Lord Protector, but within eighteen months Charles II was heading for the throne.

The momentous and revolutionary abolition of the monarchy in the middle of the seventeenth century failed because, in spite of the constitutional revolution, there was no structured party system. There was no machinery that could control jealousies or at least contain them beneath a recognized label. And where Oliver Cromwell had understood and coped with the jealousies of the army commanders, his son, Richard, could not and, indeed, fell victim to them. The army liked him and he was likeable, but he had no dictatorial powers, a fact that at first he did not understand. The irony was this: Cromwell needed Parliament just as monarchs had; even though Parliament was still imperfectly formed, it had enough personality to exercise what authority it had or could assume – against anyone. Remember, Parliament was not yet a permanent body. It was called when the Head of State either considered or was forced to consider that it had to be consulted. And although Cromwell, the Republic and Parliament are often lumped together, they were not one and the same. Cromwell fought Parliament just as earlier monarchs had done. Parliament fought the powers of the Protector, just as earlier Parliaments had fought the monarchs. Parliament was rather like an elected extraordinary general meeting of a corporation. And it was up to the Commons to grab back all those powers that it believed Oliver Cromwell had taken over. Parliament sensed that the army had become a new estate of the realm and therefore regarded itself immune to any democratic control

The army, or rather its lower echelons and therefore majority, were demanding the sort of revolution popular in the developing world of the twentieth century. The army wanted a proper republic – not an experiment. Richard Cromwell had none of the guile, style, ruthlessness or support of his father. He was overthrown by the army, which resurrected the old guard of the long rejected and ridiculed Rump Parliament. But these were the death days of the great experiment in constitutional reform. The army was once more dividing, but for reasons of powerful ambition rather than monarchist and republican dogma. The rift at the top of the army grew and this sent shivers of disunity throughout the senior ranks who, to a man, started to have doubts about their hardline actions against Parliament. It was December 1659.

George Monck, Commander-in-Chief of the army, had been one of the Parliamentary commanders in Ireland. His secret neutrality agreement with the Ulster Irish had made Cromwell's suppression of Ireland that much simpler. Now, he marched south from Coldstream in the Scottish borders to London. But he marched with no personal ambition; Monck opposed the notion of army rule. He therefore accepted the need for free Parliamentary elections and free elections meant that those who had never really wanted a Republic came back to both Houses of Parliament. This did not mean they accepted without question the rule of the monarch, but they did accept, on reasonable terms, the institution of monarchy. So it was from this point that the Restoration of the monarchy was inevitable.

Imagine the excitement that an ordinary change of government causes in our modern society and then guess what it might have been like in 1660 when the news spread of Monck's arrival and the introduction of free elections. Certainly Samuel Pepys, opening his diary in 1660, was impressed.

February 3
I and Joyce [Mrs Pepys] went walking all over Whitehall, whither General Monck was newly come and we saw all his forces march by in very good plight and stout officers.

Perhaps Pepys meant Monck's officers were stout hearted rather than portly.

> February 7
> Boys do now cry 'Kiss my Parliament' instead of 'Kiss my Arse' so great and a general contempt is the Rump come to among all men, good and bad.

> February 11
> I walked in Westminster Hall, where I heard the news of a letter from Monck, who was not gone into the city again, and did resolve to stand for the sudden filling up of the House; and it was very strange how the countenance of men in the Hall was all changed with joy.

The big debate in the 1650s may have been for the Republic, the Commonwealth, to have or not to have a monarch, to be Roman Catholic or Puritan, but at the same time as the political and social upheaval, a scientific and artistic revolution, which frightened the political leaders, was under way.

By the end of the Republic, with Cromwell gone and Charles II about to ascend the throne, a different style of writing began to appear. It may be that people were adjusting to the new freedoms, trying to see who they were, rather than being told who they were and what they ought to be. Certainly the Restoration writers, for all their scallywag style, described what they saw around them and they had long abandoned the so-called metaphysical seriousness of their Elizabethan predecessors.

Literature was constantly debated, and scientists were starting to prove that accepted ideas were bunkum. John Donne, in *An Anatomy of the World*, published in 1611, grappled with the new ideas.

> The new philosophy calls all in doubt,
> The element of fire is quite put out

And even when Donne had taken holy orders, his poetry still reflected what the Oxford scholar, Maurice Ashley, called 'an awareness of the mighty riddles of human life'. The seventeenth century was a century when writers and poets were categorized by their religious persuasions: Jeremy Taylor, Henry Vaughan and, of course, Donne were seen as Church of Englanders; John Dryden and Richard Crashaw were Roman Catholics; and John Bunyan and John Milton were Puritans. It was also a century that saw the introduction of a new industry.

Until now something like 80 per cent of the population had worked in agriculture. The biggest industry was cloth, but the dark satanic mills were yet to come; the cloth industry was still a cottage industry. So imagine the consequences of the Civil War: the land had been ravaged and therefore so had the staple industry.

But by the Restoration in the seventeenth century, the new industry that took root was coal. In the sixteenth century coal was a poor man's fuel but in the first half of the 1600s there was a thirteen-fold – perhaps as high as a fifteen-fold – increase in coal production. Coal was not a cottage industry; it needed organized gangs of fit men to mine it. This is the beginning of private enterprise, with industry that produced collective, structured employment.

By the end of the seventeenth century, the population of England and Wales stood at 5.25 million. London had doubled its size from 200,000 to 400,000. The next biggest town was Norwich, followed by Bristol, York and then Newcastle. The poor continued to be poor and the well-off lived very well. When the common people complained about their lot they were rarely listened to; and there was no one to represent them – at least no one they wanted to be represented by. They certainly wouldn't have chosen Thomas Hobbes as their representative. In *Leviathan*, Hobbes's treatise on political thought published in 1651, he argued against all the doctrinal notions that people were good and had the right to much better things. Hobbes argued that people were not at all good. They were, he thought, purely selfish creatures, out for what they could get, not for others, but for themselves.

And Hobbes thought that notions of 'right and wrong, justice and injustice, have there no place'. The only way to maintain society, he said, was to establish a total ruler, a dictator and to make everyone obedient. Hobbes argued that the extent of that obedience should be subject to various conditions, one of which was that the people should obey only as long as the sovereign was able to protect them.

And so, according to Hobbes, the price of sovereignty was protection. And, in the year 1660, that concept was about to be tested once more. Across the water in Holland, King Charles II waited and drafted his promise that on his return he would grant 'liberty to tender consciences'. By the end of May he entered London, and unlike his father, he did so in triumph and little fear for his life.

The barely begun Republic was discarded and the people lined the streets to welcome, after what may have been to them an unconscionable time, the Restoration of the monarchy and Charles II for his coronation.

CHAPTER TWENTY-FIVE
1660–81

Before Charles II could return to England from his exile in Holland, one significant announcement, a concession almost, was needed. And it had to come from Charles himself because it had to do with the fear of revenge and the settlement of old scores, and something close to the army's heart: backpay.

If the returning monarch demanded retribution for all the acts committed against the Crown during the Civil War it would be a catastrophe. So a document, which became known as the Declaration of Breda, was drawn up. It was a finely drafted balance between what Parliament wanted and what Charles was willing to concede, and it reminded the people that the Crown was the King's as God's anointed. Equally, it was clear that revenge may be the Lord's but not the King's. With certain conditions, there would be a general pardon – a clean constitutional slate. Thus, the Declaration of Breda might well be subtitled the Declaration of Let Bygones be Bygones. Charles II put his name to the document, probably written by his Chancellor Edward Hyde (whose granddaughter incidentally would one day become Queen Anne), which meant that he could and would return to England. The constitutional tidying up could begin. On board the significantly named *Naseby* with Charles were his brothers the Dukes of York and Gloucester, his aunt Elizabeth, who was the Queen of Bohemia, his sister Mary, who was now the Princess Royal, and her son, William, who was the Prince of Orange and who would one day be King of England himself. It all seemed a quiet social occasion during the short voyage from the Netherlands. That sense of ordinariness evaporated as the *Naseby* headed towards Dover on 25 May 1660. The people who had once chased the King and his followers from England now lined the coast to wave him ashore. With the Restoration came the first signs of an emerging democratic system of government. Within forty years the first political parties appeared. Monarchy was supposed to be supreme, but it has been argued that when the monarchy returned, it did so with few powers. And the conflict of the past decade had begun because Parliament believed that the King had too many powers – or at least claimed them – and that the King saw himself above the rule of Parliament. We should remember that Royalists believed, with some proper authority, that the Commonwealth had no legal standing and that Charles II's reign did not start in 1660 but at the death of his father, in 1649. Therefore, all the Parliamentary Acts that Charles I had agreed were now legal under Charles II. Everything else was illegal and therefore dropped. Take, for example, the Cromwellian practice of selling off the Church and royal estates: they were all restored. And Parliament didn't have any greater role in the central government of the land than it had had before the rebellion.

However, the power of the King and his advisers was contained, even reduced, by increasing regional and local responsibilities. More people would take part in the governing of the realm – it was the beginning of what is now called power-sharing. But in the early days of the Restoration, one fundamental difficulty remained: money and how to get it. And the first person to want money was, as ever, the King himself. This wasn't simply the usual demands of the monarch: he wanted Parliament to pay his debts. And since the agreement was that he had been King since his father had died, Parliament must pay, and pay a great deal, because the debts included those of his father, King Charles I, which he, as monarch, was obliged to clear. The bill was dropped on to the dispatch box within four months of the King's return. The present King's debts were yet to come. Charles and his secretary, Edward Hyde, recognized that they would have to come to a compromise over the amount Parliament could afford to pay their King. But not all the debts were settled in gold. Breda had promised that none should be threatened by their guilt. But some were. There had been sixty names on Charles I's death warrant. Twenty were dead and another twenty had gone into exile. Of the others, nine were executed. The remains of Oliver Cromwell were taken from Westminster Abbey and hanged at Tyburn and his long-dead head spiked for all to witness.

The blood-letting done, Charles and his Parliament got on with the governing of the realm. And it was Charles's Parliament: he, after all, could say when it should and should not be called. The Triennial Act meant little and, in truth, Parliament meant not much more. There was no great bureaucratic reformer as Thomas Cromwell had been in Henry VIII's time. But Charles felt safe with his Parliament of Cavaliers. He judged that they would be as loyal as any other group and so for eighteen years they governed together, although, it must be said, not very well and sometimes with little clear idea of who was in charge. Moreover, it was a period when the King was not inclined to champion causes, to take on political commitments, to depart from an instinct of compromise (all this is so typical of people who have been in exile for long periods). Certainly the King appears to have been someone who did not want anything to happen; anything, that is, that would disturb what he considered to be a very agreeable lifestyle. Charles II was, by all accounts, charming, considerably lazy and passionate. A man of pastimes, he was known as the Merry Monarch. He was tall, dark, handsome and athletic. He was also, in the romantic sense, a rogue. He took many mistresses (Nell Gwyn was only one of them), and fathered at least fourteen bastards. In between times he had a duty to rule, which at first he did through his Privy Council – or attempted to; unfortunately this Privy Council, or inner government of the King, would make policy at one private meeting and unmake it at another. However, it was soon made even less effectual when all important matters were first discussed through Privy Council committees, the most powerful of which was probably the origin of Cabinet government.

From 1668, five men assumed the most important portfolio. They were: Clifford, Arlington, Buckingham, Ashley Cooper and Lauderdale, known from their initials as the 'Cabal'. Parliament itself was ill-tempered, with the Lords and Commons at odds and with much time spent talking about what to talk about. Yet this was a long Parliament. It lasted eighteen years, from 1661 to 1679, and was known as the Cavalier Parliament. The Cabal was swayed by two forceful personalities. One was Clarendon who was Charles II's chief minister but not a member of the Cabal. He was the austere Edward Hyde, created Earl of Clarendon by Charles. He had been a member of the Short Parliament, served the King's father at the start of the Civil War (although he was never quite trusted) and after-wards worked diligently as Charles II's adviser in exile. Clarendon's daughter, Anne, married the King's brother, the Duke of York, who was to become James II. Hyde (Clarendon) was, therefore, a figure of considerable power and, hardly surprisingly, often openly disliked. The other influential figure was a member of the Cabal: Anthony Ashley Cooper, later the Earl of Shaftesbury.

Clarendon should have been the more powerful of the two. It was not Ashley Cooper's Cabal influence that began to dislodge him but the intrigues of the King's mistresses for whom the serious Clarendon had scant regard. Furthermore, he never understood the complexities and the importance of managing Parliament, and the need to build a political base among the old guard of Parliamentarians and Royalists. He had been blamed when the Thames froze over during the winter following the Great Fire of London, 1666. And so when the Dutch sailed up the Medway to draw to an end the disastrously managed war with them in 1667, it may not have been Clarendon's fault, but he took the blame.

What could not be slain was the dragon of suspicion that Catholicism was attempting to gain hold of the King and country. It wasn't just continuing paranoia. Charles clearly believed that if a gentleman wanted to be religious, then Rome was a more satisfying persuasion than most. And his wife, Catherine of Braganza, was a Portuguese Princess and a Catholic. His brother James, the Duke of York, was a convert to Catholicism, and because Catherine had not given birth, James was next in line for the throne.

There was also a treaty negotiated in secret with Louis XIV of France. It was called the Treaty of Dover. It provided England with a much-needed bolster to Charles's Treasury and Louis with a promise that England would help him in a third war against the Dutch. Within that treaty there was a secret clause which was not published at the time. That clause was the most damning. It said: 'The King of Great Britain, being convinced of the truth of the Catholic faith, is determined to declare himself a Catholic as soon as the welfare of his realm will permit.' In 1673, the King was forced to sign a Test Act; as the title of the legislation suggests, this was the law to test the religious persuasion of any person who held office in the service of the monarch. A soldier, for example, could be called upon under the Act to swear not simply his allegiance, but to swear also his disbelief in transubstantiation – the Catholic assertion that the consecrated bread and wine at Holy Communion or Mass are transformed into the body and blood of Jesus Christ. A declaration of disbelief was, obviously, a total denial of Rome. This 1673 Test Act went a great way towards destroying the Cabal of senior ministers.

But what about James, Duke of York? His wife Anne, the daughter of the Earl of Clarendon, and a Protestant, was dead, and the Duke, a Catholic convert, had married a Catholic, Princess Mary of Modena. He was Charles II's heir and Lord High Admiral. He refused to take the Test and therefore resigned his post as Lord High Admiral. Yet James was very likely to become King. If he refused to sign the Test, it meant that whatever the circumstances he would refuse to give up his Catholic faith and therefore Britain would have a Catholic monarch – an unthinkable proposition for the nation, or at least for those who actually governed. So it was at this point that those who really held power, and who held it not necessarily as staunch Protestants but certainly as staunch anti-Catholics, knew that a Protestant monarch would have to be found. However, there were many important Catholics willing to go to extremes to secure a Catholic monarch. Religious conflict wasn't simply something that started with the Puritans and the Royalists. Who was and who wasn't a Catholic, for example, had tormented political reformers for at least five monarchs and one dictator. In the late 1670s there had been allegations of a papist plot to kill the King. Charles's Catholic wife was vulnerable to the charge that she was involved against him, but she was not. The plotters planned to replace Charles with his Catholic brother, James, Duke of York. Here lay the continuing fear of Roman Catholicism, which extended beyond religious matters to continuing suspicions that the Catholic French would attempt to unseat the monarch. On top of this was the failure of Charles's court to produce a great statesman, a wise administrator. Thus the pervading fear of Catholicism and the argument about whether the monarch should or should not be a Catholic continued without any much needed attempt to control the rights of the monarch and confrontation between two political groupings.

On one side was the first Earl of Danby who had been the King's minister and who used his influence (and bribes) to build what was called the Court Party. On the other was Shaftesbury, a sometime Cromwellian and also, separately, Lord Chancellor to Charles; he was led the emerging Country Party. Shaftesbury believed there should be a free Parliament, free that is, from the Crown. He was against standing armies, which he rightly feared could take over the country. He also wanted religious tolerance without which, he said, there could be little chance of political stability.

Between 1679 and 1681 Shaftesbury and his Country supporters organized petitions and fought three elections. The campaign was intense and the Parliamentary grouping was well organized. And this organization changed the nature of politics completely. Shaftesbury had, in effect, started the first political party in English history: the Whigs, as the Country party became known. And the gentry of the Court party, the opposition to the Whigs, became known as the Tories.

Whiggamores were the miserable money-minded Scots who had marched on Edinburgh just a few years earlier. One hundred years later Samuel Johnson remarked that he had always thought the first Whig was the devil. So 'Whig' was a pejorative term. 'Tory' came from the Irish word, *Toraidhe*, for a small-brained and ugly outlaw or robber dispossessed by the Anglo-Irish. So both sides adopted scathing descriptions with not a little humour and indeed some pride. More importantly, here for the first time, Parliament was divided into political parties. The Whigs and the Tories had arrived.[1]

Shaftesbury's Whigs, or members of the Country Party as they were still more formally known, were formed to exclude James from the throne in a Bill appropriately named, the Exclusion Bill. There were in fact, three Bills. In 1679 Parliament was dissolved on the second reading of the first Bill. In 1680 the Lords rejected the second Bill. In 1681 the third Bill fell when the King dissolved the Parliament at Oxford. The supporters of the Bills were hardly as one; some Members took up violent tactics and could not agree on who should rule if not James. Some wanted James's daughter Mary, who was, in spite of her father's conversion, a Protestant; others wanted Charles's bastard son, James, Duke of Monmouth.

---

1   David Ogg, *England in the Reign of Charles II* (Oxford: Clarendon Press, 1934).

Moreover, Parliament could be dissolved and summoned more or less at the King's pleasure. This, and Charles's in-built majority in the Lords, meant that the Exclusion Bills were never likely to get through. The most important personal mistake made by Shaftesbury and his Whigs was their inability to understand that Charles would never give in on what he thought was a point of principle: that he ruled by Divine Right. And in this the country supported the King and not Shaftesbury.

Meanwhile, the King's senior adviser had fallen. The man Charles had come to rely upon, Danby, was a schemer who relied on bribery and patronage, rather than an innate sense of chancellorship. Danby had managed to get an agreement for the marriage of Mary, the daughter of James, Duke of York, to William of Orange. For the moment, because he had been exposed while trying to get a bribe from the French and Dutch in return for getting a British signature on a European treaty, he had to be sacrificed and sent to the Tower. His crime was hardly one to threaten his head and indeed he later returned as minister to William of Orange.

None of this was of much interest to Charles's subjects. They had more mundane difficulties. In one week in 1665, more than 7,000 people died in London. Most of those people, including their physicians, died of bubonic plague. Twelve months later, to the very week, almost 14,000 houses burned to the ground. The Great Plague and the Great Fire have often been linked. It is said that the fire destroyed the plague – or its source – and so saved further misery. It is a convenient hypothesis, but it's one that doesn't stand up. Of course, London knew all about plagues. It had suffered them for more than three centuries since the Black Death. The plague had simply never gone away. It was said that the carriers were not rats but soldiers, whose dirty coats and linen were infested with the plague flea. When the fire started, it was a convenient sign that the plague might literally burn out. In less than five days the City of London, between the Tower and the Temple, was destroyed. And the bubonic plague died out. But it is unlikely that the fire destroyed the plague because, by 1666, the epidemic was already almost played out. The breeding ground was the slum area beyond the City walls and this wasn't much touched by the fire, and therefore wasn't rebuilt. Undoubtedly the change in building style that followed the fire (from wood to brick and from straw floors to carpets) helped, although there's no evidence of any radical change in hygiene.

What the fire most certainly did, apart from destroying eighty-eight churches and St Paul's Cathedral, was to give Londoners the chance to change the shape of their city. It was a maze of crooked streets and alleys with more twists and turns than the mind of the most devious courtier. But, despite the fact that this was the age of Christopher Wren, the City remained unchanged. Wren planned a new City of London but London didn't want to be replanned. So Wren and centuries of his admirers had to be satisfied with a commission to build fifty-one churches and, of course, the new great Cathedral of St Paul's. Wren didn't start his professional life as an architect. He was born in the year the painter Anthony van Dyck came to live in England, 1632. He first studied mathematics, which led to astronomy, and by the time he was twenty-eight he was Professor of Astronomy at Oxford University. The inscription over the north door at St Paul's is said to have been written by his son: *Si monumentum requiris, circumspice* – If you would see his monument, look around.

As the great cubes of Portland stone began to be shipped from the Dorset quarries for Wren's buildings, so there was an even more urgent sort of construction taking place: ship building. While London had struggled with the plague and then with the fire, Charles II and his ministers had sent England to war. As London buried its dead, the admirals and sea generals fought the Dutch. They fought them in the Far East over possessions and the lucrative spice trades. They fought them off West Africa as trade was used to grab possessions. At home, they fought them off Lowestoft with a victory down to English artillerymen rather than good sea tactics. In June 1666 when the Dutch and British fleets engaged off North Foreland, the sound of battle reached London. This time the Dutch were the victors but within two months the fleet was refitted, put to sea and triumphed. But the war was not at an end. The French joined in, and it became clear that the once-superior Royal Navy could not protect the islands. It was time to sue for peace, especially as the Dutch sailed up the Thames estuary and the Medway and captured the King's battleship, the *Royal Charles* – the very ship (but then called the *Naseby*) that had brought Charles II back from exile in 1660. But peace came and with it a new city was christened: it had been laid out by the Dutch who ceded some of their New World territory to Charles. The city had been called New Amsterdam but Charles renamed it after his brother, the Duke of York.

CHAPTER TWENTY-SIX
1682–5

The Restoration period is for many summed up in the often saucy scenes from Restoration comedy – the men powdered and beauty-spotted, the women flighty and full-bosomed. And if, as seems likely, Restoration comedy reflected life under the Merry Monarch, how are two of the most important works of all time, *Paradise Lost* and *The Pilgrim's Progress*, explained?

In the early years of the seventeenth century, writers saw Godliness as a text. Political writers referred to God's involvement in everyday life. But by the closing years of the century, the Church of England was no longer able to make people members of it by the force of law. The Church of England came to be regarded as spiritually impotent and literature, especially the literature of political thought, reflected this.

During the seventeenth century thinkers, intellectuals, became preoccupied with the question of the boundaries of the Church and the State. John Milton saw God leading his people through the conflicts of the 1650s and then abandoning them in the 1660s – the Restoration. In 1658, the year Cromwell died, Milton started to write *Paradise Lost* in which the common man is allowed to fall to evil. By the time he wrote *Samson Agonistes* (1671), he was preoccupied with man's failure to use his God-given gifts. The Republicans were Samsons, distracted and failing to do God's good works. And when Bunyan's *Pilgrim's Progress* – the search for salvation – appeared in 1678, there was an emerging belief in a God whose text was less mysterious. Preachers searched the congregations more for goodliness, for kindliness and for tolerance, and less for transformation.

But when Charles returned to England, he wanted to settle the religious question. He wanted to restore the Church of England.

Charles had no theological conviction, simply a sense of history, and in order to achieve religious tolerance he offered to make some of the moderate Puritans bishops. In October 1660, his Worcester House Declaration was a stopgap arrangement which weakened the power of the bishops and made some of the *Book of Common Prayer* optional – a sort of early Alternative Service Book. For eighteen months Charles tried to convince the Anglican majority in the Cavalier Parliament, but Charles's religious reformation appeared doomed. The King's hope now rested with his closest adviser, Edward Hyde, the Earl of Clarendon – whose daughter Anne (1637–1771) was the first wife of James, the future king. Clarendon's name, by his right as chief minister, entitled the Acts of Parliament (the Clarendon Code) that confirmed the established Church, the Anglican Communion over the non-conformists and certainly the Catholics. Yet Clarendon was reluctant to endorse this legislation. He would have preferred to avoid the direct breach in the different Churches. The Code finished any chance there had been of ecumenism. The Prayer Book Act left nothing to chance. Its draughtsmanship was a model of uncompromising recognition of an Established Church which left no room for dissenters to remain within the Anglican communion. There could be no excuse allowed. Furthermore, the Act ordered the parishioners themselves to be responsible for making sure that the Prayer Book was available, and paid for, in every church – including the Church in Wales. Inevitably, the Prayer Book was to be used to promote English as the tongue of the Welsh people.

Article 22 of the Prayer Book Act, gave direct instructions for the Book's display and use:

A true printed copy of the said book entitled the Book of Common Prayer, shall at the cost and charges of the parishioners of every parish church and chapelry, cathedral church, college and hall, be attained and gotten before the Feast Day of Saint Bartholomew in the year of our Lord, 1662, upon pain of a forfeiture of £3 by the month for so long time as they shall then after be unproved thereof, by every parish or chapelry, cathedral church, college and hall remain default therein.

Behind Charles's hope for religious tolerance was something of his need to protect himself politically. Whereas the Puritans in his father's time were protected by Parliament, the Non-conformists now needed protection from Parliament, and the King was the person to do that. The legislation upset religious groupings, which upset political stability. Furthermore, Charles didn't have a political agenda. Consequently his ambition, perhaps very simply put, was for a quiet life. Also, although not a Catholic (until, possibly, his deathbed) he was inclined to Catholicism. Imagine the political upheaval if he'd converted to Rome during his reign, instead of during his final hours. It was this combination of a King without a vision, yet with a belief in his Divine Right to rule, that produced an outward appearance of tolerance. It was a curious combination in a century full of anything but tolerant political systems, institutions and professions.

In the mid-seventeenth century a triad of professions – the priests, the physicians and the lawyers – kept their knowledge firmly under lock and key. The Latin of their textbooks helped maintain the mystery. But Nicholas Culpeper (1616–64) had noted, 'The Liberty of our Commonwealth is most impaired by three sorts of men, priests, physicians and lawyers,' and was determined to change this. Culpeper was a radical and a Republican and his translation of one of the medical mysteries, the *Pharmacopoeia Londinensis*, was made in protest against the withholding of knowledge. Culpeper and many like-minded men were reflecting a suspicion, even a hostility, that existed in the lower classes of British society. The physicians especially were protected by monarchs and so when, during the Republic, Culpeper feared the return of the monarchy, it is likely that his ideas had much support among those of the same persuasion. And just imagine how easy it was for people, without the tongue of learning, Latin, to believe Culpeper's view that this language was the mark of a conspiracy much deeper and more sinister than even the mark of breeding, which he loathed. Thus, one consequence of Culpeper's translation of the *Pharmacopoeia Londinensis* was the growth of physicians without professional qualification – something that was illegal before 1640 but encouraged in the atmosphere of Republican revolution. As one critic remarked, by the Restoration, 'Stocking weavers, shoemakers, millers, masons, carpenters, brick-layers, gunsmiths, porters, butlers etc., are admitted to teach and write physic.' And George Fox, the founder of the Quakers, reflected 'whether I should practise physic for the good of mankind, seeing the nature and virtues of things'. Yet Fox had no medical training, simply inspiration. And Fox is a good enough example of the many who were attempting to do for religion what Culpeper had tried to do for medicine. Fox, who when imprisoned for blasphemy told the judge to 'quake at the word of the Lord' (so giving the Quakers their name), wanted medicine and religion to shake off their mysteries.

The closed shop of the medical profession was controlled by the College of Physicians. In London, the college licensed just fifty physicians. In the countryside some boroughs paid for physicians but others, especially the poorer ones, turned to the apothecaries and white witches. Quacks they may have been, according to the College of Physicians, but cures they did make, with one exception. Surgery remained a mystery that could not be solved by the translation of a Latin text.

And what of the third member of the triad, the lawyers? The common law was rewritten in the seventeenth century. Relative peace meant that people had time to settle disputes, to trade, and to make claims of land and riches plundered in more violent times. And every claimant, every negotiator, needed a new style of contract and therefore a lawyer, and the rewritten common law often favoured commercial interests. Also delays and obfuscation favoured the rich and, of course, the lawyers. And there was no police force, so everything had to be proved by the lawyers and the official informer, the forerunner of the private detective.

The law became such a lucrative profession that a father was quite willing to spend £40 a year to send his son to one of the Inns of Court. As few had £40 a year, 90 per cent of law students were sons of gentlemen and peers.

So, in the closing years of Charles II's reign, there was a clamouring for the reform of the practice of medicine, the law and the Church. Science soon reformed medicine but the law and the Church held their ground against reformation. However, the important point here is the rebellion itself.

And what of education? In the seventeenth century the two great universities were, largely, theological colleges and finishing schools for gentlemen. Yet the rebellion came because more people were thinking, writing, being read, followed and not so easily written off as eccentrics. However frightening to some, it is clear that Cromwell's decade made certain that the intellectual radical was here to stay. Furthermore, the gay atmosphere of Restoration

England was changing. Even the mood of the King himself was changing. The lazy, sometimes detached Charles became the protector of his great belief, the Divine Right of his dynasty to rule. It was a sober Charles II who emerged from the fear of another Civil War that followed the papist plot and the downfall of Danby. And while the King fought the anti-Catholic rising at home, his brother watched from a distance, in exile, knowing that little would induce the King to betray the succession. Charles believed it his sacred duty to pass the Crown to a brother whose virtues and whose vices alike rendered him, of all others, the man, as the King knew well, least fit to wear it.

Men voted against James, the Duke of York, becoming King as the Protestant tide again swept the country. Earnest and venerable divines tried to induce James to return to the Church of his fathers and his future subjects, but he remained obdurate. But his exile was short. In May 1682 James returned to England and the whole nation feared the coming to the throne of a Catholic monarch.

The following year another plot was discovered, real or otherwise, to assassinate the King. The story told was that the King and his brother, the Duke of York, loved horse racing. They planned to go to the races at Newmarket (followers of the turf will know that by 1683 Newmarket was well-established as a racecourse). The royal party would travel along the Newmarket Road and pass Rye House in Hertfordshire.

Either on their way there or on their way back (it's not quite clear which) the bodyguard would be overpowered and the King done to death. But – and here's another of history's critical buts – there was a fire at Newmarket, and the royal racegoers left earlier than expected for London and arrived safely. The person who lived in Rye House was Hannibal Rumbold, a former Roundhead officer. Immediately suspects among the Whigs were arrested. One of them, Lord Howard, confessed. Another, the Earl of Essex (a title often found in court intrigue), committed suicide. Two other Whig leaders, Lord Russell and a prominent opponent of the monarchy, Algernon Sidney, were put on trial. The Whigs had tried convincing the people that the King was in danger of being assassinated by Catholics. Here now was a Whig-approved plot to have the monarch done away with. Russell and Sidney were executed. The importance of the manner of their death must not be underestimated. These two men were the first to go to the scaffold for political differences. They died for their party belief. That had never happened before.

So Charles was triumphant and, for the final two years of his reign, lived seemingly contented with his lot at home.

This period also saw the restoration of the gentry as the social leaders of the nation. The Commonwealth had set aside the upper-class systems of hereditary right to a position in society. When the Restoration came along, the landowners, the gentry, moved easily back into their old positions of benevolent and social power. Through this comfortable merging of gentry and parish responsibilities came the social structure of English Church life and often that of a whole community which would survive as an obvious parochial pecking order into the twentieth century.

How the rest of the people lived, we can generally guess. According to one observer at the time, 20 per cent of the nation occasionally needed parish help. At the same time, modern critics of the social welfare system may or may not take comfort from the fact that seventeenth-century spongers were just as capable of fiddling the system as their twentieth-century descendants.

At the time of the Restoration, not much short of £1 million (in seventeenth-century money) a year was needed for parish handouts – and the figure was rising. On the parish or not, the staple diet of a less-than-well-off family was meat, bread and beer and very few vegetables. Meat was eaten at least twice a week, even for the one million on poor relief. For a comfortable family the main meal was at midday and it was enormous – lots of meat and fish every day.

At the time of Charles II's death, the population was more than five million. Part of the breakdown of the population is provided by figures produced from taxes. For example, there were probably about 7,000 lords, temporal and spiritual; 7,800 knights; 70,000 lawyers; 52,000 clergymen; and 250,000 shopkeepers. There were 750,000 farmers; two-and-a-half million labourers, outservants, cottagers and paupers. And, as the record tells us, 30,000 vagrants described variously as gypsies, thieves and beggars.

The end of the reign of the restored monarchy came in February 1685. King Charles II died from natural causes and he is said to have apologized to those at his bedside for taking such 'so unconscionable a time in dying'. His reign had been a period in which the emergence of party politics became apparent, and a period when to be in an opposing party wasn't necessarily revolutionary and certainly not treasonable. Charles had been an unconscionable time in dying, although perhaps not in the way he meant. Maybe the Restoration would have been better served by a shorter reign, if not by a more reforming governance. Yet he left behind a people who shared his overriding belief in the Divine Right of Kings.

CHAPTER TWENTY-SEVEN
1685–6

James II came to the throne in 1685. He was the first Catholic monarch of England since Bloody Mary (Queen 1553–8), the daughter of Henry VIII and Catherine of Aragon, more than a century earlier. James reigned for three eventful years in which Protestant fears of Catholic domination and autocratic government led to Revolution. As we have seen, James was the second son of Charles I and Henrietta Maria so he was Charles II's brother and, by his first marriage to the Earl of Clarendon's daughter Mary, he had two daughters, Mary and Anne. He had the uncompromising belief of the Catholic convert. There were those at court who feared his religious ambitions for the country, but that was perhaps a sophisticated view of power-brokers. The 'people' did not seem to fear the new King. Certainly James did not fear the power-play in his palaces. He believed that the court and politics were secondary to his judgement that he should have a standing army – that is, a permanent army – and an efficient navy that would be the equal of the awe-inspiring France. If he, James, could establish Britain's military grandeur then the security of the islands would be guaranteed and his leadership respected.

With this Divine Right to rule as his standard, then James could see it possible to restore to Britain the true faith of Catholicism. Would that not inevitably lead to his throne being the icon of Catholic Europe? In his own house of England, theory was with him. The Whigs, for example, were a bowed and even a spent force. During Charles II's closing years he had ruled without Parliament, therefore there was no challenge in the House from the Whigs and so the Crown had the power to clean out the places where the Whigs could build powerful committees and alliances. And this wasn't confined to Parliament: the local corporations were cleared, so were the powerful livery companies in the City and the bench of judges. Also many of the Whigs capable of mustering support were now gone. Algernon Sidney and William Lord Russell had been executed. The Earl of Essex had committed suicide in the Tower (or was he pushed?) and Shaftesbury had died in exile. So, when Parliament did come together, in May 1685, it was not a balanced political group. It was dominated by the Tories (although James hardly cared for them either).

There were 513 MPs of whom only fifty-seven were Whigs. There was a genuine celebration at the arrival of James on the throne in spite of fears of some at Westminster. Bonfires were lit, church bells rung and parties were held everywhere when James was crowned on, of course, St George's Day. And when, six months later, James celebrated his fifty-second birthday on 14 October (the anniversary of the Battle of Hastings), the bells rang out once more, fresh bonfires were lit and parties started all over again. James had put down the great Monmouth Rebellion that summer, so there was little doubting his strength, if not his popularity, for the time being anyway; it was clear that James, believing in his own authority and caring less than a fig for the constitutional view, would rule without consent for his opinions and style. For example, he ordered the release of imprisoned Catholics and had their fines repaid. And when more than 300 MPs asked him to enforce the laws against dissenters from the Church of England, he refused because dissenters included Catholics.

The first real challenge to James II came with the Monmouth Rebellion. It was named after James, Duke of Monmouth, whose mother was Lucy Walter, one of Charles II's mistresses, and whom Charles had always believed was his son. He certainly treated him as one. There was even a claim that Charles II and Lucy Walter had married in secret. Monmouth was thirty-six and married to Anne, the rich Countess of Buccleuch. He was handsome and dashing, had fought in the third of the wars with the Dutch and in 1679 had overcome Scottish Presbyterian rebellion on the Clyde. Most important of all, Monmouth was a Protestant and during the protest against the succession of James II (while Charles II was still alive) Monmouth had been an alternative choice as King. But for the moment he was in exile in Protestant Holland.

In the summer of 1685, Monmouth was persuaded that the time was right for him to mount a rebellion. He was encouraged by, among others, a fellow exile, Archibald Campbell, the Earl of Argyll, who promised to invade Scotland in support of him. So, hardly had James been crowned than Monmouth decided the time for rebellion was right. But the young Duke wasn't very bright. In June he landed at Lyme Regis, with a motley crew of eighty or so followers and picked up an army of 7,000 poorly led, untrained peasants and yeomen. He had a cavalry of sorts mounted not on chargers, but carthorses. He headed towards Taunton, not east towards the capital, where he denounced James as a usurper and accused him of having murdered Charles II. It is now that we hear of the first of the famous Churchills.

James ordered his relatively small forces, including cavalry and dragoons under the command of Louis de Duras, the Earl of Feversham, to deal with the uprising. John Churchill had command of the dragoons and, leaving the other commanders way behind, force-marched his men to track and harry Monmouth's squadrons and regiments until the main body of the King's men caught up. When Monmouth, who probably knew his game was up anyway, surprised Feversham's headquarters at Sedgemoor, it was Churchill who attacked, slaughtered and scattered Monmouth's ill-disciplined yet nonetheless brave troops. Churchill's action did not reflect the poor standard of the majority of the King's army, or more correctly, his militia, which did not press advantage and had on occasions run before the Monmouth rabble. Churchill's forces, more fierce and less compromising than the others, once more set about Monmouth's forces, who knew the horrible consequences of defeat and were liter-ally fighting for their lives. Monmouth abandoned his men to the uncompromising butchery.

Monmouth's stupidity was his timing. James was enjoying what today would be called his political honeymoon. If Monmouth had waited, even a year, he might have had more support. One person in particular watched the goings-on in England with more than passing interest. And he watched from the Netherlands. William of Orange knew well the imperfections of Monmouth's plan. He knew also that, with the Protestant Monmouth executed, he was, through his wife Mary, now closer to the throne.

It is said that Monmouth proclaimed himself King so that, by a statute of Henry VII, his followers might be protected because they had obeyed a King de facto. This did not much impress the King's

Chief Justice, George Jeffreys, Baron of Wem, better known simply as Judge Jeffreys (1645–89). Monmouth was captured and executed; and so were more than 200 of his followers. Another 800 were sent off to Barbados as slaves. It is said that the ladies (the royal mistresses and those in-waiting) of James's court made a handsome profit out of it: white slaves commanded good prices in the seventeenth century.

One of the most vivid records of the period, *A History of His Own Time,* was written by Gilbert Burnet (1643–1715), sometime Bishop of Salisbury. He'd been educated in Scotland, appointed chaplain to King Charles II and then dismissed when he criticized Charles for his social behaviour. Burnet understood well the stupidity of Monmouth for attempting a rebellion while James was at the height of his popularity, in the first months of his reign. But Burnet also believed that had James shown mercy, then his popularity might have lasted:

> But his own temper, and the fury of his ministers, and the maxims of the priests, who fancied that nothing could now stand before him: all these concurred to make him lose advantages that were never to be recovered. The army was kept for some time in the western counties, which both officers and soldiers lived in as in an enemy's country, and treated all that were believed to be ill-affected to the king with great rudeness and violence. Kirke [Colonel Kirke who, with Churchill and Feversham, had defeated Monmouth] ordered several of the prisoners to be hanged up at Taunton, without so much as the form of law, he and his company looking on from an entertainment they were at. At every new health [spa] another prisoner was hanged up. And they were so brutal that observing the shaking of the legs of those whom they hanged, it was said among them that they were dancing: and upon that, music was called for.

These were brutal times and James was shifting his political chess-men. He told his council of advisers that he wanted an immediate repeal of the Test Act and the Act of Habeas Corpus. Both Lord Halifax, the Lord President of the Council, and Lord North coun-selled caution, especially in the confirmation of Catholic military appointments. Halifax was sacked. North died. James was in confi-dent mood after the crushing of Monmouth, even though the King's militia had nearly failed him. Moreover, he was content with the Church of England's policy of non-resistance. Now he sought to gather about him like-minded souls, and then to make his move against the one institution on which he could not rely upon: Parliament. The year was 1685, the month, November. When Parliament met he declared that he wanted military superiority over any potential enemy. He said, remembering their dubious perform-ance against Monmouth's untrained army, that his militia was unreliable and therefore unacceptable. James demanded a fully trained standing army. Did he mean an army to impress European enemies or an army to keep him in power? Furthermore, he made it plain that his appointments of Catholic officers in the army had strengthened the formations. These men would stay. Imagine Parliament's reaction. These Catholic appointments threatened the authority of the Church of England. The thought of a standing army reinvigorated the fear of absolute control and, for some, Cromwellian nightmares. Parliament felt its very position challenged and the King's authority to take such steps legally questionable. This mattered not. When James heard that his authority was being chal-lenged, he did what none could stop him doing: he went to Parliament and shut it down. Parliament was prorogued and stayed so for the rest of James's albeit short reign.

It was now the Church, the Anglican Church, which led the oppo-sition. The Church opposed the King's policies, but did not make a downright attempt to dethrone him. But this was the beginning of the end. Sermons and pamphlets and slim books started to appear – all opposing Roman Catholicism. The centre for the opposition was London, led by its Bishop, Henry Compton. He was a thoughtful, powerful man, much respected by the clergy. He had voted for James when the Lords had debated the Bill of Exclusion, but now he and his clergy preached against popery. James issued his famous 'Directions to Preachers' which told the clergy to stick to less contentious matters. They refused. He then set up his Commission for Ecclesiastical Causes, which immediately suspended Bishop Compton. Two years later, Compton's signature appeared on a secret letter sent to Prince William of Orange, inviting him to bring his army to England. Little wonder that any friends James imagined he might have kept melted into the shadow he had cast over his court. James disregarded the signs. When Clarendon fell he was replaced by a Catholic. The eighteen-year-old Duke of Berwick, the son of James II and his mistress, Anne Hyde, found himself Governor of Portsmouth. Equally, the King still had a few supporters who were not Catholics. Some of them such unlikely characters – Whigs even – that they were seen as collaborators. There was no saving the throne. Only a few years before, the first political parties in British history had been formed and the Tories had supported James's right of succession. Now they were against him.

And across the sea, the thin, asthmatic, hump-backed Prince William of Orange still watched. He was son-in-law to the King of England and, should James fall, his wife would have a right to the English throne.

CHAPTER TWENTY-EIGHT

1687–8

It's a truism that there's no believer so dogmatic, so intolerant, so narrow-minded as a convert, perhaps particularly a religious convert. But James II had crossed the line between devotion and unbending evangelism. Many Catholics understood this and some of them saw that the King would bring about catastrophe rather than the return of the nation to Rome. Now there would be open rebellion, and James would be the last Catholic King of Britain.

His people believed that what was happening in England was part of the wider return of Catholicism and that it was a symptom of the advance of France's Catholic Louis XIV. Indeed, Charles II had made secret agreements with Louis, and he had been converted to Rome – albeit on his deathbed and doubted even at the time. Louis's power had grown in less than a decade and had given many Protestants in England cause to believe that what they saw taking place on the Continent could spread to England. England was vulnerable. It was not powerful. It had few friends in Continental Europe, whereas Louis of France was confident enough to believe that he was successor to the power of the Charlemagne empire. He fell to war with the Popes and flayed the Huguenots, the French Calvinists, of whom so many fled to England and Ireland that it could be said that the biggest migration en bloc into these islands came from the Walloons and Huguenots. Louis organized the Church, its priests, coffers, authority and, most significantly, patronage.

It was now assumed by some that the British King presented the same uncompromising determination. This was the James, once Duke of York, whose succession to the throne had been opposed but who, when the Whigs were routed, had been cheered in the streets. This was a King who had been crowned with vows of religious tolerance and who now swept them away. And so by 1688, the islands were so divided in what they expected from the throne that the nation was once more on the brink of civil war.

During the previous twelve months, sides had been taken. In April 1687 James had made a Declaration of Indulgence. This was a decree which suspended the laws against dissenters and Roman Catholics. He was probably quite successful in taking some, perhaps many, dissenters into his camp. Even the Quakers, who had refused to acknowledge a similar Indulgence of Charles II, were among the eighty or so groups which proposed formal addresses of thanks to the King. Even Whigs supported the King, including James Vernon, Francis Winnington, Lord Brandon and William Sacheverell who had opposed his right to succeed his brother. Others had good reason to give thanks to their monarch. William Williams, for example, had been made Solicitor General. Thomas Cartwright and Samuel Parker had been made bishops. But they were exceptional. William Sancroft, Archbishop of Canterbury, attacked the Indulgence; he believed it would lead to a law that could never be repealed.

There was also a strong group of moderates, led by the Marquess of Halifax and the Earl of Nottingham. Halifax was known as the Trimmer, so great was his reputation as a moderate. He was obviously good at balancing political weights because later he became Lord Privy Seal and the chief minister. The group most impatient to be free of the King was headed by Charles II's former chief minister, the Earl of Danby. This was the very man who had been impeached for his part in negotiations with, of all people, Louis XIV, and sent to the Tower. Danby joined the conspiracy to bring Prince William and an army to England.

Yet James II believed he had his own army on his side. But did he? What about Churchill, his general and agent? Or Kirke, who had been with Churchill when Monmouth's rebellion had been put down in the West Country? Were they disillusioned or could they see the writing appearing on the wall of constitutional change? And when the bishops challenged his authority, James was furious and demanded that the bishops should be sent for trial on the grounds of seditious libel. But even Judge Jeffreys thought that trying bishops was going too far. James would not listen and the bishops were sent to the Tower.

And then, on 10 June 1688, an event occurred which Danby and his friends believed was the moment they'd been waiting for.

The Queen gave birth to a son who later became known as the Old Pretender. The significance was obvious: the Catholic line would be continued. It was now that Danby and his group of conspirators wrote to Prince William of Orange. He, through the line of his wife Mary, was offered the throne – without anyone actually saying so, of course. But with this document, British history twisted in another direction. For William of Orange to plan, or to agree to a plan, to usurp the throne of his wife's father was not to be taken lightly. But William of Orange was a Protestant and Protestant desperation was high.

The Protestants really did believe that the newborn Prince was not the son of the King and Queen. It was even suggested, and believed for many a year after, that the baby had been smuggled into St James's Palace in a warming pan. James, it was said, must have an heir, by any means. Danby's letter to William of Orange was signed by, among others, Shrewsbury, Devonshire, Russell, Sidney and the Bishop of London. And it was written on the day that the seven bishops who'd been taken from Westminster Hall were found not guilty. The people cheered the news. Surely, William would hear those cheers?

But William's own lands were threatened by the French. If they gave any sign of attacking, there was no way in which William's own Parliament, the States-General of the Netherlands, would allow him to sail for England. The Prussians supported William and Marshal Frederick Schomberg (1615–90), said to be the most able soldier in Europe, was sent as his second-in-command and indeed was to remain at William's side for the battles in Ireland that drove James II into exile. Spain, a Catholic State, made no real objection to dethroning an avowed Catholic monarch because they saw him as a political and eventually as a military threat. This sense of realpolitik established what in our day of instant global communications would be seen as a major European crisis.

Imagine what it must have been like at the time. Most people could remember back forty years or so, or they had parents who could. In that time alone, they had seen Charles I have his head chopped off in Whitehall (or at least heard about it); witnessed Cromwell's Roundheads ruling the country in the name of a Republic, a Commonwealth; and then seen, and cheered, the return of the monarchy in the form of Charles II. They had heard all sorts of

stories about papist plots to kill that King and then they had celebrated the arrival of a new one, James II, even though he was a
Catholic. And now the country was about to be pulled apart by yet
another civil war and the King was trying to make his kingdom a
Catholic State. He wasn't trying to hide what he was doing. He
had put Catholics in prominent positions, including in the army and
the navy.

Thus the chessmen of Europe had to be in exactly the right positions before William had the clear line he needed to take the King,
and everything depended upon the French. If Louis decided to
strike at the German coalition rather than the Netherlands, then that
freed William.

Ironically, the solution to the dilemma was in James's hands, not
Louis's. The French, if they were to invade the Netherlands, would
need the English on their side. If James had aligned himself with
Louis, then he might have saved himself, because then William
would probably not have left the country. But James did nothing.

By now there was so much dissent and uncertainty, together with
rumour of war, that by the late autumn of 1688 even the unbending
Judge Jeffreys tried to persuade James to reverse his reforms. He
had, for example, banned Protestant dons at Oxford whom he saw
as political as well as religious agitators; there were now Catholic-
only schools; the county lords-lieutenant were disbanded; the
'wrong' type of magistrates were banned from the benches. The
country was on the edge of panic. James had no option but to heed
Jeffreys and reverse these so-called reforms. James had given in,
but he was hopelessly late in doing so. The people in high places
knew that the matter of William of Orange was advanced and that
little could stop a Dutch invasion to unseat the King. The signatories to the invitation to William had tried to protect themselves from
implication in any plot (still a treasonable matter), but the King's
men knew perfectly well what was happening, hence the efforts to
change. Intelligence reports had been flooding from the Continent
ever since September 1688. They had reported troops being gathered, ships being stored, anchorages being cleared. This was an
armada: sixty warships; 500 smaller vessels; 14,000 men made up
of Dutch, Scandinavian, Scottish and English regiments, and
displaced Huguenots. By the third week of October, William of
Orange had put to sea.

William planned to land in the north of England but the elements took control. A gale blew up and the fleet had to sail through the Dover Straits and then west, not so far from where Monmouth had made his landing three years before. The fleet got as far west as Torbay before putting its army ashore. Even then, James had hoped to stop his son-in-law, not by diplomatic persuasion – he knew it was too late for that – but by sheer force. James had a large army, perhaps 40,000 men, but they were in different parts of the country. Also, the London garrison had to stay where it was to protect the capital. This still left the King with approximately 25,000 men.

By 19 November, two weeks after William's landing, James joined his army at Salisbury. But many officers, already seeing the way the military wind was blowing, began to move towards William's camp. Churchill, at whose home the young Princess Anne, the future Queen, had been staying, had already pledged his intentions to William. In a letter written to the Prince in Holland, he made clear his treasonable intent:

> Mr Sidney will let you know how I intend to behave myself; I think it is what I owe to God and my country [and to Churchill]. My honour I take leave to put into your Royal Highness's hands, in which I think it safe. If you think there is anything else that I ought to do, you have but to command me, and I shall pay an entire obedience to it, being resolved to die in that religion that it has pleased God to give you both the will and the power to protect.

Churchill wasn't a major player in what followed but he was typical, and somewhat influential. He had also clearly chosen to usurp the power of his monarch to whom he had sworn complete loyalty and obedience: realpolitik was not the prerogative of the Continental power players. James might have followed his instincts and had Churchill arrested but he did not. In any case, by this time it would have made little difference to the outcome and would not have frightened those against him. Such an action may even have strengthened resolve. By the end of the year it was all over. England didn't want James. There was no question of another regicide: he had been allowed to escape from England and, for the moment, he was still King. Two years later James landed in Ireland with French troops and laid siege to Londonderry. About 30,000 Protestants were trapped, but they held out for three months and were rescued, an occasion still celebrated in Ulster. Later James was defeated at the Battle of the Boyne (see Chapter Twenty-Nine) and retreated to France where he relied on a pension from Louis XIV. He died in France on 6 September 1701.

When William of Orange landed in England in 1688 not everyone intended that he should be King even though he had been in the thick of the conspiracy to remove James. The Whigs, the party formed to fight for the exclusion of James, as a Catholic, from his right to the Crown, were not unexpectedly on William's side. The Tories were the party of the Crown. Even the Anglican Tories were not all for William's accession, although they welcomed his invasion.

But once William had arrived in London, and once James had escaped (probably with William's help: he needed his father-in-law out of the way, but not as an assassinated or executed martyr), there seems little doubt that William wanted to be King – he certainly wanted the English army to help fight his own battles. And the solution was obvious: William's wife, Mary, would be Queen and William could be Regent. Better still, Mary could insist that they should rule together: King and Queen. Perhaps that had been the Dutchman's idea all along. For all his weak appearance, humped back and sickly nature, William of Orange had considerable cunning. He was a Calvinist but he wasn't single-minded. He was on good terms with the Pope. He took advice from Catholics. He is said to have hated the French Catholics, but perhaps not because they were Catholics but because they were French. Besides, William could very well say that his actions were solely on behalf of his wife. After all, he would hardly have undertaken them for the English, the Irish, the Welsh and the Scots. He didn't like any of them.

William's adroitness and timing were very obvious during the first few weeks after he arrived in England. Conspirators against King James II implied to William that he could be King (although some of them, including Danby, denied this). What they really wanted was a compliant and Protestant monarch. William worked quickly: James left England on 23 December 1688 and arrived in France on Christmas Day. On Boxing Day William called a meeting in London. In front of him were some of the surviving members of Charles II's last Parliament. Joining them were the aldermen, the

Lord Mayor of London and men from the common council of London. William didn't invite the Tories from James II's Parliament, which meant that the group was dominated by Whigs – the people who didn't want James to be King in the first place.

One month later a Declaration of Rights was made which offered the Crown to William and Mary. And twelve months after that the Declaration became an Act of Parliament. But what about lawful succession? During the winter of 1688 bishops didn't mind James being King as long as he was legally bound to the Church. But in January 1689 the Tories decided that they wanted William's wife, Mary, to rule as Regent, but on James' behalf, so that James remained King. That proposal was defeated, but only just. Then the Tories said that James's flight from the country amounted to abdication and since too many people believed that James II and Mary of Modena's son, also James, was not actually theirs, then James II's daughter Mary was the obvious successor. It was then that William showed his intentions. He didn't want to be, as he called it, 'a gentleman usher' to his wife. The Declaration of Rights provided the form of words for Mary to declare that she wished to rule as Queen with her husband, William, as King. So the succession was arranged because, whatever the feelings towards James, his daughter was still next in line. But there was something else to be resolved: perhaps, just perhaps, the most important section of the Declaration of Rights. It declared that, in future, no Catholic could be monarch. The issue remains sensitive to this day, even when it does not involve a Catholic. When Lieutenant Philip Mountbatten became engaged to Princess Elizabeth, the Archbishop of Canterbury advised that although the future husband of the future Queen was Greek Orthodox, it would be better if he were received into the Church of England. Just two weeks before the wedding, in 1947, he was.

So William, who had little regard for these islands and their peoples, was to be King of England, Ireland and France. It would seem that William accepted, indeed wanted, the Crown for two reasons. Firstly, as his wife, Mary, the beautiful daughter of James II, had a hereditary claim on England, then she (and he) should exercise it. Secondly, England's wealth and military power would be an invaluable weapon in his real ambition: the submission of France.

King William was regarded as an oaf, a bore, an uncouth King. Yet he was well-educated, could speak six languages, including fluent Latin, and bewildered London society by his artistic learning. As William of Orange, he had used a mixture of cunning, astute diplomacy and military nous; he had rid his country of the French by 1674, formed an Alliance with Lorraine, Brandenburg and Spain to deter the French, and had become the head of what was then called the United Provinces. But the steady march of Louis XIV was yet to be checked.

Seventeenth-century London did not really understand the dangers as William saw them. Given the character of the new King and what he regarded as his special sense of vision it was inevitable that William thought so little of his new people. And just imagine how this new regime went down with a society that still remembered, with some fondness perhaps, the easy going times of the Merry Monarch, Charles II. And, also, think what it must have been like to see armed Dutch infantry, not English soldiers, around the capital of England.

CHAPTER TWENTY-NINE
1689–1702

James was now in France and plotting to return to England with French help. The French thought that was a very good idea. War by proxy is often attractive. James, with French help including officers, men and supplies, landed in Ireland in March 1689. Not unnaturally he was welcomed by many of the Catholic Irish. He had his headquarters in Dublin and an Irish-Catholic army of tens of thousands. Only the Protestant north of the island kept its distance from what were now called the Jacobites – from Jacobus, the Latin for James. The support for James was not confined to Catholic Ireland. The most widespread support for the King, or more accurately, his cause, was in Scotland. William's arrogance – at best, insensitivity – towards the Scots did not help his popularity. In the year William and Mary came to the throne, the Jacobites mounted a rebellion.

On 27 July 1689, John Graeme of Claverhouse, Viscount Dundee, led his Jacobites against William's men at the Pass of Killiecrankie. The King's men retreated, but Dundee, a veteran of Charles II's army, was wounded and later died. It was this soldier who was remembered in song and poetry as Bonny Dundee. This Jacobite Rebellion was important for what didn't happen. Few rallied to Claverhouse's standard, the Jacobite cause. Not until William showed that he was willing to massacre the Scots to get his way did the Jacobite cause grow. Two decades later, after an Act of Union between England and Scotland had been passed, the Jacobite determination to continue their fight would not be dampened. The battle at the Pass of Killiecrankie would not be the last.

Meanwhile, further south, the French were beginning to dominate the sea-lanes in the English Channel (or La Manche, as the French would prefer). Yet the French did not have exceptional flexibility in the unpredictable seaway that was subject to variable winds until the predominantly south-westerlies settled in the autumn. There was good opportunity to harry the English coast particularly as, after Scotland, William was preparing to fight James in Ireland. Equally, many French resources were reserved for landing James in Ireland and keeping him and his troops (mostly French) resupplied and generally acting as guard ships. The considerable support of the French and the Catholic Irish was not enough to save England for James at the Battle of the Boyne in July 1690. By some accounts it was far from being one of the famous set-piece engagements in European military history, especially considering what was at stake – not only the Crown of England but the future religious and constitution pattern, too. It was an altogether casual affair that ran into a second day. Bit by bit, William's guards and cannon scared the Jacobites away, rather than the great slaughter of many earlier royal encounters. James escaped, or was allowed to. Immediately, he demanded the French give him safe escort for his escape to France.

Had James stayed longer in Ireland, the French frigates would have been bettered deployed interrupting William's supply lines – all of which were seaborne. Instead, the Battle of the Boyne set William III's rule over Ireland not James II's. Moreover, with James dealt with, William could now use the British soldiers for his original purpose – not to chase off James II, but for his own pursuits in Continental Europe, more exactly, in the Nine Years' War, also known as the War of the League of Augsburg. It was a war fought by a coalition of, among others, German princes who were determined that Louis of France's march through Europe should cease. William III's determination was second to none, and so with his British and Dutch troops in a not altogether happy alliance, he led the charge. But William was lacking one of his most able commanders, one who was eventually called genius: John Churchill, by now Earl of Marlborough. William had replaced him partly because he wanted his Dutchmen, under Count Solms, to direct the campaign, and partly because he didn't trust Marlborough's links with James. The result was disastrous. Solms was never in the same league as a commander as Marlborough. Parliament proclaimed its disgust. Never again, said the Lords, should a Dutchman command the English contingent. King William's contempt for the English was endorsed when the Commons accepted, nevertheless, the argument that Solms had been the best man available and even voted more money for more war. But like a more famous battle to come, William's demand was a close run thing. The war chests were all but empty.

Two years earlier one of the Lords of the Treasury had proposed a government loan of £1 million which was accepted and became known as the National Debt. That same financier had another idea, but one for which an altogether more complicated arrangement was needed: a company was set up. It had 1,268 shareholders and together they raised £1,200,000 which they then loan to the government. They charged the government 8 per cent interest a year and for good measure charged another £100,000 a year to administer the loan. But it was illegal to lend the King money without the agreement of Parliament so it was decided to pass an Act that would give these moneylenders a legitimate charter.

In 1694, a Royal Charter was issued. Its title was 'The Governor and Company of the Bank of England', which is why we have a Bank of England today and why its director is called the Governor. The man who invented the National Debt and the Bank of England was a Whig by the name of Charles Montagu.

The throne was as ever financially supported by Parliament as well as by the private landings and rents of the Royal Household. This support, more carefully organized, is what is commonly known as the Civil List. Although an Act of Parliament for the Civil List was not passed until 1697, it had, in practice, existed for some time. It was always controversial. For example, a speech by Sir Charles Sedley in the Commons, six years earlier, made it clear that the debate sometimes heard today is little different from the one taking place 300 years ago. He said the Commons provided for the navy, for the army and now for the Civil List. 'Truly, Mr Speaker,' bemoaned Sir Charles, 'it is a sad reflection that some men should wallow in wealth and places [large houses], whilst others pay away in taxes the fourth part of their incomes.'

Much of the money went not to royalty but to the senior officers of the Crown. The first Great Officer was the Lord High Steward of England, or Viceroy; then the Lord High Chancellor; then came the Lord High Treasurer; the Lord President of the King's Privy Council, an office dating back to King John; the Lord Privy Seal; the Lord

Great Chamberlain; then the Constable; the Earl Marshal; and the last of the Great Officers of the Crown, the Lord High Admiral, so trusted that the holder was often the King's son or near kinsman. And they, and theirs, were always well paid.

William's inner circle was a chain of remarkable men, mostly unremarked in history. Apart from a couple of great deeds, Sidney Godolphin (1645–1712), gambler, racehorse breeder at Newmarket and the man who would become Lord Treasurer, is barely remembered. Likewise Thomas Wharton (1648–1715), the Comptroller of the Household and the author of the dirge-cum-ditty, 'Lilly Bolero'. The words are Irish but the song was contemptuous of the papists and, among the soldiers of the time, was as popular as, say, 'It's a Long Way to Tipperary' was among twentieth-century troops. It lives on as the signature tune of the BBC Overseas Service news bulletin. There was also Charles Talbot, the Duke of Shrewsbury (1660–1718), who was William's Secretary of State, and even John Churchill, the Earl of Marlborough, is hardly known until later when he became perhaps the most remarkable general in English history. This is not simply a ready reference for names who served William. These men were noteworthy figures whose lives are well-worthwhile remembered to better understand the phenomenon of what was happening in the reign of William and Mary – one of the too much overlooked periods in the history of these islands.

Some are never remembered outside historical reference, but their legacy survives into the twenty-first century. For example, Robert Spencer, Earl of Sunderland (1640–1702) made a contribution to the way in which English government works, which has survived to this very day. Sunderland was an opportunist and, like many who swayed perilously on the upper boughs of the tree of State, he was a survivor, a man who could change religions and courtly allegiance with remarkable dexterity. He understood court politics and, most usefully, European politics. He became an ambassador and then Charles II's Secretary of State. Then he supported the attempt to exclude James, Duke of York, from succeeding Charles, and promoted the Protestant cause of William of Orange.

When James became King, Sunderland claimed that he too was a Roman Catholic and he was soon reappointed Secretary of State, and helped James in his attempt to establish Catholicism in England. When James was chased out of the country Sunderland came back, abandoned Catholicism, reverted to Protestantism, became William's closest adviser and, through his own skills of intrigue and political management, convinced the new King that it was possible to govern with a small inner group. Sunderland's idea of a small inner group has had an influence that has lasted to this day. The Earl of Sunderland, an all but forgotten figure, was in fact creating what is now called Cabinet Government.

Here, then, was a small group who would influence not only the King, but would set the basis for English government. In their own time, they had more immediate concerns than posthumous legacy. They were truly worried about the succession: William and Mary were childless. The anxiety increased when, shortly after Christmas 1694, Queen Mary died. Apart from being the daughter of the deposed James II, she is rarely mentioned for doing anything at all. It's almost as if the monarch had a hyphenated name: William-and-Mary. And yet without Mary, William would not have been King. She was beautiful and graceful in contrast to her husband who was not a physically appealing character. They married for political reasons and it was only later that William appears to have recognized the importance of his wife in much that he did, and they grew to love each other.

Bishop Burnet, in his memoir of the times, says Mary was gracious, modest and gentle. But this ignores the determined way in which she broke with her sister, Princess Anne, and Anne's confidante, Sarah Churchill, the wife of the Earl of Marlborough, when William fell out with Anne's husband, Prince George of Denmark. On 28 December 1694, all thoughts of reconciliation between the daughters of James II disappeared. The thirty-two-year-old Queen was dead from smallpox. She had come to the throne during warfare, and she had died while much of Europe was still at its conflicts that would continue in that phase until 20 September 1697 when France signed, the Treaty of Ryswick with England, the Holy Roman Empire, Spain and the Netherlands. But the Peace of Ryswick was not peace in Europe. It was a truce.

What happened in England is what always happens at the end of a long confrontation; nowadays the term is 'peace dividend'. At the end of the seventeenth century, the jargon was different, but the sentiment the same: cut back the numbers of troops, save money. It was perfectly understandable. As ever on these occasions, the nation was fed up with paying taxes for a war not everyone was convinced was in the people's interest. Taxes had been raised in the easiest ways, including a levy on birth, marriages and funerals. In 1697, the seventeenth-century peace dividend had to be paid. The army of nearly 90,000 men was to be cut to fewer than 10,000. The navy was to be reduced to a point where it could hardly defend the shores. Demobilization, just as it was in 1918 and 1945, became an almost unmanageable process. Certainly seventeenth-century Britain did not have a system for coping with sudden change. Sending home tens of thousands of troops presented a social conundrum to a government and a country which was, just as it would be more than two centuries later in 1945, poor from paying for war. One result was a large increase in crime: many soldiers became footpads and highwaymen. Even before the war an Act of Parliament described these outlaws as an infestation. The Act was not simply to put robbers outside the law – that is, to declare them outlaws – but to encourage the population to catch them. This was necessary because it was believed – with good reason – that many of the people supported them.

Inevitably, England became isolationist. Not that William wanted it to, it was simply that Parliament and the people were fed up with paying for a war that by and large they didn't want. There had been fears of a French invasion and it might even have happened while James II was still trying to get his throne back, but it didn't. William realized that if, instead of showing his contempt for the English and their ruling classes, he had tried to use the political system then he would have had the support he wanted for his crusade against the French. But he did not and in the end, the two parties, the Whigs and the Tories, proved that they were now far more powerful than he had ever understood they could be. Parliament was now determined to take an even stronger hold on the powers of the English monarchy. For a start, there was the matter of who would succeed not only William, but also Anne. The Act of Settlement declared that through a line descending from the daughter of James, the throne should pass to the House of Hanover. More importantly, it declared that every sovereign had to be a member of the Church of England. Furthermore, and after the experience of William, the Act stated that no foreign-born monarch could go to war without Parliament's absolute permission.

The next test came while William was still alive. And it came about not because of the ambitions of William, but because of a crisis in the future of the Spanish monarchy. This was not some simple domestic dispute: Spain had an empire. But more important to Europe than the Spanish possessions in the so-called New World was that part of the Spanish Empire that included parts of Italy and the southern Netherlands – what is now called Belgium.

The King of Spain was Charles II. The reason for the dispute was that Charles was childless. There were three claimants to his throne: the first was France, through either the Dauphin or his second son, Philip, the Duke of Anjou, Louis XIV's grandson; the second was the Emperor of Austria, Leopold, who had visions of reviving the grander days of the Habsburgs; and the third claimant was the Emperor's grandson, the Electoral Prince of Bavaria.

William and Louis produced a plan, the Partition Treaty of 1698, to share the empire. They said they would recognize the Prince of Bavaria, but the young Prince of Bavaria died, suddenly. Another treaty was produced. The Emperor's second son, the Archduke Charles, was selected by William and Louis, but not by the King of Spain. A decision had to be reached. However, on 1 November 1700 Charles died and his will stated that his throne was to go to the Duke of Anjou. What was Louis XIV to do? Endorse the treaty and stand alongside the British and the Dutch? If he ignored the terms of the treaty and preferred the will he would have to go to war with anyone who challenged his grandson's claim. He chose to support his grandson and part of the reason for doing so was his inability to judge if the English would support him. In that, he was probably wise.

The English were not to be trusted. Moreover, the English had good reasons not to join forces with the French. They had never trusted them, nor would they ever properly do so – not even when they were on the same side during the two world wars of the twentieth century and the political European wars of the twenty-first century. Secondly, there was evidence that the French were thinking of invading England to help James II regain his throne. James II was still alive at his Jacobite court at St Germain. But he was not to linger and when he died at the age of sixty-eight in 1701, his son, James Edward Stuart, was proclaimed by his father's court as James III of England and VIII of Scotland. That was no surprise, of course, but the significant point is that Louis XIV of France announced that he recognized the son, the Old Pretender as he became known, as King of England. Here was evidence for the English that they had been so right not to trust the French. Louis's support for the Pretender was a declaration of hostility if not direct war. William was never to see the war through. On 20 February 1702, he fell from his horse and broke his collar-bone. He was a tired, weak man and in this second year of the eighteenth century medicine had no remedy.

So Anne became Queen and the long-term significance of England's involvement in the War of Spanish Succession was that England, a reluctant player, was led into a decade of war. It was a war of ruthless battles, and a war that gave Britain the island of Minorca and also a tiny colony: Gibraltar.

CHAPTER THIRTY

1702–6

Queen Anne, the last of the Stuart monarchs, came to the throne in 1702. She was the daughter of James II; her mother was his mistress, Anne Hyde, whom he married. Anne married Prince George of Denmark and, although she was pregnant eighteen times, they had no surviving child. She has been described as unhealthy, dull-witted and, like her father, a bigot, although Anne was a Protestant whereas James was, of course, a Roman Catholic. Her connection with and affection for John Churchill, whom she made Duke of Marlborough, developed while she was still Princess Anne. Marlborough's wife, Sarah Churchill, was her lady of the bedchamber – her closest confidant. Anne, like her sister Mary, was quite disloyal to her father. During the 1688 revolution, Anne joined the rebellion at Nottingham.

Yet if this all sounds like disaster for England, it wasn't. Close to the throne were the two most able people of the new century: the first Duke of Marlborough (1650–1722), perhaps one of the most celebrated army commanders in English history, and Sidney Godolphin, who had served Charles II and James II and who, until 1707, had control of the Treasury and the ear of the Queen. His support was crucial to Marlborough's military appetite for resources to fight the War of Spanish Succession. Marlborough had believed that if England didn't join the war, Louis would win it. There was another matter: Marlborough (and the Whigs were with him on this) believed that whichever power had military domination of Europe could, and even would, have control of the distant colonies. Trade with far away Newfoundland was well-established; smuggling from Continental Europe was already big business and the Royal Navy was already deploying squadrons in Canadian waters. Importantly, the foundations of the British Empire in India were now dug by the hard work (and profits) of the English East India Company whose origins lay in the East Indies cargoes first shipped back to England in 1603.

The new Queen's mind was occupied with far more than a strategic understanding of what war might mean for her people. Having lived through one rebellion and even taken part in it, she was well aware of the possibility of another such uprising. Furthermore, like Marlborough and Godolphin, the Queen was a high Tory and strong Anglican. This conviction in her religious persuasion was seemingly the single comfort in her guilt at having usurped her father's position. Anglicanism must reign above Catholicism. Catholicism was synonymous with France and it was clear that the Catholic Louis believed that with the death of King William, the English resolve to join the Grand Alliance against him was weakened. This war was crucial to the history of these islands. If Marlborough could command the Grand Alliance against Louis XIV and beat him, then the threat to Europe of dangerous domination by one nation would recede. Also, while Louis remained uncurbed, there continued to be a real threat of invasion. There is little doubt that one of France's ambitions during the War of Spanish Succession was to invade Britain on behalf of the Catholic Pretender to the throne, James Edward Stuart.

In May 1702 the Grand Alliance of England, the Dutch Republic and the Holy Roman Empire in support of the Habsburg, Charles III, declared war on the France–Spanish Alliance. In September Bavaria joined the French. Later, the Portuguese and the Germans, or some German States, since Germany wasn't united then, joined the Grand Alliance. But by 1703 (the year Samuel Pepys died), in spite of initial success, the Grand Alliance was losing ground to the French and here was the beginnings of the French and Spanish advance on Vienna. The English and Dutch armies were on the defensive in the Netherlands. Many of the Alliance leaders grumbled that Austria was too far away for them to worry about. Marlborough didn't think so: he saw the survival of Austria as essential to the Alliance and its fall as the main ambition of the French.

Marlborough began secret preparations to move part of his army away from the Netherlands towards the Danube. He didn't want the French to know what he was doing but, more than that, he didn't want the Dutch to realize what he was doing: they would not have agreed. They would have seen it as leaving them undefended. But the Danube was a 250-mile march across Europe, with French troops heavily entrenched west of the Rhine. Marlborough had 21,000 men, a very obvious force and difficult to hide. On 20 May 1703 he left Bedburg, saying that he was going to fight on the Moselle, which he wasn't. He picked up 5,000 Hanoverians at Koblenz and 14,000 Danish and Germans at Mainz, eleven days later.

The marvel of this march was Marlborough's logistical planning. The weather was appalling: rain and mud. He marched his men for four days, then rested for one. Fresh boots and equipment were pre-positioned. Marlborough was a calculating tactician, marshal and quartermaster-general rolled into one man. By the end of June, Marlborough had 40,000 men, had lost only 900 and had Prince Eugene of Savoy at his side. In September, at Höchstadt on the Danube, Marlborough earned his most memorable victory. The English attacked a small village called Blindheim. It is now remembered as Blenheim. After setbacks and advances, Marlborough's forces savaged thousands of French troops. That night he wrote to his wife: 'I have not time to say more, but to beg you will give my duty to the Queen, and let her know her army has had a glorious victory. Monsieur Tallard and the two other Generals are in my coach and I am following the rest.' Tens of thousands lay dead or wounded.

This wasn't simply a terrible battle. Before it, there had been a sense that France was invincible. Now there was shock in the court of Louis XIV. Blenheim was more than a defeat, it was the ruin of a greater part of Louis XIV's army. And there was more to come. In May 1704, the English Admiral George Rooke arrived in the Mediterranean with his Anglo–Dutch fleet. In July, he was joined by a squadron commanded by Sir Cloudesley Shovell. Reinforced by a land assault, Rooke bombarded a garrison at the mouth of the Mediterranean. This was the prelude to the famous battle for Gibraltar. And, after mixed fortunes, an event occurred in 1706 that was to have even greater consequences than Blenheim. The arena this time was the Low Countries, in what is now Belgium. Near the village of Ramillies on 23 May, Marlborough launched 25,000 of his British, Dutch and Danish troops against the French army. It broke and so was won for the Alliance the whole of Belgium. Yet there was, for Marlborough, a harder campaign to come. It would not take place in Flanders but in a bloodier cockpit: the trenches, defiles and ramparts of Whitehall and Westminster. Marlborough's honeymoon with the Queen's inner circle was coming to an end.

CHAPTER THIRTY-ONE

1707–14

It is now 1707. The war against France and Spain continued, but an event whose consequences have lasted to the present day occurred in these islands. 1707 was the year the Act of Union with England and Scotland became law; or, more accurately, the Act linked Scotland with the 1536 Union of England and Wales. Although James I had, in 1603, styled himself King of Great Britain in the Union of the Crowns (Scotland and England) and anyone born in Scotland was also an English citizen, it had taken a full century for Great Britain to become a legal fact.

The Act of Union, 104 years after James I's succession, united the two Parliaments. As long as Scotland and England had separate Parliaments it was always possible that the Scottish Parliament could follow, for instance, a totally different foreign policy. And, at the time of the War of the Spanish Succession, this was important. Imagine the difficulties if Scotland chose to support a different side, particularly as it had always enjoyed a special understanding with France.

Also, and perhaps more significant, the Scottish Parliament could choose a different monarch if it so wished – and it might well. In 1701, the Act of Settlement promised the throne to the Hanoverians once Queen Anne was dead. (Elizabeth, daughter of James I and Anne of Denmark, married Frederick, Elector Palatine. Their daughter married Ernest-Augustus of Hanover; George – later George I – a Protestant, was their son.) But the Scottish Parliament didn't accept that at all and many in the English Parliament thought that the Scots might support Anne's half-brother, James Edward Stuart, the Old Pretender, even though he was a Catholic, because first and foremost he was a Stuart.

However, before the Act of Union could become law, there were differences to resolve. For the Scots, the massacre at Glencoe, which took place in 1692, had done little to convince them that anything much would be gained by the Union. Campbell of Glenlyon had slaughtered nearly forty MacDonalds, including the Jacobite chieftain, Alexander MacDonald. The Scots believed the Glencoe massacre was carried out on the orders of King William and so Union was impossible under him.

The English Parliament was dominated by High Church Tories. For those Tories, the Scottish Presbyterian Church was beyond the Pale and they did not want its followers in the English, or single, Parliament. So they did not want the Union. Equally the Scottish Parliament was dominated by the Country party and the extreme views of the Episcopalians, who were Jacobites, and the Presbyterians.

The Scottish Parliament forced through four Acts which the Queen's men could never accept. The first Act more or less outlawed the Episcopalians. The second stopped the Queen going to war without the Scottish Parliament's agreement. The third allowed French wines to be imported, thus breaking the trade embargo on the French with whom England were at war. The fourth was the ultimate hold over England – in theory at least. It said that if the Queen died without an heir, then Parliament could appoint her successor. Queen Anne was told to veto this fourth Act, the Act of Security. She was advised that if she didn't, there could be two monarchs after her death. The veto secure, the Scottish Parliament adjourned for a month but in the following year, 1704, the Bill came up again, and the Scots refused to pay taxes unless it went through. For hundreds of years English monarchs had paid lip-service to the crudest forms of democracy for the simple reason that monarchs need money for war. And at the point when the Scots were refusing to pay taxes unless the Act of Security was passed, Marlborough was planning his great campaign against the French. So the Queen, and her advisers, backed down. The Act was passed just as Marlborough was beating the French at Blenheim. However, in 1705 the English Parliament passed the Alien Act.

The Alien Act stated precisely what would happen if the Scottish Parliament refused to pass its own Act along the lines of the English Act of Settlement: one nation, one monarch. It said that a commissioner would be appointed to negotiate a Union of Scotland and England and unless the Scots produced such a law, then, after

Christmas Day 1705, Scots would become aliens in England with all that meant for citizenship and trade. The success of this Act was helped by the disunity among the Scots themselves. The English government agent in Scotland was the man who, fifteen years later, would win lasting memory as the author of *Robinson Crusoe*, Daniel Defoe.

Defoe reported back that he thought the Act would succeed. 'There is,' he reported cynically, 'an entire harmony in this country, consisting in universal discords.' Very simply, the Presbyterians and Episcopalians may have disliked Union with England and Wales, but they disliked each other even more. However, when a Bill was passed which secured the Protestant religion and Presbyterian Church government within the kingdom of Scotland, the Scottish Parliament agreed to the Act of Union.

Many believed that unless the differences between the two kingdoms were sorted out, then there could be another war, not with France and Spain, but between England and Scotland. And so it was that on 16 January 1707 the Scottish Parliament, as E. N. William, the historian, wrote, 'signed its own death warrant by passing the Treaty of Union'. Scotland was to be united with England and Wales. After Anne's death, the throne was to descend to the Hanoverians. There was to be but one Parliament in which the Scots were to be represented by forty-five Members (only one more than Cornwall) and sixteen peers. The Scots would keep their own legal system, including the feudal private law courts and, most attractive to many in Scotland, the Scots would now have the freedom to trade on equal terms with England and the colonies. And in June, 1707, a famous proclamation was issued.

Anne Regina
Whereas in pursuance of the two and twentieth article of the Treaty of Union, as the same hath been ratified and confirmed by two Acts of Parliament, the one passed by the Parliament of England and the other in the Parliament of Scotland, we, for many weighty reasons, have thought fit to declare by our royal proclamations . . . do hereby appoint our first Parliament of Great Britain shall meet and be holden at our City of Westminster on Thursday the twenty-third day of October next, whereof the Lords Spiritual and Temporal, and knights, citizens and burgesses, and the commissioners for the shires and

burghs of our said first Parliament of Great Britain, and all others
whom it may concern, are hereby required to take notice.

   Given at our Court at St James's, the fifth day of June 1707, in the
sixth year of our reign.

On 23 October 1707, the first ever Parliament of Great Britain met at
Westminster. The Act of Union brought together Churches, politics
and religion, albeit shakily.

   In that same year, 1707, the War of Spanish Succession rumbled
across Europe until it appeared finally to conclude and so, for the
moment at least, Marlborough was a national hero. The nation gave
him his own palace, Blenheim, at Woodstock in Oxfordshire. Later,
Capability Brown designed the gardens to resemble the layout of the
troops, their regiments and squadrons, as they formed up for the
Battle of Blenheim itself.

Meanwhile, the British had captured Gibraltar and the Earl of
Peterborough had captured Barcelona. Families were leaving for the
New World to join the children of the Pilgrim Fathers who had sailed
for America more than eighty years earlier. Daniel Defoe was now
editing his own newspaper, the *Review*, and masons were working
on John Vanbrugh's Castle Howard in Yorkshire. A treaty had been
signed with Portugal to allow port wine to be brought into England
at reduced customs rates. Commerce had expanded and harvests
were good. Trade was gaining an importance that had not always
been there and it was uniting people's interests even if religion split
them. Rivers were deepened and widened and locks were built,
which suggests that roads were poor and trade good, although the
first canal, the Bridgewater, was not cut until 1761.

   The people lived much as before: the north tended to be poor, the
south prosperous. Defoe thought the Lake District wild, barren and
frightful. People lived in buildings little better than cowsheds, yet
this was changing. Cloth weaving was bringing a new prosperity to
the region and child labour was not seen as a disgrace, but a sign of
industry. Defoe wrote about one town where, 'There was not a child
in the town or in the villages round it of about five years old, but, if
it was not neglected by its parents and untaught, could earn its bread.'

   And poverty shouldn't be confused with early eighteenth-century
ignorance. Further north, in Northumberland for example, more of

the population could read than in the financially secure south. The Scots produced more books and, not surprisingly, the Lowlands had more in common with the north than did the southern counties.

Wherever the traveller went in the kingdom, the one thing to be found was beer. It was certainly safer than the water and drunkenness was commonplace. The more prosperous of London had other pastimes. Since Charles II, the fashionable had taken coffee, tea and, later, chocolate. By Queen Anne's time it was possible to pick and choose company at the different houses in St James's. Whigs were to be found at the St James's Coffee House, Tories at the Cocoa Tree, the clergy went to Truby's, the very smart to White's. Here then was the beginning of the London gentlemen's club. And there was one chocolate house that was to become greater than them all; it was run for the commercially minded in Lombard Street by a man called Edward Lloyd.

London may have been fashionable, but it was disgusting to some, including the monarch. The population of England was about five million, nearly 700,000 of whom lived in London. And the city, with its huge coal fires, was a hellhole for almost every invalid. Anne suffered from gout and preferred Bath of Windsor. She certainly avoided having every sore joint shaken by official carriage rides through London's roughly laid streets. John Macadam, although born in the eighteenth century, wouldn't be laying his smooth roads for another 100 years – and then he chose Bristol anyway.

Whitehall itself was in a sorry state; almost every building had been burned to a shell in 1698; only the Banqueting House had survived. But Parliament had grown stronger, power had shifted and the monarchy was weaker. The result was that the power of the court (but not yet of the monarchy) was waning.

Marlborough, for example, still put great store in his influence with the Queen, which was exercised through his wife, Sarah Churchill. But now, because of the new influences at Westminster, especially the re-emergence of the Whigs, that was changing. By 1707 the arrangement was under considerable strain. The Queen's dislike for the Whigs was partly taken out on Sarah, probably because Marlborough did not share his monarch's distaste, if only for very practical reasons. Certainly it was hard to see how any war could be executed without the Whigs, especially as the Tories did not form a powerful enough group to overcome any Whig opposition. This was far more than party politics. The Queen was quite definite in her views about the Whigs – most of whom were to her mind without any religious backbone. Equally she understood perfectly that she had to have the Whigs on side to finance the war. Sarah Churchill was reasonably persistent in her opinion and since she was far more than a lady of the bedchamber – but what we today would call almost a Prime Minister (an appointment that did not then exist) – the stress of the Churchill–Queen relationship was not to be underrated. An almost exhausted Sarah Churchill introduced to Anne's court her relation, Abigail Hill, who was also a cousin of the Whig Earl of Sunderland. Sunderland was also Marlborough's son-in-law. The Whigs, knowing they were important to the Queen's government, wanted a greater say in Cabinet. They put forward Sunderland and Anne most certainly didn't want him. But the Whigs, by threatening to withdraw their support from the war effort, forced Marlborough and his closest political friend, Godolphin, to insist that Anne should allow Sunderland public office. It was not such a good scheme but she gave way.

There was now another cousin of the increasingly influential Abigail Hill in the political picture. He was Robert Harley, who had gone into Parliament as a Whig but became a Tory when Anne ascended the throne in 1702 and became her Chancellor of the Exchequer. Within two years there would be what was called a Whig Junto. Junto comes from the Spanish word *junta*, which means council. Sunderland was part of that Junto, so was Marlborough. Harley soon overhauled them in prominence when, or so it has often been claimed, the Queen sent a message via one of her gardeners to come into her parlour of intrigue. He did so and immediately brought together a group of Tories and Whigs who would support the Queen in Parliament. If this group succeeded, Harley had to assume that Godolphin would fall. Thus, the intrigue and ruthless nature of politics at the start of the eighteenth century and the parts played by long famous men including Marlborough.

As we saw earlier, Sidney Godolphin had been minister to Charles II, James II and now Queen Anne. He'd been instrumental in getting through the Act of Union with Scotland; but most important to Marlborough, and therefore the Queen, Godolphin was Lord Treasurer, the government's financial manager, the man who could manage the flow of war expenses. So, and even leaving aside their friendship, of course Marlborough would try to protect Godolphin. In doing so, he knew that Harley, the Queen's favourite minister, would have to go. Therefore, Marlborough was indirectly challenging the nerve as well as the authority of the monarch.

All this assumed that Marlborough's own standing was not challenged. Sarah Churchill, Marlborough's wife, was no longer an influence with the Queen and it would only take a poor campaigning season at the war to reduce Marlborough's stock – which is exactly what happened in 1707. On the Rhine, the French commander Marshal Villars took and pillaged large parts of Germany. In Spain, the Alliance generals split their forces. It was a disastrous decision. Everything that had been gained the previous year was now lost. In the Low Countries Marlborough was stuck simply trying to hold what he had got. He had allowed many of his forces south for what he'd hoped would be the taking of the French port of Toulon. It failed. Worse still, the British fleet was wrecked off the Scillies and 1,500 sailors drowned. And although he made it ashore, the finest of England's admirals, Sir Cloudesley Shovell, died. And, at the same time, one of Robert Harley's clerks passed Harley's correspondence to a French agent. The clerk swung at Tyburn for it. As for Harley, his was a Parliamentary lynching.

Marlborough had said that Harley should be dropped from the Queen's Cabinet. She of course refused this demand. So Marlborough said he could not sit at the same Cabinet table as Harley and left London. Anne had lost Godolphin and Marlborough and this was no private matter; here was an issue which could generate a lack of public confidence in the monarchy. Harley understood this and could no more than step aside, taking with him his closest political ally after the Queen, Henry St John – more famously remembered as the first Viscount Bolingbroke (1678–1751). So Marlborough and Godolphin appeared triumphant but the real winners were the Whigs. From now on there would be increasing distance between the monarch and the man who had once been her favoured general and friend. With this dismal prospect and in some depression, Marlborough returned to the war.

Yet the nation grew weary of the conflict. 'A fruitless carnage – so much death but not peace' – that was the charge, and Marlborough had to face it. But although the Duke was now without royal favour, no politician dared put him down. Many coveted his political influence, but none felt brave enough to challenge his generalship. And, for the moment, Marlborough had more pressing matters, soon to be terrible matters. He was with his great friend and fellow campaigner, Eugene of Savoy, preparing once more to fight the French, this time at a bridgehead on the River Scheldt outside the obscure Netherlands town of Oudenarde.

During the next few hours, 20,000 men or so would die. Prince Eugene of Savoy had command of the right, Marlborough of the centre. The Dutch allies behind them would cross the river to their left. Before them was the French army. It was 11 July 1708. It was a battle of confusion and seemingly hopeless slaughter. The French would be decimated: 18,000 of them would be killed. But it wasn't over. Marlborough and Eugene laid siege to the great fortress of Lille, defended by 15,000 Frenchmen. They held out until December. Then Bruges fell and then Ghent. At the same time, the navy took the Mediterranean island of Minorca and, as a bitter, freezing winter covered Europe, all military sense suggested that the French were beaten. Louis XIV talked peace with the Dutch. Marlborough talked terms, but in great secrecy, with his nephew, the Duke of Berwick. The Duke was the illegitimate Jacobite son of King James II. He was a general of the French army and had fought with distinction against Marlborough's armies in Spain and now in the Lowlands. Thus were the families at war in eighteenth-century Europe – and the war would continue for many more winters for, if nothing else, the reason for the War of the Spanish Succession had not been truly resolved. And there was a reasonable fear that if the war against Spain continued while France was allowed to withdraw quietly, then the French might get back their military breath and once again threaten the Alliance. The French protested that the war was really over and that they would no longer defend Philip, Duke of Anjou, Louis XIV's grandson, in his claim to the Spanish throne. They would withdraw from Spain and even give over French fortresses to the Alliance. But what Louis XIV wouldn't, and couldn't be expected to do, was actually go to war against his grandson. And it was on this point that the peace broke down.

The combined armies of the Alliance once more gathered their guns and men to face the French south of what would, in the twentieth century, become a notorious battlefield, Mons. But this was 1709 and the place was the pretty wooded countryside of Malplaquet.

Some 90,000 Frenchmen faced 110,000 allied soldiers. The French cavalry, in spite of outstanding gallantry, were put to death and the infantry ran. Marlborough wrote, in seemingly great sadness as well as hope, to Sarah his wife:

> I am so tired that I have but strength enough to tell you that we have had this day a very bloody battle; the first part of the day we beat their foot, and afterwards their horse. God Almighty be praised, it is now in our powers to have what peace we please.

But the following year the armies were greater than ever and the war continued.

When a weary Marlborough returned to London it was to find the politicians at their own war and the Queen seeking vicious revenge. She was determined to rid her government of Whig domination. The political order was about to change. Sunderland was sacked, so was Godolphin and Harley returned as a Tory government leader with his Secretary of State, Henry St John, a Jacobite sympathizer and no stranger to personal scandal. The Queen had them back, nestled to her dull, but political, bosom. But what to do about Marlborough? The answer, as ever, was war. For the tenth year Marlborough returned to the war in Europe, which was exactly what the Queen, Abigail Hill, Harley and St John wanted: Marlborough was out of the way. Did this royal cabal succeed? Harley, as Chancellor of the Exchequer, created the ill-advised South Sea Company, partly to balance the English books by trading slaves and goods in Latin America. Harley and St John also attempted to win peace with France, with the utmost secrecy.

Although Harley and St John were political manipulators, both men were important draughtsmen in the treaties which would end the war. And unlike Marlborough, Godolphin or Prince Eugene, both found it difficult to suppress their jealousies. What's more Harley's position, socially, politically and nationally, was about to be boosted in the most unexpected manner. In one moment of silliness, Harley became a national hero. A French refugee stabbed him with a tiny knife. Nothing serious, but the people rose to their Chancellor of the Exchequer – not a common emotion in any century. And the Queen made him Earl of Oxford and Mortimer, and gave him Godolphin's old post as Lord Treasurer. Everything seemed in place for a successful political period other than word got about that England was in secret negotiations with that oldest enemy, France. Those at Westminster who were negotiating with France wanted Marlborough out of the way and instigated an investigation into the way he had used war funds. He was accused of using something in the order of a quarter of a million pounds for his own use. He said it was to pay for Intelligence. Marlborough's real allies were the other leaders of the Grand Alliance, the countries he had led to so many victories. The King of Prussia and the Elector of Hanover set out their belief in his innocence in a solemn document in his defence. Prince Eugene went to London to plead the cause of Marlborough. The Tory government ignored the princes of Europe. And Eugene returned, downhearted, to the war. Having previously appeared beaten, Louis XIV of France rallied his people at the news of the downfall of the man they had almost believed invincible in any warfare. The French found a surprising ally in the British government. In 1712, at the siege of Quesnoy, the Tory government sent instructions to the British commander to, in effect, not get involved in the battle.

And so, between 1713 and 1714, a series of nine agreements that came to be known as the Treaties, or more correctly, the Peace, of Utrecht brought the War of Spanish Succession to an end. Europe was carved up, boundaries drawn, territory handed over. From the Spanish Empire Britain was given Gibraltar and Minorca. From the French, Hudson Bay, Nova Scotia, Newfoundland and the island of St Christopher were handed over. So the war was over and Europe was at some sort of peace with itself. Marlborough, like the Old Pretender, was hounded into exile and in London the celebration of exile and victory was marked by squalid and spiteful scheming for the power of both throne and government.

CHAPTER THIRTY-TWO

1714–20

The last months of Queen Anne's reign found Great Britain in a bad-tempered political mood, with the Queen full of gout and rotten temper even less capable than before of controlling her government; Harley and St John, now styled Viscount Bolingbroke, were at each other's throats and the Tories were seeking spiteful revenge over the Whigs they had displaced. The government was on its last legs. Bolingbroke, who resented being only a viscount and wanted to be an earl, was bent on getting rid of Harley. The ruling Tories were split. Some didn't like the terms of the Treaties of Utrecht. Others wouldn't agree the orderly succession of the throne. Some wanted James Edward Stuart, the Old Pretender, the son of James II, to be King. Others wanted George of Hanover. As for Harley, he was in a sad state; he drank too much. He was incapable of managing the government (he had never been very good at it, drunk or sober) and he was politically and mentally befuddled. Above all, he was showing less and less respect for the Queen. At the Cabinet Council on 27 July, in apparent and terrible distress, she dismissed Harley as Lord Treasurer and ordered him to surrender his white staff of office. It looked as though Bolingbroke had won. He had not. The Queen was hardly long for the world and her more sage ministers said that she should make Charles Talbot, the Earl of Shrewsbury (1660–1718) Lord High Treasurer – in all but name what is now called First Lord of the Treasury and Prime Minister. Shrewsbury was one of the seven signatories of the document inviting William of Orange to come to England in 1688 and so he was no stranger to intrigue at Westminster and court.

The Tory Party had also set themselves the task of prosecuting the exiled Marlborough and making him repay the hundreds of thousands of pounds which he said he had spent on spies – a statement supported by the European Princes. The Tories were in spiteful mood. They said he had pocketed the money for himself. However, Marlborough was not without his friends. The Whigs, in opposition, kept in touch with him and had a common interest: siding with the Hanoverians in the matter of the succession. They got ready to put the fifty-two-year-old George, the Elector of Hanover (who had written in defence of Marlborough), the great-grandson of James I, on the throne of England. Elector was the title given to a German Prince entitled to vote for, or elect, the Emperor. And the reason this Prince, the Elector of Hanover, was next in line to the throne of Great Britain was that the 1701 Tory-dominated Parliament had passed the Act of Settlement which proclaimed that no Catholic could ever be monarch, and, what's more, that no one married to a Catholic could be monarch. It also stated that if William III and his sister-in-law, Anne, had no heirs, then the British throne should be inherited by Sophia of Hanover (a granddaughter of James I) or her line – as long as they were Protestants. The Whigs, knowing they had the open support of the Hanoverians were making it clear that they had military as well as political support to oppose what they saw as the continuation of the Jacobite cause. This did not mean that the nation was behind the Whig position and it was reasonable to suppose that the nation, if not openly split, would be uneasy over yet another rebellion and countermovement together with the very real possibility of Catholic support coming from France. Yet again, the navy kept a weather eye for any movement of the French fleet.

On 1 August 1714, forty-nine-year-old Queen Anne breathed her last and the nation breathed a collective sigh, for no uprising came. As none of Queen Anne's eighteen pregnancies had survived beyond childhood, the Protestant George, the Elector of Hanover, waited to be called to London – not that he cared one jot for the place. He liked the British, whose language he could not speak, even less. But, for the moment, that mattered not. He was Protestant and he would become King of a firmly Protestant State. Moreover, the British were not simply proud to be Protestant, they were full of arrogance in the fact that they were not Catholics. That is not the same as anti-Catholic. It is simply an eighteenth-century British view that Protestantism was superior. The British saw themselves as different, economically prosperous and thereby superior to Continental Europe. And the nation's prosperity coincided with this assurance of Protestantism. There was a common sense that Protestantism was the free and obvious religious persuasion of the successful. And the written word had much to do with it: in 1662 Parliament had passed the Licensing Act which banned all publications that didn't conform to official Church teachings. But by 1695, just nineteen years before the death of Anne, that Licensing Act was allowed to lapse and the printing presses were freed.

In Scotland, England and Wales, printing became more than business, it unblocked the political, social and, most importantly, the religious arteries of the nations. The first London daily newspaper appeared in 1702; provincial papers carried the latest from London; and Parliamentary reporting was probably more extensive than it is today. This meant that people began to get an idea that they were part of something much greater than their provincial existence had thus far allowed them to think: Great Britain.

This then was the nation of the new monarch: the beginning of the Hanoverian reign of England, Scotland, Wales and Ireland. There were six Hanoverian monarchs from George I to Queen Victoria and it was a curious dynasty. Nevertheless, on 18 September 1714, George, Elector of Hanover, sailed up the Thames and landed at Greenwich. The people of Britain had what they wanted: a Protestant succession.

In other words, George I became King of Great Britain because it was convenient to the British. He had watched their vicious skirmishing with considerable distaste, especially when they accused his friend Marlborough of misappropriating war funds. His petition defending Marlborough had been ignored with open contempt – even though he was the heir to the throne. But, like William of Orange, he found it convenient to be King and, after all, senseless to refuse the Crown and patronizing to do so. George, like most princes, had his own rules. For example, having married his cousin he then divorced her and locked her up in Ahlden Castle for thirty-two years – the rest of her life. She was guilty of adultery and George, a Lutheran, took this very seriously. But he also took two of his mistresses very seriously. One of them he made the Duchess of Kendal, and the other became the Duchess of Darlington. He would expect the British exchequer to provide for them both (and him) and when they got into financial difficulties (as he did also) to bail them out.

He understood little of the political system and held many of its guardians in contempt, even though he needed wise political management as the previous year or so had been filled with spite, vengeance and the very real risk of civil war. What was more, the Jacobites, the supporters of the Old Pretender, were not yet done. It was said, by the Jacobites of course, that five out of six people in England supported them. This is doubtful, but certainly there were many who didn't like the idea of a German-speaking King using English resources for Hanoverian ambitions in Europe. And the gov-ernment's spies were sending in reports of plans for a landing in England, for a general uprising. Then on 1 September 1715 Louis XIV died.

Some suggest that this was a blow to the Jacobite cause. Perhaps, it was, but the Treaties of Utrecht stated that the French would no longer support the Jacobites. Yet what treaty was ever signed but to be adjusted at a later date? The Scots, as ever hopeful, raised the Jacobite standard. It was a good and under-standable rebellion against the seemingly alien Hanoverian authority in Scotland. But although it would not be the last upris-ing, it was not much likely of success. If indeed 10,000 men did fall in with the colours, there was little sign of what they could worthwhile do, nor what likely support they had elsewhere other than from a not very strong group of northern gentry in England and, more importantly, from Scottish exiles in France. The acces-sion of George I had wrecked the political ambitions of the Tories and of the Jacobite sympathizers. The Earl of Mar, who had called out his Jacobites in Perth, had been in Queen Anne's government, but was sacked by George's advisers. In France, the Old Pretender, James Edward Stuart, had been told what he wanted to hear – that now was the time to strike – but his advisers were wrong. The Fifteen, as the Jacobite rising of 1715 is known, ended with the Old Pretender escaping to France in February the following year and from there to Rome, where he died in 1766 and was buried at St Peter's. But the Fifteen uprising gave the Whigs good reason to strengthen the authority of the government, even to the extent of preventing the King creating new peerages which might have upset the balance of power. And within six years, Robert Walpole, a Norfolk squire, would become the first Prime Minister of Great Britain. The uprising was also an easy opportunity for the Whigs and government to claim that anything Tory should be seen as suspicious as they were, as a political grouping, Jacobite sympathizers and therefore potential subversives. Not surprising then that after the Fifteen, the Tories were a broken political force – for the moment.

In spite of the apparent ease with which the rebellion had been put down, there was a fear in the country that there could just be a chance of a Stuart, a Jacobite, revival and therefore the possibility of yet another confrontation with France. And there was, in any case, more to the Scottish uprising than simply wanting the Stuart line to continue. For example, many – perhaps most – Scots thought little of the Union of England and Scotland. There was little evidence of its benefit to them. The Act of 1707 which had brought England and Scotland together had demolished the Scottish Parliament. Even though that assembly had itself been largely governed from London, it had represented some semblance of a distinctively Scottish voice in the sometimes disparate Scottish nation.

Also when the eleventh Earl of Mar raised the Jacobite standard at Braemar in September 1715, he was doing so as a man who had served the last Stuart, Queen Anne, well, and had, by all accounts, attempted to make the Union work. But his motives were probably not purely those of a Jacobite. If George I had given him a profitable post, he would have stayed with the monarch. Scottish historians may dispute this point, but it's certainly true that having been rejected by George I, Mar was no longer to be counted upon. And Mar believed he could count on the Episcopalian Church in Scotland and the countryside indulgences of what was still a near feudal system based on allegiance to a family.

The Whig revenge against the Fifteen's leader was fairly mild. The Lords Derwentwater and Kenmure (who had risen in support of the Stuarts) were executed after the Battle of Preston in November 1715, but many others were allowed to escape. Even some who were condemned to death, for example at Carlisle, were never hanged. In fact, two years after the rising, in 1717, the government's Act of Grace gave free pardon to all who'd taken part, except to the Macgregors. The Macgregors didn't expect a free pardon because they didn't exist, at least not officially.

The Macgregors were considered as little more than bloodthirsty criminals and raiders. At the start of the 1600s the Macgregors had been on yet another raid, this time a very bloody one in Glen Fruin. It became known in Scottish history as the Slaughter of Lennox and the then Earl of Argyll was charged with bringing the Macgregors to account. The chief of the clan Macgregor crossed the borders to plead his case to his King, James VI of Scotland and James I of England. But Macgregor never made it. He was arrested, then hanged. And, in 1610, a government commission issued an order of fire and sword against the Macgregors – in other words, an order to hunt them down. In 1617, Parliament abolished the name Macgregor. So there was no pardon for the Macgregors who continued to oppose authority. Among their number, incidentally, was Rob Roy.

But for the moment, the Whigs were confident of their political power and there was stability at Westminster. There was, however, a little matter of a £50 million debt to be sorted out. The debt was the result of the war and taxes couldn't be raised in sufficient amounts to cover it, so when an apparent sure-fire trading opportunity was presented, even the grandest snouts slurped from the eighteenth-century financial trough. The 1711 South Sea Company had been running with some success for nine years when it offered to absorb part of the National Debt. Of course, Parliament agreed. Consequently the shares in the company rose dramatically until, like so many wonder shares, their bubble burst. Many were ruined, others accused of corruption and the perils of bad investment at court found the King's mistresses besides themselves with impending financial calamity. It was the steady figure and influence of Robert Walpole that would not save the day, but do enough for the monarch and his ladies to be every grateful. And why should he not be trusted? It was he who had warned them all that the South Sea scheme was doomed. They took little notice. They were making money, or so they thought. Walpole had himself been Chancellor, but had resigned in 1717. He had done so partly because he disliked the internal political jockeying for the position of the minister with most influence over the King, and partly because he disapproved of the government's foreign policy. The court didn't think a great deal of him especially when he boringly said that the South Sea scheme was but a bubble waiting to be pricked because instead of remaining a trading company it had become a finance house; and that was the root of its problem. Walpole should have known of course: he had himself been involved in the rush and grab for profit.

CHAPTER THIRTY-THREE

1721–6

Robert Walpole (1676–1745) was a short, stout, ruddy-faced Norfolk farmer who hunted most of the season. In 1721 he became Britain's first Prime Minister – a title quite new to government and one used pejoratively because he took so much authority on himself. A simple description of Walpole might be: the first Prime Minister and the person who managed the embarrassment and political position of court, party and government – the three victims of the greed and unwise investments of the moment. He brought political stability to Britain, and he set the style and method of government management for the rest of the eighteenth century. Walpole had been sent to Eton and then in 1696 up to Cambridge University. He was there for only two years, but would have been aware of the terrible turmoil of the country and the monarchy. In his first year, there was, or it was said that there was, a plot to assassinate King William III. In his second year, the War of the Grand Alliance against France came to an end with the signing of the Treaty of Ryswick – the accord that momentarily set the balance of power in Europe in favour of the Habsburgs of Spain and the Holy Roman Empire.

Walpole left Cambridge because his brothers died and, at the age of twenty-two, he returned to Norfolk to run the family estate. Two years later, in 1700, his father died and Walpole became head of the family, married his first wife, Catherine, and then became the Whig MP for Castle Rising and, in the following year, for King's Lynn – a seat he was to hold for most of the rest of his life. In 1708 he became Secretary of War and later Treasurer of the Navy. These were important posts: England was leading the Alliance in the War of Spanish Succession. Walpole was, by then, the established leader of the Whig Junto in the Commons. But when Queen Anne came to the throne, Harley became head of the Tory government. He needed to get rid of the outspoken Walpole and through some curious and historically unproven corruption, Walpole was actually expelled from the Commons and even sent to the Tower for six months. But by the time of George I's accession, Walpole was back in favour and, in October 1715, became Chancellor of the Exchequer. That was the year of the Jacobite uprising and Walpole helped to put it down.

Walpole's rise to power had much to do with his own authority in managing party affairs and government but also, in the early years especially, it had a great deal to do with his cousin, who was also his brother-in-law, Charles Townshend, the second Viscount Townshend and later known as Turnip Townshend: he too was a Norfolk farmer.

The brothers-in-law were clearly of similar persuasion and neither liked King George's preparations for his adventures in the Baltic (Britain's military power was one of the few attractions for the Hanoverian). Walpole said Britain could never afford the costs of personal wars and that the government could not be sure of its majority if it went ahead. He and Townshend were forced to resign.

Walpole spent his time out of government getting on good terms with the Prince of Wales (the future George II who did not like his father anyway – no Hanoverian Prince of Wales ever liked his father) and by 1720 Walpole was back in favour enough to persuade the Prince to make it up with the King. Walpole became Paymaster General. By the following year, he was First Lord of the Treasury and Chancellor of the Exchequer, and sorting out the problems left by the bursting of the South Sea Company's investment bubble. He split the remaining National Debt between the Bank of England and the Treasury and activated his fall-back, a sinking fund from taxes, in order to reduce it. His longer term aim was to have a stable monarchy, not an easy proposition given the personalities and personal ambitions of the Hanoverians.

The King was learning to trust his English advisers, especially Walpole, which was wise because the advisers held the purse-strings, almost the only thing of interest to George I. So keeping the King and his mistresses in line was not too difficult although Latin had to be a reasonable lingua franca for Walpole and the monarch. Neither was proficient and their conversations rarely touched the heart of political and economic thought, but the relationship worked well enough and it reflected the apparently bland atmosphere of the Hanoverian court in London. One of the King's mistresses, the Duchess of Kendal, was also happy to explain, if needed, Walpole's views to the King, in exchange for a reasonable commission. Walpole certainly eased the financial anxieties of the King and his mistresses, but the lives of the vast majority were uncertain. Just as none of Queen Anne's children had survived, as many as 20 per cent of babies died in their first year and one-third died before the age of five.

There were then about 6.7 million people living in England, Wales and Scotland. By the end of the century, that figure would be approximately 10.5 million. The increase in population reflected advances in medicine and the general well-being of the people. However, at the beginning of the eighteenth century, of those who survived childhood, life expectancy was thirty-five years. People died in what would now be called ordinary circumstances, not because there was some genetic reason for dying young. It wasn't a characteristic of the human race, especially the British people, to have short lives. Someone who did get through an epidemic or a war might well live to what, even now, would be called an old age. It was simply that when people did fall ill they couldn't rely on medicine to cure the simplest of ailments, and so something like measles quickly became an epidemic. Also surgery was crude; there were no anaesthetics and, although alcohol may have helped the symptoms of pain, the results of shock could be death. This meant that more people were dying than were being born.

And in 1720 another, unexpected, epidemic appeared: cheap gin. Low taxes on alcohol and a freedom to distil encouraged people to abandon beer for the much cheaper gin. It was, among the poor, a killer. And there's evidence to show that the gin epidemic was very much concentrated in London, where perhaps as many as one in ten were dying from drink. Daniel Defoe claimed that because gin used much corn, the landed classes and the traders benefited from the fashion. Parliament took its time to do something about the problem but the solution was, after all, simple: tax gin out of the poor man or woman's grasp and send them back to ale – which medically, at least, was probably less harmful than the water. The traders did not mind who paid what or what they bought. A drunk would be merry on whatever the tipple and would wake up in his or her same station in life whatever the drinking companions of the night before. That was the generalization.

Yet, overall there was a slow but perceptible shift in people's stations in life. The eighteenth-century class system was being reshaped. There was increasing prosperity and innovation. The trading classes were elevated. Walpole's first wife, Catherine, was the daughter of a timber merchant of Kent. The older families were struggling to keep their wealth. The trading classes (and at this period these would include bankers) now had the money to bail out and buy out some of the less fortunate. Here were what Daniel Defoe called, 'the richest commoners'. And Defoe was well qualified to write about the changes in the class system. He understood every nuance of the London underclass. His father's name was Foe but Daniel changed it to Defoe in about 1703 – when he was in his early forties. His father was a butcher and he, Daniel Defoe, became a hosiery trader. He was also a Protestant. Defoe joined Monmouth's rebellion against the Catholic James II and then signed for William of Orange's army in the Glorious Rebellion of 1688. He started pamphleteering and produced a notorious tract entitled, *The Shortest Way with Dissenters*. But this was hardly some popular diatribe. Defoe himself was a Dissenter, a Non-conformist. He was illustrating what he saw as the farce of intolerance.

Trade is so far here from being inconsistent with a Gentleman, that in short trade in England makes Gentlemen, and has peopled this nation with Gentlemen. After a generation or two, the tradesmen's children, or at least their grand-children, come to be as good Gentlemen, Statesmen, Parliament-men, Privy Counsellors, Judges, Bishops and Noblemen, as those of the highest birth and the most ancient families. Thus the Earl of Haversham was originally a merchant. The late secretary Craggs was the son of a barber. The present Lord Castlemaine's father was a tradesman. The great grandfather of the present Duke of Bedford, the same. We see the tradesmen of England, as they grow wealthy, coming every day to the herald's office, to search for the Coats of Arms of their ancestors in order to paint them upon their coaches. It was said of a certain tradesman in London, that if he could not descend from the ancient race of gentlemen, from which he came, he would begin a new race who should be as good Gentlemen as any that went before them

Centuries earlier the aristocracy had emerged in English society, a class that assumed rights over others by birth – an aristocracy that spread from the family of monarchs. Here Defoe was concerned with a new aristocracy, a mass migration from the bottom up. But he disliked much of what he saw. He travelled about Britain observing the old order of the island. But he did so with the sharp sense of the successful tradesman he was and that his father had been before him. What he saw was the beginning of a new revolution, the Industrial Revolution. In the 1720s the development of science and a curiosity about things mechanical, coupled with the new opportunities for the trading people, mark the track towards the term 'industrial'. For instance, in agriculture – the largest industry in Britain at the time – until the eighteenth-century farmers scattered seed by hand. In 1701, a man called Jethro Tull invented the wheeled seed drill. And because he did so, corn, for example, began to grow in rows. And the gap between those rows needed to be weeded, so Tull developed a hoe drawn by a horse.

Travelling through Yorkshire – which Defoe called a 'frightful country' – in the early 1720s, Defoe described the textile industry. This was possible, he said, because there was coal and fast running water. Even the villages were arranged to dig the coal and to catch the water to produce the cloth that the growing manufacturing masterclass and their markets demanded.

Note this use of the word manufacture. It wasn't new. It had developed as a reference to the subject Defoe was describing: cloth-making. And the place where all those lusty fellows worked was already called a factory. Originally the term was used for a place where traders worked for overseas markets. But by the 1700s the two words were acceptably joined: manufactory. And while Defoe travelled throughout England watching the ways of the new Hanoverian age, in London its protectors, Walpole and Townshend, were preparing for its next generation. At a distance the Prince of Wales also watched and waited. For the days of George I were now drawing to an end.

By the early 1700s the British monarchy had lost its sparkle. It was no longer the one element by which the nation could be governed. Furthermore, the monarchy had lost its Englishness, its Britishness. The line of kings and queens, albeit with Norman, Angevin, origins, was broken. The carefully developed responsibility of successive monarchs had been kingship – the promise to protect the people from invaders and lawmakers in return for the right to rule. When, in the past, a king or queen talked about 'My People' there was a sense of responsibility but most of all, identity. This essential part of kingship had disappeared. Now there was a German King on the throne who spoke little or no English and who cared little or nothing for his people. He was succeeded by his son who hated him, and who was unpopular with his people, too, and who would sooner have been in Hanover.

And as identification with the monarchy waned, the British Protestants saw themselves as favoured, chosen, set aside for greatness by their Protestant ethic. The only people to be feared or scorned were Catholics. The Whigs were determined to stay in power and take every opportunity to denounce the Tories as Jacobites – and therefore promoters of a Catholic monarchy. The Whigs were becoming the ruling aristocracy. Against this background the Prime Minister, Robert Walpole, determined his threefold task of stabilizing the economy, the monarchy and the Whig party.

Old enemies reappeared, or tried to: one of them was Henry St John, Viscount Bolingbroke, the Tory plotter against Marlborough who had gone into exile once George I became King. And new and rising politicians nibbled at power such as the arrogant and ambitious John Carteret; the one-time ally of Walpole, William Pulteney; and the bland Henry Pelham and his brother, Tom Pelham-Holles, the first Duke of Newcastle. Walpole was careful to exclude from his circle those who threatened, and encourage those who could never do so. The Opposition courted the Prince of Wales and bribed the King's mistresses, but in the latter case, so did Walpole and usually with more effect than the Opposition. He knew far more about the needs of the King's ladies. None of this suggests that he was in total control. There were too many factions, too many opportunities to disrupt and corrupt government, the court and the institutions – especially the Church and the law. There was a constant: the King needed the government and both needed Parliament. Furthermore, whatever their differences, the King understood that he needed his son to succeed him; but most of all, he needed Walpole. It is too easy to say that attempts by Walpole's enemies to distract the King from the Prime Minister's methods of political management were unlikely to succeed. Walpole had to constantly demand that all members of the Cabinet must totally obey him. What he couldn't control were events abroad, although he tried, by distancing the Cabinet from them.

Austria and Spain, once enemies, joined forces under the Treaty of Vienna in the spring of 1725. Spain was demanding the return of Gibraltar from Great Britain, and the Austrian Ostend Company was a direct competitor of the East India Company. Then Russia joined Austria. How to prosecute foreign policy and when necessary war encouraged a strong difference of opinion between Walpole and his trusted, but not always bright, brother-in-law, Townshend. For example, Townshend quickly organized, too quickly according to Walpole, a new alliance of Britain, Hanover, France and Prussia. To Walpole this was entirely against the delicate balance he was trying to maintain. Parliament didn't want to go to war but here was Townshend bringing together an anti-Austria cabal in the name of the House of Hanover. It never came to war, but it could have.

The ordinary people weren't particularly preoccupied with matters in Europe, but rather more with matters at home, in particular with a new tax. For centuries the nation had grumbled about the burden of taxes and rioted against the levying of them: they were usually imposed to raise money for wars. But now there were riots against local levies, toll taxes. The roads of Britain were in a sad state of repair. The roads that the Romans had built 1,300 years earlier were in better condition than roads built much more recently, because those who remained after the Romans were not builders. And, of course, there had been a massive increase in traffic.

The tenant farmers, the most frequent users of the roads, had to pay the road surveyors and, in eighteenth-century England, national attention to road building and repair was in its infancy. So, to build and repair the roads the people had to pay tolls. Daniel Defoe thought the toll taxes worked well.

> Turn pikes or toll bars have been set up on the several great roads of England, beginning at London, and proceeding thro' almost all those dirty deep roads in the Midland Counties especially; at which turn pikes all carriages, droves of cattle and travellers on horseback are oblig'd to pay an easy toll; that is to say, a horse a penny, a coach threepence, a cart fourpence, at some six to eightpence, in some a shilling. Cattle pay by the score, or by the herd, in some places more.

But in no place is it thought a burden that ever I met with, the benefit of a good road abundantly making amends for the little charge that the travellers are put to at the turn pikes.

Not everyone agreed with Defoe, especially those who had to pay. Moreover there were enough people grumpy at the charge for the mood to gather pace to the extent that in 1726 the people rioted against the charges. Not that the protest did much good for them. The turnpike had first appeared in the 1660s and from now until the end of the eighteenth century it was to be the main means of improving the road system. In the 1700s more than 1,000 turnpike acts were passed. Britain was beginning its great industrial journey.

CHAPTER THIRTY-FOUR
1727–46

At three o'clock in the afternoon on 14 June 1727 a messenger arrived from the Continent at a house in Chelsea with news for the Prime Minister, Robert Walpole. Walpole hurried to Richmond to the King's son, the Prince of Wales, and his wife, Caroline of Ansbach. It was the news they had all been waiting for: George, the first Hanoverian King of Great Britain and Ireland, was dead. George Augustus, Elector of Hanover, Prince of Wales, became George II. That night the new King made his solemn declaration to his people. Note the style and tone of the address. It is almost as if this were not an eighteenth century moment in our history, but something from the middle of the twentieth century. It could have been a statement eagerly awaited by the population as they clustered around their wireless sets. But this was June 1727.

> The sudden and unexpected death of the King, my dear father, has filled my heart with so much concern and surprise, that I am at a loss how to express myself upon this great and melancholy occasion; but my love and affection to this country, from my knowledge and experience of you, makes me resolve cheerfully to undergo all difficulties for the sake and good of my people.

In reality George II detested everything about the British and Britain. And he was not some latterday Prince Hal, impatient for the power the Crown would bring. That kind of power no longer existed, and he knew it – which was part of his frustration. By the end of the seventeenth century the constitutional power of the monarch had been limited by an increasingly influential Parliament. Traditionally, the Crown's greatest power was and remained patronage. The King's constitutional right to control who got what job in government, in

Parliament and in the Church continued. Thus the new King continued to need the government, the government needed the King and they both needed Parliament.

The keeper of the government's influence was still Walpole who was strengthened by the patronage of the new Queen, the very clever Caroline of Ansbach. Clearly, Walpole was not a favourite of George II. The King went as far as to dismiss Walpole and offer his job to Sir Spencer Compton. But only Walpole and his powerful political army of Whigs could maintain the balance of power between monarch, government and Parliament. There was powerful opposition in Parliament and more importantly, Queen Caroline convinced her husband that he had not been particularly wise when he dismissed Walpole. The King did his Queen's bidding and Walpole was called back. This royal retreat hardly improved George II's short-temper and determination to use whatever powers he had.

To get some idea of the main restrictions on royal rule we have to remember that the King was a constitutionally appointed monarch whose first qualification was his Protestantism and his second an agreement to rule within the boundaries drawn by legislators. For example, the 1689 Bill of Rights that followed the Glorious Revolution may not have controlled the prerogatives of the Crown, but it most certainly set the ideals of so-called Parliamentary supremacy over the sovereign. Equally, we must not think that Parliament and government were united. Even Walpole was proving to be unpopular because he was determined to maintain his priority of putting the nation's difficulties in good order. He wanted to avoid foreign ventures, especially those dear to the King and many of Walpole's own ministers, including his brother-in-law Charles Townshend whom Walpole regarded as being dangerously adventurous in foreign affairs. Walpole could not be doing with opposition. So in 1730, Townshend had to go. He retreated to his Norfolk farm, developed a new system of root crop rotation and that was when he earned the nickname 'Turnip' Townshend. Walpole took over his portfolio.

As unpopular as Walpole appeared to some in opposition, there was no one who could command enough support to truly threaten his position. Even Henry Bolingbroke, who had become a gathering point for opposition figures, was not so effectual as he might have been considering the wide range of political and literary figures who gathered at his house, including Alexander Pope and Jonathan Swift. Swift, the Irish clergyman, pamphleteer and author of *Gulliver's Travels*, was also a marshal of Irish patriots, a Tory, and therefore against Walpole. Bolingbroke at last saw little interest in being in opposition and so departed back to France. England held little personal interest for him and, in truth, a major cause of the opposition's failure lay in Bolingbroke himself. He had not reformed: he was still the unprincipled rascal so scorned by Harley and Queen Anne. It was discovered that he had been passing political intelligence to the French ambassador, which, considering the popular belief that France could at any time support a Jacobite rising, was unwise. Even worse was to come when it was known that he had taken money from the French to support the opposition cause against Walpole. But Walpole's skill as a political manager, his pragmatism and shrewdness served him well. Bolingbroke and his friends could never agree among themselves for long enough to sustain the pressure against Walpole and, no matter how much they mocked him as the 'prime minister', that's exactly what Walpole was.

It's generally thought that Caroline of Ansbach, George II's wife, was Walpole's strongest ally. Sometimes she might suggest policy to the King which Walpole couldn't put forward without sparking one of their not infrequent quarrels. George II and his Prime Minister could never agree the constitutional restraints imposed on the monarchy by Parliament. Worse, the King often, especially in matters of foreign policy, tried to go against Parliament and always had to give in – which didn't improve his political temper. So Walpole spent much time trying to placate the King, his ultimate patron.

But if the Queen, Walpole's ally, died and the young Prince of Wales, who was no friend to his father and mother, set himself against Walpole and came out for the opposition, then Walpole's authority might well be weakened. Maybe a more colourful figure than Walpole would have given the opposition more opportunity. But Walpole was so often dull and his style of administration was deliberately lacking drama. 'A safe pair of hands' would be a modern description. Frederick, Prince of Wales, was central to the opposition's cause. Princes of Wales would always be a disturbance in the pond-life of court and political life in London. Within that princely set were good minds, not simply social limpets, and they attracted political minnows waiting to be noticed. One was a young cavalry officer, William Pitt. In 1736 Pitt was twenty-eight. He was a member of a group known as Cobham's Cubs, the young followers of one of Walpole's critics, Viscount Cobham. He'd become part of the so-called Leicester House set, named after the place where the Prince of Wales held court. Walpole, who could not stand any public opposition, made sure Pitt lost his commission in Viscount Cobham's regiment of dragoons. But within a year, Pitt had a salary of £400 a year as the Prince of Wales's Groom of the Bedchamber. Pitt's polemics and his rhetoric excited the nation. Here was a young man to watch and Walpole knew it.

The next year, 1737, the King and Queen once more fell out with their son, Frederick, whom they disliked intensely. This time, Walpole was not able to bring about a royal reconciliation. A few months later his ally, Queen Caroline, died. She had been one of the few who understood the advantages of his tight political management and the importance to the King of maintaining his support. Under Walpole's dull routine of stability, the British thrived but were uninspired. The eighteenth-century British were supposedly confident, even arrogant in the Protestant sense of superiority; in over-simplified terms, what the British wanted was a fight.

Of course, Walpole began his ministry by avoiding confrontation. He was a quiet fixer. He had smoothed over the financial scandals of the South Sea Company rather than risking the outcome of a Parliamentary inquiry. He had withdrawn a patent for making halfpennies to be distributed to Ireland, not because it was a bad idea, but because there was well-organized public resentment of it. And he pulled back from excise on wines and tobaccos. More dramatically, but very telling was Walpole's reaction to the Porteous affair. Captain John Porteous, the Commander of the Edinburgh City Guard, had fired on a crowd watching the public execution of four smugglers. Porteous was sentenced to death, reprieved and then strung up by the Scottish mob. London called the Scots judges to the bar of the House, humiliated them and proposed fines on Edinburgh. The protest was loud, and not only from Scotland: Walpole backed down, again.

The prosperity of Britain suggests that Walpole's eighteenth-century pragmatism worked. But in foreign relations his belief that all disputes should be settled by negotiation, rather than after hopeless fighting, was perhaps naive. What Walpole, for all his skills, didn't understand was that France did not see things his way. France believed that the differences of France, Spain, Austria and Britain could be settled only by war. France was right. By the mid-1730s, Austria (Britain's ally) was fighting Spain and France (also Britain's allies). And very shortly Britain too would be at war. By the late 1720s the British who, in 1714, had forced the French and the Spanish to make trading concessions under the Treaties of Utrecht at the end of the War of Spanish Succession, had turned these limited treaty concessions into a complete trading invasion of the Spanish-American colonies. It amounted to economic piracy. But by this time Spain was once again stronger and started to take action. Spanish ships stopped and searched British vessels (admittedly illegally trading) and British merchants demanded retaliation. And also, by this point, Britain believed unswervingly in its Protestant right and these were Catholics interrupting British passages on the high seas. Even so, Walpole avoided every possibility of overseas confrontation. He saw no future in getting involved in conflicts which would unbalance the British domestic economy and political system. In 1731 Walpole decided negotiation was the best way to resolve the matter. It may have stayed that way if a certain British captain had not claimed that he had his ear cut off by a Spaniard. Unlikely? Yes, but it started a nine-year war.

Captain Robert Jenkins was in command of the English brig, the *Rebecca*, in 1731 when it was boarded by the Spanish, who were said to have sliced off one of the ears of Jenkins (perhaps for the gold earring). Seven years later, with many in Parliament looking for war with the Spanish, Jenkins was taken to Parliament were he recounted the 'insult' and supposedly displayed a bottle with his pickled ear. Taken with other matters both political and military, this was considered enough to go to war with Spain. The confrontation, which was really about far more, was known as the War of Jenkins' Ear. The war was absorbed into the much wider conflict, the War of the Austrian Succession (1740–48). Before its outbreak, Walpole had achieved at least an outline agreement, the Convention of Prado – a much discredited protocol that was supposed to settle disagreements between Spain and England. True, Spain agreed to compensations but it certainly refused demands that it gave up its rights to stop and search British vessels. Britain at first said it would withdraw its vessels from the disputed area. The Spanish were happy at this. The

British decided they were not and changed their mind. They broke the treaty almost before the ink was dry.

Clearly the Convention of Prado would not let Pitt keep Britain from war; nor would it put off the so-called Patriots. They were a Whig opposition group which included Pulteney, a former ally of Walpole, as well as Carteret, whom Walpole had dispatched to Ireland, Viscount Cobham, and the young William Pitt. On 6 March 1740, Pitt got up in the Commons and verbally ripped the Treaty of Prado to pieces. He told Walpole that Britain must defend her trading rights or 'perish': 'Is this any longer an English Parliament, if with more ships in your harbours than in all the navies of Europe; with above two millions of people in your American colonies, you will bear to hear of the expediency of receiving from Spain an insecure, unsatisfactory, dishonourable Convention?'

More ships than anyone else? Mostly, that was true. Certainly the British believed that they should rule the waves. It was their right as Protestants to rule whatever and whomsoever they wished. They thought so and they would learn to sing so in perhaps the most famous song of all British time. James Thomson had written a masque, called *Alfred*, about Alfred the Great, the father of the navy. And the opening lines fitted perfectly the mood of the year 1740:

> When Britain first, at heaven's command,
> Arose from out of the azure main,
> This was the charter of the land,
> And guardian angels sung this strain:
> Rule Britannia, rule the waves;
> Britons never will be slaves.

Note that it is not 'Britannia *rules* the waves' as is sometimes sung in the Albert Hall, but 'Rule Britannia, *rule* the waves'. It was not a statement: it was a declaration that Protestant Britons were chosen by heaven to rule. Walpole was sound on ruling the British economy. He was not perfect. He was a manager of peace, not of military conflict, and his Parliamentary support was deserting him. In 1741 the opposition had rarely felt so sure of itself. On 13 February the MP for Worcester, Samuel Sandys, rose in the Commons to speak for the motion to remove Walpole from office.

According to our constitution, we can have no sole and prime minister: but it is publicly known that this minister, having obtained sole
influence over all our public counsels, has not only assumed to sole
direction of all public affairs, but has got every officer of state
removed that would not follow his direction . . . He has made a blind
submission to his direction the only ground for hope for honours or
preferments. Has not this minister himself not only confessed it, but
boasted of it? Has he not said, and in this House too, that he would be
a pitiful fellow of a minister who did not displace any officer that
opposed his measure in Parliament?

It was in this same Parliamentary debate that Walpole declared that
he was not the 'Prime' Minister.

While I unequivocally deny that I am the sole and prime minister, and
that to my influence and direction all the measures of government
must be attributed, yet I will not shrink from the responsibility which
attaches to the post I have the honour to hold. And should, during the
long period in which I have sat upon this bench, any one step taken
by government be proved to be either disgraceful or disadvantageous
to the nation, I am ready to hold myself accountable.

Once again Walpole outwitted his opponents and the House voted
for him. But it was his last victory. In February 1742, the first Prime
Minister of Britain, Sir Robert Walpole, resigned. In the vanguard of
the opposition to Walpole was the Prince of Wales, the heir to the
throne. The Prince had left George II's court in the summer of 1737
and set up his own court. Now he and the other political dissenters,
including Pitt, attacked. The prince had as much money as he needed
and he used it ruthlessly and, in the times, quite legitimately, to buy
seats for his followers. Walpole, after twenty-one years as the first
Prime Minister and so the first to occupy 10 Downing Street, the
master of patronage and the prime figure of eighteenth-century
Parliamentary politics, was to go but not into obscurity. He was
created Earl of Orford and soon set about making sure that the Whigs
continued to rule and that the weaknesses in the opposition were
exploited. And he had a personal battle to fight. During his two
decades of office, Walpole had made his fortune. This point is usually
dismissed as unimportant to the story of Britain's first Prime Minister.

But when Walpole was accused of making money out of being head of government, men who had expected reward for their time in opposition and didn't get it were the first to demand Walpole's prosecution. For example, Lord Chesterfield (1694–1773) had wanted to be Secretary of State but was to wait until 1746 for that honour. Cobham wanted more power than the command of his regiment. Pitt felt aggrieved that he was ignored. The paradox was that while most accept that favour was a reasonable way of maintaining stability and improving office, that only worked if one were favoured. Certainly, most at Westminster were convinced that political patronage for high and medium office was the best way to stay in power. Everyone did it, and everyone made money out of office, especially the nobility. Walpole wasn't the only one who understood the workings of political corruption. At the time, not many more than 1,000 rich people influenced the governance of Britain. Little wonder few would have questioned Henry Fielding's definition of a Nobody as, 'All the people in Britain except about twelve hundred'.

About 25 per cent of the peerage had some form of official office and with them came salaries and pensions. Walpole, for example, had given his son Horace three sinecures. He was one of the Tellers of the Exchequer (that was worth £1,200 a year alone); also he was Comptroller of the Pipe and Clerk of Escheats. An escheat was land or property that was supposed to revert to the Crown, and there were profits and percentages to be made from those transactions. A Secretary of State could make perhaps £7,000–£8,000 a year. Walpole had been Paymaster General and had made his fortune from it. Commissions (backhanders might be a twentieth-century description) from contractors and suppliers alone could set up the office-holder for life. One Lord Chancellor, when fined £30,000 for misappropriating government funds, paid it within six weeks and still made a 60 per cent profit. But many of them, probably all of them, needed the money. For example, it cost Walpole £15 a day in candles to light his home, Houghton Hall. He spent £30 a week on wine.

None of this was the concern of the King. He simply needed a government capable of supporting (that meant with funds) his view that the real dangers lay not in the counting houses of Westminster, but in the ambitions of the new order in Europe. George II's particular concern was with his nephew Frederick, now King of Prussia.

Frederick's accession made George II extremely nervous. He was still a Hanoverian and Frederick could well decide to invade the King's estates. And George had no doubts about Frederick's ambitions because he knew him very well.

This then was the atmosphere as Lord Wilmington, formerly Sir Spencer Compton, became Prime Minister instead of the man who would have been a safer choice, Henry Pelham, supported by his wealthy brother, the Duke of Newcastle. Wilmington was quite incompetent. What could the King do? He needed good government. He needed also, the support – financial and political – to further his military aims on the Continent of Europe.

George II turned to John Carteret (1690–1763). Carteret was a brilliant man at a time when Walpole needed brilliance working for him and no one else. Carteret had been Secretary of State between 1721 and 1724. He was too clever not to be dangerous and so was sent to Ireland as Lord Lieutenant for six years (1724–30). George II brought him back as Secretary of State and immediately Carteret made clear that a partnership between the Electorate of Hanover (George II's domain) and England with a treaty with Austria against France (more urgently against the Franco–Prussian alliance) was the flawless means of preserving the balance of power in the War of the Austrian Succession in favourable terms for the British. Carteret indeed had a reputation for brilliance, but not always for wisdom – a gift easily usurped by arrogance. Certainly he was the power behind Wilmington. But he was an individualist who cared little for the detail of political management which was necessary to hold together all the factions at Westminster; this was especially so if Britain was once again to enter the larger stage of Continental warfare. But the King, George II, wanted none of the inhibitions of the Parliamentarians he detested. He wanted to be at war.

In 1740 the War of the Austrian Succession began. It was to last eight years. In simple terms, the war was between Britain and her allies against a Franco–Prussian alliance and Charles Albert of Bavaria. The allies fought to guarantee the succession of Maria Theresa to her father Charles VI's rule of the Habsburg Empire. This was, in modest terms, the first world war. Led by George II, the British fought on Continental Europe and against the French in India and North America (the War of American Independence did not start until April 1775). The late Charles VI had the promises of European rulers that on his death they would support the succession of his daughter in Austria, Bohemia, Hungary and the southern Netherlands. Frederick the Great ignored such promises and seized Silesia, then an Austrian province.

The House of Habsburg was one of the oldest European royal families. The name comes from Habsburg Castle which was built in Switzerland by the Bishop of Strasbourg. That was in the eleventh century at about the same time that the Normans were building in England. By the late thirteenth century, the then Count of Habsburg, one Rodolph, became the Holy Roman Emperor. And the last male in that line was Maria Theresa's father, Charles. However, that wasn't the end of the Habsburgs because Maria Theresa and the Duke of Lorraine, her husband, began the modern line of the family, the last of whom (another Charles) abdicated as Emperor in 1918. Britain engaged in the War of the Austrian Succession because it had a treaty with Austria, and the fear that its old enemies, the French, might gain the Austrian Netherlands was worrying for the Hanoverian George II. It would bring the French too close to home.

But monarchs have never had an easy time raising money for wars other than when they were already winning them, or there was about to be an invasion. Nevertheless, the war existed, Britain had obligations and George wanted to protect his Hanoverian borders, but the Prussians and the French threatened to invade if he did. George agreed to remain neutral for twelve months so Maria Theresa fought on alone – she had to. She was defending her right to the Austrian throne – the old Emperor, her father, had even changed the so-called Pragmatic Sanction to favour her right to the throne on his death. But once the period of neutrality was ended George got his money and his permission from Parliament and, under the guise of being Maria Theresa's auxiliaries (today they'd be called military advisers), 30,000 British soldiers went to the Continent. Their army was known as the Pragmatic Army. So King George II had his way and was soon to make a lasting entry in the military history books. On 27 June 1743, British, Hanoverian and Austrian troops commanded by George defeated the French and Bavarian army at the Battle of Dettingen. This was the final time that a British sovereign commanded his troops in battle.

In spite of the monarch's spectacular command and also the cheering of victory, there was little support in England for a

Continental war. Even though the French and Spanish were in some form of alliance and the Jacobites were said to be planning, with French help, a landing in southern England, the government had little chance of rousing the nation and the coffers for costly wars. Moreover, Carteret (Lord Granville), who had succeeded Wilmington as prime minister on the latter's death in 1743, was an indifferent political leader. Henry Pelham became the nation's fourth Prime Minister in 1745. Walpole had liked him: he was quiet, industrious and efficient. But the King still took a great deal of notice of Carteret and his friend Pulteney, the Earl of Bath, because they supported his military ambitions. And it was very easy for them to undermine Pelham, who was not in complete control when he became Prime Minister. The nation was still at war and the King had appointed his third son, the then twenty-four-year-old Duke of Cumberland, as captain general of the armies. Pelham was not much concerned at this news; he and his brother, the Secretary of State, Duke of Newcastle ('That impertinent fool,' as George II called him) were suffering enormous difficulty trying to hold together the differing interests of the administration.

Then in 1745, not quite out of the blue, came news of a rumour turning to fact. The Jacobites were once more on the march and the Forty-Five, as the rising became known, was in the making. Legend was also in the making: the rebellion was led by Bonnie Prince Charlie, the Young Pretender. There had been three Jacobite risings before the Forty-Five in 1708, 1715 and 1719. And they had three things in common: bad timing, bad organization and false hope. The 1708 uprising, which included a French invasion fleet, was scuppered by appalling weather, indifferent navigation and a failure actually to get ashore. The attempt in 1715 stood a better chance. The Eleventh Earl of Mar, who led the rising, soon raised support in Scotland but this time there was no French support for the Jacobites. In 1719, the year of the third Jacobite uprising, raiding parties were sent from Spain to preoccupy the British and perhaps deter them from taking sides in a European conflict that was going on at the time. It came to nothing other than a skirmish at Glen Shiel.

So, in June 1745 Prince Charles Edward, relying more on romantic ideas than support, other than from the Highlanders, landed in the Western Isles. The Highlanders and Lowlanders did not care much for each other. The clans cared for none other than their own. The rising at first went Charles's way. By the autumn, it was said that he could command most of Scotland. But any Jacobite euphoria was not long lived. The important Hebridean chiefs, Macdonald of Sleat, Macdonald of Clanranald and Macleod of Dunvegan, had refused to come out for him, although the young Clanranald did so. By the time he was at Edinburgh, the Young Pretender could begin to organize his brigade of followers: the Stewarts of Appin, the Robertsons and the Macphersons. Perhaps Prince Charles's most important ally was Lochiel, the clan chief of the Camerons, although it is said that he joined against his better judgement. When Charles's army defeated the English under Sir John Cope at Prestonpans there was national support for the not always popular George II. Unsurprising then that a rousing, patriotic song began to be sung in London. Its composer was Thomas Arne (1710–78) and it was first sung in its 'British' form after a performance of *The Alchemist* by Ben Jonson.

> God Save our noble King,
> God Save great George our King,
> God Save the King.
> Send him victorious . . .

The line 'send him victorious' meant God should send victory over the Jacobite hence one of the verse's distinctly anti-Scottish tone:

> Lord, grant that Marshal Wade,
> May by thy mighty aid, Victory bring.
> May he sedition hush and like a torrent rush,
> Rebellious Scots to crush,
> God Save the King.

The irony is that other versions of the song had been used for years by the Jacobites. But now the Hanoverians had now commandeered the song which would be called the National Anthem, but not until the nineteenth century.

So with 'God Save our King' ringing to the rafters of London theatres, rebellious Scots (more accurately rebellious Jacobites) were to be crushed. On Culloden Moor near Inverness, Cumberland killed 1,000 Scots – in not much more than half an hour. And so the legend was made. Bonnie Prince Charlie, the Young Pretender to the

English throne, disguised as a woman by Flora Macdonald, escaped in a boat to Skye. But by then he was hardly a princely figure and Flora Macdonald took him to the island with some considerable reluctance. He was torn, hunted, hungry and nibbled by lice and mosquitoes. He was, eventually, rescued and taken to France as the hero of the moment. But the moment did not last long and in later years the once Bonnie Prince ended his days in Italy, as a drunkard. And there is one often-forgotten postscript to the Battle of Culloden: it was the last land battle ever to be fought in Britain. The date was 16 April 1746.

CHAPTER THIRTY-FIVE

1746–56

Around the time of Culloden, the Prime Minister, Henry Pelham and his brother, the Duke of Newcastle, found themselves with a crisis of quite a different sort. The Pelhams wanted to improve their administration by bringing in William Pitt. But the King didn't like the Pelhams and he still fancied he could have Carteret and Lord Bath leading his government so he said no to William Pitt.

Newcastle wrote to Lord Chesterfield, who was then Lord Lieutenant of Ireland.

Newcastle House, February 18, 1746
Private

My Dear Lord,
I am now to give you an account of the most surprising scene that has ever happened in this country, or, I believe, in any other.
Some few days before the meeting of Parliament after Christmas Mr Pitt went to the Duke of Bedford, expressed an inclination to know our foreign scheme, shewed a disposition to come into it, and wished that some of us would go and talk with Lord Cobham, into whose hands they had now entirely committed themselves.

Lord Cobham was Richard Temple, Viscount Cobham, for some time one of Pitt's patrons. His young followers, Cobham's Cubs or the Boy Patrons, had been Walpole's sharpest critics. In fact Cobham himself had been stripped of the command of his own regiment: Cobham's Horse. Newcastle's letter continues:

He seemed very desirous to come into us and to bring his Boys, as he called them, exclusively (as he expressly said) of the Tories, for whom he had nothing to say. The terms were Mr Pitt to be Secretary of War, Lord Barrington in the Admiralty and Mr James Grenville [Pitt's brother-in-law] to have employment of £1000 a year. Upon this, I opened the budget to the King, which was better received than I had expected; and the only objection was to the giving Mr Pitt this particular office of Secretary of War. We had several conferences with His Majesty upon it, the King insisting for some time that he would not make him Secretary of War; afterwards that he would use him ill of he had it; and at last that he would give him the office, but he would not admit him into his presence to do the business of it.

Two long-time political enemies of the Pelhams', Carteret, since 1744 the Earl of Granville, and William Pulteney, the Earl of Bath, now sided with the King against Pitt and, of course, the wishes of the Pelhams.

The King grew very uneasy, and complained extremely of being forced. But, when the difficulty seemed in a way of being removed, my Lord Bath got to the King, represented against the behaviour of his ministers in forcing him in such a manner to take a disagreeable man into a particular office and thereby dishonouring him both at home and abroad and encouraging the King to resist if by offering him, I suppose, the support of his friends in so doing. This strengthened the King in his dislike of the measure, and encouraged, I conclude, his Majesty to think that he had a party behind the curtain [that] would either force his ministers to do what he liked or, if he did not do it, would be able to support his affairs without them.

Tho' Lord Bath was the open transactor of this affair, it is not to be imagined but that my Lord Granville was in the secret. Mr Pitt, very decently and honourably, authorized us immediately to renounce all his pretensions to the Office of Secretary of War.

But it was thought proper, at the same time, to suggest to the King that, after so public an éclat as my Lord Bath had made of this affair, it was thought absolutely necessary that his Majesty should give some publick mark of his resolution to support and place confidence in his then administration; or otherwise we should be at the mercy of our enemies, whenever they were able to take advantage of us, without having it in our power to do the King of the public any service.

In other words, the Pelhams were demanding a public vote of confidence from the King.

> His majesty was extremely irritated, loudly complaining of our conduct both at home and abroad, unwilling to give us any satisfaction of assurance of his countenance or support and plainly shewing a most determined predilection for the other party. Upon this we thought, in duty to the King and in justice to ourselves, the wisest and honestest part that we could take was to desire leave to resign our employments.

But the King's party, in other words Bath and Granville, simply did not have the Commons support to lead a government so the King backed down, at least partly. Pitt was immediately created Joint Vice Treasurer of Ireland and, a couple of months later, Paymaster General of the forces – a lucrative arrangement inasmuch that the Paymaster General could put his budget in his own bank account and keep the interest on the capital. Pitt turned down this customary bonus and lived on his salary. When news of this grand gesture reached the general public, Pitt's star shone brightly.

The scoundrels of the pamphleteering classes, the periodicals and the satirists could find much to jeer at but Pitt could not easily be lampooned with much malice. There was enough wrong in society to provide seemingly endless inspiration to the cartoonists and writers including, William Hogarth. By the 1740s, Hogarth was an artist of considerable influence. In the previous decade, his 'morality' engravings about mid-eighteenth century Britain tell us more of that society than any other work. For example, the social novel had yet to be invented and so, almost for that reason alone, literature was never to have such a lasting impact as Hogarth's *The Harlot's Progress*, *The Rake's Progress*, *Marriage à la Mode* and *The Election*. One of his most powerful images, *The March to Finchley*, was a scathing illustration of part of Cumberland's army before its march north to Culloden. The central figure is a soldier. On one side he is tugged by a dark-cloaked, haggard female with a swinging crucifix who clutches the newspapers of the day. On the other arm is a comely lady, heavily pregnant, with a basket on her arm from which peeps a scroll on which we can see the words 'God Save the King'. The soldier is Hogarth's Britain and the two women are fighting for his soul. The dark figure is Catholicism in the form of the Jacobites. The lady in white is for the monarch and the child she carries is Britain's child. This was a sickly creature as one of his most memorable engravings, *Gin Lane*, testifies to the commonplace of drunkenness in London. The gin was swigged much further than the mucky alleys of the capital, London, as a 1740s christening report from Surrey distressingly shows:

> The nurse was so intoxicated that after she had undressed the child, instead of laying it in the cradle, she put it behind a large fire, which burned it to death in a few minutes. She was examined before a magistrate, and said she was quite stupid and senseless, so that she took the child for a log of wood, on which she was discharged.

There were about 7,000 gin shops in London alone and it was to this city that Hogarth turned for his social commentary. Parliament passed the Gin Act which put up taxes on the spirit and restricted its sale through retailers. The nation continued to drink, but the gin craze was on the wane. The moral crusade of the decade was reflected by Charles Wesley who had been preaching and writing what became a collection of 7,000 hymns, and his elder brother, John Wesley, the founder of Methodism, began his open-air evangelical crusade and would eventually preach 40,000 sermons.

Small factories were being built and textile-makers were leading what one day would be known as the Industrial Revolution. John Kay invented his flying shuttle for weavers but reaped few rewards. There was still famine in Ireland; witchcraft in England was no longer a crime; and Handel finished his *Messiah*.

At the time of the passing of the Gin Act, William Pitt was mourning the passing of a powerful ally, the Prince of Wales, in 1751. The man who would have been King on George II's death would probably have guaranteed Pitt's future. It was an unexpected interruption to a political career and an even more unexpected cause of death: it is thought that the Prince died as a result of having been struck by a cricket ball.

It was the middle of the eighteenth century and the war in Europe, the War of the Austrian Succession, was about to end. Henry Fielding was finishing his fat, bawdy novel, *Tom Jones*. Robert Clive was about to establish his name forever in India. The calendar that is still used today – the Gregorian calendar – was introduced by Henry Pelham. It replaced the Julian calendar and meant that Britain, after a lapse of almost 200 years, was once more using the same calendar as the rest of Continental Europe. Dr Johnson published his dictionary and Pitt eventually became Prime Minister. The Black Hole of Calcutta became notorious; James Wolfe set off to fight, and die, in Quebec; and, in the sky, the world saw the return of Halley's Comet.

First, the war in Europe. The Austrian Succession had never been Britain's war but a series of unnecessary treaties and the King's belief that his homelands were threatened, especially by Frederick of Prussia, Frederick the Great, had involved the British. But now the war was over chiefly because Frederick the Great had got what he wanted: Silesia. Britain, preoccupied with the Forty-Five Jacobite rebellion, had once again found it impossible to fight on more than one front. And in London there was more concern for the National Debt than the outcome of the war. The conclusion was yet another peace accord which did little to guarantee peace. It was called the Treaty of Aix-la-Chapelle and dated 18 October 1748. In this treaty the title of George II is King of Great Britain, Ireland and France. The English monarchy had not formally given up its claim to France, the old enemy. However, in the treaty the French once more recognized the Hanoverian right to Great Britain, said they would not support the Jacobite claim to the British throne and gave back Madras, which had been won from the English East India Company in 1746. But the war had been inconclusive, so the treaty was similarly inconclusive. Within eight years, Britain would be once again at war.

By now Britain fully understood the difficulties of controlling its foreign interests which were stretched from India to the Americas. This was all very new and quite a difficult day-to-day bureaucratic problem for the government. There was no great foreign policy, no great office of State with a century of expertise. Acquiring bits of the world was rather like a general taking a hill from the enemy and then asking: 'Now what do I do with it? How do I hold on to it? What's it for?'

But these were the beginnings of the British Empire. And if there was to be an empire, there was an even greater need for foreign policy based beyond the traditional relations and animosities on the

Continent of Europe. However, the monarch's first interest was that he remained a German. Therefore, just as George I had done, George II was inclined to set off for war in Europe if he thought his Hanoverian interests were threatened. And he often believed they were. He was after all, a Continental European – his people would never be that in almost 300 years. The British were more interested in the commercial reach and grasp beyond the Continent. At the start of the seventeenth century, British trading distinctions shifted with the moves of the newly established East India Company into areas then occupied by the Dutch and to some extent the Portuguese and French. British alliances and interests in Europe had to be based on an understanding that trade was of fundamental interest to Britain. And even in the eighteenth century, there was the recognition of the importance of maintaining Europe as an alliance of independent states – a common eighteenth-century market, not a federation. That trade was everything gradually became clear as the imperial history of the British matured. The colonization that would eventually be known as the British Empire was almost entirely about trade, not about the desire to own territory and to rule for its own sake.

India was a perfect example of this. The East India Company had attempted to get a foothold in the sub-continent at the start of the seventeenth century because there was much trade to be done. There were no ambitions to simply rule in the name of the monarch. When in 1600 the East India Company had been given a Royal Charter to trade, it was not a free pass to India and south-east Asia. No prince was to bend at the knee when the British ships arrived. The British, regarded by many in India certainly as not much more than a nation of offshore island fishermen, had to wait literally and metaphysically in line to get permission to open even the most rudimentary trading post. The Portuguese had been the major European trading nation in south-east Asia. But Portuguese influence was declining and the English East India Company believed it could replace the Iberian commercial managers. However, the Dutch were much stronger in what were called the East Indies, and they forced out the British. The British retreated to the Indian sub-continent but it was not until 1633 that the East India Company began to establish itself in Bengal. True, the British had to establish company armies to secure and maintain centres at Madras, Bombay and Calcutta. They had to fight for dominance over, for example, the French Compagnie des Indes at Pondicherry, south of Madras. Yet we might emphasize that although the two companies were rivals there's little evidence, at this stage, that they were interested in gaining territory for imperial reasons. They were trading, not colonial, powers. They were also centuries' old enemies on the battlefields of Europe. There was every reason for the bloody animosity to overcome the cautionary tales of the trading houses.

In the past, when England and France had gone to war in Europe, traders in India maintained neutrality so that their main interest, trade, should not suffer. But with the arrival of a British naval squadron, apparently determined to undermine French shipping, the Governor of Pondicherry, Joseph Dupleix, decided to go on the offensive; although even then there was evidence that the French action was to protect their trading interests rather than simply to conquer territory. The call to British and French arms was inevitable. In English history, that conflict gave the nation yet another hero that it would later castigate as a result of his success. He would be known as Clive of India.

Robert Clive (1725–74) was the son of a Shropshire squire with not much money. He was no great scholar and showed as much at the four schools he attended. Through family and friends he was given a job in London at the East India Company and at not quite nineteen, in 1744, was sent to Madras in India as a clerk. It was here that his depression and cries for help through failed suicides suggested nothing but misery and impending failure. Yet, exactly the opposite happened. His reputation was to be made and, very quickly and dramatically, he became a military commander of more than considerable talent. In 1746, two years before the European War of the Austrian Succession ended, the French took Madras. And Clive, then a twenty-one-year-old clerk in the East India Company, was one of the defenders who escaped from the city. After an unsuccessful coup in the Deccan and the successful placement of a puppet ruler by Dupleix, the British-preferred puppet, Muhammad Ali, had to escape for his life and was besieged at Trichinopoly. The events that followed sent Clive on a path to fame if not heroism.

Clive had left his clerking duties and travelled on one expedition as the Commissary, the person in charge of victualling the army. This taught him, and very quickly, the need to understand the people of the main force, the Indians, and, most important, the logistics of keeping an army on the move and ready to fight. On his return, Clive volunteered for army service with the Company, without pay, but with the rank of captain. With most of the army preoccupied with the siege of Muhammad Ali, Clive's offer was welcomed and shortly afterwards he led a detachment to Trichinopoly. It is very likely that he met Muhammad Ali and they talked over the way in which the siege might be lifted. An attack on the French at Trichinopoly would have been foolhardy. The plan was to attack the most important outpost of French and Indian interests, the centre of the Carnatic, Arcot, because it was all but undefended. With a relatively small force – 800 Indians and Europeans – and an attack-and-hold operation that lasted close on two months, Clive began to wear down the French and in doing so attracted Indian reinforcements that had more than likely been waiting to see what side would win before joining the battle. The detail of first the fall and then the defence of Arcot is full of episodes that point to fortune, incompetence, ill luck, and then good luck. For example, Abdul Codah Khan, the commander of the Indian sepoys, had been the only one to seriously attack Clive. But he was killed and his followers lost heart. If he hadn't been killed the result might well have been different. Clive was also saved from a sniper's musket ball by the quick thinking of a friend, who died for his pains.

Nevertheless it was clear that it was Clive's determination and leadership that won the day. The French were defeated. Dupleix's ambitions for French India were finished (and so was he) and Muhammad Ali was placed on the throne to, it was hoped, dance to Clive's tune. Britain had a new military genius and in India the legend of British invincibility was born. Muhammad Ali gave him the title, Sabit Jang, which means 'steady in war'. And when he was sent on other expeditions to take the French forts at Covelong and Chingleput, the legend grew. At Chingleput, his forces were raw recruits, ill-trained and with little courage under fire. Clive was seen standing in the vanguard of the action, quite exposed to enemy fire in an attempt, a successful one it seems, to shame his soldiers into action.

Clive would have been inhuman had he not encouraged the myth. However, he was never again to have such a celebrated victory, and there is, in Clive's story, a sense that he spent too much time trying to justify his image. There's even evidence that this pressure, on a not always stable character, damaged his health.

Shortly after his celebrated victory, Clive became quite ill. It was probably gallstones, but there are hints of fits of nervous or even manic depression. He was prescribed opium as a pain-killer and another legend, that he was an opium addict, grew up. The only firm evidence suggests he took opium when he was ill and at no other time. But the growing fame of Clive brought with it sufficient enemies to encourage such rumours.

Just a few days before sailing for home in 1753, Clive married Margaret Maskelyne; but his departure from India was not the high occasion it might have been because he was later accused of making too much money out of his exploits and of pocketing a percentage of the cost of keeping his soldiers and those he had rescued from French rule. If he was not always popular with the highest in the Madras administration, Clive was popular on his return to England. England needed a hero and Clive would do. But he was a hero to be kept at arm's length and he even failed to get into Parliament when he stood for election in a rotten borough in Cornwall. Dejected, Clive had little opportunity that would satisfy him and was reasonably pleased when the East India Company asked him to serve as Deputy Governor of Fort St David, which was south of Madras, and had applied for a commission for him as a Lieutenant-Colonel of foot. In 1756, the throne of Calcutta was held by a young and vicious prince, the Nawab Siraj-ud-daula. He was hardly a household name in Britain, but he soon would be. It was at this time that the Black Hole of Calcutta took the lives of 123 Europeans, or so it was claimed.

Until the nineteenth century a black hole was the common name for a military detention cell. The Black Hole of Calcutta was the detention cell in Fort William in Calcutta. Siraj-ud-daula marched on Calcutta – the traditional headquarters of the East India Company. The Governor, Roger Drake, was a weak, arrogant man with few diplomatic talents and an even smaller sense of military appreci-ation. When the garrison was besieged by Siraj-ud-daula, it was abandoned. The families, women and children, with Drake in the middle of them, took to ships in the river, leaving the rest of the garrison to the Nawab's mercy. Many of them were shut up in the Black Hole, a room fourteen feet by eighteen feet wide. John Zephaniah Holwell, one of the survivors, wrote in his official report

that out of 146 prisoners, 123 died. Holwell probably got it wrong
– deliberately. It is possible that he dramatized the incident to foster
the desire for revenge at home. Fewer than half the number Holwell
claimed were in the Black Hole and perhaps forty or forty-five
perished, suffocating during a hot, airless, Bengal night.

Whatever the correct figure, the important fact was that this single
event would destroy any lingering belief that the British could
remain in India simply as innocent traders. Clive soundly beat the
Nawab and his French allies at the Battle of Plassey in 1757.
The British now occupied India. The age of British imperialism
was dawning.

CHAPTER THIRTY-SIX

1756–60

In 1751, while Robert Clive was making a name for himself and the British in India, William Pitt, Pitt the Elder as he became known, was still wondering if he would ever become Prime Minister. His patron, the Prince of Wales, had died. The Prince favoured Pitt and the politician fancied that he would replace the Pelhams as leader of the government. The Prince's father, however, George II, did not like Pitt. He regarded him as an enemy. After all, Pitt had made no secret of his contempt for Hanover and the way British men and finances were being used to protect the Electorate.

There's another aspect to Pitt that's sometimes overlooked. He was often quite ill. In the mid-eighteenth century, that was hardly unusual. A small gripe could easily turn into something far more complicated. Although medicine was advancing, quite rapidly in fact, Pitt and his fellow sufferers were two centuries away from small, white, cure-all tablets. And it wasn't quite out of the question that, like many great men, Pitt's illnesses were sometimes brought about by stress and a personality disorder. At different times, a cocktail of medical symptoms, including something described as 'gout of the stomach', baffled his doctors. He suffered fevers, nervous depression and insomnia. Perhaps, like Clive of India, Pitt was prone to manic depression.

Henry Pelham, the Prime Minister, was quite different. He was solid. Sanity never deserted him, politically nor mentally. Pelham was described as an honest bore, by one observer. And, with his enormously rich brother, the Duke of Newcastle, Pelham balanced the very differing factions in the administration and Parliament. When Henry Pelham died in March 1754 George II is said to have remarked, 'Now I shall have no more peace.' That was because he knew the battle for political leadership would centre on William Pitt.

Even when Henry Fox (1705–74), Pitt's political rival, joined the
Cabinet George understood that Pitt would forever be a political
thorn that could never be pulled, particularly when Pitt made it clear
that he believed that the government was doing more to defend
George II's Hanover than Britain's real interests on the Continent. In
truth, Britain's interests – both political and commercial – could not
be confined to Continental Europe. The gathering wealth in India
through the East India Company, the increasing importance of the
sugar islands of the Caribbean and the uncertain political ambitions
of those in America tested Britain's diplomatic and military acumen.
America in particular presented a complex list of decisions to be
made over territory and the right to rule that territory without offering some political say in return. In North America the issue was
territory, not trade. In 1745 the Governor of Massachusetts and the
British military commander in America was William Shirley. He
wrote a letter to the Duke of Newcastle encouraging Britain's control
of Canada:

Louisburg October 29

I took the liberty to mention in a former Letter to your Grace, that I
thought, if the Expedition against Cape Breton should succeed, a
Spirit would immediately be rais'd in the Colonies for pushing the
success as far as Canada; which observation I find was not ill-
grounded; And I trouble your Grace with the repetition of it now,
because the Reduction of that Country to the Obedience of his Majesty
seems to be the most effectual means of securing to the Crown of
Great Britain not only Nova Scotia, and this Acquisition, but the
whole Northern Continent as far back as the French settlements on the
River Mississippi, which are about 2000 miles distance from Canada,
by making all the Indians inhabiting within that Tract (who are now
chiefly in the French Interest) dependent upon the English; the immediate consequence of which would be throwing the whole fur trade,
except such part of it as the French settlements in the Gulph and River
of St Lawrence, and even the bank of Newfoundland, and securing the
whole Codfishery to the English . . . which besides the Profits arising
from that part which the French lately had of it amounting to near £1
million sterling, would be further Beneficial to the British subjects by
the great consumption of Rum, and Cloathing [*sic*] necessary for the
Men in carrying on Fishery, and the greater quantity of Shipping,

small Craft and fishing Gear of all Sorts necessarily employed in it, which would in such Case be all British.

Competition – political, military and commercial – with the French was a centuries-old concern for the British. Shirley's letter reflects two great powers not vying for global superiority but for every advantage in the reachable world. North America was by then the most attractive proposition. It was vast, the riches were rumoured to be great and the territorial expansion seemingly endless.

In truth, though, both the English and French knew that the real potential had to lie in the East. The English most certainly had been attracted to eastern trade for reasons other than spices and peppers, in themselves compelling reasons to trade. By this time, the mid-eighteenth century, the fascinations of eastern culture that intrigued European senses of history and grandeur, were centuries old, whereas America had been always seen as a land of opportunity for the individual but in no way a mysteriously sophisticated society. Savages and land were there to be conquered. Shirley's letters to Newcastle reflected this reasoning. There were no princes and silken viziers to intrigue as there were in the near and far-eastern lands of Asia.

By the second half of the eighteenth-century Britain had more than doubled its overseas trade largely because of exports to the American market that Shirley had been so keen to encourage. And this import and export trade even survived a decade of war. The British had broken France's commercial grip on India and America. The Spanish (exhausted, said Shirley) had lost influence in the West Indies. By the 1750s, the British Merchant Fleet was more than half a million tons. Twenty years later, it was 30 per cent bigger, a measure of the developing trade particularly with the growing population of the 'Northern Continent'.

At the start of the century there were about 300,000 settlers living in America. By the 1770s there were three million. And that increased population generated industry, including those needing imports. America wanted, for example, iron and wool. So the stagnant wool industry in Britain was revived and the young iron industry boomed. Then, in 1756, the uneasy peace in Europe slipped away. The diplomatic revolution that had set new allies against old friends now meant war. It was called the Seven Years War: Britain and Prussia against France, Russia, Austria, Sweden and Saxony. In truth, Britain hadn't been at peace for some time. The War of Austrian Succession ended eight years earlier, but France and Britain had continued their conflicts in India and North America.

During the Seven Years' War France tried to invade Britain; Britain lost Minorca (which resulted in the execution of a British Admiral by the name of Byng), but won Martinique, St Lucia, St Vincent, Grenada, Tobago, Havana and Manila (some of which was given back to the French and Spanish). The Black Hole of Calcutta became an infamous entry in British colonial history and General Wolfe died famously at Quebec. But most significantly, this war was the first world war and the beginning of the British Empire.

And so everything should have pointed to a successful period in British government but it was not. The Duke of Cumberland (or the Butcher as he was known after the Battle of Culloden) was no strategist, and the Duke of Newcastle, now Prime Minister, at least nominally, demonstrated expected incompetence. This opened the way for William Pitt the Elder who, although not Prime Minister, became Britain's war leader, an early day Churchill, c.1940–45. Pitt's opportunity to lead came through what twenty-first-century Britons might think a preposterous incident.

Britain lost one of her possessions – Minorca. The Spanish had owned Minorca but handed it to Britain (along with Gibraltar) as part of the War of Spanish Succession reparations under the 1713 Treaty of Utrecht. Minorca was a symbol of British military virility and the feelings of the British at the time were similar to the feelings that would have erupted in Britain more than 200 years later if the Task Force Commander had backed away from trying to retake the Falkland Islands after the Argentinian invasion. On the occasion of the loss of Minorca, Admiral John Byng (1704–57) failed to relieve the British garrison on Minorca. He was tried for cowardice, which was a nonsensical claim by the disgraced British government, and shot on his own quarterdeck. In April 1756, Byng had been sent to relieve the English garrison at Fort St Michael, which was then besieged by the French army commanded by the Duc de Richelieu. Byng's fleet was not in best condition and the Admiral himself had a reputation as a commander who could find reasons why a mission was far more difficult than his instructions suggested. But in the case of relieving Minorca, he may well have been correct. He engaged the French fleet, but little came of it and the siege went on. Byng then left the region without landing British reinforcements and without blockading the French logistics line between Toulon and Minorca.

In the British fleet, as well as in Parliament, there was a sense of hopelessness and injustice. News, claim and counter-claim took days, often weeks, to reach home. So by the time the report of the loss of Minorca reached London the chattering crowds, the superior officers who had kept back ships and, most of all, the King all wanted the head of the man who had failed to bring them Minorca.

This incident in the Seven Years' War is hardly discussed today, but in the mid-eighteenth century it was celebrated in long articles in the growing numbers of newspapers and journals. And one of the most telling quotes of the Byng affair remains common currency. It comes from Voltaire in his novel *Candide*: 'Dans ce pays-ci il est bon de tuer de temps en temps un amiral pour encourager les autres' (In this country it is thought well to kill an admiral from time to time to encourage the others).

A scapegoat was needed and so Byng was shot. But the incident, and the other inefficiencies of this war, reinforced the fact that no matter how much the King disliked William Pitt, he needed this man who was capable of marshalling the people, the military, Parliament and government if the wider war, the coming world war, was to be won. The people wanted Pitt and so they had him.

In 1757, Pitt introduced a Militia Act which laid down who would be called up, who would be trained, for how long and when. It was a system that lasted until the twentieth century and the introduction of the Territorial Army of 1917. For the first time, the militia would be raised by ballot. This meant that almost anyone, rich or poor, would be trained, county by county; would be subject to the Mutiny Act; and would, in theory at least, be the Home Guard or the second line of defence against invasion – and this is important – or any rebellion in Britain.

Pitt's attention now turned to America. Lord Loudoun had command of the British forces in North America but he wasn't much good at it; his planning was bad, he had poor tactical vision and he had unrealistic expectations. So he was replaced by General James Abercromby. And Pitt, who was wise enough to bring the colonial governors into his confidence, wrote to those of Massachusetts, New

Hampshire, Connecticut, Rhode Island, New Jersey and New York. He had a plan: he was going to invade Canada and this would be the start of a campaign which, although not immediately successful, led, eighteen months later, to the conquering of Quebec and, more famously, the death of General James Wolfe and the beginnings of Canada as part of a British Empire.

Pitt wanted to attack on three fronts. It was an ambitious plan. The first thrust would be the St Lawrence River, Louisburg and Quebec; the second through Ticonderoga and the Great Lakes; and the third into Ohio. Louisburg fell in the summer of 1758 and Fort Duquesne in the November. (Incidentally Fort Duquesne was soon renamed Pittsburgh.) By 1758, the tide of war was beginning to turn. A central policy of this war was to keep the enemy – that is, France – occupied. One way to achieve this was to subsidize the Prussian war effort in order to make them more enthusiastic about taking on the French. This allowed British forces to attack the French in India and North America, knowing that the enemy would be stretched on more than one front. It also allowed the Royal Navy to raid the French coast, thereby stretching the French resources even further. However, these ideas, which looked good on paper, weren't always successful.

Many of the British Americans were by now second, third and fourth generation Americans. The reasons they left Britain are well-documented: poverty, disillusion, adventure and opportunity. The circumstances of life in America were little understood in the Royal Closet and in the halls of Kensington, Westminster and Whitehall. The efforts of British commanders in America had never been impressive, and there was little real reason for these people not to be united against the government of Britain. America was more than 3,000 miles away and no British leader had ever been asked to execute a war over such vast distances. And, as the Romans had found, the more roads their legions marched along, the more vulnerable they became. Pitt understood this, especially with regard to America. Years later, in his last speech to the House of Commons, he would plead for an understanding of the colonists. But he would be ignored.

And as Jeffrey Amherst and James Wolfe prepared their battle plans in Canada, Britain was only twenty years away from a war that would result in American independence. In 1759 Wolfe was dead, killed taking the Heights of Abraham. He was a casualty of victory. Such fickleness turns on a single moment. Wolfe's death provided a hero. The King's death would provide a political conundrum. In the autumn of 1760 George II, the last man who could keep Pitt in power, died. He was seventy-seven and, for the thirty-three years of his reign, Britain had flourished. As much as George disliked Pitt, he had learned to trust his abilities. And he recognized the wisdom of supporting the combination of Newcastle managing the finances with Pitt managing the war, a war in which Pitt had gained Canada and with it the assurance that France would not rule from the Arctic to the Gulf of Mexico. Political leaders who insist that victories do not remove dangers of war have never had much of a hearing in any century, including the twenty-first. Pitt was no exception and on 5 October 1760 he resigned.

CHAPTER THIRTY-SEVEN
1760–68

During the three decades of George II's reign the system of constitutional monarchy was established: the monarch no longer reigned by Divine Right. There were rules of succession and the powers of the monarch, although still considerable, were governed by political expediency. The monarch needed the Prime Minister; the Prime Minister needed the monarch; both needed Parliament.

Into this, now established, system came the twenty-two-year-old George III, in 1760. He was George II's grandson, the son of Frederick, the Prince of Wales who died. The third Earl Waldegrave observed the young George shortly before he became King and remarked that it would be unfair to decide upon his character in the early stages of his life. But he observed that there was room for improvement. George III was not bright, perhaps even a little backward. He was nevertheless seen as a conscientious man with ideas (not always his own). Mostly he relied on John Stuart Bute (1713–92), the Earl of Bute, for his political education. Bute had joined the royal circle during a downpour at Egham racecourse. The rain had driven the then heir to the throne, Frederick, Prince of Wales, into a sporting marquee. The Prince's party needed a fourth at cards; Bute was their man, and from that moment he became an intimate member of Frederick's set. When the Prince died Bute befriended his widow, Princess Augusta. In fact, it was thought they became very close friends indeed. Bute became indispensable to Prince George – the future King. He was a father figure and the new King George relied on him.

Pitt, on the other hand, although not Prime Minister, was the most powerful politician in the land – but not at court, and it was at this point that he found himself isolated. The Seven Years War trundled on. Britain's successes against the French in India, in North America and its support for Frederick the Great of Prussia had brought victories and commercial dividends. Now there was, to Pitt and Newcastle, the Prime Minister, a case for declaring war against Spain. The Cabinet said no and Pitt resigned. The Duke of Newcastle was not much good without Pitt, and Bute – a man with no political, only courtly, experience – became Prime Minister in 1762. He would not last. He was not a great political plotter or manipulator.

Inside three months of Pitt's going, Britain was at war once more with Spain. It was not a disastrous affair for the British. They captured Havana and Manila, and could then say they had toeholds throughout the northern world. From such a strong point, in 1763, it seemed the time was right to sign a peace treaty with France. Pitt's reading of history suggested to him that there was a danger, a very real one, of concluding not a peace treaty, but a truce. In other words, he felt that unless France was hobbled and not allowed to regain its possessions, regroup its resources and then its forces, a new war between the two nations would come soon. But Pitt was no longer in command. Bute really had little perception of what he was getting into yet, in spite of Pitt's cries of anger from the sidelines, Britain was achieving the formality of treaty rather than truce that she craved. True, Britain formally now had Canada, Nova Scotia, Cape Breton, Grenada, St Vincent, Dominica, Tobago and, from the Spanish, Florida. But in return, Britain gave France the lucrative sugar island of Guadeloupe, Martinique and St Lucia. Such a prize was Guadeloupe that at one stage the British thought it might be worth letting the French have Canada instead. The worst part of the treaty for Britain was the giving away of fishing rights that were even in those years considered to be worth £1 million a year.

The British public were less than impressed and the terms of the Paris Treaty, together with new and unpopular taxes in the spring of 1763, brought about mob protests on the streets of England and newspaper articles condemned the government and Bute in particular. Bute was not a political pugilist and within weeks he was heading for a nervous breakdown. He resigned and the new chief minister, the new First Lord of the Treasury, was George Grenville (1712–70), William Pitt's brother-in-law. But the King still regarded Bute as his Prime Minister. So, effectively, there were two Prime Ministers: Grenville and, behind the curtain, the Earl of Bute.

Bute was, and remained, George's mentor, his father confessor, his 'dearest friend', and although Grenville might have become a fine office manager for Britain, he was no managing director. He was an isolationist. And he had an ambition to reduce the tax burden. He did so by making the British Americans pay more. In doing so, and in doing so diligently, Grenville may perhaps be accused of hastening the American War of Independence.

The administration of Britain was going through the agony of the King's dislike and mistrust of his Prime Minister, of the Prime Minister's mistrust of the King, and of Parliament's mistrust of both. As Dr Johnson remarked, 'Most schemes of political improvement are laughable things'. Bute was a laughable character by now whose effigy was burned in the streets. And the fire-raisers could have burned effigies of any number of public figures at the time. In the early 1760s the seven million or so people of England and Wales knew that the ruling society was as corrupt as it was thoughtful even if some of the practices were not seen as unusual at the time. For example, the buying and selling of votes and seats was commonly practised; few thought that wrong. It was simply the system. After all, here was a society that had only very recently decided that witchcraft wasn't a crime; a society that treated its poor as outcasts, commonly practised religious and racial bigotry, still accepted slavery without question (the Slave Trade Act did not come until 1807 and Abolishment not until 1833) and treated backhanders and bribes as a way of everyday life and office. For years, the engravings of Hogarth and others, and the writings of many, had shown how badly, at least by twenty-first-century standards, children were treated at this time. And although Defoe talks of five-year-olds working at machinery, and praises this as good, industrious order, Jonas Hanway, in 1766, wrote in a pamphlet, 'An Earnest Appeal for Mercy to the Children of the Poor':

> Never shall I forget the evidence given at Guildhall, upon occasion of a master of a workhouse of a large parish, who was challenged for forcing a child from the breast of a mother, and sending it to the Foundling Hospital. He alleged this in his defence, 'We send all our children to the Foundling Hospital; we have not saved one alive for fourteen years.'

Jonas Hanway wanted an Act of Parliament that would make London parishes and poor children under the age of six in the country to be nursed. Hanway was not much interested in the Englishness of the infants, only that 47 per cent died before the age of two.

While social pleading depended on debate and Parliament's whim, the industrial upheaval brought added miseries. Take, for example, the plight of hand spinners. In 1765 James Hargreaves, a carpenter and weaver, produced his most famous invention and named it after his wife. It was to be called the spinning-jenny. By using eight spindles driven by a great wheel, Hargreaves revolutionized the methods of the textile industry. And just like those who, 200 years on, viewed automation with dismay, the spinners understood perfectly that their livelihoods would never be the same again. This era was the beginning of what is now called the Industrial Revolution. And inventiveness was not confined to the industrial drawing board: musicians, writers, painters and diarists were prolific, and to be found at every coffee house, salon and studio. Among them were Thomas Sheridan and then his son, Richard, Thomas Tyrwhitt, Joshua Reynolds, Tobias Smollett, James Boswell, Samuel Johnson, Laurence Sterne and Oliver Goldsmith.

Smollett published *Peregrine Pickle* and *Sir Launcelot Greaves* and then he decided to produce a political magazine. Smollett's *The Briton* was in direct opposition to John Wilkes's *North Briton*. Where Wilkes lambasted the King's closest friend and political mentor, the Earl of Bute, Smollett supported Bute. But it was neither a well-produced journal nor a popular cause and *The Briton* folded. It was Laurence Sterne who called Smollett 'Smelfungus', and it was now Sterne who achieved a great following through his volumes of *Tristram Shandy*.

But Sterne, like many of his time, was a moralist. Horace Walpole said that the sermon in the third volume of *Tristram Shandy* was the best part of the novel and Voltaire regarded it as required reading. Perhaps William Pitt thought so, too – the first two volumes were dedicated to him. Another Irishman (Sterne was born in Clonmel, Co. Tipperary), Oliver Goldsmith, became a friend of Samuel Johnson. It was Johnson who sold the manuscript of *The Vicar of Wakefield* for Goldsmith. Johnson got £60 for it and probably saved Goldsmith from the debtors' prison.

But for the King there was a more complicated book balancing to be performed: the sombre business of balancing his own ambitions for government with the reality of eighteenth-century politics was uppermost. Grenville was Prime Minister, with George Montagu, Earl of Halifax, and Charles Wyndham, Earl of Egremont, as the two senior secretaries of state. When, after Egremont's death, the King tried to persuade Pitt to become Prime Minister, Pitt said no. Two years later, George III tried once more but the result was the same and Grenville felt himself more secure in office, to the extent that he threatened to resign unless the King agreed to get rid of a number of Bute's admirers. He was challenging the monarch, telling him there could not be two governments of Britain. Most distinctly, he was saying that the King could not have two Prime Ministers. And, for the time being, Grenville won.

Grenville was dedicated to the good of the nation even if he was unimaginative. He was a diligent economist and the arch tax collector of the eighteenth century. By 1765 the Grenville administration had angered the colonists by limiting by law their westward expansion in North America. Now there was to be a new tax – the Stamp Tax – and it would be remembered as one of the main catalysts for the American War of Independence, of which more later. Grenville had not worked out the consequences of the tax and by the summer of 1765 he was gone. His successor, Charles Watson-Wentworth, the Marquess of Rockingham, whose secretary was Edmund Burke, who was to become one of the most influential thinkers in eighteenth-century political history. Rockingham's administration was not really to the King's liking. Not much was, especially when he was in puritanical and preachy mood. Consequently, this was not a happy period for the King. There was already a talk of war with the American colonies.

Rockingham perceived the need for a change in Whig politics. He believed in a proper party programme of government, one that would be supported by a wider electorate, especially among traders. He saw the need for a group that would act on party principle rather than simply do anything to stay in power. And in this the beginnings of a system of party politics – not just the parties themselves – began to change the climate. One of the longer term victims of party politics would be the monarch's role in government. But let us not put down too many plaudits at Rockingham's political feet.

Although he was both a party and economic reformer, Rockingham was not a Parliamentary reformer; he did not stay in power long enough for that to happen. Also, reformers need energy and he was probably too lazy. He much preferred horseracing to the everyday business of government. Once he actually forgot to attend his own Cabinet meeting. Add to this the double-dealings of the King and the campaign to persuade Pitt the Elder to return, and it was inevitable that Rockingham would not survive. At Westminster there were more or less three groups. First there were the Royalists who would support the government if that's what the King wanted. Then there were the squires, the landowners who were not ambitious for public office, and who wouldn't blindly support the government because the King said so; but they would give it a fair hearing if the monarch did. The third group contained those who were ambitious for public office and who would swing with the prevailing mood and hang upon the court's coattails.

What was missing in Parliament was a formal 'Opposition'. There were opposition groups, but no organized opposition. Certainly, during the early part of his long reign, it is unlikely that any opposition would have made much impression on George III. He thought in the Hanoverian manner, if that is indeed the characteristic shown as attention to detail but not much wider perception of the consequences of policy-making. He was wholly committed to the role of sovereign rather than the grandeur of his office. He took Parliament at its word; any rebellion within the American colonies would be resisted by force and in doing so, he, George would thus support the constitutional rights of Great Britain and its commercial interests.

The constitutional debate was by and large an uninteresting subject for a nation stirring to the call of another revolution – that of the opportunity of industry. At the start of the eighteenth century England and Wales had a combined population of almost five-and-a-half million. Illness, a very high child mortality rate and, in London, an adult death rate accelerated by cheap gin until the 1750s, meant that the population grew by only one million in the first half of the eighteenth century. In the next fifty years, partly due to huge increases in medical science, it grew by something approaching three million, ending the century at about nine million. Scotland, over the same period, went from little more than one million to nearly three million by the end of the century.

Most people expected to live until they were about thirty-one or thirty-two. By the end of the century that expectation had risen to thirty-nine. But that doesn't mean there weren't any old people – after all, George III himself was on the throne for almost sixty years.

As the population grew so, of course, did towns and cities. For example, at the start of the eighteenth century, about 10,000 people lived in Glasgow. By the middle of the century there 25,000 and, 100 years on, there were more than 200,000. Bigger city populations meant bigger, sometimes redesigned, towns. In 1767 Edinburgh's Town Council approved James Craig's plan for the development of new buildings and for what was called feuing. A feu was a perpetual lease at a set rent. The pavement on each side of the street would be ten feet wide, not more than a foot higher than the road and there would be free access between pavement and road. Moreover, the city fathers were to 'execute a common sewer' in the middle of the street. Most importantly, anyone with a house in the street should be allowed to put their own drains in and connect to the public sewer. So there was no longer any need to empty chamber pots from the upstairs window and good drainage meant better health and there-fore the possibility of lower death rates. Edinburgh would become one of the finest cities in Europe with modern planners determined that it should be so.

Not that there was too much interest in the south of Great Britain. London, as ever, was contemplating only power; in the 1760s it was more interested in the ailing Pitt, now the Earl of Chatham, who was suffering terribly from gout and from bouts of desperate depression. Gossip too surrounded the founding of the Royal Academy in 1768, the taxes to be imposed on the Americas and the likely consequences, and the authorship of the Junius Letters. Here, for three years between 1769 and 1772, were seventy of the most vicious attacks – published in London's *Public Advertiser* – on major political figures, particularly the Prime Minister, the Duke of Grafton, and even the monarch, George III.

If Junius (probably Sir Philip Francis) thought all pedestals should be toppled, he did not include a new hero of the day, Captain James Cook who would be remembered, without malice, as one of the great adventurers of the eighteenth century. James Cook was a navigator who had learned his trade well enough in east-coast colliers and then in the Royal Navy that he would become a fine explorer and hydrog-rapher. Cook began the first of his three great voyages in 1768, and in a decade he sailed to Tahiti, New Zealand, Australia and Hawaii;

plotted the exact positions of the Easter Islands and Tonga, New Caledonia and Norfolk Island; surveyed the North American coast; and charted the extreme coast of Siberia before sailing south again to Hawaii. It was in Hawaii that he was murdered in 1779. He was mourned by a nation hardly at peace with itself and moving inexorably towards war with its American colonies.

CHAPTER THIRTY-EIGHT
1769–70

The political atmosphere of 1769 was full of the signs of the beginnings of a dissolution of the then British Empire. But geographically there was still enormous ignorance of what lay south of the equator. Everyone knew about Europe, something of China, India and North America, but not much about the southern hemisphere.

Two centuries earlier, Columbus, Magellan and, by 1587, Drake, had shown that the world was far larger than most had imagined and that there was plenty of room for other continents. In 1606, a Dutch admiral, William Jansz, had discovered Australia. A few years later Abel Tasman and the Dutch navigator, François Visscher, found Tasmania and New Zealand in their search for a commercial route to South America. But very little detail was known, hence Cook's expedition in the *Endeavour*.

The true nature of the expedition was classified. Cook had two sets of instructions: the first, entirely public, were given him by his masters, the Admiralty, with guidance from the Royal Society. He was to sail via Cape Horn to what was then called King George's Island and what is now called Tahiti. He was to observe a transit of Venus in June 1769. It wasn't until this had been done that he was allowed to open his second set of instructions, or Secret Orders. The Orders were not published until as late as 1928.

Secret

Whereas the making Discovery of Countries hitherto unknown, and the Attaining a Knowledge of distant Parts which though formerly discover'd have yet been but imperfectly explored, will redound greatly to the Honour of this Nation as a Maritime Power, as well as the Dignity of the Crown of Great Britain, and may trend greatly to the advancement of the Trade and Navigation thereof; and Whereas there is no reason to imagine that a Continent of Land of great extent, may be found to the Southward of the Tract lately made by Captain Wallis[1] in His Majesty's Ship the *Dolphin* . . . or the tract and any former Navigators in Pursuits of the like kind; You are therefore in Pursuance of His Majesty's Pleasure hereby requir'd and directed to put to sea with the bark you Command so soon as the Observation of the Transit of the Planet Venus shall be finished . . . You are to proceed to the southward in order to make discovery of the Continent above-mentioned until you arrive in the Latitude of 40 degrees, unless you sooner fall in with it.

The latitude forty degrees south runs roughly through Southern Australia and Tasmania and the southern end of New Zealand's North Island. The furthest point north in the 'Continent', now known as Antarctica, mentioned in the Secret Orders is more than sixty degrees south. Cook's Secret Orders instructed him that if and when he discovered the continent, he must measure it, survey the coastal waters, shoals, currents, tides and harbours, headlands and rocks. He was to look for fish, plants, minerals, precious stones, beasts and fowl and bring examples back to England so, as the Orders stated, 'We may cause proper examination and experiments to be made of them.'

And, after a further list of orders, this most secret document concludes that the consequences of the voyage should remain secret and that when he returned he should take any notes, diaries or logs from his crew members and tell them they had not to breathe a word of what they had seen. He would, with all sealed reports, go straight to the Admiralty.

Cook did as he was asked but he didn't find the great southern continent. However, he did experiment with shipboard medicine and it's popularly said that Cook found the cure for scurvy – the fatal disease of many a long-distance sailor. It's said that he gave every-one the juice of lemons and limes and that was that. In fact, the Admiralty had already done a great deal of research into keeping sailors healthy and the person who probably did more to cure scurvy was a naval surgeon called James Lind. More than twenty years

---

1   Samuel Wallis (1728–95), circumnavigator. The Polynesian island group Wallis and Fortuna are named after him.

before Cook sailed Lind had carried out a series of anti-scurvy tests using sailors as guinea pigs. On Cook's second voyage, which lasted three years, he recorded the loss of only one man through disease. However, Cook observed that although lemons had their value, they were impractical to keep on board.

Cook should have died a hero, preferably of old age. He did not. Cook was killed by islanders in Hawaii in 1779. It was not a premeditated act although the manner of his killing and dismemberment was sickening. By the time of his death, Cook had explored the edges of the Antarctic, staked the English flag across islands of the peaceful ocean, disproved the hypothesis of the great southern continent and developed charting and marine surveying to a level that was barely improved until modern echo and satellite technology. Most of all, Cook honoured the central ambition of George III, an ambition contained in those first Secret Orders. He opened a route that would allow English-speaking peoples to one day colonize the south-west Pacific.

Meanwhile, in the towns and countryside of these islands people believed themselves to be overtaxed. One adjustable form of revenue, the window tax, had existed since 1696. The formula was simple: each house was charged a single sum for the building itself and then so much per window. The idea was to raise millions, and millions were raised – and not a little opposition. It is still possible to see older houses where windows have long ago been bricked up to avoid the tax.

Of course, there was nothing new in taxation but at the start of the 1700s the government was taking £4.3 million a year from the people in taxes. By the end of the century it was nearly £32 million. As the country advanced, someone had to pay. Britain now had organized government and organized government was costly. The National Debt was rising. In 1700 it was about £14 million but by the end of George III's first decade it was £129 million. By the end of the century it would be £456 million. The interest alone was £9 million a year and taxation had doubled.

And when the population wasn't being taxed, some of it was being robbed in a more traditional manner. The magistrate Sir John Fielding wrote to the Secretary to the Treasury, Charles Jenkinson, to inform him of several recent robberies. Fielding wrote that the mugging and robbing often took place near the fields of Tyburn and Tottenham Court Road in London and that he had sent a foot patrol to search the area but 'before they got out of the coach which carried them to the spot, they narrowly escaped being murdered by three footpads, who without giving them the least notice fired two pistols immediately into the coach'. At the time, there wasn't a police force. Sir John's only help came from the Bow Street Runners who were the nearest thing to an organized force. The Runners, as they became known, were set up in 1748 by Sir John's half-brother, Henry Fielding, now better known as the author of *Tom Jones*. The year before *Tom Jones* was published, Henry Fielding was the Chief Justice of the Peace at Bow Street Magistrates Court. There was, in government, a considerable debate on what powers existed to maintain law and order. For example, in 1768 there was a mob riot in St George's Fields, part of what is now south London, and the troops were called out. In a debate following the riots, Edmund Burke told the House of Commons that liberty was all and a police force must be treated with suspicion, yet must be considered. Burke would not trust certain law-makers with the code of liberty he endorsed and he was wary that a regular force was the beginnings of a police state unless its role was tightly monitored. In an increasingly affluent society, the question of how to maintain law and order brought considerable stress upon the government of the day. At the same time there was a need to reduce the cost of government and a need to find new ways of raising taxes, while the new methods of law and order should not threaten the security and liberty of the people.

The rate of change in the nation in the 1770s was rapid enough to frighten people who were used to the slow rates of change characteristic of previous generations. Perhaps every generation argues that case, but during this period the reasons were, to many of the eight or so million people in England, Wales and Scotland, coming to mean revolutionary rather than evolutionary change. There were technological and scientific innovations and the first tentative steps towards the Industrial Revolution were taken.

In the first decade of the century, twenty-two new patents were registered. By the 1760s the figure was 205. By the last decade of the eighteenth century there would be more than 900 new inventions. In 1769 a one-time barber and wigmaker patented a machine that would make him a famous, rich, dark satanic mill-owner. His name was Richard Arkwright and his invention was a spinning frame powered by water.

In the same year, James Watt patented his steam engine and Josiah Wedgwood opened another pottery. The Royal Academy had just been established and its first president, Joshua Reynolds, gave the first of his *Fifteen Discourses*, in which he claimed history painting to be the most noble form of art. Tobias Smollett left England for ever, William Smith, the founder of English geology, was born and, in the summer of 1769, the men of Hambledon were having a lean season on the cricket field.

Perhaps Britain was not a poor nation. Certainly the level of gambling suggested that the rich were very rich and that the not-so-rich thought gambling a simple way to become so. But the sums involved were sometimes enormous, even by twenty-first-century standards. In the eighteenth century, thousands of pounds were bet on a horse or the turn of a card and, perhaps more surprisingly, bets of around twenty-thousand guineas were not uncommon at the more fashionable cricket matches. However, there was still a need for foundling homes, charity schools, parish workhouses and the burial of those who had died undernourished and badly cared for.

At the same time, the courts were recognizing that new schemes, inventions or processes were just as much part of a man's property as was his house or livestock. The courts were having a harder time with the question of religion. There was no question that the English could have anything but an Established Church of England. Therefore, the term dissenters covered other religions, everything from Protestants to Catholics to breakaway groups such as the Congregationalists. In Scotland, the question of religion would become simpler. There was no Established Church. The Church of Scotland was the majority church, but not established in law and answerable to Parliament as was the case south of the border. There were too the smaller groups, particularly the Episcopalians. These were the devotees who refused to go along with the 1690 'victory' of Presbyterians in the Church of Scotland. Episcopalians were minority worshippers to the degree that in 1705, when they first had bishops, consecration took place in secret. Politically, Episcopalians were linked to a losing but sensitive cause – that of the Jacobites. In 1712 the Toleration Acts made clear that being an Episcopalian was fine as long as worshippers did not support Jacobite claims to the throne. Few would agree to that and after both the 1715 and 1745 Jacobite risings, Episcopalians were further persecuted.

The position of the Catholic Church was even harder to come to terms with for any political administration. Very simply put, Catholics were potential enemies of the State. There was no question of having a Catholic monarch. Nor could a monarch marry a Catholic. Even in the twentieth century, when Prince Michael of Kent married a Catholic, he had to give up his right to the English throne – he was eighth in line of succession at the time. Moreover, because Roman Catholics in the eighteenth century made up three-quarters of the population of Ireland, there would always be a suspicion, especially from the Anglican ruling class, the so-called Protestant (more accurately the Anglican) Ascendency, that Catholics would harbour ambitions for dramatic rather than token Emancipation. Indeed, at the time of the French Revolution, Dissenters in Ireland, of which Catholics made up a considerable majority, went about calling each other 'Citizen'. Catholics had been subjected to suppressive laws dating from the 1570s. Although in the eighteenth century some of the restrictions were relaxed, they still had no right to vote or to sit in Parliament. Even when they could vote, because of restrictions on membership of the Parliament, Catholics could only vote for Protestants. And so Catholic Emancipation did not come about until 1829 and even then it was not a freedom without fences.

The Whigs, even though they had what could be described as Non-conformists within their noble ranks, had been the controlling group that had organized the Protestant succession and, since then, they'd had an unshakable grip on government. Every British Prime Minister but one (Bute) had been a Whig.

But now as the year 1769 moved to a close, the reign of the Whigs was about to be broken. The political climate was one of radical thinking, public opposition to Crown and government, and growing rebellion in America and in Ireland. Furthermore, in spite of the picture of rich and healthy Britain painted by Arthur Young, and the industrial innovation, there was an increasingly obvious economic depression settling over the management of Britain's affairs.

By 1770 George III had been on the throne for ten years. He was thirty-two years old and his first decade as king had been one of political instability. He wanted to change the political system. He wanted to get back control of political patronage – the key to government.

By the time George III came to the throne, the Whigs had broken into Old Whigs and New Whigs (although that's not a term found in history books). The Old Whigs were the followers of Pitt, Grenville and Newcastle, while the New Whigs said the King was a tyrant, seeking more political control than was good for the country. They said he corrupted Parliament and ignored the views of the people. They claimed he was trying to return to the age of the Stuarts and absolute power.

It was now that a stout, loud-voiced earl became Prime Minister. His name was Lord North and his task was to bring about political stability. Frederick North, Baron North and Earl of Guildford, was fat, thick-lipped and had bulging eyes. He had an apparently inexhaustible good humour and the knack of explaining in the simplest terms the most complex matters of national economics. From 1770 until 1782 he was Tory Prime Minister and so ended the Whig domination which had existed since the death of Queen Anne in 1714. Although the Tories had gone along with the 1688 Rebellion, which eventually got rid of James II, they had been seen as supporters of the Catholic Jacobite Pretenders to the throne.

During Lord North's twelve years, attempts were made to reform Parliament; Adam Smith published his great work, *The Wealth of Nations*; Jeremy Bentham published his *Fragment on Government*; and Joseph Priestley discovered and isolated oxygen. The actress Sarah Siddons appeared with David Garrick at Drury Lane and became the darling of theatregoers, and Gainsborough painted her. The Sunday School movement started; Britain lost the American War of Independence; and the first Derby was run at Epsom Racecourse.

Lord North's constituency, Banbury, was owned by his family and thus his family could say who would be MP: such an arrangement meant that it was an example of what was called a 'pocket' or 'rotten' borough. Although his ministerial career was prompted by family and friends, North was no political charlatan. He was a good debater and he had a sharp and amiable mind which could unravel tangled policy problems. The movement towards Parliamentary reform was partly prompted by growing mistrust of the very system which had made North an MP. In 1770, William Pitt (the Elder) proposed in the House of Lords an increase in County Members. Pitt had set out on his Parliamentary career by becoming the Member for Old Sarum, a family borough which was nothing more than a mound of earth in Wiltshire. He had sat for Seaford in Sussex and Aldborough in Yorkshire, both owned by the Duke of Newcastle. He'd also been the Member for Okehampton which was owned by his old school chum George Lyttleton. But the rottenness in the election system by bought or even non-existent (other than on paper) boroughs could not forever last. The constitutional integrity of the Parliamentary system resided in the metropolitan regions with their potentially important voters. The potential was there, but not for the moment. Curiously, the urge for reform was not simply in the hands of far-seeing political leaders. Certainly from the second half of the eighteenth century there was more evidence of change in the Churches and from those changes, mostly through evangelical movements, reform was demanded. It was a sense of social reform that extended from the very rights of mankind to the abolition of slavery movement to Parliamentary reform that would take place in that period leading to the end of the Hanoverians. Just three examples demonstrated this era of reforming movements: in 1807, the slave trade was banned by the British. In 1832 the first of the Parliamentary Reform Bills was passed. In 1833, slavery was abolished.

In 1770, one person who most definitely did not want Parliamentary supremacy was George III. George demanded that Parliament took its cue from him, not from the nation. The way it worked was simple: the King handed out jobs, contracts, offices of State and fat pensions to those who did as they were told, in other words, those who voted for his policies. For those who didn't there were punishments which included loss of pensions and jobs. There was nothing new in this; it was the centuries-old practice of royal patronage and, for the first twenty years of his reign, George III followed the path of Parliamentary, and official, corruption. Some of the great personalities of the age – almost every wit and radical, every stoic and pragmatist – stood on their feet in both Houses during George's reign: the National Debt, taxes and a badly thought-through war inspired even the dullest Parliamentary speaker. However, that is not to say that Parliament was not still in the possession of the King and in Lord North, appointed in 1770, he now had a leader who would be the obedient agent of his business; in other words, His Majesty's most loyal subject. George III held Parliament, the Cabinet and policy in his hand. His ambition was fulfilled. Effectively, the King was his own prime minister.

However, although power was his, the blessing of all his people was not. The people had always looked to other heroes. Marlborough had been one. Clive of India was the most recent and when, in 1774, Clive committed suicide, there was doubt, conjecture, intrigue and even uneasiness throughout the land. There were stories that Clive had died from an apoplectic fit, or that he had taken an overdose of opium. But the truth seems to be that on 22 November 1774, he could stand the agonies of his ongoing stomach illness no longer and, as one observer has said, 'In a paroxysm of agony, he thrust his penknife into his throat.' Perhaps he had not been comforted by the accusations from home that he had diverted East India Company funds into his own pockets. The irony, of course, was that Clive was desperately needed by the Company to root out corruption at all levels. Indeed, Clive the reformer was perhaps more spectacular than Clive the general and his reforms were drastic. Their success prompted the Mogul Emperor to invite Clive to extend a British protectorate to Delhi and all northern India. This is a useful reminder that, at that time, British interests only covered Bengal. The reason was that when the East India Company established itself in India, Bengal became the capital of its trading interests. (The popular image of the British Raj is a nineteenth-century phenomenon.) So, in the 1760s, Clive had to decide whether to expand the Company administration or to stay put. To expand would require an enormous bureaucracy, complex communications and a ruthless army – and it would have been a Company army, not a British army. So he refused the Mogul's request. The princes would have liked the British to run much of India but the British were fighting the Seven Years War against the French, and had insufficient interest and certainly neither the manpower nor the organization to take over from the Company.

In fact, Clive was far from certain that the Company could any longer run its own business in India and he had suggested to Pitt that the government should take it over. The British government refused and continued to refuse until the Sepoy Rebellion in 1857. In 1767, when he returned to England, it was so evident that Clive had done well out of India that he was accused of doing too well. Just as an earlier British hero, Marlborough, had been accused of lining his pockets, so Clive was now subject to the same accusations. Clive mounted a counter-offensive as bold as any skirmish he'd led or organized in India. And he reminded Parliament that after the horror of the Black Hole of Calcutta, it was he, Robert Clive, who had defeated Siraj-ud-daula, the man the British held responsible, at the Battle of Plassey. By the end of a Parliamentary committee's interrogation, it was clear to everyone that although he had received great gifts and had made a minor fortune, his profits were never so great as rumour would have wished. The Commons passed a motion declaring that Clive had 'rendered great and meritorious services' and that as far as Parliament was concerned, the matter was done with. Yet it is doubtful if Clive properly recovered from his inner torments.

Similar torments to be faced by his successor in India, Warren Hastings (1732–1818). Hastings came from a wealthy Worcestershire family that had fallen on hard times. The family home, Daylesford, had been sold many years earlier and Hastings intended to make his fortune and buy it back. At the age of sixteen he went to India, like Clive, to be a clerk in the English East India Company. Eleven years later he had risen to be a member of the Bengal Council and, after a four year interval in England, became a member of the Madras Council in 1768.

In theory, all should have been well in the coffers of the Company but by 1770, it was close to bankruptcy. North went to Parliament in 1773 with his Regulating Act, which left all the commercial operations of the East India Company in the hands of its Directors, but the government of Bengal was to be administered by a governor general and a four-man council, and Britain was to appoint a justice of the Supreme Court. Seemingly it was inevitable that with his success, Warren Hastings was made the first Governor General, with a salary of £25,000 a year. Hastings achieved a great deal and laid the groundwork for what became the British Raj. He also gathered terrible enemies of his own side. He quarrelled with his own Council, appointed not by him but by London. One of the members, who had hopes for governorship, fought a duel with him. Hastings was also accused of making the mistake of confirming Maharaja Nandakumar's sentence of hanging for forgery. When Hastings went back to England in 1785, it was to face up to allegations that he was a bad and partial ruler and was corrupt. His opponents were formidable – Charles James Fox, Richard Brinsley Sheridan and Edmund Burke. That trial went on for seven years. In the end, Hastings was acquitted. And in spite of the cost of defending himself, there was still enough left to realize his ambition. He bought back the family home,

Daylesford. By this time at Westminster there was growing support for the proper governing of India. Hastings, certainly no saint, had gone a long way to lessen the corruption and maladministration that had been the Company's way in India. He had effectively laid the ground rules for what became the Indian Civil Service. Above all, he had preserved British rule of one empire while the wise Councils of Westminster had managed to lose another in America.

CHAPTER THIRTY-NINE
1770–81

The Boston Tea Party did not start the American War of Independence, but it did inflame an already sore relationship between Britain and her colonial interests in America, which had come to the boil under Grenville's premiership of the 1760s. At the time there were thirteen colonies in America. Parliament declared that Britain had a right to tax those colonies because they were subjects of the Crown just as much as any county in England. But most, although not all, British taxpayers were represented in Parliament. No colonist was, and so their argument was based upon 'Taxation without representation'. Even Pitt the Elder had argued in the Commons that Britain had no right to tax the colonies because, although they were supposedly subjects of the Crown, they were not represented in Parliament.

The cost of the colonies and the lack of money to pay for them was a constant factor in assessing the British Empire. For example, after the war with France the National Debt was about £150 million and the interest on that sum was more than £4.5 million a year. Nothing after the war occurred to ease the debt problem, which meant the prosperity of the nation was in doubt. The huge benefits of reconstructed finances plus those which came from the highlights of the Industrial Revolution were still to come. Although the figures may not impress in the twenty-first century, seen in context of government spending the price of having colonies was prohibitive in the 1760s.

For example, the cost of running the government was estimated at some £10 million. Within that figure, the bill for the colonies – mainly keeping the troops to protect them – was £350,000 a year, a considerable percentage of the total. Prime Minister Grenville may have been uncertain how to meet these costs, which were over and above those incurred by the commercial investors, but he was sure that his only source of income would be, at the very least, maintaining taxes and in some ways introducing new ones. The accounting system made it very difficult to know what benefits the taxpayer got from the import/export trade between the West Indies and the North American colonies. Should people in Britain foot the bill for defending those colonies that were not protected by company militia? In 1765 Grenville's arithmetic suggested that if he imposed so-called stamp duties on the American and West Indian settlements he might raise as much as 15 per cent of the overall administrative costs.

We should not see this tax-raising proposal in the same way as budgets are presented today. There was no threshold for tax-paying nor was this income tax as we know it. That was not introduced until 1799 by William Pitt the Younger to help finance the war against France. That rate was two shillings (10p) in the pound. Grenville's tax would come from the rich through their businesses. The stamp duty would be imposed as a percentage of the value of, for example, contracts, licences and even playing cards. This was already a feature of the British tax system. Grenville accepted that people in Britain would be extremely unhappy to pay for the colonies. The colonists would surely see that it was only fair that they should make a contribution to their own administration and defence because by paying for security, stability would be guaranteed and that would allow them to be protected and go on to make more money for themselves and a better way of life. The logic of this escaped the colonists who were independently minded, saw the Governor and his administration as a wasteful extravagance of the Crown and believed that Grenville's proposal was nothing more than a method of getting yet more money out of the colonists who got very little in return. They demanded rights by being British, even though they paid no more than 1 per cent of the taxes. They accepted that the Crown had a right to tax, but only in general terms. The colonists said that any specific taxes had to be endorsed and then ratified by their assemblies. Moreover, when, in 1765, Grenville introduced stamp duties, colonists understood that by combining in opposition to the taxes, they would make them uncollectable.

The opposition to paying more tax began in Virginia and in the autumn of 1765 there was general disorder throughout the colonies. Some of the colonists rioted simply because of the financial effect the stamp duty would have on everyday life; some were inflamed by the lack of representation in the far-away Parliament; but some frontiersmen were riled by any interference from a land, its State and established Church, that they had sought to escape. The Stamp Act provided a means of focusing their joint efforts. Thus in October 1765, the thirteen colonies agreed a plan for opposition to the new taxes and even an outline to boycott British goods. Imagine the consternation in London where the trade balance was an essential element in the government's economic plan for the North American colonies. By that October, Grenville had gone from office.

The new First Lord of the Treasury was the Marquess of Rockingham, who disliked the idea of a stamp duty. It was not a simple task to repeal the Act. To do so would have financial implications, although if the tax could not be collected and the consequences of the opposition to them unacceptable, they indeed had to go. An equally important conundrum for Rockingham was protection of the monarch's dignity. George III had approved the Stamp Act. The balance had to be a repeal of the Act and, at the same time, an assertion of the Crown's authority.

So in March 1766, exactly twelve months after stamp duties had been introduced by Grenville, Rockingham's administration abolished them. The face saver was the Declaratory Act. In February, in the Lords, Augustus FitzRoy, the Duke of Grafton (who would soon be Prime Minister and who was said to have a more conciliatory attitude towards America) had proposed a motion which insisted that Parliament did indeed have the authority to bind the colonies to any laws. On 10 February 1766, Lord Mansfield got to his feet in that debate to express two propositions about the relationship between Parliament and Empire:

> First, That, the British legislature, as to the power of making laws, represents the whole British Empire, and has the authority to bind every part and every subject without the least distinction, whether such subjects have a right to vote or not, or whether the law binds places within the realm or without.
>
> Second, That the colonists, by the condition on which they migrated, settled and now exist, are more emphatically subjects of Great Britain than those within the realm; and that the British legislature have in every instance exercised their right of legislation over

them without any dispute or question till the fourteenth of January
last . . . In every government the legislative power must be lodged
somewhere, and the executive must likewise be lodged somewhere.
In Great Britain the legislative is in Parliament, the executive in the
Crown . . . When the Supreme Power abdicates, the Government is
dissolved. Take care my Lords, you do not abdicate your authority. In
such an event, your Lordships would leave the worthy and innocent,
as well as the unworthy and guilty, to the same confusion and ruin.

Power, Supreme or otherwise, had decreed that the taxation of
Americans was legitimate and the consequences understood.
Benjamin Franklin, who then lived in London, made his view known
that Parliament should restrict its colonial law-making to mercantile
issues. It was a debate that would last ten years.

During the next few years, the American colonists lived in uneasy
state with the British government. When confrontation came,
it demonstrated that no part of the worldwide empire could be
seen in isolation.

In every school textbook of British history there used to be a scene
of the Boston Tea Party. Colonists dumped tea into the harbour, thus
creating the brew that would begin the war between Britain and the
thirteen states of America. Like all over-simplifications there is an
element of truth. With that truth came the connection between one
part of the Empire and another. What was going on in India had an
effect on what would take place in America.

In one hemisphere were the sometimes disparate colonists of
the North American continent; in another was the well-established
East India Company. The government in London tried to force the
American colonists to import cheap East India Company tea because
the Company was suffering hard times. That really is the basis of the
Tea Act which caused the trouble; how did all this come about and if
it could have been avoided, would America have remained British?

The answer to the latter question is 'No'. Independence from the
Crown was inevitable. To see how the Boston Tea Party occurred
when it did, we have to see what was going on in Britain and, by
extension, in India during the 1760s and 1770s.

We have already seen that Grenville went in 1765, to be replaced
by Rockingham. Rockingham lost his job in the summer of 1766

having repealed the Stamp Act, but having failed to sort out much else. Pitt the Elder did not wish to become Prime Minister once more. He was unhealthy and could not expect to control the Commons. Pitt had been made Earl of Chatham, thus losing credibility as the people's Prime Minister. The Marquess of Rockingham had tried to run Parliament from the Lords and had failed. Pitt was not going to be any more successful, especially as he had not the physical, never mind the political, stamina. Almost from the time he assumed office in 1766 until October 1768, Pitt, or Chatham as now he was, provided no sure leadership. During this period, with Parliament losing its way, the American colonial opposition was even more difficult to judge and therefore handle.

The Chancellor of the Exchequer between 1766–7 was Charles Townshend (1725–67). Townshend exploited the colonial notion that they were willing to accept Parliament's authority to legislate on issues of trade. Townshend, through his 1767 American Import Duties Act, put heavy import duties on glass, paint, paper and tea entering America. No one doubted that he simply wanted to raise money to cover the cost of administering the North American colonies. The Act caused more trouble than it was worth. Not much money, if any, was collected and the colonists became even more displeased with Parliament. By 1769 most North American assemblies had come close to challenging the authority of the Crown. This stance verged upon treason.

Pitt the Elder survived until by the autumn of 1768 when he became too ill to carry on in office. The Duke of Grafton, Augustus FitzRoy (1735–1811) replaced him, but he had no more idea of what to do than had Pitt. Moreover, Grafton was really a Pittite and therefore was not going to produce radical policies. He would have wished to be more understanding towards the American colonists, but pressing political difficulties at home didn't allow time to fully concentrate on thinking through and implementing any conciliatory colonial policy. His administration was preoccupied with the so-called Wilkes affair. John Wilkes (1727–97) was a Radical accused of seditious libel and in 1768, although elected MP for Middlesex, was imprisoned as an outlaw.

Lord North replaced Grafton in 1770. North's was a courtesy title (he was heir to the Earldom of Guildford) and he sat in the Commons. One of his first decisions was to remove all but the tea tax put in place by Grafton's Act. At first North, who would be Prime Minister for twelve years, appeared self-assured and able to exploit the fact that, in spite of the influence of George III, he was running Parliament from inside the Commons. This may not have satisfied all the American colonists, but for the moment it eased transatlantic tension. Now from London to Bengal.

As discussed, Warren Hastings had become Governor General of India in 1733. Later a tragic figure, who was impeached for corruption, he established what would become known as the British Raj. If Hastings settled, if not resolved, many of the diplomatic and administrative difficulties of the Crown and the Company he failed, inevitably, to balance the Company books. British interests were verging on insolvency. It was at this point in the 1770s that the Crown thought it could resolve some of the Company's problems by using the American colonies. The answer, so the government thought, was in tea. The East India Company had seventeen million pounds of tea that it could not sell. The price of tea in Britain was inflated by the import duty of more than 100 per cent. The Americans, however, paid much less in import duties. But we have to remember that the independently minded American colonists were, as it suited them, boycotting goods from Britain and refused to be used by the Crown. The government ignored these sentiments. It decreed that the duty on tea imports to Britain would remain at the present level. However, tea exported or re-exported to America would only be liable for the much lower American tax rates. The Crown then, in its belief that it could impose its will, announced that seven million pounds of the Company's tea surplus could be shifted into America.

At this point some of the American colonists, reading what they believed to be subterfuge by the British, asserted their independence. Sam Adams organized the dumping of the tea imports over the side of the ships. This defiance on 16 December 1773 became known as the Boston Tea Party. Parliament in London announced that by law it was closing down the government of Boston and promised to exact compensation for the East India Company from the people of that town. Parliament had underestimated the reaction to this legislation, which became known as the Intolerable Acts. The Acts asserted in the Boston Port Bill that the harbour would be closed until compensation had been paid. The Massachusetts Government Act revoked the charter of the colony. The Quartering Act gave the governor of

Massachusetts authority to billet any of his troops in the homes of any settlers he so chose. Moreover, a piece of Parliamentary legislation, which at first sight had nothing to do with Boston, was also seen as an assault on the independence of the settlers. This was the Quebec Act of 1774, which fulfilled promises that Roman Catholics should have greater freedoms and that Catholics would be allowed, for the first time, to be members of the Quebec Council. It might be remembered that Quebec was a colony where all but fewer than 10 per cent of the population were Catholics and French-speaking. Catholics were not allowed to sit in Parliament in England and so the British settlers in Montreal could not see why they should be threatened by an overwhelming majority of Catholics. Moreover, the 1774 Act increased the territory of Quebec. What had this to do with the Boston Tea Party? Settlers far beyond that port saw this as an example of George III's government imposing its will and even driving a wedge into the prejudice that insisted Catholics were lower class citizens. In other words the social, religious and even administrative structure of the colonists was threatened.

This new, and to the colonists, threatening legislation was the catalyst for the action which resulted in twelve of the colonies (Georgia was absent) meeting in Philadelphia, in the autumn of 1774, for the first of what became known as a Continental Congress.

Thomas Jefferson (1743–1826) argued at that Congress that the assemblies should have as many rights of legislation as the Parliament in London. There was a sense that the American colonists had an instinctive appeal to the ancient practice of kingship. In one of its forms, kingship is when the people declare allegiance to the monarch in return for the monarch's protection. That protection is against invaders and, most importantly, against government, for the monarch is supposed to be above government and is the patron of all the peoples. The colonists' instinct was that George III would protect them against Parliamentary authority.

In the second half of the eighteenth century, Parliament believed it had considerable sway over the monarch. It was only partially right in this judgement. The weakness in Parliament's assumption was that George III did not trust his senior ministers. Thus, this monarch asserted his constitutional authority and insisted that his Prime Minister, Lord North, gave it expression through Parliament. Here was the basis of how Britain and its monarch dealt with the

American colonists and therefore the charge that it was George III who lost America.

The 1774 Congress in Philadelphia was the basis of turning the feelings of those rebellious colonists into practical opposition to the British government. Immediately after Philadelphia, British spies began amassing evidence that what had been a political rebellion was turning into a military opposition. This led to the opening shots in the American War of Independence. In April 1775, British troops were sent to Concord. Their task was to seize an arms cache held by the rebels. In May 1775, the second Continental Congress met (now including Georgia). It took the overwhelming decision to raise an army against the British in Massachusetts. The congressional members had an uneasy time of it. At that point it is doubtful that the majority wanted independence, but they refused to accept the unexamined will of the British Parliament. There was still hope for a compromise. This was expressed in the Congress's so-called Olive Branch Petition to the King, by which America would remain loyal to the Crown if either trade or tax controls were lifted. The petitions' sincerity was questioned and the King rejected it. George Washington was tasked with raising the army. Even the offer of a token arrangement of British sovereignty was now unlikely, even impossible, to achieve.

In spite of the importance of the event it is not the place of this book to describe in detail the American War of Independence. For our purposes it should be sufficient to give a brief description and a recapitulation of causes. The American Revolution began in 1775 and ended in 1783. There were thirteen American colonies at the time. They were: Connecticut, Delaware, Georgia, Massachusetts, Maryland, New Hampshire, New Jersey, New York, North Carolina, Pennsylvania, Rhode Island, South Carolina and Virginia. Collectively they claimed that the population was continuously angry over the British Parliament's insistence that it had the right to tax in all departments, the settlers. There were three illustrations of this antagonism. Firstly, in 1770, five colonists were killed and many more wounded when British troops opened fire on the settlers at Boston. Secondly, on 16 December 1773, there were the events surrounding the Boston Tea Party. Thirdly, in 1774 Britain imposed Intolerable Acts. From this point major confrontation seemed inevitable.

In April 1775 the War began at Concord and Lexington. On 4 July 1776, a congress of the American colonies made the Declaration of

Independence. George Washington was shortly after defeated by the British forces commanded by General William Howe at White Plains. The following year, 1777, saw the famous battle of Saratoga. General John Burgoyne's British army of some 5,000 troops was forced to surrender to the superior sized army of General Gates.[1] This single victory inspired the French to join the Americans in the war against their old enemy, the British. Until the beginning of 1781 the British forces, both at sea and on land, did well but their downfall soon came. On 19 October 1781 General Charles Cornwallis, later the first Marquess Cornwallis,[2] and his British forces were surrounded at Yorktown in Virginia. American and French troops, commanded by George Washington, controlled the land approaches to the peninsula and French ships had command of the sea lanes. Cornwallis was forced to surrender.

Yorktown probably did more than any other incident to convince British public opinion that the war against the American colonists could not be won. The naval confrontations, especially in the West Indies, by and large went Britain's way. However, naval battles do not decide wars. He who holds the land mass commands the future. In 1783 America became independent of Britain by the Treaty of Versailles (sometime known as the Treaty of Paris).

And what happened to that territory north of America that most certainly had not been part of any revolution? Canada had become a secure British territory. By 1763, the decade before the American Revolution, the British controlled Hudson Bay, Newfoundland, Nova Scotia, Quebec (and had done for half a century), Prince

---

1   Burgoyne (1722–92) commanded the British troops who headed south from Canada. In 1777 he famously captured Fort Edward and Ticonderoga, but the logistical support he had been promised failed to materialize, hence his surrender at Saratoga. Gentleman Johnnie, as he was popularly known, was also a playwright. Before the war he had written a country comedy, *The Maid of the Oaks* (1774) and, in 1786, *The Heiress*. George Bernard Shaw studied him and Burgoyne's character can be found in *The Devil's Disciple*. Horatio Gates (1728–1806) was an Essex man from Maldon who joined the English army. He bought an estate in Virginia and became a Patriot. Cornwallis took British revenge on Gates at the Battle of Camden in 1780 and the latter lost his command. He died in New York having freed his Virginian slaves.

2   Cornwallis (1738–1805) suffered mixed sentiments because he was against the blanket taxing of the colonists. He recovered from the disaster of Yorktown and became Governor General of India from 1786 to 1793. He was once more appointed Governor General in 1804 and died in India. He was also Lord Lieutenant of Ireland (1798–1801) and was credited with putting down the 1798 Irish Rebellion.

Edward Island and Cape Breton Island. There would be rebellion, but not for decades. None of this meant that Canada might not join the revolution, or certainly watch with interest: after all, at the time of the Boston Tea Party, Canada was 95 per cent French-speaking and Catholic. The advantage to the British was that the territory was sparsely populated and often preoccupied with its seasonal interests. For example, Newfoundland was mainly fishing. The important area of Nova Scotia was almost barren. Fur trapping and trading meant that there was enough to get on with battling the elements and little energy left for fighting bureaucracy.

Given the climate and pickings, part of Canada functioned properly only during seasons. Yet it was hardly a backwater of British interests in North America, although it was not at the centre of the Crown's plans for colonial expansion. Just as the emerging North American settlements had been populated by economic, religious and political refugees from Britain, now after the American War of Independence Canada provided the haven for tens of thousands of settlers who did not wish to live under the government of the United States of America. That the territory should be populated by loyalists was, of course, to the Crown's advantage. Equally, loyalty comes at a price and the new settlers in Canada needed extravagant land grants and bursaries to succeed. Nor could the new Canadians simply sweep aside those settlers already in place. With certain and obvious exceptions the British English-speaking migrants settled alongside French-speaking Canadians. Whatever their instincts and origins, both French and British Canadians were united in their suspicions, and sometimes outright antagonism, towards republican Americans south of the border. The original settlements were north of New England and in the young territory of New Brunswick. However, it was hardly any time at all before the trappers and traders inched westwards. The boundaries were shifting and the sometimes ill-defined settlements around the Great Lakes existed in some fragile peace. By the time that Britain was at war once more with France in 1794, the differences between the North American straggle of British loyalists and those already in Canada were already sharply defined. For example, the North West Company formed in 1785 was in direct competition with the eastern-based traders, such as the Hudson's Bay Company.

North America was, by the final decade of the eighteenth century, abuzz with new exploration. The hero of this period in British colonial history was probably the Stornoway man, Alexander Mackenzie (1764–1820). It was Mackenzie who became the first European to cross Canada from the east and then the Rockies to the Pacific. This was not the beginning of the Scottish 'occupation' of Canada, but it was certainly a reminder to us of what Michael Fry has called 'the building of the Scottish Empire'.[3] Here was the genesis of the notion that the English found themselves with an empire run by the Scots.

Scotland was never big enough to have its own empire. It had neither the history of government and monarchy that would allow that, nor the financial institutions to encourage it. The picture after 1603 and the Union of the Crowns is confusing because although the Stuarts were then on the English throne, they did not speak for Scotland in isolation. The concepts of settlement and trade as being distinctive components of empire were not options for the Scots alone. The Union, not of the two Crowns, but of the two constitutions in 1707 blurred the financial and administrative minds that meant the two nations could not have similar ambitions. Individuals such as Donald Macdonald, James Murray and Mackenzie left more than a mark on eighteenth-century colonialism. Yet behind their efforts were financial and constitutional possibilities that emanated not from Edinburgh but from London. Earlier in the century Colonel Samuel Vetch (1668–1732), the Scottish governor of Nova Scotia, had sought support from the Crown for his idea that Canada should be claimed by the British. His case was made in his paper *Canada Survey'd*. His argument was that Canada could be a base for the fish and fur trade as well as the eastern seaboard being a centre for victualling for the navy. Whatever sense was seen in London was always difficult for people on the ground to follow, even when instructions came as a result of their own suggestions.

There was a conflict between those who had to run an outpost of empire and those left behind in London. It mattered not the origins of the administrator. The mood and perception of the Crown and its officers supposedly decided the way of governance. We might consider Quebec, captured by mainly Highlanders in 1759 when it was governed by the Scot, James Murray. Murray wanted to be a liberal governor because he thought that was the simplest way of

---

3   Michael Fry, *The Scottish Empire* (East Lothian: Tuckwell Press, 2001).

avoiding conflict. There was a great sense in what Murray proposed. The irony that the American settlers had included religious tolerance among their reasons for fleeing Europe, particularly England, was hardly lost on the French Catholic majority in Canada. Murray thought religious tolerance should be utterly acceptable and that furthermore, it would inspire loyalty, if inspiration were needed, against the Americans. This was sensible anticipation because the American War of Independence had not yet been fought. We can imagine his chagrin when the British government told Governor Murray that they wanted nothing to do with a multiracial society and that the territory of Quebec should be anglicized forthwith. Murray thought this a silly as well as unjust instruction and so was recalled. That the 1774 Quebec Act allowed for religious toleration was rather late payment of compensation for the original oppression. Yet Canada was no different from earlier colonies. Decisions made elsewhere, too frequently never allowed for local circumstances. A territory was to be used as a dumping ground of those in Britain who were considered surplus to requirements. So it was in Canada during the second half of the eighteenth century. Emptying the Scottish Highlands appeared to be something of a priority and, in 1773, 200 Highlanders arrived in Nova Scotia. It was all very well providing masses of land, but where was the money to come from necessary to support the new settlements? There was precious little money available, but the migration had begun and yet again the determination of not just the few but quite many converted opportunity into relative success.

The Scots took with them more than a tartan. Gaelic was commonly spoken in parts of Canada well into the twentieth century. The clan allegiances survived the transatlantic crossings; indeed many hardships were overcome because of those family loyalties. Migration helped preserve clan and Highland identification. Less successful, although attempted, was the British vision of colonial settlement whereby the atmosphere and custom of the home counties might be faithfully reproduced and supported by the social, legal and constitutional framework of England. For much of the year Canada was an inhospitable place, as indeed were the Highlands, and in a few places 'little Scotlands' flourished. Certainly before the American War of Independence, migration from Scotland was, in terms of percentage of population, as great as it was from England. The profits to be made were no less important than those to be fetched from India. Little wonder that in the second half of the eighteenth century some 200 companies had been established in Canada with investors registered in Scotland. By the end of that century the most prosperous effort in Canada would appear to have been in the hands of the Scottish merchants of Montreal. Fry argues that the Scots themselves in Canada wanted to control immigration. They wanted to protect their interests: 'their trade, principally in furs, could indeed only continue as long as it [Canada] remained empty since tilled land yielded no furs'.[4]

The North West Company was formed in 1779 as an experiment in trading. There were other companies, many of which had uncertain ethics and origins. Many of these characteristics would have been recognized at Glencoe. The value of the North West Company was to draw the disparate together in order to create harmony by letting different factions benefit from the fur monopoly thus created.

These were true frontiersmen who conformed to every modern image of bear-killing, snow-trekking individuals whose log cabins would be decorated with leather-bound books as well as gun racks. Alexander Mackenzie was far more than an intrepid explorer. He was a man of great reading as well as courage. Like many leaders, courage took strain on his character. His bouts of depression in a land often bereft of comfort told on this brilliant explorer. It was not enough to be in a successful enterprise such as the North West Company. Mackenzie was not alone in realizing that to inspire the support of the Crown in London, the Company had to expand and identify new opportunities. And so he explored mountains and big rivers (the Mackenzie is named after him) while he continuously pressed westwards. As he and his men headed for the Rockies so the Company established trading posts in his wake. This was the truly rapid expansion of a commercial empire, while his motive was partly the centuries-old ambition to find a shortcut to Cathay. Here was an obsession. He was successful. He was the first to cross Canada from the Atlantic to the Pacific. George III knighted him. It should all have been a great success for the Scottish migrants. Instead, they fought among themselves over the spoils and possibilities that Mackenzie had opened.

---

4   Fry, *The Scottish Empire*, 101.

Others would come and make their fortunes and reputations, yet the wildernesses of Canada meant that even the famous would perish. Thomas Douglas, Earl of Selkirk (1771–1820), for example, had persistent hopes that Scots would farm Canada. This was at a time when the Canadian Scots did not want migrants ruining the fur trade. Douglas failed and was ruined both physically and financially. He brought 800 Highlanders to Prince Edward Island and into Manitoba's Red River Valley (later to be famous). Such was the opposition of the fur traders that the North West Company soldiers were sent to evict Douglas and his community. Others were far more successful during more or less the same period. James McGill (1744–1813) arrived in the 1770s and he was part of the so-called Scotch Party whose members established fortunes. He also established a reputation for philanthropy and when he died he left much of his money to education in Montreal, where McGill University is named after him.

The establishment of Canada, like any other colonial system, was to rely on far more than the brilliance and determination of its trading. With the independence of America, the diverse ambitions of the Canadians and constitutional legitimacy had to be resolved. The loss of America encouraged political minds in London to look at individual holdings abroad rather than to imagine there could be a sweeping policy that would do for India, Africa, the West Indies and British North America, that is, Canada. Militarily, the British had done badly against the Patriots. The British still did not understand that it was not possible to fight a war using the strategy that might have well suited a conflict in Continental Europe. They could not successfully use tactics, logistics and the uncertainty of holding territory against an enemy with whom there was no geographical or political trade off to be negotiated. The British had never fought a war at such a distance. (The wars in India were not controlled from London or Paris.) They did not understand the environment of this theatre. Equally, the British government still had little political grasp of what it was trying to do other than not lose America. They at least understood that they should not make the same political and then military mistakes in Canada.

The 1791 Constitution split Quebec into Upper and Lower Canada. It took until 1840, the year after Lord Durham's report on 'The Affairs of British North America', for there to be a union of

Upper and Lower Canada and the year after that, 1841, for a fully fledged Canadian Parliament. Durham's 1839 study of British North America was perhaps a template from which future colonial reform came, even with the understanding that that reform anticipated independence. So although we might think of the British Empire as a long-lasting and sometimes even as an oppressive commercial as well as strategic enterprise, Durham's thinking suggests that colonial development, even in the first half of the nineteenth century, understood that for it to succeed then the colonies had to have a superior form of self-government.

This thought may be further examined in the philosophy of one of Durham's colleagues, Edward Gibbon Wakefield (1796–1862). At the time Durham was sorting out what he saw as the future of Canada, Wakefield was one of the founders of New Zealand as a colonial settlement based on some form of structured emigration of the surplus population of the British Isles. The early colonists in sixteenth-century North America had claimed migration was essential because Britain could not feed its population. Two-and-a-half centuries later the same reasons were being given to encourage emigration from Britain to Canada and New Zealand. For the moment, it was enough for the British to reflect on the consequences of losing the thirteen states. It is not unreasonable to describe the American War of Independence as having a devastating effect on Britain's constitutional and imperial history.

The conflict between hanging on to the settlements as a source of pride perhaps, taxation and territorial authority became the responsibility of Charles Rockingham in March 1782, when he became Prime Minister after Lord North's forced resignation. It will be remembered that he had become leader of the Whigs twenty years earlier. It was Rockingham who had repealed the maligned Stamp Act. With the Whigs in opposition, Rockingham had promoted the idea of letting the American colonists have their way. The conundrum was how to balance the territorial loss in North America, which had provided a base for British forces both land and naval, and the continuous uncertainty about the other colonies in the West Indies.

Rockingham died, in office, before peace with America was signed, although that's what he wanted. William Lansdowne, Earl of Shelburne (1737–1805) saw out the end of the war. Shelburne had, even in the late 1760s, opposed the pressures that were put on the

American settlers. He believed in conciliation and that the alternative would be the loss of the colonial loyalties. And so in July 1782 when Rockingham died, Shelburne was his natural successor and it was he who oversaw the successful Treaty at Versailles. Yet this was the end of Shelburne's political career. He was a victim of the not inconsiderable axis of Lord North and Charles James Fox (1749–1806). Fox and North refused to serve with Shelburne. George III could stand neither Fox nor North and he thought their coalition unprincipled. The King's feelings were hardly hurt when the Fox–North administration collapsed within months. What survived was the emergence of the Earl of Chatham's son, William Pitt the Younger (1759–1806), at twenty-four the nation's youngest Prime Minister. The coincidence of a new administration and the loss of America was the end of the first British Empire.

CHAPTER FORTY

1782–93

The Treaty of Paris, in 1783, officially ended the American War of Independence. Within six years the United States of America, as the new country was already being called, would have its first President, George Washington. America may have been free of Britain but this did not mean transatlantic trade stopped. The politics of the war had nothing to do with the bare bones of commerce. By 1786 the US dollar had been adopted as currency and in the Coinage Act of 1792 the dollar was defined as a basic unit of financial accounting and its worth in relationship to silver officially declared. The first US silver dollar appeared in 1794. The Spanish silver dollar had been in use in the thirteen colonies since early sixteenth-century settlers and this was a simple extension of the centuries old European *daler* – there was even a Sword Dollar struck by James VI of Scotland (later James I of England) and so the authority of the dollar as an international unit of trading (in some cases even in the twenty-first century the only unit to be used for certain commodities, such as oil) was established within a decade of the Paris Treaty. Bankers and traders in the British Isles were happy to trade with anyone with the money to buy what was offered or, better still, the willingness to pile up credit. That was the reality of commerce. The reality of British politics was not so easily settled. The wind of change had first blown on 4 July 1776, with the Declaration of Independence.

> When in the Course of human events it becomes necessary for one people to dissolve the political bands which have connected them with another and to assume among the powers of the earth, the separate and equal station to which the Laws of Nature and of Nature's God entitle them, a decent respect to the opinions of mankind requires that they should declare the causes which impel them to the separation.

We hold these truths to be self-evident, that all men are created equal, that they are endowed by their Creator with certain unalienable Rights, that among these are Life, Liberty and the pursuit of Happiness. [Author's italics]

That to secure these rights, Governments are instituted among Men, deriving their just powers from the consent of the governed, – That whenever any Form of Government becomes destructive of these ends, it is the Right of the People to alter or to abolish it, and to institute new Government, laying its foundation on such principles and organizing its powers in such form, as to them shall seem most likely to effect their Safety and Happiness. Prudence, indeed, will dictate that Governments long established should not be changed for light and transient causes; and accordingly all experience hath shewn that mankind are more disposed to suffer, while evils are sufferable than to right themselves by abolishing the forms to which they are accustomed. But when a long train of abuses and usurpations, pursuing invariably the same Object evinces a design to reduce them under absolute Despotism, it is their right, it is their duty, to throw off such Government, and to provide new Guards for their future security. – Such has been the patient sufferance of these Colonies; and such is now the necessity which constrains them to alter their former Systems of Government. The history of the present King of Great Britain is a history of repeated injuries and usurpations, all having in direct object the establishment of an absolute Tyranny over these States. To prove this, let Facts be submitted to a candid world.

He has refused his Assent to Laws, the most wholesome and necessary for the public good.

He has forbidden his Governors to pass Laws of immediate and pressing importance, unless suspended in their operation till his Assent should be obtained; and when so suspended, he has utterly neglected to attend to them.

He has refused to pass other Laws for the accommodation of large districts of people, unless those people would relinquish the right of Representation in the Legislature, a right inestimable to them and formidable to tyrants only.

He has called together legislative bodies at places unusual, uncomfortable, and distant from the depository of their Public Records, for the sole purpose of fatiguing them into compliance with his measures.

He has dissolved Representative Houses repeatedly, for opposing with manly firmness his invasions on the rights of the people.

He has refused for a long time, after such dissolutions, to cause others to be elected, whereby the Legislative Powers, incapable of Annihilation, have returned to the People at large for their exercise; the State remaining in the mean time exposed to all the dangers of invasion from without, and convulsions within.

He has endeavoured to prevent the population of these States; for that purpose obstructing the Laws for Naturalization of Foreigners; refusing to pass others to encourage their migrations hither, and raising the conditions of new Appropriations of Lands.

He has obstructed the Administration of Justice by refusing his Assent to Laws for establishing Judiciary Powers.

He has made Judges dependent on his Will alone for the tenure of their offices, and the amount and payment of their salaries.

He has erected a multitude of New Offices, and sent hither swarms of Officers to harass our people and eat out their substance.

He has kept among us, in times of peace, Standing Armies without the Consent of our legislatures.

He has affected to render the Military independent of and superior to the Civil Power.

He has combined with others to subject us to a jurisdiction foreign to our constitution, and unacknowledged by our laws; giving his Assent to their Acts of pretended Legislation:

For quartering large bodies of armed troops among us:

For protecting them, by a mock Trial from punishment for any Murders which they should commit on the Inhabitants of these States:

For cutting off our Trade with all parts of the world:

For imposing Taxes on us without our Consent:

For depriving us in many cases, of the benefit of Trial by Jury:

For transporting us beyond Seas to be tried for pretended offences:

For abolishing the free System of English Laws in a neighbouring Province, establishing therein an Arbitrary government, and enlarging its Boundaries so as to render it at once an example and fit instrument for introducing the same absolute rule into these Colonies:

For taking away our Charters, abolishing our most valuable Laws and altering fundamentally the Forms of our Governments:

For suspending our own Legislatures, and declaring themselves invested with power to legislate for us in all cases whatsoever.

He has abdicated Government here, by declaring us out of his Protection and waging War against us.

He has plundered our seas, ravaged our coasts, burnt our towns, and destroyed the lives of our people.

He is at this time transporting large Armies of foreign Mercenaries to compleat the works of death, desolation, and tyranny, already begun with circumstances of Cruelty & Perfidy scarcely paralleled in the most barbarous ages, and totally unworthy of the Head of a civilized nation.

He has constrained our fellow Citizens taken Captive on the high Seas to bear Arms against their Country, to become the executioners of their friends and Brethren, or to fall themselves by their Hands.

He has excited domestic insurrections amongst us, and has endeavoured to bring on the inhabitants of our frontiers, the merciless Indian Savages whose known rule of warfare, is an undistinguished destruction of all ages, sexes and conditions.

In every stage of these Oppressions We have Petitioned for Redress in the most humble terms: Our repeated Petitions have been answered only by repeated injury. A Prince, whose character is thus marked by every act which may define a Tyrant, is unfit to be the ruler of a free people.

Nor have We been wanting in attentions to our British brethren. We have warned them from time to time of attempts by their legislature to extend an unwarrantable jurisdiction over us. We have reminded them of the circumstances of our emigration and settlement here. We have appealed to their native justice and magnanimity, and we have conjured them by the ties of our common kindred to disavow these usurpations, which would inevitably interrupt our connections and correspondence. They too have been deaf to the voice of justice and of consanguinity. We must, therefore, acquiesce in the necessity, which denounces our Separation, and hold them, as we hold the rest of mankind, Enemies in War, in Peace Friends.

We, therefore, the Representatives of the united States of America, in General Congress, Assembled, appealing to the Supreme Judge of the world for the rectitude of our intentions, do, in the Name, and by Authority of the good People of these Colonies, solemnly publish and declare, That these united Colonies are, and of Right ought to be Free and Independent States, that they are Absolved from all Allegiance to the British Crown, and that all political connection between them and the State of Great Britain, is and ought to be totally dissolved; and that as Free and Independent States, they have full Power to levy War, conclude Peace, contract Alliances, establish Commerce, and to do all other Acts and Things which Independent States may of right do. – And for the support of this Declaration, with a firm reliance on the protection of Divine Providence, we mutually pledge to each other our Lives, our Fortunes, and our sacred Honor.

Britain had lost her first major colony and the colonists had accused George III of plundering more than their seas. He had plundered their rights. George III talked of giving up his crown and of retreating to his homelands in Germany. The mood in Great Britain was one of anger and, when North left the House of Commons in March 1782, he was a vanquished figure. There were no excuses in his famous response to the news of defeat at Yorktown, 'Oh, God, it is all over.' North's going was more than the departure of a prime minister. When he went he did so because of something unique in Parliamentary history. Up to that point, monarchs had accepted, reluctantly, the mood of the nation. Monarchs had sometimes accepted the decisions of their prime ministers. But now the House of Commons had the voting power to force the resignation of a prime minister and all but a few of his colleagues. And for that reason North's going can be seen as a milestone in Parliamentary history.

There were only two men capable of succeeding him, of rallying support for a new ministry. One was Charles Watson-Wentworth, the second Marquess of Rockingham, who'd already been prime minister for a short spell in the 1760s. The other was William Petty-FitzMaurice, the second Earl of Shelburne. Both had advocated an end to the war and had even opposed it in the first place, and both were Whigs. However, Shelburne couldn't maintain a majority without the help of the Rockingham Whigs, and they were unlikely to give him any support, so George III called for Rockingham. But by July Rockingham was dead and Shelburne became leader. The difference between the two was in the style and composition of their Cabinets. By and large, Rockingham, with Edmund Burke, had seen Cabinet government as a group of like-minded individuals who would present a unified front to the King. Shelburne didn't think like that. He was – or posed as – an intellectual and he was politically inept. Most importantly, Shelburne thought little of party government. He gathered together politicians of differing views and supported the King's right to choose his ministers – a concept conveniently dear to the King's heart.

And so from this came William Pitt the Younger. He was twenty-three. A year on and he would be Prime Minister. Of the rest, North hoped to return, but how could he? Few cared for Shelburne and Charles James Fox was volatile and a factionalist. Fox and Shelburne never got on. In fact, Fox detested Shelburne. Even when Rockingham was alive they would competed with each other for the right to hand out offices and general patronage. They disagreed over the way in which peace might be negotiated. Fox had long abandoned the illusion that the thirteen colonies were in fact colonies. He and Shelburne even had different envoys to the Paris talks. Animosities and schisms are the stuff of politics in any century. The 'Long Century' from the French Revolution to the outbreak of the First World War, as defined by the Marxist historian Eric Hobsbawm, was no different and indeed probably a sturdier than most examples of this truism.[5] Britain was witnessing its own Age of Revolution from the loss of America to a period of industrial and technological innovation, when seemingly every conceivable task of labour was not necessarily eased but certainly revolutionized, that was to last a hundred years and more. Less easily sat the political changes within the islands and especially the shifting relationships between England and Ireland. The historical differences between the English and the Irish had not disappeared or become any less important simply because Britain had been at war across the Atlantic Ocean.

For example, Lord Shelburne had criticized the North administration for its attitude to Ireland, especially for its restrictions on trade with the colonies during the war. To be fair, North had attempted to make concessions and it was English merchants who had opposed him (which explains something of the political realities of the day and particularly why it is wrong to think in simple terms of Whigs, Tories and the power of political majorities).

The Speaker of the Irish House of Commons, Edmond Sexton Pery (1719–1806), reported in 1779 that the restrictions were 'one

---

5   For the story of the Long Century see the three seminal works on this hypothesis: Eric Hobsbawm, *The Age of Revolution 1789–1848* (London: Abacus, 1988); Eric Hobsbawm, *The Age of Capital 1848–1875* (London: Abacus, 1988); Eric Hobsbawm, *The Age of Empire 1875–1914* (London: Abacus, 1989).

general Cause of Distress in the economy and the people'. The laws, he believed, were cruel and short-sighted, and the interests of the English merchants repressive. He claimed history suggested that whatever the motives of the English, by which he particularly meant the Anglican Ascendancy,[6] Ireland 'must continue in a state of poverty, frequently of misery'. He continued:

> It seems to be equally obvious that it is not in the interest of Great Britain to keep her in that state, in the view of commerce only. Great Britain must be the loser by it. Little is to be got by trading with a poor country . . . At present the people of Ireland are taught by partial laws to consider themselves as separated from the inhabitants of Great Britain. Were that fatal obstacle removed, they would be united as much in affection, as they certainly are in interest; and it would not then be in the power of malice to disturb their harmony. But the seeds of discord are sown, and if suffered to take root, it is feared will soon overspread the land.

By 1780 the suffering of Ireland and the Irish, particularly from the restrictions on trade, began to have some political effect, yet solutions were not really obvious. Two Bills went through the Westminster Parliament which allowed the Irish export of woollens and glass, and an expansion of trade with America, the West Indies and Africa. But not much actually changed. Industry did not attract investors. Both the hard cash necessary to build these industries and shipping were in short supply. And so, in spite of the joy with which the new legislation was greeted in Ireland, reality soon descended, and Edmond Pery's hoped-for economic miracle and calming of animosities barely materialized.

In Scotland in the eighteenth century, there was an unprecedentedly strong export trade, especially in sturdy clothing and iron tools and, thanks to the increasing demand for glass, high investment there meant bigger potential export markets, which in turn supported an expanding fleet. And Scottish entrepreneurs appear to have been more imaginative than those trading from or through Ireland.

---

6   For the best explanation of this phenomenon, see R. F. Foster, 'The Ascendancy Mind', *Modern Ireland 1600–1972* (London: Allen Lane, 1988).

Yet even in Scotland the effects of the war were catastrophic. Just before the war, the Scottish Tobacco Lords, as they were known, were bringing in some forty-six million pounds of tobacco. More than 90 per cent of it was then re-exported, much of it to France. Halfway through the war, the Scottish import-export trade was down by 40 per cent, but the resilience of the Scottish traders meant they survived. In 1783 Glasgow set up a group to examine potential markets. It became the first Chamber of Commerce in Britain and it worked. Within seven years Scottish trade figures had recovered to their pre-war levels.

But it was at the centre of British power where reform was most needed. Its symbol was the action of George III in asking Pitt the Younger, then twenty-four years old, to form an administration in December 1783. This was the fifth administration in under two years. At that time, ministers still owed their loyalty first and foremost to the monarch, not to their party. In fact, there probably wasn't a Whig or a Tory party political position on many major matters at the time. There was a political instinct, yes, but not a manifesto in the way they exist today. And the Cabinet was not single-minded: it was a coalition. The King had the right, which he exercised, to appoint his ministers but George didn't like political parties. To him a party meant a faction and therefore a danger. Sometimes that faction imposed its will: Rockingham's administration did. So did the coalition of Fox and North. What about Pitt?

In May 1782 he had spoken in the House on Parliamentary reform, although he didn't outline the best way forward. However, he pointed out that there wasn't a Member of Parliament who wouldn't, as he put it, agree with him 'that the representation, as it now stood, was incomplete'. (In fact, he was wrong on that. Many would disagree with him.) He concluded that there should be a committee to 'enquire into the present state of the Representation of the Commons of Great Britain in Parliament'. Pitt's proposal was rejected, but only by twenty votes. The King was not sorry.

George III had reigned for two decades and had been through, and often suffered from, almost every form of political intrigue. He had watched, fought and compromised at every opportunity to keep control of his administrations and, in some cases, to lead them. Furthermore, his reputation, once the immediate loss of the colonies was out of the way, was high enough for this Hanoverian to be called

Good King George by his people. His reputation was helped by the low public esteem in which politicians were held, and by the antics of the Prince of Wales.

In 1784, shortly after George III appointed Pitt, there was an election that produced a political confrontation between North and Fox on one side and the King and Pitt on the other. The result represented a show of support for George III's decision to send North and Fox packing and to appoint Pitt as his Prime Minister. George was satisfied especially as Pitt never had more than fifty MPs supporting him and so was compelled to rely on the King and his supporters. One consequence of this was that most of the ministers owed more allegiance to the Crown than to the Prime Minister.

But Pitt had advantages of his own. First, he was a Pitt and he carried the family name with ease. He was conscientious, honourable and, despite his age, he had already been Chancellor of the Exchequer and was formidably bright. Above all, he was not associated with the old group of politicians and so it followed that he had no close cronies. He also recognized that he had to accept political change, and even defeat, rather than risk causing more damage by open confrontation. He was a man who could take stock to analyse, after success, why he had been successful and, after failure, how to avoid repeating the experience. If there existed an advantage in defeat, or an unrecognized one in success, Pitt knew how to make that advantage work for him. One of his key advantages was his understanding with the King. They were never friends in the social sense but their relationship worked. Pitt needed the King and the King needed Pitt – particularly in matters of finance and economic reform. For example, the nearly seventy different forms of customs and excise duties were revised so that the bureaucracy no longer had the right to multiply the duty gathered by charging it in different forms – on the same import. The further revisions began to be set out as household accounts. Pitt was producing for the first time what we now call the Budget. The King was, or should have been, pleased. But the King was not always in an understandable state to give good judgement on anything put before him.

In the autumn of 1788, George III was showing visible signs of erratic behaviour that has unfairly been diagnosed as insanity. He suffered from porphyria, a lack of haemoglobin production. The symptoms were sometimes unbearable itching, skin pain and purple urine. His pain and increased pulse brought out exclamations, so easily dismissed as ramblings. Imagine how his suffering may have increased when he was bound, gagged and tied to furniture – a reminder that even the royal physicians had little medical learning. Certainly George III was not the first member of a British royal family to suffer from some form of porphyria. Mary Queen of Scots displayed some symptoms as did, in the twentieth century, the late Prince William of Gloucester.

The medical condition of the King was of intense concern because of his political authority. The King's followers needed his support especially against Fox and his friends who had taken up with the Prince of Wales, who would become George IV in 1820. The Prince, in 1788, was following the path of most Princes of Wales by setting up in opposition to the monarch. Fox in particular had nothing to lose in opposing George III. There was no chance, after the antagonisms of the Fox–North coalition, that George would ever admit Fox as his first minister; but the heir to the throne might. Fox was an opportunist and he was older than Pitt, so he felt his chances of becoming prime minister were fading. When there were rumours that the King might die, this was good news to Fox's ears. The new King would get rid of Pitt and give his post to Fox. He could hardly have guessed that, ill or not, George III would outlive the lot of them. In fact, with Pitt the Younger as his Prime Minister, George III was about to witness a remarkable decade in England's political and social history. The Norfolk pamphleteer, Tom Paine, was writing *The Rights of Man*, Edward Gibbon was finishing *The History of the Decline and Fall of the Roman Empire* and the working environment was radically changing because industrial society was shifting (and not because there was deep anxiety about the ways and circumstances of people's lives). Furthermore, here was a period that demonstrated that events elsewhere, and not at home, might excite the society in which radical thought germinates. For example, Tom Paine's ideas about England were triggered by the American revolt and then the French Revolution.

In the year following the King's illness, the Revolution started in France, Fox once again misjudged the mood of the country. It is easy to see why. Pitt thought it best to have no great opinion on the Revolution other than to believe that the spirit of the French would not cross the Channel. Fox, on the other hand, heard the cry Liberty as a rally to break Pitt's grip on power. It was not. Nevertheless, for three years, the Revolution in France could not be ignored by those who governed the British Isles. The British were no strangers to revolution, but what was happening to France, with the very real possibility of regicide, was no casual moment at a time when the British were feeling their own way towards reforming systems and even Catholic Emancipation, albeit on a limited scale. Americans had rebelled against being ruled and taxed by another nation; theirs was an anti-colonial rebellion. The English Revolution of 1688 had not been against monarchy and nobility, but against a particular monarch, James II, and Roman Catholicism. And no one tried to return to the Cromwellian model, to a republic. But in France, almost without warning to those preoccupied with their political, commercial and colonial ambitions, that was what was happening.

In eighteenth-century France the King governed from Versailles, surrounded by his courtiers. However, the courtiers, the French nobility, had been stripped of power. They were landlords who simply took revenues from their distant estates and as a class, or, more accurately, as a caste, did nothing to help govern the country. They certainly weren't as powerful as the Church, nor were they as powerful as the peasants. The French peasantry was a European phenomenon: peasantry with power. They were depressed by high rates of taxation but they also owned half the land in France and their lot was getting better. They were potentially dangerous.

There was also in France an influential group of extraordinary people not to be under-rated. They carried no guns, received no patronage and had no crude plans for the downfall of the monarch. Nevertheless, their names have survived longer than many of the revolutionaries themselves. They were the philosophers: Diderot, Rousseau, Voltaire.

On 14 July 1789 the royal prison in Paris, the Bastille, fell. It held only a handful of prisoners, one of them mad, but it represented the absolute rule of the French monarch. The revolution was well under way. At the start, Britain appears to have assumed that the outcome would be an English-style Constitutional monarchy. Pitt quietly welcomed this idea: he believed a reformed French throne would be less of a military threat.

Fox and the so-called Whig opposition were excited by the prospect of change. But there was no fear that the revolutionary ideas would spread to Britain. Perhaps this short-sightedness had a lot to do with the fact that few people anywhere in Europe, perhaps even in France, understood the implications of what had been started. In Britain in particular, judging the French Revolution's effects was probably influenced by the satisfactory outcome of the nation's own revolution, the centenary of which was being celebrated. It was 100 years since the English Bill of Rights was published. The Glorious Revolution of 1688 could have been mistakenly assumed similar to what was going on in France.

Fox got up in Parliament and sang French praises. Edmund Burke, however, was pessimistic. He supported the idea of change, but he thought that what was actually happening was potentially dangerous.

Furthermore, Burke, a devout Christian, believed the outcome would be, at least, civil war on a scale more ferocious than the old wars of religion. The consequences of 14 July for many of the Non-conformists in the British Isles were imagined to be far more exciting than the content demeanour of the Anglicans. For example, in Ireland, Irish Catholics greeted the news of the opening of the Bastille as a huge act of change. As for Burke, he could not accept that the French were merely shuffling their society. Burke saw the Revolution as a prelude to something quite frightening: a creeping threat to the institutions of Christian Europe. For that reason, Burke wanted Pitt to make troops ready for war against the French. But it's doubtful if he expected Pitt to do as he advised. He thought the Prime Minister was a man of no imagination and little vision.

Pitt did nothing. Burke wanted intervention, and a few Whigs, if not exactly in agreement, took serious note of what Burke was saying; and Fox (even though he understood the instinctive British mistrust of the French) supported the Revolution. But the differences between Fox and Burke were so great that the two men quarrelled in public (in the House of Commons, ironically during the Canada Debate), and Burke broke from the party.

And, by the late summer of 1792, the French Revolution had spread beyond the French borders. The French monarchy was no more. News of mass murders of the aristocracy crossed the Channel. What had been seen as constitutional reform was turning into bloody dictatorship. And dictatorship was turning into war.

British radicals, poets, writers and, in some cases, the constituents of the new working men's clubs were all in touch with the French extremists, the Jacobins (the Jacobin Club existed between 1790 and 1794 and was a club for those with radical ideas). The Jacobins shouldn't be confused with the Jacobites, the old supporters of a Stuart pretender to the English throne. Jacobinism in Britain was strong enough for the French to believe they had support for the export of the Revolution. They turned out to be wrong, but at the end of January 1793, the French announced the annexation of the Austrian Netherlands. The next day, 1 February, they declared war on Holland and on Britain. And so now, with the declaration of war, Pitt, with his do-nothing policy shredded, expressed his misery to the Commons.

> The contempt which the French have shown for neutrality on our part most strictly observed; the violations of their solemn and plighted faith; their presumptuous attempts to interfere in the government of this country and to arm our subjects [a comment that could have been read in almost any of the previous four centuries], to vilify a monarch, the object of our gratitude, reverence and affection, and to separate the Court from the people; does not this become, on our part, a war of honour, a war necessary to assert the spirit of the nation and the dignity of the British name? We are at war with those who would destroy the whole fabric of our Constitution. In such a cause as that in which we are now engaged, I trust our exertions will only terminate with our lives

So Britain was once more at war with France and would continue to be for more than two decades.

CHAPTER FORTY-ONE
1793–1800

In 1793 a young artillery lieutenant was responsible for the capture of the Royalist fortress seaport of Toulon. In Paris, Robespierre took note of this young Corsican officer whose name was Napoleon Bonaparte. France would need an imaginative commander. An alliance of Europeans against France was set up. It was called the First Coalition and consisted of Britain, Holland, Spain, Austria and Prussia. But it was not a success because each member was too busy looking after its own interests. In the British Isles, Pitt's apparent lack of immediate concern was not reflected in, for example, assaults on freedoms when he suspended habeas corpus, sacred to the British code of the rights of man. *Habeas Corpus* (Latin: you may have the body) was a thirteenth-century writ that was mainly used to settle legal conflicts between the courts of equity and common law. It demanded that anyone who detained (imprisoned) a person should produce that person at court within a specific time together with the reason for the detention. By the time of Henry VII (1457–1509) the writ was used, in theory, to protect the individual from wrongful imprisonment. Like most Acts, this was amended, particularly in 1679 when loopholes in the law were removed and, going on from our immediate period, in 1816 and again as late as 1960 when the Act was strengthened; for example, the occasions when the Act could be set aside were limited.

Of course, any government had the power to suspend habeas corpus in extreme situations of national security. In 1794, with the French Revolutionary War under way, Pitt thought the security of the nation threatened enough to suspend habeas corpus. Why would he do that? He was concerned about sedition and espionage, and therefore felt the need to lock up a suspicious character and deny that person access to the law until the administration felt it safe to let the detainee have access to that freedom. Thus, it was a sure sign that Pitt's administration felt the King's rule was threatened. The situation in Europe was no safer because of promises of coalitions against France. Promises were empty. The partners in the First Coalition against France were in disarray. The Low Countries, with one British ally, the Prussians, were more interested in sharing the partition of Poland with the Russians. The Prussians then made a peace agreement (to consolidate their Polish gains) and sat out the war in selfish neutrality. The Austrians followed to pick over the Polish bones while the French armies drove into Spain and Holland, which became known as the Batavian Republic. The Spanish, sensing the course of the war, also deserted the First Coalition. If all this wasn't enough, the British Royal Navy failed to dominate the sea-lanes. And the navy mutinied twice.

In April 1797, conditions of service in the navy were so bad that the Channel Fleet, at Spithead, refused to put out sea. Within a few days, many of the demands of the ratings were granted. This encouraged the North Sea Fleet to mutiny at the Nore, and so, for weeks, it was the Royal Navy and not the French that virtually blockaded the Thames. The conditions in which ratings lived on the lower decks in the eighteenth century were appalling. Pay was often infrequent (partly to prevent sailors leaving the ship and never returning). The ships themselves were riddled with disease. A wounded man was often put ashore without any compensation and not even pay. And so the men mutinied. There were hangings aplenty. The French were in the Channel and a squadron was heading for Ireland, so the Admiralty Board responded quickly in order 'that the Fleet should speedily put to sea to meet the enemy of the country'. The Board said that it understood the grievances and wages were raised to four shillings a month extra for petty officers and able seamen, three shillings a month extra for ordinary seamen and two shillings a month for landmen. Wounded sailors would continue to be paid. But the Spithead sailors weren't satisfied. They pushed once more at the Board's eagerness to reach agreement before there was another disagreement with the French. The demands of the Spithead sailors were coped with but those of the North Sea Fleet were not settled so easily. The Nore mutineers, as they were known, did not surrender for four weeks. But it was clear that England, as ever, needed its navy. When the fleet finally put to sea, they won the Battle of Camperdown and stopped the Dutch invasion of England.

But for one man in particular, the Nore and Spithead mutinies were of little immediate interest. In 1797, Commodore Horatio Nelson had just been promoted to Rear Admiral, was about to be knighted and, within months, he, the nation and the wife of Sir William Hamilton would be celebrating his destruction of the French fleet at the mouth of the River Nile; this ruined Napoleon Bonaparte's ambitions to invade Egypt and thus interrupt British trade routes to and from the Far East, threaten British India and extend his empire to the sub-continent. Like Bismarck in the next century, Napoleon saw the taking of territory as a mark of progress. Nelson knew well the naval role of disrupting enemy ambition, ideally by stopping the enemy fleet from putting to sea and, when they did so, defeating them and taking ships as prizes. (Hence the many French names on ships of the Royal Navy.)

Nelson's story is the tale of a typical British hero. Not well born, he overcomes disabilities and he is criticized by superiors, the victim of jealousy, unconventional and loved by the people better than he is regarded by authority; he then dies in a crucial battle and so achieves his finest hour and legendary status.

Nelson was born in Norfolk in 1758, two years after the Black Hole of Calcutta and in the same year as Halley's Comet was seen. He was twelve when he joined his first ship, the *Raisonnable*, a ship captured from the French in the days when the Royal Navy rarely changed ships' names. She was a fine ship for Nelson and for her captain, Maurice Suckling. Suckling just happened to be Nelson's uncle, otherwise Nelson, who was a feeble child, might never have been taken into the navy at all.

In the summer of that year, 1771, Nelson transferred to the *Triumph*, and then to a merchant ship bound for the West Indies. When England went to war with the American colonies, so did Nelson. By 1787, he had commanded four ships and had married Frances Nisbet. But the following year he was unemployed. In those days, if an officer didn't have a ship, then the best he could hope for was to go ashore on half-pay. It wasn't until January 1793, only four weeks before France declared war, that the Admiralty called Nelson back. He took command of the *Agamemnon*, the ship he loved more than any other, including the *Victory*. The following year he was wounded in his right eye in the Corsican campaign at Calvi, and eventually lost its sight. In 1797 he became a rear admiral, a knight of the Bath and, at Santa Cruz, lost his right arm. And so now, in 1798, it was a half-sighted, one-armed, diminutive, glory-seeking, prone-to-sea-sickness junior admiral who hoisted his pennant in the *Vanguard* and started searching the Mediterranean for the French fleet as Bonaparte rampaged through Continental Europe.

The northern provinces of what we call Italy (it did not become a single State until 1861) had fallen; Venice was degraded into a separate province of Austria. Napoleon would soon have an idea to invade Britain. He was already thinking of doing what only the Norman had done. Napoleon wanted to turn a murky tidal river at Boulogne into a massive invasion port. He did not abandon this idea until the summer of 1805. Pitt knew this. No wonder, outward appearances aside, Pitt was taking the war with France far more seriously than some imagined. And it was not as if England had no other worries. There was real rebellion in Ireland. The concept of Catholic Emancipation was a major issue that could destabilize the politics as well as the constitutional stability of the British.

However, in 1798 the single British ambition was to bring about Napoleon's defeat. Nelson believed that could be best achieved at sea. The French fleet of thirteen capital ships, each armed with 74 guns, and four smaller vessels was commanded by Admiral François-Paul Brueys d'Aigailliers, usually referred to as Admiral Paul Brueys. Nelson found the fleet at anchor midstream in the shoals at Aboukir Bay, just to the east of Alexandria. The French thought themselves safe among the shoals. Nelson, his flag in the *Vanguard*, went in shortly before sunset with six ships to one side of the French line, six the other. The battle went on through the night until shortly after six in the morning.

It was a grand and an awful spectacle. Admiral Brueys was seen flopped in a chair, both legs shot off, still trying to direct operations. A further salvo saved him further pain. His captain refused to leave the deck. His ten-year-old son was trapped below in the fire. Four French vessels managed to escape to sea including the *Guillaume Tell*, commanded by Rear Admiral Pierre-Charles Villeneuve who would face Nelson once more, at Trafalgar as commander of the whole French fleet. As Nelson wrote in his dispatch, 'My Lord, Almighty God has blessed His Majesty's Arms in the late Battle by a great victory over the Fleet of the Enemy.' The importance of his battle was that it stopped Napoleon building a communications line between France and Asia. And the Royal Navy was now in Malta, and so could stay in the Mediterranean all year round instead of returning the fleet to home waters every winter. However, in spite of the naval victory, the land battle was very much going Napoleon's way. Britain had allies but they were not very good against the superior strategy of the Corsican. Moreover, the war was taking a lot of money and the allies demanded even more to take on the land role that the British felt they themselves could not pursue at a large scale. Britain's main contribution was at sea, with Nelson hunting for the new Mediterranean fleet and, later, the brilliant admiral William Cornwallis blockading the main French fleet in Brest – for two years.

It was a problem for the government that many of those shopkeepers, their customers, suppliers, landlords and tenants were not making a big enough contribution. Money had been raised by barons from their peasantry and by counties from the landowners, and even windows had been taxed. Pitt had already tried to raise money by trebling the taxes on luxuries – for example, on hair powder, horses and servants. But now, Pitt – a politician, not a monarch – proposed the most obvious and universal means of raising money for war. On 3 December 1798, William Pitt gave the House news of the first graduated income tax.

> It is my intention to propose that a general tax shall be imposed upon all the leading branches of income. I trust that all who value the national honour and the national safety will co-operate in obtaining by an efficient and comprehensive tax upon real ability, every advantage which flourishing and invigorated resources can confer upon national efforts. It is my intention to propose that no income under £60 a year shall be called upon to contribute and the scale of modification up to £200 a year shall be introduced.

Income tax had arrived at two shillings in the pound. Pitt wanted 10 per cent from everyone earning more than £60 a year. And at the end of the eighteenth century there was a larger population to be taxed.

The century began with a population of less than six million, but by the end of the century it was more than ten million. And by 1800 the National Debt, which had been about £19 million at the beginning of the century, was closer to £500 million. However there had been a 400 per cent increase in cotton output and a four-fold increase in coal mining; the steam engine was invented, the first canal opened and the first edition of *The Times* was printed. And it was the century of the Georges, the third of whom they said was insane.

However, the momentous event at the end of the century was the Union of Great Britain with Ireland. It was more than a significant constitutional moment. Ireland and Britain joined together because Ireland was, to the British, fast becoming a failed State in rebellion. The object of that rebellion was the so-called Protestant Ascendancy that ruled Ireland and therefore the British rule itself. The Protestant Ascendancy was the almost entirely Protestant/Anglican organiza-tion that ruled a nation island that was 75 per cent Roman Catholic. The rebellion came not from the Catholics but was initiated from a Presbyterian-based movement known as the United Irishmen (see p.405). This group was the spearhead for those who wanted change and even a republican rebellion against the British – the period was within a decade of the French Revolution. A further issue was the role of religion in the politics of both Ireland and Britain that would eventually bring about Union through the 1800 Act of Union.

The short answer is that religion identity in Britain and Ireland influenced political and social reform at the time of Union between the two kingdoms. Every faction in Ireland, unlike the rest of the British Isles, had religious labelling. From this alone, the easy paral-lels with the late twentieth-century Troubles in Northern Ireland become obvious.

During the second half of the eighteenth century, Protestant England appeared confident in its own identity and its peoples displayed a global colonial and Protestant arrogance so much so that they characterized predominantly Catholic states as poverty-ridden; the British were showing that only Protestants could enjoy a true and lasting prosperity. Recently, historian Linda Colley has written, 'British Protestantism was not a matter of faith but their assumed superiority of their Christian denomination. Therefore, the Protestant Ascendancy in Ireland existed because the ruling class were Anglican Protestants. They had no role as religious proselytizers.'[1] Colley's

---

1   Linda Colley, *Britons: Forging the Nation, 1707–1937* (London/New Haven, CT: Yale, 1992).

accepted view should be read with the anxieties of Britain's ruling classes. Protestant arrogance could only palliate a formidable mix of not always successful British experiences, as follows: the American War of Independence (1775–83); the strengthening of the Evangelical movement and its political influences; Papal recognition of the Hanoverian monarchy and therefore a tentative relaxation of restrictions on Catholics (1776); the refusal in the 1780s of the Irish Parliament to contribute to the Royal Navy and ease trade restrictions; the French Revolution (1789–99); the Society of United Irishmen (October 1791) inspired by the French Revolution; the execution of Louis XVI (1793), England being no stranger to the consequences of regicide; war with France (1793–1815); the constant fear of French invasion through Ireland (a token landing at Killala in August 1798) and via Boulogne to the English southern coast (Napoleon did not abandon his plan to launch the invasion of England until August 1805); and finally, the Irish Rebellion (1798).

By the 1790s, the three main reasons for political anxieties were: an overstretched war economy; war with France; anarchy in Ireland.

Pitt's solution was Union with Ireland and a form of Catholic Emancipation (with voting powers but no representation in Parliament). Protestant England was acknowledging the political influence of not so much Roman Catholicism as a faith, but the majority of the islanders who opposed Protestantism as a ruling elite rather than a religious persuasion. Pitt did not see constitutional and political Union as any form of religious ecumenism.

England and Ireland had been in personal Union – when two states may share the head of state and legislation but are recognized internationally as separate states – since 1542, when Henry VIII became King of Ireland under the Crown of Ireland Act. A similar arrangement existed between Scotland and England following the accession of James VI of Scotland as James I of England (1603) until the 1707 Act dissolved the personal Union and created Scotland and England as the Kingdom of Great Britain. This might have been the opportunity constitutionally to tidy up the British Isles and two years later, 1709, the Irish House of Lords unsuccessfully petitioned for Ireland to join a Kingdom of Great Britain.

The petition was complicated by Irish insistence on effective representation in the English Parliament along the lines reasoned by William Molyneux (1656–98), an MP for Trinity College

Dublin who had insisted that Ireland should not be legislated by Westminster without proper representation in London – the model used by the American colonists in their demand 'no taxation without representation'.

Throughout the Seven Years War (1756–63) Britain saw Ireland as a backdoor for a French invasion and so, Union became attractive to Britain – but not to Ireland. Henry Grattan (1746–1820) and his Patriot Party led the opposition. Instead of Union, Grattan achieved limited legislative independence in 1782. Grattan was part of the Protestant Ascendancy and supported the Crown but wanted Parliamentary reform and Catholic Emancipation (which George III did not).

By the 1790s, Ireland was becoming a failing State and breeding open rebellion by a mix of Presbyterian and Catholic Defenders. The Defenders dated from the 1780s. They were Catholic vigilantes formed in Armagh to defend their people against the Protestant Boys (later the Orange Order). Following the Ulster cleansing of Catholics in the mid-1790s, the Defenders moved with other Catholics to Leinster and Connaught. They were natural allies of rebellious Presbyterians against the ruling Protestant Ascendancy.

In 1791, Wolfe Tone (1763–98) and other Protestant radicals in Belfast, inspired by the French Revolution and republican democracy in America, founded the Society of United Irishmen. This was not a Catholic led group. For example, the twelve backers of the Society's own newspaper, the *Northern Star* were almost all Presbyterians. Here was a reminder that the mix of Christian Churches throughout the British Isles could not be simplified in terms of the Established Church of England versus Roman Catholics and Dissenters in some continuous quasi-religious war.

The Established Church of England was (and remains) the State religion under Parliamentary control. In the 1600s the increased authority of the High Church (almost Anglo-Catholics) unwittingly encouraged anti-Episcopal sentiment and had much to do with the confrontation between Parliament and Charles I. During the Commonwealth, a form of Puritanism was preferred; the *Book of Common Prayer* was withdrawn and Puritans were found throughout the New Model Army. With the Restoration (1660) Puritanism became part of the Non-conformist churches and by the mid-1700s the Evangelical movement was building on the traditions of the

Puritan beliefs surviving in the Anglican Church and was increasingly seen as influential in campaigning for political reform. Its
influence was also part of the transatlantic revival in the 1730s.[2]

Unlike the Irish Roman Catholics, the 80,000 English Catholics
were led by a secular aristocracy rather than its clergy, who numbered
not many more than 400, and were not a political consideration. If
there were any political concerns, they had more to do with how
English Catholics might react to Irish Catholic Emancipation.

Scotland's religious communities had an altogether different tint
with four main Christian persuasions: the Roman Catholics; the
Episcopalians; the Presbyterians; and a myriad of Non-conformist
Churches. In 1188 Pope Clement III (1130–91) declared the Scottish
Church no longer a subject of the Archbishop of York, but the
Daughter of Rome thus separating the Scottish Church from the
English Church. This uneasy alliance survived until the establish-
ment, led by the Calvinist convert, John Knox (c.1512–72), of the
reformed Church of Scotland in 1560 and the decision of the Scottish
Reformation Parliament that the Church, the Kirk, was Protestant
and to outlaw the Catholic Mass. Seven years on, 1567, the government recognized the Established Church of Scotland as the official
Church. By 1689 the Scottish church had become Episcopalian and
very much a minority persuasion beneath the Church of Scotland,
Established but not in the English sense where the Church of England
was controlled by Parliament. The Episcopal and Roman Catholic
denominations may have been in the minority, but were not without
political influence. A further significance of the Scottish Presbyterians
was that influence extended to Northern Ireland communities and
the Irish were present at the 1707 ceremonies for Scottish Union.

Here then, was the religious wiring diagram of the British Isles
suggesting that with the exception of Wales – Anglicans under the
see of Canterbury and Non-conformists – religion had a political
history and remained very much in the political consciousness of
government. Therefore, it followed that structured religion, by the
period of introspection and political fear in the 1790s, was ever
likely to be at least a serious consideration in the political thinking
of Pitt and others if for no other reason that all other religions

2   David W. Bebbington, *Evangelicals in Modern Britain: A History from the 1730s to the
1980s* (London: Unwin Hyman, 1989).

(particularly the Catholics) were suspected of political ambitions encouraged by England's historical enemies.

For the English establishment, religious identity could not be separated from politics and security of the State. For example, there was a constitutional difference between Pitt as Prime Minister, who saw Catholic Emancipation as a practical political reform, and the King, George III, who was against Catholic Emancipation because he believed it compromised his coronation vows as head of the one Church, the Established Church of England. Moreover, the King saw no good reason for Catholics in Ireland to vote for Parliament. In 1801 Pitt offered his resignation on this point of principle and because he had promised Emancipation for the vote on the Union.

In Ireland, established Catholic families sensed that Emancipation could mean more than votes, for example: legal right and status could threaten the pockets and holdings of the Protestant Ascendancy – something not imagined in the Pitt-led debate. Catholics were already reclaiming lands they said had been taken or plundered by Protestants in earlier times. It was an observation raised by Lord Minto (1738–1805), sometime Lord Lieutenant, in the Lords: 'The Catholics of Ireland not only claim a participation in the civil franchises enjoyed by their Protestant countrymen but they foster claims on the Property of Protestants, the present possession of which they treat as mere usurpation; and these claims are of no trifling extent.'

While right and tenure were difficult to distinguish (and litigants argued this into the twentieth century) the constant was clear: Protestants (ruling classes) had taken land from Catholics (then largely, non-ruling classes). Again, the religious (but not necessarily the devout) persuasions could rarely be separated from political argument.

In ordinary times each of these distinctions, may have had only local significance. But there were no ordinary times in Ireland. Furthermore, the religious make-up of Ireland and the uncompromising position of the English Established Church could not be ignored as a base for anti-British exploitation. Prime Minister Pitt understood the extent that religion (not faith) was an influence on the politics of Ireland and therefore Britain. To Pitt, Ireland in constitutional Union rather than personal Union was the only way in which stability could be maintained. The Irish Rebellion in 1798 did nothing to weaken this conviction.

Rebellion in Ireland was no novelty. The Gaelic Uprising in 1641 led to the massacre of thousands of English and Scottish settlers, who had been given prime estates three decades earlier in Ulster and reduced the Gaelic population to peasant status. It took Cromwell's ruthless campaign in 1649 to successfully put it down. Nor should the relatively minor confrontations be overlooked. For example, when in 1778 the British repealed some of the harsher anti-Catholic protocols in the 1698 Popery Act, anti-Catholic sentiment in England increased – as senior Catholic laity had feared that it might. The animosity towards the Catholics was so inflamed that in 1780 Lord George Gordon (1751–93) and his followers in the Protestant Association descended on Westminster to demand the 1778 Act's repeal. Two 'No Popery' marches, involving perhaps tens of thousands of people, produced rioting. Others outside the protest joined the marches and the rioting. Britain's economic state was parlous and hardship everywhere.

The 1798 rebels wanted at least a reformed Parliament and believed that in Tone's republican-minded United Irishmen they had the vehicle to get it. Tone emerged in Irish politics at a time when Roman Catholicism and Protestant Dissenters showed they could be in sympathy. Tone claimed that he believed that if the Irish expected to right what they saw as wrongs imposed by the Protestant Ascendancy, then one essential action had to be the merging of religious lines – ecumenism for political ends. This was the original motive of the United Irishmen: to unite Catholics and Protestants to achieve political ambitions. Indeed, Tone's *The Argument on Behalf of the Catholics of Ireland* was directed at an Ulster Presbyterian audience.

The British suppressed the organization until it became an underground movement in 1794. From this suppression, the Society attracted more support than it might have had and so became an even greater threat as a secret oath-taking society with the notional support of the French – who sent an invasion fleet to southern Ireland (with Tone embarked). It might have landed if it had not suffered a storm.

The British successfully infiltrated the Society as well as encouraging the Orange Order's excessive treatment of collaborators. But the Rebellion was not yet defeated. In May 1798, the United Irishmen rose in Dublin – but without the result it had imagined.

The response in the capital was at best disorganized and tepid. Some suggest that because the Dublin rallying call was not enthusiastically followed, then the provincial Societies were left to carry the main rebellion standard. This is only partly so. The seat of the uprising was in Wicklow, south of Dublin, and Wexford; it was almost exclusively Protestant led. The Catholics of Munster and Connaught, who might have been expected to join forces, never did on any meaningful scale. This was not a Roman Catholic uprising – majority against minority rule. In fact, the zealous and successful militia that helped put down the rebellion was three-quarters Roman Catholic. The Rebellion failed its architects but it was an unquestionable lesson for Pitt: Union had to come.

With the Rebellion came the anticipated fury of those who saw it as an inevitable consequence of religious inclination caught in political rebellion. For example, Dr Patrick Duigenan (1735–1816), a Catholic-born lawyer-politician who supported Pitt's notion for Union but opposed Catholic Emancipation, was uncompromising in his belief that the Catholic majority (his wife was a practising Catholic) could not be tolerated.

> The great cause of disorder is, that a large proportion of the inhabitants are Roman Catholics, the most ignorant, and consequently, the most bigoted in Europe; their hostility to a Protestant British government, from the very tenets of their religion is uncurable [sic]. This enmity to all Protestant governments is innoxious [sic] in other European Protestant states, because such states are all despotic governments, in which the body of the people have but very little power or influence, and in which the number of Romanists bear but a small proportion to the bulk of the people; but in a popular Protestant state, Romanists become dangerous subjects in proportion to their numbers, rank, and property; their religion obliging them, as a point of faith, to deny the supremacy of the state, (that is the power of the state to bind its subjects by its own laws) and compelling them to acknowledge and submit to the supremacy of a foreign tribunal. The Romanists in Ireland, on the very best calculation, do not, in number, amount to two-thirds of the people; as to property, they do not possess the fiftieth part.

Nor was this a matter of simply how to deal with Catholics. The Anglican wealthy and noble in Ireland, were in a social and religious minority; but they held the political ground and so were nervous that Union would take away their power. They would argue the political case against Union and leave the militia to put down the Rebellion.

Where Pitt and the Protestant Ascendancy merged was in their common concern for a gathering threat from peasant Catholics and petty bourgeois Non-conformists that supposed 'the fight of Protestant against Catholic, quiescent for a century, seemed likely to recommence'. No one forecast the twentieth century.

But did this mean that religion did indeed have a major influence over Anglo–Irish politics at the end of the eighteenth century? Pitt seems to have believed this to be a given in his search for a settlement with Dublin. His assertion that Catholic Emancipation should go hand in hand with Union was politically motivated. Equally, it was not to enhance Catholic political power and only agitators sought that anyway. There is no evidence to suggest that apolitical Catholics – some 70 per cent of the Irish population – had any interest in Union. Laws made at Westminster or Dublin were laws wherever they were drafted and would not significantly change their circumstances and few would come out to speak in their favour. For example, in spite of fighting for the rebellious cause, an influential part of the non-republican Presbyterian congregation believed most Catholics who fought in the 1798 Rebellion were fierce and bloodthirsty and, not much more.

> All the Protestants of Ireland, that is, almost the whole property of the kingdom, would find it in their interest to join the King's standard. The bloody remorseless cruelty, and insatiable thirst for plunder, of the rest of their countrymen [Roman Catholics] would soon convince them [the Protestants] of using their arms against them.

The Union cause, perhaps because of the Rebellion, was in the ascendant. Yet because of the status quo, as represented by some of the Protestant Ascendancy, it was not to be given clear passage. Moreover, the opposing opinion in Dublin was well represented in London. Some, like Richard Brinsley Sheridan, then a Whig Member of Parliament, could never believe Union to be a proper way forward. Sheridan tried to amend the Committee Stage of the Bill in 1799 by suggesting that the cure for Anglo–Irish instability was Emancipation of *all* the faiths (including the Established Church).

That it be an instruction to the Committee to consider how far it
would be consistent with justice and policy, and conducive to the
general interests, and especially to the consolidation of the strength
of the British Empire, were civil incapacities, on account of religious
distinctions, to be done away throughout His Majesty's dominions.

Sheridan had no possibility of getting Parliamentary support for his
amendment – it amounted to an unconstitutional instruction to the
Committee and was nothing more than a delaying tactic. Union
would take more than a year to debate, but it would go through in
spite of the Anglican anxieties.

What could the Protestant Ascendancy hope for in Union?
Protestant nationalism had long been based on the autonomy of the
Irish Parliament and so had acted as a barrier to Unionism. But the
Catholic Relief Acts of 1791–3 had had a 'formative impact on Irish
Protestant opinion'. Moreover, attitudes among British and Irish
political elites began to move in the same direction. By having legislative control entirely in the hands of the London-based interest,
including the Established Church, then the Protestant Ascendancy
might less fear the growing influences of the Catholic and Dissenting
churches. In an exchange between Lord Cornwallis (1738–1805),
the Lord Lieutenant in 1798, and Alexander Ross (1742–1827) saw
Union and Catholic Emancipation as travelling one and the same
political route. Cornwallis was 'fully convinced that until the
Catholics are admitted into general participation of rights (which
when incorporated with the British government they cannot abuse)
there will be no peace or safety in Ireland'.

Here surely was the answer to the question of the influence of
religion on political thinking. While religion was not faith, there
was no doubt that at least one of its persuasions did have a direct
influence – ironically, far more than the majority of Irish Catholics
understood, or maybe cared.

The Catholic position did not divide the debate on religious lines.
The Catholic laity and clergy in Ireland, including Thomas Troy
(1739–1823), the Archbishop of Dublin, had considerable political
powers on two fronts: they had a lobby in the Irish Parliament and
they had a voice from the pulpits. That partly suited the Protestant
government even though it never trusted the Church and so, when
Archbishop Troy condemned the Rebellion (because he believed it

would lead to atrocities on both sides), the government in Dublin suspected his motives. When Troy was called to Dublin Castle to explain himself, his Catholic followers were suspicious that he might be in collusion with the government – such were the suspicions of all parties even though it was obvious that the Irish Catholic gentry had no less desire for a quiet society than the English.

There was agreement on one important point: Pitt would lend his authority to a Catholic Emancipation Bill only if it went through a Union Parliament. The Catholic leadership in Ireland believed they held a political sway and so agreed to this, with the exception of a group of lawyers led by Daniel O'Connell (1775–1847). O'Connell's first speech against Unionism and, more significantly, for Emancipation was made in 1800. But his time was not then. O'Connell's significance came during the following quarter of a century when his campaigning was influential in the 1829 Catholic Emancipation Act.

In January 1799, Parliament prepared for a Union with Ireland Bill uncertain what support it would have in Dublin. Certainly in the Irish capital, it was a coffee house subject – with pen as well as *craic*: 'Pamphlet writing is such a rage at present that all classes are scribbling upon the Union. It is a common question in the streets; are you writing a pamphlet against the Union.'[3] Pamphleteers (often anonymous) were indeed writing – for both sides of the argument: 'In every other country where religious distinction has been made the test of office, the majority has constituted the establishment. In Ireland, the case is reverted in favour of the minority.'

Few cared for this argument. Colonial Britain was used to ruling over the majority. Furthermore, British colonial and imperial history suggests that Catholics were excluded not entirely for religious reasoning but more simply: they were the natives beyond the Pale.

The question of whether religion had a political influence, even a political identity, was being answered in every political and even rebellious action. From the grandeur of the Protestant Ascendancy to the miserable poverty of the majority of Catholics, one common point stood out: no political or social interest in Ireland was without a religious label. Even moderate opinion was religiously identifiable.

---

3   *Freeman's Journal* (13 January 1799).

When the Union Bill arrived in the Dublin Parliament, in 1799, it fell by just 107 votes to 105. Sheet writers, pamphleteers and editors had little time for divides, statistics and who voted what. Instead they bunched all non-Established Church, including the Catholics, together.

> The uncommon zeal and activity with which the Dissenters have endeavoured to decimate their political principle, and to overturn the established Constitution in Church and State, are notorious . . . they have attempted to promote their designs by means of religion and by sending forth missionaries of their doctrines under the name of Dissenting Ministers.[4]

The *Express and Evening Chronicle* had few doubts that the missionaries were political agents and that Pitt's anticipated Catholic Emancipation, after Union, could be nothing but divisive: 'It is certain that Catholic Emancipation can never be attained completely while a Protestant is suffered to exist in Ireland.'

Pitt, acknowledged the insecurities of both Catholics and Protestants when faced with the prospect of Union when he spoke in Parliament in January 1799:

> It must ever be a question of the greatest difficulty to say what shall be the rights of the Catholics, or what securities are necessary for the Protestants . . . the Protestant feels that the claims of the Catholic for power and privilege (for this now is all) threatens his ascendancy and the Catholic considers his exclusion as a grievance.

Equally, Pitt was suspicious of the motives of those who used this religious argument to reach a political conclusion:

> When questions of this nature have been agitated in this House by those who pretended a regard for the privileges of the Catholics, it was ever my opinion that the questions were direct attacks on the independence of the Irish Parliament.

His disappointment was clear that such big questions as Union 'are more likely to be decided upon by passion than by judgement' and

---

4 *St James Chronicle.*

that religion, national pride and instinct 'influences political decisions'. There seemed little doubt that radical politics then originated
in religious heterodoxy.

The Act of Union between Ireland and Great Britain was passed on
2 July 1800 in Britain and 1 August in Dublin. The two kingdoms
were united on 1 January 1801 as the United Kingdom of Great Britain
and Ireland. Of the eight Articles and protocols in the 1800 Act, two
were direct references to the position of the Established Church.

Article 4 allowed: 'the lords spiritual and temporal and the
commons, to serve in the Parliament of the United Kingdom on the
part of Ireland'. There were to be four Protestant Irish bishops in
the Parliament but, until amended, not with the same authority as
English bishops: 'all lords spiritual of Ireland shall have rank next
after the lords spiritual of the same rank of Great Britain'.

To show that the Irish Anglican Church and the bishops were not
left to flounder among other denominations, Article 5 established the
position of the combined Churches:

> Article Fifth.
>   That it be the fifth Article of Union, that the Churches of England
> and Ireland, as now by law established, be united into one Protestant
> Episcopal Church to be called, The United Church of England and
> Ireland; and that the doctrine, worship, discipline and government of
> the said United Church shall be, and shall remain in full force for
> ever, as the same are now by law established for the Church of
> England; and that the continuance and preservation of the said United
> Church, as the Established Church of England and Ireland, shall be
> deemed and taken to be an essential and fundamental part of the
> Union; and that in like manner the doctrine, worship, discipline and
> government of the Church of Scotland shall remain and be preserved
> as the same are now established by law, and by the Acts for the Union
> of the two kingdoms of England and Scotland.

Anglican persuasion was established and controlled by political
decree, not by doctrine. Doctrine was not an exceptional division in
many of the Churches and even liturgies were not so far apart – even
in the Established Church of England and the Roman Catholic
Church. The true divisions and impressions were in what religion
represented politically.

The Protestant Ascendancy was not obnoxious because it was Protestant and obedient to the Established Church of England. It was offensive because it was a ruling majority class. The United Irishmen supporters were Presbyterians and Catholic Defenders, but this did not mean that all Presbyterians and Catholics were in republican rebellion. Yet, in late eighteenth-century Ireland exacting political party identity was a thing of the future. The Protestant Ascendancy was as much a label as any given to the supporters of the Defenders and the United Irishmen.

Consequently, while religious faith was not an effect on political thought and action, religious denominational labelling had a long-lasting political influence. Ireland's subsequent history carried on religious labelling. In the late twentieth-century Troubles in Northern Ireland, it became commonplace for political and paramilitary groups to be too easily labelled Catholic or Protestant. This convenience did little to help the cause of power-sharing. In late eighteenth-century Ireland and Britain, the opposite was true.

CHAPTER FORTY-TWO

1800–1805

And so the nineteenth century, opened with Britain at war: the French Revolutionary War. Britain would cope with that affair and within fifteen years Napoleon would be defeated and on his way to his final exile on St Helena. A much longer term conundrum was gathering a new storm in Britain's history and one which would continue to blow into the twenty-first century: Ireland. In the late eighteenth century, the rebellious nature of parts of Ireland and the prospect of the Catholic majority – 75 per cent of the population – caused the British to suspend the Irish Parliament and bring its authority back to Westminster. Pitt wanted to give the Catholics more rights and threatened to resign when George III said this was impossible because it would be against his Protestant Coronation Vows. As for the British Catholics, they were very much a gentle minority. Yet nothing could be settled easily in Ireland, nor had it ever been so since English conquest began with Henry II in 1155. His son, John, was called Lord of Ireland. During the next 150 years or so, the Irish took back some of their land, while the descendants of the invaders merged into Irish society. By the sixteenth century, England had no real control beyond the small area round Dublin called the Pale. Even so, Henry VIII took the title King of Ireland.

Elizabethan Ireland became a military threat and it wasn't until the end of the 1500s that some sort of English rule was established. Land was confiscated and given to the so-called new-English aristocracy which, of course, was Protestant. In Ulster, the Lowland Scottish Presbyterians arrived to take the confiscated lands.

In 1641 there was an awful rebellion and it took the ruthless mind of Cromwell to once again bring order. Cromwellian terror added to the legend of English brutality. And so to 1654 and the Act for the Settlement of Ireland. Two-thirds of landed property was taken and given to Protestants. The dispossessed were transported to the far west of the island. In the Revolution of 1688, James II escaped to Ireland. He held a council to restore property. William of Orange then defeated him at the Battle of the Boyne and the property changed hands once more. James's supporters had their land confiscated and handed over to personal friends of William.

In 1707, the year of the Union with Scotland, the Irish House of Commons, in their loyal address to the then Queen, Anne, prayed, 'May God put into your royal heart to add greater strength and lustre to your crown by yet a more comprehensive union.' But by the 1770s and 1780s, political and economic stability had sent the Irish in completely the opposite direction, and there was an increasing demand for independence. But ideas of independence were Protestant ideas. The Roman Catholics were stripped of almost every chance to prosper. They could not vote, couldn't become lawyers or join the army. They weren't even allowed to own a horse of any value. And if they had property it could only be left to the eldest son if he became a Protestant.

In 1782, Ireland received a new Constitution but the King could veto anything he didn't like. And in London there was always the fear that a truly independent Ireland might endanger England's security. It might even give too many concessions to the Catholics whose peasantry in the south was considered one of the two dangerous groups in Ireland, the other being the Protestants in the north. The Scottish settlers from Stuart times were the ancestors of the Ulster Protestants, and it was in Ulster that Wolfe Tone and his fraternity of United Irishmen campaigned for independence. The members of the Society of United Irishmen weren't Catholics, they were Protestant radicals. Tone had helped set up the United Irishmen in 1791, in Belfast, but they were far more instrumental in the south than the north. Tone was outlawed and fled to France. Inspired with French Revolutionary zeal, he and his radicals organized a rebellion. Tone, who in fact had arrived too late for the fighting, was captured and sentenced to death. He committed suicide.

This then is the briefest of backgrounds to the troubles at the turn of the century, and perhaps to others that followed. By 1800 Pitt had pushed through the Act of Union with Ireland. On 1 January 1801 it became law. The Act of Union did not settle the sense of unrest. In fact, there were many who believed it was a signal for more concessions. The notion that a French-style revolution could so easily inspire others to rebellion had not gone away, especially as the British still had the insecurity of being at war with France and understanding too well the history of French ambitions to use Ireland as a springboard to at least unsettle, if not invade, England. Moreover the Act of Union did not truly draw together the two peoples. Not even the fifth article of the Act of Union and its uncompromising settling of the status of the Established Church of England and Ireland could satisfy the religious conflict that seemingly remained an instinctive connection between religion and politics in Ireland and England for the entire nineteenth and twentieth centuries.

But where was the Article for Catholic Emancipation? George III believed it unthinkable. 'I shall reckon any man my personal enemy who proposes any such measure,' he said.

So the Act of the Union with Ireland immediately alienated the Catholics, but it did more than that. The wording of the fifth article that describes the United Church as 'an essential and fundamental part of the Union' meant that the Irish would have to pay dues to what they saw as some Established Heretical Institution.[1] Furthermore, the Catholic priests would have to rely on their parishioners for money. So any radical, in almost any parish, had simply to encourage anti-British feeling on the most fundamental of grounds – religion.

There is little evidence that the people of England supported Catholic Emancipation. In fact, the previous decades had seen a decline in Catholicism in Britain. A priest by the name of Joseph Berington (1743–1827), in his *State and Behaviour of English Catholics* written towards the end of the eighteenth century, observed that Catholics – from all walks of life – were giving up their religion and, in some counties, there were hardly any at all:

In the West, in South Wales, and in some of the Midland counties, there is scarcely a Catholic to be found. After London, by far the greatest number is in Lancashire. In Staffordshire are a good many also . . . Excepting in the towns, and out of Lancashire, the chief situation of the Catholics is in the neighbourhood of the old families of that persuasion. They are the servants, or the children of servants, who have married from those families, and who chus [*sic*] to remain

---

1   E. N. Williams, *A Documentary History of England* (Vol. 2, London: Penguin, 1965).

round the old mansion, for the convenience of prayers, and because
they hope to reserve favour and assistance from their former master.

The issue of Catholicism would never be far from Pitt's mind. His
failure to bring it forcibly to the minds of others over the Irish question had the inevitable consequence. Pitt the Younger, at the age of
forty-two, resigned as Prime Minister. For half his life he had been
an MP and for most of that time he had been Prime Minister. And
now his stamina was almost gone. For nearly twenty years Pitt had
struggled with the Irish problem. When the Irish Parliament was
given apparent independence in 1782, there were those in power in
London who believed, or said they believed, that the constitutional
conflict was now settled but it was not. The French Revolution
had inspired radical Irish opinion into believing that non-sectarian,
independent government was a possibility. A rebellion in 1798 had
needed to be put down.

But what Pitt saw as the fundamental challenge went unanswered:
he had argued for Catholic Emancipation; he wanted to give Catholic
freeholders the vote, but this was unacceptable to King George. Irish
Catholics were seen as a threat to the security and the social and
political structure of Ireland and England. Pitt fully understood
that his liberal ideas could not survive the legislative process at
Westminster. The waverers, so necessary to Pitt's ambition, would
not challenge the King.

Pitt must have been at a low mental and physical ebb. It is very
possible that he was already suffering from the cancer from which he
would perish five years later. And he was up against the most experienced politician in England – the King. Pitt must have known that
there was little chance of creating legislation that would satisfy
Dublin, London and, most important of all, the court. That he could
not rely on his Cabinet did not signify disloyalty in the way it would
today. The administration – the government ministers – had a clear
understanding of constitutional duty. Ministers would probably
accept what would now be called collective responsibility on
defence, foreign and economic policy, but on other matters they
would expect to make their own judgements. Catholic Emancipation
was as much a matter of conscience as of politics. Furthermore,
George III's victory over Pitt (and that's what it was) reinforced his
belief that he had the right to appoint and dismiss anyone he wished.

Most politicians of the time accepted this right to some extent. So, at the start of the nineteenth century, the monarch remained an essential part of the institution of government.

The war with France was a matter of foreign policy, so the Prime Minister could expect collective responsibility in the Cabinet, but the question of how to bring the war to an end split the Cabinet. At that time, Henry Dundas was Pitt's closest colleague in government and, in a memorandum, Dundas set out the reason for the Cabinet division: on one side there were those who wanted to restore the Bourbon monarchy; on the other were the realists who were saying that however much the British disliked what was happening in France, they had to accept that the new French administration was in control of the country. The French were still in a revolutionary state and so control on a wide scale was essential, certainly uncompromisingly desirable. Britain, in spite of the contradictions between religion and politics within the islands, was by and large a stable State.

The government, however, was in itself less than that. When Pitt went, so did Dundas, and the following year he was created the first Viscount Melville. Henry Addington (Pitt's successor who would become the first Viscount Sidmouth) was not a great inspiration in politics. In fact Dundas had thought Addington so lightweight that he could never expect him to hold together a Cabinet, whatever its constitutional loyalties. Despite the sceptics at Westminster, Addington, who had been Speaker of the House of Commons for the previous two years, did become Prime Minister and Pitt's resignation had not meant a sweeping change in the administration of British political life. This was not a collective Cabinet dismissal, rather what would now be called a Cabinet reshuffle. True, Dundas, Grenville, Castlereagh, Cornwallis, and Canning all went with Pitt but the Cabinet's patronage was limited and most owed their jobs to the Sovereign. The internal politics meant that many went, returned and went again. The constant was the threat that Napoleon would be brave and assured enough to invade southern England. His preparations to build his invasion embarkation port at Boulogne may have been more successful if he had accomplished six major tasks: understood better the size and vessel construction needed for his invasion fleet; listened to advice from those who knew how to dredge Boulogne, build the port and deploy the shallow-drafted but keeled vessels he would need to invade and resupply the invasion; stuck to one or two plans rather than produce more than a dozen that could not come to anything anyway; thought of a way to break Cornwallis's blockade of Brest where the French Channel fleet was stuck; chosen better admirals – including perhaps being bold enough to make a Spaniard commander of his fleet instead of Villeneuve; understood that his attention and resources should be concentrated on what he really understood, land armies.

By the summer of 1805 Napoleon had abandoned his invasion plan and would never revive it. However, the British could not be certain of this. Moreover, they had much more on their political minds than a land war on the Continent over which they had little influence. For while doors in the corridors of Westminster and Whitehall opened and slammed on the hypothesis of a newly emerging political science, there were danker alleys and closets rarely if ever seen by the likes of Addington, Dundas and Pitt. They ran through that nineteenth-century institution of horror: the workhouse. Perhaps there is a connection. Addington, Dundas, Pitt and their political friends may not have recognized the conditions the workhouse rules were meant to maintain, but the disciplinarians of the workhouses may have recognized what it would take to maintain law and order at Westminster during the coming decade.

It was now the year 1805 and one of the most celebrated battles of the nineteenth century, the Battle of Trafalgar, was about to take place. To the Royal Navy it was, and is still, its finest moment. The enemy was vanquished and Nelson was killed, and he became a national hero for ever. The significance of what happened on 21 September 1805 has continued to this very day.

The peace treaty that was signed to end the French Revolutionary War, the Treaty of Amiens, was, in military and indeed political terms, not a peace agreement but a truce. Another war with France was inevitable. The treaty was signed on 27 March 1802 but it was simply a recognition that France controlled the land and Britain the seas. Napoleon did not withdraw his troops from the Italian regions. He appeared determined to renew his ambitions in Egypt and what is now called the Middle East. And so Britain did not withdraw her troops from Malta, the pivotal point of Mediterranean power. It was, to paraphrase a future Prime Minister, George Canning, the peace everyone wanted and of which no one was proud. Incidentally, in the wording of the document, for the first time in hundreds of years, an English king was not described as King of France. That point of principle had finally been abandoned.

War broke out again in 1803 and about 10,000 British tourists, those who had travelled to 'gaze upon the scenes of Revolution', were interned, accused of spying. In Paris in the following year Napoleon had the Pope crown him Emperor of the French.

In London, the hapless Prime Minister Addington, who had reduced the navy while restructuring the army, must have recognized that his administration lived on borrowed time. On 26 April he told the King that he was resigning. The King was persuaded that Pitt should be brought back. But Pitt believed Fox should be in his administration if there were to be an all-party government to manage the war. The King refused to accept Fox.

On 2 May 1804, Pitt wrote to the Lord Chancellor, Eldon. In effect he was writing to the King:

> The present critical situation of this country, connected with that of Europe in general, and with the state of the political parties at home, renders it more important and essential than perhaps at any other period that ever existed, to endeavour to give the greatest possible strength and energy to His Majesty's Government, by endeavouring to unite in his service as large a proportion as possible of the weight of talents and connections, drawn without exception from parties of all descriptions, and without reference to former differences and divisions. There seems the greatest reason to hope that the circumstances of the present moment are peculiarly favourable to such an union, and that it might now be possible (with His Majesty's graces approbation) to bring all persons of leading influence either in Parliament or in the country to concur heartily in a general system formed for the purpose of extricating this country from its present difficulties, and endeavouring if possible to rescue Europe from the state to which it is reduced.

Effectively Pitt wanted the right to choose his own Cabinet and to demonstrate this right by having Fox in it. He was saying that the country was in bad shape and threatened, therefore the best people should be in government – for that reason alone, it should include

Fox. The collection of people described in his letter would be a Ministry of All the Talents – something that could not be achieved until after Pitt's death in 1806 when there was a hiatus, with no party in a position to form a government. George III did not care for Fox's behaviour by attending what the King believed to be 'factious meetings'. He sent Fox packing from the Privy Council and so was 'astonished that Mister Pitt should one moment harbour the thought to bring such a man before his royal notice'. George III did not like innovators in his form of politics. Few did. The age of reform was not so far-fetched from the age of rebellion. Moreover, the King and his advisers were not being so unreasonable given Fox's objections to any further war, together with his open dislike of Addington. Fox appears to have become tired of the whole affair and told his friends that they should join the administration without him. So Pitt, in spite of his belief that the Prime Minister should be able to choose his own Cabinet, respected the King's wishes, returned to office and went about reorganizing Britain's defences.

Napoleon, as we have seen, planned to invade southern England; Nelson was in the Mediterranean trying to find the French southern commander, Villeneuve, but he was already in the Atlantic, joined by six Spanish ships, and was sailing westward. By the middle of May 1805, Villeneuve was at Martinique – coincidentally, the birthplace of Napoleon's wife, Josephine. Three weeks later Nelson reached Barbados. Villeneuve heard of this and set sail: he was seen heading towards the Bay of Biscay. The French were then intercepted, not by Nelson, but by a squadron commanded by Vice Admiral Sir Robert Calder, which forced them south. If Calder had destroyed Villeneuve's fleet instead of being more interested in prize ships, the Battle of Trafalgar would not have taken place, Nelson would not have been killed and British history would have been quiet differently recorded. We might remember that although Trafalgar was a remarkable battle, it was the culmination of a campaign spread across hundreds of thousands of square miles of ocean, and conducted without the benefit of modern technology. It is worth pausing to see the mischief to history that Calder's action caused.

By 22 July 1805 Villeneuve was disillusioned and tired. Led by this frightened and inept man who, to be kind, could be described as a realist, the combined Franco–Spanish fleet was making little headway towards the imagined safety of El Ferrol when, late that morning, its guard ships reported that a British line of warships lay ahead. This was a considerable part of Calder's reinforced squadron.

The importance of this part of the story is fog or, at least, a July Atlantic mist from the cold sea and a sun which had yet to burn off the haze. This was not quite naval blind man's bluff. There was no indication around noon that day that Villeneuve behaved anything else but correctly. Because neither fleet could properly see each other, it meant the mist was relatively settled. This tells us that there was very little wind. That being so, it must have been extraordinarily difficult to deploy as a fighting force and manoeuvre into any position that could effectively make or counter an attack. They probably did not really know the size and gunnery of each other. The best commanders in these circumstances make the higher assessment. Reasonably, they both decided that the other had about the same number of ships.

Villeneuve had twenty ships of the line, that is, big ships, and seven frigates in three columns. This was not a so-called battle-line. This would have been a cruising formation. Calder's fleet was slightly smaller but better equipped. Calder was in the *Prince of Wales*. At precisely noon, the *Prince of Wales* signalled to form up into battle stations. The fleet then came into two lines and shortly after that, into a single line of battle. That manoeuvre alone took more than an hour which, given the poor conditions, was a very respectable time. Villeneuve ordered his combined fleet into one long line of battle, with not Villeneuve, but Admiral Don Federico Gravina's *Argonauta* closest to the enemy.

Some time after three that afternoon, we would have seen two lines of ships facing each other about seven miles apart. If you stand on a beach on a hazy but not foggy day, you probably will not see much further than this. The English fleet was on a starboard tack. This meant that the wind was coming from the right-hand side. Therefore, Villeneuve's fleet, ostensibly going the other way, would have had the wind on the port side, the left side. This is important when realizing how difficult it is to manoeuvre to engage the enemy. This is not team formation sailing. With the rigs of these huge ships, it could take hours not minutes to simply turn left, sail on for a little and then turn right to resume the line in order to get close enough to engage. In what might have been variable wind conditions with mist coming and going, commanders and sailing masters threw all their expertise into carrying out the famous naval order to engage the enemy more closely.

When Villeneuve altered course, presumably to stop Calder attacking him at the rear, Calder had to also alter course to keep parallel to the Frenchman's fleet. The concept at that time was that a broadside of gun bombardment was the only effective way of dealing with a fleet engagement. Getting as close as possible made the likelihood of that broadside being more effective. Also, we have to remember that these ships were not dead in the water. They were still sailing. The light winds meant the whole positioning exercise was taken slowly. The mist, which came and went and varied between haze and fog, added to the puzzle of how to engage the enemy or to avoid it.

It was not until 5.15 that afternoon that the first shots were fired in the Battle of Cape Finisterre. The order to fire came from Gravina and it was his flagship, the *Argonauta*, which blasted away with her eighty guns at the British fleet. It took half an hour after *Argonauta* had fired on the Royal Navy's *Hero* before the British ship could manoeuvre into a position to return the fire. Also, because of the weather conditions, especially the mist, it was necessary to lose ships out of the order of battle so they could get close enough to the commander-in-chief to tell him what was happening. We can begin to see the complexities of this naval warfare, even before the disaster and panic that followed spars and rigs being shot away and men blown to pieces. By the time darkness came and the mist had settled heavily, neither commander could possibly have known the whereabouts exactly of the other ships, nor of some of their own vessels.

Calder was facing four fogs. The first was the natural mist of temperature and sea. The second was the fog of all warfare, the uncertainty of what exactly was going on. The third was created by the two fleets. Imagine the effects of dozen upon dozen of cannonballs being fired. Constant firing produced masses of gun smoke. Disabled, even dismasted vessels produced a fourth fog, that of inboard chaos. If we take one example of that chaos, the big ninety-eight-gun *Windsor Castle*, we can see the confusion. The weather, the inability to manoeuvre at will and the fact of being in a position so easily seen, when others were obscured, meant that all enemy gunfire was trained on her. A ship in that state could not continue under its own efforts. Therefore, it had to be taken in tow. However, the *Windsor Castle* was a large vessel. Consequently, Calder could not delegate one of his smaller ships to do the job. Thus, the dismasting and casualties suffered by the *Windsor Castle* meant that another large vessel, desperately needed in the line of battle, was taken out of the offensive to look after her. The combined fleet suffered similar damage and at least one of the Spanish ships simply drifted into enemy lines.

There was quite a lot of firing and killing. The British at first seemed to have come off worst. The first estimates suggested Calder had lost about eighty men. A later count suggested about forty had been killed and somewhere in the region of 168 wounded. By the Atlantic grey dawn, the French and Spanish fleet appeared to have lost 149 men and almost twice that number wounded. Interestingly, most of the casualties were Spanish. Villeneuve's flagship, the *Bucentaure*, had little damage and just a handful of casualties. It is not a difficult assessment that it was Gravina and not Villeneuve who had done most of the fighting. They had also lost two Spanish ships and, of course, the 1,200 men who were on board. The ships were not much good and so no great prize for the British. Moreover, the capture of more than a thousand Spanish presented a logistical headache. What was Calder expected to do with them? Also, taking two enemy vessels in tow was not an easy task. It would slow down Calder's fleet and limit its ability to manoeuvre. But those ships were worth money. Calder clung to them and in doing so lost advantage and, eventually, his honour and his command.

With hindsight, Villeneuve had all the advantages on his side and should have at least attacked the rear of Calder's joint squadron and rescued the Spanish ships. Given the high casualties in the British fleet, Villeneuve could easily have tested Calder's will. Calder himself had taken a beating. Nevertheless, as Villeneuve did not immediately attack, Calder should have judged the Frenchman's indecisiveness and nervousness. Equally, we may make a judgement about Villeneuve, but Calder would not have had our insight to his character. Moreover, there was certainly nothing wrong with the seamanship and tactical judgement of Gravina. On balance, Calder should have attacked as quickly as possible and Villeneuve should have taken the same decision. For once in his life, Villeneuve had naval superiority if not supremacy. Neither admiral was a Cornwallis, a Nelson, a Ganteaume, a Missiessy, a Cochrane or a Collingwood.

Villeneuve did not decide until after lunch the following day to go after Calder, who was quite clearly by that time in no fighting mood. Having made the decision, because of the poor winds it took Villeneuve another two hours to get his combined fleet into a battle formation. Wind and sea state were certainly not going to change just because Villeneuve had finally made a bold decision. Calder, in the meantime, was by now far away on the horizon and occasionally disappearing in the mist or haze. He wanted to escape rather than put Villeneuve to the sword. It was a decision which changed naval history.

At first glance, we had here a naval farce: a weak French admiral apparently deciding to go in pursuit of a British fleet commanded by an admiral more interested in protecting his dubious prizes and having had a bloodied nose from the combined fleet.

Calder, it still appears, was guilty of lack of purpose. The Franco–Spanish combined fleet was known by the British to be the biggest at sea. He had been given instructions by the Admiralty to engage Villeneuve. These orders were not transmitted in order for there to be a high seas skirmish. Calder's task was to send Villeneuve, Gravina and as many of their ships and men as possible either to the bottom of the Atlantic or in tow as prisoners and prizes. In admittedly difficult circumstances, Calder ran away from his implicit instructions. There can be no doubting that he knew the importance of this engagement. He was a vain man. Therefore, he knew that success here would have given him everything that he could have wanted for the rest of his career. It would even have put him above Nelson – one of his supreme ambitions. Yet he still failed to track after Villeneuve, to wait for the right conditions to attack and then attempt to deliver the blow that would have finished the war at sea with France.

Nelson reached the eastern Atlantic, discovered Villeneuve was to the north and so, on 23 July, he sailed for England. On the same day Napoleon arrived at Boulogne. By the middle of August Nelson was in Portsmouth. Villeneuve was trying to meet up with Admiral Honoré Ganteaume and break into the Channel, but the latter was boxed in by Britain's southern squadron and so Villeneuve turned back, heading for Cadiz.

On 15 September, Nelson sailed south from Portsmouth in his flagship, the *Victory*. At dawn on 21 October, Nelson stood on his quarterdeck and watched as the Spanish advance squadron of twelve ships under Admiral Gravina and twenty-one French ships under Villeneuve hove into sight. The war had started two years earlier, but this was the first time that Nelson had seen the enemy. It was to be the only time. The combined Franco–Spanish fleet was decimated and Villeneuve was captured along with his flagship, the *Bucentaure*, but Nelson was fatally wounded.

Nelson had confirmed what Napoleon now had to accept. Britain really did rule the sea-lanes. But the war did not stop at Trafalgar.

CHAPTER FORTY-THREE

1805–8

Napoleon had planned to invade Southern England with his Grande Armée of some 177,000 troops. In August 1805, Napoleon arrived at Boulogne to review his army and the strategic situation. The question was simple: invade or not invade? Firstly, neither of his two major fleets was in support. One was bottled up in Brest. The other was still in the western Atlantic. Secondly, and most decisively, the news from the East and the grand coalition of European States forming against him meant his armies needed his attention. That August, Napoleon's umpteenth grand plan for invasion – there had certainly been fourteen – was abandoned. This was a full three months before Trafalgar, a battle that would have meant he had no reinforcement fleet, nor one that could continue to protect the continual supply line and, if necessary, cover a retreat – although the Emperor never imagined that for long. This was the end of his invasion plan, it was not the end of the war. That would rumble for a further full decade until Waterloo in 1815 when Wellington nailed him to his mast of battle honours. For the moment, with Trafalgar two months off, Napoleon marched his divisions to the Danube.

In the year of Trafalgar, a coalition, the so-called Third Coalition, had been formed between Sweden and the Russian, Austrian and British empires. Their aim was to put down the French Empire led by Napoleon who just the previous December had been crowned Emperor. Here we have a simple reminder that war at the start of the nineteenth century was different than at the beginning of the twenty-first century, with all the amazing communications of the latter era. To control such a coalition of forces was an almost impossible task. To know what other armies were doing and the circumstances that might change those plans was a difficult strategic as well as tactical task for any commander, especially when there was unlikely to be one overall commander, general staff and political agreement on how a war would be prosecuted and where that might be done. So there should be little surprise that the single command of Napoleon, by now joined by the Bavarians, should have had certain military advantage.

The Austrians under General Karl Mack von Leiberich (1752–1828) took pre-emptive action. Mack ordered his 77,000 troops to protect the Alpine passes – probably because he thought Napoleon's thrust would enter northern Italy. His support for this badly judged action was the Russian army that was still in Poland but Napoleon saw the opportunity to literally outflank Mack's army by cutting it off from the Russians. Mack came face to face with the French VI Corps at Elchingen on 14 October (still, incidentally, a whole week before Trafalgar). He lost 2,000 troops and two days later surrendered. This, the Ulm campaign of Napoleon, was a turning point in his war. But Napoleon's supreme moment of tactical genius was to take place two months later. On 2 December, with Nelson not yet buried and so the British popular mood distracted from the great military campaign unfolding in Continental Europe, Napoleon defeated the combined Austro–Russian armies commanded by Tsar Alexander I near Austerlitz in the modern-day Czech Republic. This was the end of the coalition of Sweden, Britain, Austria and Russia. It also meant the end of the Holy Roman Empire. This would not satisfy the ambitions of any of the European States, nor their fears – especially Prussian anxieties that managed another alliance, the Fourth Coalition and set off for war against France the following year, 1806.

As for Pitt, he had little time left and would die in February of that year, supposedly uttering at his end, 'Oh, my country! How I leave my country!' Before death, his deep sorrow was for his close friend Henry Dundas, the first Viscount Melville (1742–1811). Melville was to be impeached for maladministration in the Admiralty where he had been First Lord between 1804 and 1805. It was said he misappropriated funds. He did not, but the accusation finished him.

There was far more to this than a minister's maladministration. And the Melville case gives a good insight into the political animosities of the time. Pitt had to submit to the King's right to appoint ministers, and Addington had been returned to government, this time as Lord President. It was claimed by Addington and his colleagues that Melville was guilty of malversation, that's to say corrupt practice or behaviour in public office. Melville most probably was guilty of negligence – but nothing much more. This difficulty might have been overcome if it hadn't been for the third grouping in politics: the Foxites, the people Pitt had wanted in government; the people the King had turned away. If Charles James Fox and his followers could fuel the charges against Melville, then the fight between Addington and Pitt would be noisier, and the Foxites could claim that they displayed the unity the country so much needed. The charge was made and Melville was impeached. Pitt wept openly; some said that he was overcome for his old friend, particularly as their other friend, William Wilberforce, spoke against him. But also Pitt was, by then, terribly ill. He was dying of cancer and his stamina, his resourceful-ness and his emotions were all stretched to breaking point. Fox, Pitt's great political rival, observed that death 'was a poor way of getting rid of one's enemy'. And although he voted against a Commons motion for a Pitt memorial in Westminster Abbey, Fox readily agreed that Pitt's debts should be met by the Exchequer. Fox, just eleven years older than Pitt, would not survive him by many months.

In addition to seeing the death of two English statesmen, 1806 was another year spent at war. It saw the British taking the Cape of Good Hope, but for those in other circumstances perhaps none of this meant much, especially in the more wretched reaches of British life. Hard by Westminster, in the Parish of St James's, a perfect illus-tration of these extremes could be found in an official Government document.

General State of Poor Children under the care and management of the Governors And Directors of the Poor of the Parish of St James's, Westminster.

Number of children transferred from preceding years:	650
Born and received this year:	565
Of whom have died in the workhouse:	56
Removed and discharged:	273
Above age six, apprenticed out:	113
Left in the care of the Parish:	712

This workhouse was considered for its day to have been neat and even 'commodious'. Yet none of the inmates was allowed out with-out permission from the master and when they were out, they had to be back on time otherwise they were 'gated' – refused permission to go out. Children in the workhouse were regularly beaten by the master. Anyone pretending to be ill to escape work would have their food ration cut and even thrown into the dungeon. None of this was thought unusual and, anyway, the people who may have given the nation legislation against such treatment had other and apparently mightier decisions to make.

With Pitt's death, George III was faced with a limited choice of politicians from whom to form the next administration. He sent for William Wyndham, Lord Grenville. Grenville was Pitt's cousin, but his political alliance with Charles James Fox had led to a break with Pitt two years earlier. By calling on Grenville to form the next administration, the King was tacitly accepting Fox.

Fox's mind raced across every political idea in England in the latter part of the eighteenth century; his pedigree suggested someone who would never be ordinary. Nor was he. His great-grandfather was the first Duke of Lennox, who was the son of Louise de Kéroualle, the mistress of Charles II. So the Stuart King and the Hanoverian George III cannot have been unaware of them. And should anyone have forgotten, Charles James Fox's Christian names were obvious reminders. Fox's father was the first Baron Holland who, as Paymaster General, made a fortune by siphoning funds. With this background, it is hardly surprising that Fox is remembered as a far from ordinary figure. He was a rebel, a gambler, a piercing critic of what he saw as George III's political and fiscal oppression of the American colonists, a supporter of the French Revolution and, when the King suffered temporary loss of his faculties, a leader of the movement to have him replaced by the Prince of Wales. Fox was also Great Britain's first Foreign Secretary. Now, in 1806, the coalition of politicians produced the Ministry of All the Talents – a misleading description inasmuch that not all the Ministry was talented. The close supporters of the late William Pitt knew they could never be part of the administration. Addington (now created Lord Sidmouth) was Lord Privy Seal, and Lord Henry Petty was Chancellor of the Exchequer. Charles Grey, a friend of Fox, was his successor as Foreign Secretary, and was soon to become Prime Minister; but for the moment he was Grenville's First Lord of the Admiralty. The Pittites, Hawkesbury, Castlereagh and Canning were left to fume on the backbenches. And there was little vision in the

British approach to ending the war. It is probable that there could be no end until the French wanted it, or had been beaten, but when Fox died, in September 1806, there was no one left with his political agility to negotiate the peace anyway.

This does not mean that Britain was in some dreadful political hiatus. A good example of serious work particularly pushed forward by judicious lobbying was the abolition of the slave trade in March 1807. This only went some way to stop the trade, which by some estimates had seen some twelve million Africans shipped to the Caribbean and the Americas and about a third of them in British ships, the majority from Liverpool. Most of the African slaves were destined for the British-owned sugar plantations in the West Indies or the cotton and tobacco farms of the southern provinces in America. Not all countries decided to stop the slave trade, or even contemplated doing so. The British did so partly through the emergence of an evangelical movement in the British Isles from the second half of the eighteenth century. Pamphleteers, especially from Quaker-based groups, fought slavery and tried to influence opinion formers such as William Wilberforce. Although Wilberforce was the leading political campaigner, it was Thomas Clarkson and his like that urged him to take up the challenge. Certainly when the Society for the Abolition of the Slave Trade was formed in the late eighteenth century, it was Quaker led with Wilberforce as much a target as any other opinion-maker.

But it was more than campaigning that turned the slave trade into something no longer deemed acceptable. This was the period that would lead to a reforming society, and perhaps most famously towards the Reform Act of 1832 that signalled the complete political reformation in England. More visible, and therefore pertinent to public debate, was the increasing sense that not all was right with colonial slaving custom. After the American War of Independence, many of the black slaves who had been encouraged to take the British side were homeless and stateless. The British gave them refuge in Canada – effectively only the eastern seaboard; in the free state of Sierra Leone; and in England – mainly that meant London. At one point it was thought that 10,000 slaves were in London and many, if not most of them, were on the streets.

We have also to consider the now famous court case brought about by the neglected historical figure of the slavery abolitionist, Granville

Sharp (1735–1813), the grandson of an archbishop of York. He was living in London with his surgeon brother when in 1765 Jonathan Strong, a black man, was brought to the house for treatment. He had been so badly beaten by his master, David Lisle, that he was close to death and his injuries took four months to heal. Lisle tried to recapture Strong, but Granville Sharp arrived at the house. Sharp went to law and said the slave was no longer in slavery as he was in England and not in his master's service. In 1768, the court found in Strong's favour. Later, Sharp did this again with an escaped slave, James Somersett. The then Lord Chief Justice in 1772 was Lord Justice Mansfield. He decided that once in England, the slave could not be forced to leave against his or her wish unless a crime could be proven. The consequences of that effectively ended slavery in England. It was also Lord Mansfield who heard the case in 1783 of the *Zong* – a slave ship sailing out of Liverpool. Crossing the Atlantic, the ship was in difficulties and the captain, Luke Collingwood, had 133 African slaves thrown overboard. Bizarrely, the case was not about murder or injustice. It was about an insurance claim. The owners tried to claim the insurance for loss of cargo – the description of the Africans. The public outrage at the inhumanity of the event added considerably to the greater realization that the British could no longer condone this trade.

There was another event that added to the bubbling cauldron of freedom. The French Revolution of 1789 had many a knock-on that was not envisaged and is sometimes forgotten. In 1791, slaves in Saint-Domingue in Haiti rebelled and won their rebellion. The British sent in the Royal Navy and the army but was defeated – as many as 40,000 British troops perished. Imagine the result. The African slaves had succeeded in demonstrating that it was possible truly to throw off their chains. The plantation owners and slave masters in the Caribbean trembled.

The anti-slavery movement gathered strength and in March 1807 the trade was banned. The Royal Navy was given the task of intercepting the slavers, but of course other States had no intention of giving up. Moreover, it took until 1833 for the abolition of slavery (rather than just the slave trade) to pass through both Houses and only after a compensation fund of £20 million had been agreed.

Within a year of the 1807 Act abolishing the slave trade, the Ministry of All the Talents was no more. It had been formed by

Grenville when George III reluctantly accepted that Charles James Fox should be in an administration. Grenville had even included some of the followers of the Prince of Wales, the radical opposition to so much that was dear to the monarch. The administration had foremost in its mind the war with Napoleon. Yet it fell not because of the war with Napoleon but because the mix of political views simply could not be united. Certainly with the death of its most powerful figure, Fox, in September 1806, the government had not long to go. A deciding factor was the poorly managed attempt to return to the matter of Catholic Emancipation. Viscount Sidmouth, Henry Addington, had been a less than successful Tory Prime Minister between 1801 and 1804. His reputation was made a decade later when as Home Secretary he used draconian measures to counter the Luddites. Now, in 1806, his biggest influence was against Grenville's proposal to allow Catholics to become senior officers in the army – a further step towards Catholic Emancipation. But the Parliamentary draughtsmanship was poor; the Commons said so, and the King became suspicious that his government was on the road to Catholic Emancipation without telling him. Yet little or none of this was political manipulation; it's simply that the Ministry of All the Talents was not actually very talented at all – certainly not without Fox – and it fell in 1807.

The new Prime Minister was the elderly third Duke of Portland. He'd been a member of the coalition government of Fox and North in the 1780s and later, for seven years, Pitt the Younger's Home Secretary. At sixty-nine, he was the same age as George III and neither man was at the height of his powers. However, Portland's Cabinet did include four men with undoubted and sometimes explosive talent. The Home Secretary was Lord Hawkesbury, Spencer Perceval was Chancellor, Viscount Castlereagh was War Secretary and George Canning was Foreign Secretary. It was not a time for unimaginative government towards the end of 1807. Britain was about to embark on another conflict and by the following year, 1808, the Peninsular War had begun. It would continue for six years.

The Peninsula of the war was the Iberian Peninsula – Spain and Portugal – and this was Britain's part in an otherwise ineffectual European campaign against Napoleon. The Peninsular campaign is significant because it meant a change in tactics and, eventually, in

strategy in Britain's determination that Europe should not be controlled by Napoleon. The threat was not imagined. After all, Napoleon, as
would Bismarck towards the end of the century, measured success by
the amount of territory taken. Moreover, the British had watched
Napoleon build Boulogne from creek to embarkation port to invade
the nation of shopkeepers. Furthermore, this was the age of innovation, of commercial and industrial development; absolute control over
Europe could bring about the political and economic domination of
Britain by foreign interests. As if that was not enough concern to the
British, the government of Portland was going through difficult times.
A certain Mrs Anne Clarke published allegations of corruption in army
administration and directly implicated the Duke of York – the King's
son and Commander-in-Chief of the army. The Duke was not a very
good soldier (it was this Duke of York who marched them up and
down again) but he was a conscientious administrator and had tried to
improve the soldiers' lot. Perhaps the fact that Mrs Clarke had been,
but no longer was, the Duke's mistress coloured her allegations.

The Duke of York was forced to resign as Commander-in-Chief
although Mrs Clarke was later discredited. But the real importance
of this event is that it allowed the opposition to revive charges of
corruption in high places. It also provided the right atmosphere for
an independent MP named John Curwen to bring forward a Bill to
stop the sale of Parliamentary seats. Until this Bill, selling and
buying a seat in the House was quite common practice and few
thought it a dishonourable way in which to get a Commoner or a
peer into the House.

Elliot, the Irish Secretary to the then Prime Minister, Grenville,
wrote a letter in 1806 which insists that the money for a seat be paid
in English money and not Irish, which was very important because
the Irish pound was worth less.

November 4, 1806
    Parnell states that he believes Lord Portarlington will let us have
his seat for £4000 *British*, provided he is given to understand that he
is to have the support of Government for the representative peerage
on the second vacancy after Lord Charlemont's election.

The Bill that became known as Curwen's Act eventually restricted
the influence of the Crown as well. So it was at this point that

something close to the way MPs are elected today began to evolve. Curwen's Act wasn't Parliamentary reform but it was one layer of it. And for some, it wasn't the actual buying of seats in the House that angered them, but the way they were bought. The bulk buying-up of seats meant that ministers controlled votes and individuals. One of the seat brokers, Sir Christopher Hawkings, cleared his entire stock to ministers and there was well-founded suspicion that the money for them came out of the Privy Purse, in other words was financed by the King himself.

A peer who owned a seat would put an MP into Parliament and then tell him how to vote. So to be independent, a would-be MP had to have money of his own – but even then there was no telling how safe that seat might be. Certainly a majority of votes did not always guarantee a seat. For example, Sir Samuel Romilly paid for his seat, thought that he had won it but then found a petition was raised against him in spite of his having paid £2,000. Buying a seat eventually faded from the electoral system, but not for a long time. Even in the twenty-first century the method of payment to support political parties and even the amount that could be spent at general elections continued to demonstrate that the apparent democratic Parliamentary process was less than perfect.

CHAPTER FORTY-FOUR

1809–19

While Parliamentarians discussed the price of representation, the war rumbled on. In one battle alone 40,000 died. Another battle was staged for political rather than military reasons and, as a result, two Cabinet ministers duelled and the Prime Minister suffered a stroke. And, at the end of the first decade of the nineteenth century, a famous general was, for the moment, giving up his political ambitions.

Sir Arthur Wellesley was the son of an Irish peer. He was born in Ireland but insisted that he was English and was said to have asked if the fact that he had been born in a stable meant that he was a horse. After service in India he had become a Tory MP. By 1809 he was back in command of the British forces in Portugal and, at the Battle of Talavera, he earned his first title, Viscount Wellington. (He wasn't created Duke of Wellington until 1814.)

Elsewhere in Europe, one British expedition ended in disaster. The British tried to send its army up the River Scheldt to take Antwerp. When the French reinforced Antwerp, the British commander left a garrison on an island called Walcheren in July 1809. The British were destroyed, not by French muskets, but by malaria; as in so many wars, including those of the twentieth century, disease and infection account for most casualties. The British public wanted French blood, not infected corpuscles of their own troops. What they got was a group of British transports ferrying more than 25,000 Frenchmen to freedom in France, ready to fight another day. If the French were to be beaten, then it would have to be Wellington's role to do so. But Wellington did not have a large and well-disciplined army; something he could not take for granted in 1809. He thought his army a rabble of plunderers but they served him, if not well, then eventually successfully.

By 1810, Wellington and his rabble had mauled the French army at Busaco and then allowed them to follow him to the seemingly impregnable Lines of Torres Vedras, the lines of fortifications he'd built to protect Lisbon. If they had the strength and imagination, the French might attack. The British were vulnerable but the great chain of Torres Vedras, and the prospect of a bleak winter with few resources, were too much. Come the spring, and leaving behind thousands of their dead, the French retreated from Portugal and into Spain. Wellington took his time. He refused to hurry for those who demanded spectacular victories. He wanted to take the war to France itself. In 1811 the British held the enemy at Fuentes d'Oñoro and Albuera but still Wellington waited; the waiting paid off. The French generals began to quarrel. Troops were withdrawn for the campaign in Russia. Wellington advanced on the frontier strongholds of Ciudad Rodrigo and Badajoz and prepared to face the French Marshal Auguste de Marmont. At Salamanca, Marmont's military calcula-tions failed him and Wellington had his first significant victory of the Peninsular War. But the war was far from over. Another army force under Marshal Nicolas Soult, who had fought Sir John Moore at Corunna in January 1809, was already on the march. Wellington was forced back to the Portuguese frontier.

In London, the government and the court were forced to address George III's illness. In 1810 the King became apparently incurably eccentric in his behaviour. As long ago as 1788 his sanity had been questioned and Pitt had said that Parliament should provide legis-lation for a limited Regency. In 1810 the Prince of Wales, Prince George, became Regent, but his powers were restricted for one year. There were limitations on what appointments he could make. He couldn't, for example, create new peerages – often done for political reasons. Now, the King was placed in the care of Queen Charlotte and a council of advisers. And, in 1811, to make it very clear that this was Parliament's doing and therefore the Regent was bound by it, a Regency Act became law. The Act was the answer to the constitutional question: would the Prince bring his Whig friends into government, particularly Grey and Grenville, and discard the Tories? Grey and Grenville had gone four years earlier when the King had refused what was called 'a measure of Catholic relief'. The Prince had no reason to change government policy or to be seen to do so. Furthermore, the quiet and, in many ways, unre-markable Spencer Perceval, who had become Prime Minister in October 1809, now had his Cabinet under control. But then, in May

1812 Perceval was murdered. It was not an assassination in the political sense. A bankrupt businessman called John Bellingham, armed with a grievance and a gun, shot him dead in the House of Commons lobby. So Perceval, who had achieved more than most recognized, went into the history books as the only British Prime Minister to be assassinated.

As if all this wasn't enough for the new Prime Minister, Robert Banks Jenkinson, Earl of Liverpool, Britain now found herself at war with the United States. It became known as the War of 1812. It started because the Royal Navy seized American ships trying to run the blockade against Napoleon, and because the British presence in Canada still annoyed the Americans. A plan to avert war was agreed, but it had to be carried more than 3,000 miles across the Atlantic by sailing ship, and then across land to the Americans and then, if agreed, to all the waiting commanders. Very simply, the plan didn't arrive in time and the war began, continuing until January 1815.

At sea, Britain was in control. But ashore it was another matter, although the British did burn the White House to the ground. Peace, in this unnecessary war, was signed on Christmas Eve 1814, but perhaps its most famous battle took place a fortnight later: the Battle of New Orleans. In just thirty minutes the Americans, commanded by Andrew Jackson (1767–1845)[1] killed or wounded 2,000 British troops and lost just thirteen of their own. Jackson was a hero (and became the seventh United States President, 1829–1837) and a new legend grew up: the war of 1812 was the Second War of Independence.

The war with the Americans was, in European terms, a diversion. Napoleon had been pulling back his troops from across Europe for a great assault on Russia. The Tsar, once Napoleon's admirer, now believed that peace in Europe was impossible while Bonaparte marched. And in June 1812, the Emperor marched for Moscow. He believed his military strength would have the Tsar calling for peace – that is, capitulating. The Russians would not do so and at Borodino, just west of Moscow, a quarter of a million Russians and French fought the bloodiest battle of the whole century. True, Moscow fell, but the Russians did not. The severest of winters closed in on

---

1   Not to be confused with the Confederate commander, General Thomas 'Stonewall' Jackson (1824–63).

Napoleon and he started his retreat. Fewer than 20,000 of his once invincible army made it to Warsaw.

By the spring of 1814, Wellington had driven the French out of Spain and was in Bordeaux. Napoleon's allies had abandoned him and some were now opposing him. In April that year, Napoleon abdicated and went to Elba. A Bourbon, Louis XVIII, brother of the beheaded King, was now on the throne. From his Mediterranean island, Napoleon saw that there were differences of opinion among his allied enemies. Also, his friends brought news that the King of France did not really command the respect of the people. On 26 February 1815, Napoleon sailed for France. Three weeks later he was back in Paris and the Bourbons were running.

Meanwhile, the allies decided the time had come to destroy Napoleon. They prepared to invade France but Napoleon didn't wait for their invasion. He moved on Belgium where Wellington now commanded Dutch, German and Belgian troops as well as his own. The Prussian army under Marshal Gebhard von Blücher was defeated at Lugny on 16 June. Wellington withdrew to Waterloo.

The Battle of Waterloo lasted one day. Wellington had 68,000 troops but Napoleon had 72,000 and attacked three times between the late morning and late afternoon of 18 June. Blücher arrived in the early evening with a further 45,000 troops to support Wellington, and a last French attack at about seven o'clock failed. Napoleon's army retreated, leaving 25,000 dead and 9,000 captured. Wellington is thought to have lost 10,000.

Napoleon escaped to Paris; he had visions of making a great stand on French soil but none shared his enthusiasm. On 22 June 1815 he abdicated and by the end of the month he had escaped to Rochefort on the Biscay coast. He imagined he would go to America. He did not. Instead, he was taken aboard a British warship, the *Bellerophon*, perhaps in his belief that he would be received as an Emperor and allowed to live in considerable style and dignity in England, the country that he had longed to invade and subjugate its people. Instead and, apparently to his surprise, he was put aboard another ship and on 26 July set sail for the island of St Helena in the Atlantic where he would die six years later.

Throughout the long campaign, Waterloo was the only time Napoleon and Wellington met in battle and both would be remembered for this one day, although neither thought it their finest. Now all that remained was to draw up a treaty of Europe that would manage the peace as successfully as Wellington had managed the last days of the war. There was now the chance of a long-lasting peace with France for the first time since the days of the Normans. The allies went to conference rather than war but skirmishing continued in the negotiating chamber. Rather like the post-First World War conference on the future of Europe and the degree to which France insisted the Germans had to pay for the war, so now the Prussians demanded France suffered. Castlereagh had a wiser formula for peace. It was a lesson that we had forgotten by the time of the 1920 Versailles Treaty. Castlereagh understood that the war was done and the best way of avoiding grievance and animosity, which could lead to a further rising, was to be moderate in the settlement terms. The French would pay a financial penalty but more testing would be a British army of occupation with Wellington as an imperial figure in command for three years. Churchill, in his *A History of the English-speaking Peoples*, thought the agreements and protocols, 'the last great European settlements until 1919–1920'.[2]

Meanwhile the style of early nineteenth-century clothes, furniture and buildings – the style of Regency Britain – began to establish itself. This was the period of Jane Austen, of the construction of, appropriately, Regent Street in London, of gas lighting in fashionable places and of Davy's safety lamps in the coal mines. It was also the period of continuous unrest among the newly named working class.

In 1799 a Leicester youth called Ned Ludd is said to have smashed machinery that had been installed by a stocking maker because the machinery did the jobs of many who had worked by hand. Then, in 1811, organized machine-smashing occurred in the textile factories of the Midlands and Yorkshire. In 1813 the Luddites, who took their name from Ned Ludd, were executed at York.

The end of the Napoleonic Wars meant peace in Europe, but in England there was now no need for huge numbers of sailors and soldiers: 300,000 servicemen were discharged from the war at a time when the combined British population was perhaps no more than thirteen million. And the labour market was already overcrowded,

---

2   Churchill, *A History of the English-speaking Peoples*, 310.

inflation was high, perhaps artificially so, and taxation was at wartime levels.

Manufacturers who thought that the war's end would bring increased export markets were wrong: there was now no war from which to make profits. Iron production is just one useful indicator: the price of iron was now £8 a ton, whereas during the war it had been £20. Thousands of iron- and coal-workers lost their jobs and many of them took to the streets. A year after the war ended there was considerable evidence that the government could lose control of the country. This was the atmosphere in Britain on 16 August 1819 when between 60,000–80,000 people attended a meeting in St Peter's Fields in Manchester. The speaker was Henry Hunt, known as Orator Hunt and described as one of the extremist leaders. The local yeomanry was sent in by magistrates to arrest him but they failed so the magistrates, instead of sending in the army, ordered the cavalry of the Hussars to do the job. There was panic and hundreds in the crowd received sabre wounds; eleven died.

The name given to this massacre was Peterloo – a popular irony derived from the British success at Waterloo. The rights and wrongs of that day are debated still. However, in spite of the threat of sedition, treason and uprising, the increasingly prosperous British had more confidence than ever in the very institutions that had been threatened. And the governing caste was just as confident of its right to govern. Perhaps it was a sign of this confidence, and of a faith in future prosperity, that in the year of the Peterloo Massacre the East India Company was arranging to buy a tiny area of Asia called Singapore.

CHAPTER FORTY-FIVE
1820–23

George III died in 1820 and Britain's fourth Hanoverian monarch was another George. George IV, although intelligent, was given to pleasures rather than statesmanship and, as Prince of Wales, he had been incautious in some of his friendships. For example, he had been very much under the influence of the best-remembered dandy of early nineteenth-century England, Beau Brummell. Brummell and the Prince of Wales parted company not long after George III was declared insane and incapable of ruling. By 1820 Brummell was hiding from his creditors in France and later perished in an institution for the insane.

However, before the Prince of Wales assumed the responsibilities of Regent, he took easily to the fashion of drinking and whoremongering, often, it is said, at Carlton House, close by Pall Mall. He attracted an odd baggage of creditors, debtors, madams, officers on half-pay, bucks and society wits, and the likes of Letitia Lade, once the mistress of the highwayman Sixteen-String Jack, who was hanged. And then, in 1784, the young Prince had lost his heart to a twice widowed commoner, but more importantly, a Roman Catholic, Maria Fitzherbert, six years his senior. Worse still, he was a strictly Protestant heir who wanted to take a Catholic wife – an utterly illegal proposition under the Royal Marriages Act. It could never be a public union, but it is largely accepted that a ceremony did take place in Mrs Fitzherbert's Mayfair drawing room. Robert Burt, an Anglican clergyman, officiated. Under law, this was not recognized, but both the Church of Rome and the Established Anglican Church of England recognized the union.

However, there had to be a public marriage, but not between the King and Mrs Fitzherbert. In the last decade of the eighteenth century, Mrs Fitzherbert was the love of the Prince's life and the embarrassment of the court. And so, as seemed best in the circumstances, a royal wedding was arranged – to a royal princess. In 1795, George miserably married Caroline of Brunswick and promptly got drunk for the rest of the day. The only child of this unhappy union, Princess Charlotte, was born the following year. But that young Princess died when giving birth to her own child, who was stillborn. If either of them had survived, one or other of them would have become Queen and there would have been no William IV, perhaps no Queen Victoria and perhaps no Elizabeth II.

George and Caroline's marriage was made in Brunswick and St James's, not in heaven. George called the Princess of Wales, 'the vilest wretch this world was ever cursed with'. He absolved her of all marital obligations, which was a nice way of saying that she was to be kicked out of his life – or so he thought. In 1806 a committee of the Privy Council began what was called the 'Delicate Investigation'. It certainly was. Its brief was to examine rumours that the Princess of Wales had given birth to an illegitimate child. If this were true, there would be a constitutional crisis. After all, she was the wife of the heir to the throne. Nothing was proved although, considering her lifestyle, there was good reason why such a rumour might have gripped the Privy Council's imagination.

In 1814, George banned Caroline from court, and eventually she left England for the Continent – but still as the Princess of Wales, and as the darling of the people. As in other times, the nation took sides. The Prince of Wales was only a few years away from being King or, to put it another way, the Princess of Wales was only a few years away from being Queen. The Prince wanted a divorce. She had been having an affair with a former member of her household, Bartolomeo Pergami, and adultery by the Princess of Wales, the future Queen, was a treasonable offence. A letter from Caroline to George found its way into *The Times*. The Princess of Wales, by now the uncrowned Queen, had not written the letter. It had been composed for her by those who knew the publication would harm George and bring the people even more to her side. It did both. Not that she needed much in the way of a public relations exercise.

For example, when she returned to England her carriage was spontaneously hauled by exuberant supporters. Crowds gathered outside her London house. Her every public appearance was followed, whereas George was seen as the wrongdoer. In July 1820, a hearing was opened in Westminster Hall to examine the case against the Princess of Wales, accused of adultery. It all fell apart. The witnesses for the government were unreliable. Parliament was split. Earl Grey, the leader of the Whigs, declared that Caroline was innocent of adultery. The Cabinet was forced to drop the matter. London was delighted: flags, illuminations, minor rioting. George Canning, President of the Board of Control, who favoured Caroline's viewpoint, resigned in protest at her treatment.

But even now the matter was not done with. The final scene for Caroline came on 19 July 1821. The stage was the coronation of her husband as George IV at Westminster Abbey. She went to the Abbey and was refused entry. 'Let me pass; I am your Queen,' she cried. The pages slammed the doors on her. Her cause was finished. As Sir Walter Scott wrote, it was 'a fire of straw burnt to the very embers'. And then, the next month, she died. Of what, it is uncertain. She was fifty-three and for the government, the embarrassment of Caroline of Brunswick, Princess of Wales, and their newly crowned monarch was over.

The political theatre quickly, if not quietly, moved on. Collective party responsibility was still confined to military, foreign and, some-times, economic affairs. And apart from the fact that Parliamentary systems and collective responsibilities were still developing, the Duke of Wellington was not simply a run-of-the-mill politician-turned-soldier-turned-politician. Wellington, like many of his col-leagues at the head of the governing classes, was an exceptional personality. He was someone who regarded his own counsel as the correct one. He watched, waited, planned and was cautious. In other words, his instinct was that of the conservative thinker. In a letter to the Prime Minister, Robert Banks Jenkinson, Earl of Liverpool, on 1 November 1818, Wellington outlined very clearly his idea of how government should perform without what he called factious opposition.

> The experience which I have acquired during my long service abroad has convinced me that a factious opposition to the Government is highly injurious to the interests of the country; and thinking as I do now I could not become a party to such an opposition, and I wish that this may be clearly understood by those persons with whom I am now about to engage as a colleague in Government

This is a Commander-in-Chief making it clear that he is loyal, but equally, he remains his own man. Within a week, Liverpool was telling Wellington that he understood and accepted the conditions for Wellington's return. After all, Liverpool could hardly afford to lose the nation's one living hero.

And so Wellington joined Liverpool's Cabinet with the simple ambition of being part of a political system united in preserving the order of things. Not everyone went along with this view. In 1820, the threat of insurrection was considered very real. Twenty Radicals led by a middle-aged man called Arthur Thistlewood met in a hayloft in Cato Street in Marylebone, London. Their plan, or so it was said, was to assassinate the Cabinet and take over government. It came to nothing and they were arrested. Five of them, including Thistlewood, were hanged.

The immediate result was the Parliamentary Statutes, known as the Six Acts, which, among other things, banned gatherings of more than fifty people at a time. And a heavy stamp duty was imposed on newspapers, the idea being that the Radicals wouldn't be able to afford to print their own.

The Acts weren't much more than political gestures, in theory to strengthen the authority of the magistrates. Nevertheless, confidence in the government's ability to cope with civil disorder appears to have been restored, although there is some evidence to suggest that Radicalism was not as threatening as was supposed. But it is important to remember that this was a society which didn't have an organized police force and much of the information came from paid spies. Spying was a lucrative occupation. Here's a bill for spying services sent to the Home Office from the Bolton magistrate.

Mr C and his agents:	£71
Mr W and his agents:	£122.11s.3d
LF and his agent B:	£34.17s
Postage and various expenses:	£6.1s
Total:	£234.9s.3d

At these rates, spies were on to a good thing. So a lot of the intelligence about the Radicals might have been spiced up to keep their paymasters happy.

While the greased palm of domestic bureaucracy kept regular hours, the oil lamps burned nightly in Castlereagh's understaffed and overstretched Foreign Office. Castlereagh became overworked. He had guided the nation's foreign policy through seven dangerous years which had included the rewriting of the political and diplomatic laws of Europe after the defeat of Napoleon. He had hoped for a safer Europe. But much militated against that: revolutions in Portugal, Spain and the Two Sicilies; suspicions of Russian ambitions; threats from Austria to existing treaties; the Greek War of Independence and the threat to Turkey. Castlereagh became deranged, and on 13 August 1822 he went into his dressing room and cut his own throat. Some have suggested that on top of these professional stresses, Castlereagh was being blackmailed.

CHAPTER FORTY-SIX

1824–7

The 1820s began and ended with George IV on the throne. It was a decade of change, a decade of four prime ministers: Liverpool, Canning, very briefly Lord Goderich and the Duke of Wellington. This was the decade of the opening of the Stockton and Darlington Railway, of the bridge over the Menai Strait, of the death of Lord Byron who had gone to fight in the Greek War of Independence. It was a period in which the term 'reform' was being taken more seriously.

The Reform Acts were three nineteenth-century Bills designed to allow more people to vote and to change the voting method. The First Reform Act was in 1832, the second in 1867 and the third in 1884. But back in the 1820s there were other reforms: reforms of how to react to political necessity and moral indignation that produced, for example, the 1829 Catholic Emancipation Act. There were also new laws that would allow freer trade and tariffs; reforms that moved towards active trades unions and changed attitudes to the way, and the conditions in which, people worked. One example came in 1823 with the repeal of the Combination Acts that had made it illegal for two or more people to combine in trying to get better conditions at work and more money. Without the Combination Laws the passage towards active trades unionism became clear – at least with the benefit of hindsight. And there actually was an attempt – an unsuccessful one – to establish something called the Grand National Consolidated Trades Union.

Reform did not suddenly come upon the British conscience. The French Revolution nudged any complacency among the people and their so-called representatives. MPs did not represent the people, of course; the best that we can judge, Members of the Parliament simply represented the right to rule and, at best, would take up a mood. That was what Pitt had done when he threatened to resign over Catholic Emancipation in Ireland; that was what Clarkson *et al.* encouraged the MP William Wilberforce to do when he took up the cause to abolish the slave trade and then slavery altogether in the British colonies. So we can see there was no single reason for the British to look at themselves and judge if they were a fair or unfair society. A series of sometimes startling, even unnerving, events and movements would set in motion an era that would move society to look at its institutions and their functions, exclusive or otherwise, for the next two centuries. There were so many wrongs by twenty-first century standards that needed reforming. In the period we have reached, the British had been subjected to political trauma rather than pangs of social conscience.

The Protestant arrogance of the eighteenth century reflected how the British saw themselves in the world and, increasingly, how the world saw the British and their treasured institutions, particularly banking and the law. In fact, the institutions were icons for the British and how others saw them. They had colonies, the makings of an empire in India, powerful fleets, industrial and technological achievement, a 'safe' monarchy, an enviable and evolving Parliamentary system and a government that, although still subjected to royal whim and persuasion, was indeed edging towards a recognizably sound form of modern democracy. There was, too, a religious revival although the Established Church was not threatened by dissident Christianity. The evangelical movement was confident and increasingly regional. For example, the Anglican Bishop of Chester would often remark that there were more Non-conformist worshippers in the see than Anglicans. As for Catholicism, it was not longer a threatening umbrella for French and Spanish ambitions on the British throne. In Scotland, the churches had reached their own conclusion how best to live together and although the Church of Scotland was not an Established Church it was the accepted 'official' Church. The Episcopalians were in the minority but of no great threat to the orthodoxy.

In Ireland, there was an altogether different form of social discontent. The United Irishmen of Protestants founded by Wolfe Tone had indeed agitated for dramatic reform and independence by the inspiration of the French Revolution. The Catholic Church – some three-quarters of the population – may not have been an organized threat to the Protestant Ascendancy in that island, but they nevertheless reflected a platform from which Parliamentary and social grievance might be mounted against the British. Certainly, Pitt the Younger had wanted Catholic Emancipation in Ireland even though the King refused on the grounds that this would be against his own coronation vows as defender of the faith of the Established Church.

The United Irishmen rebellion of 1798 may have fizzled out, but it certainly convinced Pitt that political control had to be concentrated in Westminster and therefore there had to be an act of political union. This was enacted as the Union of Great Britain and Ireland on 1 August 1800. (Northern Ireland is still referred to as Great Britain and Northern Ireland.) That Pitt failed to achieve a Catholic Emancipation Act at the same time was simply a step too far for the moment. It would come, but not in his lifetime. The Roman Catholics had been governed by the 1571 Penal Laws in England and in Ireland, the 1695–1727 Penal Code. Why then, if Pitt had failed to convince the monarch in 1798, could Prime Minister Wellington and King George IV get a Catholic Emancipation Bill on the statute book in 1829? Simply, there was an urgency in the fear of both men that Catholic disturbance really would lead to a break up of the Union led by the formidable figure of the Irish MP David O'Connell (1775–1847) whose Catholic Association demanded that Catholics had a right to be MPs.

However, we should not see reform in terms of big issues. Often they were matters of small conscience, almost uneasiness. For example, Robert Peel, the new Home Secretary in 1822, began work to change the criminal law, prisons and even the very public display of punishment. If villains were executed in the Port of London area, then the wretched remains were placed on a particularly gruesome form of display and left for all to see. It was called gibbeting. The idea was that the sight of these remains should act as a crime deterrent. But there's no evidence that it did. One William Sykes was moved to write to Robert Peel that: 'the scare-crow remains of the poor wretches who, long since expired by death of their crimes, now hang upon gibbets It is said that "Persecution ceases in the grave". Let these poor remains find a grave, and the remembrance of their offences pass away.' A woman could still be burned alive for some crimes, even something as simple as coining. Public flogging of females was still a spectator sport. Neither burning, hanging nor flogging appeared to be a deterrent to criminals.

Peel may have been impressed with the plea from Sykes but the practice of gibbeting continued in London until 1834. But those like Peel who wanted criminal law reform were not liberals, in modern terms, although it was at this time that the distinctions between political ministries were beginning to become clearer. And during this time of experiment with reform perhaps the most important change was the evolution of political positions as Westminster. There wasn't yet a clear ideological distinction between those who claimed party labels, but Parliament was definitely moving towards what would now be called the party system and an official opposition.

When Lord Liverpool had a stroke in 1827, he had been Prime Minister for fifteen years. Some say that Liverpool was a nonentity but he had governed during the final years of the Napoleonic Wars; the considerable economic and social changes that followed; evidence of rebellion; scandals in the royal household at a time when the monarch's credibility was essential to the political stability of the administration; and the suicide of his Foreign Secretary. And through all this, he had little direct control of the House of Commons because he sat in the Lords.

And the system under which Liverpool governed in the 1820s, although moving slowly towards the two-party system, was far removed from what now exists where two main parties lay out their promises and then the nation votes for one lot or the other.

In the 1820s an election was the time when the King and his government (which the King chose) asked for a vote of confidence. And so a general election wasn't much fought by an opposition trying to replace the government, indeed most seats weren't even contested. The biggest influence on the outcome of the election might well turn out to be a public display of confidence not by the people, but by the monarch, in the government.

From this it is easy to see how Liverpool could be judged as someone who had done little more than keep apart the two powerful government factions of George Canning and the Duke of Wellington, while clinging to the memory of Pitt the Younger. That judgement would be too simple and would not acknowledge the way in which ministers set their own agendas, even if this meant ignoring those of their own government. For instance, there had long been a debate on the extent of Catholic Emancipation. Some of Liverpool's ministers were as much opposed to this idea as others were in favour. Therefore, the chances of success were almost nil. There was no way in which Liverpool could simply say, 'This is Government policy, therefore I insist everyone agrees,' especially as the King wouldn't have agreed with him anyway. The best he could hope for was an agreeable Parliament, rather than an agreeing one. Every time there was a new idea, his job was to reassure many of his colleagues that it was an evolutionary concept, rather than a radical departure.

Thus Liverpool ruled for fifteen years (probably longer than most had expected him to), but he couldn't have survived without the support of the Regent, the Prince of Wales (the future George IV). Second, the way in which government worked meant that it couldn't be judged in the way that government is judged today by its legislative programmes.

When, in 1827, Liverpool went (he was to die the following year), the King reluctantly appointed his successor: George Canning. Canning had been Foreign Secretary during the previous five years and now his political thinking grew in a direction that would have been recognized during and after the Second World War, when plans were laid for a transatlantic alliance. This was hardly surprising considering that, as Foreign Secretary, he had been deeply involved in events in Spain, where he had supported a Spanish rebellion against the ruling junta. Canning may have said the rising was justifiable, but there was a definite anxiety throughout Continental Europe where a rising against authority could be taken as inspiration to overthrow Holy Alliances. No wonder Austria and Russia were going to intervene. No wonder Canning saw intervention in the affairs of others as an unwise act. Britain had rarely got off lightly when drawn into a conflict that was not really its own. Yet in Britain, volunteers lined up to go to Spain to support the liberal armies – just as they would in 1936. Effectively, the volunteers made no difference. The Liberals in Spain were beaten down. If anything should be remembered from this it is the word Liberal. The events in Spain at the start of the nineteenth century so inspired Radicals in Britain that they adopted the word Liberal as a political title.

The interests of the Europeans in the early nineteenth century turned to Latin America. The Spanish had colonies, the Portuguese were in Brazil and the British traded there. While the Spanish had been distracted by the Napoleonic Wars, many of their South American colonies had gone their own ways – or tried to. The Spanish were now keen to re-establish control. There was every chance of a series of colonial wars. Canning wanted the Americans to help Britain oppose European intervention. This was in the American interest: it didn't want wars on its continent, no matter how far south they were fought. But the then President, James Monroe, was persuaded not to involve America in unworkable alliances. On 2 December 1823, the fifth President of the United States addressed Congress. His speech has become known as the Monroe Doctrine and remains the basis of American foreign policy. A summary of what he said might be that the United States would see any European attempt to influence politically the 'Western hemisphere' as 'dangerous to our peace and safety'. In 1917, it was President Wilson who, during the First World War, declared, 'I am proposing that the nations should adopt the doctrine of President Monroe as the doctrine of the world: that no nation should seek to extend its policy over any other nation or people, but that every people should be left free to determine its own policy, its own way.' So, the consequences of the Napoleonic Wars, the ideas of a British Foreign Secretary and the consequent reservations of a young United States produced a doctrine that survived into the twenty-first century.

We must judge that for his remarkable talents, Canning was never much trusted by George IV and, equally, Canning did not trust the King. He would not accept the way in which the monarch believed it still the royal right to interfere in foreign policy. Canning's grievance was harder for him to cope with because foreign ambassadors – particularly the Russian and Austrian – knew exactly how George worked and so circumvented Canning's authority. Canning knew, for example, that Prince Khristofor Lievan, the Russian ambassador, and the Austrian envoy, Prince Esterhazy, had direct access to the King and tried to persuade him to countermand the policy over South America. Canning was ready to resign over the worrying interference, or *tracasserie*, as he called it. Of course, Canning had resigned once before – on the government's treatment of his friend, the King's wife, Caroline of Brunswick. That had not made him a favourite of the King who suspected that Canning had had an affair with her. But if George IV had sleepless nights, they were few in number. Within a few months, George Canning was dead, probably exhausted by office.

To judge this period, we must remember that the sense of tumult and revolution was not a distant memory. The lessons of the consequences of the two revolutions, the American War of Independence and the French Revolution, had been difficult to understand in a British political system so influenced by the Crown. Canning, in highest office for just one summer, understood the groundswell of change. He understood too that if there were to be change, then there had to be credible systems to put in place of old ways, and that changing a system had to be seen to everyone's advantage without anyone else losing position or dignity. One such movement was Catholic Emancipation which Canning supported and which included the abolition of the Test Acts. There were three Test Acts, each dating from the seventeenth century, and each centred on the question of religion in Britain. They were called the Test Acts because they made legal tests of a person's faith. If anyone wanted to hold public office, then he (no question then of she) had to be an Anglican communicant, denounce the Roman Catholic doctrine of the Eucharist and accept that the monarch was head of the Church of England. At this point, British society was influenced by laws which restricted the social, educational and political movement of large numbers of the population. There was fundamental discrimination against most people other than male (and often house-owning) members of the Church of England. Only they had the right to university education and to hold political office. Jews, Roman Catholics, Dissenters and women were excluded.

In the early nineteenth-century political climate men believed that change would come, that great changes had to be made, but that they had to be evolutionary, rather than revolutionary. The instinct to preserve the institutions of politics meant that for the moment the government of the nation remained a matter of reacting to events rather than deliberately instigating them. This then was the political climate in Britain as it moved from the eighteenth to the nineteenth century and the next. Those in high office were very much the instruments of – rather than being entirely instrumental in – the events that would take the institutions and therefore the influences on the British character forward. The mini-volcano that preceded this change was in the Tory Party commanded by Wellington and a more effectual future Prime Minister, Robert Peel. Frederick Robinson, Viscount Goderich, had succeeded

Canning in August 1827 but could not hold the Cabinet together, and he was gone by January 1828. Now attention was focused on the new Prime Minister, a man with an immense sense of duty, the hero of Waterloo, Arthur Wellesley, first Duke of Wellington.

CHAPTER FORTY-SEVEN

1828–32

In January 1828 when the Duke of Wellington became Prime Minister of Great Britain the convenience of labelling would have it that here was another Tory leader; but that would be a simplification too far. Wellington had little notion of party politics. His political conviction was that of duty, of public service, and he became Prime Minister perhaps reluctantly and largely because he saw it as a duty to carry on the government of the monarch. His Cabinet colleagues did not share his philosophy and the mixture was soon to boil over. Someone said that the first Cabinet meeting had a sense of gentlemen who had just fought a duel. Wellington complained that too much of his time was taken with smoothing feelings.

In its first year, the Cabinet was forced to accept the repeal of the Test Acts – the laws by which anyone wanting to hold public office had to demonstrate his allegiance to the Church of England and the monarch's leadership of that Church. Peel, Henry Temple, Viscount Palmerston, and William Huskisson opposed the repeal, but changed their minds when they saw that the Commons would have it anyway. Dissenters and Non-conformists had for ages been able to claim indemnity from the Acts' punishments, but for many it was an important symbol of something else: Catholic Emancipation.

But the first serious Cabinet split came when two boroughs – Penryn and East Retford – were found guilty of corruption. The High Tories wanted to merge the towns into adjoining constituencies. Huskisson wanted the seats transferred to unfranchised towns; he said it was a resigning matter. Wellington, probably to Huskisson's surprise, accepted Huskisson's resignation although the Duke could not have imagined the result. With another Canningite gone, the old Tory Party began to crumble, and what happened in Ireland hastened their decline. Here was the time of utter contradiction among Tories

– what to do about Catholic Emancipation in Ireland where some three-quarters of the islanders were Catholics?

It was now that the lawyer Daniel O'Connell forced the political pace against the English. He did not want independence: he wanted Home Rule under the Crown. Importantly for our understanding, O'Connell was a Catholic. At that time, anyone appointed to a government office had to go through a by-election. The man who was now given one of the vacant government jobs, at the Board of Trade, was an Irish Protestant called William Vesey-FitzGerald. The election was to be in County Clare. Daniel O'Connell, who five years earlier had formed the Catholic Association in Ireland, decided to stand in the by-election. But the law said that as a Catholic he couldn't hold office and so couldn't be an MP. But he won the election. Peel was against Catholic Emancipation in any form and could not support any electoral revision. Wellington was a political pragmatist. He had a potential rebellion in sight and most certainly did not want to launch yet another military campaign in Ireland to put down any form of rebellion. Peel was not so understanding and Wellington did not want to lose him from government. Peel would have resigned from the Cabinet if Wellington had not made it clear that he was absolutely vital to the administration's survival. To support Wellington, Peel felt that he would have to give up his seat in High-Tory Oxford, where he had been elected as an anti-Emancipation campaigner, and bought himself a seat in Wiltshire. It was this act of loyalty to Wellington, together with the King's horror of the Whigs in power, that persuaded George to agree to a Bill for Catholic Emancipation. Peel steered it through the House the following year, in April 1829. What this meant practically for Irish Catholics was that all the Irish offices, other than the posts of Viceroy and Chancellor, could now be held by them. For those in Ireland who wanted to repeal the Union with England, there was a long way to go. Any agitation for Home Rule was viewed with great suspicion, even by some of the senior clergy of the Roman Catholic Church. Moreover, not all Irishmen who wanted a degree of autonomy fancied the idea of an Irish Parliament dominated by O'Connell. The differences within the island itself were stark – of a kind recognizable today.

In the south-west of Ireland, the Catholics wanted more freedom from England. In the most northerly of the five ancient kingdoms, the people of Ulster (descended from English settlers) had little desire to seek independence – even though it had been the Protestant community who attempted to get Home Rule in the eighteenth century, long before Catholics were powerful enough to try. And in England itself there was little political satisfaction at the outcome of the Emancipation Bill. The Catholics themselves, largely centred on old families, were far from agitators. The Tories were split three ways into what today is called the right, who had voted against the Bill; the followers of the late George Canning, who were no longer in government; and, in the middle, the support-ers of Wellington and a pragmatic Peel. The Whigs were also divided because some of them had been Canning's supporters, and had therefore voted for the legislation; other Whigs had opposed it. A further complication arose when some Tories started campaigning for Parliamentary Reform precisely because they thought a more balanced Parliament would not have let the Bill through. This impossible political confusion encouraged a writer in the *Quarterly Review* to suggest that the time had come to forget the political labels Whig and Tory. He believed that the political conflict was not between two parties trying to control government, 'but between the mob and the government . . . the conservative and subversive principles'.

Meanwhile Robert Peel had other matters on his mind – law and order. He wanted to organize the 'thief-takers' who had existed since the first half of the 1500s into a police force. Thief-taking was a busi-ness, and the money came from the reward for every thief. In the countryside, local villains were known and the system worked. In the towns and cities, unpaid constables and thief-takers might work for a parish or a ward.

But many law-abiding people didn't want an organized police force. There was a very real fear that it could, and would, be used to usurp public liberty. The Parliamentary view at the start of the nineteenth century was that public morality was the best form of protection. However, in London, although constables and watchmen were commonplace, they did most of their work in the daytime. They were often reluctant to seek out footpads and muggers once it was dark. Peel, as Home Secretary, decided to change all this. By December 1828, Peel was considering appointing a police authority that would take charge of London by night and for the existing police authorities to switch their allegiance from joint control of Home Office and Bow Street to a larger unit within his own Home Office. This would mean a slow handover of powers and so he decided to centre the new policing group on Charing Cross and five parishes within it parochial boundaries. Peel referred to the need to make 'changes in the Police of the metropolis'.[1] Peel's metropolis police – or Metropolitan Police as it would become known – did not include the jealously guarded jurisdiction of the City of London.

The extra money for the new services would, Peel suggested, come out of the local rates. There was already a tax, or a rate as it was called, to pay for the watchmen. This was called the Watch Rate. The new tax would be a Police Rate and from this emerged the term Police Watch Committee, still in the twenty-first century used by local authorities. Here are the beginnings of the Metropolitan Police Force, which, in 1829, Robert Peel set up with a Commissioner of Police and his Assistant Commissioner, in an office in Scotland Yard. The policemen became known as Peelers or Bobbies after Robert Peel. Ten years later a Royal Commission said there should be wider police areas, but many people didn't want to pay a national tax for policemen. Others insisted that policing was an entirely local matter. And so county justices were allowed to appoint men who would organize local forces; these men were to be known as Chief Constables.

For the nation, the important moment of this time was June 1830 when George IV died with a miniature of Mrs Fitzherbert round his neck. George IV, a lumbering and increasingly ugly fellow, was not missed. The new King, William IV, was not another Prince of Wales, but the Duke of Clarence, the late George IV's brother. He had been a fine naval man and, at one time, a patron of the young Nelson. For some time, Clarence had lived with his mistress, Dorothy Bland, an actress who was more popularly known by her stage name, Dorothy, or Dora, Jordan. The arrangement was perfectly reasonable. Their behaviour frightened no horses and they lived happily enough and, indeed, had ten children. However, the Royal Marriages Act of 1772 stated that the monarch's approval was necessary for a prince (or a princess), under the age of twenty-five, to marry a commoner. George had always disapproved and so William and Dora had never married.

---

1   Letter from Peel to Henry Hobhouse, MP, 12 December 1828.

Occasionally William found pleasures in other women, but as he said, 'Mrs Jordan is a very good creature, very domestic and careful of the children. To be sure she is absurd sometimes and has her humours. But there are such things, more or less, in all families.' But money (or the lack of it), boredom perhaps and the prospect of a younger wife meant separation. Dorothy Jordan was given £4,400 a year, and she moved from their home, Bushey House. She died alone, hiding from her creditors, just outside Paris.

William had been a naval officer for more than thirty years, the first British monarch to have a whole career in the senior service and by chance, which death is, came to the throne. He had remained the Duke of Clarence, all but obscure on the royal list, until the death of Princess Charlotte (George and Caroline's only child) in childbirth in 1817. Next in line was his older brother, the Duke of York, but he was in uncertain health, and there had been a keen hunt for a bride for this naval duke who might one day be King.

Courtiers found Amelia Adelaide Louisa Theresa Caroline, the unmarried daughter of the Duke of Saxe-Meiningen who was twenty-five years old and not particularly pretty. But then the Duke of Clarence was fifty-two and even less pretty. It must have been a daunting prospect for her. In 1818, she had arrived in London to be greeted by the grossly fat Prince Regent, the news that her future father-in-law (George III) was locked in Windsor Castle and the expectation that she would sort out William's finances. But the marriage worked. However, it did nothing for public approval of the monarch. Wellington may have organized the approval of the new King among courtiers, or some of them, but he could not control the sentiments of the electorate. In fact, Wellington was to discover that even with a very limited electoral suffrage (of a population of about 20 million, fewer than 435,000 had the vote) even he, the hero of Waterloo, had no exceptional gift when it came to the return at the general election. Furthermore, it was a big Parliament: 685 Members from the forty English counties and 179 English boroughs, twenty-four Welsh counties and boroughs, the two universities, the twenty-four cities, and the Scottish and Irish constituencies. But there was an imbalance between population and Members. Cornwall, for example, had a population of only 300,000 but had forty-two MPs. Lancashire had one million more people, but only fourteen Members. And for all of them, the prospect of a new Parliament was complicated by a further distraction: a rebellion in Paris in July 1830.

The July Revolution threw out Charles X, the last of the restored Bourbon monarchs, and Louis Philippe became King of the French, a constitutional monarch. Perhaps seeing what was possible, the Belgians rebelled against the Dutch, their rulers since 1815. The condition by which people who have lived in servitude become willing to rise up when there is a demonstrated possibility that rebellion may be successful spread through Europe. Wellington and his Tories grew nervous as news from the Continent reached London. Wellington's suspicions allowed his opponents to suggest that the former commander-in-chief was planning yet more Continental military excursions. There seems little evidence that Wellington was planning anything at all, but political rumour assumes an authority above gossip. It was said that these events influenced the outcome of the general election. They certainly had an effect on what happened in Britain after the election.

Wellington was defeated and the man asked to form the new government was the Whig leader, Charles Grey, the second Earl Grey. The Revolution in France had aroused his interest. He had campaigned, unsuccessfully, for changes in Parliament since the 1790s and now he saw his chance. Political reform was certainly a way to calm rebellious instincts. Grey agreed to be Prime Minister only if Parliament would accept a Reform Bill. It did. The reform-minded Whigs now had power for the first time in half a century. It was not an easy time to be in power. The events in the Continent made military spending a high priority but not a popular one. No one who might govern was to be popular. All the more important then to note the vents of March 1831 when the government leader in the Commons rose to present the Reform Bill, which would by the following year become one of the most important political and social milestones of the nineteenth century.

It is said that the Industrial Revolution created inequalities among the peoples of Britain. But the Industrial Revolution simply made the existing inequalities more obvious. In the 1830s almost everything in society was unequal. There were restrictions on the economic, social, educational, religious and democratic development of the people that made sure that one group remained in charge and another remained almost entirely without influence.

Charles Grey began his programme of reform by getting rid of the so-called rotten or pocket boroughs – the constituencies owned, and therefore controlled, by the wealthy. And then he gave the vote to more people. Grey was the natural leader of the Whigs. He was an aristocrat, to the right of the Whig party and he respected the old institutions. And although he was a Reformer, his instinct was to balance the relationship between the governing aristocracy and the general public. He believed reform was the way to stop the Radicals getting their hands on government. In the 1830s, the government that was pushing through this Reform Bill was the most aristocratic Cabinet of the century.

However, the Reform Bill didn't make it through the Lords first time. But thanks to the Irish Members, the Bill received its second reading on 23 March at three in the morning. But in April the Tories (who held the balance of power) defeated the government at the committee stage and the King dissolved Parliament.

This meant another election and, this time, the reformers achieved a big majority. A new Reform Bill was presented in June with an important amendment: voting would be given to certain tenants in the counties. This allowed the landlords to control the votes on their estates: tenants would be unlikely to vote against their landlords' wishes. It got through the Commons in September but, in spite of the best efforts of the aristocratic Cabinet, not the Lords. In October they defeated the motion when twenty-one bishops voted against it. If they hadn't, Reform would have been on the statute book by one vote. The Commons immediately asked the King to prorogue Parliament and when the new session began the Reform Bill was put forward once again. This time the Lords, realizing that continuing opposition was not feasible, passed the Act in 1832 with various amendments. The Act abolished many boroughs and handed over seats to the shires and, to a lesser extent, to the cities. But there were anomalies: 56 per cent of the electorate lived in counties but they had only 31 per cent of the seats; fifty-six boroughs were told they could no longer have Members; thirty boroughs were allowed just one Member each and twenty-two new boroughs could have two Members each. The vote was given to men who were freeholders of property that was worth forty shillings a year, or those with land worth £10 annually, or who were leasing £50 properties.

In truth, the Reform Act didn't change people's lives and rights to the extent some had feared and others had hoped. Yet, whatever the argument about the worth of the 1832 Act, the way the people of Britain would be governed in future had changed.

CHAPTER FORTY-EIGHT

1834–7

In 1834, with Britain just three years away from the start of the Victoria era, the sense of reform was still strong and full of expectation. The previous year, government had got through the Abolition of Slavery Bill. The 1807 Act had banned the slave trade to British colonies. The 1833 Act banned slavery in those colonies; £20 million of compensation to the plantation owners and slave masters helped the abolitionist medicine go down. Reform and discovery were talked about almost as if there was a wide awareness that a whole new era in British constitutional, legal, political and cultural history was in its dawn. It was now that a twenty-five-year-old Charles Darwin was sailing with Captain Robert FitzRoy in the *Beagle* on the voyage that would visit the Galapagos Islands. Charles Dickens was twenty-two and about to become Parliamentary reporter for the Whig journal, the *Morning Chronicle*, and in two years' time the first episode of *The Posthumous Papers of the Pickwick Club* would appear.

Grey was, until the summer of 1834, Prime Minister; Palmerston was Foreign Secretary; William Lamb, Viscount Melbourne, the man who was to tutor the young Victoria, would replace Grey. It was all very exciting and even romantic. It was not, however, a time of so much comfort for the poor and enlightenment for those with responsibility for legislating to relieve the worst effects of poverty. When the Poor Law was amended in 1834, there was loud rejoicing. Not much of it was heard in the slums and alleyways. The Poor Law may have been considered an improvement by some, but it defied the evidence of a desperate need for something more liberal and less dogmatic. There had been a Poor Law since the 1530s; money came from voluntary payments in the parishes. By the end of the sixteenth century magistrates were allowed to raise money – in other words, funding poor relief was now compulsory.

By the eighteenth century, the impoverished who weren't able-bodied had to go to the workhouses. The parishes had to provide jobs outside the workhouses for the sound of limb. But agricultural workers in particular were more and more falling on harder times (England was very much a rural society) and the parishes couldn't, or wouldn't, support the poor.

And so, when the Poor Law Act was amended boards of guardians were appointed to administer it. In theory, this was an improvement to the system; in practice, its effects were not necessarily seen that way. Instead of putting the able-bodied to work in the parishes and tending the less able in the workhouses, now all paupers were forced into the workhouses in which conditions were to be wretched – as a matter of policy. As one government commissioner put it: 'Our intention is to make workhouses as like prisons as possible.' This was the nineteenth-century version of the short-sharp-shock treatment. The idea was that the poor would do anything to avoid the workhouse. The cost of looking after the poor was about £8 million a year. Parliament had let through an inadequate piece of legislation and given those who would administer it overwhelming authority. The proposed legislation was never properly scrutinized and the Commissioners presented their evidence in a less than objective way. But MPs were simply glad to get rid of the problem by voting it into law. The Secretary of the Poor Law Commissioners was Edwin Chadwick. He was unbending, domineering, arrogant and unpopular but, apparently, unassailable for nearly two decades. The character of leadership was not much help in deciding if poverty hurt or did not. Moreover there was little prospect of champions stepping forward to improve the lot of those with so much in their lives that might have been improved.

For example, at the start of the nineteenth century the Combination Acts were passed. These said, in simple terms, that two or more people weren't allowed to 'combine' to get better working conditions and higher wages. In 1824, the Combination Acts of 1800 were repealed which meant that there were now people trying to form area and even national trades unions – in other words broadening the authority of organized labour. This movement took trades unionism from groups who wanted better conditions to groups who had an ideological, social and political agenda. That sounded like progress, but just as there was something akin to a fear of the poor, so there was a fear of organized labour. The Whigs, for example, appeared so afraid of some union movements that they were reluctant to allow Parliament to confront them for fear of rousing what some saw as a sleeping giant. Where they could act quickly, and sometimes unfairly, they did. Six labourers in Tolpuddle in Dorset administered oaths of trades unionism. In 1834, they were transported. It was a tactical mistake. The story of the Tolpuddle Martyrs was to be remembered more for its symbolism than for their punishment.

If any had wished for a sign of disapproval of the way the six labourers were treated, then it might have come in the autumn of 1834. On 16 October the Houses of Parliament burned down. By the following morning, the forum of the first Prime Minister, Walpole, of Charles James Fox, of the Pitts, of Edmund Burke, was little but dust and ashes. But this was no act of revolution. A janitor in the House was burning bundles of wooden tallies, sticks that for centuries had been used for accounting in the Treasury. He got carried away, the Palace of Westminster overheated and the ultimate result was the neo-Gothic building that exists today. That this inferno happened in the year of the Tolpuddle Martyrs, of the enactment of inadequate Poor Law reform, of an unsuccessful experiment in national trades unionism, and of three prime ministers, is coincidental; however, it's not hard to imagine the stir it caused in William IV's England.

William was not one of the nation's finest monarchs. As Duke of Clarence, he had been considered a comical figure, oddly shaped and often tiresome – but a loving father to his ten children by his actress mistress of twenty years. As a royal duke he had been a harmless enough figure; on the throne, he was a liability. He'd wanted to be King so much that he took to gargling to keep away infection and any disease that might take him before his royal time had come. His habit of spitting out of the window of his coach, of wandering about London until rescued and of making less than regal public statements didn't endear him to his ministers. And he knew it.

But once on the throne, which it turned out he didn't like nearly as much as he thought he would, William imagined revolution, the rising of the people and the importing of the principles settled by the guillotine in France. He was comforted by his Home Secretary, Viscount Melbourne. But he didn't much like Melbourne; he found him too aristocratic.

Melbourne was a Whig, and the Hanoverians never quite trusted the stylish confidence of the Whigs. William may have wanted to be King but Melbourne had never quite wanted to be Prime Minister. That was difficult for William to understand. As Melbourne remarked: 'He hasn't the feelings of a gentleman; he knows what they are, but he hasn't them.' However, politicians in the 1830s could not ignore their monarch whatever they thought of him.

When Grey retired in 1834 and Melbourne became Prime Minister, he lasted only a few months, but by the following spring he was back in Number 10. The change-about presented an interesting constitutional decision. Towards the end of 1834, the Earl Spencer died. His heir, Lord Althorp, was the Whig leader in the Commons. But now he, the most important Whig in the Commons, had gone to the Lords and Melbourne didn't want to carry on. But he thought it best for the party that he should. The King had other ideas. Even though the Commons was against him doing so, he sacked Melbourne and so, for a few months, Peel was Prime Minister. William IV was the last King to appoint a Prime Minister against the wishes of the Commons.

Melbourne and the King had one thing in common: a wariness of the growing trades union movement. Melbourne said that employers shouldn't sack men just because they were trades unionists, the danger lay in the taking of secret oaths. He, and William IV, believed that the move from simple bargaining for wages and conditions could lead to political, ideological and social groupings. The mass demonstration against the sentencing of the six Dorset labourers was not in principle wrong to Melbourne but it was the size that he could not accept. To bow to an argument was reasonable, to a crowd was unthinkable. However, it was Melbourne's government which, two years later, did pardon the Tolpuddle Martyrs.

Melbourne was a member of what was generally called the Whig ruling class: a world of people who could, and did, take for granted their mansions in London and the country, their right to provide ambassadors abroad and political leaders at home, and the ease with which they achieved their purpose in life.

Melbourne's family name was Lamb. The Lambs revolved about his mother Elizabeth, Lady Melbourne, whose lover was the very influential George Wyndham, the third Lord Egremont. In fact, Egremont was probably Melbourne's father. Certainly Melbourne's brother George was fathered by the Prince of Wales.

If Melbourne's elder brother Peniston hadn't died of consumption Melbourne would probably have become a writer rather than a statesman. But as heir to the title, his life took a different route. He became an MP and married Caroline Ponsonby. She, now Lady Caroline Lamb, was erratic, capricious and often unbalanced. She fell in and out of love. And then, most famously and destructively, she fell in love with Lord Byron – or perhaps in love with the idea of being in love with him. By 1825, Melbourne and Caroline were separated. She was dead by 1828.

By 1835 Melbourne was Prime Minister for the second time. It was hardly an ideal time to be leader. The Whigs were, as ever, split among themselves. They were disliked by the Lords and there never had been a Hanoverian who really trusted them. In Parliament they were more or less a minority and needed the Radical and Irish benches' support in the lobbies.

But important legislation did go through, including, in 1835, the Municipal Corporations Act. This set out to be the first reform of city and urban government. Councillors would be elected and therefore, indirectly, so would mayors and the city and town aldermen. But the biggest change in Melbourne's rule came not with political reform, but with the death of the King. William IV died in 1837.

Twenty years earlier, the Duke of Kent (the fourth son of George III) had married simply because any child of the marriage was likely to be the future monarch. The Duke married a widow, Princess Mary Louisa Victoria of Saxe-Coburg-Gotha. In 1819, a daughter, Alexandrina Victoria, was born. She became fifth in line to the throne, after her father and her uncles, and in the early hours of 20 June 1837, she became Queen Victoria.

CHAPTER FORTY-NINE

1837–41

At nine o'clock on the morning of 20 June 1837, Viscount Melbourne, the Prime Minister, wearing the dress of a Privy Councillor, was ushered into Kensington Palace. He was escorted to a small receiving room. There, quite alone, stood a blue-eyed girl, not five feet tall, dressed in mourning black. Melbourne bowed and kissed her hand. She was eighteen years old, her name was Alexandrina Victoria, and she was now Queen of Great Britain. Melbourne would be her mentor.

That same morning, her Privy Council stood in a horseshoe and listened to her speech of declaration which had been written for her by Melbourne. Late in the evening, he returned to Kensington Palace and for an hour or so, the two talked. That night she noted in her diary, 'I had a very important and very comfortable conversation with him.' Her mother, the Duchess of Kent, and her private secretary, Sir John Conroy (who appears to have been more than private secretary), had longed for her succession and hoped either for an earlier death of William IV or for an extension – a delay – of Victoria's coming of age. Both would have raised the question of a Regency, and thus the chance of even more power for Victoria's mother and Conroy. Victoria was defended from the prospect by her governess, the Baroness Louise Lehzen. In the journals of Charles Greville (1794–1865), who according to Benjamin Disraeli was the vainest man he had ever met, there's a note which tells us how the new Queen dealt with Conroy.

It is not easy to ascertain the exact cause of her [Victoria] antipathy to him, but it has probably grown with her growth, and results from divers causes. The person in the world she loves best is the Baroness

Lehzen, and Lehzen and Conroy were enemies. Her manner to the
Duchess is, however, irreproachable, and they appear to be on cordial
and affectionate terms.

Once Victoria was Queen, the dubious ambitions of her mother and
Conroy were defeated.

Victoria's coronation was a blaze of diamonds, encrusted scab-
bards and elderly burnished breastplates earned in some of the
bloodiest wars Europe had witnessed. It was a pageant of British
triumphalism, but for organization it would hardly have won a skirmish because, as Greville noted, few, including the Queen, knew
what was going on.

> The different actors in the ceremonial were very imperfect in their
> parts, and had neglected to rehearse them. Lord John Thynne, who
> officiated for the Dean of Westminster, told me that nobody knew
> what was to be done except the Archbishop and himself . . . when the
> orb was put into her hand, she said to him. 'What am I to do with it?'

It was said that one million people watched the procession but the
real business of royalty was not the business of pageantry. More
important to the young Queen was that she understood what was
expected of her, and for others to understand what she expected. The
Baroness Lehzen had been Princess Victoria's confidante, but Queen
Victoria now needed more than a trusted governess. Melbourne was
wary of letting anyone become the power behind the throne of the
young Queen and so he took on that role himself. This meant that he
was with her for hours at a time, every day. They wrote to each other,
sometimes three or four times a day. At royal dinners, the guest of
honour would be at the Queen's right hand, but Melbourne was
always at her left. As they came to know more of each other it
became obvious that this was no ordinary relationship between
monarch and Prime Minister.

Melbourne and Victoria were so close that London joked of a
romance – although all knew there could be none. The Prime Minister
was undoubtedly attracted to the young Queen and she to him. But
this was no affair of the heart. Victoria needed someone she could
trust and Melbourne was also her friend. And for the moment, while
Melbourne was there, Victoria believed, as she wrote to Prince

Albert, that 'The Whigs are the only safe and loyal people.' But the Whigs would not be in power for long, even though Melbourne would continue to be an influence at court.

Victoria had been Queen for just two years when she faced her first major political crisis. In May 1839 a motion to suspend the Jamaican Constitution was carried by just five votes. (Jamaica had refused to implement the 1833 anti-slavery legislation and had defied British instructions to change its prison laws.) Melbourne regarded such a tiny majority as a confidence issue and resigned. Victoria was faced with a Tory government led by Sir Robert Peel. She disliked Tories and Peel knew this, so he wanted some sign that he had her confidence. The way he went about trying to get it was a little clumsy; he said that she should sack some of her Ladies of the Bedchamber, who were the wives of the Whig ministers. The Queen was nervous and she immediately turned to Melbourne for advice. Melbourne wrote to Victoria, telling her not to worry and not be put off by Peel's cold manner. He was, noted Melbourne 'the most cautious and reserved of mankind'. The difficulty for Victoria was that she still needed Melbourne. She found him comforting and therefore reassuring, and believed she could not work with Peel. Melbourne's position was difficult. Firstly, he could not see how the Whigs could last in power for very long. Returning to government would probably mean a collapse in political confidence over one of the many issues of the day and the disgrace of being swept from power. Secondly, Melbourne believed Peel could provide the political stability that Britain needed. Thirdly, he must have known that, at this point in her reign, Victoria should not be seen as a monarch under the spell of the Whigs – or any other political group.

Melbourne told his Cabinet what the Queen had said and written to him and, to a man, they appear to have fallen under the spell of the new monarch and instructed Melbourne that she must be supported. Melbourne told the Queen that he would stay. Undoubtedly, it was this promise that encouraged Victoria to stand out against Peel. And this she did in a short letter (he called it a note) to him.

Buckingham Palace, May 10, 1839

The Queen, having considered the proposal made to her yesterday by Sir Robert Peel, to remove the Ladies of her Bedchamber, cannot consent to adopt a course which she conceives to be contrary to usage, and which is repugnant to her feelings.

Within three hours Peel was writing to the Queen making out his case and telling her that he couldn't be her Prime Minister – which is what she wanted to hear anyway. It all seemed quite simple to the Queen; Peel had assumed too much and she would call Melbourne, with whom she felt safe. But Melbourne was far from happy, particularly when the true story of Victoria's confrontation with Peel became known. Peel had not, as Melbourne had imagined and as the Queen had implied, demanded the removal of all her Ladies of the Bedchamber – only some. But it was too late to change the appointment and, anyway, Peel would not hear of it.

Melbourne's first task was to take the blame for the crisis. He could not possibly allow the country to believe that the Queen had behaved wrongly. In the House of Lords he accepted criticism that he had manipulated the matter in order to stay in office. That was far from the truth, but to protect her he made no attempt to deny the political accusations. And so Melbourne reluctantly returned to Downing Street.

Peel was not dissatisfied with the outcome. He hadn't really wanted to lead another minority government and he sensed it wouldn't be long before he could rouse a greater number of seats. For the Whigs, there was little to gain but the satisfaction of demonstrating their loyalty to their Queen who was only nineteen and may have felt vulnerable without the Ladies of the Bedchamber whom she'd learned to trust. The new Queen's kingdom was less than satisfied with its lot. And Melbourne himself was tired. He was sixty and was sometimes forgetful. His party, the Whigs, had survived for as long as they had perhaps because they were simply the most acceptable alternative to the strengthened Radical movement on the one hand and the Tories on the other. The Whigs were good at giving ground when the governing of the country required compromise, but Melbourne knew that this could not go on. Melbourne's instinct was simply to avoid the disagreeable, but that policy could not be maintained when the country faced so many difficulties. For example, there was a general recognition that the Poor Laws were not working properly or, more accurately, were too harshly administered.

But attention was increasingly focused far away from the welfare of the poorhouse tenants towards Afghanistan and China: the First Afghan War and the Opium War. Afghanistan was a land of some 245,000 square miles. In the nineteenth century it was a large and often inhospitable buffer between British interests in India and the Russians, and perhaps the Persians. Whoever controlled Afghanistan could threaten or defend their interests with some assurance. The Russians supported the claims to the Afghan throne of a man called Dost Muhammad. The British candidate was the very unpopular Shah Shuja. Afghanistan rebelled. The three Afghan Wars (1838–42, 1878–81, 1919–1921) were examples of hopeless expectation and even imperial arrogance that were inevitable in a period when, through commitment and necessity, the British believed their superior form of warfare more than capable of imposing their authority. In this assumption, the British were wrong. For example, in the first war, only one soldier of some 16,000 troops and followers who had retreated from the capital Kabul managed to get across the Khyber Pass and home into India. The lessons of those wars was hardly heeded in 2001.

Just as an interest in the poppy crop played a part in the twenty-first-century Afghan war, so it did in Victoria's early reign. A district commissioner observed that if the locals could be encouraged to grow poppies they could raise revenue and so pay taxes desperately needed by the British. As for the poppies, they could be converted to opium and sold to the Chinese, even if the Chinese did not want the British merchants to trade the cargo in China, a nation-state already damaged by the effects of opium. Little of this much mattered when it came to the profit and loss sheets in the British counting houses. And so it was with the commercial events that led to what became known as the Opium Wars. Opium farming was a profitable business for the English East India Company and although, officially, the Chinese banned opium imports, some of their officials in Canton were corrupt and opium was stored in large warehouses. A senior Chinese official was sent to Canton to have the millions of pounds' worth of opium destroyed. The Opium War began. It went on until the summer of 1842 when the heat was so intense that many of the British troops died from sunstroke. In August of that year a truce was signed, the Treaty of Nanking, and the greatest prize was not actually opium, but the ceding by the Chinese of Hong Kong, which remained a British colony until its return to China in 1997.

During all this warfare, in October 1839, Queen Victoria's two cousins, Ernest and Albert Saxe-Coburg-Gotha, arrived in England. In 1836, Victoria's uncle, King Leopold of the Belgians, had been determined that she should marry his nephew Albert. They had met and, although she liked Albert, she was not overly impressed. Then in 1837, when Victoria became Queen, she made it clear to Leopold that although Albert might be a decent enough prince, she was after all Queen. Albert was given a tutor, Baron Stockmar, who had instructions to 'bring on' the young man – as a trainer might a yearling. When Albert and Ernest arrived in 1839, and the Queen looked him over, she recorded in her diary: 'It was with some emotion that I beheld Albert – who is beautiful!' On 13 October 1839, Victoria told Melbourne that she meant to marry her cousin. On 10 February 1840, Queen Victoria and Prince Albert were married. Prince Albert was not the most educated prince in Europe. He had had eighteen months at the University of Bonn and a little travelling under the guidance of Stockmar, who commented that Albert did not concentrate very long on any one subject. And the opposition had much fun pointing out that nowhere in official documentation was it written that Albert was a Protestant – which all British monarchs and their spouses had to be by law.

Victoria had no intention of sharing her constitutional responsibilities with her husband; however, she did want Albert to have a degree of precedence and privilege which Parliament (in fact, the Lords) was not willing to grant. He would not be King but Victoria said her husband should have first place in the land after herself. Albert himself never quite knew what his constitutional position was, but what he did do, successfully, was replace Melbourne as Victoria's closest adviser. And even when he was dead, the Queen often considered what he would have advised before taking decisions. As for Melbourne, his time was done. The country had turned against the Whigs. In 1841 they lost four consecutive by-elections. In May they lost a Budget motion in the House. On 4 June, there was a motion of no-confidence in the government: Melbourne lost it by one vote. On 28 August there was another defeat and Melbourne rose in the Lords to announce that the Whig government would resign.

The end had come and, in his letter to the Queen, Melbourne allowed his emotions to show through. 'Lord Melbourne,' he wrote, 'will ever consider the time during which Your Majesty is good enough to think that he has been of service to Her Majesty the proudest as well as the happiest part of his life.'

CHAPTER FIFTY

1841–53

In September 1841, the year after the penny postage stamp was introduced, Sir Robert Peel once more became Prime Minister. Peel's Cabinet was a conservative group with a small 'c'; some in his administration had resigned from government in 1834 over Catholic Emancipation – and that was a Whig administration – but, although care must still be taken when labelling political parties, it was at about this time that the Tories began to be thought of as Conservative with a capital 'C'.

It was also at this point that a new cast stepped on to the Westminster stage; almost all the great names of the rest of the century had now taken their places and one by one they came forward: Derby, the protectionist Conservative; Palmerston, who started the Opium War and would become the first Liberal Prime Minister; Gladstone, soon to be President of the Board of Trade, and Prime Minister four times; and Disraeli, Victoria's favourite Prime Minister.

But for the next five years Robert Peel, the man who first organized the Metropolitan Police, would preside with considerable purpose over all his departments. That may now sound pretty obvious but the role of Prime Minister was little more than 100 years old and the authority of the office was still developing. Peel's predecessor, Melbourne, was regarded by the Tories as someone who gave the government no central control; he just allowed the various departments to get on with it. The importance given to the office of a twentieth-century Prime Minister hadn't really been approached until towards the end of Lord Liverpool's premiership in the 1820s. Liverpool had believed that the Cabinet should be a body for collective decision-making and not, as it had been, a number of departments and individuals who simply did what they wanted to do.

And there was another aspect of premiership that a modern-day Prime Minister doesn't have to worry about: the monarchy. Although the sovereign's powers were decreasing, he or she was still a considerable political force and often forcibly expressed fear or distaste for one or other of the political parties, as Victoria had for the Tories – especially Peel and his Tories – during her first couple of years on the throne.

Peel recognized the vulnerability of government to royal whim and the often-sensed Parliamentary politicians' indifference to the authority of almost any government leader. However, the Victorian constitutional historian, Walter Bagehot, described Sir Robert Peel as the best leader of the Commons of his (Bagehot's) time. Victoria thought him a cold fish and so he was, in public at least. He was the son of a very wealthy cotton spinner (also called Robert), retained a trace of his earlier Lancastrian accent, recognized his own superb abilities and was sometimes over aware that he was at the head of a Tory institution founded not on trade, but supposedly upper-class values. This was not something about which Peel was overawed. When it came to a tumble, it would not take an aristocrat and few upper-class values to knock Peel off balance. The question in debate may have started with land-owning classes, but it would finish with more urban debate. The question of the Corn Laws had been around for generations; they had existed in one form or another since the Middle Ages. They were protectionist laws that imposed duties on cheap corn imports to protect British grain prices. In 1815 a Corn Law banned imports until British grain had reached a certain price, indeed, an artificially high price. It was unworkable and a sliding scale was introduced, but not for a decade. But the significance of that law had nothing to do with whether it worked or not.

The Whigs controlled the interests of the majority of political decision-makers and the one interest the Whigs had in common was that they were landowners. It would not matter how many times the Corn Laws became an issue, the Whigs would never repeal them. Nor would Peel's own landowning Tories. And so when the 1815 Corn Law was pushed through the House, it was, perhaps, the last time the landowning class in England actually controlled a political decision.

The Anti-Corn Law League was founded in 1839. Its platform was simple: the League accused the protectionist system of having nothing to do with keeping down the price of bread but allowing landowners to get the best prices. Equally, cheap food meant a contented people and, in some ways, really did suppress the need for wage demands. There was also the possibility of counter protection laws in other countries – that is, export markets. This did not cheer the landowners, which was something of a dilemma for Peel who had a reputation for doing nothing until he had to. But the Anti-Corn Law League would not go away until the Corn Laws had. Moreover, the League was politically savvy. One ploy was to get people to buy forty-shilling (£2) freeholds and so get a national vote, or even two if they already had such a freehold. Under the 1932 Reform Act, a man who had a freehold worth forty shillings was allowed to vote in the General Election. At the same time, the League was not unopposed outside government. The Chartists, for example, who are sometimes called the forerunners of socialism, were agitating for political and social reform. They were not on the side of the League because they, along with many others, saw the League as a tool of the industrialists who were no friends of Chartism.

In fact, this threat of something more than legislative action may have directly encouraged Peel to agree to get rid of the Corn Laws. His obvious difficulty was that a large number of his political group were landowners. In August 1845, the potato crop failed in Ireland and Peel knew that if he were to stay in command he had to put the Corn Law reform – in reality, its abolition – to his Cabinet. He did not get the support he had expected and so he went down. His resignation was a formal affair because the person who could have formed a new administration, the Whig Lord Russell, would not do so. Peel returned. However, the protectionists were waiting for him whatever the damage they might do to the Tories, that is, to their own people. This fight to stop the repeal of the Corn Laws would strip the Tories of any cohesion Peel had hoped to preserve. And the man who led the Tory protectionists and attacked Peel was the son of a Spanish Jew who had been an MP for only nine years. His name was Benjamin Disraeli.

Chartists, protectionists, landowners and industrialists clashed in the furious debate over the repeal of the Corn Laws. The landowners said the League was backed by industrialists who wanted cheap corn, and therefore cheap bread, so that workers had one less good reason to demand higher wages. The Chartists who wanted social and political reform were against the League, saying that if prices collapsed then agricultural workers would be sacked and they would flood the already overcrowded labour market. The labourers were suspicious of the League because it was run by the middle class. Peel, who knew that lifting the tariffs was inevitable, was opposed by the Whigs, and by people in his own party – the new Tories, the protectionists. And there was Disraeli.

Disraeli had become a member of a group called Young England. They opposed Robert Peel and saw themselves as the future of Tory politics. Certainly the party was changing as Disraeli knew it was. It is from about this time that the Conservatives, in a group which might be recognizable today, began to emerge.

In 1843 the whole structure of British society was under stress. There was violence in the towns and people were killed, including two policemen. In Ireland, Daniel O'Connell and a young Irish Protestant group called Young Ireland were pushing for independence (although O'Connell, a pacifist, broke with them when they advocated what would now be called terrorist tactics).

And on 20 January Edward Drummond, Peel's secretary, was assassinated because the murderer thought he was the Prime Minister himself.

It was against this background, and supported by the editor of *The Times*, John Walter, that Disraeli saw his chance to show the public that he was wise enough to warn that the repeal of the Corn Laws would split the party, and that he was the man to speak for the land-owning and agricultural interests of the people. Disraeli knew he had the confidence of all the protectionists, particularly as they sensed victory. His own party was shambling from one internal crisis to another, but the protectionists refused to reduce hostilities with Disraeli attacking Peel not so much over the Corn Laws (that was Disraeli's vehicle) but for not leading the Tories in the direction they should be heading.

Peel was in an impossible position. He believed the economic situation demanded the repeal of the Corn Laws. It followed, to his way of thinking, that the party must therefore support these argu-ments otherwise it would be done for. He judged also that protectionism would prove so unworkable that the protectionists themselves would abandon their campaign. In this he was correct, but he never saw it happen. The Bill went forward. Its sentiment was unambiguous. It would cut all import tariffs on grain – barley, oats and wheat – to a peppercorn sum: one shilling. On 25 June 1846 the Corn Laws were repealed. But on the same night as the Bill went through Disraeli and his friends, with no regard for the party, turned on Peel. This was simple, bitter, revenge.

The subject was Ireland. Peel understood the so-called Irish Question better than most. In his twenties, for six years he had been in Liverpool's government as Secretary for Ireland. As Prime Minister, he accepted the enormity of his task. He admitted the problem of peaceably governing seven million people while maintaining intact the Protestant Church Establishment for the 'religious instruction and consolation of one million'. In other words, three-quarters or so of the population of Ireland were Catholics. A balanced social, religious and political equation was unlikely. It was a sentiment recognized by successive generations of ministers and prime ministers. But the extent of that problem would claim him as it did later politicians. In 1846, Ireland was almost destitute. The Corn Laws could do little for the people. There was a grain famine in Ireland and England, which imports could hardly replace. Then in a few months there was a new disaster. The potato famine began in the spring and the blight had spread across Ireland by the summer. Four million people in Ireland lived almost entirely on potatoes and relief work couldn't cope. Where it might have succeeded there was corruption. More than 100,000 Irish people migrated to America in 1846 alone, and in the following five years perhaps one million died. And from all this, understandably, came violence: violence from the disaffected, the poor and from the people who capitalized on it all.

It was this situation that faced Peel at the same time as the Corn Law debate in London. He was determined to act quickly and so he asked for what would now be called Emergency Powers to deal with the agrarian violence in Ireland. The legislation to get these powers was called a Coercion Act. It was reasonable to ask for such a Bill to go through the House. It should have had a bipartisan passage.

The protectionists had never opposed the idea. But on the night that Peel got his Corn Law repeal through, Disraeli and his friends wanted revenge. They voted against the Coercion Bill and Peel lost it by seventy-three votes. Disraeli and the protectionists were delighted. Four days later, on 29 June 1846, Peel was forced to resign. Peel never became the elder statesman which he, and the nation, deserved. Four years later, in 1850, he was riding in Green Park in London when he fell from his horse and died. Disraeli heard the news and thought it a great event. Yet it was Gladstone who later remarked that Peel had died at peace with mankind, even with Disraeli. 'The last thing he did,' said Gladstone, 'was to cheer Disraeli. It was not a very loud cheer, but it was a cheer.'

But the Tories – the Conservatives – were so split among themselves that there was no way they could hope to form a government. And so the new Prime Minister was a Whig – Lord John Russell. He was to be the last Whig Prime Minister because at this point a new, important, homogeneous political group began to emerge. It was a mixture of the disciples of Robert Peel (Peelites), Whigs and Radicals, all of whom, in the 1840s and 1850s, came to feel politically homeless. They coalesced into one of the two major parties in British politics between the 1860s and the 1920s – the Liberals. The Liberals didn't come into being on one particular day at Westminster, but it was then that people began talking about Liberals, particularly the disaffected Whigs, Radicals and Conservatives.

By now, Queen Victoria had reigned for a decade. She and Prince Albert already had five children, and now, after Peel's resignation, she had a new Prime Minister, Lord Russell. It was a six-year government and might be remembered as a six-year calming down period. This was just part of a period of widespread social, political and constitutional reform, which went far beyond the personal and political ambitions of men like Disraeli, Palmerston, Gladstone and Russell. This was a Britain which was changing the way it earned its living, expanding its interests abroad and expanding its social and religious consciousness. It was a Britain that was building railways, outposts of Empire and neo-Gothic churches. It was a period when men were rejoicing in progressive ideas and technologies, and when some of the worst iniquities of the nineteenth century were being questioned. For example, in the 1840s it was commonplace to find children down the pits. In Leicestershire for example, for every 1,000 males employed in coal mining, more than 400 were described as children and young persons. The figure was the same in Derbyshire, and in Yorkshire and Pembrokeshire the ratio of children to adults employed was higher. Not surprising, then, that fatal accidents were frequent. A Mines Act was passed which, in theory, stopped females going underground and said that boys under the age of ten shouldn't be employed. But the one group who might have helped the wider cause of children did not. The move to give factory children better education (its proposers had the lucrative textile industries in mind) was opposed by a petition of two million signatures from the Non-conformist Churches. They believed that education would be a chance for the Established Church to influence youngsters. The Bill that did get through the House did little more than limit the working day of eight to thirteen-year-olds to six-and-a-half hours. Nothing was done to remove the dreadful conditions in the factory schools.

The ambition of reformers was to make sure that children and females didn't have to work more than ten hours a day. But for the moment, this couldn't be allowed through because industry relied so much on these two groups that restricting their hours to ten would mean that no machinery would operate for longer than that. None of this happened in isolation of these islands. Throughout Europe in the late 1840s, there was a change in social as well as constitutional attitudes. There were revolutions in France, Germany, Austria and Italy (although Italy was still a collection of States and would not be a country as it is now until the 1860s). In Britain Charles Dickens published *Dombey and Son*, William Thackeray *Vanity Fair*, Macaulay his *History of England* and Charlotte Brontë her *Jane Eyre*. And in November 1847 two men were commissioned, at a secret meeting in London, to write 'A detailed theoretical and practical programme of the Party'. The document was written in German and translated into English by Miss Helen Macfarlane. That done, it was ready to be published in London in 1850. The two men were called Karl Marx and Friedrich Engels, and the document was called *The Manifesto of the Communist Party.* Few understood the significance of what was being published. Even fewer would begin to guess that the sentiments would occupy some of the greatest political minds not of the nineteenth century, but the one after. For the moment though, the British were faced with confrontation not so much at home, but in most inhospitable regions, beginning with the Crimea War, one day to remembered only for Tennyson's *The Charge of the Light Brigade* and an image of Florence Nightingale.

CHAPTER FIFTY-ONE

1854–7

In the late 1840s and early 1850s, the British believed implicitly in their military invincibility and in their ability to put down uprisings in far-off lands. In the 1840s, British troops had fought the First and Second Sikh Wars in India, the First Afghan War and the First Opium War in China. And now, in 1854, the Crimean War began. The Russians had moved into an area of Eastern Europe which included what is now called Romania and was then part of the Ottoman Empire.

The Ottomans were the Turks. The Russians moved in on the pretext that they were the protectors of Slav Christians as indeed they were to suggest some 125 years later in the Balkans. The French and the British saw this Russian action as a portent of Russian designs on the rest of Europe. The Ottoman Empire was huge and rickety, and the Victorians feared the instability that might follow its collapse should Russian adventurism prove irresistible to the Tsar. Moreover, and as ever, the British – never then nor later particularly successful at foreign analysis – feared the Russians had designs on India. More immediately was the inescapable conclusion that the Russians would at least go for Constantinople (Istanbul) and the Black Sea.

The most influential policy adviser to the government was Stratford Canning, a cousin of the one-time Prime Minister George Canning, whose understanding of what could happen had been obvious two decades earlier. Canning had come to the conclusion that persuading the Turks to reform the administration of the Ottoman Empire would simply delay its collapse. But other events would hasten what Canning called 'the evil hour'. And the Russian Orthodox belief that it should protect Christian Orthodox Serbs exacerbated the situation. It hardly helped British political thinking that in the thick of this analysis, the government was not at its most stable. In 1852, Lord John Russell's Whig government collapsed. In February, Edward Smith-Stanley, the Earl of Derby, became Prime Minister. By the end of the year, he too had gone and George Hamilton-Gordon, the Earl of Aberdeen, had formed the first coalition government in English political history. Russell was his new Foreign Secretary, but only for a couple of months, although he did stay in the Cabinet as Minister without Portfolio.

The new Foreign Secretary was not the one man who would have made more sense of foreign policy, Palmerston, but another earl, Lord Clarendon. However, Palmerston was influential. Canning relied on his help and on the general anti-Russian feeling in Britain. The Turks, knowing they had Canning's support and believing that any British government idea of appeasement would fall away if the Russians attacked, rejected all demands, most of them clumsily presented, from the Tsar for his claims to intervene to protect Christian Slavs under Ottoman rule. And so, on 2 June 1853, the government ordered the British fleet to sail for the Dardanelles.

But the Cabinet could not make up its mind what it really wanted to do next. And although at that point war might have been avoided, what the Turks did next (in October) made that impossible. They declared war on Russia. The Russians retaliated against the Turkish Black Sea fleet at Sinope (the birthplace of the philosopher Diogenese). Aberdeen dithered. He was called cowardly. As 1854 opened, relations between Russia and Britain worsened and the Russian ambassador was recalled in February. A couple of weeks later, the Crimean War started. There was little need for British assistance as the Turks already had some advantage in the field against the Russians, but Aberdeen, probably under enormous pressure because of his earlier vacillations, agreed that the British army under Lord Raglan (1788–1855) should be sent into the Crimea. Raglan did not think that wise.

Raglan was sixty-six years old. He had fought, and was wounded, at Waterloo in 1815 and had married Wellington's niece. He was not a distinguished general and for some reason persisted in calling the enemy the French. However, he may be remembered for more than his style of coat and raglan sleeve. Many of his commanders were about the same age and older, with the exception of his Cavalry Commander, Lord Cardigan, who, apart from leading the charge of the Light Brigade, had the woollen jacket, the cardigan, named after him. The Light Brigade charge would in twenty-first-century military affairs be considered a stupid operation. There would be no glory, only tragedy. It would be the sort of event that would have the public crying for withdrawal from the conflict.

The Charge was launched in October 1854 in Balaclava. The Russian guns were dug in. The British sent 673 cavalry along the valley to attack the Russians. They succeeded but at terrible cost in lives and wounded. Cardigan thought his men very brave, drank a bottle of champagne and went to bed. Later it was understood that the Light Brigade had charged the wrong Russians. Raglan had not been quite coherent in what he wanted his cavalry to do and when his orders reached his junior commander, Lord Lucan, he misread them. He too was born of the single-minded bravery and was later promoted Field Marshal. Obey the last order or question the value? The consequences of doing the wrong thing were considerable. William Howard Russell, the famous correspondent of *The Times*, reported, 'At twenty-five to twelve not a British soldier, except the dead and dying, was left in front of those Muscovite guns.' It was all a fine nineteenth-century example of useless military heroism. Of the 673 cavalry in that charge, 113 were killed, and 134 wounded. Nearly 500 horses were left for dead in what Tennyson would call 'The Valley of Death'. After the charge, the British and their allies were still determined to take Sebastopol, the great Russian port on the Black Sea. But before that could be achieved, the two sides met again, this time at the Battle of Inkerman. It was a ferocious affair. The British took 2,357 casualties; the French, 929; the Russians, more than 12,000. However, the matter was inconclusive as the objective of taking Sebastopol was not achieved. That would have to wait until spring 1855.

Dreadful weather took command of the campaign. The soldiers were still in their summer clothes and many had lost their kit altogether. Cholera and dysentery, withering cold and starvation took a greater number of men that enemy bullets had not. The hospital ships running between the Crimea and Constantinople were hardly safe havens for the wounded. One in ten died on that voyage and, in February, half the patients of one of them died – and by no means all of them from their wounds. And then conditions started to improve and lives began to be saved. At first the government did not know just how terrible were the conditions, but finally woke up to the disaster that would eventually bring it down. The scandal of the Crimea could no longer be hidden from the British public. A Commission of Inquiry was set up although its report was not published until the worst was over. The Secretary-at-War, Sidney Herbert, wrote to Florence Nightingale, who had arrived in Crimea with her nurses, and gave her his backing for the actions she believed necessary to relieve the suffering of the soldiers. And the evidence of neglect which faced Miss Nightingale was an equally damning example of bad planning and buck-passing – no one would accept responsibility. In the field, the consequences of poor decision-making and even worse leadership were clear at last. Raglan resigned and then, ten days later, died. In September 1855, Sebastopol at last fell and, in March 1856, yet another Paris Peace Treaty was signed.

The war was over and Britain, under its new Prime Minister, Lord Palmerston (who was born in 1784 at Broadlands, later the twentieth-century home of Lord Mountbatten) continued the family business of industrial and economic expansion. As Britain expanded its trading interests abroad, there were extra mouths to feed at home.

The population of England and Wales had grown from less than fourteen million at the 1831 census to nearly eighteen million in 1851. In the same period, Scotland's population grew from 2.2 million to 2.8 million. In Ireland, the population had fallen from 7.8 million in 1831 to 6.5 million at the eve of the Crimean War – and, for the moment, that downward trend continued. The famine had had its effect, but emigration now contributed greatly. In Scotland alone, more than 10 per cent of the population was Irish born. Famously, the biggest movement was to America, but those seeking a new life in the New World weren't all Irish. In 1850, the number of Americans who'd been born in Great Britain was reckoned to be 1.3 million.

The 1851 census provides a picture of the nation, and of what the people of Britain were doing for a living halfway through the century. The biggest single group was still agricultural workers – nearly one-and-a-half million of them. Then came domestic servants – about one million. Here, in extracts from a report in the 1851 census, is a simplified picture of the nation's workers.

1851 census:

Cotton calico, manufacture, printing and dyeing:	501,565
Boot and shoe makers:	274,000+
Hat and dress makers:	268,000
Coal miners:	219,000
Washerwomen, manglers and laundry keepers:	146,091
Errand boys, porters and messengers:	101,000
Grocers:	86,000
Gardeners:	81,000
Engine and machine makers:	48,000
Railway labourers:	34,306
Pedlars:	30,500
Horsekeepers, grooms and jockeys:	29,000
Nurses:	25,500
Straw hat and bonnet makers:	22,000
Anglican clergymen:	18,587
Policemen:	18,348
Surgeons and apothecaries:	15,163
Stay makers:	13,700
Hairdressers and wig-makers:	12,000+

The census also reveals something about one class that was expanding rapidly in Victorian society: civil servants. There were now 31,000 of them. In 1853 a commission reported to the government that there was a need to improve the upper echelons of the Civil Service. Its principal authors, Sir Stafford Northcote and Sir Charles Trevelyan, put forward the idea of recruiting by examination. They recognized that just as a man expected results if he paid any professional – a lawyer, for example – then the tax-payer had the right to a similar professional expectation from the Civil Service. The nineteenth-century Civil Service mandarins pointed out that setting an examination didn't necessarily test a man's character. And surely the best people would not care to sit for a public examination. But Northcote and Trevelyan had identified a widely recognized weakness in the nation's bureaucracy.

Reform was also under way in another area of English life associated with scandal, corruption and privilege – the Established Church. By the 1850s, the Church had undergone administrative and constitutional reform in rather the same public manner as had the Civil

Service. The Roman Catholics remained in a minority with restricted civil rights and there was a larger minority group, the Dissenters or Non-conformists: those who chose not to conform to the Established Church.

What people actually believed is hard to judge but there is a perception that in most rural areas superstition was a greater influence on lower-class countrymen and women than the parson's promises of heaven or his threats of hell. However, contemporary opinion suggests that by the 1850s the Church and the people were well pleased with each and while High and Low Churches may have striven for men's souls, the liberal wing of the Church strove for reform. This was the age of reform of almost any institution and the anomalies in Church administration made it an obvious target. Bishops had done very well from endowments, some making tens of thousands of pounds a year. One archbishop is said to have died with an estate in excess of £1 million.

Liberal churchmen were uneasy about the Church's established wealth from property, investments, patronage and donations, all of which made the Church of England an institution with greater wealth than some European States. Religious rather than secular reformers wanted reform because they believed the Church had lost its religious way although this was a continuing mood that had surfaced during the latter part of the sixteenth century and had never waned. Yet it took government-sponsored commissions and legislation to make basic changes, such as those forbidding a clergyman to hold more than two livings. The Church in all its Anglican and Non-conformist persuasions visibly thrived; between 1831 and 1851, more than 2,000 new churches were built, many of them sponsored by new money that wanted wealth and achievement to have the tallest spire and the stoutest pews as a memorial. The nineteenth-century desire to erect what would eventually become nationwide neo-Gothic memorials to God and, of course, the Victorians was under way.

As we saw above, the coalition government of George Hamilton-Gordon, the fourth Earl of Aberdeen, had collapsed largely because of the mismanagement of the Crimean War. The Cabinet refused to accept the motion in the House for a Commission of Inquiry into the 'condition of the army and the supply services'. Lord John Russell, the former Prime Minister who was, by then, Lord President of the

Council, protested and resigned. The House voted against the government by more than 150 votes. And so Aberdeen's Cabinet, which had included William Gladstone as Chancellor of the Exchequer and Palmerston as Home Secretary, had to go.

The Queen was unhappy. She liked Aberdeen and it was thanks to him that the royal family came by Balmoral Castle. Aberdeen had inherited the lease from his brother and the Castle was said to sit in one of the driest areas of Scotland – something to do with the rain clouds breaking to the west. This attracted the Queen. Without seeing anything more than watercolours of the castle, the Queen bought the lease from Aberdeen in the late 1840s. 'It was,' she wrote in her journal on first seeing it, 'so calm, so solitary, it did one good as one gazed around; and the pure mountain air was most refreshing. All seemed to breathe freedom and peace, and to make one forget the world and its sad turmoils.'

The most obvious man to be Prime Minister was Palmerston but the Queen didn't much care for that. The Conservatives held a majority in the House and so she called on the Earl of Derby. The fourteenth Earl was then in his late fifties. He had entered Parliament as a Whig in the 1820s, served as Secretary for Ireland, worked for the abolition of slavery and then joined Disraeli and the ranks of the protectionists, the Conservative group who had brought down the Peel government. Briefly in 1852, Derby had become Prime Minister. If there had to be a change, then it would have to be Derby. Disraeli was delighted. This was a chance of office. He, Disraeli, even threatened to break up the party if Derby didn't accept the challenge. But Derby knew that any government he formed wouldn't last long if it was without Gladstone, Sidney Herbert and, most important of all, Palmerston. Derby couldn't count on Gladstone. He detested Disraeli (he actually said Disraeli inspired in him a sense of revulsion) and would never sit in Cabinet with him. He and Herbert could not forgive the way in which Disraeli had brought about Peel's downfall. That left Palmerston, who wouldn't serve under Derby.

Derby failed to get the three men he needed and the Queen tried Lord John Russell. Although well regarded, there wasn't enough support for him and so the first and obvious choice, Palmerston, became Prime Minister at the age of seventy-one. Disraeli was very Disraeli about the whole affair. He described Palmerston as an imposter, an old painted pantaloon, a man utterly exhausted. But not everyone shared this sense of spite. Sidney Herbert pointed out that people may criticize and dislike Palmerston but he was, 'the only public man in England who has a name'.

Palmerston's peerage was Irish. At twenty-two he had become a Tory MP and, by the age of twenty-five, a junior minister. By 1830 he was in charge of foreign policy. He was Foreign Secretary for both Lord Grey and Viscount Melbourne. After the fall of the Peel government, Palmerston was back as Lord John Russell's Foreign Secretary, but he lost his job because he simply disregarded the wishes of the Queen and therefore the government. Now, four years after forcing Lord John Russell to sack him, the Queen had Palmerston as her Prime Minister.

How would she get on with this man she called 'Pilgerstein'? The answer was, very well indeed. Palmerston took charge of the war and proved to be a good war leader. Victoria recognized this. He, in turn, recognized her intellect and her careful enthusiasm. Furthermore, Palmerston changed his mind about Prince Albert. Until this point, he hadn't held Albert in much regard. Now he saw him as a thoughtful adviser. 'How fortunate,' Palmerston once remarked, 'it has been for the country that the Queen married such a prince.'

And by the end of Palmerston's first year as Prime Minister, and the end of the Crimean War, Victoria had completely changed her attitude towards the man she had dismissed for going his own, and not her, way. 'Of all the prime ministers we have had,' said Victoria, 'Lord Palmerston is the one who gives the least trouble, and is most amenable to reason and most ready to adopt suggestions.' What her once beloved Melbourne (by now seven years dead) would have thought of such praise can only be guessed. Victoria raised Palmerston to the Garter. Elevated to that most noble order, Palmerston did not rest in his Windsor stall. He sensed that the country wanted an inquiry into the mismanagement of the Crimean War even though he risked losing two of his Cabinet ministers – Gladstone and Herbert – in the process. A more innovative Prime Minister might have suffered, but Palmerston was at the pinnacle of his public popularity. And no matter how talented the Peelites (who included Gladstone and Herbert) were, they had no great numbers to support them. And Palmerston had a war, the supreme test of foreign policy and domestic political diversion. Furthermore, Palmerston understood how to exploit the authority of his office. The nineteenth-century constitutional analyst, Walter Bagehot, once described the office of Prime Minister as that of the nation's headmaster, a person with influence, an authority, a facility in giving a great tone to discussion, or a mean tone, which no other person had. He saw Palmerston as a headmaster with a light tone to the proceedings of Parliament.

Palmerston was twice Prime Minister, and when he won the 1858 General Election, he won it on his personality rather than his policies. Equally, the party really did accept Palmerston's opinion that no new legislation was necessary. On one occasion he was asked what new ideas he would bring before the House. 'Oh,' he said, 'there is really nothing to be done. We cannot go on adding to the Statute Book *ad infinitum* . . . we cannot go on legislating for ever.'

Within a year of bringing the war with Russia in the Crimea to an end, Palmerston, his government and most of all, his far-flung soldiers, were about to face a test of great and long-lasting consequence – the often misnamed Indian Mutiny.

CHAPTER FIFTY-TWO

1857–60

The British had been in India since 1663 when the East India Company set up in Bengal, having been chased from their other holdings in south-east Asia by the Dutch. Bengal had been ruled by the Moguls since 1576. About halfway through the eighteenth century, Clive of India defeated the ruler of Bengal at the Battle of Plassey and the Moguls ceded Bengal to the East India Company. The Company nominated an Indian prince to the throne, but in truth ruled through a British governor – whom, of course, they appointed.

The Mutiny started in 1857. For about twelve months Indians had rebelled against British rule – rule not by the British government, but by the East India Company. As well as its own governor and princes in its pocket, the Company had its own bureaucracy and, most importantly, its own army. It has to be remembered that the popular version of the Indian Mutiny, more properly, the Sepoy Rebellion, is misleading. The uprising was not about animal grease on cartridges. It was, inevitably, a far more complex matter.

During the first couple of decades of the nineteenth century the British fought what became known as the second Maratha War. The result was a further consolidation of British interests and most importantly, the merging of Gujarat with the presidency of Bombay. From there, the Company also controlled Agra, Delhi and Meerut. Here was an addition to the North-West Province. By the time of the third Maratha War, which lasted just between 1817 and 1818, the Company had amassed, by the standards of the day, a huge army. The Maharaja of Nagpur, Appa Sahib, and the leader of the Confederacy, the Peshwa Baji Rao, were roundly routed. Baji Rao was sent off to the Ganges with a pension book and his land was merged with the Bombay presidency.

Thus by 1820, the British East India Company had established the Raj in India, but it still was not government from London. It was the effective ruling of India by what we would call a corporation, but with government support. This did not mean unlimited profits. When Lord Wellesley was Governor (1797–1805) he had not much regard for the profit/loss accounts of the Company, although there were periods of excellent trading results under his rule. Wellesley's main interest was sorting out Britain's place in India. He resigned before he could be sacked, but always believed that he had done a remarkable job and should be honoured. He had his supporters. This consolidation by the Company did not mean that they could stand down their considerable forces. In the 1820s they were at war with Burma; a decade later, with Afghanistan; a decade on from that, with Sind (now Sind Province in Pakistan) and the Sikhs in Punjab. Moreover, between 1814 and 1816 there had been the Gurkha War, immediately followed until 1818 by the third Maratha War. Between 1845 and 1849 there were two Sikh wars.

The Gurkhas, who in the twentieth and twenty-first centuries became the British army's most loyal forces, had in the early nineteenth century gradually encroached into British interests in the Bengal provinces. It was decided in 1814 that these Gurkha movements threatened British interests. The Gurkhas were not confining themselves to a gradual migration of their peoples. They were sending raiding parties. The problem for the British was that the dividing and sub-dividing of the territory included the provision of certain border rights and extensions for the people of Nepal, the Gurkhas. Moreover, the British began to see the mini-invasions as more than an expected spread of Nepalese interests. They were also a direct challenge to British authority. So in 1814, under General Sir David Ochterlony (1758–1825), the British mounted an expeditionary force into Nepal. It took two years to crush the Gurkha opposition. It was a rugged terrain and far from the set-piece military campaigns on the plains and fields of European conflict. Curiously, it was this confrontation that began a partnership between the British army and what became its brigade of Gurkhas.

The following year the British were once more beset by raiding parties. This time the invaders were Pindari tribesmen reinforced by disaffected Maratha troops. This combination presented an added problem for the British army, which in that area in central and southern India had effectively about 20,000 troops. Officially the Maratha leaders supported British rule. If the two British armies wanted to beat the Pindaris, then they had to do so without worsening relations with the Maratha. They, if they chose, could put ten times the number of men the British had into battle. However, war with the Maratha was inevitable. On 21 December 1817 in the Battle of Mahidpur, 3,000 Maratha soldiers were killed. The British took nearly 800 casualties, killed or wounded. The senior commander of the British forces was General Lord Francis Rawdon-Hastings (1754–1826). He was an experienced soldier who had fought in the American War of Independence the previous century. In 1813, he was Governor-General of India and had taken part in the confrontation against the Gurkhas two years earlier. He should be remembered as the man who bought Singapore for the British in 1819 and would be, if it were not for the image of Sir Stamford Raffles.

It was Rawdon-Hastings who overpowered the joint Maratha and Pindari troops and so ended the war on 2 June 1818. This is a man who had been a soldier and administrator all his adult life. Apart from a brief interlude in London, he had, like many of his contemporaries, devoted himself to colonial soldiering and administration. So we get from a few lines, the mix of firm nineteenth-century British authority, as well as the benign reasoning that it is possible to live side by side with former adversaries, even though their instincts and characteristics are obvious enough to keep men like Rawdon-Hastings on their guard. There is one point in his journal when Rawdon-Hastings, negotiating a settlement and therefore working out the price to be paid to defeated princes, heard why the Maratha leaders preferred wider spread than consolidated influence. One of them explained, 'We Mahrattas have a maxim that it is well to have a finger in every man's dish.' Rawdon-Hastings interpreted this that as far as the Indians were concerned there was 'solid value in pretext for interference which would afford opportunities of pillage or extortion'.

The princes defeated, they had now to look to the British government for money and position in order to maintain any authority over their own people. It is here that Rawdon-Hastings' diary produces the perfect description of the British rule in India. It can be likened to the ways of a strict public school housemaster. The recalcitrant boy will be beaten. That same boy will be then encouraged to play games and even be invited to tea parties as long as the games are played by the housemaster's rules and his social courtesies observed at teatime.

> The dispersed plunderers having now no head under whom they could reunite, will look out for other modes of subsistence; and it is to be hoped that a tranquillity will prevail in central India which we may improve to noble purposes. The introduction of instruction into those countries, where the want of information and of principle is universal, is an object becoming the British Government. It is very practicable. Detachments of youths who have been rendered competent at the Lancasterian schools in Bengal under the missionaries, should be despatched under proper leaders to disseminate that method of teaching. Its progress would soon enable numbers to read and comprehend books of moral inculcation in the Hindostanee language. Lady Hastings caused a compilation of apologues, and of maxims relative to social duties, to be printed for the use of her school at Barrackpore. It was not only studied, to all appearance profitably, by the boys, but many individuals of high caste in the neighbourhood used to apply for the perusal of copies. It has all the attraction of a novelty, while the simplicity of what it recommends is likely to make impression on minds to which any reflection on the topics was ever before suggested.[1]

The First Sikh War (1845–6) and the First Afghan War (1839–42) were linked. In the summer of 1838 a treaty was signed over Afghanistan, which the British, in the form of the East India Company, either believed or hoped would stop Persian and Russian incursion in Afghanistan. The British had large interests in the kingdom. They certainly believed that there was a constant threat from the Punjab in the east and/or Persia in the west. There was also constant fear that the Russians would control Afghanistan and therefore threaten India. There were two claimants to the Afghan throne. One, Dost Muhammad, was supported by the Russians. The second, supported by the British, was Shah Shuja. Here was the source for

---

1   Marquess of Hastings, *The Private Journal of the Marquess of Hastings KG, Governor-General and Commander-in-Chief in India* (ed. Marchioness of Bute, London: Saunders and Otley, 1858).

the First Afghan war. The British army of the Indus, under Sir John Keane (1781–1844), took Kandahar. Shah Shuja was crowned. By the end of July 1839 Dost Muhammad had abandoned Kabul and had taken refuge in the north. If these animosities and regions strike a note with modern newspaper readers, this is hardly surprising. The warring of Afghanistan and the tribal defaults have not much changed in 200 years. A garrison of 8,000 East India Company troops remained at Kabul to preserve the authority of Shah Shuja. An uneasy truce lasted until 1841. The son of Dost Muhammad, Akbar Khan, roused sufficient troops and people to mutiny against this all but British rule.

The British ambassador to the court in Kabul was Sir William Hay Macnaghten (1793–1841). He was effectively the British ruler. He had no regard for the tribesmen and warlords of Dost Muhammad. However, it was his task to make sure that the apparent truce survived. If any proof were needed that Macnaghten was right in mistrusting the Afghan leaders it came two days before Christmas in 1841. He had a meeting arranged with Akbar Khan. It was supposed to be a meeting to discuss differences. Akbar Khan's senses of diplomacy were limited. The discussion did not continue for long. Akbar Khan murdered Macnaghten. Apart from the outrage, the British position was now precarious. Akbar Khan's stock was high as he himself had killed the British envoy. Amongst his people, therefore, he had nothing to prove. A couple of weeks later, in early January 1842, the British garrison at Kabul was forced to surrender. Akbar Khan promised the British that they would be able to withdraw from Afghanistan in all safety. Who would have trusted this Afghan murderer? Major General William Elphinstone was the commander who surrendered the garrison. He died almost immediately. Some 16,500 people, made up of Indian troops, British troops, wives and children, filed out of the Kabul garrison, surely with little faith in Akbar Khan's promise of safe conduct to India. The Afghans massacred most of them on the Khyber Pass road on 13 January 1842. A very few were taken prisoner and thrown into prison at Kabul.

All that was left of the British presence in Afghanistan was the garrison at Kandahar and that at Jalalabad, both under siege. General Sir George Pollock (1786–1872) was the man designated to rescue the three pockets of British survivors and their followers at Jalalabad, Kandahar and Kabul. Pollock had joined the East India Company's army at the age of seventeen. He fought at the siege of Bhartpur two years later and in the Gurkha War of 1814–6. Ten years later he was fighting in the first of the Burmese wars. He was a natural choice, perhaps the only one, to lead the rescue attempt to Jalalabad. Akbar Khan's tribesmen began the siege of Jalalabad in March 1842. Pollock did not manage to raise the siege until 16 April and then pressed on to Kabul. There were just ninety-five prisoners left. He made them safe and then destroyed the grand citadel. Pollock returned in triumph, but in a sombre mood.

By December 1842 the British, the East India Company, could no longer justify the cost and the danger of being in Afghanistan. They pulled out just twelve months after the murder of Macnaghten. The successful Akbar Khan brought his father Dost Muhammad to Kabul in triumph. Here was a lasting lesson of the feebleness of any outside force or ideology to rule over the Afghans. It was a lesson, seemingly, unlearned by the British and all who followed, including the Russians and Americans into the twentieth and twenty-first centuries. The wars of Victoria's soldiers continued. Peace seemed so far off when the smallest skirmish led to terrible reprisals. The withdrawal from Afghanistan had hardly been completed when the British entered upon the Sikh Wars (1845–9).

The Sikhs came from the Punjab. Here was a centre of loyalty to the British. Their leader at the beginning of the nineteenth century was Ranjit Singh. Partly with the help of the French, Ranjit Singh had structured the Sikh army along European lines. The competence of the Sikh army was partly responsible for the ridding of Afghans from the province of Punjab. However, Ranjit Singh had not achieved his ambition, the establishment of a Sikh State. He did overpower Kashmir and Teshawar. He really wanted the territory across the Sutlej river, the important waterway which runs, roughly, from the area of Amritsar down to Bahawalpur in what is now Pakistan, where it joins the Chenab River. In 1839 he died and with him went the Sikh support for the British. The British had annexed Sind province and there was much speculation that they would do the same in the Punjab. There was hardly any secret about the Sikh unrest nor their intentions and so when, on 11 December 1845, 20,000 Sikhs crossed the Sutlej, the British army was there. Within a week the two forces engaged at Ferozepore. There was some confusion among the

British. Sir Hugh Gough, who commanded the army, had to take orders from the Governor-General, Sir Henry Hardinge. Hardinge wanted reinforcements. What might have been a quick victory for the British turned into a slog, but it was enough to eventually have the Sikhs driven back beyond the River Sutlej. The following year, 1846, the two armies met again. This was the wretched stuff of military legend with the 16th Lancers charging full tilt at the Sikh positions. The Sikhs withdrew. A fortnight later Gough's army all but slaughtered the Sikhs. The First War was done and a truce of sorts was signed on 11 March 1846 at Lahore.

The Sikhs, a warrior caste, believed they could still overwhelm the British. The Punjab protectorate under Sir Henry Lawrence had two years' breathing space to prepare for what seemed an inevitable uprising. There were, in 1848, skirmishes. Gough, had prepared his army, but perhaps not for the casualties he was about to receive at the Battle of Chillianwala on 13 January 1849. Gough, not yet reinforced with troops on their way from Multan, was attacked by the Sikh artillery. He sent in his infantry. Fighting continued on from mid-afternoon to late evening. By then the British had taken the Sikh lines, but at an awful cost. On the British side alone, more than 2,300 soldiers were killed. Gough may have won the battle, but he had lost his command. He was told he was to be replaced by Charles Napier (1782–1853).

Napier was an experienced officer, having fought in Ireland and conspicuously in the Peninsular Wars under Wellington. It was Napier who defeated the amirs at the Battle of Meeanee in Sind in 1843 and, when in control of the province, is said to have sent this report to London: '*Peccavi*' (I have sinned). His command in the Sikh Wars was short-lived. He left India in 1851 and died in England two years later. Napier, before he left India, had warned that British tactics, especially in taking over estates and provinces, would lead to revolt. He was never to witness the dark and revolutionary change in British India history.

When Lord James Dalhousie (1812–60) was appointed Governor-General in 1847, the British developed a new policy which was hardly universally popular among the princes and even some of the British. The solemn custom of the Hindus is that a son has to be present at the funeral of the father. The reason: the successor proves the importance and success of the father who will therefore not burn in hell. But what if there were to be no surviving son? It was common enough practice for a boy or young man to be quickly adopted in order to observe this Hindu rite. This therefore meant that the son, adopted or not, would always inherit possessions, including property. If we expand this hypothesis according to rank, the whole State would be inherited. Dalhousie saw this and disapproved.

The Governor-General used the death of the Raja of Satara as a test case. The Raja had died and his heir had been adopted. Dalhousie said that if there was no proper heir then the title should lapse. The Raja's adopted heir was not proper as far as Dalhousie was concerned and the Hindu rite and tradition should be ignored. If the male line had lapsed, so had the inheritance and therefore Dalhousie would claim Satara for the Company, that is, the British. This very imperial idea of sequestration was known as the Doctrine of Lapse. The more territory Britain gained, by whatever means, produced a side effect. It is difficult to understand why Dalhousie and others did not accept that one of the costs of gaining territory is that it has to be protected: the more territory, the more protection. Britain could not provide British troops to guard its Empire. In India the solution was to enlarge the army of sepoys. So, in a short period, Britain was in danger of transforming its India interests from a commercial operation that used dubious but local practice to grease the machinery of commerce, to something more vulnerable: Acts such as the Doctrine of Lapse would so easily cause agitation, disrespect and downright resentment. An imperial army, spread across the country and made up largely of local soldiers had to be enormously disciplined and motivated, otherwise that resentment could spread to military ranks. Here, then, was one of the elements in what became the greatest test of British rule in India during the mid-nineteenth century – the Sepoy Rebellion.

The modern parallel is obvious. The idea of replacing one system of rule with another one which seems better, even fairer, does not always soothe the senses of injustice within the indigenous population. The state of Satara Nagpur in 1848, then Sambhalpur in 1849 and five years later, Jhansi and Nagpur 'lapsed' and were thus taken over. After Nagpur, the British decided that the corruption among the rulers of Oudh was intolerable. It has to be said that some of Dalhousie's own officials expressed their doubts about the policy.

Two colonels, John Low and William Sleeman, the latter the Resident in Oudh, made their opposition clear. They were overruled along with anyone else who disapproved not so much in principle of annexation, but the detail. The counter-argument to Dalhousie's policy was that it was perfectly reasonable for the British Company to assume the running of Nagpur or Oudh as long as this was not seen as robbery. Correcting maladministration was one thing; the British helping themselves to the revenues was quite another. It was the same argument that in the post-colonial twentieth and twenty-first centuries Western states and international organizations could run developing countries, but their banks and corporations should not cream off the desperately needed profits. So the argument against a complete takeover of Oudh was not against the principle of annexation, even Sleeman suggested that. He and others, however, were opposed to what would become one of the scars on imperialism, the lifting of the revenues.

The politics and accountancy came together without any fuss. Simple annexation meant taking over the whole State and virtually declaring it British. That was a difficult decision. Confining the action to Company administration only, would improve the lot of the people and, most importantly, the Company. It would of course be an expensive operation and the Company would not be expected to bear the cost. So it was up to the accountants to show that the revenues, or part of them, could be used to offset the expense of putting the house in order. But what of the surplus revenues? Who owned those? Dalhousie could well be accused of short-sightedness, but not of ambition for the wealth of Oudh. On 18 June 1855, Dalhousie declared that the Company would not annex Oudh, but it would administer it and, of course, it would take for itself any revenues it thought reasonable. In other words, the King of Oudh was simply a puppet. In reality Oudh would, or so Dalhousie and the Company thought, become their own metaphorical goldmine from January 1856. It appears that they had not imagined many difficulties with this concept although there were hints that the puppet might not necessarily dance. This proved to be true. The King refused to sign over his State. The administrator, and one of the most distinguished figures in Indian colonial history, was Major-General Sir James Outram. He received instructions to issue a proclamation that Oudh was now part of British India.

The colonels and Outram understood the connection between colonial arrogance and the overwhelming numbers of sepoys in the British army. For example, the most important army was in Bengal. Perhaps as many as seven out of every ten sepoys came from Oudh. In 1857, and the beginning of the Indian Mutiny, there were 277,000 soldiers in the armies of the three presidencies of Bombay, Madras and Bengal. In some cases, depending on regiments, 80 per cent of the force would be Indian. By itself this preponderance of sepoys was not a threat to British rule. There had been little to suggest that the vast majority were anything but totally obedient and loyal. The policies, however, excited by people like Dalhousie, added an element of uncertainty into the minds of those like Sleeman and Low who were perhaps closer to the moods of those they ruled. Dalhousie thought the imbalance between British troops and sepoys unwise. In London this was understood, but in 1857 Britain had only the year before concluded a peace to the two-year long Crimean War. Between 1854 and 1856 there had been no flexibility in the British order of battle to allow Dalhousie extra troops, or even replace those taken from India to fight in the Crimea. Certainly the imbalance of sepoy to British soldier was marked in the mutiny which began in May 1857, but it is unlikely that if it had been restored earlier the presence of larger numbers of British soldiers would have made much difference.

By now, this precarious balance between trading and governing was about to collapse. It would be recovered, but the immediate consequences were murderous. Through these three presidencies, the East India Company now ruled more than 60 per cent of India. The other territory was in the hands of the princes, but they relied heavily on direction from their British Company advisers. Even the armies of the princes were commanded by Company men.

If Dalhousie is to be loaded with any of the blame for what happened in 1857, then the irony is that he wasn't there when the discontent boiled over into rebellion. He should not be damned. The Marquess of Dalhousie is sometimes seen as, historically, the best of the British Governor-Generals in India. He was appointed in 1847 at the age of thirty-five. His record shows that it was he who planned the remarkable network of railways in the sub-continent. His engineers built 2,000 miles of road, irrigated farmland and strung 4,000 miles of telegraph cable across India. He opened up the Indian Civil

Service to any British subject, whatever their class or colour, and, as we have seen, apart from undoubtedly improving the way the States were administered, he took for Britain: Berar, Jhansi, Nagpur, Oudh, Pegu, the Punjab and Satara. All this took him just nine years. It also took away his health, which was the reason Dalhousie left India in 1856 having made his final acquisition, Oudh, and perhaps squeezing the trigger of mutiny.

Dalhousie was replaced by a man the same age who had been with him at Christ Church College, Oxford, Viscount Charles Canning (1812–62, third son of the British statesman, George Canning). Canning was to become the first Viceroy of India. When the mutiny began on 10 May 1857 at Meerut, it would become a year when the Governor-General was thought to be weak and so earned the title 'Clemency Canning'. This was an injustice. Canning was a judicious and intelligent man whose quiet courage probably was essential in bringing the rebellion to a close. He arrived in Calcutta late in February 1856 to be welcomed by the departing Dalhousie. One of Canning's first tasks was to resolve the problem of Oudh. Outram was ill and had returned to Britain two months after Canning's arrival. Canning was not at all well himself and relied very much on local advice, which is why the short-tempered Coverly Jackson, a revenue officer, replaced Outram. Jackson spent more time quarrelling than administrating. More importantly, Canning had arrived at the very time of the official annexation of Oudh and during the declining health of its King, Wajid Ali. So Britain had a new Governor-General, coping with a disgruntled King, equally dissatisfied local populations and an administrator of this crucial region who was simply not the man, certainly not the diplomat, necessary to even begin a smooth transition from regal to British rule. Canning now made one of the best decisions of his short time in India. He sacked Jackson and replaced him with the enormously knowledgeable Sir Henry Lawrence (1806–57). Lawrence was to die in the mutiny the following year. His younger brother, John Lawrence, would be equally famous in India and become Governor-General.

The mutiny was about far more than Dalhousie's policies. It was a rebellion against the British, the way in which they ruled and the arrogance among administrators, or at least many of them. Dalhousie and his policy of the taking up of lapsed titles was simply an example. So, as with all events which cause a sensation and live under scrutiny in future years, there was never one reason for the mutiny although the trigger for it was easily identifiable. The popular view is that the rebellion came when soldiers in the Bengal army, both Hindu and Muslim, refused to bite on the greased cartridges with which they were issued. The cow fat on those cartridges insulted the Hindu soldiers. The pig fat, the Muslims. If that was the trigger, it most certainly was not the cause of the mutiny; that came from a far more complex set of grievances. Nor was it simply an isolated incident. In the Bengal army there were more than 80,000 men within seventy-four infantry regiments. Fifty-four of those seventy-four regiments either mutinied or did so in part. At the time of the defiance only three infantry regiments were considered loyal to the British.

Thus, the infantry of the Bengal army became the focal point of the mutiny. The Madras army of fifty-two native regiments refused orders to serve in Bengal in the summer of 1857, but never mutinied. The Bombay army consisted of twenty-nine infantry regiments of Indian soldiers. There was open dissent, but not full-scale mutiny in three of those regiments. Now why should the mutiny have come largely in Bengal? Part of the answer is in its tradition of recruiting.

Bengal was the home of the full Indian battalions. They had been formed by Clive exactly 100 years earlier. Almost exclusively, the British recruited what we would have called agricultural workers, the judgement being that the equivalent to yeoman stock made good soldiers. There was some sense to this. They were used to living off the land, they had an easier disposition and, again a British term, were likely to see reason in reasonable instruction and order. This meant that the recruiting sergeants had to travel widely. There were not enough agricultural soldiers in the main Bengal recruiting areas – Dinapore and Burhanpur.[2] More recruits were pressed from north India. The non-Bengalis were high caste soldiers, many of them Brahmans and Rajputs. The British view was that the higher the caste (and coincidentally, the higher the stature), then the greater expected loyalty. Messing with the caste system forecast all sorts of difficulties. Curiously, it was not until this period – the nineteenth century – and the need to maintain status, that the caste system became a quasi-political difficulty in Indian society. So until this

2   For more on this see, Dr Saul David, *The Indian Mutiny 1857* (London: Viking, 2002).

confrontation between British rule and the East India Company native soldiers, the clear ordinances of the caste system were not meticulously followed even when the castes subdivided to distinguish the soldiery.

The introduction of a higher caste system in the Bengal army, not by Indians but by the British, was the seed from which insurrection grew. In short, British senses of order and ambitions for the loyalty of soldiers actually emphasized differences that hitherto had been more or less ignored by the Indians themselves. The high caste Hindus by the 1850s probably controlled more than 50 per cent of recruiting into the Bengal native infantry regiments. There were natural anxieties and annoyances among some of those regiments which, even today, are typical in barrack rooms. For example, modern soldiers are very aware of the advantages of overseas allowances. In the mid-nineteenth century some of the Bengal battalions were angry when their 'overseas allowances' were withdrawn. In 1856, Canning instructed that all East India Company soldiers would be liable for general service and therefore obliged to serve outside the areas of Company control, that is, non-British India and even overseas. This instruction appeared in the General Service Enlistment Order. It seems likely that the greatest concern came from the old serving sepoys who thought that their traditional role was being set aside. Again, just as it is common in modern armies for rumours and assumptions to spread, so did the assertions of the old guard in the regiments in the 1850s. The most common assumption was that the British were getting rid of the distinguished Bengal army. It would be, according to the barrack-room lawyers, nothing more than a general force with no distinction of caste and available for whatever task the British thought fit to give it. After all, Indian forces had gone in 1855 to the Crimea.

We have seen, above, the parallels with modern attitudes in the services. However, there is one big difference: the sepoys were mainly volunteers who saw all sorts of reasons, including position and money, for joining up. More important, unlike a modern British or Indian regiment, the Company army was made up of sepoys led by British officers. There may have been understanding, but there was no inherent sympathy of the religious sensitivities of the sepoys. There is, perhaps to us, yet another source of aggravation to be remembered. The English East India

Company formed its army and dressed it as a series of British regiments. Instead of the tribal dress and style of the traditional sepoy, he was dressed up as a model soldier in the European style. Moreover, he was armed with the heavyweight weaponry of the European. All this may seem of little consequence. It assumes importance when added to the series of aggravations and disappointments which were brought together daily under the considerably harsh discipline of a typically agricultural-born soldier being force fed on European military discipline.

Moreover, there were no great social benefits when off duty. The sepoy was expected to maintain loyalties, enthusiasms, alertness and smartness in very basic huts built of mud and thatch, and which they usually had to build for themselves. The Madras and Bombay armies were better off than the Bengalis. Here was another reason, but again not an exclusive one, for the sense of rebellion to fester. Perhaps all this could have been ignored if the overseas allowances had continued and even improved upon and, more importantly, the basic rates of pay were attractive. There was a further factor. The unfairness of the promotion system in the Bengal army presented problems for its officers. If, for example, they had poor senior soldiers, there was not much they could do to replace them. Moreover, the most effective means of military reward, promotion, could well be out of the hands of a commanding officer. Meanwhile, lower down the scale, junior soldiers felt they were not being rewarded for their capabilities. There were Indian officers. Many of these, Company men, remember, were equally dissatisfied with the nineteenth-century glass ceiling that prevented their rise, even when long-served, to anything more than junior and strictly subordinate roles. It might not be a coincidence that the mutinous regiments looked to these older and dissatisfied Indian officers for example and leadership. The differences and anomalies in the ways in which sepoys were treated were not accepted by all British administrators. There were certain examples drawn to Canning's attention that the poor conditions borne by the sepoys could cause active dissent.

This whole picture of unfulfilled ambitions amongst sepoys, the lack of understanding of what had been created within the army of castes and the inability to either think through the consequences or persuade others to do so, was exacerbated by an often not very high quality of British officer class. Ironically, the British infantry officers often had one of the same frustrations as the sepoys inasmuch that length of service decided promotion, rather than capabilities. We might add to this the restrictions of any commanding officer to impose his will on the regiment. In particular, because of centralized controls within the Company and administration, even commanding officers quite often had little authority over the regiment's discipline. A local commander might well know his sepoys and the best way to keep them on side and improve their efficiencies. Some higher command gave him little room for initiative and therefore great opportunity to witness dissent. By the middle 1850s the lack of discipline among the Bengal infantry was regarded with contempt by the other armies. It was as if the fundamental task of a commanding officer was to hold his regiment together, not to exercise it as an efficient fighting machine. By that time many of the sepoys were not at all interested in the regiment's function.

Consequently many, although certainly not all, British officers, incapable of exercising absolute control, grew even further distant from their sepoys. They, in turn, increasingly gave the impression that they would only choose to obey orders that suited them. The result was a lack of trust and respect on both sides. There were exceptions, but the above shows that the mutiny in May 1857 that began in the Bengal army had long-standing and complex origins and was certainly not about the grease on a cartridge case.

We might also remember that earlier, in 1849, there had been mutiny in the ranks of the regiments in the Punjab. On that occasion a small group of sepoys had roused their colleagues to demand more pay. This handful of men had genuine grievances. So had the sepoys in 1857. However, in the more well-known Indian Mutiny the conspirators were greater in number. The grievances were older and, on reflection, there was some conclusion that the wider agenda was to bring down the East India Company. Therefore, we must assume that the dissatisfaction and ambitions against the British went beyond the army. The Indian Mutiny may have been directly about conditions of service. Indirectly, and more seriously, it reflected an anti-British sentiment among some who could, for example, spread a rumour that the British would make everyone become Christians – and be believed. This last point should not be underestimated when making a list of grievances that brought mutiny.

The high-handed British attitude affected a broad cross-section of Indians. The biggest effect, of course, fell on those with most to lose, the princes and officials. Honours, pensions and bureaucratic titles had been forfeited as a result of British policies. Central inefficiencies within legislation of the East India Company had restricted careers and advancements in spite of 250 years of working and trading in India. Equally, we should not make comparisons with so-called business efficiencies of the twenty-first century. There were, in the 1850s, no ideas of personnel management. While they were spared the ridiculous jargon and business-speak of modern times, the running of commercial houses had not gone much beyond the fifteenth-century practices of employer-employee relations. The Company, and therefore the British, still failed to either appreciate or care for the sensitivities of caste and religion. The restructuring and recruitment within the Bengal army proved this. The pensioning off of old princes without understanding the consequences for those who expected to inherit, perhaps a generation on, reflected either British ignorance or arrogance. We should argue therefore that the Indian Mutiny was the figurehead of a movement of greater dissatisfaction among Indians.

All this dissatisfaction and its history does not explain the incident that brought about the mutiny. In 1853, as a prelude to issuing the Indian soldiers with a new rifle, the cartridges arrived in India. This was not some pre-positioning exercise. It was a climate test. The system was very simple and was the same as with an earlier muzzle loaded weapon. The cartridge came in two parts. One contained the shot. The second part was the gunpowder that exploded and sent the shot out of the muzzle. All this was normally in a strengthened paper tube, the cartridge. The basic system is ages old and in a slightly different form is still used in shotguns. In the 1850s the army was changing over to a new weapon. The cartridge was partly greased to make it easier to ram down the barrel. A dry cartridge, a paper one, could be universally used. The army needed to know how a greased cartridge would react to the temperature and humidities in India. The authorities in London were not impressed by any suggestion that the origins of the tallow grease, that is, pork or beef dripping, might offend Indian religious sensitivities. During the two years of the tests there were no complaints from the sepoys. In 1856 the new Enfield rifles arrived in India. The cartridges, apart from the initial order, were to be made by the Department of Ordnance of the Bengal army. The greasing came in three parts, the most sensitive being tallow.

Instead of thinking through the consequence of making the tallow as they did, the authorities were distracted. They were now faced with a continuing rumour which began at the beginning of 1857 that there was a move to convert India to Christianity. The extension of this rumour was that a Christian sepoy would not mind biting into a greased cartridge in order to release the powder into the barrel. Towards the end of January came the first signs that the Indian soldiers, including officers, had asked that the greased composition should be changed. Here was no difficulty. The answer was simple: sepoys should be issued with clean cartridges and they should be allowed to grease them with whatever they wished. Moreover, any tallow would be that from goats or sheep. All should have been satisfied. However, the rumour persisted that the tallow was from pigs and cows. In ordnance records there is no written evidence that this was so. It is possible to draw modern parallels. How often government departments, especially agriculture, have been either vague or evasive until the crisis has proved original accusations founded. There was, in early 1857, an almost offhand agreement from the Department of Ordnance that the tallow may indeed have been prepared from substances which native soldiers might find offensive.

From a distance of 160 years it would seem that the offer to allow sepoys to grease their own cartridges should have resolved the matter. However, the grease question was long out of the hands of the authorities. Might the paper, asked the sepoys, also contain some grease content? It must have been clear by February at the very latest that the cartridge and grease controversy was a vehicle to raise the wider grievance. The conspirators were not going to let the opportunity slip. There were visible signs of unrest. The homes and buildings of Europeans had been attacked by arsonists. The Raniganj telegraph office was burned to the ground. There was evidence of bribery among Indian officials to disrupt and exacerbate an undercurrent of unrest. The belief that the British were going to usurp the religious responsibilities of Indians and corrupt the caste system could not be countered. The unrest and movement of dissent was helped by the lack of discipline within many of the sepoy regiments. The senses of which regiments were loyal and which were not was hard to assess.

By middle to late March this was becoming clearer. Open defiance was rife throughout the 19th Native Infantry and on 31 March the regiment was disbanded. However, it was by then too late to prevent the rebellion that would begin in May. Tensions increased with growing disobedience. The partial reason for disobedience was that the sepoys believed they could get away with it because of the lack of discipline.

The Sepoy Rebellion was a cruel and wretched conflict that began in May of 1857 and was not finally put down until two years later. It is not the place of this book to go into the mutiny in great detail. Some 45,000 white British soldiers, half of them in Punjab, waited in May for the inevitable uprising. Given the distance between England and India, there was no hope for immediate reinforcement. A sense of helplessness was the order of the British soldiery spread across India. The mutiny began when the rebels took over Meerut and within three weeks the rebellion covered the Ganges valley. The successful sepoys then headed for Delhi. On 11 May 1857, they were joined by the Delhi garrison and one of their first tasks was to slaughter any Christian who came to hand. Two days later a new Mogul emperor, Bahadur Shah, was proclaimed. On 20 May, the 9th Native Infantry, close to Agra, joined the rebellion. At the same time, the British managed to disarm the Peshawar garrison, fearing it too would mutiny. On 30 May came the uprising at the Lucknow garrison and its commander, Brigadier General Isaac Handscomb, was killed. During the first two weeks of June the mutineers carried out a series of massacres as far apart as the early centre of unrest, Oudh, central India, Rajputana, the Punjab (which by and large remained loyal) and the north-west.

As this was going on, Major General Sir Henry Barnard (1799–1857) grouped his forces north of Delhi, and Lieutenant General Sir Patrick Grant arrived in Calcutta to become Commander-in-Chief of India following the death from cholera of General The Honourable George Anson(1797–1857). It is quite possible that many British casualties also came from disease rather than the fighting, a common factor in warfare at that time. By the end of June there came the notorious massacre of Europeans in Cawnpore who thought that they had been granted safe passage along the Ganges. Three days later, 30 June, the siege of Lucknow began. Later that week, now the beginning of July, Barnard also died of cholera and his place as commander of the Delhi Field Force was taken by Major General Thomas Reed (1796–1883). It is about this time, mid-July, that the British started to get a grip of their operation to put down the rebellion. On the 12th of that month, for example, Brigadier General Henry Havelock (1795–1857) overwhelmed the rebellion of Cawnpore at Fatehpur and then, three days later, at Aong and Pandu Nadi. In retaliation, Nana Sahib executed some 200 women and children. The following day Havelock advanced on Nana Sahib's positions near Cawnpore and defeated him.

By the end of July there was a sense of compromise among some of the Governor-General's staff. On 31 July, Canning made his Clemency Declaration which announced that any mutineer who had not committed murder would be spared execution. British newspapers condemned Canning's action as cowardice. By the beginning of the third week in September, Delhi was now back in the hands of British troops. By the 25th, Havelock and Sir James Outram mounted the first relief of the Lucknow Residency. There was then a setback and it was not until 17 November that the Residency was relieved yet again. One who stayed was Havelock who was to follow many heroes in the mutiny. He died of dysentery on 24 November 1857. Lucknow had become a symbol of British resistance. It was not until 24 March 1858 that the rebels were put down at Lucknow. There was not a single week without a battle or skirmish.

The final battle for Oudh did not take place until mid-June 1858. Even so, there could be no official declaration of peace in Oudh until January 1859. Finally, on 8 July 1859, Canning was able to declare, throughout India, a state of peace.

Eleven months earlier the 1858 India Act, which transferred the sub-continent to the British Crown and out of the hands of the East India Company, had come into power. That royal proclamation was displayed across India in November of that year along with an unconditional pardon to all mutineers save those who had either murdered or sheltered murderers. There was little mercy for the latter groups. Typical public execution was to be tied to cannon mouths and blown to pieces. So ended a black and seemingly unnecessary chapter in the history of the British Empire.

Although the rebellion was seen as one mass demonstration, we might really see it as a series of mutinies. The evidence is weak that

there was a masterminded national uprising. Inevitably, and therefore obviously, the mutinies would only take place where sepoys
believed the rest of the regiment were with them. The argument in
almost every case for rebellion was that the British threatened religion and caste. Whether they had a great idea what would happen
once it was all over is uncertain. The inclusion of disaffected officials and even princes suggests that a wider aim was to replace the
British rule. To do this there needed to be continuous order among
mutineers. Caste and religion may have been the excuses the rebels
spread, but there is a sense that this was almost a violent industrial
revolution where the lot of the common soldier against the boss class
of British rule had to succeed. This may well account for the fact that
the rebellious regiments did not abandon pecking orders.

Why did the Sepoy Rebellion fail? Part of the answer is that the
Punjab did not join in and therefore the European, mainly British,
troops were able to contain the uprising. Another part of the answer
contradicts the question. To some extent the rebellion was a success
inasmuch that the Indians did get rid of the East India Company's
rule, although that would have happened anyway. Their conditions
and relations with the British improved. It was a result of the rebellion that Major General Jonathan Peel, the brother of the late Prime
Minister Robert Peel, became chairman of the inquiry into the organization of the Indian army. General Peel, who was also Secretary of
State for War, worked quickly through written and oral evidence and
reported at the end of the first week in March 1859. His report
was thorough. However, to modern eyes, it would still reflect what
we might call Victorian arrogance over its subjects in the Empire.
Some of the issues were attended to. Promotion of Indian non-
commissioned and commissioned officers would – in theory – no
longer be on seniority. A man could now be rewarded for his talents.
Commanding officers were to be given more authority in order to
exercise local power based upon their regimental knowledge rather
than being overpowered from some central bureaucracy. The
question of combining military necessity with national dress was
settled. No longer were sepoys to be dressed up as a facsimile of
their British counterparts.

The main thrust of Peel's commission of inquiry was to prevent
another rebellion by restructuring the Indian army. Peel decided that
the army could no longer have so few British soldiers. Bengal had

been the centre for the rebellion. Therefore, he insisted that in future there should be no more than a two to one ratio, that is, two sepoys for every one British soldier. The army in the Madras and Bombay presidencies was considered more reliable. Here, his recommendation was that there should be three sepoys to every British soldier. Perhaps the most important recommendation was the structure of the Bengal native cavalry. There was great debate whether this should be a regular formation as with the infantry or an irregular one, that is, having their own structures and operating independently as well as, of course, being akin to what we today would call a fashionable militia. The commander-in-chief in Bombay, Lieutenant-General Sir Henry Somerset, was against irregular troops because their Indian officers tended to have a greater status and therefore power, and there was a raffishness of less formal discipline. There was always a sense of a social conceit found in a fashionable British militia well into the twentieth century. Moreover, regular soldiers tended to come from the same areas and districts, and were subject to more formal disciplines. The cavalry squadrons and regiments, certainly in the British army, had always an irregular air. Some argue this still to be the case, rather like an independent military family fighting for the common good, but in their own inimitable style.

Somerset was overruled partly by the evidence of celebrated Sind and Punjab senior officers. These officers had confidence that their experience would not be ignored. Brigadier John Jacob, who commanded the Sind Irregular Horse, his regional commissioner, Sir Bartle Frere, the celebrated Sir John Lawrence and Brigadier General Neville Chamberlain all recommended that their very successful and very loyal Punjab Irregular Force should be used as an example for the Bengal army. The voice of the Punjab military was heard and their opinions adopted. That was all right for the cavalry. The rebellion had started in the infantry. One very good reason for having irregular forces was that they did not cost as much. They would, of course, have regular senior officers, just as the modern Territorial Army has full-time senior officers. The cavalry, for example, would be commanded by a regular officer, each squadron in the regiment would be commanded by a regular officer and the adjutant and the medical officer would also be full-time soldiers. This would not work with the infantry, or at least not the whole order of battle. Canning reflected what he called the common-sense approach.

Thirty of the infantry regiments would be irregular, but the remaining twenty would be full-time. Overall there should be about 80,000 British troops in the infantry, the cavalry and the artillery, the latter entirely British.

We are not to bother ourselves with the military pros and cons of reform after the mutiny. However, we would do well to notice the continuing nervousness of the British rulers, brought about by their need to maintain large standing armies to protect their territorial possessions, and their inability to be confident that their mixed caste and religious soldiery would remain loyal. There was even, in the 1860s, a system of mixed regiments which, because it was good enough to inspire unity, was later seen as a threat. The thinking was that by maintaining social differences, then no one group would ever rally enough support for a rebellion. Thus the military aim of all commanders, a well-founded and competent team, was seen as being a potential danger to the Raj. We should never underestimate the long-lasting psychological effects of the Indian Mutiny on the British rulers of India, right up to the eve of independence in the summer of 1947.

There is a footnote to the Mutiny that points to the wider Empire. Clearly the Victorian era illustrated the need to demonstrate the British ability to hold their possessions by force if required. They had, after all, been found wanting, albeit in an earlier century, in another continent. Yet it is worth pondering that it was probably just as well that the British had been kicked out of North America because they most certainly could not have raised the forces to police the colonies that they came by after the eighteenth century.

In 1876, Victoria was created Empress of India by Disraeli and the Raj was firmly established in political as well as commercial terms in the British catalogue of imperial holdings. Various Acts of Parliament had whittled away the authority of the English East India Company and so Victoria's translation to Empress was hardly a phenomenon. Yet today, it is too easy to think that the Empire and colonies were quite simply subsumed into the British system and that London had a cogent policy for every aspect of their possessions. India is an example of the uncertainty of possessions. In the late sixteenth century English traders had come upon its markets and potential. The fear that those markets, especially spices, could be controlled by foreign agents forced the English into setting up their businesses in Asia. In the seventeenth century the interests of the Company had grown. However, it was not until the nineteenth century that the British, through at first the Company and then more direct instruction from London, had the true Parliamentary support and nearly enough resources to talk about India as being British. India, like much of the Empire, was a commercial venture to the British which offered risk and therefore opportunity. Its strategic value was minimal other than to deny it to others, particularly the Russians and perhaps Napoleon and, unless judged from a commercial point of view and in later times, the soldiery it could provide for British wars elsewhere.

In 1858 an Act of Parliament took away the East India Company's territories and their soldiers, and gave them to the Crown. A council was established, with the principal Secretary of State, and this took over full government. And to show that it was now Victoria and not the East India Company who ruled, it was at this point that the title Viceroy of India first appeared. People in Britain were encouraged to go to India, to become planters. The railways were extended, forestry commissions were set up, the judicial system overhauled, canals were dug, irrigation improved. And so a new order was established; a new era in colonial living was founded.

CHAPTER FIFTY-THREE
1861–70

1861 was to be a miserable year for Queen Victoria. On the morning of 16 March her mother, the Duchess of Kent, died at Frogmore with Victoria at her bedside. The Queen had never before witnessed the death of another human being. The deep distress was overwhelming and for six months the Queen struggled with her grief. Some of her closest friends believed that she was 'determined to cherish her grief'.

And Victoria still saw her husband as the handsome Prince she had married twenty-one years earlier, yet, by 1861, he was portly, his hair was going and his dull complexion reflected the anxieties and workload he took so seriously as Prince Consort. He was obviously ill. He suffered bouts of vomiting and high temperatures, his gums were inflamed and his glands swollen. In November, after a visit to Sandhurst to see the new Staff College, he returned to Windsor soaked through, full of rheumatic pains and quite unable to sleep for nights on end. One of the Queen's doctors explained that the Prince was suffering from 'gastric fever'. This was not true, but the reason for telling him this was more than poor diagnosis. They actually believed that the Prince had typhoid, but they well knew his terrible fear of the disease and the seriousness of his illness was hidden from him. Also, the royal physicians, for all their standing, were not particularly celebrated for their accuracy in diagnosing serious illness. It is even possible that Albert had bowel cancer.

There is also another source of Albert's illness that suggests that he was infected before the Sandhurst visit. The Queen wished their son, Albert Edward, the Prince of Wales, known as 'Bertie', to have a little more purpose and structure to his life, which was not always easy for a royal prince in the nineteenth century and certainly did not reflect the history of the Hanoverian Princes of Wales. Prince Albert decided that he needed discipline and arranged for the Prince of

Wales to join the Grenadier Guards in Ireland. Remember, this was hardly the most boring and secluded institution in nineteenth-century England. The Grenadiers were certainly not unimaginative when it came to enjoying themselves. In fact, right into the second half of the twentieth century the only real instructions a young subaltern had on joining the Grenadiers was that he should hunt two days a week and not marry until he was twenty five. This then was the environment in which the not always sober and responsible Prince was sent to, although a junior officer called William Carington would turn out to be a good influence on the Prince. William Carington was so favoured that he became an equerry to the Queen and was later Comptroller of the Household of the Prince of Wales and Keeper of the Privy Purse. However, his brother Charles Carington was not above royal suspicion, as Victoria was to point out.

The Prince got into a little trouble in Ireland. An 'actress' by the name of Nellie Clifden was slipped into the Prince's bed, probably by William and his brother Charles. Who was to blame is not entirely certain especially as the Prince was quite capable of mismanaging his own affairs. When the Prince returned to London, Nellie went too. Ever a generous man, the Prince of Wales 'shared' Nellie with his dear friend, Charles Carington. Nellie was not a passing one-night fancy. When she came to London, the affair was so blatantly conducted that in the Prince's social scene Nellie became known as the Princess of Wales. Although not an enemy of the Prince, nor of Charles, one of the lords in waiting, Lord Torrington, spread the gossip through the court so that it came to the ears of the Prince Consort, who felt it his duty to tell Victoria. There was worse to come. Nellie, it was thought, might have a child by the Prince or even claim him to be the father of a child she might have by another – even his close friend. The shock, and it was nothing less, was made worse when it became common knowledge that the arrangement, including Charles Carington's part in it, was known in Continental Europe. Moreover, it was far more than behind-the-fan gossip because it coincided with the Queen's insistence that it was time for the Prince to marry. His bride would be Princess Alexandra of Schleswig-Holstein-Sonderburg-Glücksburg.

It was this terrible constitutional and social dilemma over Nellie that sent an already ill Prince Consort to Cambridge to talk (firmly) to the Prince. His visit to the Prince's Cambridge abode – Madingley Hall, with its basic plumbing – is said to have worsened Albert's condition and within a month he lay dying. The Queen, according to the Carington papers, never really forgave Charles Carington and refused to prefer him when her then Prime Minister Lord Salisbury suggested he be sent to India as Viceroy.

On 14 December 1861, Prince Albert's breathing quickened and his doctors understood that pneumonia they could not control was with him. At some time shortly before eleven o'clock that same night, his breathing eased and then ceased. The Queen, kneeling by her husband's bed, holding his hand, waited and then whispered, 'Oh, yes, this is death; I know it. I have seen it before.'

Her father had died when she was eight months old, and with her mother dying just nine months before Albert, Victoria now experienced absolute loneliness. She went into the deepest mourning, from which she never quite emerged. And she went to the place she dearly loved, her retreat, Osborne House on the Isle of Wight. Some close to her wondered for her sanity. At first she would see no one, not even her Prime Minister Palmerston. The scene at her much delayed Privy Council meeting only added to the bizarre stories. Ministers stood in the traditional three-quarter circle, but instead of being with them, the Queen hid in an adjacent room and they had to shout to her through the door that was left just ajar.

At night she cried herself to sleep cuddling Albert's red dressing gown. Wherever she went, she was never without his watch and red handkerchief. She even carried his keys. She grew thin, became abnormally weak and sometimes could scarcely walk. On occasions, she could not speak. The Queen may have been suffering from a nervous breakdown without her staff realizing what was happening. She was to write later that year, 'For me my very misery is now a necessity and I could not exist without it.'

Gradually the sympathy of her people and her ministers turned against the Queen. Her self-imposed seclusion became too trying. People like to see their monarch. They could not. She shied away from the noise and the ceremonials that were part of her expected duties, especially those in London. She became a stranger in her own capital. In 1864, a notice was tied to Buckingham Palace railings: 'These commanding premises to be let or sold, in consequence of the late occupant's declining business.' After all, many of her people were experiencing a misery of their own.

*   *   *

1861 was the year of the new census. In the mid-1860s, there were about twenty-one million people living in England and Wales, more than three million in Scotland, and in Ireland about five-and-a-half million. The 1861 census shows that of those twenty-one million English and Welsh, more than two-and-a-quarter million were agricultural workers or domestic servants – still the two commonest occupations.

The Britain of the 1860s was prosperous but it was also a land in which there was squalor, poverty and sometimes little hope. Many believed the future was far away from the British Isles: the nineteenth century was the time of the great migration of peoples. In the 1860s alone, 1.7 million would leave. Some would return, but most would have left for good, not all of them to escape the weather. Shortly before Christmas 1860, the south of England was covered by rains, then frosts and snow. The terrible weather stopped all work on the Thames waterfront and, crucially, in the docks. Britain was by then a great ship-owning nation. There were, for example, about 160,000 seamen in England and Wales; more than 30,000 bargemen and lightermen; about the same number of dock-workers. London was one of the busiest ports in the world. Newspapers of the time report that the frost froze the London docks on 17 December and didn't ease until 19 January. And if the docks couldn't work, then neither could the hauliers nor the markets. Thousands were laid off. The Poor Laws were supposed to help but, in many cases, they failed to do so – a reminder that this was a period when the advances of the age outstripped the social needs of the people. Many of those freezing London dockers would have started their working lives loading and unloading sailing ships. Now there were vessels with steam engines even though sail was by no means finished – the famous *Cutty Sark* wasn't launched until 1869, the year the Suez Canal opened. (Sailing cargo ships were a common enough sight on the oceans.)

The railways now criss-crossed the country and, as transport spread, so did suburbs of tightly packed housing, especially small houses, 20 per cent of which often contained two families. In industry, Joseph Whitworth had patented his standard sizes in threads and screws. The Bessemer converter and then the Siemens-Martin steel-making process accelerated the change from iron to steel. And although most of British industry relied on small firms, new systems meant factories were expanding and therefore changing the shape and skyline of towns that were now becoming cities. Never before had there been such a pace of British social, political and commercial change. In less than half a century Britain had triumphed over its old enemy France and then become its ally; science, medicine and technology had altered the potential that could hardly have been imagined even in the 1790s. Slavery had been abolished in the British colonies although drudgery was hardly different in the poorhouses of towns and cities. The Great Reform Act of 1832 had set a baseline for democracy even if there was more than a century to go before an all but perfect form of universal suffrage and responsibility was in place. Over all this, Victoriana thrived now as an Empire and not simply as a colonial collection. Change was also rumbling through Europe. Italy was becoming a State, much to the suspicion of the Catholic Church in Rome where the dogma of Immaculate Conception had been declared in 1854 and where Papal Infallibility would be proclaimed sixteen years later. Germany, which had been a confederation of thirty-eight sovereign States since the 1814 Congress of Vienna had suffered a ground-swollen Revolution in 1848. Demands for reforms, including the powers of the monarchy led indirectly to Kaiser William I of Prussia appointing as Prime Minister a man who would become the most powerful politician in Continental Europe during the second half of the century, Otto von Bismarck (1815–98). In 1871, by joining the German Empire with the Kingdom of Prussia following the French defeat in the Franco–Prussian War, Germany became a unified State. That French defeat rankled so much that it brought about French refusal to ease German reparations after the First World War and so encouraged the German nationalism that led to the Second World War.

Less than a year after Prince Albert's death in 1861, Palmerston was ready to concede that he needed the late Prince Consort's advice. Albert would have known what was going on in Germany, especially what was in the mind of Bismarck. Here was a difficult political and strategic conundrum that Palmerston could not answer and it was a sensitive matter since the Queen's daughter, Victoria, was married to Kaiser William's son, Frederick, or Fritz as he was always known. It was their son who became known in Britain, especially in the First World War, as Kaiser Bill.

Palmerston did not understand what Bismarck was up to. He should have done. During Palmerston's time at the Foreign Office, he had doubled the number of dispatches coming into Whitehall from the embassies and he had read them. But back then, Bismarck was simply a Prussian ambassador to St Petersburg and Paris; now he was in a position of considerable power and, to Bismarck, absolute power was everything. Therefore, when the Poles rose against the Russians, Bismarck supported the Russians. He'd never cared for the idea of Polish independence and he looked to the future when he, in turn, might need Russian support. Britain could do little about it. Public opinion supported the Polish rebels, so too did Palmerston, but he didn't want to go to war. Worse still, neither Palmerston nor his Foreign Secretary Lord Russell seemed to remember the strategic axiom of never making threats unless you can carry them out. Militarily, Britain could not help the Poles. And when there was trouble in Denmark in 1864, during which the Duchies of Schleswig and Holstein were attached to Prussia, Palmerston ought to have been better prepared. Once more there was a royal family connection: the Prince of Wales married in March 1863. His bride was Princess Alexandria of Denmark so it was no wonder that the Danes thought it reasonable for the British to side with them.

In 1863 King Frederick of Denmark died. There was no direct successor and so the next in line was Duke Christian who would become Christian IX of Denmark. The succession was challenged by the German-leaning line of the Danish royal family. Bismarck declared war on Denmark – leading a Prussian–Austrian intervention. The Danes lost Northern and Southern Schleswig, Holstein and Lauenburg. This is the simplified version of the story. Little wonder that when asked what was the solution to the Schleswig–Holstein Question, Palmerston is said to have replied: 'The Schleswig–Holstein question is so complicated, only three men in Europe have ever understood it. One was Prince Albert [who was dead]. The second was a German professor who became mad. I am the third and I have forgotten the answer.'

The solution to the Schleswig–Holstein Question was so complicated that it became a euphemism for any subject to which there was no conclusive and textual answer in every political examination paper for the next 100 years. Britain did nothing much, even though it had a treaty with Denmark, because there was not much it could do. Moreover, Palmerston, the man so interested in foreign affairs, completely misread Bismarck's determination and ability. He called him 'crazy'. He believed the French could become involved (a lasting fear of his generation), and he believed his military advisers who said the Prussian Army was not very good. Bismarck had outmanoeuvred everybody, as he would continue to do. He had Austria and Russia on his side and a certain belief that France and Britain would not hold together as allies to do anything to stop him. Palmerston and Russell were attacked in the House and in the press. Lord Derby described the government's foreign policy as 'a policy of meddle and muddle'. But it is doubtful if the country would have wanted to go to war. Even if it had, it was hardly a realistic notion. Britain was probably incapable of sustaining an intervention without the support of its naval power and the assurances of an equally powerful allied army.

Within a few months, and while Bismarck's Prussians plotted their next moves (against Austria and then France), Palmerston had grown physically weak. This old Irish peer was in his eighties and, although in the General Election of 1865 Palmerston's continuing ability to appeal to the middle-class voters (and therefore the vast majority of those allowed to vote) won him another majority, by October of that year, he was dead.

Victoria, who never settled to him, saw his death as a sad state of affairs for the nation. Palmerston reflected a sometimes over-confident nation by his style, language and prejudices, and especially his notion that all foreigners could do with a good dose of English advice. But Palmerston took his own decisions based on his own readings of any subject. His prejudices tended to be arrived at rather than instinctive. Palmerston was not a party man, he was simply Palmerston and when he was gone so too was a remarkable age of English politicians. Palmerston's Foreign Secretary, Lord Russell (the grandfather of the philosopher Bertrand Russell), once again became Prime Minister in 1865. The country saw no great foreign policy issue to be resolved and instead expected Russell to bring a new Reform Bill to the House.

Since 1832, the population pattern had changed – there were now new industries, new towns and bigger boroughs, but the distribution of seats was the same. Russell's Cabinet decided to take one issue at a time, but without having thought it through. The Reform Bill was defeated in the House and Russell offered his resignation. The Queen refused to accept it, but a week later, she was forced to. Derby became Prime Minister again, and Disraeli his Chancellor of the Exchequer.

So with Disraeli, the Conservative, in government and with Gladstone, the Liberal, in opposition, the battle line was drawn for the debate on what would become the Second Reform Act. Disraeli took the lead. Derby was Prime Minister, but he was in the Lords; Disraeli was leader of the Commons. The Conservatives had just as much of a problem drafting their own Bill as Russell's government had had. Three ministers resigned, but eventually it went through. The Reform Act was a political success, although it could never be said to have righted all the thirty-five-year-old legislation it replaced. The urban working-class man (as long as he was a householder) was now allowed to vote, but the working-class man in rural areas was not. There was still no such thing as a secret ballot. Nor were the women allowed to vote. Forty-five new Parliamentary seats were created. The electoral boundaries were reshaped on the advice of a commission, which Disraeli made sure was loaded with Conservatives. But, as might have been expected, working-class voters found few working-class men to send to Westminster.

Disraeli, not so much interested in the detail as in the result, was triumphant. There was just one further step needed and he had not long to wait. In February 1868 Lord Derby, who had been Prime Minister for less than two years, was too ill to carry on and so Disraeli, at the age of sixty-four, took over the Conservative leadership.

His letter to the Queen accepting the Premiership quite properly offered his devotion. Disraeli played on her vanity and her undoubted experience, coloured as it was by her assumption of what Prince Albert would have done in almost any circumstance. Little wonder that Victoria rather cared for that letter and, for the moment, Disraeli was where he'd long wanted to be – in Number 10. But by December, the Conservatives would be out and Gladstone and his Liberals would be in.

The arrival of Gladstone and Disraeli at the political pinnacle coincided with the emergence of two distinct political parties, as opposed to vague labels beneath which various small groups congregated. Disraeli was a novelist before he became a politician. His father, Isaac D'Israeli, had written or edited collections of literary and historical anecdotes. Disraeli's literary education began among his father's books and he never went to university. But, when he was twenty-two, he published his first novel, *Vivian Grey*. By the time he'd become an MP, in 1837, Disraeli had published nine books. In the 1840s, his political novels *Coningsby* and *Sybil* were published. It is in *Coningsby* that Disraeli wrote his definition of what Conservatism was then. As for Gladstone, he disliked or, rather, felt bitter towards Disraeli. Yet perhaps his sharpest feeling against him was the way in which he had politically kidnapped the Queen. Gladstone was convinced that Disraeli had blatantly and unscrupulously brought Victoria into the Conservative fold. Disraeli certainly left nothing to chance, although any explanation to be found in his own writings doesn't go that far. But before the end of 1868 it was William Ewart Gladstone, not Disraeli, who was Prime Minister. And for the next half decade, Disraeli, the Queen's most devoted servant, would, once more, be on what he saw as the wrong side of the House but he would return to Number 10. Despite Victoria's reservations, he would be accepted by her as one of, if not the, most favoured Prime Ministers of her time. For all his faults, Disraeli was a man of great courage and honourable emotions – which the Queen understood even if his political enemies, and friends, refused to contemplate them. It was the Oxford historian, Llewellyn Woodward, who wrote that Disraeli 'brought politics nearer to poetry, or, at all events, to poetical prose, than any English politician since Burke'.

However, in November 1868, Disraeli's Conservatives lost the General Election. They did so because they were outwitted by Gladstone on the question of Ireland. Earlier in the year, Disraeli had hoped to shelve the Irish debate by referring the questions of education and land to a commission of inquiry. What could not be hidden, even by a Royal Commission, was the question of the disestablishment of the Anglican Church in Ireland. Gladstone put down a motion in the House to rid the State of the Church he called a 'hideous blot'. This meant that the Catholics went over to Gladstone.

On the first vote, Disraeli was defeated, but the House was adjourned for Easter. After Easter, he was again defeated, but he had anticipated that. His plan was not to resign but to dissolve Parliament. This would delay the end of the government, and give him the chance (which the Queen supported) of winning an election and staying in power. And when the government went to the country, it was defeated. Gladstone and his Liberals had a majority of more than 100 seats. For Disraeli, there were but three consolations. First, Gladstone lost his seat (but would have another, of course). Second, he asked the Queen for, and got, a title for his wife Mary Anne (she became Viscountess Beaconsfield. He became the Earl of Beaconsfield on his retirement eight years later). Third, and most important to Disraeli, he kept the friendship of the Queen.

None of this impressed Gladstone who was now Prime Minister of a Liberal government. In the first Cabinet sat eight peers and seven commoners (including Gladstone himself) and featured John Bright, the great orator and reformer, at the Board of Trade; George Villiers, the fourth Earl of Clarendon, at the Foreign Office; Robert Lowe at the Treasury; and Edward Cardwell, who was to reform the army. They were a mixture of reformers, small 'c' conservatives, Radicals and Whigs. Gladstone's first task was Ireland and when the Queen's telegram arrived asking him to form the next government, he is said to have remarked, 'My mission is to pacify Ireland.' Part of this ambition of pacification was the disestablishment of the Church of Ireland which was the official State Church in which only one-eighth of the population worshipped. The other Churches, including the majority persuasion, the Roman Catholics, found the anomaly indefensible. When the Fenian Rising occurred in 1867, Gladstone realized that he had to introduce disestablishment. On 1 March 1869, Gladstone introduced his Irish Church Bill in the Commons. It went through on the second reading by 118 votes and on the third by 114. But the real battle came in the Lords where the disestablishment of the Church of Ireland was judged to be a constitutional matter. The government had told the Lords to send back its Bill without blemish, but the Lords might well vote against it on the second reading. At this point, the Queen intervened. As much as she preferred Disraeli to Gladstone, the monarch would not put up with a constitutional crisis. The Bill went through. The Conservative peers had, for the first time in twenty years, been defeated on an important piece of legislation. But the intervention of the Queen is a reminder that the twenty-first-century debate over the power of the House of Lords has been heard many times. In the nineteenth century, a prime minister could still live in the Lords – but the real power, and the monarch's concern for that power, rested in the Commons.

Certainly for hundreds of years, the Lower House had nursed its right to take decisions, with the 'advice and consent' of the Upper House. In June 1869, the Commons, the Prime Minister and the monarch reminded their Lordships of their duty to give that advice, but above all, that consent, when the Commons so demanded. And so they did. But that, of course, was not the end of the debate. However, Gladstone's government was not a set-piece government, not the sort that had almost casually ruled Britain in the 1850s. It was a government full of imagination, an intelligent administration, a government of ideas.

The judicial system was simplified and modernized and university teaching posts were now thrown open to men of any religious persuasion. And next came the overhaul of the army, the role for Edward Cardwell. The army hated this. In truth, the army had been left to itself since Waterloo, more than half a century ago. Flogging was abolished (in peacetime anyway). And a man could now join up for as little as six years and then go on reserve for six years. But the biggest shock to the military system came when, in 1871, officers found they could no longer buy commissions and the Commander-in-Chief was, for the first time, made subordinate to the Secretary of War. The county infantry regiments were created and soldiers were gradually armed with the new Martini–Henry breech-loading rifle.

There was another question of power under discussion: the monarchy. In October, a plot to kidnap the Queen was discovered. And shortly before Christmas, the government thought there would be a Fenian (Irish Republican) attempt to capture her at Osborne House on the Isle of Wight. Nothing happened and Victoria suspected that the plots were imaginary anyway (although there had, by this time, been five attempts on her life). But since Prince Albert's death in 1861, Queen Victoria rarely visited London and she thought this was a ruse to get her to leave the places she loved, Osborne and Balmoral, and return to her public duties. To many, Victoria had become the invisible Queen.

And when, in 1870, the Third French Republic was declared in Paris, republican ideas spread, albeit momentarily, to England. A rally in Trafalgar Square demanded that the Queen should step aside. In 1871, some Radical MPs began to question the Civil List. They wanted to know why the people paid for the royal children. In Parliament, they wanted to know the reason for handing out money to Prince Arthur, the 'princely pauper' as they called him. In November 1871 the Radical MP for Chelsea, Sir Charles Dilke, said the royal family cost too much and weren't worth it. *The Times*, while condemning what Dilke had said, also noted that his definition of royalty as a 'cumbersome fiction' was, in fact, received with 'great enthusiasm'.

Five months later, Dilke got up in the House to move a motion that there 'be laid before the House certain returns relating to the Civil List'. This was nothing but a way of getting a republican debate. Dilke got his motion listened to, but only two MPs supported him. Dilke (whose father, incidentally had been a friend of Prince Albert) was not really much of a republican at heart. And by the time he spoke, the mood of the nation had shifted back to the Crown. 'A certain sympathy', it was called.

When, in December 1871, Bertie, the Prince of Wales, was struck down with typhoid – exactly ten years, almost to the day, after his father's death from the same illness – the nation waited anxiously for news. So serious was the Prince's illness that the bell ringers of St Paul's were gathered to toll another royal mourning. The Prince recovered, but the republican cause did not.

CHAPTER FIFTY-FOUR

1870–85

In the 1860s the Industrial Revolution put to sea. For shipping, it was necessary to have high-quality steel, not so much to build ships themselves, but to make boilers that could stand enormous pressures, and which wouldn't be too big. The secret that engineers needed to unlock was a technique to use the steam not once, but twice – and that could only be done if the steam was pushed through under enormous pressure.

In 1865, a Liverpool engineer-turned-shipowner called Alfred Holt built three ships fitted with engines that met the criteria and could carry 3,000 tons of cargo – twice as much as the big clippers – as well as plenty of coal, and could steam, at ten knots, for more than 8,000 miles without stopping. This meant that one of these new steamships could get to China and back in about two months. Even in good weather conditions the clippers would take three months, and carry nowhere near that amount of cargo.

And then, in the year that the *Cutty Sark* was built, 1869, the Suez Canal was opened. This gave the new steamships an advantage. By the end of the 1870s only the smaller ships were built of wood. A centuries-old tradition had died. Also about to die was one of Britain's most famous writers, Charles Dickens. In 1868 he returned from a series of gruelling public readings in America. He was in poor health but two years later he began work on his final novel, *The Mystery of Edwin Drood*. He did not live to finish it. Dickens was an optimist who believed that human nature would eventually override the power of the institutions in which he had so little trust. The extent to which he was mourned by the vast middle class suggests that he was far from alone in his belief. One of the first demonstrations of a change in social policy came in the same year Dickens died – in education. The minister who introduced the new Education Act was

William Edward Forster. His Bill was an important advance. Its purpose was to provide more schools, good and active schools inspectors, and religious freedom – a controversial subject if ever there was one. The Church schools could and did carry on, with increased grants, but no local authority money. Most important, this was to be the first time that local authorities had money for education. Local education boards could now put education on the rates. For the first time, children would not be denied elementary education because they came from impoverished families. It was a beginning.

The imaginative reforms of the Gladstone government are said to have drawn the template for the twentieth-century State: education, the law, the Civil Service. But the very brilliance of the Gladstonian changes helped bring about his government's downfall. Real reform means the reform of the institutions that make up the Establishment, and thorough reform creates enemies within the Establishment. So perhaps Gladstone tried to do too much. Certainly the reform of the army came too late to have an effect on the implementation of foreign policy. An illustration of this came in the summer of 1870.

France had declared war on Prussia. There was plenty of diplomatic posturing, but with a run-down army, there really was little that Britain could have done, and so Britain did nothing. No one supported the French, who lost, and the Emperor, Napoleon III, was captured. The Empress escaped to Britain where she made their home at Camden House in Chislehurst, south of London. But the astonishing military efficiency of the Prussian army reinforced the Gladstone Cabinet's belief that the British army had to be restructured and re-equipped as a matter of national urgency. And of equal long-term importance, as a result of the armistice treaty negotiations it was decided that all nations should now recognize William of Prussia as the German Emperor. At home, one of the reforms of the Liberal government was about to work against Gladstone. In 1872 he had introduced the Ballot Act. For the first time in British history, men would vote in secret. In theory at any rate, they would not be pressured by lords or masters, landlords or employers. The Conservatives saw the advantage of good party organization, and Conservative Associations began to appear across Britain. The Liberals began to lose by-elections.

In 1873 Gladstone was defeated in the Commons when he tried to introduce a Bill to set up a new Dublin university at which Roman Catholics and Protestants could study side by side. In January 1874, Gladstone called an election and ran on the platform not simply of tax cuts, but of the abolition of income tax altogether. The voters were not fooled. And so, perhaps thanks to the secret ballot which the Liberals had introduced, the Conservatives came back to majority government for the first time since the collapse of the Tories almost thirty years earlier – which, of course, Disraeli had helped bring about. But, Disraeli, now in his seventies, was tired, gouty and asthmatic, and had wondered aloud to the Queen whether or not he should retire. She persuaded him to stay, but sent him to the Lords as the first Earl of Beaconsfield, which she believed to be a less strenuous place, but from which Disraeli could, as she put it, 'direct everything'. But he could not direct the news of terrible Turkish atrocities in Bulgaria. What happened after the Bulgars joined the rebellion and the Turkish irregular troops, the Bashi-Bazouks, arrived, was indeed a massacre. It's been estimated that 12,000 Christian Bulgarians were killed. The exact figure was never known. Gladstone had been in semi-retirement for nearly two years – since his General Election defeat. When the massacre reports began to circulate he was at Hawarden, contemplating the writings of Thomas Aquinas. He was working on the question of religious and philosophical retribution. Bulgaria called him away from his studies and in three days he wrote what was to become his famous pamphlet, 'Bulgarian Horrors and the Question of the East'. It was this document, or rather the events which prompted him to write it, that brought Gladstone back to front-bench politics.

At the end of 1876, a conference was held in Constantinople that agreed Russian proposals for Turkish reform. The problem was the Turks didn't agree to them. The Sultan, persuaded by the Young Ottoman leader, Midhat Pasha, appears to have believed that recent history would repeat itself – that there would be another Crimean War. Then, in the spring of 1877, the Austrians, ever mindful of the rich pickings of the Balkans, agreed to remain neutral in the inevitable war between Turkey and Russia, as long as they would be given Bosnia and Herzegovina, and that the Russians would promise not to set up a Slav State at the end of the war. So, the war began. The Russians went into the Balkans – the graveyard of so many strategic ambitions. The advance should have been swift but it wasn't. At a place called Plevnia in Bulgaria, the Turks held out until starved into submission.

Gradually, the mood in Britain changed. The nasty Turks who had massacred 12,000 innocent Bulgar Christians were now the heroic defenders. It became, for some, a weekend sport to go along to Gladstone's London house and shout at his windows. By the third week of January 1877, the Russians had reached the gates of Constantinople and the British people resorted to jingoism. In the streets and in the music halls, the strident verses rang out.

> We don't want to fight, but by jingo, if we do,
> We've got the men, we've got the ships, we've got the money too.

The Royal Navy was ordered to Constantinople and Disraeli's government asked for an extra £6 million as a war fund. It all ended at the Congress of Berlin, a conference of the Great Powers. The easy and cynical solution was to carve up the region between them. Russian territory now extended to the mouth of the Danube. Bulgaria received her autonomy. Montenegro, Romania and Serbia were designated principalities. Austria was allowed to occupy Bosnia and Herzegovina, as it had originally demanded. And in a separate piece of diplomatic trading with Turkey, Britain was given charge of a Mediterranean island called Cyprus.

When Disraeli returned from the Congress of Berlin, he claimed he had brought 'peace and honour', and there was one aspect to the settlement which was to have far-reaching consequences in British history. The Russians believed they had been defeated by Bismarck manipulating the other European partners against the Tsar. Gradually, the friendship between Russia and Germany cooled. Not many years into the future this led to an alliance of France, Britain and Russia – but not Germany.

If Disraeli had gone to the country after the Congress of Berlin, he would probably have secured a huge Commons majority. But he didn't because other matters were pressing. And when he did, almost inevitably, the nation forgot Disraeli, the preserver of peace, and Gladstone triumphed. However, Disraeli had cemented a secure place in the affections of the sometimes very affectionate Queen. Disraeli had presented Victoria with the most sumptuous jewel in her Crown. On 1 January 1877, Victoria made a note in her journal that for the first time she had signed herself as Queen and Empress. The imperial Raj was confirmed. In India, it was an occasion akin to the blessing and recognition of a high priestess. The Maharaja of Cashmere, for example, believed it was indeed an auspicious day and the Empire really would be seen as a protective cloak for the people, whatever their caste. Disraeli considered the colonial impression important for Britain's world standing. Most of all, he loved the pomp of the whole affair and delighted in the pleasure his huge sweet-scented imperial bouquet gave his Queen.

Yet imperial triumphs could not hide the need for further reform in Britain. Disraeli's Conservative Cabinet spent much thought on it, and continued the reforms others had started. But, just as Disraeli hadn't been able to find a solution to the problem of the two nations, the haves and the have-nots, in his fiction, nor could he truly find one in real life.

And then, once more, war erupted on two fronts – Afghanistan and Africa – and in one year, Disraeli's popularity had more or less evaporated. There's some evidence to suggest that, even by the 1870s, with their Queen Empress of India, the British were not necessarily well tuned to the idea of imperialism. Perhaps there was too much depressing news at home. The economy was in a more or less terrible state, and there were continuing unsolved difficulties, especially in Ireland. When the election came in 1880, the result was clear enough: Conservatives 240 seats; Liberals 347. The Queen didn't want Gladstone as her Prime Minister. She didn't want anyone but Disraeli and she all but ignored the result of the election. She said that Gladstone would 'ruin the country'. Gladstone had declared that he was loyal to the Queen, that he was devoted, but the Queen could not for one moment bring herself to believe that. And so it was with enormous reluctance, on St George's Day 1880, that Victoria accepted the inevitable.

Gladstone's fight was against what he called Beaconsfieldism. He wanted to undo everything that Disraeli stood for. Disraeli could do little but watch in growing anger. He still directed his party's campaign against Gladstone in Parliament, and there were those who believed that this was the old Disraeli, but the cold white winter of 1880–81 and his asthma were killing him.

On 29 March 1881 he told his friend, Philip Rose, 'I shall never survive this attack. I feel it is quite impossible . . . this is the last of it.' On 29 April, the body of Benjamin Disraeli was entombed in the churchyard vault close by his country home, Hughenden, in Buckinghamshire. Three princes – including the Prince of Wales – six dukes, and a crammed bench of lesser nobles mourned him, as the crimson cushion, on which rested his coronet and his insignia of the Garter, was carried before the coffin on which had been placed wild primroses – flowers sent by the Queen. She was distraught. The man she had once loathed had become her closest confidant. 'The terrible void makes the heart sick,' she said. In 1881 scarcely remembered men were also dying, for their country in Africa.

The First Boer War – or, as it's sometimes known, the Transvaal Revolt – had started. On 16 December 1880, the Boer flag was raised over Heidelberg in South Africa. In February 1881, two months before the death of Disraeli, the Boers cut to pieces the British Army at the Battle of Majuba Hill. In Britain, hardly anyone had expected the revolt of the Boers to be so decisive. There would be some sort of settlement, but only a temporary one. More immediately, Gladstone's Liberal government was faced with a stiffer problem – Ireland.

The terrible storms that had swept the summer pastures and arable crops of these islands at the end of the 1870s and the early 1880s had sent the economy into further decline. Irish tenant farmers were destitute. In one year alone, there were 10,000 evictions. Fury translated into violence. The Irish Land League, formed in 1879 to campaign for the security of tenants and for Home Rule, had, as its President, Charles Parnell.

Parnell was an Anglo-Irish Protestant, who since 1875 had been an MP at Westminster. The strength of the Irish lobby, the 'Home Rulers' as they're sometimes known, was great enough to force the government to agree to put through legislation for compensation for the evicted tenants. But the Bill, at best a half-hearted piece of Parliamentary draughtsmanship, was thrown out by the Lords. The Irish reacted with violence. There were burnings and beatings, and Parnell invented a tactic whose description has remained in the English language. The Irish were not to deal with anyone who dealt with the British. Such a man suffered so effectively that his name slipped into the national dictionary. Captain Boycott could find no one to work for him, no farrier would shoe his horses and no shop would serve him. When he and his family took refuge in the Harman

Hotel in Dublin, the manager made them leave. Boycott became a noun and a verb.

The Home Rule movement wanted to repeal the Act of Union and bring back an Irish Parliament which at least had responsibility for internal government. After the election of 1874, there were nearly sixty Irish MPs sitting at Westminster. After the 1886 election, they held the balance of power. There was, for Gladstone at least, another strand to this. It was the realization that unless some constitutional solution could be found, independence might come about by violent means. The origin of that fear was found not in London, nor in Dublin, but in New York. In the late 1850s, James Stephens formed the Fenian Society in New York. Its aim was Irish independence from Britain. In 1867 the Fenians moved their campaign to Britain. They murdered a policeman and three Fenians were hanged. They then blew a hole in the wall of Clerkenwell jail. Twelve people were killed. The Fenians – or the Irish Republican Brotherhood as they became – eventually faded, but only because they were replaced in 1916 by a new organization – the IRA, the Irish Republican Army. By this time, terrorism, as it is now known, was rife. There was still a viceroy in Ireland, just as there was in India. In March 1881 a Coercion Act was passed to give him absolute power – including what was called, in the later-twentieth-century in Belfast, the power of internment.

Gladstone believed that Parnell remained the key to peace. The majority of the Cabinet believed this was akin to supping with the Irish devil. There were allegations that Parnell had been involved in – or at least approved – the assassinations, but in truth there is little evidence to say that he was. For the next couple of years there was a period of calm, but not for Gladstone. He presided over a Britain trying to recover from economic depression. In 1885, he was defeated on a Budget amendment, and resigned. He then lost the 1885 election to Robert Gascoyne-Cecil, Marquess of Salisbury, partly because his Liberal Party was split. Yet Gladstone had taken one of the most important decisions in nineteenth-century politics. He had become a convert to Home Rule for Ireland. He realized that for Home Rule to come to anything, supporting the Conservatives was more likely to bring it about than attempting to drag his own people through the lobby. What actually happened was a fiasco of political mismanagement. A new Coercion Bill was introduced, and defeated.

Salisbury was forced to resign and Gladstone became Prime Minister again. Within months his Home Rule Bill was before the House. Within days it had been thrown out and so was he. Salisbury was back. The Irish Question was still on the table.

CHAPTER FIFTY-FIVE

1886–1901

Britain had an empire, dominions and colonial dominions. Thus foreign policy occupied nearly as much Cabinet time as did domestic policy. Now, the Cabinet concentrated on the Middle East. Britain and France had joint rule in Egypt that produced an uneasy Franco–British alliance, which reflected a century of competition between the two in the territory that we would in the twenty-first century distinguish as Egypt and Sudan. In the 1880s an uprising led by Colonel Arabi Pasha (1839–1911) warned there was every possibility of a nationalist rebellion in Egypt. Arabi Pasha was an officer promoted from the ranks and came to local prominence during Egypt's war against Ethiopia in 1875. Turkey 'owned' Egypt at this time; it was part of the famous and, for the Egyptians, unpopular Ottoman Empire. Arabi Pasha led, in 1891, a rebellion against the Turkish governor in Cairo. Alarms bells rang in Paris and London and they were forced to respond when the Turks asked for help in defending the governor's position against the rebels. Arabi Pasha was defeated at Tel el-Kebir by Sir Garnet Wolseley (1833–1913), captured and exiled to what was then Ceylon, later Sri Lanka. Rebellion was not confined to Arabi Pasha's ambition. There was also a fanatic of sorts, Muhammad Ahmad, known as the Mahdi, or 'the guided one'. Very quickly the Mahdi had control of most of the Sudan. Gladstone saw the Sudanese rebellion as a 'struggle for freedom'. He decided that it was only right to leave the country, and the Egyptians were forced to agree with him.

To make the decision was easier than to execute it. But on 14 January 1884, General Charles Gordon (1833–85), who had achieved fame in the Chinese Wars of 1859–1860 and 1863–4 when he commanded the Chinese army against the Taipings, left London charged by the Cabinet with the task of evacuation. He arrived in

Khartoum in February, and once there he judged that it would be wrong to withdraw the garrisons and abandon the country to the mercy of the Mahdi's Dervishes. He accordingly asked for reinforcements and put forward plans for counter-attack. He was resolved to remain in Khartoum until his self-imposed mission was accomplished. By May of that year, 1884, Gordon was trapped in Khartoum. Public opinion demanded that he should be rescued. The government, with other matters on its mind and obviously dithering, did nothing until it was too late. At last, Gordon's dilemma became a Cabinet crisis. Gladstone gave in and General Wolseley was ordered to Cairo. He did not arrive in time. When reinforcements and rescue squadrons arrived in Khartoum on 28 October, Gordon was dead and soon would be a martyr.

That was in 1885. In the twelve months between June 1885 and June 1886, Britain had four General Elections. The obvious reason was Ireland, but there was also a lack of cohesion in Gladstone's Liberal Party; the unpopularity of his handling of the crisis in Sudan which led to the death of General Gordon; and the emergence of another generation of political thinkers in the Commons – among them the thirty-six-year-old Lord Randolph Churchill, the leader of the younger Conservatives, and, on the other side of the House, the Liberal rebel, Joseph Chamberlain. Salisbury was Conservative leader in the Lords, and was the man who became Prime Minister. But he was wise enough to understand that the chances of remaining in office were slim. He was right. By January 1886 Gladstone was back in power, armed with his now public crusade for Irish Home Rule. But he needed support and too many in the Liberal Party refused to support him.

Gladstone wanted an Irish Parliament in Dublin. An Irish governing executive was to have control over internal affairs leaving, among other things, foreign policy, defence and custom duties to London. Ireland would keep the vast majority of her own revenues, would have her own judges and a loan fund was to be set up to buy out the landlords. When the Bill was sent to the House, Joseph Chamberlain attacked it, inflicting mortal wounds on Gladstone's Parliamentary draughtsmanship. The Bill was thrown out by thirty votes and Gladstone failed. And when the General Election came, the people voted against him.

The final figures show that the Conservatives had 316 MPs, Gladstone's Liberals had 191, and Parnell 85 Irish MPs. But there were also 78 Liberal Unionists; they were Liberals who stood for the continuation of the Union with Ireland and who had pulled away from Gladstone over this single issue. What had happened was this: led by Chamberlain, the Liberal Unionists, who might well have attracted votes from the growing working-class movement, instead started aligning themselves with the Conservatives. The result was that the working-class vote had no natural home, and this meant there was a very real electoral opportunity for a third British political party. It would be called the Labour Party.

But if Gladstone had little to celebrate, the nation had. It was 1887, a year of great celebration: Victoria had been on the throne for fifty years. The editor of *The Times*, writing on the morning after the anniversary celebrations, was quite overwhelmed:

> No scene was ever depicted on canvas, narrated by historian, or conjured up by a poet's fancy, more pathetic, or more august than the spectacle of Victoria, Queen and Empress, kneeling yesterday at the foot of her throne to thank Heaven for her reign, with all its joys and all its griefs, of fifty marvellous years. The eye wandered over groups of statesmen, writers, orators, famous soldiers and sailors, ermine-clad judges, divines in rarely worn vestments, Asiatic princes gleaming with jewels, forms and faces as fair as they were royal and noble, a bench crowded with Kings and the heirs of Kings. The centre to which the gaze constantly returned as the reason and interpretation of the whole was the figure seated, solitarily [still dressed in mourn-ing] in all that sunshine of splendour, on her chair of state. On her account alone, the rest were there, whatever their degree. They were met together to attest the judgment of Great Britain and the world that Queen Victoria had redeemed the pledge she accepted on that throne, beside the altar, half a century ago.

The party over, the business of government and the closing century beckoned. And Ireland nagged at every political manifesto, partly because positions on Ireland could decide real political support in the House. Salisbury's government, for example, depended on Liberal Unionists who didn't support Home Rule and had broken from Gladstone to say so. And Salisbury's Cabinet was hardly a place of calm and cheerfulness. One of the sources of anguish was Lord Randolph Churchill, the father of the twentieth-century Prime

Minister. He was just thirty-seven and was the youngest Chancellor of the Exchequer and Leader of the House since William Pitt. He had been one of the founders, and then the leader, of the radical Conservative group of younger MPs known as the Fourth Party. It talked about Tory Democracy. This was a programme of party reform. Churchill stirred the fears of the Tory managers.

In December 1886, he presented his Budget to Cabinet. He wanted to reduce taxation but said death duties would rise, and so would estate duties on private houses; and £8 million would come out of the army and navy budget. Unsurprisingly, the War Minister refused to accept the cuts. Salisbury didn't want either to leave, but wouldn't go so far as to overrule his War Minister. Churchill threatened to resign. Salisbury, perhaps to Churchill's surprise, said so be it.

The passing of the old political order at this time was coincidental with the extraordinary shift in social and political movements. The Chartists had heralded social disquiet but had achieved little. Marxism, set to text in London, had never worried the ruling classes for long. But Radicalism now took a new regard. Keir Hardie, a Scot, came to the fore. At the age of ten, he had become a coal miner in Lanarkshire. He stayed in the pits for twelve years until he was sacked. He was an agitator they said, and so he was. By 1886 he had become the secretary of the Scottish Miners' Federation. That was the year that Gladstone was defeated and the Liberal Unionists broke away to side with the Conservatives. Working-class voters saw the popular Liberal Radicals, like Joseph Chamberlain, even though they sat on the Liberal side of the House, as Conservatives. Thus, Keir Hardie had much support when he encouraged the idea of creating a third political party, the Labour Party, instead of relying on the Liberals. And in 1892, Hardie was elected Independent Labour MP for West Ham in London and arrived to take his seat wearing a cap and supported by a brass band. The political face of Britain was indeed changing.

When the final decade of the nineteenth century opened, the Conservative Leader, Lord Salisbury, had been in power for more than four years. His government lacked the sparkle of the Disraeli and Gladstone Parliaments, yet there were achievements including the Local Government Act and the Factory Act. And because the Conservatives thought that some future Liberal administration would make all schooling free, thus destroying the position of the Church schools, they introduced a Bill to make all elementary schooling free. Some Conservative backbenchers denounced that Bill as a 'surrender of Conservative principles'. Yet 83 per cent of school-children would now get free education, paid for by the people, the taxpayers.

It would, in the wording of the Act, be 'a grant in aid of the cost of elementary education in England and Wales at the rate of ten shillings a year for each child of the number of children over three and under fifteen years of age'. Yet Britain was falling behind other nations, and its own ambitions, by not providing a comprehensive secondary education. True, there had been improvements, of sorts. During the previous quarter of a century there were more schools. But there wasn't a central government watchdog and certainly no yardstick for standards. And the new free elementary education was really concerned with overcoming illiteracy, and it wasn't until progress had been made here that secondary education became more imagina-tive. By 1889, the new County Councils were told to provide technical education. This meant new colleges and they became grant main-tained from central government. However, the Royal Commission report stated that the 'educational opportunities offered . . . to boys and girls who . . . leave school . . . are still far behind the require-ments of our times'.

The importance of this Royal Commission report is not that it directly achieved a great deal, but that it led to later reform. This was because one of the Commissioners, Robert Morant, was the draughts-man of the great Education Act of 1902. He made sure that many of the Commission's recommendations appeared in that legislation, the architecture of which survived until the Butler Education Act forty years later. And so, at the beginning of the decade, the Conservatives had introduced worthy but uninspiring legislative programmes. The party managers had wanted trusty Conservative, not Radical Conservative, government and that was what they got.

Gladstone's party seemed full of ideas, but little cohesion. So there was not much of a choice for the British people at the election of 1892, in spite of the Liberal's list of policies published the previ-ous year after the party's conference in Newcastle. It promised Home Rule for Ireland (Gladstone's last ambition), rural government, Parliaments every three years and industrial accident compensation for workers. It was enough, but only just, for a new Gladstone administration and one determined to push through its new Local Government Act that, although partially wrecked in the Lords, would lead to the creation of urban and district councils, and elections to parish councils. Gladstone could never be content with what had happened to such important legislative ambition. On 1 March 1892, Gladstone rose in the House to make a speech which, in effect, marked the end for him as a Parliamentarian. His speech accepted the Lords' amendments to the new Local Government Act, but it gave him the opportunity to wonder at the differences between the centuries-old question of balance between Lords and Commoners.

> The question is whether the world of the House of Lords is not merely to modify, but to annihilate the work of the whole House of Commons, work which has been performed at an amount of sacrifice – of time, of labour, of convenience, and perhaps of health – but at any rate an amount of sacrifice totally unknown to the House of Lords? Well Sir, we have not been anxious – I believe I speak for my colleagues, I know I speak my own convictions – we . . . have been desirous to save something from the wreck of the Session's work. We feel that this Bill is a Bill of such value that, upon the whole, great as we admit the objections to be to the acceptance of these amendments, the objections are still greater and weightier to a course which would lead to the rejection of the Bill. We are compelled to accompany that acceptance with the sorrowful declaration that the differences, not of a temporary or casual nature merely, but differences of conviction, differences of prepossession, differences of mental habit, and differences of fundamental tendency, between the House of Lords and the House of Commons, appear to have reached a development in the present year such as to create a state of things of which we are compelled to say that, in our judgment, it cannot continue.

It wasn't until the Parliament Act of 1911 that any government had the courage to deal with that issue, and curb the wrecking powers of their unelected lordships.

Gladstone had already decided to resign before he made that speech. It wasn't the issue of local government that made him go. He was perhaps angrier with his Cabinet's determination to support a building programme for new battleships. Gladstone the Radical, in old age, hard of hearing and short of sight, retreated to his Liberal instincts that money to be spent on weapons was better spent elsewhere.

But Gladstone was a totally committed European. His was the template for modern Liberal European commitment, and perhaps because of this vision, he never fully believed that the Bismarckian policy of armed peace could usurp the greater ambition of a united Continent of Europe of which, he believed, Britain had to be part.

On 3 March 1894, two days after that speech, he went to see the Queen and resigned. She cared little for him, and was not much bothered. Four years later, William Ewart Gladstone, 'the greatest popular leader of his age', was dead.

Lord Rosebery – mostly remembered as a successful racehorse owner who twice won the Derby during his sixteen months at Number 10 – was reluctant to be Prime Minister. He didn't really believe a Liberal could lead the country from the Lords but the Queen thought this was nonsense. She liked him, perhaps because he was instrumental in the creation of the Scottish Office (of which she much approved), but more probably because he was very careful to take her advice and explain everything to her. Her reign and so an astonishing era in British life was drawing to a close. Yet there was always room for one more war.

By 1896, Horatio Kitchener (1850–1916), the British Commander in Egypt, had set about the reconquest of Sudan and, at the same time, the campaign to avenge the death of Gordon. But hardly were the victory bells silent when bells of quite another calling rang out. For Britain was again at war with the Boers. It was one of those conflicts of which most have heard, yet can't quite place in the historical calendar and most certainly cannot remember why British troops were fighting in Africa. Yet a half-a-million men fought in the Boer War. One in ten were killed or wounded. Most died from disease rather than at a conventional enemy's hand. It was also the war in which the British started concentration camps – a tragedy that was not lost on Germans when a few decades later they were accused of unspeakable war crimes in similar camps. This Boer War was the second war between the British and the Afrikaners, or Boers. *Boer* is the Dutch word for farmer and the Afrikaners were farmers of Dutch origin.

There are three particular characters in the story of Africa, Britain and the Boer War: Cecil Rhodes, Paul Kruger and Dr Leander Starr Jameson. Cecil Rhodes was the man who founded the De Beers diamond company and after whom Rhodesia (now Zimbabwe) was named. He was a parson's son who, as a child, was ill and so sent to South Africa because it had a healthier climate. He made his money out of diamond mining and, in 1889, set up the British South Africa Company to develop the northern neighbouring territories of the Transvaal – which became Rhodesia. Paul Kruger was an Afrikaner. He was the President of the Transvaal. His battle wasn't directly with the British government, but the so-called Uitlanders (outlanders or foreigners), the non-Dutch Afrikaner settlers. They had grievances which he refused to acknowledge. Jameson is perhaps the least known of the three. He was Cecil Rhodes's friend and the colonial administrator. He succeeded Rhodes as leader of his Progressive Party and, in 1904, became Prime Minister of the Cape Colony.

In summary, Jameson, on behalf of Cecil Rhodes, led a raid on the Transvaal in an attempt to overthrow the President, Paul Kruger. This invasion failed, but it worsened relations between Britain and the Afrikaners and the eventual result was the Boer War. Jameson had taken 500 men when he invaded the Transvaal, but the uprising had been postponed although Jameson didn't know that until too late. He and his men were captured by the Boer army, and Rhodes was forced to resign as Prime Minister of the Cape Colony.

The Boers had believed, rightly, that their whole way of life was threatened by Britain and, under Kruger, they began to arm themselves for war. But it didn't come immediately. In London, Chamberlain believed war could be avoided in spite of the best advice he was getting from South Africa. The weakness in Chamberlain's and, to some extent, Rhodes's reading of the situation was that they both failed to understand the determination and grit of Kruger and the Boers. But in autumn 1899, all negotiations were meaningless. Furthermore, both sides had so armed themselves that the threat of war had a momentum of its own. For three years, there were sporadic talks between the British and the Boers and a gradual realization that the outcome of the failure of these discussions would be military confrontation. By the autumn of 1899, the British had reinforced their Natal garrisons to such an extent that Boer intelligence had presented to Kruger a reasonable report of the British military capabilities along the border. It was up to Kruger and his commanders to make the best judgement of the British intentions rather than just their capabilities. It was a classic example of military and political stalemate. Kruger knew what military force was facing him. He now had to decide what the British intended to do with it and how best he should respond with his own resources. Kruger brought his troops up to battle readiness and made sure that the Orange Free State would be allied to the cause. By the beginning of October 1899, he was as ready as he would ever be. On 9 October, Kruger gave the British forty-eight hours to stand down their forces. If they did not, then it would be war. The British did not.

Once again the British were to prove that, in the nineteenth century, their armies either did not have the mindset or the tactical appreciation to succeed beyond the traditional battlegrounds and scenarios of Europe – and even that assessment must be theoretical. Since Waterloo, British forces had not been tested other than in the colonies. The British fighting on a grand scale against an enemy who agrees to traditional military terms represented a considerable and feared force. The British facing an irregular opposition, especially in alien territory, was rarely impressive. British military history from the American War of Independence onwards supported this hypothesis. When adopting similarly irregular tactics, British (mostly junior) commanders could exhibit military wizardry. Now in this Second Boer War, there were moments when the British appeared to have failed to learn the lessons of 100 years of skirmishing. The highly mobile, irregular and committed Boer troops were able to take on the more formal and structured forces of the British.

Before the end of October, Mafeking and the British force led by Colonel Robert Baden-Powell (1857–1941) were under siege. The following month, November, the second famous siege by the Boers, that at Ladysmith, was underway and was not relieved until the last day of February 1900. If there is a distinguishing mark of the Second Boer War, it is a sense there was no memorable set-piece battle. The commando tactics of the Boers made this unnecessary. While not giving an analysis of this war, there are points to be considered that have a bearing on how the Empire was perceived at home and abroad. When Ladysmith was relieved on 28 February 1900, the 22,000 inhabitants of the besieged township had suffered most of their casualties by disease. The British public saw only a military success. In fact, more British soldiers died of disease in the Boer War than by enemy action.

Second, the British introduced into this campaign a draconian tactic which social and military historians would argue over through a century to come. General Kitchener, who was by now commanding the British forces, saw that the simplest way to reinforce his own military strength was to adopt a so-called scorched earth tactic. This meant moving into an area and torching it, so making it uninhabitable. The second stage of this policy was the introduction of concentration camps into which Kitchener ordered mostly civilians, including women and children. In those conditions many died.

Less than a half a century later, Britain was reminded publicly that it was they and not the Germans who had introduced concentration camps into conflict.

The British now appeared to be in the final stage of the war. By the spring, Bloemfontein, the capital of Orange Free State, had fallen and within weeks it was annexed by the British. Towards the end of May 1900, the British invaded the Transvaal and, by July, President Kruger had fled the country. But the Boers had not gone.

They now returned to the warfare they understood best. They mounted guerrilla operations and moved, apparently freely, against British targets including troops and their logistical formations. Anyone who has watched the inconclusiveness of the wars in the twenty-first century in Afghanistan and Iraq would be seeing a repetition and a lesson of the vulnerability of supposedly victorious forces to hit-and-run tactics. It was at this point and because of these tactics that Kitchener scorched the Boer lands and imprisoned the women and children into concentration camps.

When the Boers attacked in greater numbers, as they did, for example, in February 1901 in the Cape Colony, they were defeated. Kitchener pressed on and established killing zones whereby he had pillboxes within gun-sight of each other. Into these killing zones the British forces tactically drove the Boer fighters. By the end of the year there was not much Boer resistance effectively outside north-east Transvaal. By May 1902 there was none at all and a peace treaty was signed.

Having beaten the Boers, what were the British supposed to do with their victory? Around 4,000 Boers had died and about 5,774 British; tens of thousands on both sides had been wounded. The

British had got 40,000 Boer prisoners of war. Presumably, it had been worth it?

The war began in the last years of Queen Victoria. Those who surrendered were now asked to swear their allegiance to her son, Bertie, King Edward VII. That was about all the British demanded of the recalcitrant Boers. None was imprisoned; the survivors were allowed to resume their way of life. The Dutch Reform Church would be paramount, the courts and schools and councils would use Dutch as their first language. True, the Boers were very much part of the British Empire, but the way in which they were administered was to be left to a constitutional commission and even the original British objection to the Boers' treatment of blacks was to be left for further discussion. Little wonder that after the ruthlessness of the conflict there was an impression that it had come to its various conclusions by gentleman's agreement.

This was the final of the wars of the British Empire. There would be further skirmishes, battles, even campaigns that were the result of Britain having had an empire – for example, the war against Mau Mau in Kenya, Communist confrontation in Malaya, indirectly anti-terrorist campaigns in Palestine and Aden and against the separatists in Cyprus. There would, however, be nothing further on such a grand scale.

What was not finished was the consolidation of the remarkable assets of the British in the African continent. Once more we have the reflection that the Empire was built for commercial reasons. The true picture is more complex. The biographies of great industrialists often show that their expansionist ideas were developed not simply because they wanted to make money. There was more than money at stake. The profit and loss accounts reflected power. Often, the famous magnates had visions of expanding power-bases and that the commercial establishment of those bases was the way in which they knew how to work. The multinational corporation is the result of someone originally having a good idea, being even better at exploit-ing it and then finding themselves in the global market-place where people, corporations, ideas and industries are bought and sold until commercial empires emerge. The British Empire is an awesome label. Not only revisionists feel embarrassment and even anger. However, the sentiments of awe and anger are easily found when inspecting any empire, whatever its historical or commercial origins and association. It is worth considering this idea when we think not only how the whole British Empire developed, with its political and strategic imperatives as well as economic incentives, but in its individual parts.

Like the man who famously liked the product and therefore bought the company, a nineteenth-century individual emerged with that same philosophy. Cecil Rhodes could not think small. There is much in his life which suggests it should have been possible to have all of the world held in the hands and name of the monarch. For although the British were never comfortable, constitutionally and militarily in Africa, people like Rhodes appeared to claim commercial, territorial and political success in the way their ancestors might have done if the American War of Independence had gone the other way. Africa, for some, became the America that never was. Rhodes was among that number.

Rhodes represented the surviving instincts of that eighteenth-century Protestant arrogance which demanded the British rule the world and not just the waves. It was as if he believed that individual races could not be protected from broader and imperial ambitions. This was not the survival of the fittest, the corrupt version of the origins of species. Rhodes, for example, saw simply that the fittest would and should rule. The weak would be the servants. Perhaps crudely put, his ruthlessness and grabbing instincts were very useful to British governments. Governments normally prefer uncompromising characters to do their work, even, or especially, when some of it is dirty. Society can then drag down those who successfully carried out their tacit, even implicit, wishes with the charge that it was all very well, but, it might have been done differently. Thus, John Churchill, Duke of Marlborough, the most successful general in British modern history, was vilified – except by his military adversaries. Robert Clive was similarly exposed to the jealousies and high-mindedness of a generation who had grown up very pleased with the glory he had created. Rhodes would later inspire an ambivalence among those who could never quite display the stomach for fulsome exploitation of circumstances. Rhodes, never in poverty, exploited every opportunity to have more, almost for more's sake.

Rhodes was a useful tool for British policy in Africa. One example regards Bechuanaland (later Botswana). This was the home of the Bamangwato people. It lay between two great rivers, the Zambezi and the Orange, so, north of the Cape. In the late 1870s there had been much movement by the Boer settlers and from German explorers and colonists. The view in London was that if this continued, two disturbing possibilities arose: the Germans and the Boers might see the advantages of joining together to oppose British interests and, by doing so, they would control what was then thought to be huge profits to be made from exploiting minerals.

Kruger saw great advantages of having German colonists on his side, which meant making sure that the German government could be relied upon to agree Boer policies, especially against the British. We should not forget the web of dynastic lines that linked Victorian England with Germany. The German in-laws and cousins might be relied upon in Europe – for the moment – but the way of true diplomacy, politics and commerce was more realistically expressed when considering the opportunities for wealth in Africa. After all, it was this emerging Germany that looked jealously at the growth of the British Empire and felt, indeed, like a poor, well-dressed relation.

The two main British interests in Africa were commercial and religious. Rhodes, representing the counting house, saw a German–Boer axis as a direct and physical threat to his ambitions. The missionaries, representing even higher authority, saw a threat to their work. (The combined efforts of the Lutheran Dutch Reform and Calvinistic persuasions rarely ran smoothly.) Rhodes, supported by the Evangelical Church, appealed to the then Prime Minister, Gladstone. Did the British really want the Boers, maybe with the Germans, occupying Bechuanaland? The answer was obvious when, towards the end of 1884, the British moved in a small army and declared Bechuanaland a British protectorate. Bechuanaland itself had no great value; it was what led from it that particularly attracted Rhodes. Five years later, in 1889, in the great tradition of the early British colonists in the West Indies, America and India, Rhodes established the British South Africa Company (BSAC). Africa under British influence now had a series of trading organizations, each of which commanded political as well as commercial influence in London and could so easily decide the futures of whole territories in the continent of Africa. Just as the English East India Company had ruled the sub-continent on behalf of the British, so the likes of Rhodes ran corporations that were established to do exactly that in Africa.

The companies in Africa, including Rhodes' BSAC and the British Imperial East Africa Company, so clearly followed the sixteenth-century patterns of commercial authority. They controlled troops, administrators, district officers and, importantly, the judiciary. They also bought off tribal chiefs. Just as the British in India had paid off princes with lump sums, pensions and promises plus nominal authority, so the British South Africa Company bought the tribal chiefs and kingdoms. When, for example, King Lobengula of the Ndebele handed over rights to exploit the land of his people, the Mashona, he would never again have the opportunity to regain his independence. Lobengula can easily be forgiven for giving so much away. It would take a decade for his people to understand that the few hundred original settlers now ruled their lands in all but name. The consequence was the Matabele Wars. The first one took place during 1883 and 1884. By this time the advances in weaponry were considerable and the Company militia had a fearsome advantage over the traditional warriors. The biggest advantage was the Maxim machine gun. The brochure's description of this weapon's devastating fire power was reluctantly endorsed by the Ndebele. The British had a simple philosophy. The blacks had to be either killed off or herded into central Africa. It was not an exclusive philosophy. There were many in the United States of America who would have nodded sagely at this opinion. There seems to have been little compassion for those commonly (and not necessarily, then, offensively) called niggers. Rhodes thought the 1890s a time to thrash the black Africans until they learned their lesson and began saying their prayers. This did not quite conform to the Christian fellowship of the missionaries.

The lesson teaching was not confined to what was by now Rhodesia. Nor were the Company troops, financed by Rhodes, pink-faced soldiers from Britain. Mercenaries and regular forces had been brought in from outside, including Sikhs from India. Here was the spirit that the British saw as the right way to bring to heel recalcitrant parts of its almost completed empire. It was as if there was some belief of God's calling that the whole continent of Africa had been set aside to be a new Britannia. Could people have imagined a transformation of ancient lands from the Sahara to the southern ocean which, for ever more, would speak English and recognize the monarch in Windsor Castle as its paramount chief? Whether or not successive British governments puzzled over the worth of Empire, the likes of Rhodes and the imperial corporations, they founded had no doubts whatsoever.

This, of course, was not the settlement of the Victorian Empire in Africa. That tale is a bizarre expression of colonial right. The British had gone to Africa as part of the cautious exploration of the more southern latitudes and had discovered it as an economic viable business. Africa was a huge playground peopled by its own controversies of inter-tribal conflict, jealousies and discrimination. The peoples on the banks of the Niger and Congo rivers were as different as those who followed Chaka and disputed the tributaries of the Vaal. The East Africans were as philosophically and physically different as those who lived in the darker and lusher regions of the Great Lakes. Into this enormous playground came the Dutch, the Portuguese, the British and, to a lesser extent, the Belgians, the French and the Germans. The British especially brought with them the motives and capabilities of empire. They were, by then, professional imperialists, if we do not always use that term in a pejorative sense. The Industrial Revolution and expansion of the British Empire produced managers who did what Britain did best in the nineteenth century: commercial development. Even in Africa, the sense of the British had to be expansion. It mattered not that native peoples were caught in this trampling of old orders. Britain might even wish to rule the whole continent as in India and, as in that place, no prince could ever imagine being the overall king. Whatever Chaka's warlike tendencies and arrogance, he would never have been able to summon the resources to have his Zulus rule all sub-Saharan Africa. There was no need for him to do so. He did not have the knowledge of the rest of Africa nor the incentive.

When the Second Boer War ended in 1902, the terms were generous and led to the final agreement in 1906. Within a few days of the war ending, Cecil Rhodes died. Salisbury resigned and his nephew, Arthur Balfour, became Prime Minister.

At the dark point of the conflict, the so-called Black Week in December 1899, the Queen had stiffened the resolve of her government. 'Please understand,' she had said, 'that there is no one depressed in this house. We are not interested in the possibilities of defeat. They do not exist.' But when the news of the final surrender was brought to the monarch, it was brought not to Victoria. The

Queen who had come to the throne in the first half of the nineteenth century was dead.

A young Welsh lawyer, by the name of David Lloyd George, joined the minority of radicals who saw the war as an indictment of Britain's imperialist policies. Around 6,000 troops had died in action, and 16,000 had died from diseases. More than £220 million had been spent. But there was little to suggest that the public at large supported his view. For example the leaders of the Independent Labour Party and the trades unions opposed the war. But they had to accept that predictably the working class they represented was swept up in the general patriotic atmosphere, especially over Mafeking.

When, for example, the Queen visited Wellington College, news had just arrived that the siege had been lifted. Over the college arch was the slogan, 'Welcome to the Queen of Mafeking'. For Victoria, this was the time to be seen. She wanted the people to see her take her daily drives in her coach. Gone was the reclusive Queen who refused to be the people's Queen for so many years after the death of 'Dearest Albert'. And she made clear that she wanted every dispatch, every military and political report of the war, to be on her desk. It was soon known that although she was now eighty, with her eyesight failing and a tendency to nod off after lunch, Victoria read piles of war reports, questioned her ministers, wept for her 'dear brave soldiers', knitted them scarves and, in 1899, sent her troops a personal Christmas present – 100,000 tins of chocolate, many of which remained unopened and more prized than any campaign medal.

In October 1900, the British commanders appeared to believe the war was all but over, yet Victoria did not believe this. She told Lord Salisbury, her Prime Minister, as much. And she said that in the light of her 'great experience' she knew that the British always withdrew too soon and ended up having to send in more troops to sort out the mess.

But Lord Salisbury, encouraged by the advice of the Commander-in-Chief himself, Lord Roberts, decided to exploit the good news of war and called what became known as the Khaki Election. His Conservative government was returned with a big majority – the Boer War factor had done for the Conservatives what another conflict, the Falklands War, was to do for them eighty years later. But by the end of that year it was clear that the old Queen's health was dramatically failing. The first page of Queen Victoria's journal for 1901 makes sad reading: 'Another year begun and I am feeling so weak and unwell that I enter upon it sadly.'

Victoria had kept a daily journal since the age of fourteen. The last entry is dated 13 January 1901. She refers to two of her children, Princess Beatrice and Princess Helena, whom the family called Lenchen:

> Had a fair night, but was a little wakeful. Got up earlier and had some milk. Lenchen came in and read some papers. Out before one, in the garden chair, Lenchen and Beatrice going with me. Rested a little, had some food, and took a short drive with Lenchen and Beatrice. Rested when I came in, and at five-thirty went down to the drawing room, where a short service was held by Mr Clement Smith, who performed it so well, and it was a great comfort to me. Rested again afterwards, then did some signing and dictated to Lenchen.

She died at Osborne, the country home on the Isle of Wight which had remained just as it was when Albert died in 1861. Victoria had given specific instructions: hers would be a military funeral. Also, the Queen who wore widows' weeds for forty years wanted a white funeral. This was probably an idea she took from Tennyson, who once told her that all funerals should be white. And there were instructions that certain precious articles should be placed in her coffin: Prince Albert's dressing gown, a plaster moulded from his hand and family photographs. But there was one item that few ever knew existed. She had told Sir James Reid, her private physician – and no one else – that he was to place a particular photograph in her hand. Not Albert's, but that of her Scottish retainer John Brown. Reid did so, and then, being a man of great discretion and mindful that some believed Brown and Victoria had been secretly married, placed flowers on top of the photograph.

Her coffin was taken by ship, the *Alberta*, to the mainland and, close by Nelson's *Victory*, was borne ashore and thence by train to London and finally to Windsor for the funeral ceremony. The following afternoon she was buried in the mausoleum at Frogmore alongside Albert, for whom she had been in mourning for forty years. And so the Victorian age closed. The population of England, Wales, Scotland and Ireland was forty-one million. There were six-and-a-half million people living in London and more than 160,000 living in Cardiff. The population of Bolton was 168,000 and Glasgow's 900,000. When Victoria died there were more than six million registered voters and more than 1,300 unions with over two million members.

Victoria died a Queen and an Empress, the last Hanoverian, and monarch of the most prosperous nation on earth. But before the new decade was out, Edward VII would be dead and the road to the First World War would be opened.

CHAPTER FIFTY-SIX
A Question of Identity

Towards the end of the nineteenth century, Great Britain was at its colonial and imperial peak. The Empire of India Exhibition had opened in London in 1895. It symbolized much that Victorian England believed it had brought to India. The British saw themselves as beneficent masters who had delivered to the Indians prosperity, happiness, the virtues of mercy and even wisdom – almost as if none had existed before the British in India. Thus, the 1895 exhibition was an extravagant tribute to the British themselves. The sub-continent was Britain's proudest possession. Everything that was good in India was, they believed, because the British had made it so. The eighteenth-century Protestant self importance that urged Britannia to rule the waves had not dimmed a hundred years on. Lord Curzon (1859–1925), the Viceroy from 1898 to 1905, believed that his monarch ruled by God's command and as he, Curzon, was the monarch's monarch in India, then he too ruled by divine order.

George Curzon was one of eleven children of Lord Scarsdale, sometime rector of Kedleston. His family dated itself from the Normans and had lived in Derbyshire since the 1100s. The family home, Kedleston Hall, was an eighteenth-century masterpiece by Robert Adam. Curzon went through the normal education of his breed, being sent to Eton in 1872, where he came under the artistic influence of Oscar Browning, which was just as well for he showed no distinction in pastimes such as sport. Curzon was a natural academic prize winner. He carried this distinction to Oxford where he read classics at Balliol, under the college's master, the formidable Benjamin Jowett (1817–93). He picked up prizes, but confessed bewilderment at his failure to be awarded a first in Greats. His time at Oxford is perhaps an indication of his true interests that he exhibited throughout his political career, which he rather expected to culminate in 10 Downing Street. It may be that Curzon had a particular weakness as a politician in that he was not much interested in politics. Instead, he was inclined to the oratory and classical display of power. This would have made him the ideal colonial governor.

Curzon was in office, with Salisbury's government, in the summer of 1895. He went to the Foreign Office as a junior minister. It was a time when the British were yet again convinced that the Russians were trying to gain influence in India. It will be remembered that the only reason logically to defend British interests in Afghanistan was the belief that the Russians would use that country as a highway into the sub-continent. In 1895, there was quite serious discussion by the British of retreating from the north-west frontier. It was Curzon who eloquently convinced Salisbury's Cabinet that if they put into practice the withdrawal, then the Russians would come in behind. The British stayed. Curzon, in 1898, largely through self promotion and particularly towards Salisbury, was appointed Viceroy of India and created Baron Curzon. It must have seemed appropriate that Government House, Curzon's residence in Calcutta, was based on the family's Derbyshire seat, Kedleston Hall.

India under Curzon (in theory, of course, it was under the Secretary of State for India in the Cabinet) is a good example of proper governorship, rather than the social and largely ineffectual image often painted. Curzon believed he had a mission to redraw the plans and templates of British rule in that place. For much of his adult life (he was then only forty) Curzon had studied India, its history, commerce and strategic value in the whole of Asia from the Bosphorus to the Chinese borders. He fully understood that India was feudal and had to be fairly and efficiently governed, otherwise its peoples would rise against maladministration. Here was a recipe for division among the rulers, but not so much among the ruled. Not surprisingly, there was much political effort to get rid of Curzon. He disturbed administrators in India, who had a charmed way of life. He disrupted their schemes to better that life. If precedent was anything to go by, then this scheming against Curzon might have been enough for him to be conveniently recalled. He could have been given a job in Salisbury's government again, because his Irish peerage would have allowed him a seat. But Salisbury, or maybe his Secretary of State, Lord George Hamilton (1845–1927), understood clearly what was happening and that in spite of the whispering campaign against him, Curzon was right in what he was doing and there was greater silent support for him than there was dissent. Moreover, Curzon, had not gone to India for a rest before claiming higher office at home. If there was an acceptable way to rule colonial peoples, then Curzon, albeit with a reputation for arrogance, managed it. Curzon's time in India was probably the height of the whole British Empire. India was the focal point of that Empire. By 1903, Victoria had been dead two years, court mourning was over and Edward VII once more travelled to India, but this time as Emperor. The grandest of all festivities, the durbar, was held to honour the new King in January 1903. This should really have been the time for Curzon to leave India. It would have been the high note and his reputation would have protected him from most criticism.

Salisbury had retired in 1902 (he died the following year). His nephew, Arthur Balfour (1848–1930) became Prime Minister and, probably unwisely, renewed Curzon's credentials as Viceroy. If Curzon had not stayed, he might have stood more chance of becoming Prime Minister, perhaps following Balfour. Curzon did not see matters going that way. He believed he still had work to do in India and rather hoped that he would be supported from London by the new Secretary of State for India, St John Brodrick (1856–1942). At first he was supported, but the period between the spring of 1904 and 1905 would be a miserable time for Curzon and for British rule in India.

It began with both London and Curzon being faced with the need to reform the governing of Bengal. Curzon's view was that Bengal was too big and too heavily populated to be governed as one province. He wanted to divide it. At first, this might seem simple administrative logic, particularly in the hands of one who had made sure and steady decisions during his time as Viceroy. It left one part of the division with a Muslim majority. The Hindus in Bengal disliked Curzon's decision. It would, in theory, weaken their political strength. This was not a local difficulty. Curzon's reputation as a man who had been sensitive to religious balances, was damaged for all time.[1] There was more to come. This time, there were two areas

---

1   This partition was revoked in 1912. In 1947 Bengal was split between India and the new State of Pakistan.

of contention between the Viceroy, London and the Commander-in-Chief of the army in India, the recently appointed Kitchener.

If this period was the apogee of the British Empire, it was certainly one of the last times that the British felt they had the authority, both politically and morally, to teach savages that they should not mess with imperial masters. Brodrick was an old friend of Curzon's, but he saw the need to retain the ultimate authority for the governance of India in London, not in Curzon's residency. The Viceroy was losing his authority and it was yet again tested, this time by a British general. The British army in India had a commander plus a senior administrator, a sort of adjutant general. As we have seen, the Commander-in-Chief in 1904 was Kitchener (appointed 1902). Kitchener did not like the idea of having a major general as a joint administrator of the Indian army; he wanted to be commander-in-chief of everything military. The general's further objection was that the other administrator was also a member of the Viceroy's Council. This had always worked and the double authority had been strengthened by Curzon, who believed that the Commander-in-Chief should be responsible for war-fighting capabilities and that the major general on his council (the one Kitchener objected to) should be the much needed logistician. Moreover, if the Commander-in-Chief was campaigning, then the Viceroy would have at his side an immediate military adviser. Kitchener was not the sort of man to delegate the authority of his command, especially as, the way he saw it, a junior general would be in a position to influence the Viceroy while he was not there. Curzon said that the system had worked perfectly well before Kitchener's arrival in 1902 and so he rejected the famous general's demand.

Generals rarely become famous without having a grasp of tactics, both military and political. Kitchener thus lobbied the political hierarchy in London. St John Brodrick was won over. At the time that Curzon discovered what was happening, he was in England, where his American wife, Mary, was seriously ill. Kitchener had got his way, but then said he was going to resign. He was out to ruin Curzon. He knew that a threat of his resignation would be close to devastating for Balfour's unpopular administration. Curzon returned to India just before Christmas. In the following spring, 1905, he led his Viceroy's Council in rejecting any plans to scrap the military department and thus Curzon's major general. Kitchener had anticipated this and, determined to see the end of Curzon, had already primed his London supporters who forced the government, in spite of civilian and military advice, to support Kitchener. Brodrick wrote to Curzon, by now no longer his close friend, that the Viceroy's Council could no longer have anything but a very weakened military department. There now came about a curious ploy from London. It was clear that the government wanted to get Curzon out of India, but to do so without being seen to dismiss him. That would have caused ructions in India and in the British press, which the government did not believe it was popular enough to disregard.

Kitchener, still in India, appeared to be backing down from his original demands. Then, within a few weeks, he went the other way. The test came when Curzon nominated a new major general as his military member of the committee. Brodrick vetoed the nomination. Curzon had no option but to resign. He stayed long enough for a visit by the Prince of Wales, then left. Earlier, we noted that Curzon was a better orator than he was a politician. He had been politically outwitted, although it was partly his own fault. Curzon should have gone in 1903. If he had, he might have become Prime Minister. The business of publicity and Kitchener's politicking did not save Balfour's government. It went in 1905, largely due to an argument over tariffs, to be replaced by the Liberals led by Sir Henry Campbell-Bannerman (1836–1908).

That is very much a small part of the British in India. It is meant to show that even at its height, the Raj was vulnerable to personal bickerings and ambitions. Moreover, Curzon's leaving was not going to excite the sub-continent. Lord Minto (1845–1914), who replaced him, was not a remarkable man but he did make an important contribution to the government of India. Just as Hamilton, as Secretary of State, and Curzon had worked well together, and Brodrick and Curzon should have done, so Minto was supported by his Secretary for India, Viscount Morley (1838–1923). Minto had been Governor General of Canada for six years until 1904 and so he was used to colonial administration. With Morley's complete support, he put in place the Morley–Minto Reform, which set the way Indians were brought into the various ruling bodies of their own country. So, for example, elected members, both Hindu and Muslim, joined the Viceroy's Council, all the provincial councils and the Legco, the legislative council. This reform was in place by 1909 and once more reflected the political awareness of a middle class in India which had, especially following the development of the Indian National Council of the late 1880s, become an obvious part of the future governments of India. There are times when it is wrongly seen that there was no independent political movement until the arrival of Mohandas Karamchand Gandhi (1869–1948). The politics of India, as we would see them today, took on a recognizable role far long before Gandhi left Africa.

The 1909 reforms were surely clear indication that the time was not far off when the Viceroy should go for all time. It may be that two world wars delayed that moment. Equally, it would be interesting to speculate if there had been no wars, would Britain's role in the world have much changed and would the inevitable agreement for India's independence have arrived sooner? The British described India as a miracle of the world, meaning that they had created this wonder. In the early twenty-first century, we might say that the parade of elephants, silks, jewels and princely images at Earls Court in the 1896 exhibition did not include the social distinction that kept the Queen's hopefully loyal subjects at arm's length from the by then 100,000 British administrators and military. If we thought that way, then we should remember the times; that same social and bureaucratic apartheid was practised in Britain.

Officialdom and the ruling classes – whether administering the nation or industry – maintained a barrier between the ruler and commoner. Edwardian Britain was a society in which the common man would call his doctor, his parson, his schoolmaster and certainly his master, Sir. That was simply the way of the British world. There was absolutely no reason why matters might be any different in India. This was a British society, for example, which would during the Second World War stop the pay of a British merchant seaman once he took to the lifeboat having been torpedoed during the Battle of the Atlantic. The Raj reflected the character of the British, most of whom were no different in their master–servant relations than any other nationalities.

To some extent Britain was the servant. It was committed to its Empire and most certainly needed the sub-continent because it was a captive market for British industry. The nineteenth century had seen the grand expansion of British industry, particularly manufacturing. Britain was the first to take advantage of its home-developed

Industrial Revolution. Technology had made almost every process of manufacturing simpler, more efficient and, therefore, capable of greater production. Greater production capability was only viable if there were increased sales. The expansion of a modernized cotton industry needed huge markets. The history of colonization contained a continuing effort to provide tariffs and incentives for British goods to be sold into the colonies. The seventeenth-century adventures in North America had been seen as opportunities for English goods. The eighteenth century had seen enforced purchasing regulations by the colonies. The juggling of protection values had directly caused the animosities in North America that led to the symbolism of the Boston Tea Party. In the nineteenth century, British manufacturers wanted India as a market place for its goods. By the second half of the century, the British economy *relied*, not exclusively but urgently, on India. By the Edwardian period, almost two-thirds of imports to India came from Britain. Some 60 per cent of shipping in Indian ports were flying the Red Ensign. Perhaps as much as a half of the hidden services, such as insurance from India were going through the London markets.

Equally, India was not alone in supporting the British economy. Colonial holdings in the Far East, south-east Asia, Australasia and Africa were proving that without an empire, Britain would have been much poorer, perhaps even poor. Curzon may not have got it right when he claimed that God's hand was on Britain's colonial existence. He might, however, have made a reasonable case that there was some providential economic guidance. This then was the position at the start of the twentieth century when Britain ruled a quarter of the global population, carried as much as half of the world cargoes in her ships and one-third of global exchanges, finances and insurances facilities went through offices in just one square mile of the capital of the British Empire, London. It would take decades for the British to get used to the idea that striding in mastership of much of the world required an economic, political and constitutional gait that was a spectacle of an earlier, not a present age.

The British were evolving a new ruling class, which emerged as a second generation from the relatively new public schools system born from the nineteenth-century industrialists who wanted their sons to have classical and not technical educations. At the other end of the social scale, in 1904, in an effort to encourage socialist and trades union adult students the Workers' Educational Association was found by Albert Manbridge (1876–1952) to bring together existing voluntary adult education forms. Workers' education was not a new idea. Eighty years earlier, George Birkbeck (1776–1841) had established the London Mechanics' Institution (later, Birkbeck, University of London). These progressions were for a predominantly masculine-run society long questioned by women activists. For example, when Emmeline Pankhurst (1858–1928) founded the Women's Social and Political Union in 1803, she was following a calling of one of the first women's rights movers, Mary Wollstonecraft (1759–97) in 1792 with her publication, *Vindications of the Rights of Women*. The nineteenth-century movement for women's suffrage was unsuccessful in spite of the 1882 Married Women's Property Act and the championing of the cause by leading politicians and radicals of the second half of the century. What was emerging in the early twentieth century was something similar to that which came about in the early years of the nineteenth century – an instinct for reform. Trades unions were increasingly powerful, so much so that in 1906 the Trade Disputes Act appeared on the statute book to bring some order and anticipate disorder in the relatively new area of industrial relations, with management facing politically attuned and affiliated organized labour. The streets of Britain's towns and cities were changing shape with more pillar boxes, lamp-posts, kerbs, drain covers and, most of all, the common appearance of motor vehicles with the first motor buses in London in 1905.

If reform was evident in almost all the forms it had taken in the early 1800s, there was one huge difference. Many of the early nineteenth-century reforms took place in a society undergoing industrial, social and religious revolution (the 1829 Catholic Emancipation Act was an example) following a long and wretched war with France. Now, the British had to anticipate a war on a scale never before imagined.

In 1914, the Great War, or the First World War as it became called, broke out. The build-up was a long affair. It was a war between the Alliances: the Triple Alliance of Germany, Italy and Austria–Hungary on one side and the Triple Entente of Britain, France and Russia on the other. The German–Austrian alliance was obvious and reasonable being of a common language and traditional allies in Europe. Austria was in deep political and military uncertainty in the Balkans and Germany was its natural ally. Italy saw no option but to join Germany, the most powerful nation in Continental Europe. Each signed to come to another's help if that State were to be attacked – one for all and all for one. The Triple Entente was less formal. There was no treaty, only a friendly understanding. As allies, Britain and France made some sense, in spite of their history as enemies. The French were said to have a big and powerful army (it turned out that big did not mean powerful) and the British did not; the British undoubtedly had a powerful navy. As for the Russians, their inclusion in the Triple Entente was far more a factor of late nineteenth and early twentieth century values and responsibilities. Russia was tied to Britain through the blood relationship of the royal families, although similar family ties between Germany and Britain did not draw them together. If Germany had a particular fear of the British, it was the size of the Empire. Bismarck's legacy in German consciousness was that possessions were indicators of greatness and therefore power. German insecurities twitched whenever the British Empire, at its most powerful, remember, was mentioned; from all this, a drift to war, while not inevitable, did have some sense of fatalism about it.

The rivalry in the Balkans between Russia and Austria–Hungary was tripped when Archduke Franz Ferdinand, the heir to the Austro–Hungarian throne, was assassinated at Sarajevo. At the time, the event held no major interest in Europe. However, interest was heightened when Austria–Hungary declared war on Serbia. Russia, holding the notion as it had ever had that it was the guardian of the Orthodox Christian Serb tradition, allied itself with Serbia. The Germans, allies of Austria–Hungary, declared war on Russia and therefore on Russia's co-entente ally, France. Germany then invaded Belgium, which was allied to no one although Britain had an agreement to go to its aid and did so. In the simplest terms, with no apologies for its unsophisticated explanation, that is how it all began. But if this were seen as a European affair, how did it become styled as a world war?

The Turks, the Ottoman Empire, joined the Germans and so the campaign spread to the Middle East and, in particular, Mesopotamia (Iraq) in November 1914 – it was a campaign that would continue until 1918, when it was terminated by the success of General Edmund

Allenby (1861–1936). At sea, the naval war was almost exclusively between the Royal Navy and the German High Seas Fleet. The British victory off the Falklands Islands in December 1914 meant the Germans were defenceless against British advances on German territories in the Pacific and their African colonies. The main German naval threat to the British and allies came through the latest addition to naval warfare, the submarine. The German U-boats were responsible for the loss of some 6,000 vessels. This was partly Britain's fault and continued to be so until it introduced the convoy system that meant vessels could not so easily be picked off one by one.

In May 1915, the passenger ship *Lusitania* sailed from New York. On board the 32,000-ton Cunard liner were Americans. Nearing Ireland on 6 May the *Lusitania* received U-boat warnings from the British Admiralty. She was attacked on 7 May and took just eighteen minutes to sink: 1,253 passengers died – 128 of them Americans. Many in the British War Cabinet thought that would be enough to bring America into the war. It was not. Submarine warfare did bring America into the war but not until 1917 when the Germans resumed its unrestricted, shoot-on-sight U-boat policy – and sunk the American grain ship, *Housatonic*. Three weeks later, on 25 February 1917, the Germans sunk the *Laconia*; four Americans died. On 6 April, America declared war on Germany. It was the turning point the European allies had waited for.

This four-year conflict was very much a conflict of new and advanced weapons. The machine gun was not a new system, but its latest version on both sides meant infantry stood little chance and were cut down in the battalions as they went over the top. However, the most feared weapon was poisoned gas. The French used it first in the form of not entirely lethal xylyl bromide grenades. The terrible threat of gas was that it made soldiers more vulnerable to any fighting because they were encumbered in gas masks and capes and, when 'hit' by gas, could take a very long time to die so their units were not effectively fighting while coping with gas casualties. Perhaps the decisive new weapon was the tank. It added mobility although many British commanders did not like it as they saw it entirely against their cavalry instincts. The first tanks were used in the Battle of the Somme in 1916. They were not then particularly successful, but this was only the start of the tracked vehicle that would replace the charger with often devastating effect and with the added advantage that, once they took the ground, the tanks were portable artillery that could hold it.

What turned the war? Probably the American intervention. In November 1917, with American troops 'over there' Passchendaele was finally taken at the third Battle of Ypres and in September 1918, the year the Royal Air Force was formed from the Royal Flying Corps (RFC), the since vilified General Douglas Haig (1861–1928) broke through the Hindenburg Line. On 11 November 1918, the armistice was signed. Probably ten million soldiers on all sides never lived to know that.

In 1919, Lady Astor left her house in St James's Square for Parliament. She was to take her seat as the first woman to sit as an MP. It was hailed as the most significant Parliamentary moment since the Reform Act of 1832. Yet the period that followed was hardly a time of post-First World War rejoicing. It seemed clear, even as the Treaty of Versailles to formally end the war was signed, that another conflict between Britain and Germany was likely, if not inevitable. The French determination to enforce crippling economic and territorial reparations against Germany (which incidentally had been allowed to march home with its army intact) rang few bells of satisfaction among the allies. Pushing the Germans to the very brink of a new and dangerous nationalism was not really what the post-war period was best used for.

The formation of the IRA, the Irish Republican Army, seemed small beer compared with what could happen in Continental Europe. Not that the government of the British Isles was indifferent to what was happening in Ireland. In 1914, the Irish Home Rule Bill had got through Parliament, but because of the war had not been enacted. Tens of thousands of Irishmen joined their regiments to fight the Germans. Thousands of them returned home and promptly volunteered for the IRA. When, in 1920, the Government of Ireland Act offered to partition six north-eastern counties of Ireland from the rest of the island and give both sections parliaments, the southern Irish said 'No'.

In March 1920, the first units of the 8,000 soon to be notorious Black and Tans were sent to Ireland from England. This was a unit of often ill-disciplined and tormenting former soldiers (most of whom could not find jobs in post-war Britain) sent in to reinforce the

Royal Irish Constabulary in what the British government warned them would be a 'rough and dangerous task'. They were called Black and Tans because there were too few uniforms for them, so they wore a mixture of army khaki and police blue/black. The theory was that they would take on the IRA. The tried and they failed. Also, acts such as their shooting twelve civilians in Dublin at a football match at Croke Park only recruited sympathizers, if not members, for the IRA. By the following year, 1921, the Irish Free State created by the December Anglo–Irish Treaty gave the twenty-six counties of Ireland the sort of dominion status held by Canada inside the British Empire. Not surprisingly, the hard-line Republicans, including the IRA, would have nothing to do with this Free State and so Ireland burst into a civil war that lasted until 1923. As for the six north-eastern counties, they too wanted nothing of the Free State. Instead, they opted to be a self-governing province within the United Kingdom – here in 1921 was the start of what we call Northern Ireland and, the beginning of the Republican demand: 'Give us back the six counties.'

If we see Ireland during this period as a challenge to British Establishment authority, which it had been consistently since the sixteenth century, so it was a time to reassess the role of that Establishment. Britain had been ruled by its aristocracy since the thirteenth century. Aristocracy did not always mean titles and honours. The aristocracy was the group, usually families, in British society that assumed the right to rule and/or the dynastic responsibility to do so. When individuals emerged, they were never ordinary, usually powerful or stand-ins during an interregnum – the nineteenth century saw a lot of this. If there is a moment when the ruling class (a general term, but without detailed analysis, reasonable anyway) began to give way to a new style of political influence and persuasion, it was probably in 1916 when H. H. Asquith (1852–1928) failed as a Liberal Prime Minister and as a war leader. He was replaced by the Liberal munitions minister and Secretary for War, David Lloyd George (1863–1945). His reputation was made during the seven previous years as a reforming Chancellor of the Exchequer. His harsh 1909 'People's' Budget included social reforms and super-taxes on those with earnings higher than £3,000. The Lords blocked his Budget. Two elections followed but the decider was the 1911 Parliament Act that reduced the powers of the Upper House. That

Act was passed by their Lordships only when the King made it known that if they did not, then he would swamp the Lords with new Liberal peers to get the majority to bulldoze through the Bill. By voting for the Bill, the Lords were only allowed delaying powers on money Bills and they lost the authority to vote out public legislation other than Bills that would have extended the life of the Parliament – and thus the government.

Lloyd George is usually included in lists of the top three twentieth-century Prime Ministers. But he did preside over the end of the Liberals as a predominant Parliament power. When he replaced Asquith, many Liberals refused to serve under him. The Liberal–Conservative coalition was dominated by the Tories. A month after the signing of the Armistice, Lloyd George went to the country. He was opposed by his own Liberals who still favoured Asquith but, thanks to the Conservatives, Lloyd George won. It was not much of a peace. The land fit for heroes was not fit enough to find employment for four million demobbed soldiers; it was not politically peaceful because so many objected to the Irish settlement and, publicly, very many indeed were scandalized by the number of people who had received honours for making donations to the election campaign treasure chest. Then, in 1922, the coalition collapsed. The Conservatives pulled out. Lloyd George was finished as a national leader and resigned. Asquith returned as Liberal leader in 1923 for three years and Lloyd George between 1926 and 1931, but he and the Liberals were a spent force.

When Lloyd George went in 1922, the Tory, Andrew Bonar Law (1858–1923) became Prime Minister. He was not a well man. He had already retired once through ill health. Now in October 1922, having helped bring down Lloyd George, he went into Number 10 as a not particularly significant fellow and lasted only until May 1923. He died that year. Stanley Baldwin (1867–1947) followed him into office and so started a prime ministerial career of a far higher calibre national leader than many in the twenty-first century give him credit. He would steer the Tories through the hectic and uncertain years of economic decline and National Government that led into the Second World War. However, the important British political moment at the start of the 1920s was the appearance, for the first time, of the Labour Party as Her Majesty's Official Opposition when Lloyd George went in 1922. It was also all change elsewhere: that same year, Benito

Mussolini (1883–1945) became Prime Minister of Italy and Stalin (Iosif Vissarionovich Dzhugashvili,1879–1953) became General Secretary of the Communist Party of the USSR.

The strength of the Labour Party in the 1920s marked the significant political change of the twentieth century. Under Ramsay MacDonald (1866–1937) the first Labour government (1924) may have been short-lived, but it was now seen to be a party worth voting for. Baldwin was again Prime Minister when the Labour administration could not continue. Whatever the political leadership and brilliance of individuals, none could duck the force of the economic collapse that buried Britain's business and individual finances in the 1920s. The General Strike of 1926 was never as dramatic as now pictured, but it illustrated the sense of hopelessness throughout the nations. There was no big idea like the United States' New Deal to get Britain back on its feet – nor were there resources to create one. And so, officially, in 1929 the Great Depression began.

The Depression began with Black Tuesday in October 1929, when Wall Street crashed. Two years later, the world was deep in the worst economic recession in history, caused by land price collapses, too many loans to people who could not repay, too many goods made for a nation that increasingly could not afford them. In the United States, thirteen million were unemployed. The Depression disease spread. The United States had too many banks (5,000 or so closed down) making unrepayable loans in Europe, including the United Kingdom. The money had been borrowed partly to pay off debts from the First World War although Britain had for the most part used sales from its own foreign assets to pay for the war effort. Nevertheless, because it had lost so many foreign exchange assets, Britain was not immune when the American banks called in the loans and pressure was placed on European banks. They could not take the financial strain and many collapsed.

One aspect of Britain's slump in the late 1920s was a poor decision made in 1925 by the then Chancellor of the Exchequer, Winston S. Churchill – long since back in the Conservative Party from which he had jumped to the Liberals in 1904. Churchill, in April 1925, restored the pound sterling to the gold standard; but he took the Bank of England's advice and he did so at its pre-war rate of $4.86. This made British exports prohibitively expensive. Unemployment doubled to at least 2.5 million. The knock on from this was a lowering of wages. This provoked the 1926 General Strike.

By 1930, investors were running from British deals, and the briefly returned Labour government could not cope. The Labour leader, Ramsay MacDonald, had to accept that Britain had to have a National Government with the Liberals and the Conservatives. The Labour Party saw MacDonald as a traitor to the party's cause. In 1931, the General Election saw Labour decimated at the polls. But the National Government continued – with Baldwin and the dominant Conservatives. A Budget of draconian cuts in spending and wages, along with rises in income tax rates, had the opposite result than was intended. Deflation ran through industry, commerce and finances and, because of Churchill's decision on the gold standard, gold was being sold. On 21 September Britain left the gold standard and the pound dropped from $4.86 to $3.40. The pound was now more realistically priced and began a slow recovery. It was just as well; by 1936 with the rise of Hitler's Nazi Germany, there was, once more, a whiff of war in the political air. Certainly industry would benefit from the unstable nature of near foreign relations: the government started a rearmament programme.

For many economists and political scientists, the Second World War was inevitable because economic pressures (partly engineered by French demands on post-First World War Germany) and often political humiliation had encouraged German nationalism. We should always remember that Hitler was elected. Certainly the war came because the 1919 Treaty of Versailles failed and, indirectly, because the League of Nations could never survive without the United States; the historical irony was that an instinctive post-First World War United States could never follow the enthusiasm of its President Woodrow Wilson (1856–1924) for such a body – it was his idea – that could prevent war and the horrid slaughter of that witnessed during 1914–18. Also, Germany was not allowed to join the League in 1919 as it was considered to have started the First World War and therefore was an aggressor; and nor was Russia, as it was a Communist State and so therefore a potential aggressor. The standing procedures, rules and protocols amounted to a very inept piece of political and constitutional draughtsmanship. Whether or not a better format could have stopped Hitler is impossible to know; certainly without the United States enthusiastically on board, it is unlikely that it would have.

It is not this volume's place to give an account of the Second World War. It is best said that the reasons for the war and why it was a *world* war are briefly as follows:

In 1937 Japan invaded China. The victors of the First World War badly handled the European peace. German nationalism increased. In 1939 Germany invaded Poland, a State supported by the British. President Wilson's 14-point peace plan was never accepted by the Europeans and Congress never accepted his idea to join the League of Nations. There is evidence that the German people felt the peace had let them down. The liberally inclined German Weimar Republic tried to govern Germany between 1919 and 1933 although it did put down Hitler's coup attempt in 1923. Hitler assumed the Chancellorship in January 1933 and within three months had total control of Germany. In March 1936, ignoring international treaty law, Hitler took over the Rhineland. In 1938, Austria was annexed as part of Germany. The British and French had opposed the annexation (the Anschluss) but were powerless to stop it. Moreover, Hitler was demanding the integration of German-speaking Sudetenland, which included a large part of Czechoslovakia (Bohemia), with Germany. In Munich, September 1938, the British Prime Minister Neville Chamberlain (1869–1940) accepted the limited annexation so that some form of peace would be preserved. This was seen by many as appeasement. In return, Hitler promised he would make no further territorial claims in Europe. In March 1939, Germany ignored any Munich agreement and invaded Prague. In August 1939, German and Russia signed a non-aggression treaty known as the Molotov–Ribbentrop Pact after the signatories. Neither country trusted the other and were right not to do so. The Pact simply allowed Russia and Germany to divide up Finland, the Baltic States and Poland between them. Germany invaded Poland on 1 September 1939. Britain and France declared war. Russia invaded eastern Poland on 17 September. The world was at war. (This ignores the wars between Russia and Japan, Italy and Albania and so on but sets a simple timetable of events for our parochial purpose here.) A few points remain to be mentioned:

1940
Churchill becomes Prime Minister
Battle of Britain
Rationing introduced

1941
Operation Barbarossa – Germany attacks Russia
Pearl Harbor. US enters war

1942
Auschwitz exterminations start

1943
Germany surrender at Stalingrad
Allies succeed in North Africa
Battle of the Atlantic starts

1944
Anzio landings
D-Day

1945
Russians enter Berlin
Hitler suicide
Germany surrenders, 7 May
Roosevelt dies
Truman becomes US President
Labour wins British General Election
Atomic bombs on Hiroshima and Nagasaki
Japan surrenders, 14 August
War ends

The war had changed Britain visually, socially and politically. Cities
were scarred with bombsites, purple buddleia sprouting incongru-
ously from upper floors of gaping tenements. War debris, from
rusting machinery to no longer needed Anderson shelters, littered
every city, town and village in England at least. Until 1947 certainly,
women's fashion had barely shifted from the late 1930s and even the
Princess Elizabeth had to count coupons for her wedding clothes.
While horses still plodded furrows, the biggest revolutionary sight in
agriculture, the tractor, was now to be seen throughout the land, but
the new ideas of farming that the diligent but too often forgotten Agriculture Minister Tom Williams (1888–1967, later Baron
Williams of Barnburgh) was bringing about were not yet paying

dividends. Bread was rationed now, but had not been during the war. A common enough admonition to peckish mouths was muttered at kitchen and dining tables throughout the land, 'Careful! That's butter.' The people knew the value of 'bread and scrape' just as they became used to the phrase 'War Damage' as repairmen and builders scrapped for permissions and resources to patch up and rebuild the austere and make-do society that came out of the 1939–45 conflict. It was a society that understood that the cost of war had left Britain on its uppers. The adage 'To the Victors All' did not ring true. Most significantly, immediate post-war Britain was dominated by politics and ideological ambition. There had never been, in British political history, a more significant step-change than that of the election of the Labour government of Clement Attlee (1883–1967).

Attlee was not a cloth-cap caricature of the Labour Party as many of the Conservative nomenklatura would have wished him to be seen. He was a public-school man (Haileybury) who after Oxford was a London School of Economics lecturer and convert to the socialism of William Morris and John Ruskin. His political formative years were as Mayor of the London borough of Stepney and in 1922 he was elected as MP for Limehouse. He refused to serve in the National (coalition) Government but by 1935 had become leader of the Labour Party. For the first two full years of the war, he was Lord Privy Seal under Churchill and later Deputy Prime Minister and Lord President of the Council. In 1945, he became the first Labour Prime Minister with an overall Commons majority. Under Attlee, Britain's home and foreign policies changed out of all recognition. The pattern was set for colonial independence, Britain became a founder member of the North Atlantic Treaty Organization (NATO) and the United Nations (UN), and the country went to war in Korea. At home, the social revolution was accomplished by the 1950s – nationalization and the welfare state. Under Attlee, the government did everything that a Churchill government would not have done.

The story of the 1945 General Election has two strands: Churchill's political miscalculation and the British people's demand for better times. Churchill utterly misjudged the people; he totally failed to believe that the voters would abandon their hero of the Second World War. There is anecdotal evidence that many who voted Labour believed Churchill would be Prime Minister – perhaps a hangover of a generation living with National Government. However, it became manifestly clear that the British wanted change. They remembered the miserable economic times prior to the war; they had fought for freedoms and better times and Attlee offered a radical future whereas Churchill only offered Churchill and promises of a welfare state that the people did not believe he would provide if he stayed in office. Churchill was a symbol of much that was fine, but he was nothing more than that and proved so when he eventually returned to power to loud cheers but few new ideas that would continue the truly radically different way of life that Attlee had shown.

During the war, the 1942 Beveridge Report of the sometime director of the London School of Economics (LSE) William Beveridge (1879–1963) detailed the national insurance system that would fund a National Health Service (NHS), social security benefits and State-funded pensions, developed from the non-contributory and means-tested pensions of Lloyd George in 1908. Here was the prospect of a cradle-to-the-grave compassionate welfare state that swept Attlee into power. But how did the people react to Labour's idea of mass nationalization? Was there not a little thought that this was socialism too far? Certainly crusted Conservatives felt that was the case but the general electorate had just lived through five years of State control and so nationalization did not appear such a constitutional ogre. The millions of servicemen and women were far more inclined to vote Labour. They had a sense that change was all they wanted; anything but the life that had promised little or nothing.

Labour won 393 seats, the Conservatives 210 seats and the Liberals 12 seats – only 9 per cent of the vote. Attlee's team had the freedom of a massive majority. Everything they wished to do was possible. Ernest Bevin (1881–1951), the General Secretary and founding member of the Transport and General Workers' Union before the war, became a distinguished Foreign Secretary and European mastermind of the founding of NATO. Aneurin Bevan (1897–1960) was the far Left Health Minister who set up the National Health Service (and resigned over cuts in the Service in 1951). Ellen Wilkinson (1891–1947), the Education Minister, is another too often forgotten Labour figure. She failed to get the education reforms she thought essential and the right of the young English and Welsh, including raising the school leaving age to sixteen – a most radical (and expensive) idea of the time. However, she drove through much of the school reforms imagined by the Butler Report during the war.

Yet it was not enough. A sometimes erratic personality, Wilkinson died from an overdose.

The Left wing of the party did not quietly get on with the job of government. It demanded what were sometimes seen as extreme reforms and Attlee, with Ernest Bevin's help, could barely control their demands. It was as if the revolutionaries had, at last, come out of the bush and down from the mountains, only to find their leader too wrapped in a respectable cloak of burdensome office. Whatever their disappointments, the single effort of nationalization – taking industries and services into public ownership – was in the election manifesto and would not be forgotten. The coal mines, employers of 700,000 workers, fell into public ownership; so did iron and steel, transport, including the railways (almost immediately becoming inefficient), hospitals (part of the emerging National Health Service) and even the Bank of England. Here was the establishment of new bureaucracies and bewildering inefficiencies.

The institution of State-run industry should have reassured future populations. It did not. When, later on, Thatcherism sold off much of what had been nationalized, there was not glorious hope that all would be better. The British had lost interest, and therefore faith, in many of their most important institutions. That was a legacy of the Second World War. The 1945 electorate hoped that all would be well in the changed world. They soon became disillusioned, then cynical and then indifferent. By the time of the Me Society attributed to Thatcherism, the English (not the Scots, Welsh nor the Irish) were losing their identity anyway. Much of the post-1945 disillusionment had a great deal to do with the single fact that the islands were penniless. Yet there was a sense that Britain wanted to have a social revolution without really rethinking and making an effort. This was partly because of the relative lack of destruction in England especially. True, cities and industries were bombed and thousands killed. Yet, there was always something obvious in the debris. Unlike Germany, a nation and a State having to rise from its own ashes with half its people in Stalinist Eastern Europe, the British were not so crushed that too many could simply think that all they had to do was dust themselves down and carry on as before. The socialist revolution that was State-ownership, with the exception of the NHS, helped too much. In 1945, Britain may have wanted, but in economic reality did not need, the Labour socialist order of doing things. Britain would have been better off with rampant capitalism, not overwhelming socialism. The nation, having Dug for Victory, needed to get out there and dig for the peace dividend. From having to live by its wits and resources, the British were becoming a nation fast believing that they had the medals to prove that they had fought for freedom and cradle-to-grave comfort. They had not. The NHS was a brilliant concept that rightly became the envy of much of the globe; but it became a way of thinking that suggested to too many that the State would always provide and that government should pay, whereas they forgot that government coffers came only from one source.

The further irony of the revolution was that by the start of the 1950s and the need to go to the country, Attlee's government had theoretically done all that it set out to do. It had no new ideas that would inspire a nation grumpy with austerity and disturbed that it was once again at war (in Korea). Moreover, much of the funds government might have used for regeneration were being distributed back into the military system that was deployed as an occupying army in West Germany and, of greater test, throughout the colonies with huge bases and a constant throughput of an increasingly expensive National Service conscription.

If the NHS was the momentous step-change in British domestic life of that Attlee government, then the significant foreign policy event was the independence movement of British possessions in Africa and the Indian sub-continent. The 1940s truly felt the wind of change in British colonial history.

The Edwardians had ruled Britain's overseas possessions and dominions for their original purpose: the economy. The idea was simple: cheap and rare goods in and British goods out. This trading principle did not always run smoothly but by the death of Victoria and the reign of her son, Edward VII, the British Empire was at its strongest and most profitable. Without the breadth of colonial trading Britain would have been financially embarrassed. Nation-states tumble from historical peaks yet the early years of the twentieth century did not obviously suggest it was right to talk of the Empire sliding away; in fact, there is evidence to suggest that the British Empire was even expanding certainly in terms of its influence in the conduct of the Great War. The 1914–18 conflict was a world war because it was a battle of empires: the British Empire, the

German Empire, the Ottoman Empire, the Japanese and to a lesser extent, the Italian colonies. When the war ended, the colour-coding of the globe changed.

The cultural and economic swathe from Turkey down through the Levant, Syria, Mesopotamia, Palestine, Jordan to the Persian Gulf, was no longer the Ottoman Empire ruled by the Caliph of the Faithful. The San Remo conference of the 'victors' of the First World War was held in 1920 and confirmed the ruling of the newly formed League of Nations that Britain and France should have an international mandate to rule this region. France administered Syria and Lebanon. Britain administered Iraq, Palestine and what became Jordan. From 1914, Egypt had anyway been a British protectorate. The American President, Woodrow Wilson, did not want the colonial powers to expand their empires, hence the concept of mandates. The difference was lost on the British, for whom the candle of imperialism still flickered; the British were part of the global ruling class, even if they were strapped for cash.

The illusion of Empire supporting Britain was obvious to economists, but not to the industrial and political classes. Trade was reasonably good, but special rates and duties distorted the real value. Colonies were places from which the British could import goods at a profit and to which they could export at a global profit. Globalization began with the British Empire. Moreover, Britain may have been forced into sterling devaluation but, along with its white dominions, the Empire had almost overnight become yet again the most powerful trading block in the world. Exploitation of colonial markets in, say, 1631 was not much different from that in 1931. As a consequence of Britain's devaluation, similar devaluation by the dominions and preferential trading between them all, Britain was back to where the investors of the seventeenth century had always hoped to be – almost 50 per cent of British exports were going to the colonies. This was a far cry from the cynical concept of some who believed that without their colonies and the resultant imports, the British would be living in a cold and unimportant little island group, work weary and living on herrings and potatoes. Certainly that was the reputation of the British among the Indian princes when they saw the first envoys from England in the early 1600s.

The British were quite comfortable with the idea that some were inferior and then there were the British. The vision of India, the apparent success in the Boer War, Mafeking, the crushing of the German Empire, Lawrence of Arabia, the stream of features and editorials in the Harmsworth and Beaverbrook newspapers – all of this worked on the minds of the British who, of course, could metaphorically strut through a quarter of the globe at a time when, for example, 99 per cent of the people of New Zealand were British by birth and had gone out there to work and then rule the Empire; hence the irony in the determination of the political and religious leaders from India preparing to descend on Westminster in 1931. Their message was not one anticipated in British high streets. The Indians were telling the British that it was time they left the sub-continent. The 1931 Westminster Conference became one of the most important dates in the later British Empire. It was the moment when imperialism was ended.

The conference itself came about because the imperial ways were waning. The structure was theoretically the same. Colonies and dependencies were totally ruled by Britain as if they were shires. Colonies with home rule governed themselves but had little say about defence and foreign affairs. Some, like Canada were moving on from that; Canada was a dominion so decided her own foreign policy. In the Imperial Conference of 1926 and then in 1931 five other colonies – Australia, Newfoundland, New Zealand, the Irish Free State and South Africa – were offered the same dominion status. These were the white colonies. The kith and kin. The extended family refused to be treated like children. But the jewel of the British Empire, India, was excluded. Britain had a different relationship with India than it did with the rest of the Empire. For example, one-third of the British army was garrisoned in India. Who paid? India. That wasn't the case in any other colony. And although the British Crown had run India since 1858, there were few commercial concessions. So militarily and economically the British never wished to devolve real power. Furthermore, Indians were not kith and kin.

Yet how could the Third British Empire, the post-war empire, be constitutionally restructured if India were excluded? For many in India, exclusion was fine. Some wanted independence and others parity with the dominions at the very least. To them, this was very possible. And collectively they pointed to a declaration made by Lloyd George's India Secretary Edwin Montagu in August 1917.

Semantically it was as debatable as Balfour's Declaration on a Jewish Homeland:

> The policy of His Majesty's Government, with which the Government of India are in complete accord, is that of the increasing association of Indians in every branch of the administration and the gradual development of self-governing institutions with a view to the progressive realization of responsible government in India as an integral part of the British Empire . . . I would add that progress in this policy can only be achieved by successive stages. The British government and the government of India, on whom the responsibility lies for the welfare and advancement of the Indian peoples, must be the judges of the time and measure of each advance, and they must be guided by the co-operation received from those upon whom new opportunities of service will thus be conferred and by the extent to which it is found that confidence can be reposed in their sense of responsibility

August 1917 was a low point in Britain's efforts in the Great War, a war in which she needed Indian troops. Whatever the reason for the declaration, in 1931 here was the theme to the independence debate. Not that dominion status had been abandoned. Three years earlier, at a conference at Lucknow, it was clear that many in India would settle for dominion status or to have the same standing us other dominions. And in 1929 the Viceroy, Lord Irwin, declared that the goal of the political debate was for India to indeed become a dominion. So presumably the way forward seemed defined. Of course, it wasn't because Irwin, in yet another example of 'what the minister really means' instruction, was forced later to say that having a goal didn't mean it would be reached.

> I have never sought to delude Indian opinion into the belief that a definition of purpose, however plainly stated, would of itself be the enunciation of a phrase, provide a solution for the problems which have to be solved before that purpose is fully realized. The assertion of a goal, however precise in terms, is of a necessity a different thing from the goal's attainment. No sensible traveller would feel that the clear definition of his destination was the same thing as the completion of his journey; but it is an assurance of direction.

The mood in India, now in the psychological grip of Gandhi, was not much inclined to diplomatic obfuscation. The British wanted rid of Gandhi. They said no political progress could be made until his movement was stopped. Also, India was witnessing the battle between the Hindu-led politicians against the Muslim League; the princes were uncertain of their future powers and clearly the sense of nationalism, the sense of moral justice and the sense of expectation could not be set aside by speeches without promises. That London India Conference scared the British imperialist Establishment. A member of it, Brendan Bracken, would later be Winston Churchill's propagandist. So when he wrote to the newspaper baron, Lord William 'Max' Beaverbrook, Bracken was reflecting the views of Churchill:

> 8, Lord North Street, 14th January 1931
> Dear Lord Beaverbrook,
>   It may seem odd that one of the smallest of political tyros should attempt to persuade a master of politics to interest himself in a great public affair. But the memory of the agreeable lunch you gave me not long ago encourages me to write to you about the India Conference. This wretched government, with the aid of the Liberals and some eminent Tories, is about to commit us to one of the most fatal decisions in all our history, and there is practically no opposition to their policy. Disagreeing as I did, with much of your Empire Free Trade policy, I could not but admire all the force and resources which you put into your campaign, and I believe that if those great talents were devoted to combating defeatism, it would still be possible to preserve the essentials of British rule in India.

This was not a Left versus Right affair in British politics. Viceroy Lord Irwin had been right. It should not be assumed that ambition meant all was settled. But both Irwin and Ramsay MacDonald, in the chair of that meeting, were also mindful of an earlier letter MacDonald had received from the Muslim leader, Muhammad Ali Jinnah (1876–1948), who would be the first leader of Pakistan. Jinnah believed that declarations of aims and possibilities were declarations of intent. Equally, it would be naive if we didn't recognize that whatever the innocent or mischievous interpretation, the gap between self-government and independence was constitutionally enormous. Jinnah's letter to MacDonald seemed to span that gap in one paragraph: 'I must emphasize that India expects the translation and fulfilment of these declarations. There never was a more momentous or graver issue in the history of the two nations than the present one on which hangs the fate of nearly one-fifth of the population of the world.'

Certainly the Tories wanted to slow down the pace of discussion. Gandhi was insisting that Congress would speak for everyone including the princes. That was hardly a good start on the long road to agreement. Lord Peel, speaking for the Tories, showed that to his mind the Indians had better understand there was hard travelling ahead. To him the statement of the goal of independence was not the same thing as the purpose of the 1931 conference:

> I wish to state here that . . . while we are united on the goal, we may differ as to the pace or rapidity with which we may obtain that goal . . . in many ways Conservative feeling has been deeply moved by recent events in India; it has been deeply disturbed by the great non-co-operation movement. Conservatives have never believed that non-cooperation on a large scale could be non-violent. They have never believed that the experiments already tried in India some years ago with unfortunate results could be tried again in India with more fortunate results . . . we are told that independence and those declarations of independence by the Congress [of India] were due to frustrated ambition, frustrated desire for further self-government. I am not going for a moment into the psychology of those declarations. I will only say that declarations of that sort of independence and separation from the empire have been made. I regret that they have been made, but they have had some definite influence on Conservative opinion in this country.

Generally, the Indians were not much impressed with Conservative opinion even if some Indian delegates straddled the line between British and Indian views without losing respect of either. One of them was Ranjisinghi Vibhaji Jadeja, the Maharaja of Nawanagar. He is still remembered at Lord's as one of the finest cricketers ever. He was also a thoughtful reformer in his own region. When Ranji – as he was known – rose to speak, he was heard with almost universal reverence.

I have been educated in this country and have spent many years of my life here. England is almost as much my cultural and spiritual home as India; its great institutions and its political life have been to me, a perennial source of refreshment. From her I have imbibed much that is ennobling and invigorating. Mr President, my hopes centre in the perpetuation of the British connection which in my belief is a guarantee of the advancement of my country and of her future greatness . . . one thing is certain – if those who have come to this conference go back to India without the Parliament of Britain making it clear that the minimum constitutional demands of India will be conceded, not only will this conference have been held in vain, but I am much afraid that such a fiasco would strengthen beyond measure the extremist party in India.

The 1931 round table was the first of three. The third, in 1933, mattered most – although Gandhi never would accept dominion status. There is an illusion that Gandhi brought about the independence of India and the end of the British Raj. He did not. To say that he did is like saying Nelson Mandela brought about the end of apartheid in South Africa. What can be said is that, like Mandela, Gandhi became the symbol of change. Gandhi did not even achieve what he set out to do. There was no peaceful change at the end of British rule. There was no return to a national identity in 1947 – whatever that could ever have meant in a sub-continent of perhaps 400 million people with different religions and castes along with fourteen languages and as many as 200 dialects. And his policy of *satyagraha* (peaceful opposition) may have perplexed the British but it did not drive them out. It did not make India ungovernable as was its aim. In fact, there is not much evidence that even his own people saw its long-term political value. India became independent because of a series of political events that had started in the nineteenth century, because of the completely changed political mood and feasibility of maintaining old ways after the Great War, and because of political and strategic thinking coupled with the advances in communications, including worldwide radio and talking newsreels in the 1930s. What we don't know is whether independence – often chaotic and ruthlessly violent – may have taken a different course if there had not been a Second World War.

Change came because of the emergence of the Congress of India as a political party that grew to represent millions more than it had imagined it might. Change also came because of the pressures of the Muslim League and, initially at least, the leadership of Muhammad Ali Jinnah – but not later. It came because the First World War changed economies and political realities in India, the rest of the Empire and London. Furthermore, the image of the British Raj was visibly changing. For example, restructuring of the India Civil and Political Services and reforms that had begun prior to the war meant that more and more Indians were in jobs previously reserved for Europeans. By 1919 Indian ministers ran much of India's provincial government and, within ten years, certainly 40 per cent of the Civil Service was Indian. All this was unthinkable in Curzon's time as Viceroy at the start of the century when he dismissed the India National Congress as the chattering and, worse, intellectual middle classes. Thirty years later, Congress represented the broadest cross-section of Hindu society – with the chattering intellectuals at the top. Moreover, it had done so by using the imperial system of being well organized at district level.

Yet not all was simple. There was the gulf between those Indians who wanted self-government, maybe not full independence, but self-government in everything other than defence and foreign policy and the Viceregal administration. There was, too, a distance between viceroys and London politicians. The viceroys, men like Lord Irwin and Lord Reading (Rufus Isaacs, 1860–1935), recognized that change would come anyway so it was better to have it on easier terms. Consequently, between the wars, the British were forced to change their approach to imperial rule because Curzon's chattering intellectuals were being heard. The British were willing to recognize that India could one day be a dominion – with all the freedoms that suggested – a privilege so far reserved for kith and kin, that is, the white colonies. With the British government on the one side and Gandhi and the Indian National Congress on the other, most sensed (some, like Churchill, reluctantly) some sort of freedom. So came the 1935 India Act. The Act meant more self-government and a pathway to dominion status. But Gandhi didn't want India to be a dominion. He wanted the British out altogether.

I regard the status of India as unique. After all we represent a fifth of the human race. I do not think therefore, that a political status which might suit other Dominions of the British Commonwealth would

necessarily suit us. You must remember that India has been a subject
nation for a long time. If Great Britain approaches the question of the
future relations between our peoples in a spirit of friendship with no
reservations, she will not find India behind-hand in coming to meet
her proffered hand. We would be quite ready, once our right to independence has been recognized to enter into an alliance or partnership
on equal terms which would place the relations of Great Britain and
India on a satisfactory basis.

Gandhi and the Congress represented only a part of Indian opinion,
nominally that of the Hindus. There was also the Muslim League
and, of course, the princes who still 'ruled' much of India. Inevitably,
Hindus and Muslims never agreed safeguards for the Muslims in a
revised constitution. As for the princes, they certainly wanted better
than they had been offered. In the November 1931 London conference, Gandhi said Congress had the right to represent all India, even
the princes. The British were determined that India should not
become another Ireland, but sectarianism remained. In March 1930
at the All Indian Muslim Conference the president, Muhammad
Iqbal, had no doubts of the intentions of the Hindu-led Congress:
'The Congress leaders claim that they are the sole representatives of
the people of India. The Round Table Conference made it abundantly
clear that they were not. They know that the British people and the
rest of the world realize the importance of Communal Settlement in
India.'

Jinnah, who was once more emerging as a central figure, immediately rejected the idea of a federal India and an increasing Hindu
majority in any Parliament. Gandhi, unsmiling, reflected on truth
and that Hindus were expected to believe in *ahimsa*, that all living
creatures were sacred and no harm should be done to any – including
Muslims:

Tolerance may imply a gratuitous assumption of the inferiority of
other faiths to one's own, whereas ahimsa teaches us to entertain the
same respect for the religious faiths of others as we accord to our
own, thus admitting the imperfection of the latter. This admission
will be readily made by a seeker of Truth who follows the law of
Love. If we had attained the full vision of Truth, we would no longer
be mere seekers, but would have become one with God, for Truth is

God. But being only seekers, we prosecute our quest, and are
conscious of our imperfection.

The Muslim League had few moments of faith in *ahimsa* as practised in public. Considering what followed in 1947, then as painful
as it all was supposed to be to Gandhi, the real world of Muslim
versus Hindu in India ruled the hearts and the minds of the country's people and not their theology. As for the British, still uncertain
after the mutiny half-a-century earlier, they could handle old-fash-
ioned radicals leading mob violence, but a softly spoken, unrelenting
guru was much harder. Yet, as Gandhi – more influenced by John
Ruskin than John of the Cross – would point out, none of this should
have been alien to British thinking. Was not the whole British political ethic and the strength of that nation's peoples built on
Christianity? To Gandhi, his spinning wheel was, for India's starving millions, the symbol of salvation. He believed that he, Gandhi,
was that symbol.

The only other person apart from Gandhi and Jawaharlal Nehru
to survive in the public imagination outside India was Muhammad
Ali Jinnah – the man who became President of Pakistan. He was a
Muslim from a merchant's family of Karachi. Like Gandhi, Jinnah
went to London to train as a lawyer. Unlike Gandhi he returned to
India and stayed. Interestingly, his mentor was the campaigner of
the Indian National Congress, G. K. Gokhale, an activist long
before both Gandhi and Jinnah. While Gandhi was still in Africa, it
was Jinnah who led the Indian National Congress delegation to
London to lobby British MPs contemplating the Council of India
Bill. It was Jinnah who first advocated an India of absolute unity.
He understood nationalism as a dangerous concept, as well as one
that had moral might on its side. It was he who brought the All
India Congress and the Muslim League together. It was Jinnah who
negotiated in 1916 the Lucknow Agreement, which parcelled up
the numbers of reserve seats for Muslims on councils. Until the
end of 1918, the British needed to know exactly what Jinnah was
thinking. After that, he was not so important. Most certainly, the
rise of Gandhi had much to do with his decline. For example, in
1927, when the Simon Commission looked at the possibilities of
constitutional reform in India, Jinnah once more attempted to bring
the Muslim League and the India National Congress together. He

failed. He did not have control over provincial Muslim opinion. Jinnah resigned and he left India to practise law in London. He did return in 1935, when he saw new opportunities through the elections that would follow that year's Government of India Act, but he still argued with Gandhi on a crucial point: Jinnah believed that to maintain multiracial unity, then India should have self-government beneath an umbrella of British constitutional rule. Gandhi was unmoved. He wanted absolute independence.

Although he remained in Indian politics, Jinnah, who rarely got on with others, was never again a formidable figure until shortly before independence. He had no big political base. The Muslim League had not much more than a fifth of the seats at the 1937 elections. Yet it took the Second World War for the British to realize they had to build up faith in Jinnah as a leader. This was neither a constitutional nor political act of morality. Jinnah had influence with over 50 per cent of the Muslim-based Indian army. That was Britain's main concern. India and the whole Empire were again to be called to the colours – the British colours – as the world once more went to war. The Empire rallied to the Union flag and, arguably, it gained strength from this bloody conflict. In fact, the Second World War revived something that had lain dormant for a decade or more – imperialism. Of course, the 1931 Statute of Westminster should have made clear to all the dominions (but not the Crown colonies) that they had the option of war or not. Ireland for example, understood its position – it declared its neutrality. In Australia, Bob Menzies (1894–1978), usually called Pig Iron Bob, the most loyal subject of any monarch, immediately declared that Australia was in the war. His view was, he said, a constitutional one and a declaration of war by Britain was enough legality. As he told Australians on 3 September 1939, there was 'unity in the Empire ranks – One King, One Flag, One Cause'.

The New Zealand Prime Minister M. J. Savage (1872–1940) asked the Governor-General for a formal declaration of war before saying that New Zealand had signed on. 'Where she goes, we go, where she stands, we stand,' he said.

J. B. M. Hertzog (1866–1942) in South Africa was not so sure. He did not like the British but his deputy Jan Smuts (1870–1950) did. It went to a Parliamentary vote. Smuts won that vote but sixty of the 145 members voted not to go to war. Smuts then became Prime

Minister, not because Hertzog's refusal to go to war had been beaten, but because the Governor-General would not allow him to put the case before the people in a General Election. That was true imperial power, a power that would not have been exercised in peacetime.

We should not lump the rest of the British Empire in Africa in with South Africa. Sierra Leone raised war funds for Britain 'in grateful recognition of the great benefits which Sierra Leone has received during the past 135 years under the British flag'. Maybe as many as 200,000 Africans were conscripted, but not into military service. They were sent as miners and labourers to dig for the other form of victory, the natural resources needed to manufacture weapons and military systems and to feed those who would use them. Remember, this was a world war. So when Malaya fell to the Japanese, alternative sources of rubber had to be found. Nigerians provided them. By the end of the war, according to the Colonial Office, 374,000 Africans had been in the war – of those 7,000 died – not all at the front. The Colonial Office said that blacks were not to be sent to Britain for enlistment. But what happened when the Canadians enlisted West Indians? And as the war went on, the greater was the need for manpower from all over the Empire. The RAF may have recruited West Indians, thousands of them, but there was clearly a bias against coloured members of the colonies. This had long existed and showed itself in what we would now find as bizarre circumstances. Papers were written questioning what would happen if a white nurse had to attend a black wounded soldier? What would happen if a black medical orderly had to attend a white officer, or worse, the wounded wife of a white officer? These were social issues.

The bigger and lasting conundrum was the global confrontation; equally, the most important ally after the United States, the Soviet Union had few reservations about fighting Hitler and Japan. It had not joined the war to hold together the British Empire. True, the war could bring about the collapse of Empire; but that was unlikely as long as the Soviet Union bore the brunt of Hitler's firepower. Nevertheless, Stalin's army was not going to defend the British Empire in Burma and Singapore. Singapore was bought in the nineteenth century because it was a choke point for shipping and controlled the Empire's access and authority over south-east Asia as well as the Far East. Singapore, Burma, Malaya and Hong Kong all fell to the Japanese. The imperial dominoes were tumbling and so were the Empire's servicemen and women. For example, of the 30,000 or so who died in the Merchant Navy, 5,000 were from the colonies. The Canadians sent almost 500,000 men and women and the first contingents were in Britain by December 1939. Seven divisions of Australians, more than half a million men and women, were sent; 27,000 were killed. Two divisions of New Zealanders were committed to the Pacific and the Middle East. The South Africans, at first only in their own continent, fought through Italy.

In India, the Viceroy, Lord Linlithgow declared war without consulting any of the major political or cultural figures in the sub-continent. They were treated just as they had been at the start of the Great War. This very real affront didn't meant that those same leaders failed to support the war. Gandhi told Linlithgow that he viewed the war with an English heart. Nehru said he was offended by the Viceroy's proclamation but not its sentiment. He supported the war because he believed fascism had to be confronted. The Congress Party could not follow that line. Congress represented too much of India and a broad section of it. It did not withdraw from government as some members wanted to, but it hardly participated in issues that had to do with the war – Congress could not be seen to be entirely pro British otherwise its pressures for independence would weaken. This did not deter the Indian war effort. India became a pivot in the allied war in the Far East and 2.25 million Indians were in uniform. So, here were reasons that the Second World War revived, albeit briefly, the imperial nature of Empire. It expanded the authority of the dominions, each of which assumed an individual position unleashed from Britain. Inevitably, there was a sense of never again although that had been the feeling after the Great War. The Second World War changed so much in political and social life among the Western allies that it was inevitable that the imperial tableau should also be altered, except, of course, in the mind of Britain's wartime leader, Winston S. Churchill.

When Churchill went into Parliament in 1901, twelve million square miles or so of the globe was British. More than 440 million people (about the population of twenty-first century Continental Europe) lived under the authority of the Union flag. Maybe this made 1947 harder to understand for those so wedded to the commercial and strategic values as well as the images of British imperial history. Churchill, with that obvious imperial DNA he displayed so easily, could not accept the independence of India and the removal of the very jewel upon which he had gazed all his life.

The political expediency, the sell-outs, the broken promises and the horrifying violence in India in 1947 was morally and politically shocking, and not just to the British. The transition to independence was never expected to be an entirely peaceful process. The animosities between Hindu and Muslim, the rushed planning for the handover and the opposing values of Gandhi and Jinnah seemingly and inevitably all led to a transition deeply and forever stained with a level of violence between the indigenous people that had never been known under British rule. Some would blame the speed at which independence was finally granted and, in particular, the style of the man selected to see it through, Lord Mountbatten (1900–79). It is true that he was sometimes the most arrogant of almost all the viceroys that had gone before. However, he alone should not be held responsible for the carnage when a million Indians died. The British collectively failed for five reasons: they failed to set in train a reasonable form of independence before the Second World War; Churchill's Victorian imperial instincts refused to admit that independence was right and inevitable; London should not have dismissed the previous governor General Archibald Wavell (1883–1950) and his eminently sensible military plan to cover the withdrawal of Muslims to the newly created State of Pakistan (the name is an acronym from Punjab, Afghania, Kashmir, Iran, Sindh, Turkharistan, Afghanistan); the British did not give Jinnah more support until it was all too late; the British were frightened of Gandhi's influence over his people even though it was obvious he could never deliver his ambition to have an India with a single national identity.

The independence movement had found its feet in the 1940s. Colonies such as Ghana, Burma, Ceylon (later Sri Lanka) made a relatively easy transition. Others were not so fortunate. The 1952 Mau Mau rebellion in Kenya was a bloody affair and, to a lesser extent, so was the state of emergency in Cyprus. The demands or inclinations for colonial independence should not be seen in isolation from other British political and military excursions. The surest example of this occurred in 1956 when Britain, with the help of France and Israel, attacked the Suez Canal Zone. In 1875, Disraeli had bought from the Ottoman governor a controlling interest in the

Suez Canal Company. A decade later, Britain became a guarantor of the canal's neutral status. It was an economically vital waterway to so many nation-states and, given the volatile political nature of the region, was always vulnerable to closure. In the 1950s, faced with Arab nationalism, Britain gradually withdrew from its position as major military power in Egypt.

The Egyptian leader who had Britain on the run was Gamal Abdel Nasser (1918–70). Nasser was immensely popular far beyond his own Egyptian borders. Nasserism was indeed a movement, just as had been the late nineteenth-century Mahdiya Islam Brotherhood that under the 1881 holy war, the *jihad*, terrorized British interests in the Sudan. Nasser was seen by many in the region as a new *Mahdi* (guided one). When Nasser nationalized the Suez Canal Company, the British Prime Minister, Anthony Eden (1897–1977) set out to regain the canal. This single action was the last imperial charge of the British. It was also a politically divisive event in the United Kingdom. Eden, against the military advice of his chiefs of staff and, against the wishes of the United States, combined with France and Israel to invade the Suez Canal Zone. Eden was obsessed with Nasser. The operation was a disaster. It had a limited military advantage, but with no support from other States, Eden had to order withdrawal. It was also his withdrawal from British politics. He was totally discredited, much to the anticipation of his Chancellor, Harold Macmillan (1894–1986) who quietly sat waiting for Eden to leave Number 10 Downing Street, into which he, Macmillan, then entered. Suez, set British politics on another road and, it weakened its authority in the Middle East.

Macmillan, meanwhile, saw the way of the modern colonial world and in 1960 made what is now seen as one of the most important speeches on independence and freedoms ever heard in Africa. Macmillan, first, to hardly any attention in the House of Commons and then, in Africa, made his 'wind of change' speech. He was saying that the Empire was disappearing, but people within that Empire had to realize why and that it should be an evolution rather than a revolution. Of course, he was right and few, other than the hardline white ruling classes of South Africa for whom black rule was unthinkable, doubted Macmillan. What he said was not surprising. What was important was the fact that he said it where he did. In that same year, 1960, Nigeria and Cyprus became independent.

The following year, 1961, Sierra Leone joined Tanganyika as an independent state. South Africa would not budge. Apartheid was an ideology as well as an unspeakable form of self-protection for the ruling whites. Rather than even consider bending, South Africa detached itself from the debate and left the Commonwealth. The rest of the colonial world had little difficulty in seeing their future as well-supported and, in some cases, very well funded independent States. The West Indies Federation broke up in 1962 and Uganda also took its freedom. Kenya became independent in 1963 and, the following year, Zambia was created out of what used to be Northern Rhodesia. When Southern Rhodesia declared its own independence (UDI) it did so because the white settlers had watched what had happened to other newly created nation-states in Africa and believed that chaos would follow. So the march of independence continued, until the last colony to be handed over was Hong Kong. In 1997, the colony was given back to the Chinese. The British no longer mourned their Empire.

The few Crown colonies that remain too often cause pain to the British administration. Successive British governments, particularly that of Prime Minister Tony Blair, would have dearly loved to give Gibraltar to the Spanish. However, the people of Gibraltar, rather like those of the Falkland Islands, want to remain British. In some ways, the Falkland Islanders and the Gibraltarians are rather like the original seventeenth-century settlers in far-flung places. They rely on the patronage of the British monarch for their very existence.

When the then British Prime Minister, Margaret Thatcher, ordered a task force to recapture the Falkland Islands from the Argentinians in 1982, she was doing more than holding on to a bit of imperial history. During that period of the spring of 1982, there re-emerged in the British people a jingoism that is a reminder that the legacy of Empire runs deep. However, there was also evidence that it was waning.

The Thatcher act of defending a possession in true imperial style was coincidental with a step-change in British identity and the celebration that followed told us, admittedly anecdotally, something not all had recognized in the modern British character. The leaders wanted a victory parade. Although none would doubt the loyal support of the British public for the armed services, there was too a sense that that same public had moved on. There was an uneasiness about the form of celebration. Parades are fine spectacles and those who march may do so proudly, knowing that by and large they have the right to and the streets will be lined with those who agree. There was, however, a feeling that the British no longer cavorted to jingoism. When in February 2002, the *Guardian* newspaper surveyed a sample of those born during the conflict, it reported that hardly any knew anything about the war. Not one said that it had an impact on his or her life. The fact that about 1,000 had died, 255 of whom were British, meant nothing.

The Attlee government had, through social conviction, created a period of bewildering change in a society that had not seen such specific policy review in the previous years of the century in spite of two global wars. For the rest of the century, certainly from the late 1950s, the perception of Britain as a principal member of a global master-class would also change. It would do so because of the quick evolution of political and social thought in the United Kingdom and in particular its often defensive reaction to what went on in the rest of the world.

Post-Second World War Europe took decades to recover from that conflict at a time when it was still economically bruised from the market effects of the preceding decade. The UK had gone into the Second World War just a step or two ahead of the bailiffs. The war had helped some industries, particularly, for example, those involved with the constant production of war materiel. After the war, Britain was poor. The means of rapid industrial recovery, including supplies and domestic and foreign markets, were not readily available. The war had produced advances in aircraft design, communications, engineering systems and a reminder that the value of the female labour force at whatever level should not be underestimated. The revolution in social conditions for the population were applauded but beyond the means of the nation. At the same time, the United Kingdom did not have the opportunity to close its gates and sort its own difficulties. The borders of Europe had changed. When Churchill gave his Iron Curtain speech on 5 March 1946 at Westminster College, Fulton, Missouri, he did so in the knowledge that every European map had to be redrawn and every security concept rethought (NATO – the North Atlantic Treaty Organization – was not formed until April 1949):

The United States stands at this time at the pinnacle of world power. It is a solemn moment for the American democracy. For with this primacy in power is also joined an awe-inspiring accountability to the future. As you look around you, you must feel not only the sense of duty done, but also you must feel anxiety lest you fall below the level of achievement. Opportunity is here now, clear and shining, for both our countries. To reject it or ignore it or fritter it away will bring upon us all the long reproaches of the aftertime.

It is necessary that constancy of mind, persistency of purpose, and the grand simplicity of decision shall rule and guide the conduct of the English-speaking peoples in peace as they did in war. We must, and I believe we shall, prove ourselves equal to this severe requirement.

I have a strong admiration and regard for the valiant Russian people and for my wartime comrade, Marshal Stalin. There is deep sympathy and goodwill in Britain – and I doubt not here also – toward the peoples of all the Russias and a resolve to persevere through many differences and rebuffs in establishing lasting friendships.

It is my duty, however, to place before you certain facts about the present position in Europe.

From Stettin in the Baltic to Trieste in the Adriatic an iron curtain has descended across the Continent. Behind that line lie all the capitals of the ancient states of Central and Eastern Europe. Warsaw, Berlin, Prague, Vienna, Budapest, Belgrade, Bucharest and Sofia; all these famous cities and the populations around them lie in what I must call the Soviet sphere, and all are subject, in one form or another, not only to Soviet influence but to a very high and in some cases increasing measure of control from Moscow.

The safety of the world, ladies and gentlemen, requires a unity in Europe, from which no nation should be permanently outcast. It is from the quarrels of the strong parent races in Europe that the world wars we have witnessed, or which occurred in former times, have sprung.

Here then was the reasoning for the formation of NATO, said to have been described by its first Secretary General, Lord Ismay (1887–1965), as an alliance to keep the Russians out, the Americans in and the Germans down. The Americans, in the same year as Churchill's speech, 1946, formulated their policy of containment: the concept that global Communism and not just European Communism could only be contained. There was no great stomach for war until policy changed in the Far East when it was seen that a Communist advance could prove the domino theory that as one country fell, so the neighbour would. Churchill's Iron Curtain remained until November 1989 and so from 1946, if not earlier, successive British governments believed and so geared their defences to the possibility that an East–West European trip wire would snap and Soviet forces would be at the Channel ports within four to ten days.

In these forbidding times of the 1940s, the likes of Margaret Thatcher and Ronald Reagan spent their formative years. By the time they reached the heights of political power in the late 1970s, nothing that had happened during the intervening years – the Berlin airlift between 1948 and 1949, the Korean War that started in 1951, the creation of the Warsaw Treaty Organization in 1954, the suppression of the Hungarian Uprising in 1956, the Soviet lead in intercontinental warfare technology in 1957, the Cuban missile crisis in 1962, the invasion into Czechoslovakia in 1968, and so on – changed their minds about the threats to their societies. On this fact alone, we may suspect the origins of uncompromising attitudes to any form of threat during their leadership.

By the closing years of the 1950s in Britain, there was a social movement that would set a pattern for the futures of younger people who would influence the next generation, which in turn would manipulate the technological revolution that followed in the 1990s and into the twenty-first century.

In 1947, a shortage of fuel and the harshest winter since 1894 were largely responsible for yet a further band of austerity measures. However, there were stirrings that times were changing for the better. The film industry was upbeat and full of romantic storylines such as Herbert Wilcox's (1890–1977) *Spring in Park Lane*. Musicals (as opposed to revues) appeared for the first time. *Oklahoma!* made its London debut when it opened in Drury Lane in April 1947 to delirious audiences who had never before seen its like. Christian Dior (1905–57) presented his first fashion collection and lifted the industry and Western women out of their dressing up doldrums. It was called the A-Line, or as the Americans called it, the New Look. This, with the fairy-tale wedding of Princess Elizabeth to Lieutenant

Prince Philip, gave the feeling that maybe there was indeed a new life out there somewhere. For the next ten years, the pace of social and cultural change quickened in Britain. Rock 'n' roll, with its origins in blues and country music, crossed the Atlantic and with it came the idea that three or four people could plug in the phenomenon of the youth club scene, the electric guitar, and take on the world. In doing so, they could kick over so many concepts that their parents clung to – especially the idea that young people should be seen but not heard. They were being heard through mega-decibel amplifiers.

Much has been made of the social change of the contraceptive pill, and rightly so. Yet perhaps a bigger influence on the lives of a younger generation was National Service conscription. Conscription was a nineteenth-century Prussian idea. It did not find its way into British military thinking until 1916 when volunteers for the First World War had all but disappeared. Conscription ended in 1919, but returned under the National Service (Armed Forces) Act of 1939. It continued until 1960, with the last National Service soldiers emerging in 1962. From this we see a single change in the life of young people: two generations of boys had never been able to make their own way into adulthood. At seventeen-and-a-half, they had reported for National Service. From day one they had, as the phrase had it, learned to salute everything that moved and paint everything that did not. They learned to recognize authority at a hundred yards across a parade ground. They learned to value as well as to sometimes despise pecking orders and their places within that system. Equally, they learned to go with or beat the system. They learned teamwork. Most did not want to go. They learned that most senior officers did not want them to come. They also learned cleanliness (most came from homes with only rudimentary habits in the bathroom) and tidiness. If all this sounds too good, then it is equally so that most were only too glad to get out. Curiously, research suggests that while conscripts look back at their service as a complete waste of time, they also remember the two years or so with a certain pride. However, there was one aspect of conscript life that was common to all recruits: the haircut. Short back and sides was, until the 1950s, a common cut for most youths and young men. In the Services, there was no option but very short.

When conscription ended at the start of the 1960s, the first youngsters in twenty years moved from teenage to adult at their own pace. The first rebellion of the 1960s was long hair. Long lank or prettily combed after the style of whatever hero or group the youngster signed up for, hair was the first defiance and the one that would overturn most of the visible values that parents had suffered or enjoyed. This is surely a trite assumption of the nature of those entering their fun years of the so-called Swinging Sixties. Yet it is a symbol of much that was to follow.

Rock 'n' roll, flower power and the hippy generation reflected changing society. Woodstock in 1968 and 1969 may have assumed an image for a generation that was utterly hedonistic. But it was also a generation that paradoxically protested because some sense of morality was offended. It was a generation in 1968 that knew the Soviet invasion of Czechoslovakia was inherently wrong. The students marched against their universities throughout the Western and Latin American worlds. They paraded their causes with the fervour of all-consuming radicals through the streets of every continent: here were the civil rights movement in America; the New Left movement throughout Western Europe; the peace campaigners; the anti-Vietnam War demonstrations in almost every country with students forcing campuses to close for days on end; the Warsaw protesters at the Polish Theatre (protest was not confined to the so-called free States); the German student rights protests; the total disruption by thousands of anti-war protesters at the Democratic National Convention in Chicago. In that same year, Friends of the Earth was founded and so was the Northern Ireland Civil Rights movement. All this and very much more in one unforgettable year of protest: 1968. Unforgettable that is, to the thousands, perhaps millions of young people who took up the paving stones of the society that had produced them and hurled them in protest at authority.

All this was seen on arguably the most powerful opinion former in post-Second World War British society – colour television. Colour television did not appear in British living rooms until 1967 on BBC2 and 1969 on BBC1 and ITV. It was the medium that would dominate the way people believed they were seeing for themselves events as they really were. There are still those who insist that colour transmissions tipped American public opinion against the war in Vietnam. In the United Kingdom, the realism and entertainment value of the new form of television from the late 1960s was such a powerful presence in daily life that sociologists could rant that it was responsible for the breakdown in society. The claim was (and remains in some influential quarters) that television numbed the mind, made conversation redundant and isolated individuals in the same room and so corrupted family life. It may tell us something about the British that animal programmes were rarely included in the programme list of insidious broadcasting.

However dubious are the claims about influences on societies, it is always a safe assumption that the former US President Bill Clinton got it right when he said if you want to know what wins elections, tell yourself the following: it's the economy, stupid. The British were not alone in expecting to vote for a national government on the simplification of the Clinton hypothesis: will I be better or worse off if I vote for the sitting government? Personal economies or perspectives of how others live were rarely so obvious as they became in the 1980s and 1990s. When stories circulated that the French medical system was superb, it was because people in the UK were dissatisfied with their own system or, more likely, believed anecdotal evidence while ignoring the fact that their own experiences had not always been so terrible. They were forming an opinion not from first-hand experience, but on the headline principle of 'it was in the paper so it must be true'. Here was a sense of dissatisfaction in spite of near unprecedented riches in the society created by Thatcherism and then the seemingly uncontrollable asset-stripping of every basic rule of banking and money marketeering. So many people who could take fantastic decisions in everyday life – from political advisers in their twenties who could influence government decisions to bankers with little supervision – no longer needed the great institutions that had created almost a thousand years of British life. People by the twenty-first century no longer needed their history. They no longer needed the status of being British as had the Victorians or their early twentieth-century ancestors. The Protestant arrogance of the eighteenth century no longer had resonance and nor did the way of the Church that had created that illusion. The Church was so irrelevant to most people that fewer than 10 per cent of the population attended on the high day of Easter, one of the points in the Church calendar when congregations are measured. The banks were seen as increasingly corrupt, particularly after the events of 2008 and the making of the so-called world economic crisis. The law enforcers were feared rather than being of comfort to a population increasingly bewildered by violence. Government departments after the 'task force' era that followed the 1997 elections were consistently shown to be incompetent. Finally, the politicians themselves were seen to be untrustworthy. The scandal of expenses claims and ministers on the make as lobbyists would at one time have brought about enormous protests of disgust. By the close of the first decade of the twenty-first century, British society simply shrugged. By then, the British appeared to have lost faith in the great institutions. The banks, the law, the Church and government itself had failed them.

It is at this point that we should take heed that when giving such a broad view of the story of the British, we are of course Anglo-centric. In other words, we fall into the trap of lumping the nations of the British Isles together. Clearly we should not. Equally clearly, to give proper and deserved space to the histories of each of the British nations would take volumes rather than this single volume. However, having reached the crucial point in explaining the decline of the British, or Britishness, then it is a moment to set the English apart. For it is the English who are in decline.

For the Scots and the Welsh, none of this loss of faith in the institutions particularly mattered. The Scots, for example, do not have and never have had a huge problem with their Church although the debate between the different persuasions has always been vigorous. Scottish jurisprudence is to be admired. The wrecking history of the clan is often not for the weak, but equally none can doubt the individual identity of the people north of the Scottish–English border. The Welsh have been air-brushed out of most British histories and it is easy to get the impression that nothing happened in the principality after the 1284 Statute of Rhuddlan and then the abolition of Welsh civil law in the sixteenth century. In the twenty-first century, both Scotland and Wales had their devolved government, albeit on a limited scale. The importance of devolved power was the way it maintained and even enhanced national identity. It should be argued that the Scots and Welsh did not need any Westminster-designed policy and concession to tell them who they were. The English, on the other hand, were gradually losing their identity. The institutions had little influence anymore on the English persona and, more and more, the English had no idea what it meant to look up to those institutions and certainly not to be proud of what they meant and ironically, throughout the world in the former colonies, often still mean.

Modern British history is in great part the history of the British governed at Westminster. The individuals and even the organizations such as trading houses may have been run and organized by Scots, Welsh and Irish, but the Westminster stamp is an English one. Certainly since the early nineteenth century, one of the drivers of British history was Empire. Empire gave the British nomenklatura, but did not give the average Briton a purpose – politically, militarily, and most important of all, commercially. The purpose was to rule and to make money. That is not a historically Marxist hypothesis. It is an acceptable observation. People in power do things because they are in power. People in power do things for the power and, therefore, the opportunity that power presents. The Empire did that. The huge majority of the British during the time of Empire had no power whatsoever other than that which presented itself on a tiny scale within their social and working lives. In spite of outbursts of jingoism through the nineteenth and twentieth centuries, there is no evidence that the average Briton saw the Empire as anything more than an opportunity to do better for themselves and live in a style that would not be possible on the same remuneration at home. Nor is there any convincing evidence that the British at home saw the colonial servants as anything more than an extension of the ruling classes at home. Yet, because the Empire existed well into the twentieth century, so did the red bits in the school atlas and so did the global acceptance of English as a diplomatic and trading language. All this gave the British not so much a sense of superiority but a sense of identity.

Identity is about understanding that others can confirm who you are. In the case of the British, we have an anomaly of identification. Others do not confirm British identity. They see Britishness as Englishness. It is as if they know how Englishness sounds and that is enough. But the English are not so sure of their own character. They may talk about the wartime spirit, salts of the earth and particularly pluckiness – a euphemism for losing. However, thanks to the English losing or discarding their history books during the formative years of education, they know little of their history. Probably. Reading history does not let a nation as mixed and as large as the English into the secret of present identity. Yet it does tell something of what forefathers looked like. When a nation loses faith in its great institutions, however, it probably has little need to know where and how those institutions originated and developed, and why they did. Consequently, it has even less interest in its identity. The danger here is that it develops an unhealthy curiosity about those in its midst who have no such difficulties with identity. The danger comes when that curiosity develops into an understanding that what identity is left in the English is being undermined by people who know who they are. Great Britain had much purpose when it had its Empire. The twentieth-century chestnut that when it lost that Empire, Great Britain did not discover a new role is only relevant in the twenty-first century. That is because Britain does not yet know where it wants to position itself in, say, the coming thirty or forty years and into the second half of the twenty-first century. The people who ran the Empire knew what they wanted for the coming half century. But then they knew who they were, and so did everyone else.

Index

(Monarchs are those of England/Britain unless otherwise stated)